Early German Settlers of York County Pennsylvania

Revised Edition

Keith A. Dull

HERITAGE BOOKS
2007

HERITAGE BOOKS
AN IMPRINT OF HERITAGE BOOKS, INC.

Books, CDs, and more—Worldwide

For our listing of thousands of titles see our website
at
www.HeritageBooks.com

Published 2007 by
HERITAGE BOOKS, INC.
Publishing Division
65 East Main Street
Westminster, Maryland 21157-5026

Copyright © 1997 Keith A. Dull

Other books by the author:
Early Families of Berks, Bucks and Montgomery Counties, Pennsylvania
Early Families of Lancaster, Lebanon and Dauphin Counties, Pennsylvania
Early Families of Somerset and Fayette Counties, Pennsylvania
Early Families of York County, Pennsylvania, Volume 1
Early Families of York County, Pennsylvania, Volume 2
Early German Settlers of York County, Pennsylvania, Revised Edition

All rights reserved. No part of this book may be reproduced or transmitted in any form or by any means, electronic or mechanical, including photocopying, recording or by any information storage and retrieval system without written permission from the author, except for the inclusion of brief quotations in a review.

International Standard Book Number: 978-1-58549-160-5

CONTENTS

Introduction v

Additions and Corrections viii

Codorus 1

Dover 95

Manchester 176

Shrewsbury 287

Index 371

INTRODUCTION

In this book, Mr. Dull traces the lineages of a major portion of the German families of York County, giving exhaustive coverage of the townships of Codorus, Dover, Manchester, and Shrewsbury. His reference point, so to speak, was the 1762 tax list. He culled through earlier and later records, along with the great amount of published information now available, looking for data on these specific individuals and their associated families. We are pleased to publish the impressive body of knowledge he has amassed on these families.

Show below are the sources he used.

The Publisher

Sources and Abbreviations

York County Church Records of the 18th Century by Marlene S. Bates and F. Edward Wright (1991):

BLY - Blymir's (St. John's) Church
CAN - Canadochly Church
CLY - Christ's Church
ERC - Emanuel Reformed Church
FIS - Fissel's (Jerusalem) Church
FMY - First Moravian Church
FRI - Friedensaal (Schuster's/White) Church
JCS - Private record of Reverend Johan Caspar Stoever
KRE - Kreutz Creek (Trinity and St. James) Church
LIS - Lischy's (St. Peter's) Church
QUI - Quickel's (Zion) Church
RJL - Private record of Reverend Jacob Lischy
SAD - Sadler's (St. John's) Church
SHE - Sherman's (St. David's) Church
STE - Steltz Union (Bethlehem) Church
STJ - St. Jacob's (Stone) Church
STM - St. Matthew's Church
STP - St. Peter's (Yellow) Church

STR - Strayer's (Salem) Church
TLY - Trinity Church
WOL - Wolf's (St. Paul's) Church
ZIE - St. Paul's (Ziegler's) Church

Literature by Annette K. Burgert:

- BNK - *18th Century Emigrants from German Speaking Lands to North America/the Northern Kraichgau* (1983)
- BWP - *18th Century Emigrants from German Speaking Lands to North America/the Western Palatinate* (1985)
- BNA - *18th Century Emigrants from Northern Alsace to America* (1992)
- EEB - *18th Century Emigrants from Eppingen*
- BFG - *York County Pioneers from Friedelsheim and Gonnheim in the Palatinate*
- *Westerwald to America*

Literature by Neal Otto Hively (land draft maps and indexes):

- Codorus Township (1988)
- North Codorus Township (1991)
- Shrewsbury and Springfield Townships (1992)
- The Manor of Springettsbury (1993)

The 1762 and 1779 tax list of York County, Pennsylvania.

The York County Historical Society's Abstracts of York County, Pennsylvania Wills 1749-1819 (1995, F. Edward Wright).

The Unrecorded Wills of York County, Pennsylvania, 1753-1792.

David A. and Brenda L. Paup's Index to the Probate Inventories of York County, Pennsylvania, 1749-1850 (1992).

Miscellaneous church records and family histories mentioned as used.

Other Abbreviations Used

b.	-	born
bapt.	-	baptized
bro(s).	-	brother(s)
bur.	-	buried
Co.	-	County
d.	-	died
dau(s).	-	daughter(s)
exec(s).	-	executor(s)
m.	-	married
spon.	-	sponsored

U.S. Postal Service State Abbreviations

ADDITIONS AND CORRECTIONS

The following are additions and corrections to the first edition (1997) of *Early German Settlers of York County, Pennsylvania:*

ADDITION - Page 5

Binckle - Peter, son of Christian and Esbeth (Burri) Binckle, was b. Mar. 2, 1704, and d. in Bethania, NC, on Aug. 20, 1793. He m. Anna Maria Werle (Oct. 28, 1704-Sept. 1748) on Feb. 2, 1725, and Anna Maria Margaretha Geigerschemel on Feb. 3, 1749. Anna Maria Margaretha was b. Jan. 18, 1722, and d. in Stokes Co., NC, on Feb. 9, 1803. Peter arrived in Philadelphia on the ship *Princess Augustus* on Sept. 16, 1736. The following information can be added to their children (see *The Palatine Immigrant*, 1997):
 - Sarah m. Leonard Moser and Edward Bartley.
 - Margareta m. Ulrich Wolenwether.
 - Johannes m. Johanna Leedy.
 - Anna Barbara m. Mathias Meyer and Johannes Frey.
 - Johann Adam m. Maria Weller.
 - Elisabeth m. John Herbach.
 - Johann Christian m. Catharina Lecklider.
 - Johann Peter m. Susanna Dull.
 - Frederick m. Elisabeth Dull.

ADDITION - Page 16

Gantz - Frantz and Margaretha were sponsors to the baptism of Margareta, dau. of Georg Leonhardt and Elisabeta (Schneider) Manchen, at Zion Church in Baltimore (now Carroll) Co., Manchester, MD, on May 1, 1768, and Frantz was sponsor to the baptism of an infant of Georg Phillip and Elisabetha Manchen at Zion Church on Jan. 30, 1774.

ADDITION - Page 76/77

Schmidt - Carl was a signer to a petition for a school on Sept. 17, 1762, according to records of Zion Church in Baltimore (now Carroll) Co., Manchester, MD. He and his wife were alive on Nov. 13, 1766, when they acted as sponsors to the baptism of Anna, dau. of Nicholas and Anna Elisabeth (Noll) Schlotthauer, at Zion's Church. The following additional information on their children is recorded at Zion Church in Manchester, MD:
 - Matthaus was b. about 1742. He and his wife, Anna Margaretha,

had the following children (in addition to those previously mentioned):
- Anna Barbara, b. Jan. 12, 1764, bapt. on Ascension Day, 1765, and spon. by Johan Jacob Faubel, Anna Barbara Hopmann, and Anna Barbara Schmidt.
- Maria Magdalena, bapt. on Dec. 27, 1766, and spon. by Antony and Maria Magdalena Noll.
- Michael, b. about 1744, and m. Anna Maria. He d. before Sept. 14, 1766, when his widow had the following child bapt.:
  - Michael, b. Aug. 27, 1766, and bapt. Sept. 14, 1766.
- Anna, b. about 1746, was a sponsor to the baptism of Johan George Schaefer on June 17, 1764. She m. Daniel Lang about 1765, and had the following children:
  - Johann Antonius, b. Aug. 18, 1766, bapt. Sept. 14, 1766, and spon. by Johann Anton and Maria Magdalena Noll.
  - Anna Maria, b. Apr. 31, 1770, bapt. June 24, 1770, and spon. by Matthaus and Margaretha Schmidt.
- Anna Barbara, b. about 1748, and was a sponsor to the baptism of Anna Barbara Schmidt in 1765.
- Johann Anton, bapt. Apr. 2, 1762, and spon. by Anton and Maria Magdalena Noll.

ADDITION - Page 86

Trorbach - Michael, son of Wilhelm and Margaretha (Veipers) Trorbach, was bapt. at Kleinich Rheinland, Pfalz, on Mar. 31, 1709, m. Maria Elisabetha, dau. of Hans Adam Herrman, at Sohren, Germany on Apr. 20, 1723, and immigrated to America on the ship *Patience* on Sept. 9, 1751. He d. in York Co. in October 1771.

ADDITION - Page 87

Trorbach - Jacob and Nicholas, sons of Michael Trorbach, were taxed in York (now Adams) Co., Huntingdon Township, PA, in 1762.

Trorbach - Wilhelm moved to VA sometime after 1770, when he acted as exec. for his bro. Adam's will. He was taxed in Rockingham Co. in 1788, and had 291 acres in 1789. He had the following children:
- William C., b. in 1771, and was a confirmant at Trorbach's Church on May 20, 1804.
- Jacob, b. about 1773.
- Michael, b. about 1775.
- Adam, b. about 1778, m. Catherine Pence in Rockingham Co., VA,

on Dec. 3, 1799/Jan. 1, 1800. He appeared on a list of muster fines for the 58th Rockingham Regiment of the Militia in 1816.
- John, b. about 1783, m. Elisal Tafelmeier in May 1806.
- Mary, b. in 1785, and was a confirmant at Trorbach's Church on May 20, 1804. She m. John Wedig/Werdict on Nov. 6, 1801.
- Anna, b. in 1786, and was a confirmant at Trorbach's Church on May 20, 1804.
- Henry, b. about 1788, m. Eve Noll in Aug. 1809.
- Barbara, b. about 1791, m. Frederick Kessler in Rockingham Co. on May 12, 1812.

CORRECTION (see BNK) - Page 105

Fink - Christina Margaretha, dau. of Johann Nickel Fink (tailor at Kusel), m. Johann Henrich, son of Johann Ludwig Walter (clothmaker of Herborn), at Kusel on Oct. 25, 1735. Henrich was a clothmaker, and immigrated to America on the ship *Glasgow* in 1738. Henrich and Christina had the following children at Kusel:
- Maria Elisabetha, b. Sept. 30, 1736.
- Anna Maria, b. Jan. 19, 1738.

ADDITION - Page 113/114

Gansert - Andreas had the following daus. (bapt. at Muddy Creek Lutheran Church in Lancaster Co., East Cocalico Township, PA):
- Anna Maria Margaretha, b. Jan. 29, 1747.
- Margaretha Barbara, b. Mar. 12, 1749.

CORRECTION - Page 153

Quickel - Anna Maria, b. in 1768, m. Phillip, son of Phillip and Juliana (Wintermeyer), Gentzler. It should also be noted that she is the dau. of Michael and Anna M. (Freytag) Quickel, and granddau. of Michael and Barbara Quickel.

ADDITION AND CORRECTION - Page 201

Gentzler - Conrad was naturalized on Mar. 22, 1761. He may have had two or more marriages. The following information can be added to his children (see research of Stella Cansler Haggerty):
- Phillip W., was naturalized in York Co. on Aug. 20, 1763. The following information can be added to his children:
  - Anna Gertrout (not Catharina) m. Valentine Cline. Phillip's will, or transcripts of his will, mistakenly name his dau. Catherine Cline. Gertrout d. in Lincoln Co., NC, in July 1822.

- Maria Catharina (Katie), m. John Finger, and Gerhard Georg Gerding on Mar. 14, 1804, after her sister Mary's death.
- John, m. Barbara Rudisill, and d. on Sept. 28, 1828.
- Phillip, b. May 2, 1766, m. Anna Maria, dau. of Michael and Anna M. (Freytag) Quickel, in Lincoln Co., NC, on June 12, 1790, and d. in Lincoln Co., NC, on Feb. 29, 1854.
- Mary, m. Gerhard George Gerding, and d. between 1801 and 1804.
- Georg, b. Jan. 31, 1770, m. Magdalena or Margaret, dau. of Peter Finger, and d. Oct. 2, 1830.
- Barbara, m. Henry Troutman and William Wiles.
- Conrad, d. in Monroe Co., TN, in 1846.
- Elisabeth, b. in 1778, and resided in the home of Walter Douglas in Alexander Co., NC, in 1850. She was of "unsound mind."
- Conrad, was shot and killed in 1776 on his way home after being discharged from his military service in the Revolutionary War.

ADDITION - Page 238

Miller - Hans Jacob was b. to Hans and ____ (Schneider) Miller in 1628, and m. Vrenilli Gubleman. This information comes from David Sprinckle of AL. However, a query from *Mennonite Family History* (Jan. 1994) indicates that Jacob Jr. was b. in Friedenstadt, Germany, in 1663 to Hans Jacob and Tryne (Meili) Muller (also noted: a Martin Meili (b. in Duhren, Germany, in 1665) m. Anna Rutgen, and arrived on the *Maria Hope*) (these families were Mennonite):
- Rudliffe, b. in 1658. He m. Barbara, and d. in Lancaster Co., Conestoga Township, PA, in 1732. Rudliffe's wife d. sometime after that date. In 1719 Rudliffe was listed as an English settler in Conestoga Township. In 1720 he is listed as Rudith Miller (and son); in 1721, on the English assessments as Rudy; in 1722 as Ralph (and son); in 1724 as Rudall (and son); and in 1725/26 as Rudy (and son). His will was written on Nov. 27, 1731, and probated on Feb. 1, 1732. Perhaps Barbara is the Bru Miller whose estate was filed at Lancaster in 1740. Rudliffe and Barbara had the following children:
- Henry, b. about 1696, and was taxed in Conestoga in 1719, 1721, 1722, 1724, 1725, and 1726. Letters of administration were granted to his widow, Barbary Miller, in Chester Co., PA, on Mar. 9, 1727/28.
- Jacob, b. about 1698 (possibly the Jacob whose estate was filed in Lancaster Co. in 1737).
- Anna Margaretha, b. about 1700, and m. Michael Sprinckel (see

entry). He was taxed in Conestoga Township in 1724 and 1726.
- Hans Jacob, b. on Mar. 20, 1663. He m. Magdalena on Apr. 2, 1693. He immigrated to America from Durnten, Gruningen district, Switzerland, on the ship *Maria Hope* from London on June 29, 1710, and arrived at Philadelphia in Oct. 1710. In 1710 he had 1,000 acres surveyed in the Pequea Valley (+ 6% for roads). He was taxed in Lancaster Co., Conestoga Township in 1718; as Jacob and son in 1719; and as Jacob Elder in 1725. He was naturalized in 1717. He d. on Apr. 20, 1739, and is bur. in Tchantz Graveyard. His estate was filed in Lancaster Co. in 1740. They had the following children:
  - Hance, b. about 1796, and taxed in Conestoga in 1718 and 1719.
  - Martin, b. in 1699, and was taxed in Conestoga in 1719, 1725, and 1726. He was naturalized in 1717, and his estate was filed in Lancaster Co. in 1743.
  - Michael, b. about 1700, m. Barbara. He may be the Michael Miller that resided in York Co. on Oct. 16, 1727. His will was written on Mar. 23, 1737, and probated on Aug. 26, 1739. He was taxed in Conestoga in 1718, 1719, 1720, 1721, 1724, 1725, and 1726. In May 1718 he had 1,200 acres on the northwest side of the Conestoga River. His will was probated in Lancaster Co. in 1739. He had the following children:
    - Jacob.
  - Jacob, b. in 1702. He was taxed in 1719 as a freeman with his father; Jacob Jr. in 1720, 1724, 1725, and 1726. He was naturalized in 1717. On Nov. 19, 1754, Jacob deeded 100 acres (part of a 1,000 acre patent to Jacob Miller on June 30, 1711) to his son, Martin in Strasburg Township. This land was adjacent to Jacob Miller, Jr., Amos Strettell, and Jacob Miller. He m. Catharina and had the following children:
    - Jacob.
    - Martin, b. in Switzerland about 1720, m. Margareth Neff, and d. in Strasburg Township between Jan. 7 and Mar. 15, 1773 (will dates). On Dec. 1, 1744, Jacob and Catherine Miller deeded 100 acres in Strasburg Township to Martin that was part of the 150 acres that had been granted to them on Apr. 29/30, 1731.

CORRECTION - Page 315

Haman (Homan) - Michael was taxed in Shrewsbury Township in 1762. He received a warrant for 100 acres on June 1, 1762, that was surveyed as 188 acres on June 2, 1755. His will was written in Shrewsbury Township on Jan. 11, 1765, and probated on Jan. 3, 1769.

It was executed by his widow and Michael Kleinfelter. He m. Elisabeth and had the following children (other children were mentioned, but not named in the will):
- Godleap.

ADDITION - Page 317

Kleinfelter - Hans Peter, son of Hans Jorg and Margaretha Kleinfelter, was b. in Floersbach, Hesse, on Apr. 2, 1702. Hans Jorg was b. about 1673 (1678), and m. Margaretha Rheinhardt of Mittlesinn, Bavaria, in 1693. She was b. about 1672. Hans Jorg was Prince Forest Ranger and Game Warden at Floersbach, Germany, and d. there on Jan. 8, 1743. Margaretha d. in 1749.

CODORUS TOWNSHIP

Amspacher (Hamspacher) - Johan Georg was b. in Kolbering, Germany. He m. Anna Barbara, dau. of Melchior Reppert of Bonfeld, on Jan. 30, 1720. They immigrated to America on the ship *William and Sarah* in 1727. He received a warrant for 150 acres in Manchester Township on Oct. 30, 1736 (Blunston License), that was assigned to Georg Ness on Feb. 11, 1744. They had the following children at Eppingen (see EEB):
- Anton, b. on Nov. 16, 1720.
- Anna Margaretha, b. on Nov. 7, 1721, and m. Johan Georg Ziegler on Jan. 17, 1738 (see entry in Manchester section).
- Anna Barbara, b. on May 30, 1723.
- Johan Georg Stephen, b. on Apr. 5, 1725.
- Maria Elisabetha, b. about 1732, and was a sponsor to the baptism of Johan Adam Fissel in 1756.
- Anna Catharina, b. on Sept. 27, 1734, bapt. at CLY on Apr. 1, 1735, and spon. by Anna Maria Schmidt.
- Susanna, b. on Sept. 5, 1736, bapt. at CLY in Nov. 1736, and spon. by Reinhardt and Susanna Hammer.
- Johan Georg, b. on Sept. 28, 1738, bapt. at CLY on Nov. 12, 1738, and spon. by Johan Georg and Margaretha Ziegler. He m. Catharina, dau. of Hans Martin and Maria Eva Merckel (see entry in Shrewsbury section). They had the following children (recorded at FRI):
  - Christina, b. on July 9, 1767, bapt. on Aug. 2, 1767, and spon. by Michael Gerberich and Margareta Hess.
  - Johann Heinrich, b. on Aug. 26, 1771, bapt. on Sept. 28, 1771, and spon. by Heinrich and Juliana Merckel.
- Maria Eva, b. on July 26, 1740, bapt. at CLY on Sept. 18, 1740, and spon. by Valentin and Maria Eva Schultz. She m. Georg Wampler, and had the following children:
  - Johan Georg, bapt. by RJL on Apr. 23, 1758, and spon. by Georg Ernst and Eva Meyer.
  - Maria Catharina, b. on Aug. 17, 1760, and bapt. at CLY on Aug. 24, 1760.
  - Elizabeth, b. on June 19, 1762, bapt. at TLY on June 19, 1762, and spon. by Nicholas Schaeffer and wife.
  - Jacob, b. on Jan. 12, 1769, and bapt. at CLY on Jan. 29, 1769.
  - Christina, b. on Sept. 7, 1771, and bapt. at CLY on Sept. 22, 1771.
  - Margaretha, b. on Feb. 27, 1774, bapt. at TLY on Apr. 10, 1774, and spon. by Ludwig Fridlein and wife.
  - Infant, b. on July 27, 1776, bapt. at TLY on Aug. 24, 1777, and spon. by Gottfried Gruber and wife.

- Maria Magdalena, b. on Mar. 8, 1744, and bapt. at CLY on Mar. 17, 1744.

Amspacher (Hamspacher) - Tobias received a warrant for 200 acres in North Codorus Township on Sept. 20, 1762. He also received a warrant for 50 acres in North Codorus Township on Mar. 9, 1753, that was surveyed as 84.80 acres on Mar. 9, 1754, and 84.80 acres on Mar. 29, 1750. He had the following children:
- Elisabeth, b. about 1710, and m. Jacob Rudisill about 1731 (see entry in Manchester section).
- Rebecca, b. about 1720, and m. Carl Eisen in the Codorus region on Apr. 29, 1740 (recorded by JCS). She was a sponsor with her father to the baptism of Eleanora Hearken in 1740 (CLY).
- Tobias, b. about 1722, m. Sara, and had the following children:
  - Elisabeth, bapt. by RJL on Dec. 8, 1745, and spon. by Jacob and Elisabeth Rudisill.
  - Samuel, b. on June 14, 1768, and bapt. at CLY on June 11, 1769.

Apfelman (Eppleman) - Johann received a warrant for 50 acres in North Codorus Township on Nov. 28, 1750, that was surveyed as 111 acres to John Hileman (see entry) on Jan. 18, 1754. His will was written in Paradise Township on Jan. 11, 1786, and probated on Feb. 25, 1786. He m. Anna Margaretha, dau. of Heinrich Bott (see entry in Manchester section), at CLY on Nov. 4, 1751, and had the following children:
- Magdalena Margareth, bapt. by RJL on Aug. 23, 1752, and spon. by Anton and Anna Margareth Mahl.
- Philip Ludwig, b. on Mar. 1, 1754, and bapt. at CLY on June 2, 1754.
- Catharina Elisabeth, bapt. by RJL on Feb. 1, 1756, and spon. by Peter and Catharina Elisabeth Wolff.
- Anna Christina, b. in Mar. 1760, bapt. at WOL, and spon. by Peter and Maria Magdalena Mohr.
- Johannes, bapt. by RJL on June 6, 1762, and spon. by Johannes and Catharina Bott.
- Johann Henrich, b. on Aug. 15, 1764, bapt. at WOL on Sept. 9, 1764, and spon. by the grandparents, Johann Henrich and Anna Catharina Bott.
- Conrad
- Jacob
- Katherine, probably the Catherine, who m. John Closs at TLY on May 11, 1794.

CODORUS TOWNSHIP

Aumuller - George warranted 150 acres in Codorus/Manheim Township on Mar. 2, 1768. He m. Elisabetha Margaretha, and had the following children:
- Johan Georg, bapt. by RJL on June 20, 1762, and spon. by Johan Georg and Elisabeth DeHoff.
- Son, b. on Jan. 12, 1767, and bapt. at STJ on Mar. 25, 1767.

Baer - Jacob was taxed in 1762. He warranted 150 acres in Codorus/Manheim Township on Feb. 26, 1773. He also received a warrant for 50 acres in 1749, and 65 acres on Dec. 16, 1758. His probate inventory was filed in 1782. He m. Anna Maria, and had the following children:
- Anna Margaretha, b. on June 2, 1754, and bapt. at CLY on Sept. 8, 1754.
- Georg Jacob, bapt. by RJL on Sept. 1, 1756, and spon. by Michael and Maria Peterman. He m. Christina about 1785.
- Daniel, b. on Sept. 9, 1756, and d. on Mar. 31, 1837. He is bur. at STJ.
- Anna Elisabetha, bapt. by RJL on May 22, 1763, and spon. by Johan Michael and Anna Elisabetha Bricker.
- Johannes, b. on Apr. 23, 1766, and bapt. at STJ He m. Catharina about 1797.
- Johan Georg, b. on Apr. 12, 1773, and bapt. at STJ on May 9, 1773. He m. Margaretha about 1793.

Bartemess - Adam received a warrant for 50 acres in North Codorus Township on Jan. 27, 1757, that was surveyed as 31.80 acres on Mar. 16, 1757 (see entry in Dover section).

Bauman - Johann m. Maria Barbara. He received a warrant for 100 acres on Mar. 20, 1767, that was surveyed as 98.51 acres called *Broad Valley* on Apr. 17, 1767. He also received a warrant for 50 acres on Apr. 6, 1768, that was surveyed as 25.92 acres called *Broad Hallow* on Dec. 19, 1768. His will was probated on Aug. 17, 1799. He had the following children:
- Johannes.
- Elisabeth, b. on May 13, 1757, and m. Henrich, son of Ulrich and Ursula Hess (see entry in Shrewsbury Township section).
- Anna Maria, b. on Oct. 28, 1759, d. on May 3, 1821, and is bur. in Friedensaal cemetery. She m. Abraham, son of Andreas and Anna Margaretha Swartz (see entry in Shrewsbury section). Anna Maria's will written on Mar. 21, 1818, and probated on Feb. 12, 1821. It named her sister, Eve (deceased), and her sister's daus., Elizabeth, wife of Josophine Young, Catharina, Eve, Barbara, and Christina Bop.

- Eve, m. Bernhard Bopp (see entry in Shrewsbury section).
- Heinrich.
- Johan Jacob, b. on June 22, 1772, bapt. at FRI on July 5, 1772, and spon. by Johan Jacob and Anna Sophia Heibel.

Becker - Adolphus, was the son of William (d. 1785 York Township) and Christina Becker. His probate inventory was filed in Codorus Township in 1769. He m. Christina Barbara, and had the following children:
- Catharina Dorothea, b. on May 12, 1763, and bapt. at CLY on May 12, 1763.
- Anna.

Becker - Wilhelm was taxed in Codorus Township in 1779. He received a warrant for 50 acres in Codorus Township on Apr. 22, 1767, that was surveyed as 49 acres called *Gun Powder Springs* on Apr. 20, 1779. He m. Anna Catharina. He and had the following children (recorded at STJ (except the first)):
- Johan Wilhelm, was b. about 1758, and was taxed in Codorus Township in 1779.
- Johan Jacob, b. on Nov. 22, 1764, and bapt. on Apr. 4, 1765.
- Johann Peter, b. on Mar. 27, 1767, and bapt. on June 21, 1767.
- Christian, b. on May 4, 1769, and bapt. on July 30, 1769.
- Johannes, b. on Jan. 10, 1772, and bapt. on May 7, 1772.

Behler - Jacob was taxed in 1762. He is probably the Jacob Pegler that received a warrant for 50 acres in North Codorus Township on Apr. 4, 1754, that was surveyed as 62 acres on Dec. 1, 1753. He served in Captain John Myer's Company in the Revolutionary War (1778). He m. Eva Maria, and had the following children:
- Maria Margaretha, bapt. by RJL on Oct. 6, 1754, and spon. by Ulrich and Maria Margaretha Vollenweiller.
- Anna Christina, bapt. by RJL on June 26, 1760, and spon. by Johan Christoph and Anna Margaretha Gray.
- Christian, bapt. by RJL on Feb. 27, 1763, and spon. by Christian and Elisabetha Fass.
- Johan Jacob, bapt. by RJL on Sept. 6, 1765, and spon. by Jacob and Anna Maria Barr. He m. Catharina, dau. of Jacob and Anna Maria Runkle, about 1781. He served in the Revolutionary War in Captain John Myer's Company (1778).
- Johan Martin, b. on Mar. 12, 1771, and bapt. at STJ on Apr. 6, 1771.
- Johan Georg, bapt. at STJ on Feb. 27, 1774.
- Johannes, b. on June 4, 1779, and bapt. at STJ on June 20, 1779.

CODORUS TOWNSHIP 5

Behler - Michael received a warrant for 50 acres on May 19, 1774 that was surveyed as 36 acres on Oct. 13, 1774. He also warranted 200 acres on Oct. 3, 1767, that was surveyed as 101.80 acres called *Chestnut Grove* on Mar. 6, 1768 (patented on Jan. 19, 1790). He warranted 50 acres on Dec. 4, 1764, that was surveyed as 94.138 acres on May 13, 1766, and 50 acres on May 14, 1767.

Bernard - Balser was taxed in 1762.

Binckele - Peter was taxed in 1762. He was b. in Kuckischberg, Canton Berne, Switzerland, on Mar. 2, 1704, and m. Maria Werle on Feb. 2, 1723 and Anna Margaretha Geiger on Feb. 3, 1749. Maria was b. in Steinthal, Alsace on Oct. 28, 1704. Anna Margaretha was b. in Entz, Wurtemberg on Jan. 18, 1722, and had a child, Johannes Werner (see entry), on Sept. 20, 1746. Peter received a warrant for 150 acres in North Codorus Township on Sept. 10, 1750, that was surveyed as 274 acres (no date), 16 acres (no date), and 142 acres on June 11, 1822. He ?(John) received a warrant for 100 acres in North Codorus Township on Dec. 18, 1751, that was surveyed as 224 acres on Oct. 23, 1752. Peter had the following children (recorded at FMY):
- Maria, b. on Dec. 26, 1725.
- Catharina, b. on Mar. 25, 1727.
- Peter, b. on June 25, 1728, and d. before 1753.
- Christian, b. on Sept. 27, 1729, and d. before 1751.
- Anna, b. on June 26, 1731.
- Sarah, b. on Feb. 24, 1733.
- Margaretha, b. on July 24, 1735.
- Christiana, b. on Feb. 21, 1738, m. ____ Fischer, and resided in Wachau, North Carolina.
- Elisabetha, b. on Feb. 16, 1740, and d. before 1749.
- Anna Barbara, b. on May 26, 1741.
- Johannes, b. on Mar. 15, 1741, and bapt. on Mar. 26, 1741.
- Johan Adam, b. on Aug. 2, 1744, and bapt. on Aug. 13, 1744.
- Infant (twin), b. on Sept. 1, 1745, and d. unbaptized.
- Infant, b. on Sept. 1, 1745, and d. unbaptized.
- Elisabetha, b. on Dec. 8, 1749, and m. ____ Herbach.
- Christian, b. on Jan. 28, 1751.
- Johan Peter, b. on Jan. 30, 1753, bapt. at FMY on Feb. 1, 1753, and spon. by Frederick Rohmer, Adam Hoff, Jacob Christman, John Beitzel, and John and Daniel Heckedorn.
- Anna Maria, b. on Feb. 22, 1755.
- Frederick, b. on Nov. 4, 1757.
- Joseph, b. on July 9, 1761, bapt. at FMCY on July 11, 1761, and spon. by Melchior Schmidt, Peter Feiser, and Ludwig Brotzman.

Bischoff - Matthaus was an innkeeper of the Lowen Inn, in Wallhalben, Germany, and m. Anna Barbara. They immigrated to America on the ship *Two Brothers* in 1747, and had the following children (recorded at Wallhalben Lutheran Church (see BWP)):
- Johannes, b. on June 30, 1720, and d. in 1725.
- Johan Velten, b. on Jan. 10, 1723.
- Frantz Michael was taxed in 1762. He was naturalized on Apr. 10, 1760. He was b. on Sept. 17, 1724, and m. Anna Elisabeth, dau. of Heinrich Schmidt (see entry), before 1760 (sponsors at the baptism of Johan Philliph Stambach), and had the following children:
  - Anna Catharina, bapt. by RJL on Apr. 2, 1763, and spon. by Johannes and Anna Catharina Schultz.
- Johan Jacob, b. on May 25, 1727.

Bollinger - Isaac's will was written in Codorus Township on Apr. 1, 1770, and probated in 1770. He m. Catherine, and had the following son:
- Frederick.

Bollinger - Jacob received a warrant for 50 acres in North Codorus Township on Sept. 6, 1749, and 70 acres on Feb. 18, 1773 (interest began Mar. 1, 1761), that was surveyed as 112.71 acres called *Acorn Hill* on Mar. 20, 1773. He also warranted 150 acres in Heidelberg and North Codorus Township on Dec. 6, 1766, that was surveyed as 160.81 acres called *Addition* on Jan. 23, 1767. His probate inventory was filed in Manheim Township in 1777 (will written on May 31, 1777). He m. Anna Maria. Her will was written in Manheim Township on July 15, 1780, and her probate inventory was filed in 1781. They had the following children:
- Abraham served in Captain John Myer's Company during the Revolutionary War (1778). He m. Elisabeth, dau. of Peter Runk (see entry), before 1773.
- Johan Jacob, b. on Feb. 20, 1755, m. Anna Maria, dau. of John and Elisabeth (Wanner) Hershey, on Aug. 29, 1780, and d. on Aug. 11, 1821. She was b. on Nov. 1, 1762, and d. on Apr. 18, 1846.
- Christian, m. Maria Margaretha, dau. of Peter Runk (see entry), before 1789.
- Michael, m. Catherine before 1781.
- Catherine.
- Maria Eva, b. on Sept. 16, 1753, and m. Jost, son of Peter Runk (see entry).

Bombariere - John received a MD warrant for 200 acres in Heidelberg, Jackson, and North Codorus Township on Feb. 22, 1733 (surveyed to Andrew Hershey with his acreage on Mar. 2, 1733).

Bortner - Balthasar was b. in Oberhockstadt, Germany, in 1698, and confirmed at Niederhochstadt in 1710. He d. in Berks Co., Tulpehocken Township, PA, in 1748. He immigrated to America on the ship *Adventure* and arrived in Philadelphia on Sept. 23, 1732. He m. Maria Elisabetha, who was b. in 1695, and d. about 1750. They were the parents of the following children:
- Johan Jacob, b. in 1722, bapt. at Niederhochstadt on Aug. 10, 1731, and spon. by Jacob Sauter and Apollonia Meyer. He m. Sara Balt, and resided in Berks Co., Tulpehocken Township, PA.
- Hanna Mela, b. in 1724.
- Anna Barbara, b. about 1727. She m. Henry Kann in Berks Co., Tulpehocken Township, PA, on Feb. 17, 1748 (see entry in Dover section).
- Georg was taxed in 1762. He was b. in Oberhockstadt in 1732. He m. Maria Appolonia Floucher, who was b. in 1731. Georg d. in 1801. They lived in York Co., Codorus Township, PA, where they had the following children:
  - Christina, b. Dec. 22, 1759. She was bapt. at St. Jacob's about 1759, and m. Abraham, son of Michael Hassler (see entry), about 1782. Abraham was b. on Oct. 4, 1761, and d. on May 17, 1803. Christina d. in Morrow Co., OH, and is bur. in St. John's Evangelical Lutheran cemetery.
  - Johan Georg, b. on Feb. 6, 1761, bapt. by Reverend Jacob Lischy on Mar. 1, 1761, and spon. by Georg and Elisabeth Gaumuller. He m. Margaretha, dau. of Franz Heinrich and Anna Margaretha (Ruhl) Gans (see entry), in York Co., PA, on Jan. 3, 1785. Georg d. in Codorus Township (Bonnaire, PA) on Apr. 8, 1843, and Margaretha on Jan. 17, 1842. They are bur. in Fissel's cemetery. Georg purchased land in Codorus Township from John Gerberich on Oct. 11, 1785. He later sold this land to Abraham Hassler on Mar. 14, 1788.
  - Ludwig, b. on May 15, 1762. He was bapt. by Reverend Jacob Lischy on June 20, 1762, and spon. by Ludwig and Anna Catharina Krebs. He m. Elisabetha Margaretha, dau. of Franz Heinrich and Anna Margaretha (Ruhl) Gans (see entry), about 1783. Ludwig d. in Codorus Township on Dec. 12, 1815, and Elisabetha d. there on Sept. 15, 1820. Ludwig is bur. at St. Jacob's. Ludwig patented a 54.38 acre tract and a 82 acre tract in Codorus Township on Dec. 22, 1809. He patented a 67.80 acre tract in the same Township on Dec. 20, 1809. On Apr. 4, 1806, he purchased 53. 109 acres from Jacob and Catharine Hassler.
  - Maria Catharina, bapt. by Reverend Jacob Lischy on Feb. 24, 1765, and spon. by Michael and Maria Catharina Schultz.
  - Maria Elisabetha, b. about 1766, and bapt. at St. Jacob's on Oct. 5, 1766.

- Johannes, b. in 1768. He m. Julianna, dau. of Franz Heinrich and Anna Margaretha (Ruhl) Gans (see entry), at York Co., St. Matthew's Lutheran Church on Nov. 16, 1790. Johannes d. in York Co. in 1859. Julianna d. there on June 27, 1824.
- Johann Peter, b. on June 3, 1770, and was bapt. at St. Jacob's on June 19, 1770. He m. Elisabeth.
- Michael, b. on Nov. 20, 1780, and d. in Shrewsbury Township on Oct. 21, 1870. He m. Margaret Markle.
- Peter, b. in Berks Co. in 1734.
- Maria Elisabeth, b. in Berks Co. on Mar. 8, 1738, bapt. at Little Tulpehocken on Apr. 30, 1738, and spon. by Johan Wilhelm Leitner and wife.

Brillhardt - Peter was taxed in 1762. He received a warrant for 200 acres on Jan. 16, 1747 that was patented as 331.5 acres on Sept. 16, 1773. He also received a warrant for 100 acres on Mar. 22, 1775 (interest began on Mar. 1, 1750). His will was written on May 25, 1782, and probated on Oct. 16, 1782. He m. Ottilia. They were sponsors to the baptism of Christina Bunckely at the First Reformed Congregation in Lancaster in 1738. They had the following children:
- Peter, b. about 1737. He received a warrant for 300 acres in Springfield Township on Jan. 14, 1767, that was surveyed as 261.3 acres called *High Land* on Aug. 9, 1767, and patented on August 11, 1787. He received a warrant for 50 acres in Springfield Township on Aug. 6, 1753, and 150 acres on June 1, 1767, that were surveyed as 262 acres called *Red Spring* on Oct. 22, 1767 (patented to Peter Brillhart, Jr., on Aug. 11, 1787). He received a warrant for 60 acres in Shrewsbury Township on Mar. 23, 1775. He m. Cary, dau. of John Myer of York, before 1757 (see entry). His will was written in Shrewsbury Township on Dec. 25, 1801, and probated on Apr. 23, 1804.
- Elisabeth, b. about 1741, m. Samuel, son of John Bixler of Manheim Township. He was taxed in Heidelberg Township in 1779.
- Maria, b. about 1743, and m. Joseph Grabell.
- Eve, b. about 1745, and m. Samuel Flickinger, son of Andrew Flickinger of Manheim Township. His will was written in Heidelberg Township on Sept. 9, 1816, and probated on Dec. 9, 1816. He was taxed in Manheim Township in 1779.
- John, b. about 1747. He was taxed in Heidelberg Township in 1779.
- Anna, b. about 1749.
- Barbara, b. about 1751, and m. Benjamin Yount.
- Jacob, b. about 1754. He was taxed as a single man in Codorus Township in 1779. He received a warrant for 15 acres in Springfield Township on Apr. 21, 1772, that was surveyed as 20.6 acres on Mar. 23, 1792. His will was written in Shrewsbury

Township on Feb. 7, 1811, and probated on May 16, 1811. He m. Margaret.
- Christian, b. about 1756.

Brodbeck - Heinrich was taxed in 1762. He warranted 87 acres in Codorus/Manheim Township on June 3, 1767, 50 acres in Codorus Township on May 16, 1769, and 150 acres in Codorus Township on May 30, 1768. He m. Eva, and had the following children:
- Anna Helena, b. about 1745 (a sponsor in 1760).
- Johannes, b. about 1748, and m. Anna Margaretha (he was a sponsor in 1763) about 1773. His will was written in Manheim Township on Jan. 12, 1796, and probated on Apr. 18, 1801.
- Elisabetha, b. about 1750 (a sponsor in 1763).
- Anna Barbara, bapt. by RJL on June 16, 1753, and spon. by Jacob and Anna Barbara Hubman.
- Melcher, bapt. by RJL on Jan. 29, 1756, and spon. by Melcher and Ursula Werner.
- Matthias, b. on Jan. 27, 1760, and bapt. at STJ. He m. Maria Catharina, dau. of Georg Keller (see entry). She d. in Manheim Township on May 15, 1840, and is bur. at STJ.

Brotzman (Protzman) - Ludwig was taxed in 1762. He was b. in Wittgenborn in the Domain of Wachtersbach, Germany, on Mar. 26, 1718, and immigrated to America in 1750. He was taken into the Moravian Church at York on Mar. 5, 1752, and first communed on May 4, 1753. On Apr. 17, 1764, he moved to Frederick Co., Monocacy, MD, and joined the Moravian Congregation there. He d. of Jaundice on Apr. 5, 1778, and was bur. in the Moravian Churchyard on Apr. 7, 1778. He m. Anna Maria Heylmann in Hasseldorf in Wachterspach in 1746. She was b. on Sept. 23, 1723. They had the following children:
- Anna Maria, b. on Aug. 17, 1747.
- Johannes, b. on Feb. 26, 1749, and d. in Monocacy, MD, on Mar. 12, 1811 (bur. in the churchyard on Mar. 13, 1811).
- Johan Lorentz, b. on Aug. 4, 1751, m. Elisabeth, and resided in Monocacy, MD.
- Johan Ludwig, b. on Dec. 10, 1753, and m. Maria Elisabeth, dau. of Martin and Sarah Rauser, in 1787. She was b. on Feb. 22, 1772, bapt. on Oct. 8, 1794, and d. of ardent nerve fever on Aug. 29, 1809 (bur. on Aug. 30, 1809). Ludwig was a shoemaker.
- Gertrude, b. on Mar. 21, 1756, and m. Johan Ludwig Moller.
- Justina, b. on Nov. 28, 1756.
- Johan Henrich, b. on June 1, 1764, and bapt. on June 3, 1764.

Brotzman - Lorentz was b. in Witgenborn, Waechtersbach, Germany, in July 1721. He moved from York Co. to Frederick Co., Monocacy,

MD, before Oct. 8, 1758, when he was a communicant in MD, and d. on
Dec. 9, 1767 (bur. in the Monocacy Churchyard). He m. Maria
Elisabetha, dau. of Philip Hoehns (see entry). She was b. in Cassel,
Zweibrucken, Germany, in Feb. 1726, immigrated to America in 1738,
and d. on May 2, 1806 (bur. in the Monocacy Churchyard on May 4,
1806). They had the following children:
- Jacob, b. about 1747, m. Johanna, dau. of Frederick and Elisabeth
  Leinbach, on May 10, 1768, and resided in Frederick Co.,
  Monocacy, MD.
- Daniel, b. in York Co. on Nov. 16, 1749, m. Gertrude Baumgartner
  in Lancaster, PA, on Nov. 26, 1780, and Maria Buhler, widow of
  ___ Spieker, after 1789. Gertrude was b. in Lancaster Co., PA, on
  June 22, 1752, moved to Lilitz in 1763, Bethlehem 1773, and
  returned to Lancaster before her marriage. She d. of childbed fever
  on Apr. 27, 1789, and was bur. in the Monocacy Churchyard on
  Apr. 30, 1789.
- Anna Margaretha, b. on Jan. 11, 1754, m. John Williard, and d. on
  Mar. 3, 1844.

Christy - Hans warranted 50 acres in Codorus Township on Apr. 25,
1747. Hans and Anna Christie were sponsors at the baptism on
Heinrich Jaeger at TLY in 1745.

Danner - Henry received a warrant for 150 acres in Heidelberg and
North Codorus Township, that was surveyed as 175.127 acres called
Grevious Valley on Jan. 19, 1767.

Danner - Michael received a warrant for 280 acres in Codorus and
Manheim Townships on June 2, 1762, that was surveyed as 259.56
acres on June 6, 1767 (interest began on Mar. 1, 1755).

DeHoff - Heinrich wrote his will in Manchester Township on Mar. 28,
1785, and it was probated on July 27, 1785. He m. Anna Maria, and
had the following children:
- Anna Maria, bapt. at the First Reformed Congregation at
  Lancaster on Dec. 15, 1745, and spon. by Lorentz and Anna Maria
  Weber. She m. Nicholas Weyant, and had the following children:
  - Frederick, b. on Feb. 2, 1781, and bapt. at CLY on Mar. 18, 1781.
  - Jacob, b. on July 31, 1784, and bapt. at CLY on Sept. 26, 1784.
- Johan Georg, b. on Sept. 8, 1733. He was taxed in 1762. He was
  warranted land in Codorus Township on Aug. 28, 1766 (surveyed as
  93 acres and 11 perches called *Court House Ridge* on Nov. 13,
  1766), and 50 acres on May 31, 1762 (surveyed as 98.62 acres
  called *Nimble and Quick* on Nov. 13, 1766). His will was written on
  Aug. 20, 1803, and probated on May 1, 1810. He m. Anna

Elisabetha Kislin. She was b. in Aug. 1732, and d. on Sept. 1, 1805. He d. on Apr. 18, 1810. They are bur. in STJ cemetery. They had the following children:
- Anna Catharina, b. on Mar. 16, 1757, and bapt. at STJ. She m. Samuel Glassick (see entry).
- Susanna, b. about 1758.
- Johan Niclaus, bapt. by RJL on June 1, 1760, and spon. by Johan Niclas DeHoff and Anna Helena Brodbeck.
- Georg Philip, b. about 1763, and m. Margaretha about 1783.
- Johannes, b. on May 7, 1765, and bapt. at STJ on May 27, 1765. He m. Elisabeth.
- Christian, b. on July 27, 1766, and bapt. at STJ on Sept. 5, 1766. He m. Hanna about 1788.
- Johan Jacob, bapt. at STJ on Apr. 2, 1768.
- Elisabetha, b. on Oct. 10, 1769, and bapt. at STJ on Oct. 24, 1769. She m. Abraham Painder.
- Maria Barbara, b. on May 9, 1772, and bapt. at STJ on May 17, 1772. She m. Elias Reinhardt.
- Maria Eva, b. on Nov. 5, 1773, and bapt. at STJ on Nov. 15, 1773.
- Christina, b. about 1775, and m. Jacob Shawer.
- Johan Niclaus, b. on Apr. 14, 1743, bapt. at Trinity Lutheran Church in Lancaster Co. on May 10, 1743, and spon. by Nicholas Muller and wife. He was a sponsor to the baptism of Johan Niclaus DeHoff in 1760. He served in the Revolutionary War in Captain John Myer's Company (1778). He m. Anna Maria, and had the following children (bapt. at STJ):
- Johan Adam, b. on June 9, 1772, and bapt. on June 21, 1722.
- Elisabetha, b. on Jan. 9, 1775, and bapt. on Feb. 5, 1775.
- Anna Maria, b. on Dec. 25, 1776, and bapt. on Jan. 19, 1777.
- Johan Georg, b. on Aug. 23, 1779, and bapt. on Sept. 18, 1779.
- Johan Jacob, b. on Aug. 16, 1782, and bapt. on Oct. 9, 1782.
- Christina, b. on May 11, 1787, and bapt. on May 20, 1787.
- Catharina, b. on May 13, 1791, and bapt. on June 5, 1791.

Detweiler - Martin was taxed in 1762.

Dick - Abraham received a warrant for 150 acres in North Codorus Township on Mar. 7, 1754, and 100 acres in Jackson Township on Mar. 7, 1754, that was surveyed as 105 acres on Feb. 6, 1756. He was taxed in Germany Township in 1762.

Dillman - Jacob received a warrant for 200 acres on May 14, 1767.

Earhart - Johann Peter was b. to Johannes Earhart about 1687. He m. Anna Margarethe, dau. of Nicholas Becker, in Staudennheim on Feb. 3, 1708 and had the following children:
- Johann Heinrich, bapt. at Staudennheim on Nov. 19, 1713, and immigrated to America on the ship *Samuel* on Aug. 27, 1739.
- Maria Elisabeth, bapt. at Staudennheim in the Palatinate on Nov. 30, 1716, and m. Carl Adam Diehl (see entry in Shrewsbury section).
- Maria Christina, bapt. at Staudennheim on Aug. 17, 1721.
- Johan Wilhelm, b. in 1721, and immigrated to America with his uncle, Wilhelm, on the ship *Friendship* on Oct. 12, 1741. He was taxed in 1762. He m. Anna Catarina Schreiner in Lancaster Co., Warwick Township, PA, on Dec. 1, 1746 (JCS). They resided in Shrewsbury Township in July 1766. Wilhelm's will was probated in York Co. on Feb. 27, 1781, and executed by Thomas and Jacob Ehrhardt. Wilhelm and Catharina and had the following children:
  - Thomas, b. on Apr. 24, 1749, and bapt. at Christ's Lutheran Church of York on May 14, 1749. He m. Rosina Michael
  - Johan Peter, b. on May ?, 1751, and bapt. at Christ's Lutheran on June 16, 1751.
  - Eva Elizabeth, b. on Aug. 22, 1753, and bapt. at Christ's Lutheran on Sept. 9, 1753.
  - Johannes, b. about 1755. He m. Margaretha, dau. of Johan David and Anna Catharina (Simon) Schaffer (see entry in Shrewsbury section).
  - Maria Dorothea, b. about 1757. She m. Michael Zech. Michael Zech's will was written in Shrewsbury Township on Oct. 19, 1810, probated on Aug. 30, 1817, and executed by William Zeck and Jacob Falkinstein.
  - Jacob, b. about 1760.
  - Catharina, b. about 1762.

Emig - Johan Philip was taxed in 1762, and received a warrant for 100 acres in North Codorus Township on Jan. 27, 1757, that was surveyed to George Emig and Lawrence Kramer on Oct. 9, 1767. On Jan. 27, 1757, he received a warrant for 60 acres in North Codorus Township (interest began on Mar. 1, 1749/surveyed with son's land in 1767). He m. Anna Maria, dau. of Johann and Margaretha (Adam) Hahn, on Apr. 11, 1724. She was b. in Dannenfels Nassau-Weilburg, Germany, in 1706, and d. at 4 p.m. on Aug. 10, 1762 (obituary at CLY). They immigrated to America in 1743. They had 3 sons and 3 daus., and two of each were alive at the time of her death. They had the following children:
- Johan Philip was taxed in 1762. He received a warrant for 100 acres in North Codorus Township on Mar. 6, 1767 (interest began

on Mar. 1, 1752), that was surveyed with his father's 1757 warrant as 189.80 acres called *Stoney Ridge* on Apr. 7, 1767. He received a warrant for 50 acres in North Codorus Township on Mar. 9, 1775, that was surveyed as 32.110 acres called *Chesty Burgh* on May 24, 1775, and a warrant for 50 acres in North Codorus Township for 50 acres on Mar. 9, 1775, that was surveyed as 66.80 acres called *Green Tree* on May 24, 1775. His will was written on Nov. 14, 1797, and probated on Oct. 25, 1819. He m. Maria Anna, and had the following children:
- Jacob.
- Lorentz.
- Philip.
- Georg Carl, b. on Sept. 17, 1760, and bapt. at CLY on Nov. 2, 1760 (exec. of father's will).
- Johan Michael, b. on Aug. 4, 1762, and bapt. at CLY on Sept. 26, 1762 (did not appear on father's will).
- Johannes.
- Catharina.
- Eva.
- Elisabeth.
- Anna Maria, b. on Apr. 9, 1771, bapt. at FRI on May 9, 1771, and spon. by Jacob and Eva Catharina Folckner.
- Dewald, b. about 1730, m. Susanna Maria, and had the following children:
  - Maria Magdalena, bapt. by RJL on Jan. 1, 1751, and spon. by Dieterich and Magdalena Meyer.
  - Johan Conrad, bapt. by RJL on Apr. 20, 1753, and spon. by Conrad and Catharina Muller.
  - Maria Elisabeth, bapt. by RJL on Feb. 15, 1761, and spon. by Georg Geisselman and Maria Elisabeth Haugin.
  - Johan Philliph, bapt. by RJL on July 31, 1763, and spon. by Philliph Emig and Maria Elisabeth Gecklerin.
- Georg, b. about 1745.

Eppley (Eppli) - Jacob was b. on Apr. 23, 1741. He received a warrant for 50 acres on Oct. 15, 1774, that was surveyed as 53.75 acres on Oct. 12, 1774. He also surveyed 130 acres called *Christianna* on Nov. 11, 1766. He served in the Revolutionary War in Captain John Myer's Company in 1778. He m. Christina before 1767, and Elisabetha about 1774. Elisabetha was b. on May 24, 1755, and d. on Mar. 24, 1835. He d. on Apr. 9, 1820. They are bur. in STJ cemetery. He had the following children:
- Susanna, b. on Aug. 5, 1767, and bapt. at STJ on Oct. 11, 1767.
- Catharina, b. on Dec. 25, 1770, and bapt. at STJ on Apr. 6, 1771.

- Johannes, b. on July 3, 1775, bapt. at STJ on Oct. 1, 1775, and d. on Dec. 30, 1836. He m. Julia Ann Bricker. She was b. on May 10, 1782, and d. on July 18, 1856. They are bur. in STJ cemetery.
- Christina, b. on Jan. 12, 1778, and bapt. at STJ on Apr. 4, 1778.
- Frederick, b. on July 11, 1780, bapt. at ZIE on Oct. 16, 1780, and spon. by Carl Friedrich and Anna Maria Wildbahn.
- Johan Peter, b. on July 14, 1784, bapt. at ZIE on Sept. 19, 1784, and spon. by Peter and Barbara Krebs.
- Elizabeth, b. on Oct. 29, 1786, bapt. at ZIE on Feb. 17, 1787, and spon. by Anton Wild and wife.
- Anna Barbara, b. on Oct. 18, 1790, bapt. at ZIE on Dec. 5, 1790, and spon. by Peter Kerbs and wife.

Eslinger - Johan Georg warranted 56.106 acres on Oct. 31, 1766, and 150 acres on May 16, 1769. He appeared as a sponsor with Veronica Neukommer on the baptism of Johannes Neukommer in 1762 (RJL). He m. Veronica (?possibly Neukommer?), and had the following children (recorded at STJ):
- Maria Magdalena, b. on Oct. 24, 1765, and bapt. on Nov. 30, 1765.
- Anna Maria, b. on Dec. 16, 1767, and bapt. on Dec. 13, 1769.
- Elisabetha, b. on Apr. 13, 1770, and bapt. on Apr. 22, 1770.

Feeser - Wendel was taxed in 1762. He m. Susanna, and they were sponsors at the baptism of Susanna Stambach in 1751, and Susanna Hellman in 1756.

Fissel - Fishbogh was taxed in 1762.

Fissel - Killian was taxed in 1762. He was the son of Killian and Christina Fissel of Paradise Township (see entry in Dover section). He m. Catharina about 1751, and Barbara about 1760. Killian and Barbara were sponsors at the baptism of Catharina Siegrist in 1762 and Barbara Kessler in 1779. His will was written on Jan. 17, 1785, and probated on Feb. 4, 1790. Killian had the following children:
- Anna Elizabeth, bapt. by RJL on June 14, 1752, and spon. by Anna Elisabeth Fissel.
- Heinrich, bapt. by RJL on Sept. 2, 1759, and spon. by Heinrich Beisser and Anna Maria Schmahlin.
- Catherine.
- Adam.
- Margaret.

Frienst (Frensch) - Phillip was taxed in 1762 (this was probably his estate). He m. Maria Magdalena, dau. of Adam Schleppi (see entry). Philip d. before June 11, 1752, and by that date, his widow, Maria

Magdalena, m. Johann Heinrich Gerlach (see entry in Shrewsbury Township), and had moved to Shrewsbury Township. Phillip and Maria Magdalena had the following children (Adam Schleppi were appointed guardians of Phillip's minor daus. in 1752):
- Philip, b. about 1740. He was taxed in 1762. He m. Anna Elisabetha, and had the following son:
  - Jon Christoffel, bapt. by Reverend Jacob Lischy on Apr. 12, 1761.
- Maria Eva, b. in York Co., Shrewsbury Township, about 1745, and m. Solomon, son of Casper Glattfelter (see entry).
- Anna Maria, bapt. in Codorus Township by Reverend Jacob Lischy on Nov. 2, 1747, and spon. by Abraham and Eva Elisabeth Welschans.
- Maria Magdalena, b. about 1749, and m. Johan Frederick Altvater in York Co. on Dec. 31, 1769. They had the following son:
  - Heinrich in Shrewsbury Township on Oct. 23, 1770, and by May 26, 1786, resided in Washington Co., MD.

Frasher (Froescher) - Friedrich was b. on Sept. 26, 1732, and was taxed in 1762. He was sponsor to the baptism of Susanna Maria Kann in 1762. He warranted 125 acres on May 11, 1776, and 100 acres on Apr. 30, 1765. He m. Philippina, widow of Carl Schaffer (see entry) about 1761 and Catharina about 1782. His will was written on May 7, 1809, and probated on Jan. 12, 1811. Catharina's probate inventory was filed in 1815. Catharina was b. on May 6, 1751, and d. on Dec. 29, 1814. Friedrich d. on Dec. 30, 1810. They are bur. in STJ cemetery. Friedrich had the following children bapt. at STJ:
- Margaretha, b. about 1763, and m. Johannes Ehrman (see entry in Shrewsbury section).
- Johann Ludwig, bapt. by RJL in Dec. 1763, and spon. by Ludwig and Margaretha Kieffer.
- Johan Ludwig, b. on Mar. 7, 1765, and bapt. on Apr. 4, 1765. He m. Catharina about 1791.
- Maria Catharina, b. on Oct. 24, 1767, and bapt. on Dec. 13, 1767.
- Anna Maria, b. on Sept. 30, 1769, and bapt. on Oct. 24, 1769.
- Barbara, b. about 1771.
- Johan Peter, b. on Jan. 11, 1774, bapt. on Mar. 6, 1774, and d. on Mar. 26, 1852. He m. Anna Barbara. She was b. on Jan. 11, 1786, and d. on Apr. 9, 1853. They are bur. in STJ cemetery.
- Charlotta, b. on Feb. 10, 1776, and bapt. on Mar. 17, 1776. She m. Georg Peter, son of Peter Gerberich (see entry).
- Rosina, b. on June 24, 1778, and bapt. on July 5, 1778.
- Maria Christina, b. on Mar. 28, 1781, and bapt. on Apr. 22, 1781. She m. Peter, son of Georg and Margaretha (Gerberich) Baehli (see Shrewsbury section).
- Maria Elisabetha, b. on May 21, 1783, and bapt. on June 22, 1783.

- Johannes, b. on June 5, 1785, and bapt. on Aug. 21, 1785.
- Eva Barbara, b. on Sept. 29, 1787, and bapt. on Nov. 7, 1787.
- Magdalena, b. on Feb. 19, 1790, and bapt. on Mar. 20, 1790.

Frisher - Peter was taxed in 1762.

Fultz - Adam warranted 60 acres on Mar. 18, 1775 (tax payments began on Mar. 18, 1765).

Gantz - Frans Heinrich was taxed in 1762. He was b. in Pferdsfeld, Germany, on Aug. 22, 1723 to Johannes Friederich Gans (May 1686-Dec. 24, 1743) and Elisabetha Margaretha (1698-Jan. 12, 1729-30). He m. Anna Margaretha, dau. of Peter and Anna Catharina Ruhl about 1752 (see entry). Frans immigrated to America on the ship *Two Brothers*, and arrived at Philadelphia, PA, on Oct. 13, 1747. The German emigration lists indicate that he left Germany with Anna Elisabetha Gantz, and possibly another Frans. These Gantz' may have been a wife and child to Frans Heinrich, but no other information has been obtained on them. Possibly, they d. en route or shortly after their arrival in America. Anna Margaretha d. in York Co., Codorus Township, PA, sometime before 1790. Frans Heinrich was a farmer in Codorus Township. On June 23, 1768, he was warranted 200 acres in Codorus Township. On Apr. 25, 1771, this warrant was surveyed at 242.25 acres and called *The Fancy* (patented to his son, George on June 14, 1809). He added onto this with 57 acres in 1785. On June 11, 1789, he was warranted 15 acres in Codorus Township. This land was surveyed on Sept. 9, 1789, and consisted of two tracts adjoining The Fancy which were 12 acres and 9 acres (patented to George Gantz on Nov. 29, 1809 for 3.63 acres and 9.138 acres). On Aug. 20, 1793, he deeded all of his land to his son Johan Georg. In 1779, Frans had 200 acres, two horses, and eight cattle; in 1780, 150 acres, two horses, and three cattle; in 1781, 240 acres, two horses and twelve cattle; in 1782, 200 acres, two horses, and seven cattle; and in 1783, 250 acres. During the Revolutionary War, he was a member of the 2nd Class of Inhabitants of Codorus Township for requisition of recruits. He d. on Nov. 27, 1809, at the age of 85, and was bur. in Fissel's (Jerusalem) Union Church cemetery. Frans and Anna Margaretha had the following children:
- Elisabetha Margaretha, b. on Oct. 24, 1753, and m. Ludwig Bortner (see entry).
- Margaretha, b. on Feb. 3, 1758, and m. Johan Georg Bortner (see entry).
- Johannes, b. on Dec. 22, 1759. He was bapt. at St. Jacob's (Stone) Union Church on Feb. 3, 1760, and spon. by John Zeel and Christine Mueller. He was a farmer in Codorus Township, and

served as a Private during the Revolutionary War in 1775, 1776, and 1780 in Capt. Shreyer's Company, York County Militia. He was taxed as a single man in 1781, and in 1783, as a single man with 130 acres. In 1786, he m. Esther, dau. of Johan Jacob, and Esther (Sprenckel) Keller (see entry). Johannes d. on Oct. 15, 1792, at age 32, and was bur. in Fissel's (Jerusalem) Union Church cemetery. After their marriage, Esther was publicly bapt. at Fissel's on May 27, 1787. Esther never remarried, and raised her children, as well as a foster child, Jacob Blaize. For thirty pounds silver, Esther and her father purchased 131 acres, 120 perches called *Cherry Corner* from Henry Rockey on Mar. 5, 1802 (Esther was referred to as a widow of Baltimore Co., MD). The bond was transferred to John Blocker, and came due on Aug. 8, 1808. This land was situated in Codorus Township, adjacent to the land of Christopher Rockey, Dewalt Schneider, Georg Wibeling, Michael Kleinfelter, and Frans Gantz. Between 1808 and 1816, Esther deeded Cherry Corner to her son Johannes. Esther was b. in Codorus Township on Aug. 16, 1762, d. in Manheim Township at the age of 65 on June 16, 1828, and is bur. in St. Jacob's (Stone) Union Church cemetery near Brodbecks, PA.

- Johan Georg, was bapt. by Reverend Jacob Lischy on Aug. 21, 1763, and spon. by his uncle, Georg Ruhl, and Elisabeth Brodbeckin. He m. Margaretha about 1785, and Catrina in 1795. Margaretha was b. on Nov. 10, 1764, and d. in York Co., Codorus Township, PA, on July 10, 1795. Catrina was b. on Feb., 25, 1766, and d. in Codorus Township on Sept., 28, 1841. Georg was a blacksmith and d. on Nov. 29, 1815 in Codorus Township. Georg, and Margaretha are bur. in Fissel's (Jerusalem) Union Church cemetery. On Apr. 9, 1791, Georg purchased 14 acres and 71 perches, part of a tract called *Square Compas* from John and Helena Ruhl. In June 1809, Georg patented the land that his father had warranted. On Apr. 6, 1790, he surveyed 120 acres in Codorus Township called *The String* (patented on Apr. 10, 1809, for 70.75 acres). On Apr. 7, 1808, he patented 70 acres and 70 perches called *Long Side* in Codorus Township. On June 12, 1809, he patented 21.91 acres in Shrewsbury Township. In 1802, Georg built a stone house on *The Fancy*. The house consisted of two main floors, a walk-up attic, about four fireplaces, a walk-out basement area, and many windows on the south side. The basement had spring water piped into it, which emptied into stone troughs, used for cooling milk, etcetera. It was still standing in 1976, but had been vacant for years, vandalized, and had a small fire in the kitchen. It might have been restored, but when highway 216 was built, they placed the road about five feet from the corner of the house. The house was considered too expensive to move, and was

demolished by 1994. According to Delbert Gantz, Carroll Gantz has possesion of the dated stone from the wall of the house.
- Georg Wilhelm, b. on July 2, 1765. He was bapt. at St. Jacob's on July 30, 1765, and spon. by his uncle, Wilhelm Ruhl, and Anna Margaretha Schwartz. He m. Maria Catherina, and bapt. a son at Sherman's (St. David's) Lutheran Church in West Manheim Township in 1792.
- Juliana, b. about 1769, and m. Johannes Bortner (see entry).
- Barbara, b. about 1771, and was the sponsor at the following baptisms: her niece Barbara Bortner, in 1784, Barbara, dau. of Lorentz and Catherine Schulz in 1788; her niece, Christina Bortner, in 1791, and her nephew, John Gantz in 1792.

<u>Gerberich</u> - Hans Kasper m. Appolonia Voltz/Volz at Unterfranken, Altfeld, Marktheidenfeld, Bavaria, on Apr. 24, 1683. He d. on Mar. 6, 1720. They had the following children:
- Georg, b. on Dec. 12, 1684.
- Andreas, b. on Sept. 23, 1686, and d. sometime before 1697.
- Anna Katharina, b. on Sept. 25, 1690.
- Johannes, b. in 1692, and d. sometime before 1701.
- Hans Thomas, b. on Apr. 17, 1695.
- Andreas, b. on Apr. 20, 1697.
- Martin, b. on July 3, 1698.
- Johannes, b. on June 9, 1701. He m. Christina, dau. of George and Anna Barbara (Krauss) Schuch, on Feb. 25, 1727, and Christina Emmerich. Christina Schuch was b. at Remlingen, Bavaria on May 14, 1703, and d. on Apr. 4, 1736. Johannes is said to have d. from the plague just a few days after his arrival at Philadelphia on the ship *Phoenix* on Nov. 2, 1752. He had the following children at Spessart, Altfeld Bei Marktheidenfeld, Bavaria, Germany:
- Andreas, b. on Feb. 28, 1729. He d. sometime before 1734.
- Peter, b. on Aug. 12, 1730. He arrived at Philadelphia on the Duke of Bedford on Sept. 14, 1751, with his bros., Andrew and Johannes, and his uncle, Michael. Peter settled in Berks Co., Tulpehocken Township, for a time, and between 1761 and 1766 moved to York Co., Codorus Township, PA. He received a warrant for 75 acres on Feb. 26, 1773, and 100 acres on June 8, 1786 (interest began on Mar. 1, 1771). On May 7, 1773, a portion of this warrant was surveyed as 46.15 acres called *Gerbrick's Rocks*. Peter m. Anna Margaretha Rudolph, possibly a dau. of Andreas Rudolph of Altfeld, Bavaria, in Berks Co. on Feb. 9, 1755, and Margaretha Berge, widow of Clement Ruhl (see entry), and dau. of Henrich Berge, sometime between Mar. 30, 1777, and Apr. 1, 1778. Peter d. in Codorus Township on Aug. 13, 1805,

and Margaretha in Dec. 1800. He was the father of the following children:
- Margretha, b. about 1760, and m. Georg Baehli (see entry in Shrewsbury section).
- Johannes, b. on Aug. 13, 1761. He m. Anna Margaretha, dau. of Johannes and Helena Ruhl (see entry), in York Co., PA, on Oct. 1, 1786. She was bapt. at St. Jacob's on June 9, 1767, and spon. by her uncle and aunt, Frans and Anna Margaretha Gans. Johannes d. in Shrewsbury Township on Nov. 6, 1846, and Anna Margaretha d. in Codorus Township on Mar. 31, 1836. Both are bur. in Steltz Union cemetery.
- Maria Elisabeth, b. about 1763.
- Frederich, b. in 1765, and m. Eva.
- Catherina, b. in 1766, and bapt. at St. Jacob's in Apr. 1766.
- Michael, b. about 1767, and m. Barbara Miller.
- Susanna Philippena, b. on July 26, 1769, and bapt. at St. Jacob's on Aug. 8, 1769.
- Susanna, b. on June 26, 1771, and bapt. at St. Jacob's on Aug. 4, 1771.
- Georg Peter, b. on July 4, 1774. He was bapt. at St. Jacob's on July 29, 1774. He m. Charlotta (Feb. 10, 1776-Nov. 8, 1825), dau. of Friedrich and Philippina Froescher (see entry). She was bapt. at St. Jacob's on Mar. 17, 1776. George d. in Codorus Township on Dec. 6, 1838.
- Jacob, b. in 1778. He m. Sophia. Jacob d. in York Borough in 1814.
- Barbara, b. in 1781.
- Eve, b. in 1787, and m. ___ Stich.
- Joseph, b. on Feb. 2, 1791, and bapt. at Fissel's on Feb. 27, 1791. He was spon. by Johannes Kleinfelter and wife. He m. Elizabeth, dau. of Johann Jacob and Maria Christina (Dehoff) Scherer (see entry), and moved to Centre Co., Marion Township, PA, sometime before 1813. Joseph d. on July 26, 1841, and is bur. in the Emanuel Reformed cemetery in Marion Township. Elizabeth d. on Feb. 27, 1856, and is bur. in Zion cemetery in Centre Co., Walker Township.
- Andrew, b. on July 17, 1734, m. Barbara Babb (1733-1816) in Berks Co., PA, in 1758, and resided in Lebanon Co., East Hanover Township, in 1769. Andrew d. in 1795.
- Apollonia, b. about 1736.
- Margaretha, b. about 1738.
- Johannes, b. on July 28, 1740, and Catharine. They resided in Berks Co., PA, in 1763, and Dauphin Co., Derry Township, in 1782.
- Anna Barbara, b. in 1743.

- Maria Margaretha, b. about 1745.
- Johan Michael, b. in 1748.
- Maria Elisabeth, b. on Mar. 26, 1752.
- Philip, b. on Sept. 10, 1703.
- Hans Michael, b. on July 2, 1710. He immigrated to America with his nephews, Peter, Andrew, and Johannes Gerberich, and arrived at Philadelphia in Sept. 1751. Michael settled in Berks Co., PA, and m. Christine (Gertrude?). Michael d. before 1765, and Christine was residing in York Co., PA, in Mar. 1765. They had the following children:
  - Anna Margaretha, b. on Mar. 29, 1738, and m. Johannes Kleinfelter (see entry in Shrewsbury section).
  - Anna Barbara, b. about 1745. She was a sponsor with Ludwig Hahnawaldt at the baptism of Anna Barbara, dau. of Jacob Baehli, on May 10, 1766. She is presumed to have m. Ludwig Hahnawaldt and bapt. the following children at St. Jacob's:
    - Anna Margaretha, bapt. on July 12, 1767.
    - Anna Elisabetha, b. on Dec. 23, 1768, and bapt. on Apr. 2, 1769.
  - Michael, b. about 1748. He m. Maria Margaretha, and settled in York Co., Shrewsbury Township, PA, with his cousin, Peter Gerberich. Michael and Margaretha were the parents of the following children, b. in York Co., PA:
    - Maria Magdalena, b. on Feb. 28, 1772, and bapt. at Friedensaal on Apr. 12, 1772.
    - Maria Margaretha, b. on Sept. 1, 1774, and m. Johannes Ruhl (see entry).
    - Susanna, b. on Oct. 2, 1782, bapt. at Fissel's on Aug. 27, 1783, and spon. by Susanna.
    - Johan Michael, b. on Mar. 28, 1789, bapt. at Fissel's on May 21, 1789, and spon. by Johannes and Margaretha Kleinfelter.
  - John, b. about 1750.
  - Elizabeth, b. about 1752, and spon. a baptism in York Co. in 1769.

<u>Gerecks</u> - John was taxed in 1762.

<u>Glasick</u> - John was taxed in 1762. He received a warrant for 150 acres on Mar. 11, 1765, that was surveyed as 190.127 acres on Jan. 14, 1766. His will was written on Nov. 24, 1775, and probated on Jan. 29, 1776. He had the following children:
- Rachel.
- Mary.

- Samuel m. Anna Catharina DeHoff (see entry). Her probate inventory was filed in 1822. They had the following children, bapt. at STJ:
  - Johannes, b. on May 21, 1777, and bapt. on July 6, 1777.
  - Dau., b. on July 23, 1782, and bapt. on Sept. 5, 1782.

Glattfelder - Casper was taxed in 1762. He was b. to Felix and Barbara (Glorius) Glattfelter in Glattfelden, Switzerland, on July 8, 1709, and bapt. on July 25, 1709. He came to America in the ship *Francis and Elizabeth* on Aug. 30, 1743 (he is listed as sick) (came with his bro., Peter Glatfelter's family (see entry in Shrewsbury section), and settled in York Co., PA. He m. Elisabetha, dau. of Hans Jacob Lauffer (born in 1673), at Glattfelden on Apr. 3, 1731. She was b. in Glattfelden in 1709, and is presumed to have d. en route to America in 1743. Sometime prior to 1747, Casper m. Anna Maria. Casper d. in York Co., Codorus Township, in Mar. 1775 (he is bur. in Bupp's Union cemetery). His will was probated in Codorus Township on Apr. 3, 1775. Anna Maria was alive when Casper wrote his will, and d. in 1775. On Apr. 3, 1770, Casper received a land warrant for 100 acres in Springfield/North Codorus Township. The interest on this land started on Mar. 1, 1758. It was surveyed to Casper as 127.143 acres called *Beaver Dam* on Apr. 19, 1770, and patented to Mary Glattfelter on Apr. 29, 1864. On Oct. 4, 1771, he warranted 50 acres in Springfield Township. This land was surveyed as 72.74 acres, and patented to Mary Glattfelter on Apr. 29, 1864. Casper was naturalized on Apr. 3, 1763. He had the following children:
- Felix b. in 1731/32, bapt. on Feb. 2, 1731/32, and d. on Feb. 6, 1731/32.
- Anna Margaretha, b. in 1732/33, bapt. on Jan. 13, 1732/33, and d. on Feb. 23, 1732/33.
- Margaretha, b. in 1733/34, bapt. on Jan. 17, 1733/34, and d. in York Co., PA, on Mar. 31, 1779. She is bur. in Bupp's Union Church cemetery.
- Solomon, b. in 1736, and d. in 1737.
- Solomon, b. in Glattfelden, Switzerland, on Feb. 1, 1738, and bapt. on Feb. 23, 1738 (eldest son). He was taxed in Manchester Township in 1762. Solomon was a blacksmith, and m. Maria Eva, dau. of Phillip Frensch/Friend of Codorus Township (see entry). She was b. in York Co., Shrewsbury/Codorus Township, PA. Solomon received £25 from his father's estate. They moved to Frederick Co., MD, about 1768, and Somerset Co., PA, in 1776. Solomon d. on Aug. 13, 1818.
- Anna, b. in Glattfelden, Switzerland, in 1740, and bapt. on July 5, 1740. She was a single sponsor with Solomon Glattfelter to the baptism of Solomon Walther on May 14, 1758, and Solomon

Walther on Oct. 9, 1763. She received £20 from her father's estate. She probably m. Isaac Jauler (see entry in Manchester section).
- Johannes b. in 1742, bapt. on Oct. 18, 1742.
- Felix, b. in 1747, and was a single sponsor in 1768 and 1769. He m. Maria Elisabeth, dau. of Daniel and Maria Elisabetha Rennoly (see entry). She was b. on May 19, 1752, bapt. by Reverend Jacob Lischy on May 19, 1752, and d. in Codorus Township in Jan. 1827. He received his father's plantation, and d. in Codorus Township on Apr. 1815. They are bur. in Bupp's cemetery.
- Johannes, bapt. by Reverend Jacob Lischy on July 30, 1751, and spon. by Johannes Hildebrand. He m. Catharina.
- Jacob, bapt. by Reverend Jacob Lischy on July 30, 1751, and spon. by Jacob and Elisabetha Rein.
- Heinrich bapt. by Reverend Jacob Lischy on Nov. 12, 1752, and spon. by Heinrich and Dorothea Walther. He m. Anna Margaretha, dau. of John Heilman in York on Aug. 20, 1782, and d. in 1847.
- Michael, b. in 1758. He m. Anna Maria, dau. of Ulrich Hess in York on Sept. 5, 1780, and d. in Washington Co., PA, in 1824.
- Casper, b. about 1759. He m. Maria Eva, and d. in Nov. 1823. She was b. about 1765, and d. about 1851.

Groff - Frantz was taxed in 1762. He m. Anna Siegrist. They had the following children:
- Johannes, bapt. by RJL on Oct. 7, 1760, and spon. by Balthasar and Elisabeth Koll.
- Johan Georg, bapt. by RJL on Jan. 1, 1763, and spon. by Georg and Anna Barbara Kleinfelter.
- Johan Michael, bapt. by RJL on Feb. 22, 1767, and spon. by Jacob and Susanna Kroh.
- Johannes, b. on Aug. 12, 1769, bapt. at FRI on Sept. 24, 1769, and spon. by Johannes Failler and wife. He m. Julian about 1791.
- Heinrich, b. on Mar. 27, 1774, and bapt. at STJ on May 10, 1774.

Groff - Jacob was warranted 50 acres on June 27, 1754, which he deeded to Joseph Groff on Feb. 11, 1765.

Haber - Jacob was taxed in 1762.

Haentschi - Jacob was killed by savages at Bethel on the Swatara (Lancaster (now Lebanon) Co., PA) on June 26, 1756. He m. Barbara Spitler. She was b. in Benwyl, Canton Basel, Switzerland, on Mar. 30, 1728, m. Johannes Heckedorn after 1768 (see entry), and d. in York Co. on Nov. 11, 1793. Jacob and Barbara had the following children:

CODORUS TOWNSHIP 23

- Catharina, b. at Bethel on June 15, 1755, and bapt. on June 20, 1755. She m. Christian Gottleib, son of Johannes Heckedorn (see entry).

Haffner - Jacob m. Catharina. He received a warrant for 100 acres on Dec. 18, 1751, that was surveyed as 160 acres on Nov. 15, 1785, and patented on Sept. 10, 1789 (interest began on Mar. 1, 1746). He was warranted 50 acres on June 1, 1762. They had the following children:
- Jacob was taxed in 1762. He served in the Revolutionary War in Captain John Myer's Company (1778). He m. Elisabetha. They had the following children:
  - Johan Philipp, bapt. by RJL on Apr. 2, 1760, and spon. by Philipp Katzenbach and Maria Catharina Reberin.
  - Maria Catharina, bapt. by RJL on Feb. 27, 1763, and spon. by Frantz Hartmann and Maria Catharina Reberin.
  - Maria Elisabetha, bapt. by RJL on Sept. 1764, and spon. by Daniel and Maria Elisabetha Renolly.
  - Johan Michael, bapt. by RJL on Apr. 3, 1767, and spon. by Michael and Catharina Bohler.
  - Andreas, bapt. by RJL on Oct. 16, 1768, and spon. by Andreas and Barbara Muller.
- Maria Catharina, bapt. by RJL on Apr. 29, 1746, and spon. by Daniel and Maria Catharina Heckedorn.

Hammer - Frantz was taxed in 1762. He received a warrant for 100 acres in Codorus and Springfield Townships on June 1, 1749. He m. Rebecca. They had the following children:
- Tobias, bapt. by RJL on July 28, 1756, and spon. by Tobias Rudisill and Elisabeth Wolffin.
- Maria Eva, bapt. by RJL on Apr. 15, 1759, and spon. by Andreas and Anna Margaretha Swartz.
- Johan Michael, bapt. by RJL on Oct. 7, 1760, and spon. by Johannes and Maria Magdalena Keller.
- Anna Maria, bapt. by RJL on Aug. 14, 1763, and spon. by Ludwig and Margaretha Kieffer.

Hassler - Michael m. Margaretha. He was b. in Canton Berne, Switzerland, in 1730, and arrived at Philadelphia on Sept. 28, 1749. Michael d. in York Co., Codorus Township, in Mar. 1774. His will was written in Codorus Township on Feb. 5, 1774, and probated on Mar. 26, 1774. They had the following children:
- Joseph, b. on Sept. 8, 1750, m. Anna Maria, dau. of Johann Frederick and Anna Dorothea (Mueller) Roemer (See entry in Manchester section), in York Co. on May 30, 1775, and d. in

Franklin Co., Peters Township, PA, in 1798. They moved to Franklin Co. in 1793.
- Michael, m. Christina Maria, dau. of Johan Michael Geisselman (see entry in Shrewsbury section), on Dec. 1, 1777.
- Christian.
- Magdalena m. Johan Georg, son of Peter Lau (see entry in Manchester section).
- Georg.
- Abraham, b. on Oct. 4, 1761, and m. Christina, dau. of Georg Bortner (see entry).

Hauck (Haug) - Bernhard was a sponsor as a widower with his son Bernard to the baptism of Johannes Michael Hauck in 1755 (SLC). His will was written in Manheim Township on Aug. 30, 1762, and probated on Nov. 1, 1762. His wife d. before 1755. He had the following children:
- Eva Barbara, b. on Oct. 12, 1701. She was considered an unmarried spinster when she spon. the baptism of a dau. of Jean Craddy in 1749 (STM). She was still unmarried in 1762. She was bur. at SLC on Sept. 28, 1784 (age 83 years minus two weeks). This age may be a mistake for 63 years, Bernhard Sr. m. an Eva between 1755 and 1762, or he had a much earlier wife. There is no wife mentioned in the will, but Eva (presumably his spinster dau., or his son, Jacob's wife) Hauk and Jacob Hauk are execs. of his will.
- Georg, b. about 1723 (not mentioned in the will), and m. Maria Catharina (before 1745, when they were sponsors at the baptism of Maria Catharina Kessler (TLY)). He d. in 1763/64 (mentioned as deceased at son's baptism). She was alive in 1777, when she spon. the baptism of Maria Elisabeth Hauk at STM. They had following children:
  - David, b. on June 14, 1747, bapt. at STM on July 8, 1747, and spon. by David Lau and Anna Maria Lau (spinster).
  - Bernhard, bon on July 29, 1748, bapt. at STM on May 26, 1749, and spon. by Bernhard Hauck, Jr., and wife.
  - Johan Georg, b. on July 29, 1750, bapt. at STM on Oct. 9, 1759, and spon. by Bernhard Hauck, Jr., and wife. He m. Maria Magdalena.
  - Maria Elisabeth, b. on Feb. 27, 1752, bapt. at STM on Apr. 5, 1752, and spon. by Michael Fiser and Elisabetha Milton.
  - Johannes Michael, b. on Sept. 29, 1755, bapt. at SLC on Dec. 26, 1755, and spon. by Bernard Houck, Sr., and Bernard Houck, the widower's son.
  - Johan Jacob, bapt. by RJL on Oct. 10, 1761, and spon. by Jacob and Maria Ester Kessler.

- Johan Friedrich, b. on Jan. 16, 1764, bapt. at SLC on Feb. 2, 1764, and spon. by Friedrich and Margaretha Berling (both single).
- Bernhard, b. about 1725 (not mentioned in the will). He was taxed in 1762. He m. Eva about 1746, and Catharina Barbara about 1759. Eva was alive in 1756, when she and Bernard spon. the baptism of Eva Elisabeth Furhman at SLC. He had the following children:
  - Bernhard, b. on Apr. 10, 1747, bapt. at STM on June 23, 1747, and spon. by David and Anna Maria Lau.
  - Maria Elisabeth, b. on May 22, 1749, bapt. at STM on May 26, 1749, and spon. by Nicholas Honig and wife.
  - Maria Magdalena, bapt. by RJL on July 24, 1760, and spon. by Michael and Maria Magdalena Haug.
  - Maria Elisabetha, bapt. by RJL on May 23, 1762, and spon. by Michael Vogel and Elisabetha Haugin.
  - Johan Niclaus, bapt. by RJL on July 15, 1764, and spon. by Johannes and Catharina Wolffgang.
  - Johan Peter, bapt. at STJ on May 17, 1767.
- Michael, b. about 1727 (not mentioned in the will). He was taxed in 1762. He m. Magdalena, and had the following children:
  - Michael, bapt. by RJL on May 26, 1751, and spon. by Michael Schuster and Susanna Voglerin.
  - Petrus, bapt. by RJL on Oct. 29, 1752, and spon. by Casper and Anna Barbara Kuffer.
  - Johan Georg, bapt. by RJL on May 4, 1755, and spon. by Wilhelm Gander and Catharina Barbara Gilgen.
  - Barbara, bapt. by RJL on May 1, 1757, and spon. by Georg and Barbara Meyer.
  - Bernhardt, b. on Mar. 6, 1761, and bapt. at CLY on Mar. 24, 1761.
- Johan Jacob, b. about 1729. He was a sponsor to the baptism of Maria Magdalena Lau in 1753 (SLC), and received a warrant for 100 acres in Codorus and Manheim Townships on June 16, 1763. His will was written in Hanover Township on Jan. 9, 1790, and probated on Mar. 25, 1790. He m. Anna Eva before 1751 (sponsors to baptism of Eva Catharina Gettier in 1751 (RJL)), and Christina before 1779 (sponsors to the baptism of Jacob Reissinger at ERC in 1779). He had the following children:
  - Maria Christina, b. on Apr./Feb. 10, 1759, bapt. at SLC on Apr. 16, 1759, and spon. by Michael and Maria Christina Scheifele.
  - Johannes, b. on Mar. 2, 1761, bapt. at SLC on Maunday Thursday, and spon. by Stephen Fuhrman and wife.
  - Elisabeth, b. on June 27, 1779, bapt. at STM, and spon. by Johannes and Magdalena Reissinger and wife.

- Jacob, b. on June 25, 1786, bapt. at ERC on Sept. 3, 1786, and spon. by Christian and Catharina Muhlheim.
- Philip, b. about 1739, and was a sponsor to the baptism of Philip Ziefer at SLC in 1760. He m. Maria Magdalena Fuhrman at STM on Feb. 14, 1764, and had the following children:
  - Maria Christina, b. on Jan. 11, 1765, bapt. at SLC, and spon. by Peter Ohlinger and Christina Furhman.
  - Johan Jacob, b. in 1767, bapt. at SLC on Feb. 22, 1767, and spon. by Jacob and Maria Margaretha Nonnemacher.
  - Johannes, b. on Dec. 19, 1774, bapt. at SLC on Apr. 2, 1775, and spon. by Leonhard and Margaretha Jenewein.
  - Dau., b. on May 7, 1772, bapt. at SLC on Aug. 30, 1772, and spon. by Georg and Anna Elisabeth Gotty.
  - Rachel, b. on Dec. 2, 1784, bapt. at SLC on Apr. 17, 1785, and spon. by Catharina Gennwein.
- Elisabeth, b. about 1741.

Hauser - Johannes was taxed in 1762. He m. Mary. His will was written in Codorus Township on Dec. 18, 1762, and probated on Mar. 19, 1763. They had the following children:
- John, m. Elisabeth, dau. of Sebastian Herleman (see entry), about 1778.
- Peter.
- Henry.
- Jacob.
- Georg, m. Philippina, dau. of Sebastian Herleman (see entry) about 1785.
- Elisabeth.
- Yuleyane.

Headrich (Hetterich) - Jacob, m. Elisabeth. He warranted 50 acres called *Jacob's Lissey* on Jan. 16, 1769, and 200 acres called *Duck Hill* on June 2, 1767. He was a Lt. in Captain George Hoover's Company, 1st Battalion in 1776, and the 7th Battalion of Captain Schearer's Company in 1778. He was constable in 1771, and supervisor in 1774. His will was written in Codorus Township on June 16, 1779, and probated on Oct. 13, 1781. They had the following children:
- Johan Jacob, bapt. by RJL on July 3, 1763, and spon. by Jacob and Elisabeth Amman. He served in the Revolution.
- Christian, b. on Feb. 12, 1765, bapt. by RJL on Feb. 24, 1765, and spon. by Christian and Elisabeth Fass. He m. Catharina Barbara, dau. of Bernard Bobb/Bopp (see entry in Shrewsbury section). Catharina was b. on Sept. 26, 1763, and d. on Aug. 4, 1838. Christian d. on Apr. 24, 1827. They are bur. in STJ. He served in the Revolution.

CODORUS TOWNSHIP 27

- Maria Elisabetha, bapt. at STJ on Oct. 5, 1766, and m. Nicholas Wolfgang.
- Catharina, bapt. at STJ on Mar. 22, 1768, and m. Michael Schack/Schauck.
- Maria Margaretha, b. on Sept. 8, 1769, and bapt. at STJ on Sept. 24, 1769.
- Johannes, b. on Dec. 4, 1770, and bapt. at STJ on Jan. 11, 1772. He m. Barbara about 1791. His will was written in Manheim Township on Aug. 23, 1810, and probated on Nov. 21, 1810.
- Apollonia, b. on Oct. 21, 1773, and bapt. at STJ on Nov. 15, 1773. She m. Jacob Lammot.
- Abraham, b. on Sept. 15, 1776, and bapt. at STJ on Oct. 20, 1776. he m. Sarah.

Heck - Frederick received a warrant for 200 acres in North Codorus Township on Mar. 12, 1767, that was surveyed as 159 acres (with the remainder in Springettsbury lands) on May 7, 1771. He is probably the Friedrich Heeg that m. Anna Catharina, and were sponsors at the baptism of Anna Catharina, dau. of Conrad and Elisabeth Heeg on June 8, 1755 (RJL) (see entry in Dover section).

Heckedorn - Hannes was b. in 1685, and d. in York Co. on Nov. 14, 1749 (death recorded at FMY). He immigrated to America from Langenbruck, Switzerland, on the ship *Princess Augustus* in 1736. He m. Margaretha. She was b. in Nunbrum, Switzerland, in Jan. 1688, and d. in Lebanon Co., Lebanon, PA, on Dec. 27, 1754. They had the following children:
- Johannes, b. in Langen Brot, Switzerland, on Apr. 7 (5), 1716, immigrated to America in 1736, and was taken into the Moravian Congregation at Lancaster Co., Warwick, PA, on Feb. 9, 1749. He moved to York on Mar. 31, 1761, and d. on July 12, 1788. He m. Catharina Scheubel of Oberdorff, Switzerland, on Nov. 1, 1739, and Barbara Spitler, widow of Jacob Haentschi (see entry), at FMY on Oct. 12, 1769. Catharina was b. on Feb. 17, 1717, immigrated to America in 1736, and d. on Aug. 12, 1768. They had the following children (recorded at the FMY):
- Anna Barbara, b. on Aug. 22, 1740.
- Margaretha, b. on Apr. 16, 1743.
- Johannes, b. in Northampton Co., PA, on Oct. 12, 1744, and bapt. on Oct. 23, 1744.
- Johannes, bapt. at TLY on Mar. 17, 1745, and spon. by Hannes and Margaretha Heckedorn.
- Catharina, b. on May 18, 1747, bapt. on May 29, 1747, and d. on May 29, 1781.

- Anna Maria, bapt. by RJL on Mar. 12, 1749, and spon. by Peter and Margaretha Binckele.
- Anna Elisabetha, b. on Aug. 25, 1749, and bapt. on Sept. 5, 1749. She m. William, son of Jacob and Juliana (Kramer) Lanius (see entry on Kramer family in Dover section), at FMY on Dec. 26, 1769. He was b. on Sept. 12, 1748, and bapt. on Sept. 23, 1745.
- Johannes, bapt. by RJL on Feb. 10, 1751, and spon. by Casper and Maria Agnes Keiffer. He m. Barbara. His will was written in York on Dec. 5, 1774, and probated on Oct. 14, 1785.
- Anna Maria, b. on Apr. 13, 1752, bapt. at FMY on Apr. 24, 1752, and spon. by Elisabeth Hohns, Anna Maria Muller, Juliana Hoff, Margaretha Heckedorn, and Christina Meurer.
- Christian Gottlieb, b. on June 10, 1754. He m. Catharina, dau. of Jacob Haentschi (see entry), at FMY on Mar. 1, 1778.
- Anna Rosina, b. on Mar. 16, 1758, and bapt. on Mar. 18, 1758.
- Anna Rosina, b. on Apr. 8, 1761, and bapt. on Apr. 12, 1761.

- Barbara, b. on Apr. 7 (5), 1716, and m. Jacob, son of Jacob Christman, at the First Reformed Congregation at Lancaster, PA, on Oct. 1, 1742. They moved to Lebanon, PA, and had the following children:
  - Johannes, bapt. at TLY on May 23, 1745, and spon. by Hans and Catharina Heckedorn.
  - Hans Jacob, bapt. by RJL on Oct. 27, 1745, and spon. by Johannes and Margaretha Heckedorn.
  - Catharina, b. on Nov. 25, 1751, bapt. at FMY on Nov. 29, 1751, and spon. by John and Daniel Heckedorn, and Peter Binkele.

- Daniel, b. on May 26, 1720. He was taxed in 1762, and received a warrant for 150 acres in North Codorus Township on Dec. 18, 1751, that was surveyed as 182 acres on Oct. 22, 1752. He moved to Lebanon Co., Lebanon, PA, with his mother and sister in 1753. He m. Maria Catharina Denen at STM on Apr. 8, 1744, and Susanna Etter, widow of Rudolph Kunzel, in Lebanon Co., PA, on Jan. 12, 1753. He d. before 1784. Catharina d. in 1752. They had the following children:
  - Johannes, b. on Nov. 12, 1744, bapt. by RJL on Mar. 17, 1745, and spon. by Peter and Maria Salome Binckele. He m. Maria Catarina Hammann in Lebanon on Aug. 21, 1770 (JCS).
  - Johan Ehrhardt, b. on Sept. 9, 1746, bapt. by RJL on Sept. 28, 1747, and spon. by Ehrhardt Heckedorn and Magdalena Heckedorn. He m. Catharina Meiley in Lebanon Co. on Sept. 8, 1770.
  - Maria Magdalena, b. on Jan. 22, 1748, and m. ____ Heller.
  - Daniel, b. on Oct. 21, 1749, and m. Elisabeth about 1777.
  - Susanna Catharina, b. on Mar. 31, 1750.

- Johan Peter, bapt. by RJL on Dec. 4, 1763, and spon. by Peter and Catharina Runck.
- Maria Eva, bapt. by RJL on Nov. 17, 1765, and spon. by Frantz and Maria Eva Hoff.

Heln - Georg was taxed in 1762.

Herleman - Sebastian was taxed in 1762. He m. Maria Magdalena. His will was written in Codorus Township on May 11, 1791, and probated on Feb. 11, 1794. They had the following children:
- Johan Conrad, b. on Sept. 29, 1742, bapt. at Augustus Trappe Lutheran Church in Montgomery Co., PA, on Oct. 17, 1742, and spon. by Johan Conrad and Anna Maria Schrimer.
- Maria Elisabetha, b. on Mar. 5, 1747, bapt. at Augustus Trappe Lutheran Church in Montgomery Co., PA, on Mar. 31, 1747, and spon. by Jurg and Maria Elisabetha Sauer. She m. Johannes Hauser (see entry).
- Barbara, b. about 1759, and was a sponsor to a baptism in 1779.
- Philipena, m. Georg Hauser (see entry).

Henig - Johan Peter was taxed in 1762. He was warranted 253 acres on Jan. 15, 1768 (surveyed on Oct. 23, 1768 as *Hennig's Rest* (improved for 12 years)). He m. Veronica. They had the following children:
- Johan Peter, bapt. by RJL on Oct. 10, 1763, and spon. by Johannes Brodbeck and Catharina Rothermel.
- Petro, bapt. at STJ on May 16, 1766, and m. Barbara about 1795.
- Son, b. on Mar. 15, 1769, and bapt. at STJ on June 4, 1769.

Henig - Michael m. Maria Margaretha before 1758. He was warranted 100 acres in Shrewsbury/Codorus Townships on Dec. 2, 1768.

Henig - Niclaus m. Maria Elisabetha, and had the following children:
- Johan Ludwig, bapt. by RJL on Dec. 26, 1760, and spon. by Ludwig and Maria Magdalena Kieffer.
- Maria Elisabetha, bapt. by RJL on June 20, 1762, and spon. by Johannes Kleinfelter and Anna Maria Hanewald.

Heriter (Heeritter) - Johannes was taxed in 1762. He received a warrant for 250 acres on Mar. 28, 1767, that was surveyed as 183.51 acres called *Large and Poor* on Mar. 31, 1769. He m. Catharina Ulrich at STM on Aug. 20, 1753, and had the following children:
- Jacob, m. Elisabeth before 1786.

Hetchler - Martin was taxed in 1762.

CODORUS TOWNSHIP 31

Hoehns (Heintz) - Johann Philippus, son of Johannes and Maria
Elisabetha (Petter) Heintz, was b. in Kusel, Germany, on Mar. 19,
1692. He was a potter, and immigrated to America on the ship
Glasgow in 1738. He m. Susanna Maria, and had the following children
(BWP):
- Johan Marx (Marcus) was b. in Kusel, Zweibrucken, on Sept. 17,
  1719, and immigrated to America in 1738. was taxed in 1762. He
  m. Anna Elisabetha, dau. of Johan Casper Kerber (see entry in
  Manchester section), on Mar. 22, 1748. He was naturalized on
  Sept. 24, 1762. They moved to Wachau, North Carolina on May 2,
  1774, and had the following children (recorded at FMY):
  - Anna Eva, b. on Feb. 22, 1749, and m. Johan Jacob Beroth at
    FMY on Feb. 5, 1771.
  - John, b. on Oct. 26, 1750, and bapt. on Nov. 6, 1750.
  - Philip, b. on Nov. 21, 1752, bapt. on Nov. 26, 1752, and spon. by
    Francis Lewis Beroth, John and Daniel Heckedorn, Jacob Lanius,
    and Francis Jacob Miller.
  - Catharina, b. on Oct. 20, 1754, bapt. on Oct. 27, 1754, and spon.
    by Anna Maria Engel, Catharina Heckedorn, Juliana Hoff,
    Susanna Beroth, and Anna Maria Muller.
  - Christina, b. on Oct. 20, 1756, bapt. on Oct. 24, 1756, and spon.
    by Catharina Heckedorn, Eva Barbara Ebert, and Anna Maria
    Muller.
  - Rosina, b. on Nov. 11, 1758, bapt. on Nov. 12, 1758, and spon. by
    Rosina Schmidt, Catharina Heckedorn, Anna Maria Miller, and
    Eva Weller.
  - Johanna, b. on July 21, 1761, bapt. on July 26, 1761, and spon.
    by Barbara Schlegal, Eva Weller, Anna Paff, and d. on May 29,
    1762.
  - Anna Maria, b. on June 10, 1763, bapt. on June 19, 1763, and
    spon. by Eva Weller and Eva Barbara Ebert. She d. young.
  - Christian Henry, b. on June 14, 1766, bapt. on June 15, 1766,
    and spon. by Martin Ebert, Georg Weller, and Philip Rothrock.
- Philipps Henrich, b. on Nov. 25, 1720. He was taxed in Manchester
  Township in 1762 (as Henry Heans). He m. Anna Graibill about
  1753, and Christina Jost on July 23, 1771. Anna was b. in
  Lancaster Co., Conestoga Township, PA, on Sept. 7, 1732, and d.
  on Nov. 2, 1770. Christina d. in 1779. He d. on Dec. 5, 1777. He
  had the following children:
  - Maria Catharina, b. on Jan. 2, 1753, bapt. by RJL on Dec. 23,
    1753, and spon. by Jacob and Maria Catharina Ob. She m. Peter
    Ob on May 6, 1777 (see entry in Dover section).
  - Susanna Maria, b. on Nov. 23, 1755, bapt. by RJL on Jan. 1,
    1756, and spon. by Maria Catharina Grebiel.
  - Johan Jacob, b. on July 14, 1757.

- Christian Gottleib, b. on Oct. 20, 1753. He m. Veronica about 1781.
- Johan Jacob, b. on Sept. 29, 1754.
- Anna Maria, b. in 1757.
- Rudolph, b. on Jan. 1, 1759.
- Rosina, b. about 1761.
- David, b. about 1763.
- Elisabeth, b. about 1765.
- Ehrhardt, b. on Aug. 11, 1726, and was a sponsor to the baptism of Johan Ehrhardt Heckedorn in 1747. He m. Felicitas Grosch in Forsyth Co., Bethabara, North Carolina, on July 18, 1762.
- Magdalena, b. on May 1, 1729, and was a sponsor to the baptism of Johan Ehrhardt Heckedorn in 1747. She m. Georg Schmidt in Northampton Co., Bethlehem, PA, on Jan. 25, 1756, and moved to Wachau, North Carolina.
- Martin, b. on Dec. 24, 1730.

Heilman - Johannes was taxed in 1762. He m. Anna Maria. His will was written in Codorus Township on Nov. 7, 1786, and probated on Jan. 3, 1787. They had the following children:
- Catharina Barbara, b. on Jan. 14, 1750, and bapt. at CLY on Jan. 21, 1750. She m. Peter Kuntz.
- Johan Philip, b. on Jan. 29, 1752, bapt. at CLY on Mar. 5, 1752, and m. Dorothea about 1774.
- Anna Rosina, b. on Sept. 22, 1754, and bapt. at CLY on Nov. 10, 1754. She m. Gottfried Kleindinst (see entry).
- Magdalena, b. about 1756, and was a sponsor to a baptism in 1776.
- Johan Michael, b. about 1758, and m. Mar. about 1785. He served in the Revolutionary War in Captain John Myer's Company (1778).
- Elisabetha, b. on Aug. 30, 1764, and bapt. at CLY on Sept. 30, 1764.

Heinrich - Jacob was taxed in 1762 (see entry in Shrewsbury section).

Hellman - Sebastian was taxed in 1762. He received a warrant for 100 acres on July 3, 1773. that was surveyed as 101.120 acres called *Chestnut Hill* on Sept. 1, 1773 (patented to Peter Hellman on Mar. 24, 1801). He also warranted 70 acres on Sept. 28, 1774, that was surveyed as Long Run on Sept. 1, 1773 (patented to Peter Hellman on Mar. 24, 1801). He m. Anna Margaretha, and had the following children:
- Elisabetha, bapt. by RJL on Nov. 4, 1752, and spon. by Barnhardt and Elisabetha Sponhauer.
- Michael, bapt. by RJL on Mar. 7, 1756, and spon. by Michael Kron and Maria Barbara Helmanin.

- Philip, b. on July 5, 1759, bapt. at FMY on July 7, 1759, and spon. by Marcus Hoens, Martin Ebert, Christopher Haller. He d. on July 19, 1759.
- Barbara, b. on June 24, 1760, bapt. at FMY in July 1760, and spon. by Barbara Schlegel, Elisabeth Hoens, Eva Weller, and Juliana Lanius.
- Philip, b. on Feb. 24, 1763, bapt. at FMY on Mar. 9, 1763, and spon. by Maria Hoens, Frantz Jacob Muller, and Georg Gump.
- Elisabeth, b. on Apr. 11, 1765, bapt. at FMY on Apr. 14, 1765, and spon. by Anna Elisabeth Hoens, Anna Herr, Anna Maria Muller, Barbara Hoeneise, and Catharina Heckedorn.
- Christina, b. on Feb. 6, 1768, bapt. at FMY on Feb. 10, 1768, and spon. by Anna Elisabeth Hoens, Catharina Heckedorn, Sesanna Beroth, and Juliana Lanius.
- Eva, b. on Oct. 28, 1770, bapt. at FMY on Nov. 3, 1770, and spon. by Eva Hoens, Mrs. Marx Hoens, Sister Ebert, and Anna Maria Muller.
- Maria Catharina, b. on Aug. 25, 1722.
- Juliana Elisabetha, b. on Dec. 6, 1724.
- Maria Elisabetha, b. on Feb. 18, 1726, and m. Lorentz Brotzman (see entry).
- Johan Bernhard, b. on Jan. 19, 1728, and d. in 1732.
- Juliana Susanna, b. on July 26, 1730, and d. in 1732.
- Johan Nickel, b. on July 20, 1733. He m. Sophia, and had the following children:
  - Johann Jacob, bapt. at STR on Sept. 5, 1761, and spon. by Johan Jacob and Maria Catharina Ob.
  - Andreas, bapt. by RJL on Aug. 26, 1764, and spon. by Jacob Weimer and Margaretha Kreberin.
- Maria Barbara, b. on Nov. 24, 1736.

Hoff - Adam was taxed in 1762. He was b. in Friedelsheim near Durkheim, Germany, in 1704, taken into the Moravian Congregation at Lancaster, PA, on Feb. 11 (22), 1752, and d. on Nov. 20, 1785 (bur. Nov. 22). He m. Juliana Seib of Ebingen about 1736. She was b. on Feb. 18, 1720, and taken into the Moravian Congregation at Lancaster on Feb. 9, 1752. He received a warrant for 100 acres in North Codorus Township on Feb. 15, 1749, that was surveyed as 108.16 acres called *Youlian* on Mar. 13, 1768. He also warranted 120 acres on Oct. 13, 1767, that was surveyed as 125.48 acres called *Sipe* on Mar. 31, 1768. His will was written in Codorus Township on May 5, 1776, and probated on Dec. 24, 1785. They had the following children (recorded at FMY):

- Johan Ludwig, b. on Sept. 3, 1736, bapt. at the First Reformed Church of Lancaster, Lancaster Co., PA, on Oct. 3, 1736, and spon. by Ludwig Seib and wife.
- Francis, b. on Feb. 4, 1739. He was taxed in 1762, and received a warrant for 25 acres in North Codorus Township on Jan. 12, 1767, that was surveyed as 16.120 acres called *Mary Eve* on Apr. 22, 1767. He m. Maria Eva. They had the following children:
  - Anna Elisabetha, b. on Oct. 7, 1761, and bapt. at STJ.
  - Maria Eva, b. on Dec. 25, 1763, and bapt. at STJ on Jan. 22, 1764.
- Johan Adam, b. on July 29, 1740 (according to the First Reformed Church in Lancaster, Lancaster Co., PA, he was b. in 1739, bapt. on June 29, 1739, and spon. by Johan Adam Muller). He m. Dorothea, dau. of Geret Hummel, and Eva before 1810. His will was written in Codorus Township on Feb. 8, 1810, and probated on Jan. 15, 1811. He had the following children:
  - Christina, bapt. by RJL on Oct. 18, 1765, and spon. by Peter Hoff and Christina Harnisen.
  - Lowis, bapt. at STY on Nov. 17, 1769, and spon. by Lowis Gartnerin.
  - Johannes, b. on June 25, 1771, bapt. at QLC on Sept. 1, 1771, and spon. by Geret Hummel (grandfather) and wife.
  - Catharina, b. on May 2, 1775, bapt. at QLC on Aug. 27, 1775, and spon. by Catharina Bayer.
  - Johann Adam, b. on Oct. 24, 1777, bapt. at QLC on June 28, 1778, and spon. by Adam Muller.
  - Johan Jacob, b. on July 17, 1780, bapt. at QLC on Sept. 3, 1780, and spon. by Gerhard Hummel and wife.
  - Andreas, b. on June 27, 1782, bapt. at QLC on Oct. 5, 1782, and spon. by Michael Leidig and wife.
- Johan Peter, b. on Oct. 29, 1742. He m. Christina. They had the following children:
  - Daniel, b. on Apr. 30, 1771, bapt. at QLC on Sept. 22, 1771, and spon. by Stophel Kobel and wife.
  - Catharina, b. on Good Friday, bapt. at QLC on Aug. 8, 1773, and spon. by Michael Miller and Catharina Hummelin.
  - Abraham, b. on Feb. 5, 1775, bapt. at STY, and spon. by Christoph Kowel.
- Johannes, b. on Feb. 2, 1744.
- Christina, b. on Oct. 28, 1745, bapt. by RJL on Nov. 8, 1745, and spon. by Ludwig and Christina Seib.
- Johan Jacob, b. on Dec. 15, 1747, and bapt. on Dec. 26, 1747.
- Daniel, b. on Feb. 4, 1750.

- Andreas, b. on Nov. 23, 1751, bapt. on Nov. 30, and spon. by Jacob Christman, Francis Jacob Muller, John Heckedorn, and Daniel Heckedorn.
- Godfrey, b. on Nov. 25, 1753, bapt. on Dec. 6, and spon. by Godfrey Engle, Francis Jacob Muller, and Peter Binckel.
- Son, stillborn on Nov. 23, 1755.
- Dau., stillborn on Nov. 23, 1755.
- Philip, b. on Feb. 5, 1757.
- Johan Heinrich, b. on Aug. 6, 1760, bapt. on Aug. 13, and spon. by Melchior Schmidt, Francis Lewis Berot, and Peter Binckele.
- Juliana, b. on Mar. 30, 1762, and d. on May 13, 1765. She was bapt. on Apr. 2, and spon. by Eva Weller, Anna Maria Prozman, and Margaret Binckel.

Hoffacre - Michael warranted 100 acres before Oct. 14, 1768 (survey date).

Hoffman - Adam m. Anna Barbara, dau. of Michael and Anna Margaretha (Miller) Sprenckel (see entry), in York Co., PA, on July 17, 1743 (after Adam's death, she m. Ludwig Treiber (about 1753)(see entry). Barbara d. in York Co. sometime before Apr. 9, 1781, when her son, Michael Trieber was granted letters of administration for her estate. Adam and Anna Barbara had the following children in Codorus Township:
- Adam, b. about 1747, and m. Maria Barbara.
- Johann Conrad, bapt. by Reverend Jacob Lischy in Mar. 1749, and spon. by Conrad and Catharina Elisabeth Muller.

Honig - Niclaus was a weaver from Lusan (possibly Lobsann, Soultzsous-Forets) Northern Alsace. He m. Catharina, widow of Jacob Stambach (see entry), in Niederkutzenhausen on Nov. 17, 1733. They immigrated to America on the ship *Robert and Alice* in 1739. On Dec. 25, 1739, Niclaus m. Maria Elisabetha Fischer at Trinity Lutheran Church of Lancaster, Lancaster Co., PA. His will was written in York Co. on Feb. 18, 1751, and probated on June 11, 1752. Niclaus and Catharina had the following children (see BNA):
- Anna Maria, b. on Nov. 26, 1734, and d. in 1738.
- Johannes, b. on June 3, 1736, and bapt. on June 5, 1736.

Huber - Georg m. Magdalena. He was warranted 200 acres on June 23, 1768, that was surveyed as 227.80 acres on Apr. 12, 1768 (interest began on Mar. 1, 1756). They had the following son:
- Johan Georg was taxed in 1762. He m. Maria Margaretha, dau. of Jacob Scherer. They had the following children:

- Johan Georg, bapt. by RJL on Feb. 24, 1765, and bapt. by Georg Huber, Sr., and Magdalena.
- Eva Elisabetha, bapt. at STJ on Mar. 21, 1767.
- Christian, b. on June 24, 1769, and bapt. at STJ on July 4, 1769.
- Anna Maria, b. on Sept. 10, 1771, and bapt. at STJ on Oct. 4, 1771.

Huber - Johan Ulrich immigrated to America on the ship *Mortonhouse* on June 21, 1729, and received a warrant for 226 acres on Jan. 22, 1733. He was taxed in 1762. He received a warrant for 50 acres on Dec. 18, 1751, which he deeded to Conrad Supinger on Nov. 24, 1760. He m. Anna Maria. They had the following children (see History and Families of the Black Rock Church of the Brethren by Elmer Q. Gleim (1988)):
- Ulrich was taxed in 1762. He was b. on Mar. 24, 1734, and d. on Oct. 5, 1805. He m. Susanna about 1760, Eva Linafelter about 1772. Eva d. on June 16, 1820. He served in the Revolutionary War in Captain John Myer's Company (1778). He had the following children:
  - Ulrich, b. about 1761, and m. Catharina about 1782.
  - Michael, bapt. by RJL in Dec. 1763, and spon. by Michael and Catharina Bohler.
  - Maria Barbara, bapt. by RJL on Dec. 27, 1765, and spon. by Michael Noll and Anna Margaretha Fischbornin.
  - Anna Catharina, b. on Aug. 7, 1767, and bapt. at STJ on Aug. 11, 1767.
  - Johan Jacob, b. on Aug. 4, 1769, and bapt. at STJ on Aug. 8, 1769.
  - Eva, b. on Dec. 31, 1773, and bapt. at STJ on Jan. 2, 1774.
  - Johan Georg, b. on Jan. 10, 1776, and bapt. at STJ on Mar. 3, 1776.
  - Jacob, b. on Aug. 20, 1778, and bapt. at STJ on Oct. 4, 1778.
  - Son, b. on Sept. 26, 1780, and bapt. at STJ on Oct. 25, 1780.
  - Peter, b. on Oct. 3, 1785, and bapt. at STJ on Dec. 18, 1785.
  - Maria Elisabeth, b. on Dec. 18, 1788, and bapt. at STJ on Jan. 29, 1789.
  - Anna Maria, b. on May 30, 1791, and bapt. at STJ on July 10, 1791.
  - Barbara, b. on Mar. 12, 1793, and bapt. at STJ on July 10, 1791.
- Jacob, bapt. by RJL on Feb. 10, 1754, and spon. by Jacob and Ester Keller.
- Daniel, bapt. by RJL on Aug. 8, 1756, and spon. by Daniel and Elisabetha Renolly.
- Johan Daniel, bapt. by RJL on June 26, 1760, and spon. by Daniel and Elisabetha Renolly.

36   *EARLY GERMAN SETTLERS OF YORK CO., PA*

- Anna Maria, bapt. by RJL on Aug. 15, 1762, and spon. by Georg and Anna Maria Lickenfelder.

Huckenberger - Reinhard was taxed in 1762.

Hupp - John received a warrant for 100 acres on Oct. 28, 1746.

Isler - Johann Georg received a warrant for 40 acres on Mar. 9, 1753 that was surveyed as 26.49 acres in May 1753. He also received a warrant for 40 acres on Mar. 9, 1753, that was surveyed as 91 acres on May 15, 1755. He m. Susanna Siegrist, and immigrated to America in 1749. They had the following children:
- Abraham, b. in the wooded section (Gebuesch) of Canton Zurich, Switzerland, in July 1743, and d. in York Co., PA, on Nov. 11, 1761 (CLY).
- Johann Heinrich, b. on Apr. 24, 1759, bapt. at TLY on Oct. 12, 1762, and spon. by Friedrich Basler and wife.
- Jacobus, b. on June 24, 1754, bapt. at TLY on Oct. 12, 1762, and spon. by Conrad Wirtz.
- Regina, b. on Mar. 26, 1757, bapt. at TLY on Oct. 12, 1762, and spon. by Adam and Juliana Pott.

Jung - Carl was taxed in 1762. He m. Elisabetha. They had the following children:
- Carl, b. on Feb. 15, 1748, bapt. at SML on May 14, 1749, and spon. by the father and John Luffolt, a widower.
- Anna Catharina, bapt. by RJL on Sept. 26, 1762, and spon. by Peter and Anna Catharina Schneider.
- Henrich, b. on Dec. 26, 1763, bapt. at SML on Jan. 15, 1764, and spon. by Henrich Eckart and Catharina Wildasin.

Kaltreiter (Kalckreuter) - Georg received a warrant for 150 acres on June 29, 1767, that was surveyed as 140 acres called *Chestnut Valley* on June 2, 1768. He m. Ursula, and had the following children:
- Dewald, was taxed in 1762. He m. Elisabetha Catharina, and had the following children:
  - Christina, bapt. by RJL on Sept. 9, 1760, and spon. by Georg and Catharina Keller.
  - Maria Catharina, b. on Sept. 13, 1762, bapt. by RJL on Jan. 1, 1763, and spon. by Ludwig and Maria Catharina Rudisill. She m. George, son of Stefan Petry, and d. on Apr. 13, 1815. He was b. in Strousbourg, France, on Aug. 1, 1762, and d. on June 1, 1832. They are bur. in Chestnut Grove cemetery.
  - Elisabetha, b. on May 27, 1769, and bapt. at STJ on June 3, 1769.

CODORUS TOWNSHIP 37

- Georg, b. on Mar. 3, 1775, and bapt. at STJ on Apr. 16, 1775.
- Barbara, bapt. by RJL on Mar. 5, 1755, and spon. by Magdalena Meyerin.

Keller - Georg had a land warrant for 100 acres in York Co., Manheim and Codorus Townships, PA, on June 13, 1754, and 100 acres in Codorus Township on June 25 (23), 1768 (the Codorus tract was surveyed to Georg Jr. as 88.130 acres on June 22, 1788, and patented to Henry Wherly on July 26, 1809). His 1754 warrant was surveyed as 102 acres to Jacob Keller on Dec. 19, 1785, and patented to Jacob on Aug. 10, 1790. On May 31, 1768, Georg warranted 100 acres in Codorus Township. This land was surveyed on May 10, 1769 as 98.120 acres called *Squirrel Valley*, and patented to his grandson, Jacob, on June 19, 1810. He appears on the York County Militia lists in 1777/78 as being over age in Capt. John Meyer's Company, 1st of the 5th Battalion. Georg appears on tax lists of Codorus Township to 1781, and is presumed to have d. then. In 1779 and 1780, he is taxed in Codorus Township for 200 acres, two horses and three cattle. In 1781, he has 200 acres, four horses, three cattle, and two mills. Georg is believed to be the father of the following Keller's of Manheim and Codorus Township (his son, Georg, is specifically named as Georg Jr.):
- Johan Jacob, b. about 1729. He was taxed in 1762. He m. Esther, dau. of Michael and Anna Margaret (Miller) Sprenckel (see entry), about 1751. Jacob and Esther were sponsors at the baptism of Jacob, son of Ulrich and Anna Maria Huber, on Feb. 10, 1754, by Reverend Jacob Lischy. Jacob received a land warrant of 40 acres in Codorus Township on May 31, 1762. On Dec. 10, 1789, he received a warrant (interest beginning on Nov. 1, 1769) for 40 acres in Codorus Township (adjacent to Georg Keller, Sr.). This land was surveyed as 52 acres on June 1, 1790, and patented to Jacob on June 21, 1810 (Jacob Jr.). On Dec. 19, 1785, he had a survey done on his father's 1754 100 acre patent in Manheim and Codorus Township, which was patented to Jacob on Aug. 10, 1790. On Apr. 20, 1751, Jacob received a warrant for 100 acres in North Codorus Township. This land was surveyed to him as 178 acres on May 15, 1755, and patented to Daniel Renolly on Dec. 12, 1785. On Jan. 14, 1767, he warranted 100 acres in Codorus Township, that was surveyed as 75.40 acres called *Bottomless Springs* on Apr. 24, 1771, and patented on Mar. 25, 1791. On May 31, 1762, he warranted 40 acres in Codorus Township, which was patented as Bush Hill for 109.2 acres on Nov. 13, 1766, and patented on Mar. 25, 1791. Jacob served during the Revolutionary War as a Private in the York County Militia in 1776, 1777, 1778, and 1780. In 1777/88, he was in Capt. John Myers Company, 1st of the 5th Battalion. He was a farmer in Codorus Township with 170 acres,

two horses, and four cattle in 1779; 100 acres, one horse, and four cattle in 1780; 170 acres two horses, and three cattle in 1781; 170 acres, one horse, and four cattle in 1782; and 170 acres in 1783. In 1801, Jacob deeded his land to his son-in-law, Jacob Busser, in return for supporting Jacob and Esther in their old age. Jacob d. in Codorus Township in Mar. 1810, and Esther d. sometime after that date. Jacob and Esther had the following children (George is presumed to be Jacob's son, but it has not been confirmed) in Codorus Township:

- Catherine, b. about 1752, and m. Jacob Bossert. In 1783, they were taxed in Shrewsbury Township with nine inhabitants. Jacob was a Revolutionary War Private from 1778 to 1781. Jacob and Catherine deeded land to her cousin, Jacob Scherer, on May 1, 1809. Jacob was the administer of his bro.-in-law, Jacob Busser's, estate in 1818. On Apr. 7, 1798, Jacob and Catherine Bossert of Codorus Township deeded land to John Ruhl.
- Jacob, b. about 1755. He m. Elizabeth, dau. of Hans Georg and Anna Maria Keller. Jacob was taxed as a single man in Codorus Township in 1779, and 1780 (as Jr.).
- George, b. about 1758 (presumed to be Jacob's son). He m. Veronica. George had 100 acres, two horses, and three cattle in Codorus Township in 1782, and 100 acres and seven inhabitants in 1783. George wrote his will on Feb. 23, 1792, and it was probated in Codorus Township on Mar. 26, 1792. Christina Rohrbach witnessed and executed his will.
- Esther, b. on Aug. 16, 1762, and m. Johannes Gans (see entry).
- Maria, b. about 1765. She was unmarried in 1807.
- John, b. about 1769. He d. sometime after 1807. His father disapproved of his "irresolute and extravagant" lifestyle, and withheld his inheritance until he amended it. He was unmarried in 1807.
- Elizabeth, b. about 1772. She m. Jacob Busser. He was a tailor and yeoman in Codorus Township. On Dec. 8, 1791, Jacob received 40 acres 66 perches in Codorus Township from John and Anna Justina Sharer. On Dec. 29, 1797, Jacob received 18 acres and 20 perches, and 75 and one fourth acres in Codorus Township from his in-laws, Jacob and Esther Keller. On Dec. 3, 1801, Jacob received 109 acres 20 perches, and 3 acres in Codorus Township from Jacob and Esther Keller in return for supporting them in their old age. Jacob d. intestate in Codorus Township in Apr. 1814, owning 245 acres, and Elizabeth d. sometime after that date. The estate was administered by Elizabeth Busser and Jacob Bossert on Apr. 8, 1814.
- Johan Georg, b. about 1731. He m. Anna Maria about 1752 and Christina about 1758. He received a land warrant for two 50 acres

tracts, one in Manheim Township, and one in Codorus Township on Dec. 16, 1758. The Manheim Township tract was surveyed as 54.157 acres to Georg on Dec. 19, 1785, and patented to his son, Jacob on Aug. 10, 1790. The Codorus tract was surveyed to Georg as 90 acres on June 6, 1759, and patented to Henry Wherly on July 26, 1809. Georg had 50 acres in Codorus Township in 1779 (listed as Jr.); 50 acres, two horses, and two cattle in 1780 (listed as Jr.); 100 acres, three horses, and four cattle in 1781; 150 acres, two horses, and three cattle in 1782; and 50 acres and six inhabitants in 1783. Hans Georg and Anna Maria were sponsors at the baptism of Johan Georg, son of Niclaus and Anna Elisabeth Brigner, by Reverend Jacob Lischy on Jan. 26, 1755. Maria was alive on Dec. 3, 1757, and the name of Georg's wife was not specified on his dau., Maria Catherine's, baptism. Georg d. in Manheim Township in Apr. 1798. His will was written on Dec. 9, 1791, and probated on Apr. 13, 1798. His execs. were Michael Miller, and Ulrich Huber. Georg had the following children in Codorus Township:
- Johannes Jacob, b. in 1753. He m. Anna Maria. Jacob d. in York Co. on Nov. 11, 1828, and is bur. in St. Jacob's cemetery.
- Abraham, b. on Jan. 29, 1756. He was bapt. by Reverend Jacob Lischy on Jan. 29, 1756, and spon. by Jacob and Barbara Ubman. He m. Elizabeth. Abraham is taxed as a single man in Codorus Township in 1779 and 1780. In 1781, he has one head of cattle, and in 1782, he has 150 acres, one horse, and one head of cattle.
- Elizabeth, b. about 1757, and m. Jacob Keller, Jr.
- Maria Catherine, b. on Dec. 25, 1759, bapt. at St. Jacob's, and spon. by Maria Catherine Meng. She m. Mathias, son of Heinrich Brodbeck (see entry). Mathias was b. on Jan. 27, 1760, and bapt. at St. Jacob's.
- Maria Barbara, bapt. by Reverend Jacob Lischy on Apr. 25, 1762, and spon. by her uncle and aunt, Jacob and Barbara Scherer. She m. Christian Leib, who was b. in 1755, and d. in 1847. Barbara d. in 1831.
- Maria Eva, b. on Oct. 10, 1764, bapt. by Reverend Jacob Lischy on Feb. 24, 1765, and spon. by Frantz and Maria Eva Hoff. She m. Abraham Miller. He was b. in 1761, and d. in 1829. She d. on Feb. 15, 1845.
- Anna Maria, b. on May 17, 1767. She was bapt. at St. Jacob's on June 24, 1767, and spon. by Maria Peterman. She m. Michael Miller.
- Johannes Georg, b. on Nov. 2, 1769, bapt. at St. Jacob's on Feb. 2, 1770, and spon. by Georg and Elizabeth Dehoff. He d. before Dec. 1791.
- Christina, b. on Dec. 6, 1771. She was bapt. at St. Jacob's on Mar. 8, 1772. She m. Nicholas Ehrhardt

- Johannes, b. on Aug. 18, 1782, bapt. at St. Jacob's on Oct. 9, 1782, and spon. by John and Maria Barbara Baumann. He d. sometime before Dec. 1791.
- Johannes, b. about 1733, and d. in Manheim Township in Dec. 1806. He m. Maria Magdalena, sometime before 1754. In 1762 he was residing in Codorus Township. They were sponsors at the baptism of Johannes, son of Adam and Anna Margareth Hellwig, by Reverend Jacob Lischy on Jan. 20, 1754; John, son of John and Elizabeth Ott on Dec. 27, 1759; Johan Michael, son of Frantz and Rebecca Hammer, by Reverend Jacob Lischy on Oct. 7, 1760; Mary Magdalena, dau. of John and Elizabeth Ott on Jan. 22, 1764; Johannes, son of Jacob and Elisabeth Linckefelder, by Reverend Jacob Lischy on Jan. 28, 1764; and Anna Magdalena, dau. of Peter and Catharina Runk, by Reverend Jacob Lischy on Apr. 8, 1764. Johannes will was written on Feb. 14, 1806, and probated on Dec. 8, 1806. His execs. were his bro., Johan Jacob Keller, and Jacob Bossert. He was said to be an old and single man. He was taxed in 1762.
- Maria Barbara, b. about 1735. She m. Hans Jacob Scherer (see entry).
- Johan Heinrich, b. about 1740. He was taxed in 1762. He m. Anna Margaretha. They both d. sometime after 1764. They had the following children:
  - Engela, bapt. by Reverend Jacob Lischy on Nov. 7, 1761, and spon. by Christoph and Engela Rothermel.
  - Johan Frederick, bapt. by Reverend Jacob Lischy on Aug. 28, 1764, and spon. by Johan Friedrich and Catharina Hausman. He may be the Frederick Keller that m. Elizabeth Peter, and d. in Juanita Co., PA, on Feb. 22, 1848.

<u>Kercher</u> - Jacob was taxed in 1762.

<u>Kerchner</u> - Casper was taxed in 1762. He received a warrant for 100 acres in North Codorus Township, that was surveyed as 50.80 acres on Mar. 29, 1768.

<u>Kergerick</u> - Jacob received a warrant for 50 acres on May 25, 1774, that was surveyed as 77 acres called *Jacob's Lot* on Oct. 20, 1774, and patented on Dec. 6, 1808 (interest began on Mar. 1, 1765).

<u>Kessler</u> - Michael received a warrant for 50 acres on Oct. 3, 1767, that in combination with Christian Snyder's 100 acre warrant was surveyed as 154.46 acres called *Hawanow* on Apr. 16, 1767, and patented on Oct. 3, 1767 (improved 13 years in 1767).

Kieffer - Hans Leonard Kieffer m. Anna Margaretha. They had the following children (see BWP):
- Johann Casper, b. on May 1, 1704, and bapt. at Breitenbach, Germany. He immigrated to America with his bro., Abraham on the ship *Two Brothers* in 1748. He received a warrant for two 75 acre tracts on Mar. 9, 1753. He m. Maria Agnes Glocker, and had the following children (recorded at Breitenbach Reformed Church):
  - Abraham, b. on Feb. 7, 1728, and bapt. on Feb. 11, 1728. He was taxed in 1762. He m. Christina, dau. of Michael and Anna Margaretha (Miller) Sprenckel (see entry), sometime before Mar. 1754. Abraham was alive in Nov. 1762, and probably deceased in 1764, because he did not sign the release to George Sprenckel with his wife. Abraham's widow m. Jacob Welschans at the First Reformed Church of York on May 13, 1766. Abraham and Christina had the following children:
    - Johan Ludwig, bapt. by Reverend Jacob Lischy on Apr. 13, 1755, and spon. by his uncle, Johan Ludwig Kieffer, and Anna Margaretha Sprenglerin.
    - Johan Henrich, bapt. by Reverend Jacob Lischy on Sept. 22, 1756, and spon. by Heinrich and Margaretha (his grandmother) Eberhardt.
    - Catharina, bapt. by Reverend Jacob Lischy on Feb. 4, 1759, and spon. by Jacob and Catharina Pfluger.
    - Georg Freidrich, bapt. by Reverend Jacob Lischy on Jan. 25, 1761, and spon. by Georg Freidrich and Margreth Pflieger.
    - Jacob and Christina (Sprenckel) Welschans had the following children:
      - Anna Maria, b. in Mar. 1768, bapt. at Wolf's on May 1, 1768, and spon. by Jacob and Anna Maria Welschans.
      - Johan Jacob, bapt. at Wolf's on Oct. 12, 1769, and spon. by Georg and Anna Margreth Gerbach.
  - Maria Barbara, bapt. on July 26, 1733.
  - Maria Elisabetha, b. on Aug. 10, 1735, and bapt. on Aug. 14, 1735. She was a sponsor to the baptism of Michael Fink in 1760.
  - Johann Ludwig, b. on Mar. 14, 1737. He was taxed in 1762. He was naturalized on Apr. 7, 1765. He m. Anna Margaretha, dau. of Michael and Anna Margaretha (Miller) Sprenckel (see entry) (m. sometime before Feb. 1756 (on Mar. 17, 1756)). She was b. on Jan. 1, 1736. They had the following children:
    - Michael, b. about 1757.
    - Abraham, b. about 1759.
    - Johan Jacob, bapt. by Reverend Jacob Lischy on Sept. 9, 1760, and spon. by Jacob Schaffer.
    - Caspar, bapt. by Reverend Jacob Lischy on July 18, 1762, and spon. by Caspar and Agnes Kieffer.

- Johan Jacob, bapt. by Reverend Jacob Lischy on Nov. 17, 1764, and spon. by Friedrich and Maria Margareth Pfluger.
- Margaret, b. about 1766, and m. Henry Sprenckel.
- George, b. about 1768.
- Barbara, b. about 1770.
- Maria Margareth, b. on Nov. 1, 1739, and was a sponsor with Ludwig Kieffer to the baptism of Philliph Ludwig Grimm.
- Anna Maria, b. on Dec. 21, 1742.
- Abraham m. Anna Barbara, dau. of Nickel Gerhard of Liedersweiler, Oberamt Lichtenberg at Breitenbach, Germany, on Feb. 2, 1734. He immigrated to America with his bro., Casper, on the ship *Two Brothers*, in 1748. He settled in Berks Co., Rockland Township, PA, and was living there in 1757.

Kleindinst - David received a warrant for 100 acres in North Codorus Township on Nov. 22, 1766, that was surveyed as 87.120 acres called *David's Addition* on Apr. 15, 1767. His will was written in Codorus Township on Feb. 3, 1798, and probated on June 30, 1798. He m. Magdalena, and had the following children:
- Gottfried, m. Rosina, dau. of John Heilman (see entry) before 1785, and Margaret, dau. of Michael Hengst, before 1789. Margaret's probate inventory was filed in Codorus Township in 1850.
- David, had his will written in Hanover Township on Aug. 16, 1798, and probated on Sept. 5, 1798. He m. Elizabeth.
- Christian, m. Eva before 1785.
- Andrew, m. Magdalena before 1795.
- Michael.
- Eve.
- Barbara.

Kneier (Kneyer) - Leonhartt was taxed in 1762. He m. Barbara, and had the following children:
- Leonhartt m. Margaretha, and had the following children:
  - Christian, b. on Jan. 1, 1766, and bapt. at STJ on the first Sunday after Easter.
- Catharina Elisabetha, bapt. by RJL on June 6, 1762, and spon. by Frederick and Catharina Rohmer.

Konrath (Conrad) - Johan Georg m. Catharina and had the following children:
- Adam was taxed in 1762. He was b. on Aug. 5, 1738, and bapt. at CLY on Dec. 1, 1738. He m. Maria Christina. They had the following children:
  - Catharina Margaretha, b. on Nov. 9, 1761, and bapt. at CLY on Jan. 17, 1762.

CODORUS TOWNSHIP

- Johan Heinrich, b. on Jan. 6, 1763, bapt. at TLY on Apr. 4, 1763, and spon. by Heinrich Conrad and wife.
- Heinrich m. Anna Catharina, dau. of Martin and Anna Catharina Schmidt. She was b. in Fenershausen in Osingen, Germany, (recorded in death records of CLY) on Dec. 1, 1722, and d. on June 8, 1759. She was the widow of Valentine Alt, who d. in 1755 (see entry in Shrewsbury section). After Catharina's death, Heinrich m. Elisabetha Stohten. He had the following children:
- Child, b. about 1757.
- Johan Frederick, b. on Jan. 17, 1763, bapt. at CLY on Apr. 4, 1763, and spon. by Heinrich Kuhn and wife.
- Anna, bapt. at TLY on Aug. 2, 1744, and spon. by her parents.

Kramer - The following Kramers appear to be siblings, and children of an unknown Kramer:
- Daniel was taxed in 1762. He m. Anna Margareta Schmidt, probably a dau. of Heinrich Schmidt (see entry). Daniel was b. in Germany in 1730, and d. in York Co. in 1780 (his will was probated on Mar. 7, 1780). He warranted 109.126 acres on Oct. 14, 1768. Anna Margaretha d. in York Co. in 1815. They bapt. the following children at St. Jacob's (except the first two):
  - Johann Helfrig, b. in Sept. 1753, and d. in York Co. on Sept. 22, 1833. He m. Henrietta Sophia Neidig in York Co. on Apr. 5, 1785. She was b. in Montgomery Co., PA, on Sept. 19, 1761, and d. in York Co. on Nov. 20, 1839. He served in the Revolutionary War in Captain John Myer's Company (1778). They are bur. at STJ.
  - Johan Daniel, bapt. by Reverend Jacob Lischy on Oct. 7, 1760, and spon. by Daniel and Maria Elisabeth Diehl.
  - Anna Maria, b. on Aug. 21, 1762, and bapt. on Aug. 29, 1762.
  - Eva Elisabetha, b. on July 4, 1766, and bapt. on July 20, 1766. She m. Frederick, son of Peter Wilhelm (see entry).
- Helfrich, m. Eva Elisabetha, dau. of Jacob Scherer (see entry). His will was written in Manheim Township on Apr. 27, 1794, and probated on June 5, 1797. They had the following children:
  - Henrich, b. on June 13, 1761, bapt. at SLC on June 27, 1761, and spon. by Mathias Scherer and Margareth Krah.
  - Maria Margaretha, b. on May 5, 1763, bapt. at SLC on May 20, 1763, and spon. by Georg and Maria Margaretha Huber.
  - Anna Maria, b. on Dec. 15, 1765, bapt. at SLC on Dec. 25, 1765, and spon. by Georg and Anna Maria Marter.
  - Philip, b. on Mar. 17, 1767, bapt. at SLC on Mar. 25, 1767, and spon. by Philip Cramer and Barbara Scherer.
  - Johannes, b. on Oct. 21, 1768, bapt. at SLC on Oct. 28, 1768, and spon. by Johan and Justina Scherer.

- Lorentz was taxed in 1762. He m. Anna Maria. They had the
following children:
  - Anna Margareth, bapt. by RJL on Jan. 21, 1761, and spon. by
  Daniel and Anna Margaretha Kramer.
  - Johannes, b. on Aug. 17, 1762, and bapt. at STJ on Sept. 26,
  1762.
  - Anna Maria, b. on Sept. 4, 1770, bapt. at FRI on 15th Sunday
  after Trinity, and spon. by Peter Ehrhard.
  - Maria Magdalena, b. on Aug. 1, 1773, bapt. at FRI on Sept. 11,
  1773, and spon. by Georg Emig and Maria Magdalena Kramer.
  - Johann Friedrich, b. on Apr. 1, 1775, bapt. at FRI on May 14,
  1775, and spon. by Friedrich and Anna Maria Fissel.
  - Johann Georg, b. on Jan. 11, 1778, bapt. the 2nd Sunday in Lent,
  and spon. by Georg and Barbara Kleinfelter.
- Philip was a sponsor to the baptism of Philip Kramer in 1767.
- Maria Magdalena was a sponsor to the baptism of Maria Magdalena
Kramer in 1767.

Krebs - Ludwig was taxed in 1762. He immigrated to America on the
ship *Isaac* in the fall of 1749, and m. Anna Catharina Zimmerman in
York Co. in May 1752. He received a warrant for 200 acres on Jan. 14,
1767. This land was surveyed as 180.6 acres called *Fishbogh* on May
29, 1767. He received a warrant of 100 acres on May 27, 1773 that was
surveyed as 105.25 acres called *Round About* on Sept. 22, 1773. He d.
in 1784. His will was written in Codorus Township on Apr. 8, 1783, and
probated on Apr. 6, 1784. They had the following children:
- Johan Peter, b. on Feb. 21, 1753, and bapt. at CLY on Mar. 11,
1753. He m. Barbara Sappell about 1778, and d. on Feb. 25, 1842.
She was b. on Aug. 11, 1757, and d. on July 24, 1835. They are
bur. at STJ.
- Johan Georg, b. on May 6, 1754, and bapt. at CLY on June 9, 1754.
He m. Catharina about 1787, and d. on May 7, 1842 (bur. at STJ).
- Maria Elisabetha, b. in 1760, and d. about 1847. She never m.
- Heinrich, b. about 1762, and m. Margaretha about 1782.
- Catharina, b. about 1764, and m. Adam Wertz.
- Christina, b. about 1766, and m. Jacob Canto.
- Jacob, b. about 1768, and m. Christina about 1790.
- Ludwig, b. about 1770.
- Maria Margaretha, b. in 1773, m. Peter Shultz, and d. in 1817.
- Jeremiah, b. about 1775.

Kroll - Johannes was taxed in 1779, and d. in Codorus Township in
Nov./Dec. 1823. During the Revolution, he served as a Private in the
7th Battalion (1778). His probate inventory was filed in 1824. He m.
Deborah. She d. before Dec. 1828. They had the following children:

CODORUS TOWNSHIP 45

- Jacob, b. on Oct. 25, 1772, and bapt. at CLY.
- John, b. in 1773, m. Elisabeth Stuck, and d. in Feb./Mar. 1817.
- Barbara, b. about 1775, and d. in Dec. 1828. Her probate inventory was filed in Codorus Township in 1828
- Georg, b. on Mar. 1, 1777, bapt. at CLY on May 15, 1777, and m. Sarah.
- Margaretha Elisabeth, b. on Mar. 7, 1779, and bapt. at CLY on May 3, 1779. She m. John Welsch.
- Catharina, b. on Mar. 25, 1781, bapt. at CLY on May 3, 1781, and m. Solomon Drexler.
- Susan, b. on July 27, 1783, bapt. at CLY on Aug. 17, 1783, and m. Jeremiah Hess on June 11, 1812.
- Maria, b. on Oct. 17, 1785, bapt. at CLY on Dec. 10, 1785, and m. Frederick Shotter.
- Sarah, b. on June 6, 1788, bapt. at CLY on July 13, 1788, and m. Conrad Pudding.
- Samuel, b. on Aug. 7, 1790, bapt. at CLY on Sept. 12, 1790, and m. Catharine Kaufman in July 1811.
- Solomon, b. on May 29, 1794, bapt. at CLY on June 29, 1794, m. Catharina, and d. before 1830.

Kron - Lorentz had the following children (an Anna Catharina Erwin, widow of ____ Cron, m. Philip Schmeiser at CAN on Oct. 19, 1756):
- Lorentz, was taxed in 1762. He m. Rosina, dau. of Heinrich Schmidt (see entry). They had the following children:
  - Heinrich, bapt. by RJL on Dec. 24, 1752, and spon. by Heinrich and Margaretha Schmidt.
  - Catharina Elisabetha, bapt. by RJL on July 7, 1754, and spon. by Antoni and Catharina Elisabetha Ehler.
  - Michael, b. one week after New Year, 1764, and bapt. at STJ on Mar. 25, 1764.
  - Maria Elisabetha, bapt. by Reverend Jacob Lischy on June 1, 1766, and spon. by Philliphine Kronin.
- Johannes, m. Anna Maria Paulus at CAN on Dec. 2, 1755, and resided in Hellam Township. They had the following children (recorded at CAN):
  - Johann Jacob, b. on May 21, 1756, bapt. on July 4, 1756, and spon. by Johann Jacob and Anna Maria Leber.
  - Anna Maria, b. on June 12, 1757, bapt. on July 3, 1757, and spon. by Peter and Anna Christina Attich.
  - Johannes, b. on Jan. 11, 1759.
  - Christina, b. on Apr. 4, 1760.
  - Lorentz, b. on May 13, 1762.
  - Henrich, b. on Apr. 16, 1764.
  - Conrath, b. on Mar. 10, 1766.

46 EARLY GERMAN SETTLERS OF YORK CO., PA

- Michael, b. on Nov. 23, 1768.
- Henrich, b. on June 18, 1770.
- Maria, b. on Apr. 28, 1772.
- Friedrich, b. on Apr. 3, 1774.
- Catharina, b. on Oct. 22, 1775.
- Simon m. Maria Catharina Gohn at CAN on Feb. 18 (15), 1757, and had the following children (recorded at CAN):
  - Johann Melchior, b. on Aug. 10, 1758, bapt. on Aug. 20, 1758, and spon. by Johann Melchior and Catharina Elisabetha Loray.
  - Simon, b. on Dec. 10, 1759, and spon. by Philip Schmeiser and Anna Catharina.
  - Johann Henrich, b. on Jan. 28, 1769, bapt. at WOL on Feb. 12, 1769, and spon. by Johannes Cremer and Maria Elisabetha Cremerin.
  - Michael, b. on Jan. 10, 1771, bapt. at WOL on Aug. 11, 1771, and spon. by Michael and Catharina Glasser.
- Phillip m. Maria Elisabetha, and had the following children:
  - Christina, b. on Sept. 28, 1755, bapt. at FMY on Oct. 31, and spon. by Francis Jacob and Anna Maria Muller.
  - Johan Philip, b. on Nov. 3, 1757, and bapt. at CLY on Aug. 30, 1761.
  - Simon Jacob, b. on Oct. 5, 1760, and bapt. at CLY on Aug. 30, 1761.
  - Johan David, bapt. at WOL on Aug. 2, 1767, and spon. by Matheus and Catharina Bayer.
  - Johann Daniel, bapt. at STY on June 3, 1770, and spon. by Daniel and Anna Messerle.
- Anna Maria, b. on Apr. 5, 1744, bapt. at SML on May 15, 1744, and spon. by Jacob and Anna Ursula Stambach.

Kuhn - Johan Frederick received a warrant for 50 acres in North Codorus Township on Aug. 1, 1766. His will was written in Berwick Township on Mar. 22, 1778, and probated on Apr. 4, 1778. He m. Anna Catharina, and had the following children:
- Mary.
- Jacob.
- Susanna.
- Anna Barbara, b. on Mar. 9, 1753, bapt. at CLY on Mar. 11, 1753, and m. Jacob Small.
- Johan Georg, b. on Feb. 7, 1755, bapt. by RJL (CLY) on Feb. 16, 1755, and spon. by Georg and Anna Barbara Barth. He m. Catherine, dau. of Casper Reinecker before 1789.
- Maria Catharina, b. on Oct. 31, 1757, bapt. at CLY on Nov. 6, 1757, and m. John Keawey.

CODORUS TOWNSHIP 47

- Anna Margaretha, b. on Nov. 6, 1759, and bapt. at CLY on Nov. 11, 1759.
- Johan Frederick, b. on July 28, 1761, and bapt. at CLY on Aug. 2, 1761. He d. on Mar. 11, 1762, and was bur. on Mar. 12, 1762 (CLY).
- Johan Henrich, b. on Aug. 17, 1763, and bapt. at CLY on Aug. 21, 1763.

Kuntz - Johannes, was taxed in 1762, and received a warrant for 100 acres in North Codorus Township on Mar. 9, 1753, that was surveyed as 203.80 acres on Jan. 18, 1754 (interest began on Mar. 1, 1749). His will was written in Codorus Township on Feb. 19, 1784, and probated on Apr. 7, 1791. He m. Catharina, and had the following children:
- Abraham.
- Anna, m. Adam Michael.
- Peter.

Lau - Christian received a warrant for 150 acres in Jackson Township on Apr. 10, 1750, that was surveyed as 347.80 acres on Jan. 22, 1763 (see entry in Manchester section). He also received a warrant for 150 acres in Jackson Township on Apr. 10, 1750, that was surveyed as 347.80 acres on Jan. 22, 1763.

Lau - Peter received a warrant for 150 acres in North Codorus Township on May 11, 1752, that was surveyed as 281 acres on Mar. 15, 1753 (see entry in Manchester Section).

Lidey - Jacob was taxed in 1762. He received a warrant for 50 acres on May 31, 1762, that was surveyed as 94.80 acres called *Elbow* on Nov. 12, 1788. He also warranted 100 acres on Oct. 3, 1767, that was surveyed as 31.36 acres called *Elbow's Neighbor* on Nov. 9, 1768. He was naturalized on Apr. 4, 1764. He m. Ursula and had the following son:
- Jacob, m. Maria Eva, and had the following children:
  - Jacob, b. on Mar. 20, 1778, and bapt. at STJ.

Linglefelder (Linckefelder) - Johan Georg was taxed in 1762. He m. Anna Maria. They were probably the parents of the following children:
- Jacob, was taxed in 1762. He m. Elisabetha. They had the following children:
  - Maria Eva, bapt. by RJL on Feb. 8, 1756, and spon. by Michael Trorbach and Maria Eva Wigand.
  - Anna Catharina, bapt. by RJL on Dec. 10, 1757, and spon. by Peter and Anna Catharina Runk.

- Elisabetha Barbara, bapt. by RJL on Mar. 16, 1760, and spon. by Abraham Keller and Barbara Bernerin. She may be the Elisabeth that m. Philip Holl on June 12, 1783.
- Anna Maria, bapt. by RJL on Mar. 3, 1762, and spon. by Georg and Anna Maria Linglefelder.
- Johannes, bapt. by RJL on Jan. 28, 1764, and spon. by Johannes and Magdalena Keller.
- Jacob, b. in June 1766, and bapt. at STJ on July 27, 1766.
- Johan Joseph, bapt. at STJ on June 9, 1768.
- Michael, b. on May 4, 1769, and bapt. at STJ on June 4, 1769.
- Daniel, b. on Nov. 24, 1771, and bapt. at STJ on Dec. 25, 1771.
- Anna Margaretha, b. on Dec. 28, 1773, and bapt. at STJ on Jan. 2, 1774.
- Valentine, was taxed in 1762. He m. Elisabetha. They had the following children:
  - Anna Maria, bapt. by RJL on Apr. 18, 1762, and spon. by Johannes Eyseck and Anna Maria Lischy.
  - Georg Michael, bapt. by RJL on Mar. 2, 1765, and spon. by Georg and Catharina Ehrhardt.

Lischy - Jacob was taxed in 1762. He was b. in Switzerland (now France) in 1719, and immigrated to America in 1742. He was ordained by the Moravians in 1743, and was the Lutheran minister for the German families in the Codorus region. He received a warrant for 100 acres on Oct. 28, 1746, that was surveyed as 110 acres on Apr. 15, 1747 (sold to Christopher Rothermel on Apr. 11, 1759). He received a warrant for 188 acres in North Codorus Township, which was surveyed as 180.80 acres on Nov. 1, 1811 (patented on Dec. 12, 1750). He also warranted 100 acres in North Codorus Township on Mar. 14, 1755, that was surveyed as 98 acres on Apr. 23, 1755. He received a warrant for 15 acres in North Codorus Township on June 7, 1776, that was surveyed as 27.33 acres on Oct. 8, 1778, and was warranted 100 acres on Oct. 25, 1746. He m. secondly, cum lla sua at SML on Jan. 13, 1756. He had the following children:
- Jacob, b. about 1739. He m. Magdalena, and had the following children:
  - Maria Magdalena/Margaretha, bapt. by RJL on Dec. 13, 1761, and spon. by Adam and Maria Catharina Hubert.
  - Johannes, b. on Oct. 26, 1765.
- Magdalena, b. about 1741, and was a sponsor in 1760.
- Anna Maria, b. in 1743, and m. Killian, son of Philip Ziegler (see entry in Manchester section).

Lohr - Georg was taxed in 1762. He immigrated to America with his bro., Conrad, on the ship *Edinburgh* on Sept. 30, 1754, (and

CODORUS TOWNSHIP 49

apparently, his step mother-an Anna Maria Weissmueller, (Geschwy) (?widow) of Georg Lorr, had her death recorded at FMY on Feb. 2, 1755. She had been b. in Ewrach, Alsace, in the Catholic religion on Feb. 2, 1719, m. Georg Lorr in 1746, was widowed after two years, and so remained. She was bur. on Wuttring's (Votrin) land on Feb. 3). Georg Jr. m. Maria Margaretha. In 1755, they resided in York Co., Codorus Township, PA. They moved to Washington Co., MD, about 1766 (possibly to Frederick Co., Monocacy area with other Moravian families of York Co. Georg d. in Washington Co., MD, about 1766, and Maria Margaretha returned to York Co., where she m. Johan Heinrich, son of Hans Ulrich Zauck (see entry), about 1766/67. Heinrich Zauck was b. in Hoffenheim, Sinshein, Elsenz (Baden), Germany, about 1696, and m. Elisabetha, dau. of Martin Schwartz (citizen), in Hoffenheim on June 29, 1717. He immigrated to America on the ship *Dragon* on Sept. 30, 1732 (listed as sick), and settled in York Co., PA. Heinrich was granted 200 acres in York Co., Manheim Township, on Nov. 25, 1745, which he deeded to John Solomon Miller, a nailsmith of Manheim Township, on Oct. 12, 1762 (he was residing on the land at the time). In this deed, he is referred to as a tailor. Henrich's will was written on July 4, 1775, and probated in York (now Adams) Co., Germany Township, PA, on Sept. 13, 1775. In 1779, Margaret is taxed in Germany Township with 100 acres, 2 horses, and 2 cattle; in 1780, with 50 acres, 2 horses, and 2 cattle; in 1781, with 100 acres, 2 horses, and 2 cattle; in 1782, with 100 acres, 2 horses, and 2 cattle. For some reason, she is taxed in Germany Township in 1783, as widow Lore, with three individuals in her household, and 100 acres. On June 29, 1798, she m. Georg Adam Stump. Margaret Stump, formerly Zouck, widow of Georg Stump, of Heidelberg Township, wrote her will on Dec. 31, 1798, and it was probated on Mar. 30, 1799 (executed by Conrad Steiman and Michael Bear). The will named sons, Balthasar Lohr, Joseph Lohr, Henry Zauck, dau., Margaret, wife of Michael Bear, and grandchildren, David and Margaret Bachman. Presumably, after Georg's death, and Margaret's remarriage, their sons, Baltasar and Joseph went to Lebanon Co., to live with their uncle Conrad, and their son, Georg, later moved onto his father's holdings in Washington Co., MD. Georg and Maria Margaretha Lohr had the following children:

- Margaret, b. about 1754. She m. Michael Baer about 1774. His will was written in York Co., Manheim Township, PA, on May 1, 1815, and probated on Oct. 2, 1815 (executed by Henry Baer and Philip Kromer). He was b. in 1741, and d. in Manheim (now Penn) Township on Sept. 6, 1815. Michael served in the Revolutionary War, and is bur. in Mumma's cemetery. Margaret was alive in 1815.
- Johan Georg, b. at York on Sept. 13, 1755, bapt. at the First Moravian Church of York on Sept. 16, 1755, and spon. by John and

Catharina Heckedorn. He resided in Washington Co., MD, in 1790.
In 1800, he resided in Washington Co., Elizabeth Hundred (he may
have moved to Allegheny Co., MD).
- Johan Peter, b. at York on Jan. 25, 1757, bapt. at the First
  Moravian Church on Feb. 7, 1757, and spon. by Peter Binckele,
  John Heckedorn, Philip Rothrock, and John Daniel Votrin. In 1783,
  he resided in Washington Co., Marsh Hundred, with 4 horses and 3
  "bc." He m. Catherine, and d. in Augusta Co., VA, in 1841. He
  enlisted as a Private in the Revolutionary War at Hagerstown, MD,
  in 1776. According to his pension, he marched to Fort Washington,
  New York, and fought in the battle of White Plains in Captain
  John Ronald's Company. His pension also stated that he was b.
  within seven miles of Little York, PA, and moved to MD when very
  young.
- Baltasar, b. at Stouchburg on Sept. 9, 1757 (according to pension).
  He enlisted in the Revolutionary War with his bro., Joseph Lohr, at
  Lebanon, PA, in Nov. 1775. They marched to Reading, PA, thence
  to Philadelphia, thence to Fort Washington to help construct the
  fort, thence to New York, where they fought in the battle of Long
  Island. After the battle, they returned to Fort Washington where
  they were taken prisoner at the fort's surrender. They were
  released after about nine weeks, and then went to Philadelphia,
  where Baltasar was honorably discharged on Jan. 21, 1777. He
  appeared on the tax lists of Cumberland Co., Letterkenny
  Township, PA, from 1778-82. In 1780, he reenlisted in the war in
  the 6th Class, 3rd Company, 4th Battalion, Cumberland County
  Militia. From 1781-92 (1781-82 he was single), he appears on the
  tax list of York Co., Germany Township, Littletown, PA. In
  1799-1800, he was taxed in York Co., Mount Joy Township, and in
  1810, he resided in Franklin Co., Fannet Township, PA. In 1819, he
  resided in Montgomery Co., MD, and d. in Frederick Co., MD, on
  Mar. 4, 1827. He m. Lena Elisabetha, dau. of John and Elizabeth
  Knauf, on Mar. 15, 1787. She was b. in Germany Township on Aug.
  15, 1763, bapt. at Christ's Church at Littlestown, spon. by Adam
  and Anna Elisabeth Graeber, and d. on Mar. 20, 1841.
- Michael, b. at York on Oct. 6, 1758, bapt. at the First Moravian
  Church on Oct. 9, 1758, and spon. by Daniel Votring and wife,
  Adam Hoff and wife, and Melchior Schmidt. He m. Catharine
  Schriner in Washington Co., MD. Michael enlisted as a Private in
  the Revolutionary War in Washington Co., MD, in 1778 (he had
  moved there when small). After the war, he returned to MD, and
  was residing in Washington Co., MD, in 1783. He moved to Berkley
  Co., VA, for six years, and then moved to Rockingham Co. Michael
  d. there in 1835. His estate was administered on Feb. 19, 1838.

- Joseph, b. in Berks Co., Tulpehocken Township, Stouchburg, PA, on Nov. 26, 1759, while his parents were visiting his uncle. Joseph was bapt. at Christ's Lutheran Church of Stouchburg on Dec. 2, 1759 (to Georg and Maria Margaretha Lohr). His pension states that he was b. within 7 or 8 miles of Lebanon, PA, on Nov. 26, 1758. He enlisted in the Revolutionary War with his bro., Baltasar Lohr, at Lebanon, PA, in Nov. 1775 (possibly 1776). He spent the first year as a Private in Captain Soull's Company, Colonel Shee and Cadwalder's Pennsylvania Regiment. They marched to Reading, PA, thence to Philadelphia, thence to Fort Washington to help construct the fort, thence to New York, where they fought in the battle of Long Island. After the battle, they returned to Fort Washington where they were taken prisoner at the fort's surrender. They were released after about nine weeks, and then went to Philadelphia, where Balthasar was honorably discharged on Jan. 21, 1777. On Jan. 16, 1777, Joseph reenlisted, and served three years as a Sergeant in the 4th Pennsylvania Line under Lieutenant Colonel Butler, in Captain John Connelly's Company. Joseph fought in the battles of Brandywine, Germantown, and Monmouth, and was honorably discharged in 1781. After the war, Joseph returned to York Co. (now Adams Co.), PA, where he appears on the tax list of Germany Township, Littletown, as a single man in 1782. He m. Anna Maria about 1782/83 (possibly a dau. of Jacob and Anna Maria Feeser/Fuesser). She was b. in 1756, and d. in Aug. 1822. In 1783, they are presumed to be two of the three inhabitants, residing with Widow Lohr (Zauck). Joseph moved to York Co., Heidelberg Township, PA, where he appears on the tax lists from 1795-99. From 1800-10, he resided in Frederick Co., Pipe Creek, Taneytown, MD, from 1811-15 in Frederick Co., Monacacy, MD, and from 1816 till his death on Jan. 5, 1837, he resided in Frederick Co., Emmitsburg, MD. In 1795, he purchased 167 acres in Heidelberg/Germany Townships from John Will, and in 1800, purchased 6 additional acres from John Will. In 1802, Joseph and his wife sold 126 acres of his 1795 purchase. In 1801, Joseph purchased part of *Ross Ranger* and *Brothers Agreement*, which consisted of a 210 acre tract in Frederick (now Carroll) Co., near Taneytown, MD. This land was later mortgaged. Joseph was allowed Pension in Emmitsburg, MD, on July 15, 1828. Joseph and Anna Maria are bur. in Emmitsburg Lutheran cemetery.
- Anna Magdalen, b. on Aug. 24, 1760, and bapt. at Christ Evangelical Lutheran of York on Mar. 24, 1761. She m. Henrich Bachman about 1791, and d. before 1798.
- Anna Maria, bapt. by Reverend Jacob Lischy at York on July 28, 1765, and spon. by Jacob Welshantz and Anna Maria Kontzin.

- Heinrich Zauck and Margaretha (widow of Georg Lohr) had the following son:
- Johan Henrich Zauck, b. about 1767. He m. Ann, dau. of Frederick and Eva Mary Buchanan of Germany Township before Jan. 21, 1789, and Barbara about 1790.

Lorich - Jacob received a warrant for 50 acres on June 26, 1764, that was surveyed as 145.93 acres on Feb. 14, 1766. His will was written in Codorus Township on Apr. 1, 1806, and probated on July 25, 1807. He m. Eva, and had the following children:
- Barbara, m. Philip Grunblad.
- Maria Gertraut, m. Frantz, son of Adam Roser (see entry in Shrewsbury section).
- Eva, m. Wilhelm Ratscher before 1795.
- Michael, m. Christina before 1776.

Maak - Hans Nicholas received a warrant for 150 acres in North Codorus Township on Sept. 10, 1750, that was surveyed as 292 acres on Oct. 23, 1751 (interest began on Mar. 1, 1741). His will was written on Oct. 31, 1756, and probated on Dec. 7, 1756. His widow, Jacobina renounced her administration right in favor of her son-in-law, Jost Streithof.

Mayer (Meyer) - John warranted 100 acres in Heidelberg, Codorus, and North Codorus Townships on Nov. 5, 1750, that was surveyed as 226.14 acres called *Cleared Valley* on June 1, 1768 (patented on Sept. 4, 1773). He received a warrant in Codorus, Heidelberg and North Codorus Townships for 100 acres on Nov. 5, 1750, that was surveyed as 226.14 acres called *Clear Valley* on June 1, 1768. His son, John received a warrant for 150 acres in North Codorus Township, that was surveyed to John on July 23, 1743 as 136 acres called *Peasable Burgh* (patent as 138 acres on July 24, 1767). His will was written in York Township on May 3, 1756, and probated on Nov. 2, 1757. He had the following children:
- Johannes was taxed in 1762. He received a warrant for 50 acres in Codorus and North Codorus Townships on June 17, 1767, surveyed as 157.153 acres called *Fox Hallow* on Jan. 6, 1768, and patented to Frederick Myers on Sept. 11, 1811 and Matthias Myers on June 30, 1818. He received a warrant for 100 acres in Manheim Township on June 17, 1767. His will was written in Codorus Township on Sept. 10, 1769, and probated on Feb. 24, 1770. It mentions his plantation in Codorus and Manheim Township. He m. Magdalena. Her will was written in Codorus Township on Mar. 27, 1779, and probated on Apr. 8, 1780. They had the following son:

- John received a warrant for 200 acres in Manheim Township on July 17, 1767. He received a warrant for 150 acres on Feb. 6, 1767, that was patented as 138 acres on July 24, 1767.
- Christian was taxed in 1762. He m. Catharina Margaretha, and Elizabeth between 1763 and 1777. His will was written on Mar. 20, 1777, and probated on July 19, 1779 (witnessed by Peter Brillhart). They had the following children:
  - Hannes, b. about 1740, was taxed in Codorus Township in 1762, and Shrewsbury Township in 1779.
  - Christian, b. about 1742, and was taxed in Shrewsbury Township in 1762 and 1779.
  - Andreas, b. in 1753, and was taxed in Shrewsbury Township in 1779. He served as a Private in the Continental Line during the Revolution. He d. in 1833, and is bur. in Meyer's burial ground in Springfield Township.
  - Elisabeth, b. about 1748, and m. ___ Rothfan.
  - Maria, b. about 1750, and m. ___ Rosh.
  - Magdalen, b. on Apr. 23, 1752, and bapt. at CLY on May 17, 1752.
  - Johan Michael, bapt. by RJL on May 11, 1755, and spon. by Michael and Anna Elisabeth Neuman. His will was written on Oct. 26, 1781, and probated on May 13, 1782 (executed by Peter Brillhart). His will named his mother (step-mother) Elisabeth; younger bros., Henry and Abraham; sister, Maria Rosh.; bros. Hannes, Christian, Andreas; and sister, Elisabeth Rothfan.
  - Christine, b. on July 20, 1762, and bapt. at CLY on Sept. 12, 1762.
  - Henry, b. about 1764.
  - Abraham, b. about 1766.
- Barbara, m. Jacob Coffman.
- Cary, b. about 1736, and m. Peter Brillhart (see entry).
- Catherine.
- Henry. His will was written in York Township on Apr. 20, 1783, and probated on May 20, 1783 (witnessed by Jacob Brillhart and John Meyer). He m. Magdalena, and had the following children:
  - John.
  - Barbara.
  - Henry.
  - Magdalena.
  - Jacob.
  - Samuel.

<u>Meyer</u> - Michael was taxed in 1762. He m. Anna Catharina, and they were sponsors to the baptism of Anna Catharina Walter at FRI in 1760, Johann Jacob Kraut at FRI in 1766, and Johan Michael (?Kraut)

at FRI in 1770. His second wife was probably Elizabeth, and they were sponsors at the baptism of Johann Michael Muller at FRI in 1772. Michael and Anna Catharina had the following children:
- Susanna, b. about 1742, and m. Conrad Free/Fruh (see entry in Dover section).
- Elisabeth, b. about 1744, and m. Johannes Muller (see entry in Shrewsbury section).
- Michael, b. about 1761, and was a sponsor to the baptism of Johann Michael Muller at FRI in 1780.

Meyer - Peter wrote his will in Codorus Township on Feb. 2, 1795, and it was probated on Aug. 24, 1795. He m. Elisabeth, and had the following children:
- Conrad m. Margaretha Magdalena, dau. of Daniel Renolly (see entry).
- Regina.
- David.
- Christina, b. about 1768, and m. Johannes, son of Henrich Herring (see entry in Dover section).
- Peter.
- Elisabeth.
- Adam.
- Henrich.
- Mathias. He m. before 1795.
- Frederick. He m. before 1795.

Miller - John Charles received a warrant for 125 acres in North Codorus Township on Sept. 23, 1767 (interest began on Mar. 1, 1777), that was surveyed to Andrew Miller as 159.78 acres on May 10, 1771.

Miller - Leonard received a warrant for 100 acres on Jan. 14, 1767, that was surveyed as 121.76 acres called *Miller's Choice* on July 27, 1767 (interest began on Mar. 1, 1762). He received a warrant for 100 acres on Jan. 14, 1767, that was surveyed as 59.124 acres called *Humorous Dale* on July 27, 1767.

Miller - Michael was taxed in 1762. He m. Eva, dau. of Michael Sprenckel (see entry in Manchester section). A Michael Mueller m. Gertrude Gruen in the Cordorus region on May 25, 1739 (JCS), and (the same or another Michael) m. Barbara Stucker in the Codorus region on Apr. 7, 1742 (JCS). Neither have been proven to be related to the Michael who was taxed in 1762.

CODORUS TOWNSHIP

Moul - Anthony received a warrant for 50 acres in North Codorus Township on Sept. 25, 1751, that was surveyed as 118 acres on Nov. 18, 1828, and patented on Jan. 15, 1829.

Muller - Andreas was b. in 1716, and immigrated to America on the ship *Samuel* on Dec. 3, 1740. He received a warrant for 50 acres on Apr. 1, 1751, and d. before 1762. He had the following children (see History and Families of the Black Rock Church of the Brethren by Elmer Q. Gleim (1988)):
- Georg was taxed in 1762. He received a warrant for 100 acres on June 1, 1762, that was surveyed as 225 acres called *Poplar Spring* on Apr. 23, 1767. He served in the Revolutionary War in Captain John Myer's Company (1778). He m. Maria Barbara, dau. of Johannes Stambach (see entry), and widow of Johan Georg Schmeisser (see entry in Manchester section), in 1748, and had the following children:
  - Petrus, b. bapt. by RJL on July 2, 1749, and spon. by Peter and Catharina Stambach. He received a warrant for 50 acres on Dec. 6, 1773, that was surveyed as 39.8 acres called *Owl Hill* on Apr. 15, 1774. His will was written in Codorus Township on Nov. 9, 1780, and probated on Jan. 13, 1781. He m. Anna Elisabeth.
  - Andreas, bapt. by RJL on Mar. 14, 1752, and spon. by Andreas Muller and Magdalena Brendlerin. He served in the Revolutionary War in Captain John Myer's Company (1778).
  - Adam, bapt. by RJL on Jan. 4, 1761, and spon. by Andreas and Barbara Muller.
  - Michael, bapt. by RJL on Jan. 4, 1761, and spon. by Jacob and Elisabetha Haffner.
- Andreas was taxed in 1762. His will was written in Codorus Township on Nov. 7, 1772, and probated on Jan. 2, 1773. He m. Barbara Noll. Her will was written in Codorus Township on May 2, 1796, and probated on May 17, 1817. They had the following children:
  - Jacob, b. about 1758. He served in the Revolutionary War in Captain John Myer's Company (1778).
  - Maria Catharina, bapt. by RJL on Mar. 16, 1760, and spon. by Mattheas Schmeisser and Maria Catharina Reberin.
  - Johannes, bapt. by RJL on Mar. 3, 1762, and spon. by Johannes and Catharina Reber.
  - Andreas, bapt. by RJL on Oct. 24, 1763, and spon. by Georg and Barbara Muller. He m. Anna, dau. of Henry and Elisabeth (Kehr) Danner, on Oct. 29, 1785, and d. on Oct. 12, 1835. She was b. on May 6, 1768, and d. on Dec. 23, 1808. After Anna's death, he m. Elisabeth, dau. of Daniel and Elisabeth (Flickinger) Utz. She was b. on Jan. 12, 1781, and d. on Nov. 6, 1860.

- Maria Elisabetha, bapt. by RJL on Oct. 18, 1765, and spon. by Daniel and Maria Elisabetha Renolly.
- Elisabetha, bapt. by RJL on Mar. 6, 1768, and spon. by Jacob and Elisabetha Haffner.

Muller - Felix received a warrant for 100 acres in North Codorus Township on Oct. 28, 1746. His will was written on Mar. 18, 1748, and probated on June 6, 1748 (executed by George Myer, Christian Low, and Michael Hafner). He had the following children:
- Elizabeth.
- Francis Jacob was taxed in 1762. He was b. in Leimen in the Palatinate, near Heidelberg on Oct. 20, 1719, and immigrated to America in 1732. He was brought into the Moravian Congregation in Lancaster Co., Warwick, PA, on Feb. 9, 1749. He m. Anna Maria Bohn (FMY)/Anna Elisabeth Boehl (records of the First Reformed Congregation at Lancaster, PA) on Jan. 8, 1745, and Anna Maria Spiess, dau. of Anna Maria Busch by her first marriage in 1774. Anna Maria Bohn was b. in Salliendorf, near Siegen on Apr. 14, 1726, immigrated to America in 1744, taken into the Moravian Church at Bethlehem, PA, on May 15/26, 1749, and d. on Dec. 8, 1773. Anna Maria Spiess was b. in PA on Mar. 3, 1750, and was alive in 1781. Francis had the following children (recorded at FMY):
  - Frederick, b. on Nov. 16, 1745, and bapt. on Dec. 5, 1745. He and Anna Margaret, widow of John Henry Schoerder, bapt. their illegitimate dau., Anna Maria at FMY on Nov. 18, 1764 (born on Oct. 29, 1764).
  - Dau., b. on Nov. 16, 1746, and d. after an hour.
  - Son, b. on Dec. 8, 1747, and d. after a few hours.
  - Elisabetha, b. on Mar. 7, 1749, and bapt. on Mar. 18, 1749. She m. Peter Schneider (see entry in Manchester section).
  - Anna Maria, b. on Nov. 19, 1750.
  - Felix, b. on Dec. 30, 1751.
  - Maria Catharina, b. on Feb. 9, 1753.
  - Johannes, b. on Feb. 2, 1754.
  - Godfrey, b. on Mar. 11, 1755.
  - Anna Maria, b. on Nov. 4, 1756, and bapt. on Nov. 7, 1756.
  - Anna Maria, b. on Oct. 30, 1759, and bapt. on Oct. 31, 1759.
  - Johannes, b. on Nov. 10, 1760, and bapt. on Nov. 10, 1760.
  - Rosina, b. on Sept. 22, 1764, and bapt. on Sept. 25, 1764.
  - Francis Jacob, b. on Aug. 2, 1765, and bapt. on Aug. 4, 1765.
  - Benjamin, b. on Jan. 31, 1777, bapt. on July 13, 1777, and d. on July 14, 1777.
  - Catharina, b. on Nov. 15, 1777, bapt. on Nov. 16, 1777, and d. on Aug. 19, 1778.
  - Francis Jacob, b. on Aug. 25, 1779, and bapt. on Aug. 29, 1779.

- Johannes, b. on July 19, 1783, and bapt. on July 20, 1783.
- Anna Dorothea, b. in Leimen in Oct. 1725. She m. Johann Frederick Roemer (see entry in Manchester section).
- Frederick.

Mullheim - Georg warranted land in Codorus Township on Oct. 20, 1766. He m. Catharina, and had the following children:
- Catharina Barbara, bapt. by RJL on Mar. 6, 1768, and spon. by Peter and Catharina Study.
- Anna Maria, bapt. at STD on Nov. 10, 1769, and spon. by Jacob and Anna Maria Runkel.
- Jacob, b. on Jan. 16, 1780, bapt. at ERC on Apr. 30, 1780, and spon. by Jacob and Christina Hauck.
- Johannes, b. on Feb. 10, 1782, bapt. at ERC on Apr. 21, 1782, and spon. by Johannes and Rosina Eppley.
- Eva, b. on May 24, 1784, bapt. at ERC on Aug. 1, 1784, and spon. by Georg and Anna Maria Matter.
- Rosina, b. on May 24, 1784, bapt. at ERC on Aug. 1, 1784, and spon. by Daniel and Rosina Dubbs.
- Johan Michael, b. on Mar. 30, 1787, bapt. at ERC on June 25, 1787, and spon. by Michael and Margaretha Ehrhard.

Mochler (Mockler) - Peter was taxed in 1762. He warranted 100 acres on Apr. 30, 1765, 100 acres on Jan. 14, 1767, and 61.138 acres on June 29, 1767. He m. Elisabetha. They probably had the following dau.:
- Catharina Elisabetha, was a sponsor to the baptism of Catharina Elisabetha Becker in 1760.

Neucommer - Frantz was taxed in 1762. He m. Regina, and had the following children:
- Maria Magdalena, bapt. by RJL on Apr. 24, 1763, and spon. by Heinrich and Maria Magdalena Gerbach.

Neucommer - Heinrich, m. Catharina. He received a warrant for 50 acres on Nov. 25, 1767, that was patented as 35.5 acres called *Secound Spring* on Apr. 12, 1768. He was taxed in Codorus Township in 1779. They had the following children:
- Johannes, bapt. by RJL on Nov. 7, 1762, and spon. by Johan Georg Esslinger and Veronica Neukommer.
- Anna Catharina, bapt. by RJL on Nov. 4, 1764, and spon. by Daniel and Anna Maria Jonas.
- Maria Magdalena, bapt. at STJ on Nov. 29, 1766.
- Maria Elisabetha, b. on Apr. 20, 1770, and bapt. at STJ on May 18, 1770.

- Johan Jacob, b. on July 23, 1772, and bapt. at STJ on Aug. 16, 1772. He may be the Jacob that m. Maria Newcomer on Apr. 1, 1798.
- Margaretha, b. on Oct. 5, 1774, and bapt. at STJ on Oct. 30, 1774. She may be the Margaret Newcomer that m. Johannes Miller on July 31, 1798.
- Johan Georg, b. on Feb. 3, 1777, and bapt. at STJ on Mar. 2, 1777.

Neucommer - Veronica, was probably a sister to Henrich, and was a sponsor to Johannes Newcomer in 1762. She may have m. Johan George Eislinger (see entry).

Neucommer - Jacob, b. on Aug. 31, 1748, and d. on Apr. 4, 1831 (bur. at STJ). He was taxed in Manheim Township in 1779. He m. Anna Margaretha. She was b. on Mar. 1, 1755, and d. on June 17, 1827 (bur. at STJ). They had the following children (bapt. at STJ):
- Elisabetha, b. on July 14, 1774, and bapt. on July 29, 1774.
- Catharina Elisabetha, b. on Jan. 21, 1776, and bapt. on Apr. 4, 1776.
- Anna Margaretha, b. on Mar. 8, 1780, and bapt. on May 15, 1780.
- Johannes, b. on Nov. 19, 1782, and bapt. on Jan. 29, 1783.
- Elisabetha, b. on June 5, 1785, and bapt. on July 17, 1785.
- Johan Christian, b. on Apr. 11, 1788, and bapt. on July 13, 1788.

Neuman - Michael was taxed in 1762. He received a warrant for 200 acres and 150 acres in North Codorus Township on Jan. 14, 1767, that was surveyed as 111.70 acres and 80.137 acres called *Masnum* on Apr. 8, 1767. He also received a warrant for 40 acres in North Codorus Township on Apr. 14, 1772, that was surveyed as 59 acres called *Cherty Burgh* on May 22, 1772, and patented on Aug. 20, 1772. His probate inventory was filed in Codorus Township in 1778, and his administration bond was dated Apr. 11, 1778. He m. Anna Elisabeth before 1755. He had the following children (see orphans court dockets/partition documents for listing of children (Feb. 24, 1779)):
- Susanna, b. about 1755 (not a minor in 1779). She m. Conrad Klein before 1775.
- Georg, b. about 1757 (not a minor in 1779).
- Michael, b. in 1763.
- Margaret, b. in 1766.
- Andrew, b. in 1767.
- Catharina Elisabetha, bapt. at WOL on June 25, 1769, and spon. by Jacob and Catharina Elisabeth Gottwald.
- Eve, b. in 1774.

Neyswanger (Newswanger) - Joseph was taxed in 1762. He received a warrant for 100 acres on June 25, 1769, that was surveyed as 73.80 acres on July 21, 1831. Joseph was the exec. for the will of Peter Neischwanger on Aug. 25, 1775. Peter's probate inventory was filed in Shrewsbury Township in 1775. Peter Neuschwanger m. Agnes Mueller on Dec. 12, 1769 (JCS) (she was from Bethel). Joseph's probate inventory was filed in Codorus Township in 1777.

Nutz (Notz) - Johan Leonhardt was b. in 1700, and immigrated to America on the ship *Two Sisters* in 1738. He was naturalized on Sept. 24, 1746. His estate was administered in Lancaster Co. in 1758. He does not appear to have lived in York Co., just owned land there. He received a warrant for 100 acres in North Codorus Township on Feb. 15, 1749, that was surveyed as 343 acres on Nov. 25, 1775, and 337 acres on Mar. 8/9, 1750. He also received a warrant for 100 acres in North Codorus Township on Feb. 15, 1749, that was surveyed as 50.82 acres on Mar. 8/9, 1750. He m. Maria Eva Barth on Nov. 16, 1723, and Anna Catharina, dau. of Henrich Keydel, on Oct. 26, 1734. He had the following children at Zuzenhausen, Germany (see BNK):
 - Johan Georg, b. on Jan. 28, 1726, and d. before 1735.
 - Anna Dorothea, b. on Apr. 22, 1733 (at Durlachishen), m. Christian Gunther in 1752, and d. of consumption in Lebanon Co., PA, on Aug. 31, 1799 (see Salem Lutheran Church records). He d. in 1785. She was a communicant at the First Reformed Congregation at Lancaster in 1750.
 - Johan Georg, b. on Dec. 18, 1735, and d. before 1738.
 - Johan Michael, b. on Jan. 24, 1738, and d. in 1738.
 - Elisabeth, b. on Feb. 9, 1753, bapt. at the First Reformed Congregation in Lancaster on Feb. 18, 1753, and spon. by Christian Vogt and wife.

Ott - Johannes was taxed in 1762. He received a warrant for 50 acres on Oct. 10, 1762, and an additional 50 acres on May 31, 1762, that was surveyed as 170 acres called *Elizabeth* on Nov. 11, 1766. He also received a warrant for 50 acres on June 15, 1774, that was surveyed as 69 acres called *Scramble* on Oct. 12, 1774. He m. Anna Elisabetha, and had the following children:
 - Juliana, bapt. by RJL on Apr. 4, 1756, and spon. by Christophel and Juliana Rothermel.
 - Johannes, b. on Dec. 27, 1759, and bapt. at STJ. He served in the Revolutionary War in Captain John Myer's Company (1778).
 - Johan Peter, b. on Sept. 27, 1761, and bapt. at STJ on the 23 Sunday after Trinity.
 - Maria Magdalena, b. on Dec. 10, 1763, and bapt. at STJ on Jan. 22, 1764.

- Maria Barbara, b. on May 26, 1766, and bapt. at STJ.
- Anna Maria, b. on Sept. 11, 1768, and bapt. at STJ on Oct. 18, 1768.
- Johan Heinrich, b. on June 15, 1770, and bapt. at STJ on Aug. 12, 1770.

Pfaff - Peter was taxed in 1762. He was b. in Kaiserslautern in the Palatinate on June 24, 1727, immigrated to America in 1749, and in May 1771, moved to the neighborhood of Wachau (North Carolina). He received a warrant for 192 acres in North Codorus/York Townships on Mar. 2, 1769, that was surveyed as 228.31 acres on Sept. 14, 1858. He m. Anna Walpurga, dau. of Johann Casper and Anna Walpurga Kerber in 1750 (see entry in Manchester section). They had the following children (recorded at FMCY):
- Isaac, b. on Apr. 15, 1755.
- Anna Barbara, b. on Feb. 23, 1758.
- Anna Maria, b. on May 5, 1762.
- Samuel, b. on Aug. 14, 1764.
- Joseph, b. on Sept. 28, 1768.

Radfang/Redvan - Christian received a warrant for 60 acres in North Codorus Township on Oct. 31, 1772, that was surveyed as 76.122 acres called *Chestnut Ridge* on Nov. 27, 1772 (patented on Mar. 29, 1774). A Christian Rathfon had his probate inventory filed in Windsor Township in 1824. A Frederick Redfon had his probate inventory filed in Windsor Township in 1793.

Reber - Johannes was taxed in 1762. He received a warrant for 100 acres on Sept. 10, 1750, that was surveyed as 302.04 acres on June 8, 1759 (patented to Jonas Reber on Nov. 16, 1809). He m. Maria Magdalena, and possibly Anna Elisabetha about 1754, and had the following children:
- Maria Catharina.
- Johannes, m. Maria Catharina, dau. of Jacob Rudisill (see entry in Manchester section). He served in the Revolutionary War in Captain John Myer's Company (1778). His will was written in Codorus Township on Apr. 29, 1800, and probated on May 21, 1800. They had the following children:
  - Maria Elisabetha, bapt. by RJL on Oct. 11, 1761, and spon. by Johan Ludwig Rudisill and Elisabetha Rudisillin.
  - Christina, bapt. by RJL on Aug. 28, 1763, and spon. by Johan Jacob and Christina Rudisill.
  - Susanna, bapt. by RJL on Nov. 17, 1765, and spon. by Ludwig Rudisill and Susanna Rudisillin.

- Jonas, b. on Aug. 20, 1776, and bapt. at CLY on Oct. 14, 1776. (?the Johannes that m. Anna Margaretha, dau. of Frederick Ruhl (see entry).
- Henrich.
- Johan Abraham m. Maria Magdalena, and had the following children:
  - Johann Abraham, b. on Aug. 5, 1772, and bapt. at FRI on Sept. 13, 1772.
  - Samuel, b. on Nov. 17, 1778, bapt. at FRI, and spon. by Francis Weymuller.
  - Marie Christina, b. on Oct. 27, 1780, bapt. at FRI on Nov. 13, 1780, and spon. by Georg Geisselman and wife.
  - Jacob, b. on Feb. 25, 1786, bapt. at FRI, and spon. by Jacob and Maria Elisabeth Hildebrand.
- Maria Magdalena, bapt. by RJL on June 10, 1753, and spon. by Jean and Elisabetha Degraff.

Reibold (Rybolt) - Andrew warranted 129 acres on June 18, 1767, and 50 acres on Feb. 19, 1773. His will was written in Codorus Township on Sept. 26, 1800, and probated on Jan. 24, 1803 (executed by George Gantz and John Ruhl). He had the following children:
- Barbara, m. John Doll.
- Martha.
- Henry. His probate inventory was filed in Codorus Township in 1839.

Renolly - Daniel was taxed in 1762. He was b. on Feb. 10, 1724, and d. on Nov. 26, 1800. He is bur. in Lischy's burial ground. He received a warrant for 25 acres on June 15, 1774, that was surveyed as 25.106 acres on Oct. 18, 1774. He also received a warrant for 100 acres on Oct. 16, 1751, that was surveyed as 137 acres on Dec. 12, 1785, and 150 acres on Oct. 16, 1767, that was surveyed as 77.05 acres called *Cheese Mount* on Nov. 9, 1768. He also warranted 50 acres on June 15, 1774, that was surveyed as 53.27 acres called *Stoney Batter* on Oct. 17, 1774. He served as a Private in the York County Militia during the Revolutionary War in Captain Peter Zollinger's Company. His will was written on June 6, 1797, and probated Dec. 27, 1800. He m. Maria Elisabetha. They had the following children (recorded by RJL):
- Anna, b. about 1745, and m. Jacob Kraut about 1765. She may be the Susanna wife of Adam Erunst mentioned in Daniel's will. Anna and Jacob had a child in 1773.
- Maria Elisabetha, bapt. on May 19, 1752, and spon. by Johannes and Maria Magdalena Reber. She m. Felix, son of Casper Glattfelter (see entry).

- Johan Daniel, bapt. on Mar. 25, 1753, and spon. by Johan Wentel and Anna Margaretha Fissel. He m. Anna Maria, dau. of Peter Lau (see entry in Manchester section).
- Johannes, bapt. on July 7, 1754, and spon. by Jean and Maria Elisabetha Degranche.
- Johannes, bapt. on Oct. 5, 1755, and spon. by Johannes and Anna Elisabetha Ott.
- Johan Peter, bapt. on Sept. 27, 1757, and spon. by Johannes Reber. He m. Anna Eva, dau. of Peter Lau (see entry in Manchester section).
- Christian, bapt. on May 17, 1759, and spon. by Christophel and Juliana Rothermel. He m. Maria Catharina, dau. of Michael Lau (see entry in Manchester section), and d. in 1849.
- Johan Jacob, bapt. on May 11, 1761, and spon. by Jacob and Elisabetha Haffner.
- Barbara, bapt. on Nov. 12, 1764, and spon. by Andreas and Barbara Muller. She m. Peter, son of Michael Lau (see entry in Manchester section).
- Heinrich, bapt. on Apr. 3, 1767, and spon. by Heinrich and Catharina Scoil.
- Anna Elisabetha, bapt. on May 2, 1769, and spon. by Jacob and Anna Krauss.
- Margaretha Magdalena, m. Conrad, son of Peter Meyer (see entry). Hey had a child in 1794.

Rohrbach - Christian, son of Johann Rohrbach of Walst, Nassau-Saarbrucken, m. Maria Catharina, dau. of Hans Georg Friedrich and Anna Barbara (Schunck) Kuntz, at Webenheim, Germany, on Jan. 29, 1743. She was bapt. at Mimbach/Webenheim Lutheran Church on Jan. 17, 1717. They immigrated to America on the ship *Phoenix* in 1743. Christian was b. in Walscheid, Germany, in 1720, and his father came from Rueggisberg, Canton Bern, Switzerland, to Germany between 1700 and 1720. Maria Catharina d. in Chester Co., PA, about 1753. Christian m. Susanna, dau. of Valentine and Susanna Hause, in Chester Co., PA, about 1756. She was b. in Frederick Co., MD, in 1736, and was alive on Dec. 9, 1789. Christian received a warrant for 150 acres on Jan. 14, 1767, that was surveyed as 124 acres called *Polar Spring* on July 27, 1767 (improved for two years). Christian's will was written in Codorus Township on Nov. 24, 1786, and probated on Dec. 9, 1789. Christian had the following children (see BWP):
- Johan Christian, b. on Sept. 14, 1744, and bapt. at Trappe (Augustus) Lutheran Church in Montgomery Co., PA. He m. Christina soon after July 4, 1769. She was b. in 1750, and was alive in 1827.

- Laurentz, b. on Oct. 16, 1746, and bapt. at Trappe (Augustus) on Nov. 21, 1746. He m. Anna Catharina Grokes. He received a warrant for 200 acres on June 14, 1773, that was surveyed as 159.120 acres called *Punch Hall* on Apr. 12, 1773.
- Johan Heinrich, b. on Apr. 20, 1749, and bapt. at Trappe (Augustus) on July 31, 1749. He received a warrant for 145 acres on May 27, 1773. He m. Anna Veronica.
- Johann.

Rubel - Peter was taxed in 1762. He received a warrant for 100 acres on Sept. 10, 1750, that was surveyed as 113.11 acres on June 20, 1786 (patented to Christian Rubel on May 31, 1811). His will was written in Codorus Township on May 15, 1773, and probated on Apr. 26, 1773. He m. Anna Catharina. They were sponsors at the baptism of Eva Catharina Frey in 1749. They had the following children:
- Mathias.
- Christian, m. Barbara, dau. of Johan and Eve Weltz of Manheim Township. He served in the Revolutionary War in Captain John Myer's Company (1778).
- Abraham.
- Peter.

Ruhl - Peter was b. in Germany in 1694. He m. Anna Catharina, and immigrated to America on the ship *Samuel* on Aug. 27, 1739. He settled near Germantown, Philadelphia (now Montgomery) Co., PA, and d. between 1745 and 1748. In 1748, Peter's widow and children were residing in York Co., PA. Anna Catharina witnessed the baptism of Anna Catharine, dau. of Georg Martin Wagner, at St, Matthew's Lutheran Church in York Co., Manheim Township, on Mar. 27, 1748. Peter and Anna Catharina the following children:
- Anna Margaretha, b. about 1732, and m. Franz Heinrich Gans (see entry).
- Frederick, b. about 1737. He m. Maria Elisabeth, dau. of Johan Henrick and Eva (Kramer) Bahn, at Christ's Lutheran Church at York on Jan. 7, 1759. Maria was b. in York Co., Hellam Township, Kreutz Creek, PA, about 1736, and d. in York in 1769. After Maria's death, Frederick m. Catherina Eva, dau. of Henry and Anna Barbara (Bortner) Kann, in 1770. Catherina d. sometime after May 1810. Frederick was naturalized on Sept. 15, 1765. He was a cordwainer while he resided in York, and became a yeoman after he moved to Shrewsbury Township. On Dec. 24, 1770, he purchased 3 acres and 64 perches in York Township from Jacob and Barbara Updegraff. On Mar. 8, 1773, Frederick and Catherina sold this land in York to Jacob Welschantz, and moved to Shrewsbury Township. On May 7, 1773, Frederick purchased 96

acres and 9 perches called *Pleasant Ridge* from Robert and John Freeland, and on Nov. 15, 1785, added on to *Pleasant Ridge* with 140 acres purchased from John and Mary Mahon. On July 16, 1802, Frederick and Catherina deeded *Pleasant Ridge* to their son, Heinrich. Frederick served in the Revolutionary War as Private in Captain John Miller's (the third) Company of the Seventh Battalion, York County Militia, and as a Private in Captain Aquila Wiley's Company, Fifth Battalion, York County Militia in 1780. Frederick was a member of the first class of inhabitants of Shrewsbury Township, and the second class of inhabitants of Codorus Township, classified under an act of assembly passed in 1780, entitled "An Act to Complete the Quota of the Federal Army"; each class was "required to provide, in fifteen days from Jan. 30, 1781, one able-bodied recruit for the Continental Army, to serve during the war", under penalty of a fine of 15 pounds specie; both classes proved delinquent. Frederick also served as a wagoner in Captain William Lindsay's Company from Dec. 8, 1781 to Feb. 8, 1782. Frederick made his will on May 25, 1810, and it was probated on Oct. 17, 1815. The will was executed by his son John, and his son-in-law, Michael Eyrich. Frederick was the father of the following children:

- Catherine, b. on Nov. 18 (Oct. 22), 1759, and bapt. at Christ's Lutheran Church of York on Nov. 25, 1759. She d. sometime prior to May 1810.
- Heinrich, b. on Jan. 28, 1763 at 10 p.m. He was bapt. at Christ's Lutheran Church of York on Feb. 13, 1763, and spon. by his grandparents, Henry and Eva Bahn. Heinrich m. Margaretha Barbara, dau. of Jacob and Eva Elisabetha (Kleinfelter) Baehli, at the First Reformed Lutheran Church of York on Sept. 24, 1782. Margaretha was b. on July 23, 1764, bapt. in Albany Township, Berks Co., PA, at the Allemangel Lutheran Church on Sept. 2, 1764, and spon. by Andreas Kunckell and Margaretha Barbara Probst. Henry was a yeoman with 100 acres in Shrewsbury Township in 1783. He received Pleasant Ridge from his father in 1802, which he in turn deeded to his son, Johannes, on Jan. 26, 1811, along with the tract of 2Q,299 supra, which was patented to Henry on June 25, 1810. In 1828, he and his sister-in-law, Rosina (Baehli) Ruhl's, family moved to OH. Henry settled in Sandusky Township, Richland Co., where he d. between Jan. 5, and Mar. 9, 1830. Margaret d. sometime after Jan. 1830.
- Maria Elisabeth, b. on Nov. 5, 1770, bapt. at Christ's Lutheran Church of York on Dec. 23, 1770, spon. by her aunt, Maria Elisabeth Kann. She m. John Greenwalt, probably a son of Christopher and Maria (Becker) Greenwalt of Manchester Township.

CODORUS TOWNSHIP 65

- Anna Margaretha, b. on Oct. 7, 1772. She was bapt. at Christ's Lutheran Church of York on Oct. 25, 1772, and spon. by her grandparents, Henry Kann and wife. She m. Johannes Reiber/Reber (possibly a son of Johannes and Maria Catharina Reber of Codorus Township)
- Juliana, b. about 1774. She m. Michael, son of Michael and Catherine Eyrich. Michael was b. on Jan. 30, 1774, and bapt. at Christ's Lutheran on Feb. 20, 1774.
- John, b. about 1776, and d. sometime after May 1810.
- Johannes, b. on Sept. 23, 1739. He m. Helena, dau. of Andreas and Rosina (Biehlmajer) Schenck, at Christ's Lutheran Church of York on Aug. 14, 1764. She was b. in York Township on Sept. 22, 1745, and d. in Codorus Township on Aug. 27, 1826. Johannes served during the Revolutionary War as a Private in Captain George Hoover's Company of Associators of Codorus Township, and a Private in Captain John Sherer's Company (the Eighth), Seventh Battalion, York County Militia from about 1778 to 1782. He was a member of the second class of inhabitants of Codorus Township, classified under an act of assembly passed in 1780, entitled "An Act to Complete the Quota of the Federal Army"; each class was "required to provide, in fifteen days from Jan. 30, 1781, one able-bodied recruit for the Continental Army, to serve during the war," under penalty of a fine of 15 pounds specie; the class proved delinquent. John was a yeoman in Codorus Township. On Oct. 14, 1768, he surveyed 63 acres 11 perches called *Ruhl's Abode*, and 85 3/8 acres on June 18, 1767. In 1779, John owned 100 acres, two horses and four cattle; in 1780, 80 acres, two horses, and two cattle; in 1781, 235 acres; in 1782, 225 acres, two horses and four cattle, and in 1783 had 225 acres, one house, one outhouse, three horses, three horned cattle, and eight sheep. John had a 94 acre 149 perch tract called *Square Compas* patented to him by the Commonwealth of PA on May 6, 1790. On Jan. 18, 1812, John purchased 130 acres 111 perches called *George Town* and 11 acres and 12 perches in Codorus Township from Georg Philip and Loveis DeHoff. In 1794, he was one of the founders of Bethlehem Union Church. Johannes d. in Codorus Township on Jan. 23, 1825, and was bur. in Steltz Union (Bethlehem) Church cemetery beside his wife. Johannes and Helena had the following children in Codorus Township:
  - Johan Georg, b. on July 6, 1765. He was bapt. at St. Jacob's on July 30, 1765, and spon. by his uncle and aunt, Georg Ruhl and Rosina Schenck. He was confirmed on May 3, 1784, and m. Anna Rosina, dau. of Jacob and Eva Elisabetha (Kleinfelter) Baehli, in York Co., PA, in 1786. Anna Rosina was b. in Shrewsbury Township on Mar. 27, 1769, bapt. at St. Jacob's on May 28, 1769,

and spon. by her uncle and aunt, Daniel and Anna Rosina Baehli. Georg was a yeoman in Codorus Township, and he purchased 140 acres, 27 perches there on Mar. 12, 1787 from Jacob and Maria Catherina Noll. On Mar. 24, 1795, Georg and Rosina deeded to Philip Ruhl, three tracts in Codorus Township - (a) 60 acres 127 perches surveyed to Martin Anthony in 1767, called *Hard Scoffle*; (b) 79 acres 60 perches surveyed to Martin Anthony in 1768 called *Hog's Manor*; (c) 50 acres warranted to Georg Ruhl on Apr. 5, 1788. In Feb. 1794, Georg signed an agreement for the founding of a union congregation at New Freedom in Codorus Township, called *Steltz Union* (Bethlehem) Church (the actual church building was erected about 1801). He served in the Revolutionary War as a Private 5th Class. During the War of 1812, Georg served as a Private in the York County Militia. Georg and Rosina lived in the borderland region between Codorus Township, and Baltimore Co., Mine Run Hundred, MD, and appeared on census and tax records of both areas, but their sons indicate that they were b. in Baltimore Co., MD. Georg and Rosina moved to Mine Run Hundred in MD in 1795, and Georg d. there on Mar. 15, 1815. His will was probated in Baltimore Co., MD, and he is bur. in Steltz cemetery in York Co., PA, beside his parents. In his will, he mentions his land in OH, where Rosina, and her sons, Johannes and Georg, moved to in 1828. The journey was made by team with the family of Rosina's bro.-in-law, Henry Ruhl. During the trip they cut a portion of the road to Mansfield, OH, and after their arrival lived in a covered wagon until they cleared a site to build a cabin. Rosina d. on Dec. 8, 1855, and is bur. in North Woodbury Lutheran Church cemetery.

- Anna Margaretha, b. on May 20, 1767. She m. Johannes, son of Peter and Anna Margaretha (Rudolph) Gerberich (see entry), in York Co., PA, on Oct. 1, 1786. She was bapt. at St. Jacob's on June 9, 1767, and spon. by her uncle and aunt, Frans and Anna Margaretha Gantz. Johannes was b. in Berks Co., Tulpehocken Township, PA, on Aug. 13, 1761, and d. in Shrewsbury Township on Nov. 6, 1846, and Anna Margaretha d. in Codorus Township on Mar. 31, 1836. Both are bur. in Steltz Union cemetery.
- Johannes, b. on Aug. 22, 1769. He was bapt. at St. Jacob's on Aug. 29, 1769, spon. by his uncle and aunt, Clement and Margaretha Ruhl. He m. Maria Margaretha, dau. of Michael and Maria Margaretha Gerberich, in York Co., PA, on Mar. 24, 1793. She was b. in Shrewsbury Township on Sept. 1, 1774. John moved to Hopewell Township and began farming soon after their marriage. He purchased 180 and 1/2 acres situated in Shrewsbury and Hopewell Township from George and Mary

Taylor on Mar. 24, 1804. On July 24, 1812, he purchased 352 acres and 86 perches from William and Margaret McClelan. John sold 76 acres of this tract and an additional 114 acres and 103 perches to David Gorsuch on May 1, 1813. On Apr. 15, 1815 he purchased 166 acres and 38 perches in Hopewell and Shrewsbury Township from George and Magdalene Albright. John sold 113 acres and 119 perches of the 170 acre, 115 perch tract patented to him on May 24, 1809 to Peter Gerberich. On Mar. 6, 1824, John bought 88 acre acres and 73 perches, 35 acres and 80 perches, and 3 acres and 153 Perches in Hopewell and Shrewsbury Township, and 16 acres and 72 perches in Hopewell Township from Philip and Catherine Heilman. On Mar. 28, 1831, John and Margaret sold to Peter Hoffman, lot number 32 in the village of Shrewsbury, that John had purchased from Robert Fife on Mar. 1, 1828. In 1832, John and his family moved to Crawford Co., Galion, OH, where John d. on Nov. 5, 1845, and Maria Margaretha on June 6, 1850.
- Julianna, b. on Dec. 25, 1771. She m. Johann Jacob, son of Johannes and Anna Margaretha (Gerberich) Kleinfelter, in York Co., PA, in 1790. He was b. on Aug. 4, 1767, bapt. at St. Jacob's on Aug. 16, 1767, and spon. by his uncle and aunt, Jacob and Eva Elisabetha Baehli. Julianna was bapt. at St. Jacob's on Jan. 19, 1772, and spon. by Theobald Schneider and her cousin, Juliana Gantz. Jacob d. in Shrewsbury Township on Apr. 30, 1830, and is bur. in the Kleinfelter burial ground. Juliana d. in Marion Co., Marion, OH, at the home of her son Jacob on Apr. 10, 1843, and is bur. in Pleasant cemetery. They had the following children in Shrewsbury Township:
 - Elisabetha, b. on Feb. 28, 1775. She was bapt. at St. Jacob's on Apr. 2, 1775, spon. by George and Elisabetha Manchen. She m. Johann Heinrich, son of Lorentz and Anna Maria Herschner. He was b. on Feb. 12, 1776, bapt. at Canadochly Union Church, and spon. by Heinrich Liebhardt and wife. He d. in Crawford Co., Jefferson Township, OH, on June 24, 1850. She d. in Crawford Co., Jefferson Township, OH, on Aug. 11, 1853. They are bur. in Middletown cemetery.
 - Johan Peter, b. on Feb. 26, 1777. He was bapt. at St. Jacob's on Mar. 31, 1777, and spon. by Anthon Manchen and his cousin, Elisabetha Gantz. He m. Margaret Geisey, who was b. on May 9, 1784, and d. in Shrewsbury Township on Aug. 4, 1848. Peter d. in Shrewsbury Township on Mar. 10, 1834, and is bur. in Shrewsbury Lutheran cemetery.
 - Georg Michael, b. on Nov. 18, 1779, and d. in Codorus Township on May 26, 1812. He served during the war of 1812, and is bur. in Steltz cemetery.

- Rosina, b. on Apr. 17, 1782. She m. Peter, son of Peter and Elisabetha (Schaffer) Kleinfelter, about 1813. Rosina was b. on Apr. 17, 1782, and bapt. at Christ's Lutheran Church of York on May 19, 1782. Peter was b. on Oct. 22, 1778, and d. in Shrewsbury Township on Jan. 7, 1852, and Rosina on Apr. 7, 1841.
- Jacob, b. on May 1, 1784. He was bapt. at St. Jacob's on June 27, 1784, and spon. by Jacob and Maria Kreiss. He m. Elisabetha, dau. of Abraham and Christina (Bortner) Hassler. She was bapt. at Fissel's on May 12, 1788, and spon. by Elisabetha Bortner. Jacob served during the War of 1812. He d. in Baltimore Co., Mine Run Hundred, MD, on May 18, 1815, and is bur. in Steltz Union cemetery. On Feb. 14, 1816, Jacob's bro., and bro.-in-law, Henry Ruhl, and Peter Kleinfelter, were appointed guardian of Jacob's minor children. Elisabetha remarried, and moved to Richland (now Morrow) Co., Perry Township, OH, in the spring of 1833. Elisabetha d. two years later on Sept. 5, 1835.
- Heinrich, b. on Aug. 15, 1786. He was bapt. at St. Jacob's on Sept. 13, 1786, and spon. by his cousin, Heinrich Ruhl, and his wife Margaretha. He purchased 99 acres and 64 perches in Codorus Township that were part of, Hanover, and, Two Springs, tracts from his cousin, Philip Ruhl, on June 13, 1816. Henrich purchased a water right in Codorus Township from William Hinam on march 15, 1823. Henrich m. Barbara Steffie, who was b. on May 22, 1790, and d. in Codorus Township on Aug. 28, 1866. Henrich served during the war of 1812. He was a farmer, and d. in Codorus Township on Jan. 13, 1859. They are bur. in Steltz Union cemetery.
- Clement, b. about 1741. He m. Margaretha, dau. of Henrich Berge, about 1765. Clement served in the Revolutionary War as a Private in Captain George Hoover's Company of Associators of Codorus Township 1776/77. Clement d. before his son, Heinrich's, baptism on Mar. 30, 1777. Sometime between Mar. 30, 1777, and Apr. 1, 1778, Clement's widow m. Peter Gerberich. After Clement's death, his bros., Frederick and Johannes, were appointed guardians of his children. Margaretha d. in Dec. 1800. Clement owned 116 acres in Codorus Township. Clement and Margaretha had the following children in Codorus Township:
  - John, b. on Jan. 2, 1766, and d. in Centre Co., Miles Township, Rebersburg, PA, on July 8, 1842. John m. Elizabeth sometime before Oct. 28, 1792 who d. sometime after June 21, 1818. His second marriage was to Margaret sometime prior to Nov. 16, 1828. John is bur. in Rebersburg cemetery. John moved to Centre Co., Brush Valley, PA, in 1811.

- Susanna, b. on May 5 (31), 1769. She m. Johann Martin, son of Heinrich and Juliana (Saftler) Merckel. He was b. in Shrewsbury Township on Oct. 8, 1766, bapt. at Friedensaal Lutheran Church on Nov. 9, 1766, and spon. Jacob and Dorothea Kraft. Martin d. in Shrewsbury Township on July 19, 1838, and Susanna d. there on Jan. 14, 1850. She is bur. in Fissel's cemetery.
- Magdalena, b. on Oct. 17, 1771. She was bapt. at St. Jacob's on Oct. 20, 1771, spon. by her uncle and aunt, Johannes and Helena Ruhl. She never m., but had a son. In deed records she is referred to as a spinster of Hopewell Township. She transfers a bill of goods and chattels to her son on June 19, 1827. On Mar. 22, 1841, Magdalena sold part of her interest in 46 acres purchased jointly with her son, John from David Fulton on Mar. 11, 1831 to her son, John Ruhl. She d. in Hopewell Township on Jan. 29, 1856, and was bur. in Stewartstown cemetery.
- Johann Peter, b. on Dec. 8, 1774, bapt. at St. Jacob's on Dec. 16, 1774, and spon. by his cousin, Johannes Gantz, and Elisabetha Gischin. He was a blacksmith in Shrewsbury Township, and purchased lot #4 in the town of New Shrewsbury on Jan. 13, 1798, from Baltzer and Eve Faust, on condition that he build a house with a chimney within three years. Peter d. in Shrewsbury Township in Aug. 1828, and his estate was administered by John Beck on the 25th of Aug.
- Heinrich, b. on Mar. 2, 1777, bapt. at St. Jacob's on Mar. 30, 1777, and spon. by Heinrich and Catharina Manchen. He m. Margaret, who was b. in PA in 1779, and d. in Centre Co., Rebersburg, PA, on Jan. 2, 1875. She moved to Centre Co. after the death of Heinrich in York Co., about 1827. She is bur. in Rebersburg cemetery.
- Anna Lehnora, b. on Feb. 8, 1742/43, and bapt. at St. Michael's Lutheran Church in Germantown.
- Georg Wilhelm, b. on Aug. 4, 1744, and bapt. at St. Michael's. He m. Anna Maria Dorothea Siegrist, widow of Felix Albright, about 1770. Wilhelm served in the Revolutionary War as a Private in Captain George Hoover's Company of Associators of Codorus Township, a Private in Captain John Sherer's Company (the Eighth), Seventh Battalion, York County Militia from 1778 to 1782. He was a member of the second class of inhabitants of Codorus Township, classified under the Act of Assembly passed in 1780, entitled "An Act to Complete the Quota of the Federal Army"; each class was "require to provide, in fifteen days from Jan. 30, 1781, one able-bodied recruit for the Continental Army, to serve during the war," under the penalty of a fine of fifteen pounds specie; the class proved delinquent. In 1779, he owned 200 acres in Codorus Township, in 1780 he had 100, in 1781 he had 135, in 1782 and

1783 he had 200 acres. On June 18, 1767, he received a land warrant in Codorus Township for 100 acres. This warrant was surveyed as 94 acres and 92 perches called *Two Springs* on Oct. 14, 1768. On Mar. 24, 1789, he warranted 100 acres in Codorus Township, and on the same day, had 41 acres and 130 perches of this warrant surveyed. Wilhelm had 102 acres 57 perches called *Hanover* and 94 acres 92 perches called *Two Springs* patented to him on June 10, 1809. On July 13, 1785, he was warranted 150 acres in Codorus Township. 71 acres and 57 perches of this land was surveyed and patented to William on June 10, 1809. On June 10, 1809, he patented 31.5 acres in Codorus Township. He also received 6 acres 50 perches from the estate of William Smith on May 19, 1813. Wilhelm d. intestate in Codorus Township in Apr. 1815, with 200 acres. Anna Maria was b. in York Co., PA, on Aug. 9, 1747, and d. in York Co. in 1812. Wilhelm and Anna Maria were the parents of the following children, b. in Codorus Township:
- Philip, b. on Aug. 16, 1771. He m. Barbara, and d. in Darke Co., Butler Township, OH, on July, 30, 1846. She was b. in 1772, and d. on July 9, 1854. Philip purchased 60 acres 127 perches, 79 acres, 60 perches, and 50 acres in Codorus Township from Georg and Rosina Ruhl on Mar. 24, 1795. On May 9, 1812, Philip and Barbara sell 34 1/2 acres, 20 3/4 acres, parts of *Hard Scoffle* and *Hog's Manor* to Michael Zeigler. Sometime between 1813 and 1815, Philip moved to Baltimore Co., MD, where he farmed, and on June 13, 1816, sold 97 acres 85 perches in Codorus Township to his bro.-in-law, William Hinrim. On the same day, Philip and Barbara sold 99 acres 64 perches, of the *Hanover* and *Two Springs* tracts that he inherited from his father to his cousin, Henry Ruhl. Philip and Barbara are bur. in the Old Castline cemetery.
- Anna Maria, b. about 1775, and m. William Hinrim.
- Jacob, b. about 1777. He m. Anna Maria (and possibly Christina Hetrick).
- Barbara, b. about 1779, and m. Thomas Hinrim.
- Peter, b. about 1782. He m. Rachel about 1803. He d. in Codorus Township in 1815, and Jacob Ruhl was appointed guardian of Peter's children in Dec. 1815.
- Johannes, b. on Feb. 22, 1784, bapt. at St. Jacob's on May 4, 1784, and spon. by Dewald and Margaretha Schneider. He m. Elizabeth Catherine Winck in York Co., PA, on Mar. 31, 1802, and d. in Wayne Co., OH, on Jan. 27, 1849. She was b. in York Co. on Jan. 24, 1784, and d. in Columbiana Co., OH, on Sept. 29, 1854.
- George, b. on Jan. 27, 1786. He was bapt. at St. Jacob's on Mar. 26, 1786, and spon. by George and Eva Groff. Georg m.

Elizabeth, dau. of Isaac and Hannah Prosser, in Baltimore Co., MD, on Jan. 15, 1807. Isaac Prosser d. in Baltimore Co., MD, in 1827. Georg and Elizabeth moved to Richland (now Morrow) Co., Perry Township, OH, in 1814. Georg was a farmer, and d. in Perry Township, Bellville, on Nov. 12, 1842. He is bur. in Pleasant Grove cemetery. Elizabeth d. in Maryville, Nodaway Co., MO, on May 31, 1881, and is bur. in White Cloud Baptist cemetery.
- Catherine, b. on Sept. 12, 1789. She m. Peter Snyder, and d. on Sept. 30, 1869.
- Johan Jurg, b. on May 13, 1746, and bapt. at St. Michael's. In 1763, he spon. the baptism of his nephew, Johan Georg Gans, and in 1765, he spon. the baptism of his nephew Johan Georg Ruhl. He was taxed in York Co., Heidelberg Township, PA, in 1779.

Runk - Peter was taxed in 1762. He received a warrant for 100 acres in North Codorus Township on Oct. 10, 1749. The administration bond for his estate was dated June 2, 1772. He m. Anna Catharina, and had the following children (see orphans court dockets June 7, 1774, and deeds Feb. 22, 1788):
- Johan Yost, b. on July 25, 1748, bapt. at SML on Jan. 20, 1749, and spon. by Johan Yost Wagner. He m. Maria Eva, dau. of Jacob Bollinger (see entry). He served in the Revolutionary War from Codorus Township in 1780/81. She was b. on Sept. 16, 1753, d. on Aug. 9, 1821, and bur. in Lischy's cemetery.
- Peter, b. about 1750. He was named as a child in 1774, but was not mentioned in the 1788 deed.
- Elisabeth, bapt. by RJL on June 10, 1753, and spon. by Jost Wagner. She m. Abraham, son of Jacob Bollinger (see entry).
- Catharina, bapt. by RJL on Oct. 5, 1755, and spon. by Valentine and Elisabetha Linckefelder. She m. Jacob Sopach/Sepach (see entry).
- Johan Valentin, bapt. by RJL on Dec. 10, 1757, and spon. by Valentine and Elisabetha Linckefelder. He served in the Revolutionary War from Codorus Township in 1780/81, and as a Private in the 2nd Company, 7th Battalion between 1778 and 1780.
- Maria Margaretha, bapt. by RJL on Jan. 20, 1760, and spon. by Sebastian and Anna Margaretha Hellman. She m. Christian, son of Jacob Bollinger (see entry).
- Anna Magdalena, bapt. by RJL on Apr. 8, 1764, and spon. by Johannes and Maria Magdalena Keller. She was unmarried in 1788.
- Anna Maria, b. about 1766, and m. Michael Hall.

Salomonmuller (Sallmuller) - Ludwig was b. in 1711, and immigrated to America on Aug. 17, 1733. He received a warrant for 275 acres in

Manheim Township in 1752, and was taxed in Codorus Township in 1762. He m. Maria Barbara, and had the following children:
- Johannes, b. about 1739, and m. Maria Eva, dau. of Martin Hiller (see entry in Dover section), at STM on May 15, 1764.
- Juliana Salome, b. in May 1741, and m. Henrich, son of Heinrich Herring (see entry in Dover section).
- Maria Philippina, b. in July 1743, bapt. at STM in 1743, and spon. by Jacob and Maria Philippina Scherer.
- Elisabeth, b. on Feb. 8, 1745, and bapt. at STM in Feb. 1745.
- Eva Barbara, b. on Aug. 16, 1746, bapt. at SML on Sept. 15, 1746, and spon. by Eva Barbara Zasgin and Jacob Scherer. She m. Jacob Petri at STM on Apr. 3, 1764.
- Anthony Gregor, b. on Feb. 4, 1748, bapt. at SML on Mar. 8, 1748, and spon. by Anthony Nau and Eva Barbara Zanklin (spinster).
- Christina Elisabetha, b. and bapt. in Conewago (recorded at SLC), and spon. by Conrad Jost and wife.

Schaffer - Carl. He was a weaver, and purchased land in Codorus Township from Martin Uhlem on Feb. 1759. This land was sold by Carl's execs. to Georg Aumiller on Nov. 24, 1760 (a portion of Carl's land was sold by his execs. to Georg Bortner on Nov. 2, 1774). Letters of administration were issued to Ulrich Huber and Ludwig Krebs on Jan. 29, 1760. He m. Phillipina. Prior to May 26, 1761, Carl's widow m. Frederick Froescher (see entry) (orphan court dockets). Carl and Phillipina had the following children:
- Heinrich, bapt. by RJL on July 25, 1756, and spon. by Heinrich and Ann Barbara Kann.
- Carl, b. in 1758 (orphan court dockets Sept. 3, 1772).

Schaffer - Georg Jacob was taxed in 1762. He was overseer of the poor in Codorus Township in 1771. He purchased a tract of 202 acres 7 perches called *Anna Barbara* on Dec. 19, 1766. He took the sacrament on Sept. 18, 1763, and was naturalized on Apr. 10, 1765. His estate was administered by his widow, Anna Barbara, and his son, Jacob on Mar. 30, 1784. Jacob and Anna Barbara had the following children (a list of children and their spouses can be found in a deed of release between Johannes Schaffer and Jacob Schaffer, Jr., in Codorus Township, dated on Jan. 29, 1791):
- Anna Margaretha, bapt. by RJL on Nov. 20, 1754, and spon. by Niclaus Schaffer and Anna Margaretha Keifferin. She m. Peter, son of Conrad Stuck (see entry) at FRY on June 14, 1775.
- Anna Barbara, bapt. by RJL on July 8, 1757, and spon. by Johannes Andreas and Maria Margaretha. She m. Martin (he d. before 1785), son of Conrad Stuck (see entry) at FRY on Oct. 19, 1775.

CODORUS TOWNSHIP 73

- Johannes, bapt. by RJL on Feb. 4, 1759, and spon. by Johannes and Elisabeth Schaffer.
- Johan Jacob, bapt. by RJL on Jan. 10, 1762, and spon. by Abraham and Christina Keiffer. He m. Dorothea, dau. of Heinrich Walter, at FRY on Jan. 4, 1785. Letters of administration were granted to his widow, Dorothy Schaffer, and Henry Holl in Huntingdon Township on Aug. 23, 1793.
- Elisabetha, b. about 1764, and m. Bernhardt Bob/Bupp at FRY on Sept. 5, 1786 (see entry in Shrewsbury section).
- Johannes, b. in 1773, and had a guardian appointed for him on June 1, 1784.

Schaffer - Johan Niclaus was a bro. to Georg Jacob Schaffer. He m. Elisabeth Wolff. He was overseer of the poor in York Town in 1760 and 1770. He deeded land to Jacob Wolf on July 20, 1765. His patent of Sept. 23, 1762 was sold by his execs. to Isaac Gortman on May 2, 1778. His will was written in York on June 25, 1776, and probated on Aug. 6, 1776. They had the following children (4 alive in 1776):
- Johannes, b. about 1757, and had Johannes Schaffer of Dover Township appointed as his guardian in 1779 (see entry in Dover section).
- Barbara, b. on Feb. 26, 1759, and d. on Jan. 11, 1762 (TLY) (she was a goddau. of Jacob and Barbara Schaffer).
- Margareth, bapt. by RJL on Apr. 20, 1760, and spon. by Johan Jacob Wolff and Margareth Eisick.
- Maria Elisabeth, b. on Jan. 26, 1763, bapt. at TLY on Mar. 20, 1763, and spon. by Hannes and Maria Margaretha Andres.
- Philip, b. about 1764, and had a guardian appointed for him on Nov. 3, 1785.
- Jacob, b. on Aug. 6, 1766, bapt. at TLY on Nov. 10, 1766, and spon. by Kilian Tuebinger and wife. He chose John Wolf of York Town as his guardian on Aug. 31, 1780.

Scherer - Johan Jacob m. an unknown woman about 1728, and Philippina, dau. of Heinrich Zauck (by JCS) in the Codorus region on May 22, 1738. He had a 200 acre land warrant in Heidelberg Township on May 12, 1748 (surveyed to Jacob Tomas in 1785). His will was probated on July 8, 1784, and executed by Philip Grenn and John D. Sharer. (In 1780, a widow Shearer was taxed in Germany Township with 50 acres, 2 horses, and 3 cattle, and a Valentine Shearer was taxed with 20 acres, 2 horses, and 3 cattle.) Jacob had the following children:
- Hans Jacob was taxed in 1762. He m. Maria Barbara, dau. of Georg Keller (see entry), by Apr. 1749 when they spon. the baptism of George Michael and Christine Stober. He was b. in 1729, and d. in

York Co., Codorus Township, on Feb. 15, 1791 (his will was written on Apr. 10, 1786, and probated on Mar. 15, 1791). He was bur. in STJ cemetery. He was granted 50 acres in Codorus Township on May 23, 1748, and 200 acres in the same township, bounded by the lands of Jacob Keller and George Dehoff, on Oct. 15, 1768. He warranted 200 acres on June 23, 1768. They had the following children in Codorus Township:
- Maria Barbara, bapt. by Reverend Jacob Lischy on Mar. 5, 1755, spon. by Ludwig and Margareth Engelman, and m. Philip, son of David Schaffer (see entry in Shrewsbury section).
- Johan Jacob, b. on Apr. 11, 1760, bapt. by Reverend Jacob Lischy on May 6, 1760, and spon. by Peter and Elisabeth Mockler. He m. Maria Christina, dau. of Johan Georg and Anna Elisabetha (Kissel) DeHoff (see entry), and d. in Codorus Township on June 3, 1838. She was b. in Codorus Township on Nov. 8, 1758, and d. there on July 11, 1834. They are bur. at STJ.
- Johann Daniel, b. on Sept. 15, 1765. He was bapt. at St. Jacob's on Oct. 10, 1766. He d. in Baltimore Co., Alesia, MD, on Feb. 3, 1856, and is bur. in St. Peter's. Daniel m. Maria Sophia, dau. of Johan Georg and Catharina Elisabetha Schmidt (see entry). She was b. in York Co., Lower Windsor Township, on Oct. 29, 1768, bapt. at Canadochly Union Church on Nov. 21, 1768, and spon. by Henrich Gohn and Sophia Behner. Daniel bought 91 acres called *Locust Bottom* in Baltimore Co., MD, on Feb. 15, 1790.
- George, b. about 1771 (under age in 1786). He m. Rosina, dau. of Frederick and Catharina Froescher. She was b. on June 24, 1778, and bapt. at St. Jacob's on July 5, 1778. They resided in Centre Co., PA.
- Henry, b. about 1776 (under age in 1786), and m. Elizabeth (Bailey).
- Johan Heinrich, b. on Mar. 31, 1740, bapt. at CLY on May 3, 1740, and spon. by Heinrich and Elisabeth Zauck. He m. Catharina in Germany Township about 1766. He was a sponsor at the baptism of Johan Henry Mayer in Germany Township in 1753.
- Ludwig, b. about 1741, and was a sponsor at the baptism of Johan Ludwig Muller in Germany Township on Mar. 18, 1764 (not proven to be a son).
- Mathias, b. about 1742, and was a sponsor to the baptism of Heinrich Kramer in 1761.
- Maria Margaretha, b. about 1743, and m. Georg Huber (before May 1763 (sponsors to the baptism on that date)) (see entry) (named in the will of her grandfather, Heinrich Zauck).
- Eva Elisabeth, b. on Sept. 2, 1744, and bapt. at CLY on Nov. 11, 1744. She m. Heflrich Kramer (see entry) (named in the will of her grandfather, Heinrich Zauck).

- Barbara, b. about 1745, and was a sponsor to the baptism of Philip Kramer in 1767 (? single at this time?). She m. Adam Schleppi (see entry).
- Johann, b. about 1747, and m. Justina, dau. of Georg DeHoff (see entry) before 1768, when they were sponsors to the baptism of Johannes Kramer. They had the following children bapt. at STJ:
  - Maria Margaretha, b. on Jan. 3, 1775, and bapt. on Jan. 16, 1775.
  - Johannes, b. on Aug. 19, 1776, and bapt. on Sept. 15, 1776.
  - Rosina, b. on Nov. 25, 1778, and bapt. on Dec. 21, 1778.
  - Johan Jacob, b. on Dec. 31, 1780, and bapt. on Mar. 22, 1781.
  - Anna Justina, b. on Mar. 5, 1786, and bapt. on Apr. 9, 1786.
  - Georg, b. on Oct. 16, 1788, and bapt. on Nov. 9, 1788.
  - Wilhelm, b. on Jan. 8, 1790, and bapt. on Feb. 28, 1790.
- Johan Valentin, b. about 1747, and m. Anna Maria in Germany Township about 1767. They appear as sponsors to the baptism of one of Heinrich's children (not proven to be a son).

Schlesman (Slesman) - Paul was taxed in 1762. He had 68.13 acres called *High and Low* surveyed on Sept. 28, 1769.

Schlesman - George received a warrant for 100 acres on June 11, 1774, that was surveyed as 76.100 acres called *Stoney Hill* on June 23, 1774. A Georg and Margaret Schleesman had the following children:
- Georg, b. on Mar. 31, 1782, bapt. at FRI on May 5, 1782, and spon. by Georg and Catharina Walter.
- Eva Margaretha, b. on Mar. 7, 1784, bapt. at FRI on Oct. 17, 1784, and spon. by Eva Margaretha Schleesman.

Schleppi - Adam was b. to Jacob Schleppi on 1695. He was a saltzpeterseider an der lenck, berner gebiet. He m. Magdalena, dau. of Christian Pfundt, at Diedendorf, Northern Alsace on Jan. 6, 1718. He immigrated to America on the ship *Lydia* in 1741, and signed Lischy's Constitution on Mar. 17, 1745. He was a member at Trinity Lutheran Church in 1754. Magdalena was a sponsor to the baptism of a child of Abraham Welschans in 1745. Adam and Magdalena were sponsors to the baptism of Johan Adam Gerlach in 1752 and Johan Heinrich Gerhardt in 1755. Adam had the following children (see BNA):
- Elisabetha, b. about 1719, and m. Johan Jacob, son of Abraham Welschans, of Kirberg, at Rauwiller, on Oct. 27, 1740 (see entry).
- Catharina Magdalena, b. on Oct. 28, 1721, bapt. at Herbitzheim, and spon. by Stephan Hari, Bernard Rubenthal, Magdalena Beller, and Catharina Bitsche.
- Maria Magdalena m. Phillip Friest/Frensch about 1739 (see entry), and Johan Heinrich Gerlach before 1752 (see entry in Shrewsbury section).

- Adam, b. about 1735. He m. Barbara, dau. of Jacob Scherer (see
  entry) (possibly about 1768, and had another wife named Barbara
  before that date). He warranted 100 acres on June 1, 1762. Adam's
  will was written on Sept. 16, 1774, and probated on Jan. 9, 1775.
  He had the following children:
  - Anna Maria, bapt. by RJL on July 26, 1760, and spon. by Niclaus
    and Catharina Ziegler.
  - Anna Margaretha, b. on Oct. 31, 1761, and bapt. at STJ.
  - Elisabetha, bapt. by RJL on Oct. 26, 1762, and spon. by Jacob
    and Elisabetha Hedrich.
  - Johann Jacob, b. on Apr. 5, 1765, bapt. at STJ on Ascension Day,
    and spon. by Jacob and Maria Barbara Scherer.
  - Johann Friedrich, bapt. at STJ on Mar. 21, 1767.
  - Eva Elisabeth, bapt. at STJ on Aug. 7, 1768, and spon. by
    Christian Neukommer and Eva Elisabeth Welschans.
  - Helena, b. on Jan. 12, 1771, and bapt. at STJ on Mar. 3, 1771.

Schmeiser - Georg received a warrant for land in North Codorus
Township on Jan. 29, 1742, that was surveyed as 138 acres on May 5,
1743 (see entry in Manchester section).

Schmeiser - Matthias received a warrant for 100 acres in Jackson
Township Jan. 29, 1742, that was surveyed as 150 acres on May 5,
1743 (see entry in Manchester section).

Schmeltzer - Valentine was taxed in 1762. He had 342 acres in North
Codorus Township on Apr. 18, 1753. He had the following children:
  - Valentine, was taxed in 1762. He m. Catharina before 1754.
  - Adam, was taxed in 1762. He m. Anna Maria. They had the
    following children:
    - Catharina Barbara, b. on July 20, 1760, and bapt. at CLY on Aug.
      20, 1760.

Schmidt - Carl m. Anna, and had the following children:
  - Matthaus, b. about 1747. He m. Anna Maria Margaretha. He
    warranted 70 acres 75 perches called *Long Side*, on June 3, 1767,
    and 60 acres on Apr. 19, 1774. He had two horses, and two cattle
    in Codorus Township in 1779, and 50 acres, two horses, and two
    cattle in 1780. Matthaus and Margaretha bapt. the following
    children at St. Jacob's:
    - Johann Jacob, b. on Feb. 9, 1769, bapt. on Mar. 7, 1769, and
      spon. by John Jacob Vaupel and Catharine Hupmann. He m.
      Margaretha.
    - Johann Mattheis, b. on Feb. 23, 1771, bapt. on Apr. 6, 1771, and
      spon. by Johannes and Helena Ruhl.

- Carl, b. on Jan. 26, 1773, and bapt. on Mar. 7, 1773, spon. by Carl and Anna Schmidt.
  - Abraham, b. on Feb. 26, 1775, bapt. on Apr. 2, 1775, and spon. by Jacob and Elizabeth Hedrich.
  - Maria Elisabeth, b. on Mar. 10, 1777, bapt. on Apr. 20, 1777, and spon. by Jacob and Elizabeth Hubmann.
  - Anna Catharina, b. on Dec. 1, 1778, bapt. on Dec. 21, 1778, and spon. Andrew Diederich and Anna Catharine Bachman.
- Jacob, b. about 1749. He has not been proven to be a son. He was taxed in 1762. He m. Salome, and bapt. the following dau. at St. Jacob's:
  - Catharina Barbara, b. on Oct. 5, 1769, bapt. on Oct. 24, 1769, and spon. by John Nicholas and Catharine Wolfgang.
- Carl, was bapt. by Reverend Jacob Lischy on June 16, 1758, and spon. by Michel and Maria Margareth Hennig. He m. Catharina, and bapt. the following children at St. Jacob's:
  - Barbara, b. on Nov. 9, 1782, bapt. on Oct. 20, 1789, and spon. by Philip and Barbara Ulmer.
  - Catharina, b. on Oct. 29, 1784, bapt. on Apr. 15, 1789, and spon. by her parents.
  - Johann Friederich, b. on Mar. 15, 1787, bapt. on Apr. 15, 1789, and spon. by Johann Frederick Schmidt (single).
  - Solomon, b. on July 2, 1789, bapt. on Sept. 6, 1789, and spon. by his parents.
  - Jacob, b. on Oct. 20, 1791, bapt. on Nov. 27, 1791, and spon. by Jacob and Anna Maria Keller.
  - Anton, b. on Mar. 11, 1800, bapt. on Dec. 25, 1800, and spon. by Anthony and Elizabeth Miller.
- Johann Frederick, b. about 1767.

Schmidt - Heinrich immigrated to America on Aug. 29, 1730, m. Anna Margaretha about 1730, Catharina about 1753, and Maggie before 1771. He resided in York Co., Kreutz Creek, PA. His will was written in Hellam Township on June 25, 1771, probated on Sept. 20, 1771, and executed by Margaret Smith and Michael Trease. Heinrich had the following children:
  - Rosina, b. about 1728. She m. Lorentz Kron (see entry).
  - Philiph Jacob, b. about 1730. He m. Rebecca about 1753 (she was alive on Dec. 8, 1754), and Anna Margaretha in 1754/55 (she was the mother of Maria Elisabetha). He had the following children:
    - Maria Catharina, bapt. by Reverend Jacob Lischy on Jan. 6, 1754, and spon. by her grandparents, Heinrich and Anna Margaretha Schmidt.
    - Margaretha Elisabetha, bapt. by Reverend Jacob Lischy on Aug. 31, 1755, and spon. by Maria Elisabeth Stentzin.

- Philliph Jacob, bapt. by Reverend Jacob Lischy on Oct. 30, 1757, and spon. by Phillip Daniel Stentz and Maria Eva Schultzin.
- Anna Catharina, bapt. by Reverend Jacob Lischy on Sept. 17, 1760, and spon. by Peter and Catharina Stambach.
- Catharina Elisabetha, b. about 1735, and m. Anthony Oler/Ehler before 1755.
- Johan Georg, b. on Oct. 9, 1734, and bapt. at Christ's Lutheran Church of York on Nov. 10, 1734. He m. Susanna (this marriage to Susanna has not been confirmed) about 1763, and Catharina Elisabetha, dau. of Johan Philipp and Maria Sophia Gohn, about 1767. Catharina Elisabetha was b. on Sept. 16, 1744, and bapt. at Canadochly Union Church. Georg and Catharina were sponsors at the baptism of Anna Maria, dau. of Michael and Margaretha Fries, at Kreutz Creek on May 10, 1768, and Johan Georg, son of Phiellieb and Anna Liesbeta Gohn, at Canadochly Union in 1772. Georg had 150 acres, two horses, and two cattle in Codorus Township in 1779; 190 acres, two horses, and two cattle in 1780; 150 acres, two horses, and three cattle in 1781; 200 acres, two horses, and three cattle in 1782; 150 acres and ten inhabitants in 1783; and one male above 16, two males below 16, and seven females in 1790. He also had 50 acres, and one head of cattle in Manheim Township in 1781, and 50 acres, and no inhabitants in Manheim Township in 1783. His will was probated in Codorus Township on Mar. 15, 1806. His execs. were George Smith and Henry Miller. Catharina d. sometime after 1806. Georg had the following children:
- Catharina, (to Georg and Susanna) bapt. by Reverend Jacob Lischy on June 11, 1764, and spon. by Johan Jacob Klee and Catharina Fischerin.
- Maria Sophia, b. on Oct. 29, 1768, and bapt. at Canadochly Union on Nov. 21, 1768. She m. Johan Daniel Scherer (see entry).
- Johan Georg, b. on Mar. 12, 1771, m. Anna Maria, and d. on Mar. 1, 1844. She was b. on Feb. 10, 1774, and d. on July 10, 1857. They are bur. in STJ cemetery.
- Susanna, b. about 1772.
- Johannes, b. about 1774, and m. Helena.
- Anna Margaretha, b. on Aug. 27, 1776, bapt. at St. Jacob's on Sept. 15, 1776, and spon. by Daniel and Anna Margaretha (Schmidt) Cramer.
- Magdalena, b. on May 1, 1780, bapt. at St. Jacob's on June 14, 1780, and spon. by Veith and Sophia Benner.
- Anna Elisabetha, b. on Jan. 9, 1782, bapt. at St. Jacob's on Feb. 6, 1782, and spon. by George and Margaret Dehoff.
- Anton, b. on Dec. 27, 1783, bapt. at St. Jacob's on Mar. 28, 1784, and spon. by Anthony and Margaret Bruecker. He m. Catharina

- Juliana Lisbet, b. on Aug. 25, 1788, bapt. at St. Jacob's on Nov. 4, 1788, and spon. by Nicholas and Elizabeth Wolfgang.
- Anna Margaretha, b. about 1737 (or as early as 1730). She was a sponsor at the baptism of Anna Margaretha, dau. of Michael and Eva Swartz, at Canadochly Union Church on Feb. 12, 1758. She is probably the Anna Margaretha Schmidt that m. Daniel Kramer (see entry), but it has not been proven.
- Anna Magdalena, b. about 1739. She m. Johan Georg Dietz at Christ's Lutheran Church of York on Apr. 20, 1761. They had the following children at Kreutz Creek:
  - Johann Conrad, b. at midnight on July 10, 1763, bapt. on July 31, 1763, and spon. by John and Anna Maria Lebber.
  - Johan Heinrich, bapt. on Mar. 7, 1765, and spon. by his grandparents, Heinrich and Margaretha (?) Schmidt.
- Anna Elisabetha, b. about 1741. She m. Frantz Bischoff (see entry).
- Anna Susanna, bapt. by Reverend Jacob Lischy on May 23, 1745, and spon. by Susanna.
- Johan Heinrich, bapt. by Reverend Jacob Lischy on Aug. 22, 1747, and spon. by Leonhardt and Maria Vronica Comfort.
- Johannes, bapt. by Reverend Jacob Lischy on Aug. 6, 1749, and spon. by Johannes Comfort.
- Maria Elisabetha, bapt. by Reverend Jacob Lischy on Nov. 17, 1754, and spon. by Georg and Maria Elisabeth Kuntz.
- Anna Barbara, bapt. by Reverend Jacob Lischy on Sept. 19, 1756, and spon. by John and Anna Barbara Lor. She m. Jacob Harbach.
- Heinrich, bapt. by Reverend Jacob Lischy on Nov. 3, 1760, and spon. by Heinrich and Margaretha Bayer.
- Johan Jacob, bapt. by Reverend Jacob Lischy on June 24, 1764, and spon. by Jacob and Ester Banckert.

Schneider - Christopel was taxed in 1762. He is probably the Christian Snyder that received a warrant for 100 acres on Feb. 23, 1767.

Schneider - Theobald (Dewalt) m. Anna Katharina, dau. of Hermann Closter, at Saal Osterthal, Germany, on Dec. 30, 1734, Anna Margaretha about 1751, and Susanna before 1776. He immigrated to America on the ship *Dragon* on Sept. 26, 1749. Theobald's will was written in Manheim Township on June 2, 1776, and probated on Dec. 16, 1784. He had the following children:
- Theobald (Dewalt), b. about 1735. He m. Anna Maria Margaretha, dau. of Andreas Swartz (see entry). Margaretha was bapt. at Christ's Lutheran Church of York on Jan. 22, 1749, and spon. by Rebecca Hamspacker. His probate inventory was filed in 1821. They resided in York Co., Codorus Township, PA. They had the following children:

- Theobald b. about 1770. He m. a dau. of Jacob and Anna Maria Stein before 1798 (see entry in Shrewsbury section).
- Georg, b. on July 10, 1783, bapt. at Fissel's (Jerusalem) Union Church on Aug. 17, 1783, and spon. by John Gantz.
- Anna Maria, b. on Apr. 20, 1785, bapt. at FIS on May 1, 1785, and spon. by Catharina Swartzin single. She m. Adam, son of Adam and Magdalena Schmidt (see entry in Dover section). He was b. on Oct. 13, 1795, and d. on Sept. 6, 1845. She d. in Codorus Township on May 18, 1859.
- Elisabeth Margaretha, b. on 19 July 1787, bapt. at Sherman's Union Church on Aug. 26, 1787, and spon. by Georg and Margaretha Bortner.
- Magdalena, b. on Nov. 18, 1791, and bapt. at St. Jacob's (Stone) Union Church on Jan. 29, 1792.
- Maria, b. about 1737, and m. Jacob Roth before 1776.
- Johann Wendel, b. on Feb. 6, 1740.
- Anna Margaretha, b. on Mar. 21, 1743, and m. ____ Schitz before 1776.
- Johann Peter, b. on June 13, 1746, and d. on June 20, 1748.
- Catharina, bapt. by RJL on Feb. 11, 1752, and spon. by Adam and Catharina Hubert.
- Magdalena, bapt. by RJL on Sept. 14, 1758, and spon. by Leonhardt and Catharina Sabel.
- Johann Heinrich, bapt. by RJL on May 23, 1762, and spon. by Johan Heinrich and Agnes Hartman.

Schultz - Michael received a warrant for 100 acres on Aug. 20, 1773. This land was surveyed as 137 acres called *Hickory Hallow* on Sept. 23, 1773, and patented on Apr. 8, 1835. He m. Maria Catharina. They were sponsors to the baptism of Maria Catharina Bortner in 1765 (RJL). A probate inventory for a Michael Schultz was filed in Codorus Township in 1834.

Shuert - Miller was taxed in 1762.

Sopach (Sepach) - Jacob was taxed in 1762. He received a warrant for 100 acres in North Codorus Township on May 31, 1762, that was surveyed as 201 acres called *Painter Hill* on Nov. 13, 1766. He m. Christina, and they were probably the parents of the following children:
- Jacob was a sponsor in 1758, and m. Catharina, dau. of Peter Runk (see entry).
- Susanna, was a sponsor in 1768.
- Catharina, m. Henry Merschel at TLC on Oct. 1, 1782.
- Christina, m. Henry Lehner at TLY on July 15, 1783.

CODORUS TOWNSHIP

<u>Spanhauer</u> - Wernhardt was taxed in 1762, and received a warrant for 50 acres in North Codorus Township on Dec. 18, 1751, that was surveyed as 115 acres on Mar. 23, 1809. He m. Anna Elisabetha, and had the following children:
- Michael, bapt. by RJL on Feb. 4, 1753, and spon. by Lorrentz and Anna Ursula Kron.
- Johan Heinrich, b. on Aug. 5, 1762, and bapt. at STJ on Sept. 26, 1762.
- Anna Elisabetha, b. on Aug. 5, 1762, and bapt. at STJ on Sept. 26, 1762.

<u>Spessert</u> - Michael received a warrant for 100 acres in North Codorus Township on Sept. 3, 1766, that was surveyed as 45.153 acres called *Kalehousy* on Apr. 15, 1767. He also received a warrant for 100 acres in North Codorus Township, that was surveyed as 164 acres on May 15, 1766 (interest began on Mar. 1, 1753. A Michael Spessart had his probate inventory filed in Shrewsbury Township in 1815. He m. Maria Elisabetha, and had the following dau.:
- Maria Catharina, bapt. by RJL on Aug. 21, 1768, and spon. by Heinrich Horn and wife.

<u>Stambach</u> - Johannes was the son of Felix and Anna Maria Stambach. Felix Stambach d. in Kutzenhausen, Northern Alsace, on Nov. 3, 1729, aged 86 years, 3 months, and 12 days. Johannes Stambach m. Maria Catharina, dau. of Jacob and Anna Meyer, in Kutzenhausen in 1717. Jacob Meyer d. in Merckweyler on Feb. 1, 1716, aged 63 years. Jacob's widow, Anna d. in Merckweiler on Feb. 19, 1726, aged 70 years, and is bur. in Oberkutzenhausen. Johannes Stambach d. in Oberkutzenhausen on Jan. 17, 1733 aged about 57 years. After Johannes death, Maria Catharina m. Niclaus Honig (see entry) at Niederkuntzenhausen on Nov. 17, 1733. Niclaus and Catharina immigrated to America on the ship *Robert and Alice* in 1739. Johannes and Maria Catharina Stambach had the following children (bapt. at Kutzenhausen Lutheran Church (see BNA)):
- Johann Jacob, b. on Jan. 9, 1719, and bapt. on Jan. 11, 1719. He was taxed in Manheim Township in 1762. He m. Margaretha. They had the following children:
  - Maria Catharina, b. on Sept. 22, 1740, bapt. by JCS, and spon. by Johan Georg Kuntz and daus. Maria Catharina and Maria Elisabetha Morgensten.
  - Anna Barbara, bapt. by RJL on Mar. 18, 1745, and spon. by Georg and Anna Barbara Schmeisser.
  - Jacob, bapt. by RJL on June 17, 1750, and spon. by Lorentz and Barbara Stambach.

- Maria Elisabetha, bapt. by RJL on June 17, 1750, and spon. by Lorentz and Barbara Stambach. She m. John Ickes, and d. on Aug. 27, 1823. He was b. on Aug. 23, 1742, and d. on Jan. 19, 1829. They are bur. in Old Union cemetery in Osterberg, PA.
- Anna Barbara, bapt. by RJL on June 14, 1752, and spon. by Nicholas and Anna Barbara Stambach.
- Philip, bapt. by RJL on Nov. 20, 1754, and spon. by Johanna Boin and Philip Stambach.
- Maria Barbara, b. on July 25, 1721, and bapt. on July 27, 1721. She m. Johan Georg, son of Martin Schmeisser (see entry in Manchester section), at Trinity Lutheran Church of Lancaster, PA, (or CLY) on May 22, 1740. After Georg Schmeisser's death, she m. Georg Muller in 1748 (see entry).
- Nicholas, b. on Aug. 19, 1723, and bapt. on Aug. 22, 1723. He d. in 1760, and his widow was taxed in Codorus Township in 1762. He received a warrant for 50 acres in North Codorus Township on Sept. 10, 1750, that was surveyed to Jacob Stambach as 68.30 acres called *Rabet Hill* on Mar. 20, 1773. He m. Anna Barbara. They had the following children:
  - Johan Jacob, bapt. by RJL on Dec. 16, 1749, and spon. by Jacob and Margaretha Stambach. He warranted 50 acres in North Codorus Township on Feb. 11, 1773, that was surveyed as 48.92 acres called *Stambaugh's Addition* on Mar. 20, 1773. He m. Maria Magdalena, and d. on Feb. 22, 1826 (bur. in Lischey's cemetery). She was b. on May 2, 1752, and d. on Oct. 2, 1804.
  - Anna Margareth, bapt. by RJL on Mar. 29, 1751, and spon. by Margaretha Kronin. She m. George Leaseman.
  - Johan Peter, bapt. by RJL on June 14, 1752, and spon. by Peter and Anna Catharina Runk.
  - Johannes, bapt. by RJL on Oct. 14, 1753, and spon. by Peter and Anna Catharina Runck. His will was written in Paradise Township on Mar. 27, 1822, and probated on Nov. 1, 1824.
  - Anna Elisabetha, bapt. by RJL on Jan. 15, 1755, and spon. by Wernhardt and Elisabetha Sponhauer. She m. ___ Byers/Boyer.
- Lorentz, b. on Dec. 8, 1725, and bapt. on Dec. 11, 1725. He was taxed in 1762. He m. Anna, and d. in Franklin Co., Straussburg Township, PA, in 1802/03. She was alive in 1807. They had the following children:
  - Catharina, bapt. by RJL on Nov. 4, 1750, and spon. by Peter and Catharina Stambach.
  - Jacob, bapt. by RJL on Mar. 29, 1752, and spon. by Sebastian and Margaretha Hellman. He m. Elisabeth, and d. in Franklin Co., PA, in 1796.
  - Elisabetha Magdalena, bapt. by RJL on May 26, 1754, and spon. by Peter and Lowis Erb. She m. Conrad, son of Michael and

Margaret (Diller) Keinardt/Kyner. He was b. in Lancaster Co. in 1755, and resided in Franklin Co., Southampton Township, PA.
- Peter, bapt. by RJL on Mar. 7, 1756, and spon. by Peter and Lowis Erb.
- Margaretha, bapt. by RJL on June 4, 1758, and spon. by Jacob and Margaretha Stambach.
- Johan Philip, bapt. by RJL on Sept. 17, 1760, and spon. by Frantz and Elisabetha Bischoff.
- Johann Peter, b. on Feb. 11, 1729, and bapt. on Feb. 13, 1729. He was taxed in 1762, and received a warrant for 100 acres on Sept. 10, 1750, that was surveyed as 217.111 acres called *Plenty* on Apr. 14, 1774. He m. Catharina. They had the following children:
  - Anna Maria, bapt. by RJL on Apr. 30, 1749, and spon. by Emerich and Anna Maria Bott.
  - Susanna, bapt. by RJL on Mar. 29, 1751, and spon. by Wentel and Susanna Fisser.
  - Christina, bapt. by RJL on Mar. 25, 1753, and spon. by Heinrich and Catharina Gerber.
  - Maria Elisabetha, bapt. by RJL on Aug. 10, 1755, and spon. by Philip and Maria Ester Gerber. She m. Samuel Brinton/Brindel in 1776.
  - Magdalena, bapt. by RJL on Apr. 2, 1760, and spon. by Magdalena Lischyn.
  - Anna Margaretha, bapt. by RJL on Mar. 3, 1762, and spon. by Philip Jacob and Anna Margaretha Schmidt.
- Johann Philliph, b. on June 9, 1731, and bapt. on June 10, 1731. He was taxed in 1762, and was warranted land on Sept. 1, 1767, that was surveyed as 144.121 acres called *Hunting Ground* on Nov. 10, 1768. He served in the Revolutionary War in Captain John Myer's Company (1778). His will was written in Codorus Township on June 5, 1809, and probated on Sept. 12, 1811. He m. Barbara, and Anna Maria between 1767 and 1789. They had the following children:
  - Johan Heinrich, b. on May 15, 1760, bapt. by RJL on Sept. 26, 1762, and spon. by Georg and Barbara Muller. He m. Susanna, and d. on Apr. 15, 1833 (bur. at Lischey's cemetery). She was b. in 1765, and d. on Dec. 20, 1836.
  - Johan Michael, bapt. by RJL on Oct. 3, 1764, and spon. by Jacob and Magdalena Shilling. He m. Anna Maria, dau. of Philip and Maria Anna (Sprenckel) Emig, and d. before 1812. She was b. on Apr. 9, 1771, and d. on Nov. 22, 1844 (bur. at WOL).
  - Elisabetha, bapt. by RJL on July 27, 1766, and spon. by Sebastian and Elisabetha Schilling. She m. Christian Kauffman.

Steltz - Philip m. Regina. He was warranted 100 acres on July 2, 1767, that was surveyed as 73.68 acres called *Steltz Level* on Apr. 13, 1767. He received a warrant for 50 acres on Apr. 22, 1767, that was surveyed as 47.14 acres called *Overagain* on May 28, 1767. They had the following children (bapt. at STJ):
- Anna Margaretha, b. on Dec. 25, 1761, and bapt. on May 9, 1762.
- Johannes, b. on Apr. 8, 1765, and bapt. on May 5, 1765.
- Maria Elisabetha, bapt. on May 7, 1772.
- Philip, m. Margaretha before 1796.
- Susanna was a sponsor to the baptism of Catharina Hennig in 1798.
- Wilhelm, m. before 1799.

Steng - Michael warranted 50 acres on Mar. 14, 1755. A Frederick Steng's probate inventory was filed in York Co. in 1755.

Strickhauser - John received a warrant for 25 acres on May 19. 1774, that was surveyed as 7.130 acres on June 23, 1774. He also received a warrant for 50 acres on May 19, 1774, that was surveyed as 27.122 acres called *Addition* on June 24, 1774 (patented to Henry Strickhauser on May 9, 1810). His probate inventory was filed in Codorus Township in 1777. He m. Anna Elisabeth, and had the following children:
- Anna Elisabeth, bapt. by RJL on May 19, 1764, and spon. by Daniel and Maria Elisabeth Renolly.
- Johan Henrich, bapt. by RJL on Nov. 17, 1765, and spon. by Heinrich Kenner and wife. He m. Elizabeth, dau. of Joseph Herschy before 1798.
- Johannes, b. on Nov. 9, 1767, bapt. by RJL on Nov. 25, 1767, and spon. by Niclas and Maria Elisabeth Henig. He m. Anna Maria Conrad, and d. on Jan. 17, 1822. She was b. on May 5, 1772, and d. on Feb. 8, 1815. They are bur. at STJ.

Strickhauser - William received a warrant for 100 acres that was surveyed as 121 acres called *Nyawit* on Apr. 21, 1767 (patented to John Strickhauser on May 20, 1774).

Streithoff - Jost received a warrant for 100 acres on May 20, 1768, that was surveyed as 111.15 acres called *Long Hallow* on Nov. 10, 1768. He m. a dau. of Hans Nicholas Maak (see entry).

Streithoff - Frantz served in the Revolutionary War in Captain John Myer's Company (1778). He m. Ann Elisabeth, dau. of Nicholas Yost, at TLY on July 2, 1786. They had the following children:

CODORUS TOWNSHIP

- Elisabeth, b. on Sept. 22, 1786, bapt. at TLY on Dec. 25, 1786, and spon. by Elisabeth Streithoff.
- Johannes, b. on June 4, 1789, bapt. at ERC on Aug. 2, 1789, and spon. by John and Eva Streithoff.

Stuck - Conrad was taxed in 1762, and naturalized on Apr. 29, 1770. He received a warrant in North Codorus Township for 300 acres on Jan. 4, 1767, that was surveyed as 180.120 acres called *Manheim* on Apr. 8, 1767. He received a warrant for 100 acres in North Codorus Township on May 12, 1770, that was surveyed as 35.87 acres in May 1770, and patented on May 22, 1772. His will was written in Codorus Township on Aug. 11, 1770, and probated on Oct. 20, 1770. He m. Ursula and Margaretha after 1752. He had the following children:
- Peter, m. Margaret, dau. of Georg Jacob Schafer (see entry), at TLY on June 14, 1775.
- Martin, m. Barbara, dau. of Georg Jacob Schafer (see entry), at TLY on Oct. 19, 1775.
- Johan Jacob, bapt. by RJL on Nov. 3, 1751, and spon. by Johan Georg and Barbara Hoog.
- Hannah.
- Susanna.
- Eve, m. Andrew Shettler.

Stump - Peter received a warrant for 182 acres in Manheim and Codorus Township on Mar. 12, 1767 (called *Rattle Snake Swamp*). His probate inventory was filed in Manheim Township in 1791.

Summeraur - Henry received a warrant for 150 acres in North Codorus Township (in Springettsbury Manor) on May 21, 1772, that was surveyed as 28 acres (outside of Manor boundaries).

Supinger - Conrad was taxed in 1762. He received a warrant for 50 acres on Mar. 2, 1750. He m. Maria Magdalena, and they were sponsors to the baptism of Maria Magdalena Schramm in 1759.

Treiber - Ludwig was taxed in 1762. He m. Anna Barbara, widow of Adam Hoffman (see entry), and dau. of Michael and Anna Margaretha (Miller) Sprenckel, about 1753. Ludwig immigrated to America on the ship *Fane* on Oct. 17, 1749. He received a warrant for 50 acres on Mar. 6, 1767, and 70 acres on Feb. 12, 1767, that were surveyed as 150 acres called *Round Stone* on Apr. 6, 1767 (North Codorus Township). On Mar. 21, 1771, he purchased 127 acres from John and Sarah Keagy. He had 100 acres in Shrewsbury Township, that he sold to Daniel Kurfman on Dec. 26, 1760. Ludwig d. intestate in Codorus Township, and on Feb. 25, 1772, Barbara and Michael Treiber were appointed

administrators of his estate. Barbara d. in York Co. sometime before Apr. 9, 1781, when her son, Michael was granted letters of administration for her estate. Ludwig and Barbara had the following children:
- Michael, b. in 1754. He m. Barbara, and d. in York Co., PA, sometime prior to Apr. 6, 1807, when his widow, Barbara, and George Lichtenberger were made guardians for his minor children. Barbara was b. on June 11, 1757, and d. in Rockingham Co., Timberville, VA, on Feb. 11, 1812. She is bur. in Rader's cemetery.
- Anna, b. in 1756. She m. John, son of John Reiff/Rife. He d. in Rockingham Co., Timberville, VA, in Apr. 1824.
- Barbara, b. in 1758.
- Ludwig, b. on Aug. 8, 1760. He m. Barbara, dau. of Julius Burkhart (see entry in Manchester section). She was b. on June 3, 1766, and d. in Rockingham Co., Timberville, VA, on Feb. 11, 1836. Ludwig d. in Timberville on Mar. 26, 1835. He owned 440/450 acres northeast of Timberville. They are bur. in Driver/Rife cemetery.
- Anna Maria, b. on Dec. 3, 1764. She m. Peter Ocker/Acker, and d. in Rockingham Co., Edom, VA, in Nov. 1849. Peter was b. on Sept. 22, 1753, and d. at Edom on Mar. 30, 1832. They are bur. in Brenneman cemetery.
- Peter, b. on Nov. 20, 1766. He m. Dorothy Meyer, and d. in Rockingham Co., Singer's Glen, VA, on July 1, 1850. She was b. on Apr. 15, 1774, and d. on Oct. 7, 1844. In 1797, Peter purchased 112.5 acres on Muddy River, and in 1828, purchased an additional 160 acres.
- Jacob, b. in 1768. He m. Elizabeth, dau. of John Forry. She was b. on Oct. 26, 1771. Jacob is bur. in Menge's Station, PA, (six miles east of York Co., Hanover).
- Elizabeth, b. in 1771.

Trorbach - Michael was taxed in 1762. His probate inventory was filed at York in 1771. He was a communicant at the Lower Bermudian Church in Adams Co., PA, on Mar. 9, 1760, May 2, 1762, and Oct. 17, 1762 (with wife). He had the following children:
- Johan Adam was taxed in York in 1762, and received a warrant for 100 acres in North Codorus Township on Jan. 27, 1757. He also received a warrant for 100 acres in North Codorus Township on Jan. 27, 1757, that was surveyed as 125.95 acres to Matthew Trorbach on Oct. 14, 1772. He m. Katrina, dau. of Michael and Anna Margaretha (Miller) Sprenckel, about 1755. They resided in Shrewsbury Township in 1764, when they signed a release to her bro., George Sprenckel. She may have d. in 1765, because Adam and Anna Maria Trorbach spon. the baptism of Anna Maria, dau. of Adam and Catharina Hubert on Sept. 3, 1765, and Johan Adam,

son of Adam and Barbara Forny on Oct. 12, 1766. Adam and
Catharina (Scheebler) Trorbach bapt. Johan Jacob at Friedensaal
on June 15, 1766 (sponsored by Johann Jacob and Maria Barbara).
Other sources say Katharina Sprenckel was the mother to all of
Adam's children. Adam d. in Shrewsbury Township. His will was
written on Mar. 5, 1770, probated on Mar. 12, 1770, and executed
by William and Nicholas Trorbach. Adam had the following children
in Shrewsbury Township:
- Michael b. about 1756.
- Henry, b. about 1758.
- Abraham, b. about 1760.
- John Adam, b. on Nov. 13, 1763, and bapt. at CLY on Sept. 11, 1763.
- Johan Jacob, b. on Jan. 6, 1766, bapt. at FRI on June 15, 1766, and spon. by Johan Jacob and wife Maria Barbara.
- Elizabeth Catherine/Elinor, b. about 1770.
- Johan Jacob m. Maria Barbara, and had the following children:
  - Johan Ludwig, bapt. by RJL at the Lower Bermudian Church in Adams Co. on Sept. 28, 1760, and spon. by Ludwig and Anna Maria Weldner.
  - Johan Jacob, bapt. at The Lower Bermudian Church in Adams Co., PA, on May 10, 1763, and spon. by Jacob and Anna Barbara Henn.
- Mattheus and wife spon. the baptism of Johan Jacob Klemmasch in 1766.
- Michael was a sponsor to the baptism of Maria Eva Linckefelder and Anna Elisabeth Reiff in 1756.
- Wilhelm.
- Nicholas m. Anna Elisabeth, and had the following children:
  - Johan Friedrich, bapt. by RJL on Apr. 8, 1765, and spon. by Friedrich Meyer and Elisabeth Trorbachin.
  - Elisabeth Margareta, bapt. at FRI on Nov. 10, 1769, and spon. by Margareth Trorbach.
- Elisabeth, was a sponsor to the baptism of Johan Friedrich Drorbach in 1765 (a Maria Elisabetha Trorbachin was a sponsor to the baptism of Johann Jacob Muller in 1753).

Ulerich - Michael was taxed in 1762. He m. Anna Maria. They had the following children:
  - Johan Heinrich, bapt. by RJL on May 19, 1755, and Heinrich and Anna Margaretha Eberhardt.

Vogler (Vogel) - Johann Nicholas was taxed in 1762, and his probate inventory was filed in Codorus Township in 1766. He m. Susanna. After his death, she m. Nicholas Koenig at TLY on Dec. 17, 1771 (see

EARLY GERMAN SETTLERS OF YORK CO., PA

entry in Manchester section). Nicholas and Susanna Vogel had the following children:
- Hans Georg, bapt. by RJL on Oct. 27, 1745, and spon. by Georg and Barbara Meyer. He was a sponsor to the baptism of a child of Martin Hechler in 1761 (CLY). He m. Susanna about 1768, and had a child bapt. at Zion Lutheran Church in Washington Co., Hagerstown, MD, in 1774.
- Maria Magdalena, bapt. by RJL on Mar. 22, 1752, and spon. by Michael and Maria Magdalena Haug.
- Jacob, bapt. by RJL on Sept. 1, 1754, and spon. by Jacob and Barbara Schaffer.

Vollenweiler - Ulrich warranted 150 acres on June 1, 1762, and served in the Revolutionary War in Captain John Myer's Company in 1778. He m. Anna Maria Margareth, and had the following children:
- Jacob, bapt. by RJL on Jan. 20, 1754, and spon. by Jacob and Catharina Haffner.
- Johannes, bapt. by RJL on May 8, 1756, and spon. by his parents.
- Maria Eva, bapt. by RJL on July 24, 1760, and spon. by Jacob and Maria Eva Behler.
- Anna Margaretha, b. on Jan. 28, 1762, and bapt. at STJ on Feb. 14, 1762.
- Susanna, b. on Feb. 5, 1764, and bapt. at STJ on Feb. 18, 1764.
- Georg, b. on Mar. 29, 1766, and bapt. at STJ on the first Sunday after Easter.
- Anna Maria, b. on Sept. 8, 1770, and bapt. at STJ on Sept. 16, 1770.
- Elisabeth, b. on Jan. 31, 1773, and bapt. at STJ on Feb. 4, 1773.
- Peter, b. on Feb. 23, 1775, and bapt. at STJ on Mar. 6, 1775.
- Anna Catharina, b. on May 29, 1776, and bapt. at STJ on June 9, 1776.

Votrin (Wodering/Wottring) - Johan Daniel was b. in Helleringen, Lorraine (Reformed) on June 24, 1711, and immigrated to America in Sept. 1739. At age 17, he was recruited into a regiment of Dragoons in the French service, and he soon deserted and returned home. Five weeks after his arrival in America his wife, and two of his children died. He resided in Germantown, PA, for four years, and then moved to the Conewago, nine miles from York. He m. Eva Kohnz in 1733, and Anna Maria, dau. of Hans Jacob and Anna Maria Rebmann, in Apr. 1740. Eva d. in 1739. Anna Maria was b. in Uttenhofen, Alsace on June 7, 1715 (Reformed (sponsored by Hanns Jacob Reinhard, Jr., Anna Maria, dau. of Rudolph Erb, and Veronica, wife of Hans Conrad)), immigrated to America in 1739, and d. in Frederick Co., Frederick, MD, after an eye operation on Nov. 20, 1786. Johan Daniel received a

CODORUS TOWNSHIP

warrant for 50 acres in North Codorus Township on May 19, 1752, that was surveyed as 241 acres on Nov. 30, 1753 (interest began on Mar. 1, 1748). Daniel moved to Frederick Co., Monocacy, MD, in 1760, and d. of Dropsy on Apr. 15, 1786. He had the following children (recorded at FMY and BNA):
- Maria, b. on Sept. 5, 1734.
- Maria Elisabetha, stillborn on Jan. 6, 1736/37.
- Susanna, b. on Aug. 6, 1738, and bapt. on Aug. 6, 1738.
- Johannes, b. on Dec. 21, 1740, and bapt. in Philadelphia, PA, on Jan. 1, 1741. He m. Elisabeth, dau. of Nicholas and Anna Maria Glat, of Heidelberg, PA, in Berks Co., Heidelberg, PA, on Sept. 13, 1763, and d. in Monocacy on Nov. 16, 1779. She was b. on Nov. 7, 1742, and d. on Dec. 14, 1779.
- Anna Maria Salome, b. on Apr. 6, 1743, bapt. at CLY on May 28, 1743, and spon. by Peter and Maria Pengele.
- Anna Catharina, b. on May 16, 1745, bapt. by RJL on July 30, 1745, and spon. by Daniel and Catharina Heckedorn.
- Juliana, b. on Aug. 13, 1746, and bapt. on Aug. 24, 1746. She m. Philip, son of Jacob and Maria Barbara (Wilhide) Weller on Sept. 30, 1766. He was b. on June 12, 1742, and d. in Monocacy on Oct. 7, 1779. Juliana m. Henry Peitsel after Philip's death, and d. in Monocacy on Sept. 10, 1803.
- Maria Salome, b. on Mar. 18, 1749, bapt. on Mar. 29, 1749, and spon. by Johannes and Catharina Kuntz.
- Anna Elisabetha, b. on Feb. 20, 1751, and bapt. on Mar. 3, 1751.
- Maria Elisabetha, bapt. by RJL on May 19, 1752, and spon. by Johannes and Catharina Binckely.
- Maria Elisabetha, b. on Mar. 16, 1754.
- Barbara, b. on Feb. 27, 1757.

Walter - Jacob was taxed in 1762. He received a warrant for 20 acres on Sept. 15, 1774, and a warrant for 25 acres in North Codorus Township on Mar. 11, 1771, that was surveyed as 34.140 acres called *Walter's Addition* on June 25, 1772. He also received a warrant for 50 acres on June 9, 1762, that was surveyed as 114.96 acres called *Ground Oak Valley* on July 22, 1763 (patented on Oct. 19, 1767). One June 9, 1762, he received another warrant for 50 acres in North Codorus Township, that was surveyed as 42.82 acres called *Swift Run* on Nov. 13, 1766, and patented on Oct. 17, 1767. He purchased 53 in Codorus Township acres from Ulrick Fulweiler on Oct. 24, 1751. His will was written in Codorus Township on Oct. 14, 1783, and probated on Aug. 7, 1784. He m. Margaretha Gippel. He was naturalized on Apr. 3, 1763. They had the following children (recorded at FRI):
- Johan Georg, b. on May 23, 1752, bapt. on June 21, 1752, and spon. by Georg and Margaretha Ziegler. He m. Catharina, dau. of

Michael Geisselman (see entry in Shrewsbury section), and had the following children (Recorded at ZIE):
- Anna Maria, b. on Sept. 8, 1775, bapt. on Oct. 1, 1775, and spon. by Anna Maria Walter.
- Maria Eva, b. on Sept. 3, 1777, bapt. on Sept. 7, 1777, and spon. by Eva Margaretha Geisselman.
- Jacob, b. on Jan. 27, 1779, bapt. on Feb. 2, 1779, and spon. by Jacob and Margaret Walter.
- Georg, b. on Dec. 24, 1781, bapt. on Jan. 26, 1782, and spon. by Georg and Salome Geisselman.
- Michael, b. on May 2, 1784, bapt. on May 31, 1784, and spon. by Michael Geisselman and wife.
- John, b. on Sept. 16, 1786, bapt. on Oct. 22, 1786, and spon. by John Liebenstein and wife.
- Maria Catharina, b. on Oct. 20, 1790, bapt. on Nov. 6, 1790, and spon. by Margaret Walter.
- Henry, b. on Jan. 18, 1796, bapt. on Jan. 25, 1796, and spon. by his parents.
- Maria Elisabetha, b. on July 17, 1754, bapt. on Jan. 7, 1755, and spon. by Daniel and Maria Elisabetha Diehl.
- Anna Maria, b. on Oct. 29, 1758, bapt. on Jan. 7, 1759, and spon. by Anna Maria Diehl and Heinrich Hoff. She m. Georg Raus.
- Anna Catharina, b. on Nov. 7, 1760, bapt. the third Sunday in Advent, and spon. by Michael and Anna Catharina Meyer. She m. Henry Bower.
- Anna Barbara, b. on June 18, 1765, bapt. on July 7, 1765, and spon. by Georg and Anna Barbara Stely. She m. John, son of Georg Liebenstein (see entry in Manchester section).
- Wilhelmina Margareta, b. on Jan. 16, 1767, bapt. on Mar. 1, 1767, and spon. by Michael and Wilhelmina Margareta Geiselman.

Walter - Hans was taxed in Manchester Township in 1762. He received a warrant for 125 acres in North Codorus Township on Mar. 2, 1767, that was surveyed as 83 acres called *Mary-a-liss* on Apr. 14, 1767. His will probated on Nov. 8, 1784, and witnessed by Sebastian Weidman, Tobias Hartman, and Mathias Bobb. He m. Maria Elisabeth, and mentions his daus. as his two remaining heirs (he may be the father of Jacob Walter of Codorus Township, and Peter and Henry Walter of Shrewsbury Township (Henry and Jacob d. before the date John's will was probated)). John and Maria Elisabeth had the following children:
- Elisabeth, m. ___ Baer.
- Anna Barbara, m. ___ Miller (John Miller received John Walter's Bible in the will).

Waltimier (Waltemeyer) - Georg was taxed in 1762. He m. Elisabetha.
They had the following children:
- Johan Michael, b. on Jan. 8, 1773, bapt. on May 20, 1773, and spon.
  by Michael and Elisabetha Muller.

Waltimier (Waltemeyer) - Daniel (?David) was taxed in 1762.

Weidman - Mathias Sebastian was b. in Karlesruhe, Durlach,
Germany/Lancaster Co., Warwick Township, PA, in 1727 to Mathias
Martin and Maria Catharina Weidman. Sebastian wrote his will in
Codorus Township on Jan. 5, 1789, and it was probated on June 7,
1790. He m. Elisabeth Mumma, and had the following children:
- Henry, b. in York Co. in 1757.
- Jacob.
- Johannes.

Weiss - Jacob was taxed in 1762. He m. Catharina before 1763, and
Maria before 1766. Jacob and Catharina were sponsors to the baptism
of Maria Catharina Herman in 1763, and Jacob and Maria were
sponsors to the baptism of Nicholas and Ester Thiel in 1766.

Welsch - Philliph was taxed in 1762. He m. Anna Maria. They had the
following children:
- Philip Jacob, bapt. by RJL on Dec. 8, 1754, and spon. by Philip
  Jacob and Barbara Schmid.

Werner - Georg Martin received a warrant for 50 acres in North
Codorus Township on May 31, 1762, that was surveyed as 169 acres to
John Martin Werner on Mar. 17, 1757.

Werner - Johannes Georg was taxed in 1762. This Johannes may be
the Johannes, son of Anna Margaretha Geiger, that was b. before 1749
(see entry on Peter Binckele). He warranted 50 acres (55 acres called
Bushy Hill surveyed on May 23, 1776) on Feb. 20, 1775. His will was
written in Codorus Township on July 20, 1805, and probated on Aug.
16, 1805. Johannes m. Judith, and had the following children:
- Daniel, bapt. by RJL on June 19, 1763, and spon. by Daniel Jonas
  and Anna Maria Barthel.
- Maria Magdalena, bapt. by RJL on May 17, 1765, and spon. by
  Christian Cappell and Magdalena Holtzin.
- Johan Georg, bapt. at STJ on Sept. 5, 1767.
- Johannes, b. on Dec. 2, 1771, and bapt. at STJ on Dec. 25, 1771.
- Johan Christian, b. on Oct. 21, 1775, and bapt. at STJ on Nov. 19,
  1775.
- Catharina, b. on June 9, 1778, and bapt. at STJ on July 5, 1778.

- Jacob, b. on Mar. 10, 1782, and bapt. at STJ on Apr. 6, 1782.
- Elisabetha, b. on Feb. 2, 1784, and bapt. at STJ on Apr. 4, 1784.
- Jacob, b. on Mar. 16, 1786, and bapt. at STJ on Apr. 17, 1786.
- Anna Maria, b. on Apr. 4, 1790, and bapt. at STJ on May 15, 1790.
- Maria Catharina, b. on Oct. 15, 1791, and bapt. at STJ on Dec. 3, 1791.

Wertz - Johannes was taxed in 1762. His will was written in Codorus Township on Dec. 2, 1778, and probated on Dec. 16, 1781. He m. Anna. They had the following children:
- Catherine, m. John Ottman.
- Jacob.
- Elisabeth, m. Georg Steighletter.
- Daniel, b. about 1759. He was taxed as single in Codorus Township in 1779, and his probate inventory was filed in Codorus Township in 1832.
- Peter.
- Rosina.
- Johannes, b. on July 18, 1778, bapt. at Wolf's on Aug. 16, 1778, and spon. by Philip Stambach and Barbara Hauser.
- Not named in will.

Wilhelm - Peter, was taxed in 1762. He received a warrant for 30 acres on Mar. 27, 1775, that was surveyed as 33.135 acres called *Evening Song* on May 16, 1775. He also received a warrant for 100 acres on Dec. 2, 1766, that was patented as 88.17 acres called *Poverty Point* on May 16, 1775 (an earlier part of this tract was surveyed for Peter on Dec. 29, 1757). His will was written in Codorus Township on May 2, 1783, and probated on May 15, 1783. He had the following children:
- Peter, b. about 1761.
- Elisabeth, b. about 1763.
- Frederick, b. about 1765, and m. Eva Elisabeth, dau. of Daniel Kramer (see entry). She was b. on July 4, 1766, and d. on Apr. 16, 1807. She is bur. in STJ cemetery.

Zauck - Johan Heinrich was taxed in Manheim Township in 1762. He was b. in Hoffenheim, Sinshein, Elsenz (Baden) Germany, to Hans Ulrich Zauck, about 1696, and m. Elisabetha, dau. of Martin Schwartz (citizen), in Hoffenheim on June 29, 1717, and Maria Margaretha, widow of Georg Lohr (see entry) about 1766/67. Heinrich immigrated to America on the ship *Dragon* on Sept. 30, 1732 (listed as sick), and settled in York Co., PA. Heinrich was granted 200 acres in York Co., Manheim Township, on Nov. 25, 1745, which he deeded to John Solomonmuller, a nailsmith of Manheim Township, on Oct. 12, 1762 (he was residing on the land at the time). In this deed, he is referred to as

a tailor. Henrich's will was written on July 4, 1775, and probated in York (now Adams) Co., Germany Township, PA, on Sept. 13, 1775. In 1779, Margaret is taxed in Germany Township with 100 acres, 2 horses, and 2 cattle; in 1780, with 50 acres, 2 horses, and 2 cattle; in 1781, with 100 acres, 2 horses, and 2 cattle; in 1782, with 100 acres, 2 horses, and 2 cattle. For some reason, she is taxed in Germany Township in 1783, as widow Lore, with three individuals in her household, and 100 acres. On June 29, 1798, she m. Georg Adam Stump. Margaret Stump, formerly Zouck, widow of Georg Stump, of Heidelberg Township, wrote her will on Dec. 31, 1798, and it was probated on Mar. 30, 1799 (executed by Conrad Steiman and Michael Bear). The will named sons, Balthasar Lohr, Joseph Lohr, Henry Zauck, dau., Margaret, wife of Michael Bear, and grandchildren, David and Margaret Bachman. Heinrich had the following children (recorded at Hoffenheim Lutheran Church (unless otherwise noted (see BNK)):
- Maria Philipena, b. on Dec. 15, 1718, and m. Jacob Scherer (see entry).
- Eva Rosina, b. on Aug. 22, 1721.
- Maria Margaretha, b. on Mar. 4, 1724.
- Maria Eva, b. on Jan. 4, 1727.
- Anna Eva Barbara, b. on Aug. 27, 1729.
- Maria Magdalena, b. on Dec. 28, 1734, and bapt. at CLY on Feb. 23, 1735.
- Johan Henrich Zauck, b. about 1767. He m. Ann, dau. of Frederick and Eva Mary Buchanan of Germany Township before Jan. 21, 1789, and Barbara about 1790.

Ziegler - Nicholas immigrated to America on the ship *Edinburgh* on Sept. 16, 1751, and was taxed in Codorus Township in 1762. He warranted land in Codorus Township on Nov. 13, 1766. His will was written in Codorus Township on June 3, 1791, and probated on July 25, 1791. He m. Catharina Barbara. They had the following children:
- Michael, bapt. by RJL on May 18, 1755, and spon. by Michael Han and Margaretha Eisterin.
- Jacob, b. about 1757, and was taxed in 1779.
- Johan Niclaus, bapt. by RJL on June 26, 1760, and spon. by Johnannes and Catharina Barbara Wolfgang. He m. Juliana Weickel at TLY on June 8, 1784.
- Anna Elisabetha, b. on July 4, 1762, and bapt. at STJ on Aug. 29, 1762. She m. Adam Fissel.
- Catharina Barbara, bapt. by RJL on Sept. 9, 1764, and spon. by Johannes and Catharina Barbara Wolfgang. She m. John Henick.

Zimmerman - Christian was taxed in 1762. He m. Anna Barbara. They had the following children:

- Christophel, bapt. by RJL on Jan. 18, 1756, and spon. by Christophel and Juliana Rothermel.
- Maria Catharina, b. on Mar. 5, 1760, and bapt. at STJ.
- Johan Heinrich, bapt. at STJ on Dec. 26, 1763.
- Johan Christian, b. in Oct. 1765, and bapt. at STJ on Nov. 30, 1765.
- Maria Sophia, b. on May 9, 1769, and bapt. at STJ on July 30, 1769.
- Johannes, b. on Sept. 13, 1771, and bapt. at STJ on Oct. 4, 1771.

DOVER TOWNSHIP

<u>Akenbogh</u> - Barnet was taxed in 1762.

<u>Albert</u> - Carl was taxed in 1762. He m. Eva Margaretha. They had the following children:
- Maria Sophia, b. on May 2, 1762, bapt. at STR on May 31, 1762, and spon. by Johan Georg and Maria Catharina Spaar.
- Christina Elisabetha, b. on June 23, 1766, bapt. at STR in July 1766, and spon. by Philip Adam and Dorothea Spaar.

<u>Appel</u> - Johannes Elias wrote his will in Dover Township on Aug. 5, 1778, and it was probated on May 15, 1781. He m. Johanna Elisabeth, and had the following children:
- Johannes, b. on Jan. 1, 1778, and bapt. at STR on Feb. 8, 1778. He was not mentioned in the will.
- James.
- Christian.

<u>Barner</u> (Berner) - John was taxed in 1762, and d. before 1770. He had the following children:
- Barbara, m. Heinrich Richter in 1770. She was a sponsor at the baptism of Jacob Linckelfelter's dau., Elisabetha Barbara, in 1760.

<u>Bartemess</u> - Johan Adam, b. about 1732. He was taxed in 1762. He received a warrant for 50 acres in North Codorus Township on Jan. 27, 1757, that was surveyed as 31.80 acres on Mar. 16, 1757. He m. Anna Dorothea, and had the following children:
- Maria Catharina, b. on Oct. 14, 1753, and bapt. at CLY on Dec. 3, 1753.
- Johan Peter, bapt. by RJL on Sept. 7, 1755, and spon. by Peter Streher, Christian Weynand, and Maria Barbara Streherin.
- Johan Wilhelm, b. on Aug. 20, 1762, bapt. at STR on Aug. 24, 1762, and spon. by Johan Peter Spiess.
- Johan Heinrich, b. on May 2, 1765, bapt. at STR on May 16, 1765, and spon. by John and Eva Elisabeth Spaar.

<u>Bartemess</u> - Johan Peter m. Anna Maria, dau. of Johan Joseph and Helena Frantz, in 1735. She was b. in Buchenbayern Kirberger, Baden, Germany, in 1711, and immigrated to America with her son Peter, and dau. Maria Elisabeth in 1759, and d. about 1772. Peter probably d. before 1760. They had the following children in Wollnau, Baden, Schwabisch Kreis, Germany:
- Peter, b. about 1735, and was taxed in 1762.

96   *EARLY GERMAN SETTLERS OF YORK CO., PA*

- Maria Elisabeth, b. in 1738, and m. Philip Jacob, son of Johannes Zinn (see entry), in 1759.
- Eva Elisabeth, b. about 1743, and m. Johan, son of Georg Spaar (see entry), at STR on Oct. 16, 1764.
- Johann Philip, b. about 1745, and m. Anna Margaretha about 1768, and had the following children:
  - Johan Adam, bapt. at STR on Apr. 9, 1769, and spon. by Adam and Anna Elisabeth Kramer.
  - Johan Jacob, bapt. at STR on Apr. 14, 1771, and spon. by Jacob Rachhausser.
  - Maria Margaretha, bapt. at STR on Nov. 28, 1772, and spon. by Jacob and Maria Margaretha Rahausser.
  - Johann Philip, bapt. at STR on Sept. 12, 1774, and spon. by Jacob and Anna Margaretha Mey.
  - Catharina Elisabet, b. on Mar. 2, 1783, bapt. at STR on Aug. 18, 1783, and spon. by Elisabet Kramer.

Becker - Conrad was taxed in 1762. He wrote his will in Manchester Township on Dec. 19, 1794, and it was probated on Jan. 27, 1795. He m. Maria Catharina about 1754, and Catharina, dau. of Peter Ob (see entry), and had the following children:
- Anna Margareth, bapt. at STR on Dec. 28, 1755, and spon. by Mathias and Anna Rosina Lambert.
- Eve, b. about 1757, and m. Jacob Hoffman about 1777.
- Magdalena, b. about 1763, and m. Valentine, son of Andreas Kohler (see entry in Manchester section) about 1782.
- Maria Barbara, bapt. at QUI on Apr. 28, 1767, and spon. by Johannes and Maria Barbara Humrichhauss. She m. Charles Mittmar.
- Catharine, b. about 1768, and m. Christian, son of Nicholas Mohr about 1788 (see entry in Manchester section).
- Maria Elisabeth, b. on June 8, 1769, bapt. at QUI on June 11, 1769, and spon. by Peter Gess/Gus and wife. She m. Georg Eicholtz about 1788.
- Mathias, b. about 1771, and m. Elisabetha before 1792. His will was written in Newberry Township on Dec. 12, 1804, and probated on Feb. 24, 1808.
- Anna, b. about 1772, and was a sponsor to the baptism of Catharina Becker in 1792.
- Margaretha Elisabeth, b. on Mar. 5, 1773, bapt. at QUI, and spon. by Johan Kurtz and wife.
- Johan Philip, b. on Oct. 17, 1775, bapt. at QUI on Nov. 19, 1775, and spon. by Johan Philip Becker and wife. His will was written in West Manchester Township on Dec. 19, 1807, and probated on Jan. 2, 1812. He m. Elisabeth.

- Conrad, b. on Nov./Sept. 9, 1777, bapt. at QUI on Dec. 26, 1777, and spon. by his parents.
- Johan Jacob, b. on Nov. 7, 1779, bapt. at QUI on Dec. 12, 1779, and spon. by Philip Becker and wife.
- Anna Maria, b. on Jan. 11 (13), 1782, bapt. at QUI on Mar./May 3, 1782, and Apr. 10, 1797, and spon. by her parents (both instances).
- Johannes, b. on Dec. 17, 1785, bapt. at QUI on Dec. 25, 1785, and spon. by Jacob Gottwalt and wife.
- Johann Peter, b. on Mar. 14, 1788, bapt. at QUI on Apr. 7, 1788, and spon. by Jacob and Anna Maria Schmidt.
- Samuel, b. on Jan. 15, 1792, bapt. at QUI on Feb. 26, 1792, and spon. by Samuel and Elisabetha Grooss.

Becker - Johan Philip was taxed in 1762. He m. Marie Eva. His will was written in Newberry Township on Jan. 9, 1816, and probated on June 5, 1817. They had the following children:
- Johann Heinrich, b. on Jan. 26, 1766, bapt. at STR on Feb. 1, 1766, and spon. by John P. Martin and Catherine Reisinger (not mentioned in the will).
- Johan Philip, b. on June 23, 1768, bapt. at STR on July 17, 1768, and spon. by Adam and Maria Magdalena Fackler. He m. Catharina.
- Magdalen, b. on July 12, 1770, and bapt. at CLY on July 17, 1770.
- Maria Eva, b. on June 25, 1772, bapt. at CLY on Aug. 2, 1772, and m. Philip Metzgar.
- Maria Elisabeth, b. on Mar. 2, 1774, and bapt. at CLY on Apr. 3, 1774.
- Catharine, b. on Aug. 8, 1775, bapt. at CLY on Aug. 27, 1775, and m. Michael Neiman.
- Anna Magdalena, b. on Sept. 13, 1777, bapt. at STR on Oct. 19, 1777, and spon. by Martin and Anna Magdalena Reisinger (not mentioned in the will).
- Johan Jacob, b. on July 20, 1779, bapt. at STR on Aug. 22, 1779, and spon. by Conrad and Catharina Becker.
- Maria Margareth, b. on Jan. 30, 1782, bapt. at QUI on Apr. 28, 1782, and spon. by Conrad Becker and wife. She m. John Childer.
- Johannes, b. on July 18, 1786, bapt. at QUI on Sept. 24, 1786, and spon. by Conrad and Catharina Becker.

Beer - Jeremias m. Maria Elisabetha. His will was written in Dover Township on Sept. 13, 1806, and probated on Feb. 19, 1807. They had the following children:
- Ludwig, b. about 1752, and m. Maria Elisabetha, dau. of Henry Dewes (see entry) about 1773.
- Michael, b. about 1754.

- Margaret, b. about 1756, and m. Samuel, son of Nicholas Wild (see entry in Manchester section), about 1776.
- Wilhelm, b. about 1758, and m. Margaretha, dau. of Heinrich Dewes (see entry), about 1779.
- Barbara, b. on Dec. 17, 1765, bapt. at STR on Feb. 1, 1766, and spon. by Peter and Barbara Weinbrener. She m. Nicholas Lichte.
- Peter, b. on Jan. 10, 1769, bapt. at STR on Jan. 28, 1769, and spon. by Johan Philip and Esther Graber.
- Catharina, b. on Jan. 8, 1771, bapt. at STR on Feb. 16, 1771, and spon. by Johan Frederick and Anna Margaretha Majer. She m. Adam Bitner.
- Maria Eva, b. on Oct. 28, 1774, bapt. at STR on Nov. 26, 1774, and spon. by Maria Eva Spaar and Michael Spaar. She m. Philip Herring (see entry).

<u>Beitzel</u> - Johannes was taxed in 1762. He was b. in Dietenshausen in the territory of Berleburg on Apr. 12, 1712. He immigrated to America in 1737. He m. Maria Magdalena Weller of Dietenshausen in 1736 and Anna Elisabetha Eberhard of Sankt Johannes near Mayence in 1749. Anna Elisabetha was b. in Apr. 1729. His will was written in Dover Township on Aug. 10, 1786, and probated on Sept. 5, 1794. They had the following children (recorded at FMY):
- Jonathan, b. on Sept. 16, 1737. He was taxed in 1762. He m. Magdalena. His will was written in Dover Township on Sept. 4, 1807, and probated on Mar. 15, 1814.
- Johan Jacob, b. on Oct. 12, 1739. He was taxed in 1762.
- Anna Elisabetha, b. on Feb. 28, 1742, and d. before 1750.
- Anna Liese Barbara, b. on Oct. 12 (Sept. 30), 1743, and bapt. at CLY on Nov. 6, 1743.
- Magdalena, b. on Dec. 3, 1745.
- Lorrentz, b. on Dec. 20, 1747, bapt. at STR on Jan. 8, 1748, and spon. by Lorentz and Anna Elisabetha Brutzman. He m. Anna Catharina, dau. of Peter Streher (see entry), at TLY on Jan. 24, 1775.
- Margaret, b. about 1749.
- Anna Elisabetha, b. on May 17, 1750.
- Anna Maria, b. on Sept. 24, 1751.
- Louisa, b. on Nov. 15, 1752, bapt. on Nov. 27, 1752, and spon. by Dorothea Kohmer, Anna Maria Brotzman, and Catharina and Margaretha Heckedorn.
- Maria Catharina, b. on May 23, 1754, bapt. on June 18, 1754, spon. by The Engels, Franz Jacob Muller and wife, Philip Rothrock, and Lewis Brotzman, and d. on June 18, 1756.

- Johannes, b. on Dec. 14, 1755, bapt. on Dec. 22, 1755, and spon. by
  John Heckedorn, Philip Rothrock, and Lewis Brotzman. He m.
  Catharina Metzler at TLY on Aug. 19, 1788.
- Maria Catharina, b. on Feb. 15, 1758, bapt. on Feb. 22, 1758, spon.
  by Barbara Schlegel, Eva Barbara Ebert, and Anna Maria Miller,
  and d. in May 1758.
- Christina, b. on Dec. 9, 1759, bapt. on Dec. 15, 1759, and spon. by
  Eva Barbara Ebert, Eva Weller, and Elisabeth Feiser.
- Johann Henrich, b. on Sept. 9, 1761, bapt. on Sept. 16, 1761, and
  spon. by John Heckedorn, Francis Lewis Beroth, and John Fieser.
  He was not mentioned in the will.
- Maria Catharina, b. on Jan. 15, 1763, bapt. on Jan. 29, 1763, and
  spon. by Barbara Schlegel, Barbara Hoeneis and Anna Hoens. She
  d. young.
- Rosina, b. on May 20, 1765, bapt. on June 2, 1765, and spon. by
  Elisabeth Hons, Barbara Hoeneise, and Elisabeth Fieser. She d.
  young.

Benedick - Melchior wrote his will in Dover Township on Aug. 17, 1782, and it was probated on May 26, 1784. He immigrated to America on Sept. 26, 1749. He moved to York Co., Conewago Township, in 1763, and had a 106 acre farm. He m. Maria Catharina, dau. of Philip Quickel (see entry), on Mar. 10, 1752. His will was probated on May 26, 1784, and he was bur. in QUI cemetery. After Melchior's death, she m. Jacob Schaeffer. He was a widower, who d. west of Dover in 1794. Her will was dated Mar. 8, 1796. They had the following children:
- Catharina, b. on July 29, 1753, m. Antony Slothower (1752-1813),
  and d. in 1807. She is bur. at STR cemetery.
- Philip, b. on July 29, 1753, and m. Dorothea Gunther/Ginter. He
  served as an Ensign under Captain Simon Koppenhaver in 1782,
  and moved to Lancaster Co., PA, between 1785 and 1791.
- Georg, b. on Sept. 27, 1755, and m. Susanna, dau. of Frederick and
  Maria Shettel. She was b. on Mar. 31, 1763, and d. on Jan. 30,
  1848. He served in the Revolutionary War, and d. on July 27, 1816
  (bur. at QUI cemetery).
- Elisabeth, b. about 1757, and m. Conrad Stouchenberger.
- Barbara, b. about 1759 and m. Charles Grim.
- Michael, b. about 1761, and m. Susanna.
- Maria Margaretha, b. on Mar. 3, 1764, and bapt. at CLY on Apr.
  25, 1764. She m. Frederick Baker.
- Johan Peter, b. on Apr. 23, 1769, bapt. at QUI on June 11, 1769,
  and spon. by Peter Quickel and Catharina Heekin. He m. Barbara.
- Johan Nicholas, b. on May 7, 1771, bapt. at QUI on Oct. 19, 1771,
  and spon. by Peter Quickel and Catharina Hock.

- Sabina, b. on Mar. 14, 1775, bapt. at QUI on Apr. 17, 1775, and spon. by Georg Luike and wife. She m. Philip Hoffman.
- Christina, b. in 1777, and m. Joseph, son of Carl Seib (see entry).
- Johan Melchior, b. in Feb. 1780, bapt. at QUI on Mar. 29, 1780, and spon. by Michael Quickel and wife. He m. Elisabeth Spahr.

Bentz - Peter was taxed in 1762, and received a warrant for 249 acres in West Manchester and Dover Township on Mar. 5, 1767, and 300 acres in Dover Township on Mar. 5, 1767. He m. Catharina Elisabeth, dau. of Jacob Ob (see entry). They had the following children:
- Catharina Elisabeth, bapt. at STR on Oct. 14, 1759, and spon. by Philip Jacob and Catharina Ob.
- Rosina, b. on Dec. 6, 1761, and bapt. at CLY on Mar. 7, 1762.
- Anna Margaretha, bapt. at STR on Feb. 18, 1764, and spon. by Johannes Han and Anna Margaretha Bensin.
- Johan Philip, b. on Oct. 18, 1765, bapt. at STR on June 22, 1765, and spon. by Jacob and Anna Catharina Ob.

Bentzel - Johannes was taxed in 1762, and received a warrant for 150 acres in West Manchester and Dover Township on Nov. 22, 1749, that was surveyed as 176 acres on May 12, 1757. His probate inventory was filed in Dover Township in 1770. His will was written on Jan. 12, 1770, and probated on Feb. 12, 1770. He m. Maria Sophia. Her probate inventory was filed in Dover Township in 1789. They had the following children:
- Henry, b. about 1738, and m. Barbara, dau. of Leonard Immel (see entry in Manchester section), about 1765. He was taxed in Dover Township in 1779.
- Johan Philip, b. about 1740, and m. Elisabeth Haintz about 1761. He was taxed in Dover Township in 1762 and 1779.
- Casper, b. about 1751, and m. Elizabeth, dau. of Georg Herbold (see entry), at TLY on Dec. 29, 1774. His will was written in Paradise Township on Mar. 19, 1809, and probated on Mar. 27, 1809.
- Andreas, b. on May 31, 1753, and bapt. at CLY on June 17, 1753.

Bobb - Jacob was taxed in 1762.

Brauer - Henrich was taxed in 1762. He m. Barbara, and had the following children:
- Anna Margareth, bapt. by RJL on Apr. 11, 1766, and spon. by Michael and Anna Margareth Konig.

Brauer - Johannes was taxed in 1762. He m. Hannah Echelbaur/Eychelpeyer. They had the following children:

- Christian, b. on May 17, 1756, bapt. at TLY on June 24, 1762, and spon. by Georg and Margaretta Ribi.
- Johann Adam, b. on Feb. 4, 1763, bapt. at TLY on Mar. 20, 1763, and spon. by Johann Adam and Juliana Pott.
- Jacob, b. on Oct. 14, 1765, bapt. at TLY on Nov. 3, 1765, and spon. by Jacob Welschans and wife.

Danner - Tobias was taxed in 1762. He m. Anna Eva. They had the following children (recorded at STR):
- Philip Jacob, b. on May 10, 1763, bapt. on June 5, 1763, and spon. by Johan Philip and Christina Christ.
- Anna Barbara, b. on Dec. 5, 1765, bapt. on Dec. 26, 1765, and spon. by Daniel and Anna Barbara Rahauser.
- Andreas, b. on Oct. 6, 1768, bapt. on Nov. 6, 1768, and spon. by Andreas Blechart and Susanna Oberdier.

Danner - Casper was taxed in 1762. His probate inventory was filed in Dover Township in 1804. He m. Anna Catharina Barbara, dau. of Conrad Reidel (deceased before 1761), at York on June 2, 1761. They had the following children (recorded at STR):
- Susanna, b. on Apr. 8, 1762, bapt. on May 16, 1762, and spon. by Jacob Weigel.
- Anna Maria, b. on Oct. 6, 1763, bapt. on Nov. 5, 1763, and spon. by Philip Adam Spaar.
- Johan Peter, b. on Sept. 17, 1765, bapt. on Oct. 19, 1765, and spon. by Peter and Christina Magdalena Haller.
- Johan Heinrich, b. on Nov. 15, 1769, bapt. on Jan. 1, 1770, and spon. by Henrich and Maria Catharina Peter.
- Anna Margaretha, b. on Aug. 9, 1771, bapt. on Sept. 22, 1771, and spon. by Vendel and Anna Maria Gross.
- Tobias, b. on Nov. 24, 1777, bapt. on Apr. 20, 1777, and spon. by Martin and Maria Weber.

Detter - Mathias was taxed in 1762. He was b. to Nicholas (1712-1793) and Anna Catharina (Baumann) Detter, in Hirschland, France in 1732. He immigrated to America in 1749, and his father settled in Reading Township (now Adams Co.). Mathias wrote his will in Botts Town (Manchester Township) on Mar. 31, 1802, and it was probated on Apr. 30, 1802. He m. Maria Magdalena, dau. of Martin and Susanna Struecker. Her probate inventory was filed in Manchester Township in 1817. They had the following children:
- Johan Mathias, b. on Sept. 10, 1758, and bapt. at CLY on Dec. 3, 1758. He was not mentioned in the will.
- John, b. on Dec. 12, 1759, and bapt. at CLY on May 25, 1760. He m. Elisabeth.

- Maria Magdalena, b. on Sept. 14, 1761, bapt. at CLY (also the Lower Bermudian Congregation) on Oct. 18, 1761, and spon. by her grandparents, Martin and Susanna Struecker. She m. Henry Schultz at TLY on Jan. 3, 1779, and Jacob Schaffer before 1802.
- Nicholas, b. on Sept. 12, 1763, bapt. at The Lower Bermudian Congregation, and spon. by Nicholas and Catharina Detter.
- Catharina, b. about 1765, and m. Jacob Messoncopp.
- Maria Clara, b. on Jan. 12, 1767, and bapt. at CLY on Mar. 22, 1767. She was not mentioned in the will.
- Elisabeth, b. about 1769, and m. Frederick Wehn.
- Susanna, b. about 1771, and m. Jacob Erisman before 1796.

Dewes (Davis) - Heinrich was taxed in 1762. He was overseer in 1754 and 1757, and was constable in 1764. His will was written in Dover Township on Sept. 21, 1787, and probated on Sept. 8, 1788. He m. Maria Barbara, and had the following children:
- Heinrich, b. on Dec. 25, 1730, bapt. at Trinity Lutheran Church of Lancaster on Apr. 25, 1731, and spon. by Samuel Davies, Georg Nichols, and Sarah Davies. He m. Maria Elisabeth. He was a Private during the Revolutionary War.
- Sophia, b. about 1732, and m. Joseph Barkdoll.
- Catarina, b. on Jan. 6, 1741, bapt. by RJL on May 18, 1741, and spon. by Peter and Catarina Schultz. She m. Georg Herbold (see entry).
- Johannes, b. on July 23, 1746, and bapt. at CLY on Oct. 4, 1746. He m. Maria Elisabeth. His will was written in Dover Township on Dec. 12, 1784, and probated on Aug. 26, 1790. He was a Private during the Revolutionary War.
- Christina, bapt. by RJL at STR on Apr. 23, 1749, and spon. by Johannes and Anna Sophia Zin. She m. Johan Paul, son of Johan Paul Reuter, at STR on Apr. 22, 1766. Paul Reuter/Ritter, Sr., was taxed in Warrington Township in 1762.
- Maria Elisabeth, bapt. by RJL on May 18, 1752, and spon. by Johan Georg and Elisabeth Meinhardt. She m. Ludwig, son of Jeremias Beer (see entry) about 1773, and John Sturt/Stewart before 1787. Ludwig was alive in 1778.
- Dorothea, b. about 1755, and m. Wilhelm, son of Georg Herbold (see entry).
- Margaretha, b. about 1758, and m. Wilhelm, son of Jeremias Beer (see entry).

Eicholtz - Johann Friedrich, was b. to Hans Adam and Ursula (Perth/Barth) Eicholtz at Neckarbischofsheim, Germany, on May 4, 1723, and immigrated to America on the ship *Ann Galley* in 1746. His father immigrated to America on the ship *Jacob* in 1749 (see BNK). He

was taxed in 1762 (they were alive 1779). He m. Magdalena, and had the following children:
- Frederick, b. about 1743. His will was written in Dover Township on Mar. 15, 1791, and probated on Apr. 3, 1797. He m. Anna Catharina, dau. of Georg Quickel (see entry), on Nov. 22, 1763. Her probate inventory was filed in Dover Township in 1811.
- Mathias, b. about 1752, and m. Barbara, dau. of Jacob Snellbecker, about 1776.
- Johan Jacob, bapt. by RJL on May 4, 1755, and spon. by Mathias and Catharina Windnagel.

Feiser (Feusser) - Johannes Petrus m. Catharina Margaretha in Hochstenbach, Germany, on Oct. 17, 1715, and immigrated to America on the ship *Aurora* in 1744. They had the following children bapt. at Hochstenbach (see *Burgert's Westerwald to America*):
- Johannes Theiss was taxed in 1762. He was b. in Borot Hachenburg on Nov. 30, 1716, bapt. in 1716, and spon. by Johan Theil Feusser, Johannes Wirth, and Elisabetha Maria, dau. of Theil Fuchs. He immigrated to America on the ship *Samuel and Elizabeth* in 1740, settled in Salem Co. in West Jersey, and soon after moved to York Co., PA. He was naturalized on Apr. 10/11, 1761, and d. on May 14, 1781. His will was written in Dover Township on May 9, 1781, and probated on May 31, 1781. He m. Christina Schneider in Aug. 1743, and Elisabetha Schlatter in Sept. 1753. Christina d. in Aug. 1753. Elisabetha was b. in Hohmannthal Canton Schaffhausen, Switzerland, in Aug. 1723. Johannes had the following children (recorded at FMY):
  - Peter, b. on Nov. 12, 1744.
  - Catharina, bapt. by RJL on Jan. 5, 1746, and spon. by Anna Catharina Liebhard and Catharina Margaretha Feisser.
  - Anna Christina, b. on May 1, 1749, bapt. in the Society on Apr. 30, 1761, and d. in Bethlehem.
  - Maria, b. on Sept. 17, 1754.
  - Johannes, b. in Straussburg Township on Feb. 29, 1756, and d. in Jersey on Sept. 7, 1776.
  - Elisabetha, b. on Feb. 15, 1758, and moved to Lititz on May 5, 1782.
  - Bernhard, b. on Aug. 20, 1760.
  - Michael, b. on Aug. 25, 1762.
  - Jacob, b. and d. on Mar. 10, 1765.
  - Barbara, b. on May 3, 1766, and moved to Lititz on May 4, 1783.
  - Eva, b. on Dec. 21, 1768.
- Johann Adam, b. on Oct. 12, 1718, bapt. on Oct. 16, 1718, and spon. by Henrich Luckenbach, Johann Meitsch, and Elisabeth Gertrude, wife of Adam Schnug.

- Anna Christina, b. on Jan. 27, 1721, bapt. on Feb. 2, 1721, and d. on Aug. 22, 1721.
- Elsa Maria, b. on July 4, 1722, bapt. on July 12, 1722, and spon. by Maria Catharina Luckenbach, Elsa Catharina Maitsch, and Johan Peter Fuchs.
- Anna Catharina, b. on Nov. 27, 1724, bapt. on Nov. 30, 1724, and spon. by Anna Catharina Wirth, Anna Maria Fuchs, and Johan Jacob Lutsch.
- Elisabetha Catharina, b. on Dec. 16, 1727, bapt. on Dec. 21, 1727, and spon. by Elisabeth Maitsch, Maria Catharina Hoffman, and Johannes Theis Schnug.
- Johann Peter, b. on Jan. 16, 1730, bapt. on Jan. 22, 1730, and spon. by Johan Peter Croppach, Johan Peter Schneider, and Eva Catharina Hoffmann (confirmed in Germany in 1744). He m. Catharina Elisabetha Eners/Andreas in PA, on Sept. 10, 1754. She was b. in Waldmohr, Zweibrucken, in 1729, and immigrated to America in 1749. He was naturalized in the Fall of 1765, and d. in 1805/06. His will was written in York Borough on Aug. 14, 1798, and probated on Jan. 30, 1806. He had the following children (recorded at FMY):
  - Elisabetha, b. on Nov. 23, 1755, bapt. in Society on July 10, 1768, and m. Johan Tobias Bocket in Heidelberg.
  - Anna Maria, b. on Apr. 5, 1757, bapt. in Society on Oct. 29, 1769, and m. Johan Jacob, son of Johan Jacob and Maria Catharina (Schuler) Struebig. He was b. in Lebanon on Apr. 23, 1755, and was a roofer.
  - Peter, b. on Dec. 13, 1759, and bapt. in Society in 1772. He served as a Private in Captain Peter Forld's Compamy during the Revolutionary War. He d. in 1806, and was bur. in Prospect Hill cemetery.
  - Rosina, b. on Sept. 28, 1761, and bapt. in Society on July 3, 1774.
  - Anna Barbara, b. on July 24, 1763, and d. on Mar. 10, 1773.
  - Christina, b. on Jan. 23, 1766, bapt. in Society on Apr. 20, 1778, and m. Daniel Smith.
  - Johannes, b. on Jan. 30, 1769, and d. on Feb. 9, 1773.
- Johann Matthias, b. on Mar. 6, 1732, bapt. on Mar. 9, 1732, and spon. by Johan Heinrich Muller, Johan Theiss Schneider, and Anna Maria Klein.
- Johann Henrich, b. on Jan. 5, 1735, and bapt. on Jan. 8, 1735. He m. Anna Margaretha, and had the following children:
  - Michael, b. on June 5, 1761, and bapt. at CLY on June 28, 1761.
  - Johann Heinrich, bapt. at QUI on May 12, 1765, and spon. by Sebastian and Christina Fink.
  - Elisabetha Margretha, b. on Jan. 13, 1771, bapt. at QUI on Feb. 24, 1771, and spon. by Carl Ludwig Stautenhauer and wife.

- Maria Elisabetha, b. or bapt. at KRE on Nov. 7, 1784, and spon. by Maria Elisabeth Billeten.
- Johannes Martinus, b. on Mar. 21, 1737, bapt. on Mar. 25, 1737, and spon. by Johan Martin Gobler, Johan Theis Hommer, and Elisabeth Gertrude Kruger.
- Veronica Kunigunda, b. on May 17, 1739, bapt. on May 19, 1739, and spon. by Johan Henrich Schnug, Anna Kunigunda Vohl, and Christina Elss. She m. Franz Siegrist. His will was written in Hopewell Township on July 19, 1817, and probated on June 12, 1819. They had the following children:
  - Anna Maria, bapt. by RJL on Oct. 7, 1760, and spon. by Felix Albrecht and Susanna Siegristin.
  - Catharina, b. on Jan. 17, 1762, bapt. at TLY on May 16, 1762, and spon. by Killian Fissel and Catharina Fidel.
  - Veronica, b. on Feb. 10, 1763, bapt. at TLY on Apr. 3, 1763, and spon. by Anthony Gerhardt and wife. She m. Jacob Bidner at TLY on Dec. 13, 1785.
  - Johannes, b. on Aug. 8, 1764, and bapt. at CLY on Nov. 18, 1764.
  - Franz, b. on July 12, 1766, bapt. at FRI on the 18th Sunday after Trinity, 1766, and spon. by Franz and Anna Groff.
  - Michael, b. about 1768.
  - Wilhelm, b. on May 14, 1770, bapt. at BLY on June 24, 1770, and spon. by Wilhelm Reigert, Conrad and Catharina Siegrist, and John Siegrist.
  - Henrich, b. about 1774.
  - Peter, b. on Feb. 5, 1777, bapt. at BLY on June 8, 1777, and spon. by his parents.
  - Barbara, b. on Feb. 10, 1779, bapt. at BLY, and spon. by Martin and Barbara Flenschbach.

Felcker - Johan Peter was taxed in 1762. He m. Elisabetha, dau. of Anthony Keller (see entry), at Christ's Lutheran Church of York on Apr. 7, 1759, and had the following children:
- Anna Maria, bapt. by Reverend Jacob Lischy on Apr. 6, 1760, and spon. by Valentin Krantz, and her aunt, Anna Maria Keller.
- Anna Maria Elisabetha, b. on Sept. 9, 1762, and bapt. at Christ's Lutheran on Oct. 3, 1762.

Finck - Sebastian m. and unknown woman about 1717, Anna Maria, dau. of Hans Jacob Meyer, at Kirchardt, Germany, on May 14, 1726, and Christina Leibi before 1739. He immigrated to America on the ship *William and Sarah* in 1727, and was naturalized on May 19, 1739. He had the following children:
- Christina Margaretha, b. about 1714. She m. Johan Heinrich Walther, and d. before 1758. Heinrich m. Charlotte Catharina

Jeanette before 1746, and Anna Maria before 1754. He was b. in 1705, and d. on Dec. 10, 1754 (recorded at The First Reformed Congregation Register). They had the following children:
- Jacob, b. about 1735, and m. Juliana about 1756.
- Susanna, b. about 1737, and was a sponsor, with her bro., Heinrich to the baptism of Jacob and Juliana Walther's dau., Susanna at The First Reformed Congregation at Lancaster in 1757.
- Johan Heinrich, bapt. at the First Reformed Congregation at Lancaster on Oct. 28, 1739, and spon. by Johan Henrich Klein. He m. Anna Magdalena, dau. of Johann Peter and Annae Mariae Grimm, of Lancaster Co., Earl Township, at the First Reformed Church in Lancaster on Feb. 17, 1760. She was bapt. in Obermoschel, Pfalz, Bayern on June 23, 1741, and immigrated to America with her parents on the ship *Forest* on Oct. 11, 1752. They were residing in York Co., York, by July 1760, and were still there in 1779.
- Maria Magdalena, b. about 1719. She m. Ludwig Becker, and had the following children:
  - Johan Heinrich, b. on Dec. 7, 1740, bapt. at the First Reformed Congregation at Lancaster on Mar. 29, 1741, and spon. by Johan Heinrich and Anna Margaretha (Grimm) Klein.
- Johan Adam, b. about 1726. He was taxed in 1762. His probate inventory was filed in 1769. He m. Dorothea. They had the following children:
  - Dorothea, b. about 1749, and m. Johan Schodder at STR on Mar. 13, 1770.
  - Michael, bapt. by RJL on May 11, 1760, and spon. by Michael Fink and Elisabeth Kiefferin.
  - Leonhard, bapt. by RJL on Jan. 24, 1762, and spon. by Leonhard and Elisabeth Schederon.
  - Anna Margareth, bapt. at STR on Feb. 18, 1764, and spon. by Johannes and Anna Margareth Bens.
  - Johan Philip, bapt. at QUI on Sept. 18, 1769, and spon. by Valentine Krantz.
- Sebastian was taxed in 1762. He m. Anna Maria Christina, dau. of Valentine Krantz (see entry in Manchester section). They had the following children:
  - Maria Elisabeth, b. on Apr. 8, 1753, and bapt. at CLY on Apr. 22, 1753.
  - Susanna, b. on Aug. 6, 1754, and bapt. at CLY on Aug. 25, 1754.
  - Johannes, bapt. by RJL on Apr. 23, 1758, and spon. by Johannes and Maria Margaretha Emig.
  - Johann Michael, bapt. by RJL on Apr. 6, 1760, and spon. by Johann Michael Fink and Maria Elisabetha Koonsin.

- Maria Eva, b. on July 3, 1769, bapt. at QUI on July 23, 1769, and spon. by Valentine Krantz and wife.
- Sebastian, b. on July 3, 1772, bapt. at QUI on Aug. 2, 1772, and spon. by Paul Wild.
- Maria Eva, b. on Oct. 8, 1774, bapt. at QUI on Jan. 25, 1775, and spon. by Conrad Becker and wife.
- Johan Jacob, b. on Feb. 7, 1778, bapt. at QUI on May 17, 1778, and spon. by Jacob Gottwalt and wife (mother is Maria).

- Johannes, b. on Jan. 3, 1730, bapt. at Trinity Lutheran Church in Lancaster on May 3, 1730, and spon. by Johannes Bendter. His probate inventory was filed in York Co. in 1757. He m. Anna Maria Catharina, and had the following children:
  - Johan Valentine, b. on Dec. 25, 1751, and bapt. at CLY on Jan. 26, 1752.
  - Johan Georg, b. on Jan. 3, 1753, and bapt. at CLY on Mar. 4, 1753. He m. Barbara, and was taxed in Dover Township in 1779.
  - Johan Jacob, bapt. by RJL on June 8, 1755, and spon. by Jacob and Elisabeth Haas.
  - Johannes, bapt. by RJL on Oct. 30, 1757, and spon. by Johannes and Maria Barbara Humrichhaus.

- Johann Martin, b. on Oct. 6, 1733, bapt. at Trinity Lutheran in Lancaster on Nov. 11, 1733, and spon. by Johan Georg Bart.
- Anna Barbara, b. on Nov. 2, 1734, bapt. at Trinity Lutheran Church in Lancaster Co. on Jan. 1, 1735, and spon. by Johan Georg and Anna Barbara Bart. She m. Ludwig Weyer. They had the following children:
  - Johannes, bapt. by RJL on May 25, 1755, and spon. by Johannes and Maria Catharina Finck. He m. Christina Dantzler at TLY on Apr. 22, 1777.
  - Maria Margareth, bapt. by RJL on May 28, 1758, and spon. by Maria Margareth Finckin.
  - Reinhardt, bapt. by RJL on Sept. 16, 1759, and spon. by Reinhardt and Appolonica Hammer.
  - Maria Elisabeth, bapt. by RJL on Dec. 2, 1760, and spon. by Georg and Maria Elisabeth Fink.
  - Georg Michael, b. on Mar. 17, 1762, bapt. at TLY on May 16, 1762, and spon. by Michael Glink and Catharina Freytag.
  - Ludwig, b. about 1763, and m. Maria Elisabetha Miller at TLY on Apr. 12, 1785.
  - Maria Barbara, bapt. at QUI on Apr. 9, 1765, and spon. by Johannes and Maria Barbara Humrichhaus.
  - Susanna, b. about 1767, and was the sponsor (with Ludwig Frysinger) to the baptism of Ludwig Weyer in 1790 (QUI). She is probably the Susanna that m. Ludwig Frysinger before 1795.

- Johann Jacob, b. about 1769. He was a sponsor to the baptism of Anna Maria Weyer in 1788 (QUI).
- Georg, b. about 1735. He m. Maria Elisabeth, about 1758, and Elisabeth, dau. of Philip Hoss (see entry in Manchester section), about 1781, and had the following children:
  - Maria Elisabeth Agnes, b. on Dec. 12, 1759, and bapt. at CLY on Dec. 23, 1759.
  - Johan Michael, b. on Dec. 19, 1761, and bapt. at CLY on Jan. 1, 1762.
  - Barbara, b. on Dec. 4, 1769, and bapt. at CLY on Dec. 25, 1769.
  - Catharina, b. on Apr. 11, 1773, and bapt. at CLY on Apr. 25, 1773.
  - Eva, b. on Aug. 29, 1776, and bapt. at CLY on Sept. 22, 1776.
  - Johan Gottleib, b. on July 22, 1779, and bapt. at CLY on Sept. 5, 1779.
  - Jacob, b. on Nov. 4, 1782, and bapt. at CLY on Dec. 25, 1782.
- Anna Maria, b. on Mar. 2, 1737, bapt. at Trinity Lutheran Church in Lancaster on Apr. 10, 1737, and spon. by Johan Georg and Anna Barbara Bart.
- Christina, b. on May 8, 1738, bapt. at Trinity Lutheran Church in Lancaster on May 21, 1738, and spon. by Johan Georg and Anna Barbara Bart.
- Johann Michael, bapt. at the First Reformed Congregation at Lancaster on Dec. 25, 1739, and spon. by Johan Michael Barth and Barbara Klein. He m. Catharina, dau. of Jacob Berlin of Berwick Township, before 1775. He was taxed in Paradise Township in 1779. His probate inventory was filed in Paradise Township in 1782.
- Maria Margareth, b. about 1741, and was the sponsor to the baptism of Maria Margareth Weyer in 1758 (RJL).

Fissel - Killian was taxed in Paradise Township in 1762. He immigrated to America on the ship *Loyal Judith* on Sept. 3, 1742. He m. Christina, and had the following children:
- Killian, b. about 1727. He m. Catharina about 1751, and Barbara about 1760 (see entry on his family in Codorus section).
- Johannes, b. about 1729, and was taxed in Paradise Township in 1762. He m. Anna Margaretha, dau. of Martin Hiller (see entry), and had the following children:
  - Johan Jacob, b. on Jan. 3, 1752, and bapt. at CLY on Mar. 30, 1752.
  - John, b. on Jan. 28, 1754, and bapt. at CLY on May 19, 1754.
  - Johan Adam, bapt. by RJL on May 2, 1756, and spon. by Johan Adam Fissel and Maria Elisabeth Anspachin.

- Heinrich, bapt. by RJL on May 11, 1761, and spon. by Heinrich Fissel and Eva Hiller.
- Johan Philip, b. on Apr. 11, 1763, bapt. at STR on June 5, 1763, and spon. by Jacob Rahauser and Susanna Oberdier.
- Johan Wentel, b. about 1731, and was taxed in Paradise Township in 1762. He m. Anna Margaretha, and had the following children:
  - Johannes, bapt. by RJL on Mar. 24, 1754, and spon. by Johannes and Anna Elisabeth Reber.
  - Anna Margaretha, bapt. by RJL on May 2, 1756, and spon. by Anna Stammin and Michael Fissel.
  - Maria Catharina, bapt. by RJL on Mar. 20, 1761, and spon. by Philliph Fissel and Maria Catharina Reberin.
  - Anna Elisabeth, bapt. by RJL on Apr. 8, 1764, and spon. by Ulrich and Anna Elisabeth Doll.
  - Johan Heinrich, bapt. at WOL on Oct. 19, 1766, and spon. by Heinrich and Anna Barbara Fissel.
- Frederick was b. in Essenheim on the Maintz, Germany, on May 24, 1733. He m. Anna Maria, dau. of Johan Daniel Diehl (see entry on Frederick's family in Shrewsbury section).
- Michael, b. about 1737, and was taxed in Paradise Township in 1762. He m. Anna Margaretha, and had the following children:
  - Anna Elisabetha, b. on Oct. 16, 1761, and bapt. at CLY on Nov. 25, 1761.
  - Anna Barbara, bapt. by RJL on May 13, 1764, and spon. by Philliph Fissel and Anna Barbara Stiefflerin.
  - Philip, b. on Aug. 29, 1765, bapt. at WOL on Sept. 22, 1765, and spon. by Philip Fissel and Anna Maria, dau. of Georg Bender.
- Johan Adam, b. about 1739, and was taxed in Dover Township in 1762. He m. Maria Margaretha, and had the following children:
  - Johan Philip, b. on Oct. 27, 1761, and bapt. at CLY on Nov. 25, 1761.
  - Maria Elisabeth, bapt. at STR on July 7, 1765, and spon. by Johannes and Maria Elisabeth Schaffer.
  - Johann Heinrich, bapt. at STR on June 5, 1768, and spon. by Johan Heinrich and Anna Barbara Fissel.
  - Johannes, bapt. at STR on July 14, 1771, and spon. by Johannes and Elisabeth Schaffer.
- Philip, b. about 1741, and was taxed in Paradise Township in 1762.
- Johan Heinrich, b. about 1743. He m. Anna Barbara about 1764, and had the following children:
  - Johan Michael, bapt. at WOL in 1765, and spon. by Michael and Margaretha Fissel.
  - Johan Jacob, b. on Aug. 11, 1770, bapt. at WOL on Sept. 2, 1770, and spon. by Johan Jacob Stoever and Anna Maria Uhl.

Flohr - Leonard was taxed in 1762. He m. Anna Maria Barbara before 1760. They were sponsors to the baptism of Maria Barbara Gansshorn in 1760 (RJL) (both alive in 1762). They had the following children:
- Valentine was taxed in 1762. His will was written in Dover Township on July 30, 1803, and probated on Sept. 1, 1804. He m. Anna Elisabetha, dau. of Georg Zimmerman, in 1746. She was b. in Gallberg in 1724, and d. between 1763 and 1776. She immigrated to America in 1746 (STR). They had the following children:
  - Anna Barbara, b. on Sept. 26, 1750, and bapt. at CLY on Oct. 25, 1750. She was not mentioned in the will.
  - Susanna Elisabeth, b. on Apr. 27, 1752, bapt. at CLY on Oct. 15, 1752. She m. Johan Peter Jeki/Jocki at STR on Jan. 30, 1770.
  - Anna Maria, b. about 1753, and m. Johan Adam Jeki/Jocki at STR on Sept. 3, 1771.
  - Johan Georg, b. in Apr. 1754, and bapt. at CLY on July 21, 1754. He is not mentioned in the will.
  - Valentine, b. about 1756, and m. Catharina Dorothea about 1776.
  - Conrad, b. about 1758.
  - Maria Elisabeth, b. on May 13, 1763, bapt. at STR on June 19, 1763, and spon. by Georg and Maria Salome Lechner. She m. Jacob Banters.
- Leonhard was taxed in Dover in 1779. His will was written in Adams Co., Franklin Township, PA, on Nov. 29, 1714, and probated on Jan. 10, 1821. He m. Anna Margaretha, dau. of Frederick and Catharina Schaffer (see entry), and had the following children:
  - Leonhard, b. on Sept. 18, 1773, bapt. at STR on Oct. 31, 1773, and spon. by Valentine and Elisabeth Flohr. He m. Rachel.
  - Frederick, b. about 1774.
  - Valentine, b. about 1779, and m. Catharina, dau. of Conrad Suttle.
  - Sarah, b. about 1782, and m. Daniel Mickley.
  - Joseph, b. about 1784, and d. before 1814.
  - Samuel, b. on Apr. 16, 1786, bapt. at the Lutheran Church at Arendtsville, Adams Co., on June 18, 1786, and spon. by Philip and Anna Margaretha Schaffer.
  - David, b. about 1788. His will was written in Franklin Township on Apr. 22, 1823, and probated on May 3, 1823. He m. Salome.
  - Daniel, b. on Aug. 2, 1790, bapt. at Arendtsville on May 9, 1790, and spon. by Nicholas and Elisabeth Barbara Bissecker.
  - Jacob, b. about 1791.

Foucks - Peter was taxed in 1762.

Free (Fruh) - Conrad was taxed in 1762. His will was written in Shrewsbury Township on Mar. 27, 1803, and probated on Jan. 31,

1814. He m. Susanna, dau. of Michael and Anna Catharina Meyer (see entry in Codorus section), (Conrad and Susanna were sponsors to the baptism of Rosina Stormer at FIS in 1788), and Maria before 1803, and had the following children:
- John, m. Rosina before 1785 (they were sponsors to the baptism of John Peter Muller at FRI in 1785).
- Peter.
- Michael.
- Elisabeth.
- Magdalena.
- Anna Catharina, b. on Aug. 29, 1767, bapt. at FRI on Sept. 13, 1767, and spon. by Michael and Catharina Meyer.
- Maria.
- Susanna.

Frey - Martin m. Maria Magdalena Willheut on Apr. 1, 1735 (JCS). He d. before 1752, and his widow m. Isaac Roudibousch (m. before 1752). Isaac d. before 1756, and she m. Henrich Julius/Ulius before 1756. Martin's sons, Martin and Tobias Fry were minors in 1759, and their guardian was Godfrey Frey of York. Martin received a warrant for 300 acres in Dover Township on Oct. 18, 1738. Martin and Maria Magdalena had the following children:
- Tobias, b. about 1737. He was taxed in Dover Township in 1779. He m. Anna Maria, and had the following children (recorded at STR):
  - Maria Catharina, bapt. on July 7, 1765, and spon. by Samuel and Anna Maria Schultz.
  - Johan Peter, b. on Oct. 30, 1769, bapt. on Jan. 1, 1769, and spon. by Peter Streher.
  - Peter, b. on Sept. 14, 1770, bapt. on Dec. 25, 1770, and spon. by Peter and Jacobina Streher.
  - Tobias, b. on Apr. 5, 1773, and bapt. on Apr. 9, 1773.
  - Johannes, bapt. on May 9, 1775, and spon. by Lorentz and Anna Catharina Beitzel.
- Johan Martin, b. on Sept. 6, 1739, and bapt. at CLY on Nov. 14, 1739. He was taxed in York Town in 1779. His will was written in York Town on June 23, 1780, and probated on Aug. 17, 1780. He m. Maria Magdalena about 1765, and Anna Maria about 1771. He had the following children:
  - Catharina, b. on Oct. 3, 1766, bapt. at TLY on Oct. 10, 1766, and spon. by Godfrey Frey and wife. She was not mentioned in the will.
  - Martin, b. on June 9, 1769, and bapt. at TLY on June 16, 1769.
  - Anna, b. about 1770.

- Catharina, b. on Apr. 11, 1772, and bapt. at TLY on May 11, 1773. She was not mentioned in the will.
- Margaret, b. about 1773.
- Elisabeth, b. on Apr. 15, 1775, bapt. at TLY on July 5, 1775, and spon. by her parents.
- Johann Jacob, b. on May 28, 1777, bapt. at TLY on June 27, 1777, and spon. by his parents. He was not mentioned in the will.
- Johannes, b. on Aug. 23, 1779, and bapt. at TLY on Sept. 29, 1779. He was not mentioned in the will.

Frick - John was taxed in 1762. He m. Catharina, and had the following children:
- Anna, b. on Sept. 23, 1762, bapt. at STR on July 3, 1763, and spon. by Heinrich Devis and Anna Kladi.

Frysinger - Ludwig arrived at Philadelphia on the ship *Peggy* on Oct. 16, 1754, and in 1763, purchased land in York Co., Windsor Township. On Nov. 1, 1775, he is named as a mason of Windsor Township, when he purchased 37.5 acres in Dover Township. By Sept. 15, 1786, he had land in Newberry Township. In 1781, he was taxed in Dover Township with 37 acres and two head of cattle. He appears on the 1790 census of Dover Township (this area became Conewago Township in the early 1800s. He m. Elisabeth Plessen. She d. in York Co. in 1817, and Ludwig d. in Conewago Township in May 1792. They are bur. in Quickel's Lutheran Church cemetery, and had the following children in York Co., Conewago Township (except the first two in Lancaster Co.):
- Johannes, b. on Nov. 6, 1766, and m. Elisabeth. They were sponsors to a baptism at Wolf's Lutheran Church on May 19, 1799 and July 27, 1800. He briefly moved to Dauphin Co., PA, but returned to York Co., Dover Township, where he d.
- Ludwig Friedrich, b. on July 20, 1768, bapt. at the First Reformed Church of Lancaster on Oct. 16, 1768, and spon. by John and Catharine Rader. He was a mason, and d. in Dover Township. He m. Susanna (probably a dau. of Ludwig Weyer) (between 1790 and 1795).
- Anna Maria, b. about 1770, and m. Jacob Feiser.
- Jacob, b. on Oct. 24, 1773. He m. Catherine Miller.
- Elisabet, b. on July 1, 1776, bapt. at Quickel's Lutheran Church on July 28, 1776, and spon. by Elisabeth Tentzel/Fentzel. She m. John Dattesmann in Christ's Lutheran Church of York in 1804.
- Johan Peter, b. on June 30, 1779, bapt. at Quickel's on July 10, 1779, and spon. by Peter Strein and wife. He m. Susanna Catharina Colman (possibly a widow, and dau. of Johan Henry and Catharine (Worley) Acker, but this is not confirmed) at the First Reformed Church of York on Nov. 18, 1797. Susanna Catharina m.

Col. Peter Runkle in Champaign Co., OH, on Feb. 22, 1821, and d. in Champaign Co., OH, on June 25, 1852. She filed for a divorce in 1833, but dismissed the suit on may 22, 1834. She is bur. in the Christian Bodey cemetery. Susanna Catharina was b. on Jan. 12, 1773. Peter was killed during the War of 1812 in Norfolk, VA, on Jan. 4, 1815. In 1798/9, they moved to Rockingham Co., VA. Peter was a tailor, miller, and distiller, and owned 300 acres on the west side of the Shenandoah River. A survey after his death, mentions his entire holdings of 635.5 acres. During the war, Peter served with the Home Guard/County Militia, and volunteered to take the place of a neighbor. He fought in several battles, and prior to being mustered out, he was helping to take horses over a pontoon bridge. The bridge broke, and Peter helped many men and horses escape from drowning, and afterwards, couldn't be found. His body was later recovered, and he was bur. in the Old cemetery at Norfolk.
- Johan Georg, b. on Oct./Nov. 2, 1781, bapt. at Quickel's on Oct./Nov. 30, 1781, and spon. by Johan Georg Schedel and wife. He m. Elizabeth Reider/Ritter, dau. of Jacob and Magdalena (Mott) Ritter of Basle, Switzerland, in 1804/05. He worked in the iron trade, and was the manufacturer of carriages. He resided in Hanover, and was said to have been a Captain in the War of 1812.
- Barbara, b. on Apr. 21, 1785, bapt. at Quickel's on May 14, 1785, and spon. by Barbara Miller. She m. David Fettro.

Gantzert - Andreas was taxed in 1762. His will was written in Dover Township on June 8, 1776, and probated on Oct. 25, 1776. He m. Margaretha, and had the following children:
- Mattheis, b. about 1738. His will was written in Dover Township on Nov. 25, 1772, and probated on Dec. 23, 1772. He m. Catharina, dau. of Johannes Zinn (see entry), at York on Dec. 17, 1761. Her probate inventory was filed in Dover Township in 1776. They had the following children (recorded at STR):
  - Catharina, b. on Aug. 17, 1763, bapt. on Nov. 12, 1763, and spon. by Jonathan Peissel and Barbara Gansert.
  - Elisabetha, b. on July 4, 1766, bapt. on Aug. 16, 1766, and spon. by Philip Jacob and Maria Elisabeth Zinn. She m. Andreas, son of Adam Kramer (see entry), at TLY on Aug. 21, 1781.
- Catharina, b. about 1740, and m. Samuel Adam about 1761. They had the following children:
  - Johan Wilhelm, b. on Feb. 28, 1762, and bapt. at CLY on Apr. 19, 1762.
  - Greta, b. on Apr. 16, 1764, bapt. at STR on June 11, 1764, and spon. by Andreas and Margaretha Gansert.
  - Samuel, b. on June 27, 1769, bapt. at STR on Apr. 16, 1770, and spon. by Jacob and Barbara Schedderon.

- Margaretha, b. about 1742, and m. Jacob, son of Dieterich and Anna Margaretha Saltzgeber (see entry), at Dover (STR) on May 3, 1763.
- Barbara, b. about 1744, and was a sponsor to the baptism of Catharina Gansert in 1763. She m. Jacob, son of Heinrich Shedderon (see entry).

Gauff - Philip was taxed in 1762, and received a warrant for 250 acres on Aug. 29, 1765, that was surveyed as 281.100 acres on Feb. 12, 1766, and patented as 281.140 acres on June 2, 1772. His will was probated in Dover Township on Jan. 2, 1776. He m. Maria Christina, dau. of Johann Jacob Reiff (see entry). They had the following children (recorded at STR):
- Georg, b. about 1748, and m. Elisabeth Welty at TLY on Mar. 26, 1775. His probate inventory was filed in Dover Township in 1792.
- Barbara, bapt. on Mar. 25, 1750, and spon. by Georg Michael and Barbara Kann.
- Philliph Jacob, bapt. on Nov. 17, 1751, and spon. by Philip Jacob and Catharina. His will was probated in Dover Township on June 6, 1777.
- Magdalena, bapt. on Aug. 19, 1753, And spon. by Joseph and Magdalena Welschans. She m. Jacob Lauer at TLY on Sept. 28, 1779.
- Jacob, bapt. on June 8, 1755, and spon. by Jacob and Elisabetha Reiff. His probate inventory was filed in Dover Township in 1783.
- Christina, bapt. on May 28, 1758, and spon. by Joseph and Magdalena Welschans. She m. Valentine, son of Johannes Emig (see entry in Manchester section).
- Maria Catharina, bapt. on Sept. 30, 1759, and spon. by Maria Elisabetha Reiffin.
- Johann Jacob, b. on Feb. 2, 1763, bapt. at TLY on Apr. 1, 1763, and spon. by Johan Jacob Welschans and Magdalena Kann.
- Johannes, bapt. on Aug. 4, 1764, and spon. by Georg and Elisabetha Schramm.

Ginter - Dewald wrote his will in Dover Township on Oct. 13, 1774, and it was probated on Nov. 9, 1774. He m. Christina, and had the following children:
- Anna.

Gochenour (Kochenour) - Joseph was taxed in 1762. His will was written in Dover Township on Mar. 2, 1809, and probated on Aug. 7, 1810. He m. Mary, and had the following children:
- Christian.
- Samuel.

- John received a warrant for 150 acres in Shrewsbury and Springfield Township on Feb. 12, 1767, that was surveyed as 142.53 acres called *Timber Bottom* on June 19, 1767. He received a warrant for 200 acres in Shrewsbury and Springfield Township on Oct. 15, 1762, that was surveyed as 203.38 acres on Nov. 16, 1764.
- Michael.
- Abraham.
- Martin m. Maria Magdalena.
- Joseph.
- Barbara.
- Anna.
- Mary.
- Jacob m. Catharina.

Gossler - Georg Adam had 233 acres in West Manchester and Dover Township surveyed on May 11, 1757. He was taxed in York Township in 1769. His will was written in York Township on Aug. 20, 1787, and probated on July 23, 1791. He m. Anna Elisabeth, and had the following children:
- Elisabeth Margaret, b. about 1742, and m. Nicholas Anspach about 1763. He d. before 1787.
- Anton, b. about 1746. He and his wife were sponsors to the baptism of Catharina Guscha at TLY in 1767.
- Susanna, b. about 1748, and m. Nicholas Enders. They were sponsors to the baptism of Anna Maria Gossner at STR in 1791. He was a sponsor to the baptism of Nicholas Kolp at STR in 1762. His will was written in Paradise Township on Feb. 20, 1810, and probated on Mar. 14, 1810.
- Johannes, b. on Aug. 25, 1751, and bapt. at CLY on Sept. 22, 1751. He m. Catharina, dau. of Martin Hiller (see entry). He was taxed in York Township in 1779.
- Catharina Elisabeth, b. about 1755, and m. Jacob, son of Peter Streher (see entry).
- Philip Reinhard, b. on Oct. 25, 1757, bapt. at CLY on Dec. 3, 1757. He m. Anna Maria.

Gross - Andreas. His probate inventory was filed in Dover Township in 1758. He m. Anna Barbara. They had the following children:
- Michael, b. about 1739. He was taxed in 1762, and m. Anna Margaretha about 1763.
- Heinrich, b. about 1741. He was taxed in 1762, and m. Sophia, dau. of Jacob Altland, at STR on Aug. 27, 1765.
- Andreas, b. about 1743. He m. Maria Barbara, dau. of Philip Hetzer at STR on Oct. 28, 1766.

- Johan Wendel, b. about 1745, and m. Margaretha, dau. of Paul Burckhardt (see entry in Manchester section), at STR on Mar. 13, 1770.
- Carl, b. about 1747, and m. Anna Elisabeth, dau. of Herman Maurer (see entry), at STR on May 21, 1771.
- Maria Magdalena, b. about 1749, and was a sponsor to the baptism of Maria Magdalena Gross in 1771.
- Johan Georg, b. on Aug. 23, 1751, and bapt. at CLY on Sept. 29, 1751.
- Johannes, b. on Jan. 24, 1754, and bapt. at CLY on June 2, 1754. He m. Margaretta.

Haas - Johann Jacob was taxed in 1762. He m. Anna Elisabeth before 1754. They had the following children:
- Anna Maria, bapt. by RJL on July 6, 1760, and spon. by Peter and Anna Maria Weyl.

Haller - Johan Peter was taxed in 1762. He m. Christina Magdalena, and had the following children:
- Susan, b. on Mar. 12, 1762, and bapt. at CLY on Apr. 11, 1762.
- Maria Margaretha, b. on Mar. 7, 1764, bapt. at STR on Apr. 1, 1764, and spon. by Jacob and Maria Margaretha Rahauser.
- Daniel, b. on Feb. 9, 1766, bapt. at STR on Mar. 30, 1766, and spon. by Daniel and Anna Barbara Rahauser.
- Johan Jacob, b. on Apr. 16, 1770, bapt. at STR on May 13, 1770, and spon. by Jacob and Catharina Rahauser.
- Johan Peter, b. on Mar. 26, 1771, bapt. at STR, and spon. by Jacob Rahauser.
- Anna Maria, b. on Dec. 3, 1772, bapt. at STR on Dec. 13, 1772, and spon. by Georg and Anna Maria Velte.

Hamm - unknown had the following children:
- Valentine, b. about 1726, and m. Catharina, dau. of Frederick Oblad m. Anna Catharina (Foobach) Heg (see entry), at Trinity Lutheran Church of Lancaster, PA, on July 23, 1749, and Louisa about 1751. Catharina d. in Apr. 1751, and is bur. on Valentine's farm (CLY). His will was written in Dover Township on Feb. 3, 1766, and probated on Sept. 26, 1766. Louisa's probate inventory was filed in Dover Township in 1809. They had the following children:
  - Catharina Dorothea, b. on Dec. 14, 1752, and bapt. at CLY on Feb. 4, 1753. She m. Daniel, son of Jacob May (see entry).
  - Balthasar, b. on Apr. 16, 1754, and bapt. at CLY on May 23, 1754. He m. Catharina, dau. of Philip Greber (see entry in Manchester section).

- Johann Friedrich, bapt. at STR on Nov. 24, 1758, and spon. by Johann Friedrich and Anna Maria Lochman. He was not mentioned in the will.
- Christian, b. about 1760, and m. Anna Maria Hetzer at TLY on June 20, 1780.
- Johann Jacob, bapt. at STR on July 30, 1761, and spon. by Frederick and Maria Catharina Lochman. He was not mentioned in the will.
- Anna Maria, b. on Nov. 10, 1763, and bapt. at CLY on Jan. 1, 1764.
- Susanna Dorothea, b. about 1728, and m. Jacob, son of Frederick Oblad m. Anna Catharina (Foobach) Heg (see entry), at Trinity Lutheran Church of Lancaster, PA, on Apr. 23, 1749.
- Maria Barbara, b. about 1731, and m. Frederich Schindel before 1752.

Hantz - Andreas was taxed in 1762. He m. Catharina. His will was written in Dover Township on Dec. 4, 1786, and probated on Mar. 21, 1787. They had the following children:
- Johannes, bapt. at STR on Nov. 11, 1763, and spon. by Johannes and Catharina Elisabeth Spaar.
- Andreas.
- Jacob.
- Barbara.
- Maria Catharina, bapt. at STR on Mar. 30, 1766, and spon. by Nicholas and Maria Catharina Diehl.

Hartman - Matthias Albrecht was taxed in 1762. He m. Anna Catharina, and had the following children:
- Maria Dorothea, b. on Nov. 6, 1750, and bapt. at CLY on Nov. 20, 1750.

Hartman - Nicholas was taxed in 1762.

Heg (Heck) - Frederick Oblad m. Anna Catharina Foobach, and immigrated to America with their son, Conrad, on the ship *Ranier* on Sept. 26, 1749. She was b. in Rathine, Germany. He was taxed in Dover Township in 1762, and d. on Dec. 9, 1770. His probate inventory was filed in Manchester Township in 1771. They had the following children (see Hoke by Berlekamp and McConnell (1980)):
- Jacob, b. in Honau Land, Holtzhausen, Germany, and immigrated to America on the ship *Two Brothers* on Sept. 15, 1748. He settled in Codorus Township, and then moved to Manchester Township. He m. Susanna Dorothea Hamm at Trinity Lutheran Church of Lancaster, PA, on Apr. 23, 1749. His will was made on Oct. 6, 1802,

and his probate inventory was filed in Manchester Township in 1804. They had the following children:
- Anna Catharina, b. on Feb. 17, 1750, bapt. at Trinity Lutheran Church of Lancaster, PA, on Mar. 4, 1750.
- Maria Barbara, b. on Jan. 24, 1752, bapt. at CLY on Apr. 26, 1752, and spon. by Frederick and Maria Barbara (Hamm) Schindel.
- Andrew, b. on Mar. 13, 1754, bapt. at CLY on Apr. 28, 1754, and spon. by Andrew Schmidt and wife. He m. Anna Maria, dau. of Simon Wittmeyer (see entry in Manchester section). She was b. on Dec. 12, 1755, and d. on Aug. 3, 1817. He d. in 1832.
- Maria Elisabeth, b. on Aug. 11, 1756, and bapt. at CLY on Aug. 29, 1756. She m. George Neiman. He was b. on Sept. 1, 1750.
- Johan Frederick, b. on June 5, 1759, and bapt. at CLY on Oct. 21, 1759.
- Louisa, b. on Sept. 9, 1761, and bapt. at CLY on Nov. 8, 1761. She m. Jacob Barr.
- Catharina, b. on Apr. 31, 1769, bapt. at TLY on June 11. 1769, and spon. by Andreas Hock and wife.
- Elisabetha Catharina, b. on May 1, 1772, bapt. at WOL on July 5, 1772, and spon. by Jacob Schaffer and Catharina Hiller.

- Conrad was b. in Honau Land, Holtzhausen, Germany. He immigrated to America with his father in 1749, and he was taxed in Dover Township in 1762. He moved to Cumberland Co., Carlisle, PA, before 1781, and his will was written on Feb. 7, 1785. He d. Carlisle in 1785 (?Mar. 7). He m. Elisabeth, and had the following children:
- Anna Maria, bapt. by RJL on June 8, 1755, and spon. by Christian and Elisabeth Groll.
- Anna Catharina, bapt. by RJL on June 8, 1755, and spon. by Friedrich and Anna Catharina Heeg. She m. ___ Greaves.
- Christian, bapt. by RJL on May 1, 1757, and spon. by Christian and Elisabeth Kroll. He d. in Trumbull Co., OH.
- Anna Phillippine, b. on Aug. 19, 1759, bapt. at CLY on Sept. 9, 1759, and spon. by Adam and Phillippine Schettler. She m. Johan Nicholas, son of Jacob Hoffman (see entry).
- Johan Frederick, b. on July 17, 1761, and bapt. at CLY on Aug. 30, 1761. He m. Catharina, and d. in York Co., PA, on Apr. 12, 1830.
- Catharine, b. about 1763, and m. Jacob Ottenberger, and Jacob Weiser of Carlisle.
- Susanna, b. about 1765, and m. ___ Fisher.
- Jacob, b. about 1767.
- Conrad, b. about 1769.
- John, b. about 1771.

- Phillipena.
- Catharina, b. about 1728, and m. Valentine Hamm at Trinity Lutheran Church of Lancaster, PA, on July 23, 1749.

Herbold - Georg was taxed in 1762. His will was written in Dover Township on Mar. 28, 1789, and probated on Apr. 7, 1790. He m. an unknown woman, and Catharina, dau. of Heinrich Dewes (see entry) about 1767, and had the following children:
- Michael, b. about 1748, and m. Eva Catharina, dau. of Heinrich Luckenbach, at STR on Dec. 12, 1769.
- Elisabeth, b. about 1753, and m. Casper, son of Johannes Bentzel (see entry), at TLY on Dec. 29, 1774.
- Wilhelm, b. about 1755, and m. Dorothea, dau. of Heinrich Dewes (see entry), about 1779. His probate inventory was filed in Dover Township in 1816, and hers was filed in 1822.
- Leonard, b. about 1768, and m. Elisabeth, dau. of Jacob Julius (see entry), at TLY on Apr. 29, 1789.
- Johan Heinrich, bapt. at STR on Apr. 20, 1772, and spon. by Heinrich and Maria Barbara Dewes. His probate inventory was filed in Washington Township in 1843.

Herring - Johannes is presumed to be a bro. of Henrich Herring. He m. Anna Margaretha, and immigrated to PA on the ship *Neptune* on Sept. 24, 1751. In 1754, 1756, 1758, they were communicants at Trinity Lutheran Church in Bucks Co., Springfield Township, PA. They had the following children (see *History and Genealogy of the Herring-Haring-Hering-Harring Family of Pennsylvania* by Calvin Adam Herring (1962)):
- Anna Elisabeth, b. about 1720, and m. Georg Heinrich Joseph. He immigrated to America on the ship *Patience* on Sept. 9, 1751, and was taxed in Paradise Township in 1762. His probate inventory was filed in Paradise Township in 1766 (d. on Nov. 26, 1766). They had the following children:
  - Anna Catharina, b. in Feb. 1740, and m. Jonas, son of Heinrich Bott (see entry in Manchester section), at CLY on Sept. 16, 1760.
  - Christina, b. on Sept. 21, 1744, m. Johan Georg Oderman, and d. in Paradise Township on Nov. 18, 1830. He was b. on Dec. 15, 1739, and d. on May 20, 1826.
  - Johannes, b. in 1748, m. Catharina Elisabeth, dau. of Conrad Maul (see entry in Manchester section), and d. in Paradise Township in 1840.
  - Maria Elisabeth, b. on June 3, 1753, and bapt. at St. Paul's Lutheran Church in Montgomery Co., PA. She m. Johan Philip, son of Conrad Maul (see entry in Manchester section), and d. in 1836. He was b. in 1751, and d. in 1841.

- Johann Jacob, b. about 1727, and immigrated to America on the ship *Two Brothers* on Sept. 28, 1753. He m. Maria Catharina Hackmann in Montgomery Co., Upper Hanover Township, PA, on Oct. 31, 1758. He was a communicant at Zion Reformed Church in Northampton (now Lehigh) Co., Upper Milford Township. On May 17, 1777, he purchased land in Northampton Co., Allen Township, that he sold on May 14, 1787, and moved to Northampton Co., Hanover Township. He resided in Hanover Township, PA, in 1800, and d. before 1810. Maria Catharina resided in Hanover Township in 1810. They bapt. the following children in St. Paul's Lutheran Church:
  - Johann Ludwig, b. on May 1, 1759, and spon. by Ludwig Herring at his baptism.
  - Anna Elisabetha, b. on Mar. 27, 1760.
  - Anna Maria, b. on Feb. 3, 1761.
  - Maria Catharina, b. on Feb. 3, 1761, and spon. by Maria Catharina, wife of Ludwig Herring at her baptism.
- Johannes, b. about 1729. He immigrated to America on the ship *Neptune* on Sept. 24, 1751, m. Anna Elisabeth. He apparently resided in York Co. in 1763, but returned to eastern PA. Johann d. in Berks Co., PA, before 1790, and his widow d. in Bucks Co. after 1800. They had the following children:
  - Margareth Elisabetha, bapt. at St. Paul's Lutheran Church in Montgomery Co., Upper Hanover Township, PA, on Feb. 8, 1752, and spon. by Michael and Elisabeth Kabel.
  - Johann Henrich, b. on Feb. 23, 1755, bapt. at St. Paul's (Blue) Church, Northampton (now Lehigh) Co., Upper Sauccon Township, PA, on Mar. 30, 1755. He took the Oath of Allegiance in Berks Co. on June 7, 1778, and resided in Bucks Co. in 1800.
  - Johannes, b. on Aug. 18, 1763, bapt. by Reverend Waldschmidt in York (now Adams) Co., PA, at Littletown Christ's Reformed Lutheran Church on Oct. 16 (12), 1763, and spon. by John and Eva Froschauer.
- Johann Ludwig, b. about 1731. He immigrated to America on the ship *Neptune* on Sept. 24, 1751, m. Maria Catharina, and d. in Montgomery Co., Upper Hanover Township, PA, between 1765 and 1769. They bapt. the following children at St. Paul's Lutheran Church in Upper Hanover Township (except the last in Old Goshenhoppen in Upper Salford Township):
  - Johann Georg, b. on Nov. 13, 1753, and d. on Apr. 25, 1776. He is bur. at Goshenhoppen Church in Upper Salford Township.
  - Anna Christina, b. on Jan. 14, 1756, and confirmed at Indian Creek Reformed Church in 1770.
  - Jacob, b. in Montgomery Co., Marlborough Township, on Oct. 28, 1758. He m. Magdalena, dau. of Henry and Barbara (Nees)

Guttelman, at St. John's on May 27, 1783, and d. in Bucks Co., Rockhill Township, PA, on Feb. 10, 1817. She was b. on Nov. 23, 1757, and d. on Apr. 26, 1842. They are bur. in St. John's Lutheran Church, Ridge Valley. He was a cordwainer, and a Private in the 5th Battalion of Captain Schuler's Company from 1784 to 1786.

- Eva Catharina, b. on Jan. 8, 1761, and confirmed at St. Paul's on Feb. 14, 1774.
- Johan Nickel, b. on Feb. 16, 1763, and d. in 1839. He m. Maria Hersh, and d. in Montgomery Co., Marlborough Township on July 27, 1839. She was b. on Mar. 16, 1760, and d. on Apr. 23, 1842. They are bur. at St. Paul's.
- Johann Luttwig, b. on Feb. 1, 1764, and d. in Bucks Co. on Mar. 1, 1815. He is bur. in Tohickon Reformed cemetery. He m. Barbara. He was a Private in Captain Schuler's Company, 4th Battalion in 1785/86.
- Anna Margaretha, b. about 1733, and was a communicant at Trinity Lutheran Church in Bucks Co., Springfield Township, PA, in 1757.
- Margaretha Barbara, b. about 1735, and was a communicant at Trinity Lutheran Church in Bucks Co., Springfield Township, PA, in 1757.
- Maria Elisabeth, b. in 1737, and confirmed on Good Friday, 1753, at New Goshenhoppen Lutheran Church in Upper Hanover Township. She was a sponsor for a child of Georg Henrich and Anna Elisabeth Joseph at St. Paul's/Indianfield Lutheran Church on Aug. 5, 1753.
- Johann Philip, b. about 1739. He immigrated to America on the ship *Neptune* with his parents on Sept. 24, 1751. He m. Anna, and d. in Fairfield Co., Amanda Township, OH, in 1823. His will was written on May 22, 1823, and probated in 1823. She d. in Amanda Township after 1800. Phillip was naturalized in Bucks Co., Richland Township, PA, on Aug. 8, 1765. In 1769, he was taxed in York Co., Paradise Township, PA, with two horses, and 46 acres. This was part of John Brady's Warrant on the North Side of Pigeon Hills. The other portion of this Warrant had been purchased by Philip's (presumed) uncle, Henry Herring, on Jan. 2, 1759. Phillip was taxed in Paradise Township in 1783, and in 1784, he moved to Dover Township. He served in the Revolutionary War as a Corporal in the York County Militia in 1780 and 1782. In 1786,87,88, he served in the York County Militia in the 3rd Company of Foot, 3rd Battallion. Around 1803/04, he moved to Fairfield Co., Amanda Township, OH, where he had 183 acres of land. Phillip and Anna had the following children:

- Heinrich, b. about 1767. He m. Margaret, dau. of Samuel and Margaretha (Apfel) Wildasin, of York Co., Manheim Township. She was b. in 1771, and d. in Adams Co., Straban Township, PA, on Oct. 5, 1846. Heinrich served in the York County Militia in Captain John Sharp's 3rd Company of Foot, 3rd Battalion in 1786, 87, 88. He d. in Dover Township in Aug. 1825. He was a farmer and weaver. From 1824-27, he was taxed in Fairfield Co., Amanda Township, OH, as a non-resident for 61 acres that he inherited from his father. Heinrich willed this land in OH to his son, Philip.
- Elisabeth, b. about 1769, and m. ____ Siford. Her husband d. before 1823. She d. in 1833. The land in Fairfield Co., Amanda Township, she inherited from her father was devised between her heirs in 1833.
- Philip, b. about 1771. He m. Maria Eva, dau. of Jeremias and Maria Elizabeth Beer (see entry), before 1794. He was taxed in 1797 and d. before 1800. From 1824-1827, he (more properly, his estate) was taxed in Fairfield Co., Amanda Township as a non-resident for 61 acres that he inherited from his father.
- Catherine, b. in 1773. She m. ____ Schaffer about 1794, ____ Hatten about 1804, ____ Briggs between 1812 and 1819, and ____ Deeds between 1825 and 1850. She d. in Allen Co., Bath Township, OH, in 1856. Her will was written on Mar. 26, 1856, and probated on Apr. 5, 1856. She was on the 1820 census for Fairfield Co., Amanda Township, and was taxed there in 1825. She appeared on the 1850 census of Allen Co., Bath Township. ____ Briggs d. before 1820.
- John, b. about 1775. He m. Jane "Ginney" Poole in Fairfield Co., OH, on June 16, 1807, and d. in Allen Co., German Township, OH, in June 1847. She was b. in MD in 1775, and was residing in German Township in 1850. While in Amanda Township, he resided on 61 acres of land (R/T/S-20/13/14) that he inherited from his father. John Herring moved his family from Fairfield Co., Amanda Township to Allen Co., German Township, OH, in 1833, and had land in Section 21 of German Township in 1834.
- Anna Maria, b. about 1777. She m. Philip Wollet in York Co., PA, about 1799. They resided in Fairfield Co., Amanda Township, OH, until about 1833, and then moved to Allen Co., Bath Township, OH. Philip's will was written on Sept. 3, 1835, and probated on Oct. 21, 1836. Anna Maria was alive in 1835.
- Catharine Barbary, b. on Aug./June 28, 1779. She m. William, son of William Ward, and d. in Fairfield Co., Amanda Township, OH, on Nov. 5, 1850. She is bur. in Van Meter cemetery. He was b. in VA in 1780, and was alive in 1850 (he d. in Allen Co., Monroe Township, OH, between 1851 and 1859).

- Eve, b. on Feb. 27, 1783. She m. Peter, son of John and Salome (Zimmerman) Stuckey, in Fairfield Co., OH, on Oct. 6, 1805, and d. in Fairfield Co., Hocking Township, Muddy Prairie, OH, on Apr. 15, 1864. He was b. in Lancaster Co., Elizabeth Township, PA, on Apr. 4, 1770, and d. in Hocking Township on Apr. 30, 1856.

Herring - Johann Henrich was taxed in 1762. He is presumed to be the uncle of Johan Philip Herring (see entry). He m. Elisabeth Margaretha, immigrated to America on the ship *Patience* on Sept. 9, 1751, and d. in York Co., Paradise Township, PA, in May 1779. Elisabeth d. before 1767. After Elisabeth's death, Henrich m. Anna Margaretha, widow of Dietrich Saltzgeber (see entry), in Christ's Lutheran Church of York, PA, on July 6, 1767. Anna Margaretha d. before 1779. Henrich resided in Bucks Co., Haycock Township, PA, until Feb. 18, 1759, but had purchased 84 acres on the north side of Pigeon Hill's in York Co., Paradise Township, PA, on Jan. 2, 1759. This was part of a survey of 130 acres warranted to John Brady on July 5, 1745. The remaining portion of Brady's tract was deeded to Johann Phillip Herring. Henrich and his family moved to York Co. in the spring of 1759. His will was written on Apr. 20, 1779, and probated on June 4, 1779. Henrich and Elisabeth had the following children (see *History and Genealogy of the Herring-Haring-Hering-Harring Family of Pennsylvania* by Calvin Adam Herring (1962)):
- Philip Wendel, b. in 1727. He m. Elisabeth, immigrated to America on the ship *Patience* on Sept. 9, 1751, and d. in Bucks Co., Haycock Township, PA, on Jan. 28, 1812. On May 30, 1768, he purchased 183 acres in Haycock Township. He was a Collector of Arms in Haycock Township for the committee of Safety during the Revolutionary War (period ending July 10, 1776). They had the following children in Haycock Township:
  - Henrich, b. on Oct. 2, 1753. He m. Anna Margaretha, and d. in Clinton Co., Logan Township, PA, on Dec. 1, 1840. She d. on Mar. 29, 1836. He served in the Revolutionary War from 1776 to 1779. He farmed in Bucks Co., Haycock and Springfield Townships, and in 1800, moved to Sugar Valley, Northumberland Co., Miles Township, PA. This area became Clinton Co., Logan Township.
  - Johan Michael, b. on May 3, 1756, bapt. at Tohickon Lutheran on May 15, 1756, and spon. by Johan Michael Kronau and Catharina Dorothea Herring. He m. Elisabeth, dau. of Jost and Margaretta Reese.
  - Peter, b. about 1759. He resided in Bucks Co., Springfield Township, PA, in 1783. He moved to Northumberland Co., PA, and then to OH.

- Maria Susanna, b. in 1762, bapt. at Tohickon Lutheran Church in Apr. 1762, and spon. by Valentine Philipp.
- Anna Elisabeth, b. on Dec. 12, 1763, bapt. at Tohickon Lutheran on Oct. 28, 1763, and spon. by George Desch and Susanna Drach. She m. Theobald Dresh, and d. in Schuylkill Co., Lewistown Valley, PA, on Aug. 12, 1833. He d. about 1817.
- Susanna, b. on Dec. 12, 1763, bapt. at Tohickon Lutheran on Oct. 28, 1763, and spon. by George Desch and Susanna Drach. She m. Jacob, son of Nicholas and Elisabeth (Hartman) Buck, in 1790, and d. in Bucks Co., Jenkintown, PA, about 1841. He was b. in Bucks Co., Springfield Township, PA, on May 1, 1770, and d. on July 24, 1843.
- Johann, b. about 1764. He m. Maria, dau. of Johan Philip and Catharina Schreyer, and d. in Columbiana Co., Liberty Township, OH, sometime after 1850. She d. before 1850. John was a mason, sawmiller, and farmer. In 1816, he had 70 acres in Northumberland Co., Chillisquaque Township, PA, and by 1840, resided in Columbiana Co., OH.
- Adam, b. about 1768, and resided in Northumberland (now Union) Co., Mifflinburg, PA, in 1800.
- Johann Philip, b. on Sept. 7, 1772, bapt. at Trinity Lutheran Church, and spon. by John Metzger and Elisabeth Catharina Gares. He m. Priscilla before 1789, and d. in 1821.

- Maria Dorothea, b. about 1730, and m. Johann Georg Gap about 1752, and Jacob Maak about 1763. Georg's probate inventory was filed in York Co. in 1757. Jacob was naturalized in York Co. on Apr. 10, 1760, and taxed in Paradise Township in 1762. Dorothea was alive in 1779. She had the following children:
  - Maria Margaretha Gap, b. in Bucks Co. on July 3, 1753, bapt. at Tohickon Lutheran on July 22, 1753, and spon. by Henry Herring and Maria Margaretha, both single.
  - Dorothea Gap, b. about 1755.
  - Jacob Maak, bapt. by RJL on July 15, 1764, and spon. by Christian Michel and Anna Maria Mackin.
- Johann Henrich, b. in May 1732. He m. Juliana Salome, dau. of Ludwig and Maria Barbara Salomonmuller (see entry in Codorus section), in Apr. 1760, and d. in Manheim Township on June 29, 1801. His will was written on Oct. 13, 1798, probated on July 18, 1801. She was b. in May 1741, and d. on Nov. 24, 1805. They are bur. in Manheim Union Burial Ground. Heinrich purchased 100 acres in Codorus Township on Aug. 8, 1795, that he deeded to his son-in-law, Heinrich Miller on May 27, 1799. Heinrich and Juliana had the following children (7 sons and 4 daus. according to tombstone):
  - Lewis, b. about 1760, and was a communicant at STJ in 1784.

- Dau., b. about 1762, and d. before 1798.
- Johann Henrich, b. on Nov. 11, 1764, bapt. at St. Jacob's Lutheran Church on Mar. 3, 1765, and spon. by Ludwig Salomonmuller. He d. young.
- Maria Philipena, b. on Apr. 23, 1766, m. Jacob Klein, and d. on Sept. 26, 1833. He was b. on Apr. 7, 1760, and d. on Oct. 17, 1836. They are bur. in Mt. Olivet cemetery in Hanover.
- Johannes, b. on Jan. 7, 1768, and bapt. at St. Jacob's on Feb. 7, 1768. He m. Christina, dau. of Peter and Elizabeth Meyer (see entry in Codorus section).
- Johann Solomon, b. on Oct. 7, 1769, and bapt. at St. Jacob's on Nov. 12, 1769. He d. before 1798.
- Anna Maria, b. on Sept. 12, 1771, and bapt. at St. Jacob's on Oct. 4, 1771. She m. Henrich, dau. of Georg and Elisabeth (Herring) Miller.
- Johann Jacob, b. on Nov. 20, 1773, m. Eva, dau. of Michael and Margaretha (Matter) Ehrhard in York Co. in 1801, and d. in Centre Co., Gregg Township, PA, on Nov. 25, 1829. She was b. on Feb. 24, 1780, and d. on Dec. 23, 1848. They are bur. in Heckman cemetery. They moved to Centre Co. in 1801. In 1800, he was a Captain of the 5th Company, 124th Regement, 1st Brigade, 5th Division of the Adams County Militia.
- Anna Christina, b. on June 17, 1776, and bapt. at St. Jacob's on July 7, 1776.
- Henrich, b. in 1778 (under 21 in 1798), and d. in Adams Co., Conewago Township, McSherrystown, PA, in 1855. He m. Loisa, and Margaret. Loisa was b. on May 31, 1778, and d. on Mar. 6, 1842 (bur. at STM). Margaret was b. about 1782, and d. on Nov. 25, 1869 (bur. at St. John's Lutheran Church in Abbottstown). In 1810, he was residing in Manheim Township; in MD in 1820; in Adams Co., Mount Pleasant Township in 1830 and 1840; and McSherrystown in 1850. He was an Ensign in the 2nd Battalion, 61st Regiment, 5th Division of the York County Militia in 1808.
- Georg, b. on June 21, 1781, and d. on Dec. 7, 1806. He is bur. in Manheim Union Burial Ground.

- Maria Margaretha, b. about 1734. She m. an unknown man, d. in York Co., Paradise Township before 1779, and had the following dau.:
  - Maria Catharina, b. about 1757, and m. George Emler before 1779.
- Catharina Dorothea, b. about 1736. She m. Johann Nicholas, son of Johann Nickel Michel. He resided in York Co., Paradise Township in 1769, and Dover Township in 1779. Nicholas was a Captain in the Revolutionary War. Catharina d. between 1779 and 1784, and Nicholas m. Anna Maria before 1784. He d. on May 11, 1812. His

will was written on Apr. 1, 1784, and probated on Sept. 3, 1812 (it named his wife Anna Maria, son, Adam, and granddau., Anna Maria Michel). They had the following children:
- Adam, b. about 1757.
- Elisabeth Margaretha, b. in Bucks Co. on Jan. 27, 1759, bapt. at Tohickon Union on Feb. 18, 1759, and spon. by Henry Herring and wife.
- Catharina, b. in Bucks Co. on June 20, 1761, bapt. at Tohickon Union on July 5, 1761, and spon. by John Owen and wife.
- Anna Catharina, bapt. by Reverend Jacob Lischy on May 15, 1763, and spon. by Christian Michel and Anna Catharina Bergheimerin.
- Elisabeth, b. about 1738. She m. George Miller, and resided in York Co., Paradise Township in 1762, and 1769. They had the following children:
  - Henrich, b. about 1758, and m. Anna Maria, dau. of Johann Henrich Herring.
  - George, b. about 1762.
- Maria Christina, b. about 1740, and m. Adam Fauster/Tauster.

Hiller - Martin was taxed in 1762. His will was written in Manchester Township on Nov. 23, 1797, and probated on Jan. 3, 1799. He had the following children:
- Anna Margareth, b. about 1731, and m. Johannes, son of Killian Fissel (see entry), about 1751.
- Dorothea, b. about 1749 m. John Wampfler, before 1781.
- Maria Eva, b. about 1751, and was a sponsor to the baptism of Heinrich Fissel in 1761 (RJL). She m. Johannes, son of Ludwig Salomonmuller (see entry in Codorus section), at STM on May 15, 1764.
- Catharina, b. about 1753, and was a sponsor to the baptism of Elisabeth Catharina Hoock at WOL on 1771. She m. John, son of Georg Adam Gossler (see entry), about 1774.

Hoeheneise - Bernhard was taxed in 1762. He was b. in Ober-Ryxingen, Wurtemburg, on Dec. 17, 1713, came to America in 1752, and d. in Dover Township on Mar. 10, 1778. He moved to his farm in Dover Township on Nov. 26, 1773. He m. Anna Barbara Huber (Jan. 6, 1711-Oct. 1, 1789) on Martinmas 1738. She was b. in Wetterzimmer, Wurtemburg. They had the following children (born in Ober-Ryxingen unless otherwise noted (recorded at FMY)):
- Dau., b. about 1739, and d. in Wurtemburg.
- Dau., b. about 1741, and d. in Wurtemburg.
- Son, b. about 1743, and d. en route to America in 1752.

- Johan, b. on Jan. 5, 1747, and m. Margaretha, dau. of Georg Quickel (see entry), on Sept. 26, 1768. His will was written in Dover Township on Aug. 5, 1806, and probated on May 23, 1810. He d. on May 7, 1810, and she d. on May 14, 1810. They were bur. in the Old Moravian cemetery at York, but in 1908, their remains were moved to Salem cemetery.
- Barbara, b. in PA, on Feb. 9, 1755.

Hoffman - Johan Jacob was taxed in 1762. His will was written in Dover Township on Apr. 19, 1775, and probated on Apr. 29, 1775. He m. Anna Christina. They had the following children:
- Johan Philip, b. about 1746. He m. Catharina about 1766.
- Catharina, b. about 1748.
- Philip Jacob, b. on Oct. 21, 1750, and bapt. at CLY on Mar. 20, 1751. He m. Eva.
- Johan Nicholas, b. on May 2, 1753, and bapt. at CLY on June 24, 1753. He m. Anna Phillipine, dau. of Conrad Heck (see entry). His will was written in Dover Township on July 5, 1815, and probated on Oct. 13, 1815.
- Anna Christina, bapt. by RJL on Dec. 14, 1755, and spon. by Johan Nicholas and Anna Christina Herman.

Hoffman - Johan Nicholas was taxed in 1762. His probate inventory was filed in Dover Township in 1784. He m. Anna Maria Elisabeth. They had the following children:
- Cunigunda, b. on May 18, 1750, bapt. at the First Reformed Congregation at Lancaster on June 17, 1750, and spon. by Carl and Cuniginda Burckhard. She m. Philip Jacob, son of Johannes Zinn (see entry), at STR on Apr. 5, 1772.
- Anna Christina, b. on May 15, 1753, and bapt. at CLY on June 29, 1753.
- Carle, bapt. by RJL on Feb. 16, 1755, and spon. by Carle and Anna Burkhardt.
- Heinrich, b. on Apr. 24, 1758, and bapt. at CLY on May 7, 1758.
- Maria Elisabeth, b. on Nov. 23, 1763, bapt. at STR on Dec. 25, 1763, and spon. by Carl and Eva Margaretha Albert.
- Daniel, b. on Dec. 27, 1765, bapt. at STR on Feb. 1, 1766, and spon. by Jacob and Maria Margaretha Maj.
- Nicholas, b. on Mar. 10, 1768, and bapt. at CLY on Ascension Day.
- Johan Frederick, b. on July 24, 1770, and bapt. at CLY on Aug. 26, 1770.

Hoover - Johan Georg wrote his will in Dover Township on Apr. 28, 1786, and it was probated on Nov. 1, 1786. He m. Mary, and had the following children:

- Adam, b. about 1766, and m. Barbara, dau. of Peter Streher (see entry).
- Georg, b. about 1768, and m. Anna Margaretha, dau. of Peter Streher (see entry).

Ilgenfritz - Johan Georg was b. in Werentz, Anspach, Germany, on May 25, 1728. He joined the church on June 11, 1757, and left it in 1770. He m. Margaret, dau. of Peter Mohr (see entry in Manchester section), in June 1748. She was b. in Becherbach, Germany, in Sept. (Nov. 5), 1731, and d. on Apr. 6, 1769, and was bur. with her dau. on Apr. 8, 1769 (FMY). They had the following children (see FMY):
- Anna Maria Catharina, b. on Apr. 4, 1749, and bapt. at CLY on Apr. 15, 1749.
- Georg, b. on May 4, 1750. He m. Anna Maria. His probate inventory was filed in York Boro in 1810.
- Johannes, b. on Jan. 12, 1752, bapt. at CLY on Jan. 19, 1752, and d. before 1764.
- Barbara, b. on Sept. 18, 1753, and bapt. at CLY on Sept. 30, 1753.
- Elisabeth, b. on Jan. 8, 1755.
- Johan Martin, b. on Dec. 11, 1756, bapt. on Dec. 16, 1756, and spon. by John Heckedorn, Marcus Hoens, Martin Ebert, and Bernard Honeisn. He m. Catharina. His will was written in Manchester Township on Oct. 29, 1812, and probated on Nov. 20, 1812.
- Charlotte, b. on Dec. 13, 1758, bapt. on Dec. 16, 1758, and spon. by Anna Maria Miller, Elisabeth Peizel, and Barbara Hoeneisen.
- Frederick, b. on Aug. 18, 1760, bapt. on Aug. 23, 1760, and spon. by Bernhard Honeisen, Georg Ilgenfritz, and Philip Rothrock. He m. Elisabeth. His probate inventory was filed in Conewago Township in 1823. Her probate inventory was filed in Conewago Township in 1843.
- Margaret, b. on May 5, 1762, bapt. on May 8, 1762, and spon. by Catharina Hekedorn, Barbara Hoeneis, and Elisabeth Fieser. She m. John Welty at TLY on Aug. 17, 1783.
- Johannes, b. on Jan. 13, 1764, bapt. on Jan. 31, 1764, and spon. by Philip Rothrock and John Peizel.
- Juliana, b. on Aug. 7, 1765, bapt. in 1765/66, and spon. by Catharina Heckedorn, and Juliana Fischel.
- Samuel, b. on Apr. 21, 1767, bapt. on Apr. 24, 1767, and spon. by Barbara Hoeneise and Elisabeth Fieser, Sr. He m. Maria Magdalena. His probate inventory was filed in York Boro in 1835.
- Dau., b. and d. on Apr. 6, 1769 (FMY).

Julius (Ulius) - Heinrich was taxed in 1762, and naturalized on Apr. 10/12, 1762. He m. Maria Magdalena Willheut, widow of Martin Fry, and Isaac Roudiboush before Mar. 27, 1756. Heinrich immigrated to America on the ship *Two Brothers* on Oct. 13, 1747. He may be the father of Philip Jacob Julius and Barbara Julius.

Julius - Philip Jacob was taxed in 1762. During the Revolution, he was a Private 5th Class of the 3rd Company, 1st Battalion on Apr. 11, 1778. He received a warrant for 64 acres on Oct. 10, 1761, that was surveyed as 72.25 acres on Dec. 22, 1767. He m. Eva Elisabeta, and Elisabetha, widow of Jacob Miller at TLY on Dec. 26, 1776. He was alive in 1789, and had the following children:
- Philip Jacob, b. about 1760. During the Revolution, he was a Private 8th Class of the 3rd Company, 1st Battalion on Apr. 11, 1778. He was taxed as a single man in Dover Township in 1779. He m. Elisabet about 1780/81.
- Johann Georg, b. on Dec. 17, 1762, bapt. at STR on Jan. 12, 1763, and spon. by Johan Georg Kann. He m. Anna Maria Elisabeth, and d. on Jan. 7, 1848. She was b. on July 7, 1765, and d. on June 14, 1824. They are bur. in May's Meetinghouse cemetery.
- Barbara, bapt. at STR on Jan. 22, 1764, and spon. by Johan Georg Kann and Barbara Julisen.
- Johan Peter, b. on July 23, 1764, bapt. at STR on Sept. 2, 1764, and spon. by Peter and Elisabeth Kronbach. He m. Elisabeth, and d. on Mar. 3, 1833. She was d. on Feb. 17, 1867 (aged 85 years, 8 months, and 1 day). They are bur. in STR cemetery.
- Magdalena, bapt. at QUI on June 23, 1765.
- Christina, bapt. at STR on Aug. 3, 1766, and spon. by Philip and Christina Gauff.
- Elisabeth, b. about 1768. She m. Leonard, son of Georg Herbold (see entry), at TLY on Apr. 29, 1789.

Kann - unknown had the following children:
- Georg Michael m. Maria Barbara. His probate inventory was filed in Dover Township in 1762. They had the following children (recorded at STR):
  - Michael, b. about 1743, and m. Anna Maria about 1770.
  - Johan Georg, bapt. on May 23, 1745, and spon. by Georg and Maria Catharina Amend. He m. Catharina, dau. of Rudolph Spengler (see entry in Shrewsbury section), at TLY on Oct. 27, 1767.
  - Maria Elisabetha, b. on Sept. 6, 1748, and bapt. at CLY on Sept. 25, 1748. She m. John Debus at TLY on Jan. 3, 1769.
  - Anna Magdalena, b. about 1749, and was a sponsor to the baptism of Jonathan Rachhauser in 1764, and Johan Jacob Gauff in 1763.

- Johannes, bapt. on Mar. 17, 1751, and spon. by Johannes Kann and Maria Sophia Obin.
- Johan Jacob, bapt. on Dec. 2, 1753, and spon. by Jacob Reiff and Anna Maria Schultzin.
- Johan Heinrich, bapt. on Mar. 29, 1755, and spon. by Johan Heinrich and Anna Barbara Kann.
- Philiph, bapt. on Oct. 31, 1756, and spon. by Philip and Maria Christina Gauff.
- Johan Peter, bapt. on Nov. 28, 1758, and spon. by Peter and Dorothea Peterman.
- Barbara, b. about 1760, and was a sponsor to the baptism of Catharina Kann in 1775.
- Johan Heinrich m. Anna Barbara, dau. of Balthasar Bortner (see entry in Codorus section), in Berks Co., Tulpehocken Township, PA, on Feb. 17, 1748. They resided in York Co., Hellam Township, PA. Henry's will was written in Hellam Township on June 4, 1796, and probated on Apr. 24, 1798 (probate inventory in Manchester (?) Township in 1798). They had the following children:
  - Catherina Eva, b. about 1749, and m. Frederick Ruhl (see entry in Codorus section).
  - Maria Elisabetha, bapt. by Reverend Jacob Lischy on Dec. 24, 1751, and spon. by Adam and Maria Elisabeth Fischborn. She m. Philip Decker.
  - Johannes, bapt. on Dec. 9, 1753 by Reverend Jacob Lischy, and spon. by Johannes Kann and Philliphine Bortner.
  - Anna Barbara, bapt. by Reverend Jacob Lischy on June 13, 1756, and spon. by Georg Michael and Maria Barbara Kann. She m. John Heyer at TLY on Apr. 8, 1777, and Jacob Stohly.
  - Philip, b. on Jan. 15, 1759, and bapt. on Mar. 4, 1759 at Christ's Lutheran Church of York.
  - Maria Magdalena, b. on July 19, 1762, bapt. at Kreutz Creek on Aug. 16, 1762, and spon. by Joseph and Maria Magdalena Welschans. She m. Johan Kauffman at TLY Apr. 2, 1782.
  - Susanna Maria, b. on Apr. 4, 1764, bapt. at Kreutz Creek on May 12, 1764, and spon. by Friederich Frescher and Susanna Philipp Beier. She m. Michael Dersteen.
  - Henrich, b. about 1765, and m. Christina Schaefer at TLY on May 10, 1785.
  - Johan Jacob, b. on July 23, 1767, bapt. at Kreutz Creek, and spon. by Peter and Dorothea Peterman. He m. Eva.
  - Michael, b. about 1769.
  - Daniel, b. about 1771, and m. Christina.
- Johannes was a sponsor to the baptism of Johannes Kann in 1751 and 1753, and Johannes Peterman in 1756.

Kauffman - Christian was taxed in 1762. He had the following children:
- Christoph, b. about 1746, and m. Maria Charlotta, dau. of Melchior Schaffer, at STR on Mar. 10, 1767.
- Catharina Margaretha, b. about 1748, and m. Felix, son of Heinrich Leinbacher (see entry), at STR on Feb. 19, 1771.

Keller - Antony m. Maria Barbara, and had the following children:
- Jacob Jacob, b. about 1722. He was taxed in 1762. He had 295.16 acres in Shrewsbury Township surveyed on Nov. 25, 1768, that was patented to Jacob Keller (Jr.) on Apr. 12, 1822. He received a warrant for 100 acres in Springfield Township on Aug. 6, 1753, that was surveyed as 232 acres on Nov. 22, 1751. He was taxed in Shrewsbury Township with 150 acres one horse, and three cattle in 1779, and 100 acres, one horse, and two cattle in 1780. His will was probated in Shrewsbury Township on July 27, 1791. His execs. were Christian Keller and Andrew Meyer. He received a warrant for 100 acres in Shrewsbury Township on Sept. 8, 1785, that was surveyed as 77.63 acres called *Kellerin* on Oct. 30, 1786, and patented to Jacob Keller, Jr., on Nov. 23, 1808. Jacob had the following children:
  - Maria, b. about 1743, and m. Nicholas Bieri/Beery (see entry in Manchester section).
  - John, b. about 1746. He was not on Jacob's will, but he was residing in Shrewsbury Township in 1780 with 100 acres, two horses and three cattle, and 140 acres, three horses and four cattle in Shrewsbury Township in 1779. He received a warrant for 40 acres in Shrewsbury Township on Aug. 19, 1772, that was surveyed as 40.50 acres called *Addition* on Jan. 16, 1778.
  - Dau., b. about 1749, and m. Andreas Meyer.
  - Christian, b. in 1752, and was taxed in Shrewsbury Township in 1780 with two horses, and three cattle. -Henry, b. on May 13, 1755. He was not in Jacob's will, but some researchers have said that Henry and Maria were siblings. He m. Catharina, dau. of Johannes and Anna Catharina Seitz (see entry in Shrewsbury section), in York Co., PA, on Apr. 6, 1784. He was taxed as single in Shrewsbury Township in 1779, and 1780. They moved to Fairfield Co., Pleasant Township, OH, sometime between 1803 and 1810. Henry d. on Feb. 13, 1838, and Catharina on Nov. 26, 1843.
  - Samuel, b. about 1761. He was not on Jacob's will, but he had 150 acres in Shrewsbury Township in 1780, and 200 acres in Shrewsbury Township in 1779.
  - Jacob, received a warrant for 9 acres in Shrewsbury Township on Sept. 24, 1791, that was surveyed as 10.116 acres, and patented as 10.111 acres on Nov. 23, 1868.

- Peter, b. about 1732. He was taxed in 1762. He m. Barbara had the following children (recorded at the Lower Bermudian Church in Adams Co., unless otherwise noted):
  - Johannes, bapt. by Reverend Jacob Lischy on June 15, 1755, and spon. by his (future) uncle and aunt, Peter Felcker and Elisabetha Keller.
  - Johann Antony, bapt. by Reverend Jacob Lischy on Apr. 25, 1758, and spon. by his grandparents, Antony and Maria Barbara Keller.
  - Anna Maria, b. on Oct. 5, 1760, bapt. by Reverend Jacob Lischy on Nov. 23, 1760, and spon. by Johan Adam Wolf and Anna Maria Schmidin.
  - Johan Jacob, b. on Mar. 3, 1762, and bapt. at Christ's Lutheran Church of York on Apr. 9, 1762.
- Anna Barbara, b. about 1734, and m. Johan Georg Kleinfelter (see entry in Shrewsbury section).
- Abraham, b. about 1736. He m. Anna Margaretha, and had the following children:
  - Johan Phillip, bapt. by Reverend Jacob Lischy on Apr. 8, 1765, and spon. by his uncle, Johan Phillip Keller, and Elisabeth Kroin.
- Elisabetha, b. about 1738, and m. Johan Peter Felcker at CLY on Apr. 7, 1759 (see entry).
- Johan Phillip, b. about 1740. He spon. Johan Phillip, son of Lorentz and Anna Maria Kontz, at his baptism (by Reverend Jacob Lischy) on Feb. 24, 1765. He may have been the Philip Keller that m. Magdalena, and had Maria Eva, b. on Jan. 27, 1787, and bapt. at St. Jacob's on Mar. 17, 1787.
- Anna Maria, b. in 1743, bapt. at St. Matthew's in May 1743, and spon. by Isaac and Margaretha Schafer.
- Johan Michael, b. on Oct. 13, 1745, bapt. by Reverend Jacob Lischy on Oct. 24, 1745, and spon. by Johan Michael and Barbara Spar. He m. Catharina Becker in York Co., Dover Township on May 12, 1767, and had the following children:
  - Elisabetha Margaretha, b. on Oct. 9, 1768, and bapt. at Christ's Lutheran Church of York on Nov. 6, 1768.

<u>Klopfer</u> - Joseph was taxed in 1762. His will was written in Dover Township on Jan. 22, 1773, and probated on Jan. 3, 1774. He m. Anna Christina, and had the following children:
- Dorothea, b. about 1744, and m. Philip Adam, son of Georg Spaar (see entry), at STR on Mar. 24, 1765.
- Philip Jacob, b. about 1751, and m. Magdalena about 1772.
- Georg Jacob, b. about 1761, and m. Catharina about 1785.
- Frederick, b. about 1763, and m. Catharina about 1784.

- Georg Michael, b. in Dec. 1765, bapt. at STR on Dec. 26, 1765, and spon. by Georg and Catharina Spaar.

Knoertzer - Johann Balthes was b. in 1701, m. Maria Dorothea Mayer, and immigrated to America on the ship *Charming Nancy* in 1738. His was naturalized in Dover Township on Sept. 25, 1751. His will was written in York Town on Aug. 15, 1767, and probated on Sept. 18, 1769. Dorothea d. at sea in 1738, and he m. Anna Maria Catharina Wolff about 1739/40. He had the following children in Treschklingen, Germany (a stepson, Andrew Gruss was mentioned in the will) (BNK):
- Maria Catharina, b. on Feb. 9, 1725, and m. Peter Ob (see entry).
- Georg Christoph, b. about 1727, and m. Anna Marcreta, dau. of Jacob Ob (see entry). They had the following children:
  - Johan Nicholas, b. on Jan. 28, 1747, and bapt. at CLY on Feb. 30, 1747.
  - Andrew, b. on Aug. 16, 1748, and bapt. at CLY on Sept. 11, 1748.
  - Baltzer, b. about 1750.
  - Anna Margaretha, b. on Jan. 28, 1752, and bapt. at CLY on Apr. 5, 1752.
  - Maria Catharina, b. on Mar. 12, 1754, and bapt. at CLY on May 5, 1754.
- Baltzer, b. about 1729. He m. Maria Barbara about 1754, and Anna Maria about 1765. He had the following children:
  - Johan Baltzer, bapt. by RJL on Aug. 31, 1755, and spon. by Baltzer and Anna Catharina Knoertzer.
  - Georg Adam, b. on Nov. 30, 1758, and bapt. at CLY on Jan. 7, 1759.
  - Charlotte, b. on Nov. 10, 1760, and bapt. at CLY on Dec. 7, 1760.
  - Maria Eva, b. on Dec. 8, 1762, and bapt. at CLY on Jan. 23, 1763.
  - Michael, b. on Feb. 4, 1766, bapt. at QUI on Feb. 14, 1766, and spon. by Michael and Maria Barbara Quickel.
- Maria Dorothea, b. about 1731, and m. Andreas Muller (see entry in Manchester section).
- Eva Barbara, b. on Jan. 10, 1733.
- Johann Georg, b. on Mar. 29, 1735, and d. young.
- Christina, b. on Sept. 14, 1736.

Kobelet (Gobelet) - Christoffel was taxed in 1762. He m. Dorothea before 1758, and Anna Maria Margaretha, dau. of Peter Wentz, at STR on Sept. 20, 1767. He had the following children:
- Anna Margaretha, bapt. at STR on Aug. 27, 1758, and spon. by Daniel and Eva Margaretha Rachhauser.
- Elisabeth, bapt. at STR on Nov. 29, 1761, and spon. by Daniel Rachhauser and Elisabeth Bruckerin.

- Johan Philip, bapt. at STR on Sept. 26, 1768, and spon. by Philip and Anna Maria Wentz.
- Johan Jacob, b. on Oct. 29, 1771, bapt. at STR on Nov. 17, 1771, and spon. by Jacob and Anna Margaretha Majer.
- Maria Margaretha, bapt. at STR on Feb. 27, 1774, and spon. by Philip and Anna Maria Wentz.
- Johan Philip, b. on May 9, 1781, bapt. at STR on July 29, 1781, and spon. by Johan Philip and Anna Maria Wentz.

Kramer - Hans Adam, son of Johannes and Anna Elisebeth Kraemer, was b. in Essenheim, Germany, on Sept. 14, 1679. He m. Maria Elisabetha Wolff at Essenheim on Nov. 29, 1708. She was b. in Essenheim on Dec. 29, 1686. They were residing in Essenheim, Germany, in 1712, and by 1729, they were residing in Gonnheim, Germany. They immigrated to America, and arrived at Philadelphia in the ship *Pennsylvania Merchant* on Sept. 10, 1731. They were the parents of the following children (born at Essenheim until 1721, and then in Gonnheim (BFG):
- Anna Catharina, b. on Apr. 19, 1710. She m. Hans Martin, son of Gabriel and Anna Margaretha Schultz, at Friedelsheim, Germany, on Sept. 3, 1728. Martin was b. at Friedelsheim on Nov. 11, 1694, and d. in York Co., Hellam Township, PA, on Nov. 5, 1761. They immigrated to America on the ship *Pennsylvania Merchant* in 1731. Catharina and Martin had the following children in Hellam Township:
  - Henry, m. Mary Magdalena. They sold land to Harman Updegraff in Manchester Township on May 14, 1779.
  - Eva, m. George Reitzel.
  - Anna Maria Elisabeth. She m. Andreas, son of Leonhardt and Maria Veronica Comfort/Kumforth.
  - Anna Maria.
  - Christina, bapt. on July 24, 1745 by Reverend Jacob Lischy, and spon. by Johannes and Christina Schultz. She m. ____ Meyer.
  - Juliana, m. Johan Jacob Faubel, and Abraham Shineman.
  - Johannes, bapt. on Jan. 6, 1754 by Reverend Jacob Lischy, and spon. by Johannes Schultz, Jr.
  - Catharina. She m. Michael Weidner.
- Juliana, b. on Jan. (Dec.) 2, 1711/12, at Essenheim, Germany. She m. Johan Jacob Lanius in Gonnheim, Germany, on June 13, 1730. He was b. at Meckenheim on the Hart, Germany, on May 12, 1708. They immigrated to PA in 1731, and settled in York Co., Hellam Township, Kreutz-Creek, PA. On Aug. 25, 1762, the family moved to the town of York, where he d. on Mar. 1, 1778, and Juliana on Feb. 26, 1769. They were the parents of the following children, b. in Hellam Township:

- Dau., b. on June 3, 1731, and d. young.
- Jacob, b. on Aug. 14, 1732. He m. Barbara Wiest on June 29, 1762, and Barbara Buehler at Hebron on Apr. 23, 1786. Barbara Weist was b. on Nov. 25, 1742, and d. on Apr. 25, 1780. Jacob d. on Mar. 29, 1788.
- Maria Elisabetha, b. on June 29, 1734. She m. Christophel Weidner.
- Catharina, b. on June 12, 1736. She m. Friederich Rohmer (see entry in Manchester section).
- Heinrich, b. on Aug. 21, 1738. He m. Anna Margaretha, dau. of Johannes and Maria Elisabeth (Schmidt) Fischel, in Hellam Township on July 27, 1762, and Elizabeth Kuntzli/Kuensli of Mount Joy in the First Moravian Church on Dec. 8, 1772. Anna Margaretha was b. on May 18, 1745, bapt. at the First Moravian Church on May 29, 1745, and d. on Apr. 30, 1772. Elizabeth was b. on Aug. 21, 1751. Heinrich's will was probated at York on Oct. 1, 1808.
- Juliana, b. on Dec. 12, 1740. She and m. Johan Michael, son of Johannes and Maria Elizabeth (Schmidt) Fischel, on Jan. 12, 1761. Michael was b. at Essenheim, Germany, on Sept. 28 (Nov. 12), 1736, and d. on Sept. 10, 1809.
- Eva, b. on May 1, 1742, and d. in 1782.
- Anna Maria Magdalena, b. on Oct. 23, 1745, and bapt. by Reverend Jacob Lischy on Oct. 27, 1745, and spon. by Anna Maria Wolffin. She m. Ephraim Culver.
- Wilhelm, b. on Sept. 23, 1748, and m. Anna Elisabeth, dau. of Johannes and Catharina (Scheubel) Heckedorn, in the First Moravian Church of York on Dec. 26, 1769. She was b. on Aug. 25, 1749, and bapt. on Sept. 5, 1749. They moved to Lititz.
- Johannes, b. on Mar. 24, 1751.
- Johan Adam, b. on Apr. 14, 1754, bapt. at the First Moravian Church on Apr. 18, 1754, and d. on Apr. 20, 1754.
- Maria Elisabetha, born on June 3, 1714. She m. Hans Peter, son of Diebold Gaertner of Niedermodern, Germany. He m. Margaretha, dau. of Christian and Catharina Farni of Rittershofen, on May 24, 1729 (BNA). Margaret was b. on Nov. 17, 1707, and bapt. on Nov. 20, 1707. Peter and Margaretha had a dau., Catharina, b. on Feb. 11, 1730, and bapt. on Feb. 12, 1730. Peter and Margaretha immigrated to America on the ship *Britannia* in 1731, and Margaretha d. about 1732. Maria Elisabetha d. on Oct. 11, 1782. Peter was a master smith. Peter and Elisabetha had the following children:
    - Johan Peter, b. on Feb. 19, 1734, and bapt. at Christ's Lutheran Church of York on Apr. 28, 1734. He m. Louisa/Lois Erb at Christ's Lutheran Church of York on June 26, 1760.

- Johan Adam, b. on Mar. 23, 1735, and bapt. at Christ's Lutheran on Mar. 30, 1735. He m. Maria Elisabeth, dau. of George and Catharine Amendt, at Christ's Lutheran on Aug. 14 (19), 1762. His will was written on Oct. 5, 1778, probated at Yorktown on May 26, 1780, and executed by Philip Gaertner and George Maul.
- Catarina, b. on Apr. 24, 1737, and bapt. at Christ's Lutheran on Aug. 14, 1737.
- Heinrich, b. on Jan. 12, 1739, bapt. at Christ's Lutheran on Apr. 20, 1739, and spon. by his uncle and aunt, Heinrich and Eva Bahn. He m. Catharina Barbara Bolz on May 6, 1766.
- Michael, b. on Mar. 4, 1741, bapt. at Christ's Lutheran on Oct. 23, 1741, and m. Catharina Kuntz on Dec. 13, 1763.
- Johan Georg, b. on June 8, 1743, and bapt. at Christ's Lutheran on June 19, 1743, and m. Susanna, dau. of Leonard and Susanna Crow, before 1777.
- Martin, bapt. at Kreutz Creek on July 30, 1745, and spon. by his uncle and aunt, Martin and Catharina Schultz. He m. Maria Margretha, dau. of Michael and Eva Margretha (Diehl) Ebert (see entry in Manchester section). She was b. on June 21, 1753, and d. on Apr. 14, 1824. Martin d. on Mar. 30, 1818.
- Philib, b. about 1747. He m. Elisabetha.
- Johan Jacob, was bapt. by Reverend Jacob Lischy on Feb. 3, 1751, and m. Margretha, and Miss ____ Rummel in the First Moravian Church of York on June 4, 1782.
- Eva, b. about 1716. She m. Johan Hendrick Bahn. He was b. in Germany in 1708. Henrick arrived at Philadelphia on the ship *Brittania* on Sept. 29, 1731. He settled in York Co., PA, and took up 200 acres in the Kreutz-Creek Valley. Lord Baltimore claimed this region of PA for MD at this time, and the German families mistakenly allowed Colonel Cresap survey this land for Lord Baltimore. When they realized their error, the Germans sent a letter of apology to the PA government, sent a letter to Lord Baltimore, notified him of the change on Aug. 11, 1736, and voluntarily placed themselves under the PA government. Lord Baltimore issued warrants for the arrest of all 54 signers of this letter on Oct. 21, 1736, but they could not be served until favorable weather in the spring. In May 1737, Lord Baltimore's officers rode up and seized Henrick Bahn, Michael Danner, Conrad Strickler, and Jacob Welshover, who were all attending the funeral of a neighbors child. They were taken to Annapolis, MD, and thrown into jail with fourteen others, who were engaged in what the MD government considered the "Revolt of the Germans." They were all later released, and allowed to return to their homes. Henrick Bahn was one of the intended victims of the "Chester County Plot," in which some Chester Co. residents schemed to deliver the

DOVER TOWNSHIP 137

Kreutz-Creek settlement to MD, and drive off the German settlement in return for the land that the Germans had cleared. The PA government learned of the plot in time to prevent it. Henrick d. in York Co., Hellam Township, PA, in Nov. 1768. Henrick and Eva had the following children in Hellam Township, Kreutz-Creek:
- Henrich, b. in 1736, and d. young.
- Maria Elisabetha, b. in 1738, and m. Frederich Ruhl (see entry in Codorus section).
- Maria Catharina, b. in 1741. She m. Rudolph Spangler (see entry in Shrewsbury section) at Christ's Lutheran Church of York on Aug. 5, 1759, and Johan Peter, son of Peter and Catharina Schultz, sometime after 1763. Rudolph's will was written on Sept. 2, 1763, probated on Oct. 13, 1763, and executed by George Keentz and Adam Lightner. Peter was b. in 1741 (possibly in Conewago Township). Peter and Catharina were residing in Hanover (Heidelberg Township) in 1792. Peter's will was written on Oct. 2, 1815, probated on Dec. 22, 1815, and executed by Henry Shultz.
- Eva, b. on Dec. 23, 1743. She m. Jost, son of Jost Harbach. He was b. in Berks Co., PA, on Oct. 11, 1741, and d. in 1831. She d. on Dec. 2, 1794.
- Juliana, bapt. on July 27, 1746, and spon. by her uncle and aunt, Jacob and Julianna Lanius.
- Johan Adam, b. on Dec. 30, 1748. He m. Elisabeth, dau. of John and Maria Elizabeth (Mehl) Harbach (see entry on Mehl), in the First Reformed Church of York on Sept. 19, 1784. Elizabeth was b. at York on Dec. 23, 1760. Elizabeth d. in 1790, and Adam m. Catherine, widow of ___ Morgan. She was b. in 1766, and d. in 1840. Adam lived on his father's homestead until 1811, when he moved a mile northeast of his birthplace. Adam d. on July 26, 1819.
- Anna Maria, bapt. on Aug. 30, 1752.
- Johannes, bapt. on July 14, 1754 by Reverend Jacob Lischy, and spon. by Johannes and Apolonnica Kron.
- Johan Jacob, b. on Mar. 26, 1757, and spon. by his uncle, Johan Jacob Lanius.
- Christian, b. on Jan. 6, 1720/21. He m. Anna Barbara Hayer (see entry in Manchester section). Christian was residing in York Co., Warrington Township in 1762. On Sept. 7, 1773, he had 300 acres in Turkeyfoot Township, Somerset Co., PA, on Scrup Glade Run, bounded by Coxes Creek Glades. Christian d. in Somerset Co., Milford Township, PA, in 1796. They had the following children in York Co.:

- Anna Catharina, bapt. by Reverend Jacob Lischy on Aug. 24, 1747, spon. by Friedrich and Catharina Hayer. Possibly m. Johan Georg Leonhardt (see entry).
- Adam, b. about 1749. He resided in Somerset Co., Milford Township, PA, in 1796.
- Maria Elisabetha, bapt. by Reverend Jacob Lischy on Jan. 19, 1751/52, and spon. by Maria Elisabetha Lanius.
- Eva, bapt. by Reverend Jacob Lischy on July 14, 1754, and spon. by her aunt, Eva Bahn.

- Anna Maria, b. about 1723. She m. Johann Heinrich, son of Lorenz and Anna Elisabetha (Leiss) Wolff. He was b. in Essenheim on Apr. 7, 1715, and immigrated to America on the ship *Samuel* at age 25 on Dec. 3, 1740, and d. in Hellam Township about 1792. She d. in Hellam Township about 1800. They had the following children:
  - Peter, b. about 1742, m. Barbara Sitler Kaufmann about 1771, and d. in Hellam Township in Nov. 1792. She was b. in Lancaster Co., PA, about 1758, and d. in Hellam Township in 1794.
  - Johan, b. about 1744.
  - Juliana, b. on July 16, 1746, bapt. by Reverend Jacob Lischy on July 27, 1746, and spon. by Jacob and Juliana Lanius. She m. Nicholas Reib.
  - Johan Heinrich, b. about 1748, m. Catharina, and d. in York Co. about Sept. 1, 1817.
  - Anna Elisabetha, bapt. by Reverend Jacob Lischy on Apr. 26, 1752, and spon. by Elisabetha Schultzin. She m. Adam Paulus in York Co. on Apr. 16, 1762.
  - Anna Maria, bapt. by Reverend Jacob Lischy on Dec. 8, 1754, and spon. by Anna Maria Raulin. She m. Frederick Dellinger in York Co. on June 8, 1775.
  - Anna Barbara, b. on May 1, 1757, bapt. at Kreutz Creek on June 19, 1757, and spon. by Christian Kramer and wife.
  - Georg, b. about 1759.
  - Anna Catharina, b. on Jan. 20, 1763, bapt. at Canadochly Union on Feb. 6, 1763, and spon. by Philip and Anna Catharina Schmelzer. She m. Johan Peter Hack in York Co. on June 3, 1783.

- Johan Adam, b. about 1725. He m. Susanna/Anna Elisabeth Kirchner. He was residing in Warrington Township in 1762, and Newberry in 1779. He d. in York Co., York Boro, PA, in Feb. 1800. His execs. were Martin Gaertner and Adam Bahn. Johan Adam and Susanna/Anna Elisabeth had the following children in York Co.:
  - Johan Heinrich, bapt. by Reverend Jacob Lischy on June 7, 1752, and spon. by his uncle and aunt, Heinrich and Eva Bahn. He m. Eva Maria Maisch at TLY on Nov. 8, 1785.

- Andreas, bapt. by Reverend Jacob Lischy on Apr. 25, 1756. He m. Elisabeth dau. of Mathias Gantzert (see entry), on Aug. 21, 1781.
- Catharina, bapt. by Reverend Jacob Lischy on Aug. 6, 1758, and spon. by Niclaus and Catharina Schram.
- Johan, b. about 1760, and m. Margaretha Zinn at TLY on June 5, 1781. His probate inventory was filed in Warrington Township in 1792, and Margaret's was filed in 1793.
- Maria Elisabetha, bapt. by Reverend Jacob Lischy on Jan. 24, 1762, and spon. by Philip Jacob and Maria Elisabetha Zinn.
- Johan Adam, bapt. at Strayer's on Sept. 2, 1764, and spon. by his uncle and aunt, Christian and Anna Barbara Kramer. He m. Elisabet before May 1785.
- Maria Elisabetha, bapt. by Reverend Jacob Lischy on Oct. 6, 1764, and spon. by Maria Elisabetha Schultz. She m. Frederick Maysch at TLY on Aug. 17, 1784.
- Johan Jacob, bapt. at Strayer's on Aug. 2, 1767, and spon. by Jacob and Maria Margaretha Rachhauser.
- Eve.
- Abraham. His probate inventory was filed in West Manchester Township in 1821.
- Peter m. Margaretha, dau. of Wendel Michael of York, at TLY on Sept. 23, 1798.
- Catharina, bapt. at Strayer's Reformed Church on May 9, 1771, and spon. by Michael and Catharina Weidner.
- Christina Appolonia, bapt. at Gonnheim on Dec. 18, 1729. She was spon. by Christina Appolonia, dau. of Philip Heyer.

Kronbach - Johan Peter was taxed in 1762. His will was probated in Dover Township on Feb. 7, 1774. He m. Anna Elisabeth, and had the following children:
- Henrich, b. about 1750. His probate inventory was filed in Dover Township in 1777.
- Jacob, b. on Jan. 26, 1752, and bapt. at CLY on May 3, 1752. He m. Christina. His will was written in Dover Township on Jan. 8, 1797, and probated on Jan. 28, 1797.
- Johan Georg, b. on May 2, 1754, and bapt. at CLY on June 31, 1754. He m. Anna Barbara, dau. of Mary Hoffman (see entry). His will was written in Dover Township on Jan. 12, 1779, and probated on Feb. 8, 1779.
- Johan Peter, bapt. at STR on Jan. 1, 1756, and spon. by Ludwig and Varonica Gertraut Spiess.
- Elisabeth, b. about 1758.
- Eva, b. about 1760, and m. David Evans at TLY on Dec. 4, 1781.
- Philip, b. about 1762.

Kunckel (Guntel) - Johan Adam wrote his will in Dover Township on Aug. 17, 1772, and it was probated on Aug. 10, 1784. He m. Anna Margaretha, and had the following children (the will mentions that there are several children):
- Anna Margareth, bapt. at STR on Feb. 15, 1766, and spon. by Georg and Anna Margareth Schneider.

Lang - Johann Georg, son of Hans Jerg and Agnes Dorothea (Kerr) Lang, was b. in Schwaigern, Germany, on Apr. 14, 1718, and immigrated to America on the ship *Christian* in 1749 (?possibly this is a return trip STR states that he was b. on Sept. 26, 1721 in "Schweryern bey Heylbronn Grafschaft Neuberg" to Georg Lang a vinegrower and Agnes, but Georg and Elisabeth have 2 sons bapt. in CLY records before the immigration date of 1749). He was taxed in 1762. He m. Elisabeth, dau. of Samuel Esk in 1742. Georg d. on Dec. 18, 1766. His will was written in Dover Township on Dec. 13, 1766, and probated on Dec. 22, 1766. He had the following children (11 total, 6 sons and 2 daus. alive in 1766):
- Johan Andreas, b. on July 5, 1743, and bapt. at CLY on Aug. 8, 1743. He m. Veronica about 1766, and had the following children:
  - Johan Georg, bapt. at STR on July 5, 1767, and spon. by Jacob and Barbara Schederon.
- Johan Georg, b. on Oct. 7, 1746, and bapt. at CLY on Feb. 24, 1747.
- Elisabeth, b. on Mar. 25, 1751, and bapt. at CLY on Apr. 8, 1751.
- Johan Conrad, b. on Aug. 12, 1753, and bapt. at CLY on Nov. 18, 1753.
- Johannes, b. on Sept. 27, 1755, and bapt. at CLY on Sept. 22 (?), 1755.
- Frederick, b. on Dec. 10, 1757, bapt. at FMY on Dec. 14, 1767, and spon. by Franz Jacob Miller, John Peizel, and Peter Pfaff.
- Maria Barbara, b. on Aug. 20, 1760, bapt. at FMY on Sept. 25, 1760, and spon. by Catharina Heckedorn, Elisabeth Piezel, and Barbara Schlegel.
- Jonathan, b. on Sept. 15, 1762, and bapt. at STR on Nov. 7, 1763, and spon. by Jonathan and Eva Elisabeth Beitzel.
- Maria Margaretha, b. on Aug. 7, 1764, bapt. at STR on Sept. 16, 1764, and spon. by Jacob Schedderon, Barbara and Andreas Gantzert.

Leinbacher (Leinbach) - Henrich was taxed in 1762. His will was written in Dover Township on Feb. 13, 1773, and probated on Mar. 31, 1773. He m. Maria Catharina, and had the following children:
- Conrad, b. about 1744. He m. Margaretha about 1769, and Elisabeth about 1775.

- Felix, b. about 1746. He m. Catharina Margaretha, dau. of Christian Kauffman (see entry), at STR on Feb. 19, 1771.
- Maria Catharina, bapt. by RJL on Dec. 11, 1748, and spon. by Jacob and Maria Catharina Ob. She m. Gerhard Greff.
- Christian, b. about 1750, and m. Anna Maria about 1772.
- Elisabeth, bapt. by RJL on Mar. 4, 1753, and spon. by Heinrich Luckenbach and Elisabeth. She was not mentioned in the will.
- Anna Engela, bapt. by RJL on June 30, 1754, and spon. by Engela Mohrin. She m. Mathias, son of Georg Schmeisser (see entry in Manchester section).

Leininger - Georg wrote his will in Dover Township on Apr. 14, 1791, and it was probated on May 21, 1791. He m. Susanna Magdalena. Her probate inventory was filed in Dover Township in 1812. They had the following children:
- Johan Georg, b. about 1771, and m. Margaret.
- Conrad, b. about 1773.
- Maria Catharina, b. on Feb. 26, 1775, bapt. at QUI on Mar. 19, 1775, and spon. by Catharina Hokin.
- Johannes, b. on Oct. 19, 1777, bapt. at QUI on Nov. 2, 1777, and spon. by Georg Schedler and wife.
- Anna Maria, b. on July 11, 1780, bapt. at QUI on Aug. 6, 1780, and spon. by Georg Schedle and wife. She was not mentioned in the will.
- Michael, b. on Sept. 12, 1781, bapt. at QUI on Sept. 31 (?), 1781, and spon. by Friederich Eicholtz and wife. He was not mentioned in the will.
- Magdalena, b. on May 5, 1785, bapt. at QUI on May 14, 1785, and spon. by Frederick and Catharina Eicholtz. She was not mentioned in the will.
- Frederich, b. about 1787.

Leonhardt - Johann Peter was b. on May 4, 1708. He m. Maria Margaretha, and resided in Zweibrucken, before immigrating to America (according to tradition). They arrived at Philadelphia on the ship *Two Brothers* on Sept. 15, 1748, and settled in Berks Co., Greenwich Township, PA. He had land surveyed in Berks Co. on Mar. 9, 1749. Peter was a cooper, and moved to York Co., Dover Township, PA. In 1757, he was one of the organizers of the Lutheran Reformed Church in Dover Township. In 1771, he sold his Berks Co. land to his son Jacob. Maria Magdalena was b. on Sept. 28, 1715, and d. on July 1, 1777. Peter d. on Apr. 4, 1774. They are bur. in Strayer's Lutheran cemetery. They had the following children:

- Maria Magdalene, b. about 1732, and was a sponsor to the baptism of Maria Magdalene, dau. of Jacob Resch, at Dunkel's on Apr. 17, 1752.
- Philip, b. in 1734. He m. Anna Bossert (?dau. of Jacob). Philip d. in Berks Co., Greenwich Township, PA, in 1803.
- Johan Jacob, b. on Nov. 18, 1736. He m. Anna Maria (Feb. 1738-Dec. 1791), dau. of Johannes Kuhl/Keel in Berks Co., PA, on Jan. 21, 1760, and Barbara sometime after 1791. Jacob d. in Greenwich Township on Aug. 3, 1793, and is bur. in Jerusalem Church cemetery. Barbara d. in 1793
- Johann Georg, b. in 1738. He m. Anna Catharina (possibly Kramer, see entry) in York Co., PA, about 1767. They moved from Dover Township to Newberry Township between 1777 and 1779, and to Monaghan Township between 1779 and 1783. Georg served as a Private in the Revolutionary War. Between 1783 and 1784, he moved to Somerset Co., PA, and settled in Milford Township on Coxes Creek and Middle Creek. In 1784, he purchased 390 acres on Coxes and Middle Creek in Milford Township. He had 250 acres in Milford Township. Georg d. there in 1797.
- Jon Christoph, b. in 1740. He m. Anna Maria. In 1780, he served as a Private in the Revolutionary War, and resided in York Co., Dover Township, PA. Sometime before 1788, moved to Cumberland (now Franklin) Co., Southampton Township, PA. He was a communicant at Shippensburg Lutheran Church in Cumberland (now Franklin) Co., PA, on May 27, 1787, and Oct. 14, 1787. On Feb. 16, 1789, Christoph purchased lot #70 in the town of Carlisle, Cumberland Co., from his bros., Godfrey and William (they purchased this land on July 25, 1788). On Mar. 5, 1789, Christoph was a wagonmaker in Franklin Co., Southampton Township, when he (and his wife Mary) sold his lot in the town of Carlisle to Moses Thompson, and purchased a tract of land in Westmoreland Co., Mount Pleasant/Unity Township, PA, called *Pleasant Grove*, from Mathias Linn. On June 8, 1790, he was listed as a yeoman in Westmoreland Co., Unity Township, PA, when the indenture was made for this land. On Dec. 26, 1797, Christoph and Peter Lenhart purchased 100 acres in Unity Township from Daniel Collins (adjoining John Sloan, John Crawford, and the heirs of David Rankin) (this land was warranted to Christopher Lenhart in 1813). Christoph d. in Unity Township after 1810.
- Heinrich, b. in 1742, m. Catherine, and d. in Somerset Co., PA, on Mar. 21, 1837. He moved to Bedford (now Somerset) Co. in 1785.
- Wilhelm, b. on Nov. 22, 1745. He m. Anna Maria. She was b. on Sept. 24, 1751, and d. on Oct. 22, 1822. Wilhelm d. in York Co., Dover Township, PA, on Oct. 27, 1819. They are bur. in Strayer's Church cemetery

- Johan Peter, bapt. at Dunkel's Reformed Church on Jan. 30, 1749/50. He m. Catherina about 1771. Peter d. in Somerset Co., Addison Township, PA, in May 1814. Catharina was b. in 1755, and d. in 1818. They moved to Bedford (now Somerset) Co., PA, in 1794.
- Frederick, bapt. at Dunkel's Reformed Church on Mar. 7, 1751/52, and spon. by Frederick Mayer. He m. Catherine, and d. in York Co., Dover Township, PA, in 1837. Her will was written in York on Feb. 3, 1809, probated on Aug. 17, 1811, and named her dau., Elisabeth, wife of Andrew Cremer.
- Gottfried, b. on Mar. 17, 1754. He m. Elizabeth Holtzinger in the First Reformed Church of York on Nov. 14, 1778. She was b. in 1753, and d. in 1824. Some sources say that he m. Maria Elisabetha, dau. of Yost and Maria Elisabetha Harbaugh, who was b. on Good Friday, 1753, and d. on June 18, 1835. Possibly, Elizabeth Holtzinger was a widow, or Gottfried was m. twice. Gottfried was a clockmaker in York, and d. there on Aug. 15, 1819.

Lohra - Michael was taxed in 1762. His will was written in Dover Township on Feb. 29, 1764, and probated on Apr. 30, 1768 (it mentions an older bro., Georg). He m. Anna Regina Magdalena. After his death, she m. Michael Lang (see entry in Manchester section) at STR on Aug. 4, 1768 (the marriage says dau. of Michael Lohra, but I believe this was probably a mistake, because no children are indicated in the will).

Luckenbach - Johan Gerhardt was b. in Winckelbach, near Hachenburg, Nassau in 1690, and immigrated to America on the ship *Samuel and Elizabeth* on Sept. 30, 1740. The Anna Maria Luckenbach, who was b. on June 12, 1684, and d. on Jan. 10, 1750 (CLY) (bur. on the Luckenbach farm on Jan. 12, 1750) may have been his sister. He had 190 acres in Dover and Paradise Township. His will was probated in 1758 (see *Descendants of Johan Gerradt Luckenback and Conrad Hawk* by Helen King, Erwin King and Walter Hawk). He m. Anna Catharina, and they were sponsors to the baptism of Catharina Endersen in 1749 (RJL), and Anna Catharina Rudi in 1747 (RJL). They had the following children:
- Johan Adam, b. in 1713, m. a Moravian girl, and moved to Berks Co., PA. He d. in 1785, and is bur. in the Moravian cemetery at Bethlehem, PA (Northampton Co.). He was a schoolmaster.
- Johan Heinrich, b. in 1722, and was taxed in 1762. He m. Anna Elisabeth, dau. of Peter Mohr (see entry in Manchester section). He d. in Heidelberg Township in 1810. They had the following children:
  - Maria Barbara, bapt. by RJL on June 22, 1755, and spon. by Gerhardt Luckenbach and Maria Barbara Weiner.

- Anna Maria, bapt. by RJL on Jan. 22, 1758, and spon. by Johan Heinrich Endersen and Anna Maria Luckenbach.
- Johan Adam, bapt. by RJL on Apr. 5, 1761, and spon. by Adam Enderson and Maria Engela Leinbachin. He m. Anna Maria. He resided in Adams Co., Germany Township, and in 1781, was a Private in the Revolutionary War under Captain Abraham Furrey. In 1800, he was residing in Frederick Co., Emmitsburg District, MD.
- Heinrich, b. about 1762, and m. Hannah about 1782. His probate inventory was filed in Heidelberg Township in 1824.
- Johan Peter, bapt. at STR on July 7, 1765, and spon. by Peter and Anna Elisabeth Kronbach. He m. Anna Elisabeth.
- Elisabeth, b. about 1767.
- Gerhardt, b. about 1735, and was the sponsor to the baptism of Maria Barbara Luckenbach in 1755.
- Anna Maria, b. about 1738, and was a sponsor to the baptism of Anna Maria Luckenbach in 1758.

Maurer - Herman was taxed in 1762. He immigrated to America on the ship *Edinburgh* on Sept. 15, 1749. His will was written in Dover Township on May 10, 1783, and probated on June 20, 1783. He m. Anna Maria, and had the following children:
- Catharina Elisabetha, b. about 1748. She was a sponsor to the baptism of Catharina Elisabeth Schneider at STR in 1768. She m. Philip Hertzer.
- Anna Elisabeth, b. about 1750, and m. Carl, son of Andreas Gross (see entry), at STR on May 21, 1771.
- John, b. about 1754, and m. Martha Albert at TLY on Apr. 16, 1775.
- Georg, b. about 1760, and m. Eva Leidig at TLY on Apr. 17, 1781.
- Anna Margareth, b. about 1762, and m. George Schneider.
- Anna Maria, bapt. by STR on Feb. 18, 1764, and spon. by Georg and Anna Maria Weldy. She was not mentioned in the will.
- Juliana, bapt. by STR on Feb. 18, 1764, and spon. by Abraham and Juliana Rosenberger. She m. Valentine Ehrhardt.
- Johan Adam, bapt. at STR on Oct. 17, 1766, and spon. by Johan Adam and Anna Margareth Gunckel.

May - Jacob was taxed in 1762. His will was written in Dover Township on Feb. 2, 1795, and probated on May 21, 1796. He m. an unknown woman, and Barbara about 1746. He had the following children:
- John, b. about 1739. His probate inventory was filed in Dover Township in 1785.
- Jacob, b. about 1741, and was taxed in 1762. He m. Susanna Margaretha.

- Samuel, b. about 1743.
- Sarah, b. about 1745.
- Maria Margaretha, b. about 1747, and m. Jacob, son of Heinrich Rachhauser (see entry), about 1765.
- Daniel, b. on May 18, 1752, and m. Catharina Dorothea, dau. of Valentine Hamm (see entry), about 1773. His probate inventory was filed in Dover Township in 1803.

Mayer - Frederick was taxed in 1762. He m. Margaret Cunigunda, dau. of Jacob Schmidt (see entry), at STR on Nov. 28, 1758 (see entry). He was a schoolmaster in Dover Township. They had the following children:
- Johann Peter, bapt. by Reverend Jacob Lischy on Mar. 24, 1760, and spon. by Johann Peter Schmidt.
- Andreas, b. on June 8, 1762, bapt. at Christ's Lutheran and Strayer's on June 27/17,1762, and spon. by Andreas and Cathaina Haus.
- Johan Jacob, b. on Nov. 4, 1766, bapt. at Strayer's on Dec. 6, 1766, and spon. by Johan Jacob Schmidt.
- Johan Frederick, b. on June 7, 1769, bapt. at Strayer's on June 11, 1769, and spon. by Nicholaus and Maria Elizabeth Hoffman.

Mayer - Heinrich was taxed in 1762.

Mayer - Jacob was taxed in 1762. He m. Anna Margaretha. They had the following children:
- Johann Friederich, bapt. at STR on Dec. 15, 1751, and spon. by Friederich and Veronica Bassler.
- Johan Jacob, bapt. by RJL on Aug. 8, 1753, and spon. by Heinrich and Veronica Bassler.
- Johann Peter, bapt. at STR on Feb. 16, 1755, and spon. by Peter and Barbara Streher.
- Catharina, bapt. at STR on June 25, 1758, and spon. by Johannes and Catharina Rudisill.
- Johan Jacob, bapt. by RJL on Nov. 6, 1758, and spon. by Ludwig Hutig and Sabina Hutig.
- Anna Barbara, bapt. at STR on May 25, 1760, and spon. by Johannes and Catharina Rudisill.
- Johannes, bapt. by RJL on Mar. 20, 1753, and spon. by Peter and Barbara Straher.
- Johan Heinrich, bapt. at STR on Oct. 20, 1767, and spon. by Johannes and Catharina Rudisill.
- Jacob, bapt. at STR on Mar. 2, 1776, and spon. by Johannes and Catharina Rudisill.

Mayer - Johannes wrote his will in Dover Township on Sept. 3, 1769, and it was probated on Apr. 28, 1779. He m. Maria Catharina, dau. of Wendel Mittman (see entry), at STR on Aug. 24, 1767.

Mehl - Nicholas received a warrant for 200 acres on Nov. 1, 1756. His will was written on Aug. 29, 1758, and probated on Sept. 11, 1758. He had the following children:
- Anna Margretha, b. about 1733, and m. Abraham, son of David and Anna Catharina Schedderon, in 1753. He was b. in the High Bailiwick of Lautern in the Electoral Palatine on Mar. 22, 1730, and immigrated to America with his parents in 1751. He d. of a cachectic condition on July 25, 1758, and was bur. in the Reformed Churchyard at York on July 26, 1758 (CLY). They had one child.
- Maria Elisabeth Margretha, b. about 1735, and m. Johannes Herbach about 1758. He was taxed in Hellam Township in 1762, and York Township in 1779. His probate inventory was filed in York in 1800. They had the following children:
  - Anna Margaretha, b. on Aug. 13, 1759, bapt. at Kreutz Creek Lutheran Church on June 10, 1759, and spon. by Henrich Schmidt and wife.
  - Elisabeth, b. on Dec. 23, 1760, and m. Johan Adam, son of Henrich and Eva (Kramer) Bahn (see entry under Kramer), at TLY on Sept. 19, 1784. -Johannes, b. on Dec. 5, 1762, bapt. at TLY on Apr. 24, 1763, and spon. by Michael Barth and wife. He m. Elisabeth Spengler at TLY on Oct. 1, 1786.
  - Jacob, b. on Oct. 11, 1765, bapt. at TLY on Nov. 3, 1765, and spon. by Johannes Schultz and wife.
  - Juliana, b. on Mar. 30, 1772, bapt. at TLY on Apr. 26, 1772, and spon. by Valentin Krantz and wife.
  - Maria, bapt. at TLY on July 20, 1777, and spon. by Jost Herbach and wife.
- Fredrick, b. about 1738. He was taxed in York Township in 1779.
- Carl Philip, b. about 1740.
- Christina Elisabetha, b. about 1742.

Messerle - Daniel was taxed in 1762. His will was written in Dover Township on Nov. 22, 1792, and probated on Nov. 19, 1796. He m. Anna, and had the following children:
- Anna Maria, bapt. at STR on July 3, 1755, and spon. by Heinrich and Anna Maria Schedderon. She m. Jacob Huber.
- Abraham, b. about 1757. He m. Juliana.
- Petrus, bapt. at STR on Apr. 6, 1760, and spon. by Peter and Maria Catharina Ob. He m. Christina Welty at TLY on Apr. 13, 1784.

- Susanna Catharina, bapt. by RJL on June 12, 1763, and spon. by Jacob and Susanna Margareth May. She m. John Huber at TLY on Apr. 27, 1784.

Mitschele - Johann Georg, son of Johann David and Anna Catharina Mitschele, was b. in Hesslach in 1714. He came to America with his first wife, and three children in 1749 (STR). His will was written on Sept. 23, 1769, and probated on Nov. 18, 1769. He m. Catharina in 1737, dau. of Michael and Barbara (Wolff) Bauer, and Catharina Dorothea, dau. of Adolph Wentz and widow of Johan Wilhelm, at STR on May 24, 1768. Catharina was b. in Glasshutten, Wurttemberg, in 1708. He had the following children (6 total):
- Frederick, b. about 1738. He received "no more than one English shilling" from his father's will, "because he has very much offended, injured, and abused me and his mother."
- Eva Catharina, b. about 1747, and m. Johan, son of Casper Simon at STR on Dec. 13, 1768.
- Johan Georg, b. on June 5, 1769, bapt. at STR on June 8, 1769, and spon. by Peter and Jacobina Streher.

Mittman - Wendel wrote his will in Dover Township/York Town on May 3, 1763, and it was probated on May 20, 1763. He m. an unknown woman, and Maria Catarina (mother of last six children), and had the following children (his first three daus. may have been residing in Germany at the time of his death):
- Maria Elisabeth, m. ____ Bauser (was to have the majority of her inheritance in Germany).
- Margreth, m. ____ Wenen (was to have the majority of her inheritance in Germany).
- Anna Gertraut, m. ____ Bock (was to have the majority of her inheritance in Germany).
- Catarina Margretha, b. about 1743. Her will was written on Apr. 11, 1766, and probated on May 17, 1766. She left her inheritance from her father, to her mother because she cared for her when she was sick.
- Elisabeth, b. about 1745, and m. John Connel at STR on Aug. 19, 1766.
- Maria Catharina, b. about 1747, and m. Johan Mayer at STR on Aug. 24, 1767.
- Hans Jacob, b. about 1750.
- Philliph Carl, bapt. by RJL on Apr. 8, 1753, and spon. by Jacob and Anna Catharina Ob. He was taxed in Dover Township in 1779. He m. Margaret. His probate inventory was filed in Dover Township in 1829.

- Anna Christina, bapt. by RJL on Apr. 13, 1755, and spon. by Jacob and Anna Christina Hoffman.

Muller - Bernard was taxed in 1762. He m. Anna Barbara, dau. of Johannes and Maria Meyer, in 1754, and Ursula, dau. of Johan Brishler, at STR on June 24, 1766. Anna Barbara was b. in Winterlingen in 1733, and d. between 1763 and 1776. She immigrated to America in 1740. Bernard's will was written in Dover Township on May 27, 1799, and probated on Jan. 10, 1801. He had the following children:
- Georg, b. about 1753.
- Magdalena, b. about 1755, and m. Johan Herman Hellman about 1775.
- Salome, b. about 1757, and m. Georg Miller.
- Catharina, bapt. by RJL on Aug. 7, 1763, and spon. by Catharina Meyerin. She m. Philip Uppach.
- Elisabeth, b. about 1765, and m. George Styvenson.

Muller - Jacob was taxed in 1762.

Muller - Jacob was taxed in 1762. His probate inventory was filed in Dover Township in 1775. He m. Maria Elisabeth. They had the following children:
- Johan Michael, bapt. by RJL on Jan. 26, 1755, and spon. by Johan Michael Muller and Jacob Muller. He was taxed as a single man in Dover Township in 1779.
- Jacob, b. on Oct. 24, 1753, and bapt. at CLY on Nov. 7, 1753. He was taxed as a single man in Dover Township in 1779.
- Andrew, b. on Nov. 30, 1758, and bapt. at CLY on Dec. 31, 1758. He was taxed in Dover Township in 1779.
- Maria Eva, b. on Mar. 12, 1760, and bapt. at CLY on Apr. 28, 1760.
- Johan Peter, bapt. at STR on Aug. 7, 1763, and spon. by Peter and Catharina Ob.
- infant, b. on Jan. 1, 1766, bapt. at QUI on Feb. 14, 1766, and spon. by Johan Mathies and Anna Maria Meyer.
- Johannes, b. on Oct. 8, 1768, bapt. at QUI on Mar. 14, 1769, and spon. by Johannes Hummerichhauser, and Catharina Tondorn/Fondorn.
- Maria Barbara, bapt. at STR on Sept. 8, 1771, and was spon. by Johannes and Maria Barbara Humrich.

Ob - Philip Jacob was taxed in 1762. His will was written in Dover Township on May 19, 1758, and probated on Mar. 30, 1767. He m. Maria Catharina. They had the following children:

DOVER TOWNSHIP

- Johan Nicholas, b. about 1719. He was a sponsor to the baptism of Johan Nicholas Zinn in 1739. His probate inventory was filed in Manchester Township in 1754. He m. Elisabeth, and had the following children:
  - Agnes, b. about 1745, and m. Philip, son of Philip Pens (see entry), at STR on July 1, 1766.
  - Maria Elisabeth, b. on Dec. 1, 1749, and bapt. at CLY on Dec. 31, 1749. She m. Georg, son of Jacob Oberdier (see entry), at STR on May 30, 1769.
  - Niclaus, bapt. by RJL on Aug. 2, 1752, and spon. by Christian and Elisabeth Kroll. He m. Sarah Schuggart at TLY on Nov. 7, 1775.
  - Johan Jacob, bapt. by RJL on Jan. 12, 1755, and spon. by Jacob and Catharina Ob.
- Catharina, b. about 1721.
- Peter, b. about 1724. He was taxed in 1762. He m. Maria Catharina, dau. of Johan Balser and Maria Dorothea Knortzer, in 1746 (see entry). His will was written in Dover Township on Nov. 17, 1772, and probated on Dec. 1, 1772. She was b. in Troshchlingen in Gemingen in 1725, and immigrated to America with her father in 1738. Her mother d. on the voyage. They had the following children (recorded at STR):
  - Catharina, b. about 1746, and was a sponsor to the baptism of Maria Catharina Shederon in 1765. She m. Conrad Becker (see entry).
  - Sophia, b. on Oct. 9, 1748, and bapt. at CLY on Nov. 6, 1748. She m. Andrew Blechhard.
  - Dorothea, bapt. on Jan. 28, 1750, and spon. by Jonas Rudysill and Dorothea Knurtzerin. He m. Adam Metzgar.
  - Maria Margaretha, bapt. on Aug. 30, 1751, and spon. by Maria Margaretha Obin. She m. Martin, son of Martin Weigel (see entry in Manchester section), at TLY on May 10, 1772.
  - Elisabeth, b. about 1752.
  - Johan Peter, bapt. on Apr. 14, 1754, and spon. by Jacob Ob, Sr., and Catharina. He m. Maria Catharina, dau. of Philip Hoehns (see entry in Codorus section), on May 6, 1777.
  - Johan Jacob, bapt. on Dec. 28, 1755, and spon. by Jacob Ob, Sr., and Maria Catharina.
  - Eva Barbara, bapt. on July 10, 1757, and spon. by Baltazar and Catharina Knirtzer. She m. Jonathan Evans at TLY on Feb. 24, 1778.
  - Eva Margaretha, bapt. on Dec. 14, 1760, and spon. by Jacob and Maria Margaretha Lambert.
  - Andreas, bapt. on June 13, 1762, and spon. by Andreas and Dorothea Muller.

- Magdalena, b. about 1764.
- Maria, b. about 1766.
- Anna Marcreta, b. about 1726, and m. Georg Christoph, son of Balthasar Knoertzer (see entry).
- Louisa, b. about 1728.
- Philip Jacob, b. about 1735, and was taxed in 1762. He received a warrant for 275 acres in West Manchester and Dover Township on Oct. 15, 1767, that was surveyed as 275.80 acres on Apr. 4, 1768. He also received warrant for 275 acres in Dover Township on Oct. 15, 1767. His will was written in Dover Township on Dec. 19, 1793, and probated on Jan. 14, 1794. The legatees to his will were his nephew and niece, Peter Ob and Christina Heintz. He m. Agnes about 1759, and had the following child:
  - Agnes, b. on Apr. 4, 1760, bapt. at STR on June 11, 1769, and spon. by Jacob and Elisabeth Bohn. She was not mentioned in the will.
- Catharina Elisabeth, b. about 1737, and m. Peter Bentz (see entry).

Oberdier - Jacob was taxed in 1762. He m. Anna Christina about 1747, and Eva Elisabeth before 1782 (Jacob and Eva Elisabeth were sponsors to the baptism of Eva Elisabeth Reinhardt in 1782 (STR)). His probate inventory was filed in Dover Township in 1774. He had the following children:
- Georg, b. about 1748, and m. Maria Elisabeth, dau. of Nicholas Ob (see entry), at STR on May 30, 1769.
- Johan Martin, b. about 1750. He m. Eva Fronica, dau. of Michael Spaar (see entry), at STR on Oct. 20, 1771. He was taxed in Dover Township in 1779. His probate inventory was filed in Dover Township in 1812, and hers was filed in 1819.
- Philip, b. about 1752, and m. Margaret, dau. of Jacob Scharer (see entry in Shrewsbury section). He was taxed in York Township in 1779 (not proven to be a son of Jacob).
- Ludwig, b. about 1754, and m. Maria Elisabeth about 1774. He was taxed in Manheim Township in 1779 (not proven to be a son of Jacob). His probate inventory was filed in Manheim Township in 1815.
- Johan Jacob, b. on Dec. 1, 1762, bapt. at STR on Oct. 9, 1763, and spon. by Tobias and Anna Eva Danner. His probate inventory was filed in Dover Township in 1827.

Palli - Andreas was taxed in Paradise Township in 1762. He m. Christina, and had the following children:
- Andreas, b. in 1748, and bapt. ar STR on Feb. 27, 1768. He m. Catharina, dau. of Valentine Berckheimer at STR on Aug. 27, 1768.

DOVER TOWNSHIP   151

- Philippina, b. on Feb. 15, 1752, and bapt. at STR on Feb. 27, 1768.
  She m. Johannes, son of Johannes Bentz (see entry in Manchester
  section), at STR on Jan. 10, 1769.

Pawer - Georg was taxed in 1762.

Pawer - Georg was taxed in 1762.

Pawer - Michael was taxed in 1762.

Prumbach - Peter received a warrant for 200 acres on June 11, 1763,
that was surveyed as 242 acres on Sept. 1, 1764, and patented to Jacob
Cronebach on Mar. 3, 1775.

Quickel - unknown had the following children, who immigrated to
America on the ship *John* on Oct. 19, 1736 (see *Genealogical History
of the Three Quickel Brothers* by David M. Quickel (1967)):
- Johan Philip. He was a carpenter, and purchased 200 acres in
  Manheim Township on May 31, 1745. He d. in Lancaster Co.,
  Manheim Township, PA, in 1757. He m. Sabina, and after his
  death, she m. Andreas Gedlinger at Trinity Lutheran Church of
  Lancaster on Oct. 6, 1761. Philip had the following children:
  - Maria Catharina, b. about 1731, and m. Melchior Benedick of
    Zweibrucken, Germany, on Mar. 10, 1752 (see entry).
  - Michael, b. about 1735, and m. Veronica Klein and Catharina
    Gemling in 1771. On Oct. 1762, he sold his 106 acres that he
    inherited from his father, and moved to Cumberland Co.,
    Fermanaugh Township, PA. He was taxed there in 1774, and
    served in the 4th Battalion Cumberland County Militia in 1778.
    In 1780/81, he was a Private in the 7th Company, 7th Battalion.
  - Nicholas, b. in 1740, and m. Anna Miller on Dec. 22, 1761. He
    sold his 50 acre tract in Manheim Township on Dec. 1762, and
    moved to York Co., Chanceford Township. He was taxed there
    from 1772 to 1797, and then moved to Clinton Co., PA, where he
    d. in 1810.
  - Philip, b. about 1745, and m. Catharina. He was taxed in York
    Co., Newberry Township from 1768 to 1783. He was an Ensign of
    the 5th Company, 3rd Battalion, Cumberland County Militia in
    1777. He d. in Clinton Co., PA.
  - Anna Maria, b. on Dec. 5, 1749.
  - Wilhelm, b. in 1753, and served in the Revolutionary War. He
    was taxed in York Co., Chanceford Township in 1776, and in
    1782, was taxed in Cumberland Co., East Pennsboro Township.
- Johan Georg settled in Lancaster Co., Conestoga Township, PA. In
  1762, he was taxed in York Co., Dover Township. His will was

written on Feb. 6, 1784, and probated on Feb. 22, 1784. He m. an
unknown woman about 1733, and Maria Ursula Miller on Apr. 23,
1739 (JCS). They had the following children:
- Maria Barbara, b. on Aug. 30, 1734, bapt. at Trinity Lutheran
  Church at Lancaster on Sept. 15, 1734, and spon. by Leonardt
  Vier Uhr, and his bride, Maria Barbara Willhautin. She d. young.
- Anna Catarina, b. on Oct. 27, 1738, bapt. at Trinity Lutheran
  Church in Lancaster on Dec. 16, 1738, and spon. by Anna
  Catarina Quickelin. She d. young.
- Johan Georg, b. on Oct. 25, 1740, bapt. at Trinity Lutheran
  Church in Lancaster Co. on Dec. 14, 1740, and spon. by Johan
  Georg and Anna Hess. He d. young.
- Anna Catharina, b. on Mar. 23, 1742, bapt. by JCS on May 2,
  1742, and spon. by Anna Catarina Quickel. She m. Frederick, son
  of Frederick Eicholtz (see entry), on Nov. 22, 1763, and d. in
  1811.
- Philip, b. on Mar. 23, 1743, m. Eva Catharina, dau. of Andres
  Klein, at STR on Nov. 20, 1764, and d. on Mar. 18, 1821. His will
  was dated Mar. 27, 1821.
- Maria Margaretha, b. on Sept. 29, 1745, and m. Johan, son of
  Bernhard and Barbara Hoeheneise (see entry).
- Peter, b. on Dec. 16, 1746, and m. Maria Catharian Hake. He
  served in the Revolutionary War, and d. in 1776. He is bur. in
  STR cemetery.
- Eva Elisabeth, b. on June 19, 1747, and d. age 5 weeks.
- Eva Elisabeth, b. on Oct. 26, 1748, and m. Andreas, son of Carl
  Seib (see entry). She d. on Sept. 27, 1822. He was b. in
  Lancaster Co., and served in the Revolutionary War in 1781.
- Johan Adam, b. on Oct. 27, 1750, and m. Maria Barbara.
- Maria Barbara, was b. about 1753. She m. Johannes, son of
  Johannes Humrichhaus (see entry in Manchester section).
- Maria Dorothea, b. on Mar. 18, 1759, and bapt. at CLY on Apr.
  23, 1759. She m. Emanuel, son of Carl Seib (see entry), and d. in
  1830. He was b. on June 11, 1751, and d. in 1824. He had 130
  acres in Conewago Township.
- Anna Maria, b. on Aug. 28, 1761, and bapt. at CLY on Nov. 15,
  1761. She d. on May 24, 1763.
- Anna Maria, b. on Oct. 23, 1763, bapt. at CLY on Nov. 22, 1763,
  and confirmed at CLY in 1778.
- Johan Michael, b. on July 25, 1721, and m. Barbara Muller on July
  26, 1741, and Barbara Snavely, widow of ___ Bauer, at The First
  Reformed Church of Lancaster on June 2, 1761. He settled in York
  Co., Conestoga Township, PA, and moved to York Co., Dover
  Township in 1763. He purchased 418 acres from Baltzer Knertzer
  on Apr. 1, 1763, and purchased other tracts on July 14, 1764, and

Apr. 17, 1769. On Mar. 20, 1770, he deeded land that became the site of Quickel's Lutheran Church. He was a Captain in the Revolutionary War in Aug. 1776. His will was written in Dover Township on July 10, 1785. He d. on Dec. 18, 1787, and is bur. in QUI cemetery. Barbara Snavely was b. in 1739, and d. on Apr. 18, 1802. Her will was written on Aug. 5, 1795, and probated on June 29, 1802. Michael had the following children:
- Barbara, b. on Oct. 22, 1742, m. Jacob, son of Georg and Ann (Groff) Kreider, and d. on May 3, 1814. He was b. on Sept. 10, 1735, and d. on Dec. 19, 1818. They are bur. in Old Kreider cemetery in Lancaster Co.
- Elisabeth, b. in 1744, m. Michael, son of Georg and Ann (Groff) Kreider, and d. in July 1824. He was b. in 1737, and d. in Lancaster Co., Conestoga Township in 1794. They are bur. in Old Kreider cemetery.
- Michael, b. in 1746, m. Anna M. Freitag, and d. on Oct. 8, 1818. She was b. on Dec. 2, 1747, and d. on Oct. 7, 1826. They are bur. in Lincolnton, North Carolina.
- Anna Maria, b. on Sept. 7, 1752, m. Conrad, son of Henry Ensminger, and d. on Mar. 16, 1813. He was b. on Dec. 21, 1747, and d. on July 12, 1783. They resided in Manchester Township. He was a Private in Captain Quickel's Company, 5th Battalion in 1776, a Private in the 3rd Company, 2nd Battalion in 1777, and served in 1779.
- Catharina, b. on Sept. 20, 1755, m. Jacob Bar/Bear, and Henry Miller, and d. on Jan. 22, 1823. Jacob served in the Revolutionary War under Michael Quickel in 1776, and d. about 1788. Henry was b. on Sept. 10, 1751, and d. on Apr. 19, 1819. They are bur. in QUI cemetery.
- Johan, b. on June 9, 1762, m. Elisabeth Brenneman, and d. in East Manchester Township on Feb. 13, 1831. She was b. on June 12, 1763, and d. on May 7, 1830. They are bur. in QUI cemetery.
- Baltzer, b. in 1764, m. Catharina Fink, and d. in Lycoming Co., PA, in 1821.
- Anna/Nancy, b. in 1766, m. Conrad, son of Conrad Fry, and d. in Newberry Township in 1822. Her will was written on Nov. 9, 1819, and probated on May 6, 1822. He was b. on Aug. 11, 1752, and d. in 1813.
- Anna Maria, b. in 1768, m. Philip, son of Philip and Barbara (Rudisill) Cansler, on June 12, 1790, and d. in 1839. He was b. in 1766, and d. in 1840.

Rachhauser - Heinrich was taxed in 1762 (must be his widow/estate). His will was written in Dover Township on Oct. 24, 1761, and probated on Dec. 8, 1761. He m. Helena, and had the following children:

- Daniel, b. about 1737, and m. Eva Margaretha about 1757, and Anna Barbara about 1763. He was single sponsor to the baptism of Elisabeth Kobelet in 1761.
- Jacob, b. about 1743, and m. Maria Margaretha, dau. of Jacob May (see entry), about 1765.
- Maria Magdalena, b. about 1747, and m. Johan Schreyack (see entry) at STR on Dec. 27, 1768. She was not mentioned in the will.
- Veronica Barbara, b. on Sept. 7, 1753, and bapt. at CLY on Oct. 10, 1753. She m. Michael Bonge at TLY on Oct. 12, 1779.
- Anna Maria, b. about 1755.

Racki (Rockey) - Henrich was taxed in Manchester Township in 1779. His will was written in Dover Township on Nov. 27, 1784, and probated on Mar. 27, 1785. He m. Susanna, and had the following children:
- Christophel, b. about 1753, and m. Catharina about 1774. He was taxed in Manchester Township in 1779.
- Barbara, b. about 1755, and m. Nicholas Welsch about 1776.
- Wendel, b. about 1757, and m. Susanna, dau. of Philip Pather of Berwick Township, about 1778. He was taxed in Manchester Township in 1779.
- Margaretha, b. about 1759. She was a sponsor to the baptism of Abraham Veltin Welsch in 1777. She was unmarried in 1784.

Reiff - Johann Jacob, son of Benedict Reiff of Rotschweiler/Retschwiller, Northern Alsace, m. Maria Elisabetha, dau. of Bernhard Bollinger of Stinsel, in Diedendorf, Northern Alsace, on Apr. 30, 1715. He immigrated to America on the ship *Robert and Alice* in 1739. She was a sponsor to the baptism of a child of Joseph Welschans in 1746. They had the following children (see BNA):
- Johann Adam, bapt. on Apr. 19, 1716, and d. on Mar. 22, 1717.
- Maria Barbara, bapt. on Mar. 6, 1718.
- Maria Christianna, bapt. on Sept. 17, 1719, and m. Philip Gauff (see entry).
- Christina Catharina, bapt. on July 26, 1722.
- Susanna Magdalena, bapt. on Oct. 4, 1722 (?1724).
- Anna Maria, bapt. on Mar. 28, 1726.
- Elisabeth, b. about 1728. She m. Georg Schramm. His will was written in Manchester Township on Oct. 3, 1772, and probated on Nov. 10, 1772. They had the following children:
  - Anna Maria, bapt. by RJL on May 21, 1749, and spon. by Anna Maria Schrammin.
  - Johan Georg, bapt. by RJL on Jan. 19, 1752, and spon. by Joseph and Magdalena Welschans.
  - Johan Jacob, bapt. by RJL on Apr. 7, 1754, and spon. by Jacob Reiff.

- Maria Magdalena, b. on Oct. 18, 1757, bapt. at STR on Nov. 9, 1757, and spon. by Maria Magdalena Ubachin. She d. from dysentery on Aug. 17, 1758, and was bur. at Henry Wolf's place on Aug. 18, 1758 (CLY).
- Child, b. about 1760.
- Maria Elisabeth, bapt. by RJL on Mar. 22, 1761, and spon. by Nicholas and Catharina Schramm, and Maria Elisabeth Reiffin.
- Josephus, b. on Oct. 15, 1762, bapt. at TLY on Nov. 21, 1762, and spon. by Joseph Welschans and wife.
- Georg Philip, b. on Feb. 19, 1764, bapt. at STR on Apr. 1, 1764, and spon. by Philip and Christina Gauech.
- Margaretta, b. on Dec. 26, 1766, bapt. at TLY on Feb. 16, 1766, and spon. by Margaretha Graeber.
- Jacob, b. about 1730. He was taxed in Newberry Township in 1779. His probate inventory was filed in Fairview Township in 1804. He m. Anna Elisabeth, and had the following children:
  - Anna Elisabeth, bapt. by RJL on Feb. 8, 1756, and spon. by Michael Trorbach and Elisabeth Reiffin.
  - Johann Jacob, bapt. by RJL on Nov. 9, 1757, and spon. by Georg Michael and Anna Barbara Kann. He was taxed in Newberry Township in 1779.
  - Anna Magdalena, bapt. at STR on Aug. 17, 1760, and spon. by Anna Magdalena Welschans.

Reissinger - Hans Martin was b. in Schwaigern, Germany, on Apr. 5, 1685, m. Maria Ursula, dau. of Hans Georg and Maria Elisabetha (Rudel) Heiss, and immigrated to America on the ship *Charming Nancy* in 1737. He was a tailor, and d. of dysentery in Lancaster Co., Lancaster, PA, on Sept. 4, 1776 (recorded at Trinity Lutheran Church in Lancaster). She was b. on May 30, 1690, and d. on Feb. 5, 1735. They had the following children at Schwaigern (see BNK):
- Maria Barbara, b. on Dec. 26, 1712.
- Johann Gottleib, b. on June 12, 1717. His will was written in Philadelphia (now Montgomery) Co., Germantown, PA, on Apr. 15, 1776, and probated on May 28, 1776. He m. Magdalena, and had the following children:
  - Catharina, m. ___ Kiefer.
  - Gottleib.
- Maria Johanna, b. on Nov. 15, 1719, and d. young.
- Johan Martin, b. on May 3, 1722. He was taxed in 1762. He m. Anna Magdalena, dau. of Lorentz and Anna Margaretha Biegmann, at St. Michael's and Zion Lutheran Church in Philadelphia on Dec. 20, 1747. She was b. in America in 1728. They had the following children (recorded at STR):
  - Johannes, b. on Aug. 2, 1748, and m. Magdalena.

- Barbara, b. on Feb. 2, 1750, and m. Georg Richter (see entry) in 1769.
- Johann Martin, b. on Dec. 15, 1751, and bapt. at CLY on Apr. 26, 1752. He m. Anna Maria.
- Johan Conrad, b. on Oct. 26, 1753, and bapt. at CLY on Dec. 16, 1753. He m. Anna Catharina.
- Maria Magdalena, b. on June 22, 1756, and m. Frederick Laumeister at TLY on Oct. 6, 1778.
- Maria Margareth, b. on Aug. 27, 1758.
- Catharina, b. on Oct. 25, 1760.
- Anna Elisabet, b. on Mar. 7, 1762.
- Anna Maria, b. on July 20, 1763, bapt. on Aug. 14, 1763, and spon. by Adam and Anna Maria Seiffert.
- Johann Adam, b. on Mar. 7, 1765, bapt. on Apr. 7, 1765, and spon. by Johan Adam and Anna Maria Seiffert.
- Eva Margaretha, b. on Feb. 19, 1767, bapt. on Mar. 29, 1767, and spon. by Carl and Eva Margaretha Albert.
- Johan Georg, b. on Oct. 15, 1768, bapt. on Nov. 6, 1768, and spon. by Johan Georg and Catharina Mitschels.
- Christina, b. on May 27, 1770, bapt. on July 15, 1770, and spon. by Philip and Anna Maria Wentz.
- Georg Martin, b. on May 11, 1730.

Richter - Gregorii had the following children:
- Georg m. Barbara, dau. of Martin Reissinger (see entry), on Aug. 27, 1769. His will was written in Dover Township on Feb. 7, 1782, and probated on Apr. 23, 1782. They had the following children (recorded at STR):
  - Johannes, b. on July 12, 1770, bapt. on July 15, 1770, and spon. by Martin and Anna Magdalena Reisinger.
  - Johan Georg, b. on Oct. 18, 1772, bapt. on Nov. 14, 1772, and spon. by Johan and Magdalena Reisinger.
  - Johan Peter, b. on Nov. 14, 1779, bapt. on Dec. 25, 1779, and spon. by Philip Weylandt and Catharina Reisinger.
- Heinrich m. Barbara, dau. of John Berner (see entry), on Apr. 23, 1770. After Heinrich's death, Barbara m. Johan Georg Stouch (widower) (see entry). Heinrich and Barbara had the following children:
  - Anna Barbara, b. on Mar. 13, 1771, bapt. on Mar. 31, 1771, and spon. by Philip Weinand and Agnes Barnes (?Barner/Berner).
- Christina, m. Johannes Bergman at STR on July 9, 1771.

Ripfel - Ludwig was taxed in 1762. He m. Sibilla Maria. They had the following children:

- Maria Elisabeth, bapt. by RJL on May 30, 1757, and spon. by Leonhardt and Maria Elisabeth Schedderon.
- Anna Maria, bapt. by RJL on May 17, 1761, and spon. by Philip Rudisill and Anna Elisabetha Rubertin.

Rummel - Jacob was taxed in 1762. He m. Elisabetha, dau. of Casper and Elisabetha Ernst, in 1725. She was b. on Canton Berne, Switzerland, in 1694, and d. between 1763 and 1776. They immigrated to America in 1750. He and his widowed dau.-in-law, Salome Rummel, were sponsors to the baptism of Johann Jacob Schwing at TLY in 1763. Jacob and Elisabetha had the following children:
- Jacob, b. in Klerburg, Bergzabern on Sept. 6, 1726, d. in York on May 4, 1759, and was bur. in the Reformed cemetery in York (CLY). He was a carpenter. He m. Salome, dau. of Martin Schwing, on Apr. 8, 1749, and after his death, she m. Georg Gump at FMY on July 16, 1770. She was b. in Bischweiler, Alsace, on Nov. 27, 1722, and immigrated to America in 1749. She d. on Sept. 20, 1793 (FMY). Jacob and Salome had the following children:
  - Catharina Elisabeth, bapt. by RJL on Oct. 29, 1752, and spon. by Georg Rummel, Elisabeth Rohrbach, and Catharina Schedderon. She m. Georg Gutjahr.
  - Dau., b. about 1755, and m. Jacob Gartner at FMY on June 4, 1782.
  - Elisabeth, b. about 1757, and m. Johann Friedrich Stein of Nordhausen Thuringia at FMY on Dec. 9, 1783.
  - Georg Jacob, b. on Mar. 4, 1759, and bapt. at CLY on Mar. 18, 1759. He d. young.
- Georg, b. about 1737. He was taxed in Reading Township (now Adams Co.) in 1762. He m. Catharina, and had the following children:
  - Georg Jacob, b. on May 10, 1758, and bapt. at CLY on Aug. 13, 1758.
  - Johann Peter, bapt. by RJL on Nov. 29, 1761, and spon. by Jacob Hachelberger and Maria Barbara Spaarin.
  - Johan Heinrich, bapt. by RJL on Apr. 15, 1764, and spon. by Johan Heinrich and Anna Margaretha Seel.
- Frederick, b. about 1744, and m. Elisabeth, dau. of Michael Geisselman (see entry in Shrewsbury section), and widow of Adam Uhler (see entry in Manchester section), at STR on Apr. 4, 1771. He was taxed in York Township in 1779. They had the following children:
  - Johan Michael, b. on Jan. 15, 1772, bapt. at FRI on Apr. 12, 1772, and spon. by Michael and Wilhelmina Margaretha Geisselman.

- Elisabeth, b. on Nov. 4, 1774, bapt. at TLY on Nov. 27, 1774, and spon. by Michael Geisselman and wife.

Saltzgeber - Dieterich had his will written in Paradise Township on July 18, 1762, and probated on Nov. 9, 1762. He m. Anna Margaretha. After his death, Anna Margaretha m. Johan Heinrich Herring (see entry). They had the following children:
- Margaret, b. about 1734, and m. Abraham Gockelert at STM on Apr. 23, 1754.
- Jacob, b. about 1740, and m. Margaretha, dau. of Andreas Gantsert (see entry), at STR on May 3, 1763. They had the following children:
  - Samuel, b. on Apr. 3, 1764, bapt. at STR on June 11, 1764, and spon. by Samuel and Catharina Adam.
  - Barbara, b. in Mar. 1766, bapt. at STR on June 22, 1766, and spon. by Jacob and Barbara Schedderon.
- Engel Elisabeth, b. on Apr. 6, 1742, bapt. at CLY on May 18, 1742, and spon. by Engel Elisabeth Diehl. She m. Lawrence Switzgood about 1764.
- Maria Agnes, b. about 1744, and m. Philip Hommon about 1765.
- Johan Casper, b. on Feb. 28, 1747, bapt. at CLY on June 28, 1747, and spon. by Caspar Williard and wife. He m. Catharina, dau. of John Sunday.
- Susanna, b. about 1749.
- Johan Peter, b. on Mar. 8, 1751, and bapt. at CLY on Sept. 1, 1751. He was not mentioned in the will.
- Maria Margaretha, b. on Apr. 25, 1754, bapt. at CLY on Sept. 1, 1754, and spon. by Andreas and Margaret Rudisill and Maria Margaretha Bender.

Schaffer - Friederich was b. on Oct. 1, 1713, and d. in Paradise Township on Jan. 15, 1776 (bur. in Holschwamm cemetery). He m. Catharina. After his death, she m. Henrich Wehler in 1776. He was taxed in Paradise Township in 1762, and 1769. They had the following children:
- Philip, b. about 1745, and was taxed in Paradise Township in 1769 and 1779. He m. Anna Elisabeth.
- Friedrich, b. on June 15, 1747, and d. in Dover Township on June 15, 1800. He m. Susanna. She was b. on Jan. 10, 1747, and d. in Dover Township on Jan. 19, 1817. They are bur. in Holschwamm cemetery in Paradise Township. He was residing in Menallen Township (now Adams Co.) in 1776, and served in the Revolutionary War from that Township in 1780. He was taxed with 4 males and 6 females in Paradise Township in 1783, and was the

tax collector for Paradise Township in 1788. In 1790, he was residing in Dover Township.
- Margaretha, b. about 1749, and m. Leonhard, son of Leonhard Flohr (see entry).
- Gertrude, b. about 1751, and m. Andreas, son of Andreas Frederick.

Schaffer - Georg Lewis was b. on July 9, 1755, and d. in Dover Township on June 27, 1829. He m. Catharina. She was b. on Aug. 9, 1760, and d. in Dover Township on Dec. 19, 1845. They are bur. in STR cemetery. They had the following children:
- Johannes, b. on Jan. 14, 1781, and d. in Dover Township on Jan. 17, 1859. He m. Margaretha about 1807, and Rebecca about 1812. Rebecca d. on Aug. 18, 1864, aged 79 years, 3 months, and 3 days. Johannes and Rebecca are bur. in STR cemetery.
- Elisabeth, b. about 1783, and m. Andreas, son of Peter Streher (see entry).
- Jacob, b. on Dec. 23, 1790, bapt. at STR on Feb. 15, 1791, and spon. by Jacob Spahr. He was not mentioned in his father's will.
- David, b. on Aug. 2, 1793, bapt. at STR on Sept. 15, 1793, and spon. by Andreas and Elisabeth Stauch. He was not mentioned in his father's will.
- Cattrine, b. on Feb. 16, 1799, bapt. at STR on Mar. 31, 1799, and spon. by ____ Breneman. She was not mentioned in her father's will.

Schaffer - Johannes was taxed in 1762. He was Constable in 1766, and overseer of the poor in 1769. During the Revolution, he was a 1st Lieutenant of the 3rd Company, 1st Battalion in 1777/78. He was appointed guardian of Johan Nicholas Schaffer's (of York Town) son, John on May 28, 1779. He m. Elisabeth, and had the following children:
- Tobias, bapt. by RJL on May 6, 1759, and spon. by Georg Jacob Schaffer and Margaretha Schaffer. During the Revolutionary War, he was a Private in Captain Samuel Farra's Company, 5th Battalion, in 1776/77.
- Anna Barbara, bapt. at STR on May 11, 1760, and spon. by Jacob and Anna Barbara Schaffer.
- Elisabetha, bapt. at STR on July 11, 1762, and spon. by Johan Nicholas and Elisabeth Schaffer.
- Maria Margaretha, bapt. at STR on Aug. 7, 1763, and spon. by Michael and Maria Margaretha Ammann.
- Maria Margaretha, bapt. at STR on Sept. 2, 1764, and spon. by Georg Jacob and Maria Barbara Schaffer.
- Maria Catharina, bapt. at STR on Jan. 16, 1767, and spon. by Johan Adam and Margaretha Fissel.

160   EARLY GERMAN SETTLERS OF YORK CO., PA

- Michael, bapt. at STR on Apr. 9, 1769, and spon. by Georg Jacob and Barbara Schaffer.
- Maria Eva, bapt. at STR on July 29, 1770, and spon. by Johan Adam and Anna Margaretha Fissel.

Schedderon - Johan Heinrich was taxed in 1762. His will was written in Shrewsbury Township on Oct. 28, 1771, and probated on Jan. 18, 1772. He m. Anna Maria Herbach. They had the following children:
- Maria Catharina, b. in Otterberg, Germany, about Feb. 1729/30. She m. Peter Gutling (see entry in Manchester section).
- Anna, b. about 1732.
- Leonhard, b. about 1734. He was a blacksmith, and his probate inventory was filed in 1768. He m. Maria Elisabetha, and had the following children:
  - Johan Heinrich, bapt. by RJL on July 28, 1756, and spon. by Heinrich and Anna Maria Schedderon.
  - David, bapt. by RJL on Apr. 15, 1759, and spon. by Ludwig and Sibilla Maria Rubel.
  - Maria Catharina, bapt. by RJL on Mar. 22, 1761, and spon. by Frederick and Maria Catharina Huber.
  - Maria Eva, bapt. at the Lower Bermudian Church in Adams Co. on June 12, 1763, and spon. by Abraham Schedderon and Anna Maria Burckhardt.
  - Maria Catharina, bapt. at STR on July 7, 1765, and spon. by Michael Welsch and Catharina Obbin.
- Casper, b. about 1738 was taxed in 1762. He m. Eva Elisabetha Bruegger, and had the following children:
  - Casparus, b. on Jan. 23, 1763, bapt. at TLY on Jan. 27, 1763, and spon. by Heinrich Schedderon and wife.
  - Johan Jacob, bapt. at STR on June 9, 1765, and spon. by Jacob Rachhauser and Magdalena Grossin.
  - Daniel, bapt. at STR on May 8, 1768, and spon. by Daniel and Anna Messerle.
  - Heinrich, bapt. at STR on May 19, 1771, and spon. by Jacob and Anna Margaretha May.
- Jacob, b. about 1740, and m. Anna Margaretha Barbara, dau. of Andreas Gansert (see entry). They had the following children:
  - Wilhelm, b. on Apr. 8, 1767, bapt. at STR on Apr. 19, 1767, and spon. by Andreas and Margaretha Gantzert.
  - Catharina, b. on Sept. 6, 1770, bapt. at STR on Oct. 14, 1770, and spon. by Mattheis and Catharina Gantzert.
  - Margaretha, b. on Nov. 26, 1772, bapt. at STR on Jan. 1, 1773, and spon. by Georg and Catharina Kann.
  - Elisabetha, bapt. at STR on Oct. 15, 1774, and spon. by Margaretha Gantzertin.

- Johannes, bapt. at STR on July 8, 1777, and spon. by Johannes Schedderon.
- Anna Maria, b. on July 25, 1784, bapt. at STR on Dec. 12, 1784, and spon. by Johannes and Elisabeth Schedderon.
- Johan Jacob, b. on July 7, 1787, bapt. at QUI on Sept. 20, 1789, and spon. by Jacob and Christina Wagner.
- Susanna, b. on Oct. 26, 1790, bapt. at Abbottstown Lutheran Church in Adams Co. on Jan. 2, 1790, and spon. by Margaret Lingfelder.
- Margaret, b. about 1742.
- Vronica, bapt. at STR on Apr. 28, 1746, and spon. by Friedrich and Vronica Bassler.

Schenck (Shank) - Henry was taxed in Dover Township in 1762, and was an exec. to the will of Michael Lohra in Dover Township in 1768. He is probably the Henry Shank/Schenck that was taxed in Codorus Township in 1779, and wrote his will in Codorus Township on Mar. 21, 1801 (it was probated on Nov. 18, 1805). Henry of Codorus Township had the following children:
- Michael.
- John.
- Maria Magdalena.
- Margaret.
- Henry.
- Freney, m. John Meyer.
- Barbara, m. John Hershey.
- Ann.
- Elisabeth.

Schettle - Johannes wrote his will on Apr. 15, 1771, and it was probated on May 15, 1771. He m. Barbara. They were sponsors to the baptism of Johan Adam Wild in 1747 (RJL). His will mentions a son-in-law, a son's two orphan children.

Schmidt - Johan Jacob m. Maria Catharina, dau. of Johan Adam and Anna Catharina Stein, in 1726. She was b. in Hahnlein, Darmstadtisch, Germany, in 1705, and d. in York Co., Dover Township, PA, in 1776 (?said to have come to America in 1751?). His will was written in Dover Township on June 22, 1773, probated on Nov. 1, 1773, and executed by Jacob Smith. Jacob Smith administered the estate of Anna Maria Smith in Dover Township on Nov. 17, 1755 (this was probably his mother). Jacob received a 200 acre warrant of land in Shrewsbury Township on Oct. 27, 1737. They had the following children:
- Johan Adam, b. about 1727. He m. Ursula before 1752, Anna Maria before 1756, and Maria Eva, dau. of Valentine and Maria Eva

(Stocker) Schultz, in Christ's Lutheran Church of York on Dec. 25, 1760 (Adam is listed as single on this record). Maria Eva was b. on Mar. 24, 1742, and bapt. at Christ's Lutheran Church of York on Apr. 7, 1742. Adam was taxed in Dover Township in 1762. He had the following children:
- Adam, b. about 1747. He has not been proven to be Adam's son. He m. Maria Salome, dau. of Oswald and Maria Salome Dubbs about 1768. Adam resided Manheim Township in 1783, and Codorus Township in 1790, with one male over sixteen, two males under sixteen, and seven females. Adam and Salome d. sometime after 1805.
- Frederick, b. on Feb. 2, 1752, and bapt. at Christ's Lutheran Church of York on Feb. 23, 1752.
- Anna Catharina, bapt. by Reverend Jacob Lischy on June 5, 1757, and spon. by Jacob and Magdalena Corel.
- Johan Peter, b. about 1733. He m. Margaretha, and d. in Shrewsbury Township in Dec. 1785. He received a land warrant in Shrewsbury Township for 50 acres on Feb. 18, 1753, and 100 acres on May 7, 1765. He was assessor for Shrewsbury Township in 1769, 1772, and 1773. He was constable in 1769, and overseer for the poor in 1772. He was a second Lieutenant in Captain Gideon Bausley's Company in 1776. He served on Apr. 5, 1778, and as a Private in the Second Company, 5th Battalion in 1780. He had a mill in Shrewsbury Township. They had the following children:
  - Andreas, b. about 1755, and m. Charlotte.
  - Adam, b. on Mar. 10, 1757. He was a Private in the 2nd Company, 5th Battalion, in 1780, and d. in Shrewsbury Township on Apr. 24, 1830. He m. Anna Maria about 1783 and Anna Magdalena about 1798. Anna Magdalena d. on Dec. 13, 1837 aged 76 years 8 months, and 5 days. He purchased 20 acres in Shrewsbury Township on July 21, 1790, 50 acres on Aug. 19, 1788, and 15 acres on July 5, 1811.
  - Eva Elisabetha, bapt. by Reverend Jacob Lischy on Apr. 6, 1760, and spon. by Helffrich and Eva Elisabetha Kramer. She m. Heinrich Schaffer at Trinity Lutheran Church on Sept. 8, 1785.
  - Anna Margaretha, bapt. by Reverend Jacob Lischy on July 18, 1762, and spon. by Michael and Elisabetha Hooman. She m. Johan Georg Fehr/Faehr at TLY on July 29, 1782.
- Johannes, b. about 1735. He m. Anna Margaretha about 1758 and Catharina before 1763. He had the following children in Dover Township:
  - Maria Catharina, b. on Nov. 12, 1759, bapt. at Christ's Lutheran on Feb. 24, 1760, and spon. by her grandparents, Jacob and Maria Catharina Schmidt.

- Maria Eva, b. on Nov. 2, 1761, and bapt. at Christ's Lutheran on Nov. 29, 1761.
- Maria Magdalena, bapt. at Strayer's by Reverend Jacob Lischy on Jan. 22, 1763, and spon. by Adam and Maria Magdalena Diehl.
- Margaret Cunigunda, b. about 1737. She was a sponsor to a baptism in Dover Township in 1752, and m. Frederick Meyer/Mayer in Strayer's Lutheran Church on Nov. 28, 1758 (see entry).
- Johann Jacob, b. on May 4, 1743, bapt. at Trinity Lutheran Church in Lancaster Co., Lancaster, PA, on May 22, 1743, and spon. by Peter Dussing and Christina Grossmannin. He m. Margaretha, dau. of Jacob Schodder, at Strayer's Lutheran Church on Apr. 14, 1765, and d. in Dover Township in Mar. 1794. His will was written on Feb. 27, 1794, and probated on Mar. 17, 1794. In 1779, Jacob was supervisor of highways, and in 1782, was tax collector for Dover Township. In 1783, he had 240 acres, 4 horses, 5 cattle, 7 sheep, 1 still, 1 house, 1 barn, 6 males, and 6 females in his possession. Jacob and Margaretha had the following children:
- Elisabetha, b. about 1766.
- Anna Margaretha, b. on Mar. 7, 1767, bapt. at Strayer's on Apr. 5, 1767, and spon. by Frederick and Margaretha Majer.
- Adam, b. about 1768, and was a yeoman in Dover Township on Sept. 28, 1796, when he received his legacy from his father's will. Adam m. Christina, and resided in Paradise Township, where he deeded land he purchased on Apr. 20, 1796 to John Grob on Apr. 6, 1797.
- Barbara, b. about 1770.
- Anna Catharina, b. on Jan. 18, 1773, bapt. at Strayer's on Jan. 20, 1773, and spon. by Jacob Schnellbecker and wife.
- Johannes, b. on Oct. 8/12, 1774, bapt. at Strayer's on Nov. 18, 1774, and spon. by Johan Rudrauf and wife.
- Juliana, b. about 1776, and mentioned as a very sickly child in 1794.
- Jacob, b. in 1788, and chose John Henson as his guardian on Sept. 21, 1802.

Seib - Johan Carl was taxed in 1762. He was b. to Heinrich Seip (a miller at Untergimbern), in 1705, and immigrated to America on the ship *Samuel* on Aug. 11, 1732. He moved to York Co., Conewago Township, in 1749, and had a farm of 148 acres. He d. in 1768, and his probate inventory was filed in Dover Township in 1768. His will was written on Feb. 10, 1763, and probated on Mar. 28, 1768. He m. Anna Catharina (b.1703), widow of Georg Michael Peter Beller, at Obergimpern, Germany, on Nov. 30, 1728, and Judith before 1750. He had the following children (BNK):

- Maria Barbara, bapt. at Obergimpern in Apr. 1729.
- Maria Anna, b. on June 25, 1730.
- Georg Michael, b. about 1732, and d. before 1797.
- Anna Elisabeth, b. on June 23, 1734, and bapt. at New Holland Lutheran Church in Lancaster Co. She m. Henrich Six.
- Johan Leonhardt, b. on Apr. 26, 1736, and bapt. at New Holland Lutheran Church in Lancaster Co. He was not mentioned in the will.
- Johan Carl, b. on Feb. 13, 1738, and bapt. at New Holland Lutheran Church in Lancaster Co.
- Anna Dorothea, b. on June 7, 1739, and bapt. at New Holland Lutheran Church in Lancaster Co. She m. Christian Miller.
- Johanna, b. about 1741, and m. Wendel Seitz. He d. before 1768.
- Johan Peter, b. on Aug. 19, 1744, and bapt. at New Holland Lutheran Church in Lancaster Co. He was not mentioned in the will.
- Henrich, b. about 1746.
- Andreas, b. about 1748, and m. Eva Elisabeth, dau. of Georg Quickel (see entry). His probate inventory was filed in Dover Township in 1794. She d. on Sept. 27, 1822. He served in the Revolutionary War in 1781.
- Emanuel, b. on June 11, 1751, and bapt. at CLY on July 28, 1751. He m. Dorothea, dau. of Georg Quickel (see entry), and d. in 1824. She d. in 1830. He had 130 acres in Conewago Township.
- Philip Leonard, b. on Sept. 11, 1753, and bapt. at CLY on Jan. 14, 1754. He m. Rosina Hoffman.
- Tobias, b. on Apr. 10, 1756, and bapt. at CLY on June 6, 1756. He m. Anna Maria, dau. of Nicholas Wild (see entry in Manchester section).
- Christopher, b. on Mar. 25, 1758, and bapt. at CLY on Mar. 25, 1758. He m. Anna Maria.
- Anna Barbara, b. on Feb. 25, 1761, and bapt. at CLY on Apr. 30, 1761.
- Joseph, b. in 1763 (unnamed and unbaptized in his father's will), and m. Christina, son of Melchior Benedick (see entry).

Seifert - Johann Adam was taxed in 1762. He was b. to Johann Michael and Susanna (Hessenduer) Seiffert in Schwaigern, Wurttemberg, Germany, on May 23, 1723 (BNK). He immigrated to America on the ship *Fane* on Oct. 17, 1749. He m. Maria Elisabetha, dau. of Johann Frederich Schmid in Schwaigern on July 9, 1748, and Anna Maria Schwartzwaelder at St. Michael's Zion Lutheran Church in Philadelphia, PA, on Oct. 28, 1752. Anna Maria was b. in 1731. Her will was written in Dover Township on Feb. 15, 1800, and probated on July 30, 1805. He was naturalized on May 13, 1770. Johan Adam d. in York

Co., Dover Township, PA, on Dec. 28, 1787, and is bur. at Strayer's cemetery. He had the following children:
- Christina Barbara, b. in Schwaigern on Apr. 11, 1749, and d. en route to America in 1749.
- Johann Michael, b. on Sept. 26, 1753, and bapt. at St. Michael's Zion in Philadelphia on Nov. 18, 1753. He m. Maria Magdalena, dau. of Nicholas Wild (see entry in Manchester section). He d. in Washington Co., Adams Township, OH, in 1818. He had the following children (Jacob and Joseph (both went by Seifert) were illegitimate sons by his relationship with Elisabeth Straely (she resided in Washington Co., Adams Township, OH, in 1820)):
  - Johann Adam, b. on Nov. 20, 1774, and bapt. at CLY on Dec. 11, 1774. He m. Anna Maria Lauer. He d. in Dover Township in 1821, and is bur. in STR cemetery.
  - Catharina, b. on Mar. 25, 1776, bapt. at STR on Apr. 21, 1776, and spon. by Adam and Maria Seifert. She m. Joseph Buatt/Bower, and resided in Louisiana in 1818.
  - Georg Michael, b. on Aug. 14, 1777, bapt. at STR on Sept. 14, 1777, and spon. by Herman and Magdalena Hellman. He resided in Cumberland Co., PA, in 1818. He m. Anna Maria Linebaugh.
  - Barbara, bapt. at STR on Oct. 23, 1779, and spon. by Barbara Hanssin.
  - Maria Elisabeth, b. on Dec. 21, 1781, bapt. at STR, and spon. by Valentine and Maria Elisabeth Wild.
  - Johannes, b. on Dec. 22, 1783, bapt. at STR on Mar. 14, 1791, and spon. by Andreas and Catharina Honz. He m. Anna Laur.
  - Philip, b. on Mar. 22, 1787, bapt. at STR on Nov. 14, 1791, and spon. by Philip and Anna Herring.
  - Maria, b. about 1789.
  - Johann Georg, b. on Oct. 13, 1791, bapt. at STR on Mar. 14, 1791, and spon. by Georg and Catharina Fliger. He m. Mary Oberlin, and moved to Fairfield Co., Berne Township, OH, about 1820.
  - Susanna, b. on Nov. 20, 1794, and bapt. at CLY on Feb. 14, 1795.
  - Daniel, b. on Dec. 28, 1798, bapt. at STR on Apr. 9, 1798, and spon. by Jacob and Anna Maria Zin.
  - Jacob, b. in 1801. He was denied from receiving anything from his father's estate, but purchased a gun at the auction of his father's estate.
  - Joseph, b. in 1802. He was denied anything from his father's estate.

<u>Seifert</u> - Georg, m. Maria Margaretha about 1773, and had the following children:

- Johann Georg, b. on Mar. 18, 1774, bapt. at STR, and spon. by Johann Georg and Barbara Stouch.
- Johannes, b. on Dec. 17, 176, bapt. at STR on Jan. 13, 1777, and spon. by Georg and Maria Barbara Stouch.
- Samuel, b. on Jan. 17, 1779, bapt. at STR, and spon. by Georg and Barbara Stouch.

Seifert - Peter, b. about 1755, and m. Barbara about 1775, and he may be the Johan Peter that m. Anna Maria about 1791. Peter and Barbara had the following children:
- Herman, b. on Dec. 17, 1775, bapt. at STR on Dec. 31, 1775, and spon. by Herman and Magdalena Hellman.
- Johan Peter and Anna Maria had the following children:
  - Johannes, b. on May 18, 1792, bapt. at STR on July 23, 1792, and spon. by Anna Maria Michlin.
  - Anna Maria, b. on Apr. 15, 1794, bapt. at STR on Apr. 27, 1794, and spon. by Anna Maria Mezlerin.
  - Cattrina, b. on Oct. 20, 1795, bapt. at STR on Nov. 29, 1795, and spon. by Anna Maria Rahauserin.

Sohn - Johan Georg, son of Nicholas a patrician and magistrate of Osweiler, Hanau Alsace, and Anna Magdalena (Huber), Sohn, was b. on July 18, 1694. He traveled in Hungary for a time, and then m. Maria Barbara, dau. of Jacob Muller. He was a baker in York Township. In Oct. 1752, he was accused of keeping a public house/house of entertainment. He said he sold off his "living in the country" he had for nine years for an easier living in his old age. He said his bakery business was not doing well, because the town of York was so new, and he requested a license to keep a full tavern. His will was written in York on Jan. 2, 1761, and probated on Jan. 8, 1761 (execs. were John Sohn and George Keintz). After Barbara's death, he m. Catharina, dau. of Johan Peter and Salome (Apfler) Hornig, and widow of Johann Bauer, on Dec. 24, 1751. Her first husband d. in 1746, and in 1751, she immigrated to America with her three children. She was b. in Collmar, Alsace, on July 21, 1715, and d. from sphacelus and gangrene on July 2, 1759 (CLY). Georg d. on Jan. 6, 1761 (CLY). Georg and Barbara had the following children (10 total):
- Margaretha, b. about 1726. She was a sponsor to the baptism of Maria Elisabeth Pens in 1746 (RJL).
- Anna Catharina, b. about 1735. She was a sponsor to the baptism of Anna Catharina Gerot in 1755 (RJL).
- John, b. about 1728, and was taxed in Dover Township in 1762. He m. Margareth. They were sponsors to the baptism of Anna Maria Uly in 1750 (RJL).
- Jacob, b. about 1738.

- Catharina Sophia, b. on May 11, 1740, and bapt. at CLY on May 24, 1740. She was not mentioned in the will.
- Maria Elisabeth, b. on Mar. 19, 1741, and bapt. at CLY on May 10, 1742.

Sowder - Adam was taxed in 1762.

Sowder - Casper was taxed in 1762.

Spaar - Hans Georg d. in Altenburg, Germany, before 1739. He had the following children (see BNK and *Spahr Family History* by Herman G. Spahr (1994)):
- Johan Georg, b. on Dec. 11, 1699, m. Maria Catharina, dau. of Georg Michael and Anna Maria Kauffman, in 1723 (?). She was b. in Waldenburg, Hohenlohe, Bavaria, on Jan. 30, 1703 (?), and d. between 1763 and 1776. They immigrated to America from Altenberg on Oct. 23, 1740 (1737). They had the following children:
  - Casper, b. about 1741, and was taxed in 1762. He m. Anna Margaretha, and had the following children (recorded at STR):
    - Maria Barbara, b. on Sept. 17, 1763, bapt. on Nov. 6, 1763, and spon. by Johannes Welsh and Maria Barbara Peitzel.
    - Johan Casper, b. on Oct. 12, 1765, bapt. on Dec. 26, 1765, and spon. by Philip and Dorothea Spaar.
    - Johan Frederick, b. on Dec. 1, 1767, bapt. on Feb. 27, 1768, and spon. by Johannes and Maria Elisabetha Herbach.
    - Johan Jacob, b. on Nov. 11, 1769, bapt. on Jan. 1, 1770, and spon. by Casper and Elisabetha Barbara Lampert.
    - Johan Georg, bapt. on Apr. 20, 1772, and spon. by Johan Georg and Maria Catharina Spaar.
  - Johannes, b. about 1743, and m. Eva Elisabetha, dau. of Peter Bartemess (see entry) on Oct. 16, 1764, and had the following children (recorded at STR):
    - Johan, b. on Oct. 1, 1765, bapt. on Dec. 26, 1765, and spon. by Georg and Catharina Spaar.
    - Johan Georg, b. in 1767, and spon. by Jacob and Maria Margaretha Rahauser.
    - Benjamin, bapt. on Oct. 23, 1768, and spon. by Philip Adam and Dorothea Spaar.
    - Catharina Elisabetha, bapt. on July 12, 1776.
  - Philip Adam, b. about 1745. He m. Dorothea, dau. of Joseph Klopfer (see entry), at STR on Mar. 24, 1765. They had the following children (recorded at STR):
    - Maria Catharina, b. on Feb. 13, 1766, bapt. on Mar. 30, 1766, and spon. by Johan Georg and Maria Catharina Spaar.

- Johan Carl, b. on Oct. 16, 1767, bapt. on Nov. 8, 1767, and spon. by Carl and Eva Margaretha Albert.
- Philip, b. on Mar. 9, 1769, bapt. on Apr. 1, 1769, and spon. by Johan Casper and Anna Margaretha Spaar.
- Christina, b. on Jan. 19, 1771, bapt. on Mar. 6, 1771, and spon. by Jacob and Anna Margaretha Maj.
- Peter, b. on May 20, 1780, and bapt. on June 9, 1780.
- Susanna, b. on Apr. 1, 1782, and bapt. on Apr. 28, 1782.
- David, b. on Dec. 4, 1788, and bapt. on Jan. 1, 1789.

- Johan Georg, b. about 1748, and m. Maria Barbara, dau. of Johannes Rudisill (see entry in Manchester section), on Nov. 8, 1768. They had the following children (recorded at STR):
  - Johan, b. on Nov. 17, 1769, bapt. on Jan. 1, 1770, and spon. by Michael Spaar, Jr.
  - Johan Georg, b. on June 27, 1771, bapt. on July 28, 1771, and spon. by Jacob and Anna Margaretha Majer.
  - Johannes, b. on Sept. 9, 1773, bapt. on Oct. 31, 1773, and spon. by Johannes and Anna Catharina Rudisill.
  - Elisabetha, b. on Apr. 25, 1782, bapt. on June 29, 1782, and spon. by Frederick and Elisabetha Spaar.
  - Susanna, b. on Feb. 9, 1785, bapt. on Mar. 25, 1785, and spon. by Elisabeth Lampert.

- Veronica Barbara, b. on Aug. 17, 1750, and bapt. at CLY on Oct. 7, 1750.
- Johan Peter, b. on Feb. 22, 1753, and bapt. at CLY on May 20, 1753.
- Johan Michael was taxed in 1762. He m. Maria Barbara (a Catholic), dau. of Jacob Mohr of Hochhausen on the Tauber, at Sinsheim on Nov. 23, 1739, and immigrated to America on the ship *Robert and Alice* in 1743. He was naturalized on May 20, 1769. His will was written in Dover Township on Nov. 22, 1777, and probated on May 23, 1778. They had the following children:
  - Maria Barbara, bapt. at the Lower Bermudian Church on Mar. 19, 1745, and spon. by Antony and Maria Barbara Keller. She was not mentioned in the will.
  - Johan Frederick, b. on Nov. 8, 1746, and bapt. at CLY on Apr. 9, 1749. He m. Barbara Elisabetha, and had the following children (recorded at STR):
    - Anna Maria, b. on June 3, 1773, bapt. on July 11, 1773, and spon. by Barbara Gauch and Philip Gauch.
    - Johannes, b. on Aug. 14, 1775, bapt. on Oct. 8, 1774, and spon. by Philip and Christina Gauch.
    - Frederick, b. on Mar. 1, 1776, bapt. on Apr. 14, 1776, and spon. by Casper and Elisabetha Lampert.

- Johan Peter, b. on Jan. 8, 1778, bapt. on Apr. 5, 1778, and spon. by Velte and Catharina Dorothea Floor.
- Susanna, b. on Mar. 11, 1780, bapt. on May 14, 1780, and spon. by Velte and Catharina Floor.
- Samuel, b. on Feb. 16, 1782, bapt. on Mar. 17, 1782, and spon. by Velde and Catharina Floor.
- Johan Jacob, b. on Sept. 29, 1784, bapt. on Apr. 10, 1784, and spon. by Adam and Dorothea Spaar.
- Eve Fronica, b. about 1749, and m. Johan Martin, son of Jacob Oberdier (see entry), at STR on Oct. 20, 1771.
- Peter, b. about 1755, and m. Elisabeth about 1776.
- Elisabeth, b. about 1759, and m. Ludwig Schindel at TLY on Mar. 27, 1781.
- Maria Catharina, b. on Aug. 4, 1764, bapt. at STR on Oct. 9, 1764, and spon. by Georg and Catharina Spaar.

Spiess - Johan Ludwig was taxed in 1762, and received a warrant for 150 acres on July 6, 1763, that was surveyed to his heirs as 261.107 acres on July 18, 1799. His probate inventory was filed in Dover Township in 1780, but mentions Montgomery Co., MD (perhaps he was living, or visiting there at the time of his death). His will was written on Sept. 11, 1779, and probated on Jan. 23, 1780. He m. Veronica Gertraut, and Christina about 1765. He had the following children:
- Maria Eva, b. about 1744, and m. Ludwig Jost.
- Johannes Peter, b. about 1746. He was a sponsor to the baptism of Johan Wilhelm Bartemess at STR in 1762. His will was written in Dover Township on Mar. 26, 1785, and probated on Apr. 9, 1785. He m. Susanna.
- Christina, b. about 1748, and m. Engelbrecht Hertzog at STR on Aug. 27, 1769.
- Anna Elisabeth, b. on Sept. 6, 1751, and bapt. at CLY on Oct. 6, 1751. She m. Michael Herr at STR on Aug. 26, 1770. He was taxed in Manheim Township in 1779.
- Catharina, b. about 1753.
- Sophia Elisabeth, bapt. by RJL on June 22, 1755, and spon. by Peter and Elisabeth Kronbach.
- Friedrich, b. about 1757, and m. Barbara about 1782.
- Johann Ludwig, b. on July 20, 1763, bapt. at STR on Aug. 14, 1763, and spon. by Adam and Dorothea Bartmess. He m. Barbara about 1784.
- Anna Maria, b. about 1766, and was a minor in 1779.

Spitsberger - Abram was taxed in 1762.

Spodley - Frederick was taxed in 1762.

Stauedemeyer - Jacob m. Maria Dorothea. They moved to Rockingham Co., VA, between 1778 and 1784, and had the following children:
- Margaretha, b. about 1770, and was a sponsor to a baptism in 1790.
- Johan Christian, b. on Feb. 17, 1772, bapt. at Strayer's on May 28, 1772, and spon. by Christian Erek.
- Maria Magdalena, b. on Apr. 19, 1773, bapt. at Strayer's on Aug. 8, 1773, and spon. by Adam and Maria Magdalena Diel
- Bernhardt, b. in York Co., Dover Township, PA, on Aug. 19, 1774, bapt. at Strayer's Lutheran Church on Oct. 23, 1774, and spon. by Bernhardt and Ursula Mueller. He m. Mary, dau. of Georg and Elisabeth Ehrhardt in Rockingham Co. in 1798.
- Elisabeth, b. in York Co., Dover Township, PA, on Feb. 16, 1776, bapt. at Strayer's on Feb. 25, 1776, and spon. by Bernhardt and Ursula Mueller. She m. Heinrich, son of Georg and Elisabeth Ehrhardt in Rockingham Co. on June 9, 1801. He d. in Rockingham Co. on May 6, 1851.
- Maria Dorothea, b. on Nov. 30, 1778, bapt. at Strayer's on Dec. 25, 1778, and spon. by Anna Maria Diellin.
- Catharine, b. about 1780, and was a sponsor to a baptism in 1800.
- John, b. about 1782, and m. Elizabeth.
- Maria, b. on Jan. 15, 1784, bapt. at Rader's Lutheran Church in Rockingham Co., VA, in 1784, and spon. by John and Anna Roller.
- Christian, b. on Feb. 23, 1786, bapt. at Rader's Lutheran Church in Rockingham Co., VA, on May 20, 1796, and spon. by his parents.

Stouch - Johan Georg m. Anna Maria, and resided in Dettenhausen, Beblinger, Wurtemburg. They had the following sons:
- Johan Georg was b. on Oct. 14, 1719. He m. Anna Margaretha, dau. of Johann Georg and Agnes Baist, in 1741, and Anna Maria Christina, dau. of Johan Georg and Barbara Baumann, in 1753. Johan Georg Baumann was a vinedresser. Anna Maria was b. in Beblingen on July 4, 1717. Christina was b. in Hohenberg, Wurtemberg, on Dec. 22, 1719, and came to America with her parents in 1752. She d. on Jan. 7, 1772. He was b. in Dettenhausen of Beblingen Wurtemberg. Georg Stouch immigrated to America in 1752, and had the following children:
  - Maria Jacobina, b. on Feb. 9, 1745, and bapt. by Johan Georg Waldbauer and Maria Jacobina, dau. of Johan Nicolaus Reiber. She m. Peter Streher (see entry).
  - Johan Georg, b. in 1747, and d. young.
  - Maria Barbara, b. on July 2, 1749, and d. young.
  - Johan Georg, b. on June 21, 1751. He m. Anna Barbara Berner, widow of Heinrich Richter (see entry), on Feb. 18, 1772. His probate inventory was filed in Dover Township in 1803, and hers

was filed in 1824. They had the following children (recorded at STR):
- Johannes, b. on Mar. 5, 1773, bapt. on Mar. 7, 1773, and spon. by Leonhardt Stouch.
- Johan Frederick, b. on July 29 (20), 1774, bapt. on July 31, 1774, and spon. by Jacob and Margaretha Weigel.
- Christina, b. on Jan. 15, 1776, bapt. on Jan. 28, 1776, and spon. by Johan Peter and Jacobina Streher.
- Anna Elisabetha, b. on Dec. 23, 1777, and spon. by Daniel and Susanna Messerle.
- Johan Peter, b. on Jan. 1, 1780, and spon. by Peter and Jacobina Streher.
- Leonhard, b. in Mar. 1782, and spon. by Leonhard and Catharina Floor.
- Henrich, b. on Apr. 24, 1783, bapt. on June 21, 1783, and spon. by Peter and Jacobina Streher.
- Catharina, b. on Aug. 24, 1785, and spon. by Henrich and Agnes Ottinger.
- Johan Leonard, b. about 1754.
- Johan Andreas, b. about 1756.
- Johan Jacob, b. about 1758.
- Gottfried was b. at Grauenstatten on Oct. 20, 1724. He m. Anna Maria, dau. of Johan Jacob Bartel, in 1751, and Charlotta, dau. of Friedrich and Christina Kessler, in 1754. Anna Maria was b. in Rudolsheim, and d. en route to America in 1752. Charlotta was b. in Hanau Alt Cassel on Dec. 25, 1730, and immigrated to America in 1754. Gottfried immigrated to America with his bro. in 1752. His will was written in Dover Township on Dec. 18, 1792, and probated on Feb. 15, 1793. He had the following children (see records of STR):
- Johan Georg, b. in 1751/2, and d. en route to America in 1752.
- Elisabeth, b. on Nov. 17, 1759.
- Johannes, b. on Jan. 25, 1762.
- Philippina, b. on May 18, 1764, and spon. by Philip Adam Spaar and Jacobina Stouch.
- Susanna, b. on Mar. 3, 1766, bapt. at on Mar. 30, 1766, and spon. by Peter and Susanna Brunner.
- Georg Frederich, b. on Apr. 7, 1768, bapt. on May 22, 1768, and spon. by Philip Adam and Dorothea Spaar.
- Johan Peter, b. on June 5, 1774, bapt. on July 2, 1774, and spon. by Peter and Anna Maria Brunner.

Streher - Johan Peter was b. in Starkenburg Sponheim, Germany, on June 22, 1718. He immigrated to America on the ship *Patience* on Sept. 9, 1751. He had 100 acres in Dover Township. On Sept. 22/Dec.

6, 1760, he purchased land from Henry Zauck of Manheim Township. His will was written on Aug. 28, 1793, and probated on July 12, 1794. He m. Anna Barbara Burghart, widow of Johan Nicholas Hentz. Nicholas d. in 1737, leaving 4 children. Anna Barbara d. in 1764. Maria Jacobina, dau. of Georg Stouch (see entry), on Aug. 19, 1766. Letters of administration were grated for Jacobina in 1802. On May 30, 1757, he was first on the list to donate money to build Salem Lutheran Church (now known as Strayer's after this family). Peter had the following children (recorded at STR):
- Johan Nicholas, b. about 1740, and resided in Dover Township in 1790.
- Johan Matthias, b. about 1742.
- Johan Peter, b. about 1744, and d. young.
- Adam, b. about 1746, m. Maria Catharina, and was a sponsor to the baptism of Magdalena Streher in 1774.
- Johan Jacob, b. on Aug. 24, 1753, and bapt. at CLY on Sept. 23, 1753. He m. Catharina Elisabeth, dau. of Georg Adam Gossler (see entry), and d. in Rockingham Co., VA, in 1854. He served in the Revolutionary War, and is bur. in Hopewell cemetery.
- Anna Catharina, b. in 1755, m. Lorentz, son of Johannes and Maria Magdalena Beitzel (1747-1818) (see entry), and d. in 1825.
- Barbara, b. on June 30, 1767, bapt. on July 19, 1767, and spon. by Georg and Christina Stouch. She m. Adam, son of Georg Hoover (see entry).
- Johan Peter, b. on Nov. 11, 1768, bapt. on Dec. 26, 1768, and spon. by Johan Jacob and Anna Maria Werner. He m. Anna Maria (1773-1850), dau. of Johan Frederick Spaar (see entry). Peter d. in Dover Township in 1855.
- Anna Margaretha, b. on Dec. 7, 1770, bapt. on Dec. 25, 1770, and spon. by Jacob and Anna Margaretha Majer. She m. Georg, son of Georg Hoover (see entry).
- Johannes, b. on Apr. 2, 1773, bapt. on Apr. 18, 1773, and spon. by Johan Georg and Anna Barbara Stouch. He m. Elisabeth Gross.
- Magdalena, b. on Oct. 15, 1774, bapt. on Nov. 6, 1774, and spon. by Adam and Maria Catharina Streher. She m. Jacob Weigel, Jr. (see entry in Manchester section).
- Anna Maria, b. on Dec. 31, 1776, bapt. on Jan. 26, 1777, and spon. by Peter and Susanna Jeki. She m. Peter Oberdier.
- Georg, b. on Mar. 7, 1779, bapt. on Mar. 28, 1780, and spon. by Georg Stouch.
- Andreas, b. on May 18, 1781, bapt. on June 3, 1781, and spon. by Johan Philip and Anna Maria Wentz. His will was written in Dover Township on Mar. 5, 1856, and probated on Mar. 5, 1865. He d. before May 30, 1859. He m. Elisabeth, dau. of Georg Schaffer (see entry).

- Elisabetha, b. on Jan. 27, 1786, bapt. on Jan. 29, 1786, and spon. by Barbara Hanse. She m. Michael Herman.
- Eva Catharina, b. on Jan. 27, 1786, bapt. on Jan. 29, 1786, and spon. by Catharina Hauss.
- Eva, b. on May 31, 1788, bapt. on June 13, 1789, and spon. by Peter and Margaretha Trein. She m. Joseph Flohr, and d. in 1868.
- Daniel, b. in 1792.

Strehly (Straley) - Stephen was taxed in 1779. He was b. on May 1, 1751, and d. in Dover Township on July 9, 1824. He m. Barbary. She was b. on Dec. 25, 1751, and d. on Apr. 14, 1834. They are bur. in STR cemetery. During the Revolutionary War, he served in Sharp's Company 3rd Foot Battalion from 1786 to 1788. They had the following children (see Genealogy of the Straley Family by Grace Rhoads Straley Swartz (1987)):
- George, b. on Sept. 24, 1773, m. Mary, dau. of Jost and Maria Heiner, and d. in Paradise Township on Feb. 16, 1851. She was b. on Sept. 11, 1774, and d. on Feb. 6, 1858. They are bur. in Holtzschwamm cemetery.
- John, b. about 1775.
- Dau., b. about 1777, and m. Philip Ebit/Ebert.
- Jacob, b. in June 1783, m. Rebecca, and d. on July 23, 1830. She was b. on Aug. 29, 1794, and d. on Apr. 10, 1866.
- Elisabeth, b. about 1785, and m. Adam Kunckle in York Co. on Aug. 9, 1806.
- Catharine, b. in 1788, m. Abraham Lanchert, and d. on Jan. 4, 1872. He was b. on Dec. 20, 1784, and d. on Oct. 13, 1865. They are bur. in STR cemetery.
- Maria Magdalena, b. on Oct. 13, 1790, m. Daniel Seidedstricker, and d. on Feb. 29, 1866. He was b. on Aug. 20, 1780, and d. on Nov. 12, 1852. They are bur. at STR cemetery.
- Philip, b. on Feb. 24, 1793, m. Rebecca, dau. of Philip Baesel, and d. on Oct. 15, 1878. She was b. on Feb. 3, 1797, and d. on Nov. 25, 1863. They are bur. in STR cemetery.

Swartz - Mathias was taxed in 1762, and was overseer of the poor in 1772. During the Revolution, he was a Private in the 3rd Company, 1st Battalion, in 1778. He m. Maria Dorothea, and had the following children:
- Anna Catharina, b. on Mar. 24, 1765, bapt. at STR on Apr. 28, 1765, and spon. by Johan Martin and Anna Catharina Weigel.
- Anna Maria, b. on Feb. 7, 1767, bapt. at STR on Apr. 6, 1767, and spon. by Tobias and Magdalena Frey.
- Matheis, b. on Feb. 5, 1769, bapt. at STR on Mar. 24, 1769, and spon. by Johan Gerog Richter and Barbara Reissinger.

- Johannes, b. on Mar. 19, 1771, bapt. at STR on Apr. 20, 1771, and spon. by Peter Ottinger and Christina Richter.

Walck - Michael was taxed in 1762. He had the following children:
- Johan, b. on Sept. 20, 1736, and bapt. at CLY on Oct. 21, 1736. He m. Catharina. He was taxed in Dover Township in 1779.
- Johan Michael, b. on May 21, 1740, and bapt. at CLY on June 29, 1740.
- Johan Christian, b. on Oct. 30, 1741, and bapt. at CLY on Oct. 24, 1742.
- Johan Philip, b. in 1745, and bapt. at CLY on Aug. 27, 1745. He m. Maria Magdalena, and was taxed in Dover Township in 1779.

Weber - Martin was taxed in 1762. He m. Anna Maria, and had the following children:
- Daniel, b. on Apr. 18, 1763, bapt. at STR on Apr. 24, 1763, and spon. by Daniel Rahauser.
- Anna Barbara, b. on Mar. 29, 1769, bapt. at STR on Apr. 26, 1767, and spon. by Daniel and Anna Barbara Rahauser.
- Maria Catharina, b. on Sept. 20, 1769, bapt. at STR on Oct. 8, 1769, and spon. by Johan and Eva Elisabeth Spaar.

Weimer - Johan Georg was taxed in 1762. His probate inventory was filed in Dover Township in 1762. He m. Anna Catharina, and had the following children:
- Elisabeth, b. about 1748, and m. Georg, son of Valentine Krantz (see entry in Manchester section), at STR on Oct. 4, 1768.
- Peter, b. on June 24, 1754, and bapt. at CLY on Aug. 4, 1754.

Weinbrenner - Christina's probate inventory was filed in Dover Township in 1755. She is presumed to be the mother of the following children:
- Christian, b. about 1732. He was taxed in 1762. He m. Christina, widow of Jacob Weygand, before 1755 (CLY). They were sponsors to the baptism of Christina Dentzel in 1755 (RJL), and Johan Georg Fortune at St. John's Lutheran Church in Adams Co., Germany Township in 1776. They had the following children:
  - Johan Jacob, bapt. by RJL on Nov. 24, 1758, and spon. by Johan Jacob and Maria Catharina Ob.
  - Philip, bapt. by RJL on Mar. 22, 1761, and spon. by Philip and Maria Eva Kroll.
  - Catharina, bapt. at QUI on Mar. 16, 1766, and spon. by Catharina Weinbrennerin.
  - Johan Peter, bapt. at QUI on May 9, 1768, and spon. by Johan Peter Schultz and Anna Maria Schadlin.

- Johan Peter, b. about 1740. He was taxed in Dover Township in 1762, and Heidelberg Township in 1779. His probate inventory was filed in Hanover Boro in 1789. His will was written in Hanover Township on Aug. 9, 1789, and probated on Dec. 23, 1789. He m. Anna Maria Barbara, and had the following children:
  - Anna Justine Barbara, b. on July 22, 1761, and bapt. on Aug. 16, 1761. She m. Daniel Glabsatle.
- Georg, b. about 1744. He was taxed in Heidelberg Township in 1779, and his probate inventory was filed in Hanover Boro in 1780. He m. Anna Maria Catharina. Her will was written in Hanover on Dec. 21, 1789, and probated on May 9, 1781 (it named bro.-in-law, Jacob Bless). They had the following children:
  - Johan Georg, bapt. by RJL on June 1, 1766, and spon. by Georg and Anna Maria Nees. He d. before 1776.
  - Catharina, b. about 1769.
  - Johan Georg, b. on Aug. 2 (1), 1776, and bapt. at ERC on Sept. 1, 1776.
  - Johan Adam, b. on Mar. 13, 1779, bapt. at ERC on May 9, 1779, and spon. by Nicholas Neuman and Elisabeth Martz.
- Catharina, b. about 1746, and was a sponsor to the baptism of Catharina Weinbrenner in 1766 (RJL).

Wintimier (?Wintermeier) - Adam was taxed in 1762. Possibly a son of Philip, who d. before the will (see entry in Manchester section).

Zinn - Johannes was taxed in 1762. He m. Johanna Sophia, dau. of Henrich and Elisabetha Schneider, in 1726. She was b. in Plohnheim, Pfaltz, and d. between 1763 and 1776. He was b. in Kederon Pfaltz. They immigrated to America in 1738. They had the following children:
- Philip Jacob, b. about 1737, and m. Maria Elisabeth, dau. of Peter Bartemess (see entry), in 1759, and Anna Cunigunda, dau. of Johan Nicholas Hoffman (see entry), at STR on Jan. 16, 1772. He was taxed in 1762. His will was written in Dover Township on Apr. 6, 1808, and probated on May 15, 1809. Her probate inventory was filed in 1813.
- Johan Nicholas, bapt. at the First Reformed Church at Lancaster, Lancaster Co., PA, on Nov. 11, 1739, and spon. by Johan Nicholas Ob. He m. Charlotte, dau. of Wilhelm Sprenckel (see entry in Manchester section). He was taxed in 1762.
- Anna Catharina, bapt. at TLY on May 26, 1745, and spon. by Philip Jacob and Anna Catharina Ob. She m. Mattheis, son of Andreas Gansert (see entry).

MANCHESTER TOWNSHIP

Amman - Conrad was taxed in Paradise Township in 1762. He received a warrant for 300 acres in Jackson and West Manchester Township on Jan. 16, 1767. His will was written in Paradise Township on Apr. 18, 1772, and probated on Feb. 19, 1772 (?1773). He m. Catharina Mattheis, widow of Peter Mohr (see entry), in 1740. They had the following children:
- Jacob, b. about 1741, and m. Anna Barbara.
- Eva Catharina, b. on Jan. 17, 1744, bapt. at CLY on Mar. 16, 1744, and probably d. before 1772 (she was not mentioned in her father's will). She was the sponsor to the baptism of Eva Catharina Mohr in 1761.

Baner - Adam was taxed in 1762.

Baner - Martin was taxed in 1762.

Banman - Glemans was taxed in 1762.

Bauer - Hans Martin, son of Johann Martin and Margareta (Platter) Bauer/Baurer, was b. in Schwaigern, Germany, on Aug. 24, 1701, and immigrated to America on the ship *Johnson* in 1732. He was a communicant at St. Michael's Zion Lutheran Church in Philadelphia in 1733, and soon moved to York Co. He was naturalized on Apr. 11, 1751. He received a warrant for 150 acres in West Manchester and Manchester Township on May 23, 1748, that was surveyed as 183 acres on Oct. 19, 1748. He received a warrant for 200 acres in West Manchester and Manchester Township on Oct. 30, 1736 (Blunston License). His will was written in Manchester Township on Nov. 19, 1783, and probated on Dec. 1783. He m. Susanna Maria (she was alive in 1760), and Rosina before 1783. Rosina's probate inventory was filed in Manchester Township in 1784. Martin and Susanna Maria had the following children (5 children mentioned in the will (BNK)):
- Helena Christina, bapt. at Schwaigern on Mar. 25, 1732.
- Anna Elisabeth, b. on Feb. 23, 1737, and bapt. at CLY on Aug. 1, 1737.
- Johan Frederick, b. on Oct. 5, 1738, and bapt. at CLY on Nov. 19, 1738.
- Johan Jacob, b. on May 2, 1741, bapt. at CLY on June 26, 1741, and spon. by Johan Peter Wolff, Jacob Welsch, and Veronica Bassler.
- Veronica, b. on Nov. 30, 1742, and bapt. at CLY on Feb. 9, 1743.
- Susanna Maria, b. on Jan. 6, 1746, and bapt. at CLY on Feb. 9, 1747.

MANCHESTER TOWNSHIP

- Eliza Margaretha, b. on Sept. 19, 1748, and bapt. at CLY on Oct. 2, 1748.

Becker - Heinrich m. Anna Eva, dau. of Friedrich Stillinger, in 1730, and immigrated to America in 1741. She was b. in Kirchen, Poland in 1712. His probate inventory was filed in 1759 (he d. in Manchester Township in 1758). After Heinrich's death, she m. Paul Burckhart (see entry) on Aug. 29, 1758, and Philip Hoss (see entry) in 1760. She d. in 1767/68.

Becker - Frederick was taxed in 1762. His will was written in Manchester Township on Aug. 14, 1781, and probated on Apr. 6, 1782. He m. Anna, and had the following children:
- John.
- Adam.
- Maria, m. Christophel Greenwald/Grunewald (see entry).
- Anna, m. Jacob Shoemaker and resided in Bucks Co., PA.

Beer (Bear) - Abraham wrote his will in Manchester Township on Aug. 13, 1774, and it was probated on Apr. 10, 1783. He m. Fornica, and had the following children:
- Jacob.
- John Henry.
- Samuel.
- Mary m. John Fetter.
- Barbara m. Isaac Sittler at STR on May 7, 1771.

Bentz - Johannes was taxed in 1762. He received a warrant for 150 acres in West Manchester and Dover Township on Nov. 22, 1749. He m. Maria Magdalena, and had the following children (recorded at CLY unless otherwise noted):
- Johan Michael, b. on Sept. 19, 1735, bapt. on Nov. 9, 1735, and spon. by Johan Michael Bentz, and Johan Frederick and Maria Benedicta Stein. He was taxed in 1762. His will was written in West Manchester Township in 1811, and probated on Jan. 13, 1818. He m. Maria Catharina, and Margaret (after 1783), and had the following children:
  - Peter, b. about 1760.
- Johan Jacob, b. on June 24, 1762, and bapt. at CLY on Oct. 31, 1762.
- Catherine, m. John Eichingers.
- Maria Elisabeth, b. on May 31, 1760, and bapt. at CLY on Aug. 10, 1760. She m. John Schroms.

- Maria Magdalena, b. on June 8, 1769, bapt. at STR on July 17, 1769, and spon. by Catharina Margaretha Kauffman and Joseph Kauffman (not mentioned in the will).
- Anna Maria, b. on July 20, 1771, and bapt. at CLY on Sept. 22, 1771 (not mentioned in will).
- Johan Joseph, b. on Sept. 21, 1738, bapt. on Nov. 10, 1738, and spon. by Joseph Beyer, Martin Bauer, and Elisabeth Wolffin. He was taxed in Warrington Township in 1762. His probate inventory was filed in Warrington Township in 1785.
- Anna Elisabeth, b. on Jan. 3, 1741, and bapt. on Jan. 27, 1741.
- Johan Philip, b. on Jan. 14, 1744, and bapt. on Feb. 9, 1744 (bapt. at TLY on Mar. 17, 1745, and spon. by Martin and Dorothea Weigel). He m. Elisabeth, dau. of Jost Sasseman at STR on May 24, 1768.
- Johannes, b. on Jan. 14, 1744, and bapt. on Feb. 9, 1744 (bapt. at TLY on Mar. 17, 1745, and spon. by Jacob and Anna Maria Schram). His will was written in Washington Township on Aug. 4, 1804, and probated on Oct. 20, 1804. He m. Philibina, dau. of Andreas Palli (see entry in Dover section). at STR on Jan. 10, 1769, and had the following children (one dau. m. ___ Beisher):
  - Mary.
  - John.
  - George.
  - Elizabeth.
  - Henry.
  - Jacob.
  - Susan.
  - Caty.
  - David.
- Maria Dorothea, b. on June 14, 1743, and bapt. on June 19, 1743.
- Maria Margaretha, b. on Sept. 30, 1746, and bapt. in Jan. 1747. She m. Michel Uhrich at STR on May 24, 1768.
- Johan Martin, b. on Feb. 17, 749, and bapt. on Feb. 21, 1749.
- Anna Maria, b. on Apr. 8, 1751, and bapt. on Apr. 21, 1751.
- Johan Christian, bapt. by RJL on Sept. 1, 1756, and spon. by Christian and Elisabeth Kroll (mother is listed as Maria Sophia).
- Johann Heinrich, bapt. by RJL on July 7, 1757, and spon. by Georg and Barbara Hoog.
- Johan Peter, bapt. by RJL on Nov. 25, 1759, and spon. by Johan Peter and Maria Agnes Wolf.

Bieri (Beery) - Nicholas was taxed in 1762. He was b. to John and Catharina Bieri about 1697. He m. Barbara, dau. of Michael Jeremiah George and Magdalena Miller, in York Co., East Manchester Township, PA, on Dec. 1, 1728. Nicholas came to America on the ship *Friendship*

on Oct. 16, 1727, and d. on Oct. 1, 1762. Barbara was b. in the Palatinate in 1710, and d. on Dec. 2, 1791. She m. Rev. Jacob Kagy (1719-1788) on Nov. 17, 1769. Nicholas received a warrant for 100 acres in Manchester Township on Aug. 25, 1742, that was surveyed on May 6, 1743, and patented on Jan. 8, 1744. He also received a warrant for 200 acres in Manchester Township on Oct. 30, 1736 (Blunston License). Nicholas and Barbara had the following children in York Co., Springettsbury, PA:
- John, b. on Aug. 2, 1729. He m. Catherina, dau. of Hartman and Anna (Stirtz) Hunsaker, in York Co., PA, in 1748. Hartman was b. in Aargau, Switzerland, in 1695/7, and came to America on the ship *Pennsylvania Merchant* on Sept. 10, 1733. After Hartman's death, his widow m. Jacob Gochenour in Feb. 1740, and d. in 1745. They had the following children:
  - Daniel, b. in 1755.
  - Anna, b. on Jan. 30, 1768, and m. Ludwig Seitz (see entry in Shrewsbury section).
- Catharina, b. about 1730. She m. John Blosser (see entry).
- Magdalena, b. on Jan. 3, 1732, m. John Hunsaker, and d. on Aug. 9, 1796.
- Susanna, b. about 1734, and m. John, son of Christian Bixler (see entry).
- Margaret, b. about 1736. She m. ___ Forry and ___ Burkhart.
- Abraham, b. about 1738. He was taxed in 1762, and d. on May 26, 1799. He m. Elizabeth Gochenour, and had the following children:
  - Abraham, b. in 1762, and m. Magdalena Rife in Harrisburg on Sept. 28, 1786, and Barbara Good before 1802.
  - Jacob, b. on Sept. 11, 1769, and is probably the Jacob that m. Nancy Geil in Albemarle or Rockingham Co. (Edom), VA, on Nov. 27, 1794.
  - John, b. about 1773, and m. Barbara Kagy.
  - Christian, b. about 1782, and m. Catharine Frank in Harrisburg on Feb. 25, 1798.
- Nicholas, b. on June 16, 1739. He was taxed in 1762. He m. Maria, dau. of Jacob Keller (see entry), about 1763, and Mrs. Mary Good (Gro) about 1789. He d. in Fairfield Co., Rush Creek Township, OH, on Feb. 16, 1811, and is bur. in Miller cemetery. They moved to OH in 1805. Nicholas had the following children in Shrewsbury Township:
  - Barbara, b. on Apr. 6, 1764, and m. Jacob Blosser at York on Feb. 12, 1788.
  - John, b. on Nov. 4, 1765, and m. Margaret, dau. of Nicholas Shafer, in Rockingham Co., VA, on Mar. 15, 1788.
  - Jacob, b. in 1766.
  - Elizabeth, b. on Apr. 11, 1771.

- Abraham, b. on July 20, 1773. He m. Catherine Fast in Rockingham Co., Harrisonburg, VA, on Mar. 7, 1802. She was b. in Berks Co., Reading, PA, on Apr. 17, 1786, and d. in Fairfield Co., Rush Creek Township, OH, on Jan. 2, 1870. In 1803, they settled on the bluff, on the north side of the Raccoon and one mile east of Berne. Abraham d. in Rush Creek Township on June 15, 1845. They are bur. in Miller cemetery.
- Mary, b. on Sept. 4, 1775, and m. Henry Stemen (1775-1855).
- Isaac, b. on June 10, 1777.
- Nicholas, b. in 1780, and d. young.
- Henry, b. on Apr. 30, 1781.
- George, b. on Apr. 4, 1783, and m. Susanna Funk in Rockingham Co., VA, in 1796.
- Susan, b. in 1785.
- Martha, b. in 1787.
- Joseph, b. on Feb. 8, 1790, and m. Frances Garber in Rockingham Co. on Nov. 15, 1811.
- Christian, b. on Aug. 1, 1792.
- Margaret, b. on June 15, 1795.
- Francis, b. in 1796.

- George, b. about 1741.
- Barbara, b. about 1743, and m. John Gochenour.

Bigler - Hans Thomas, son of Heinrich of Leitersweyler, m. Maria, dau. of Jacob Vogler of Ingelsheim, in Hunspach, Northeran Alsace, on Jan. 7, (1702). They had the following children at Hunspach (see BNA):
- Hans Georg, b. on Feb. 10, 1703, and bapt. on Feb. 18, 1703.
- Marx was b. to Hans Thomas and Maria (Vogler) Bigler, in Hunspach, Northern Alsace, on Apr. 17, 1705, bapt. on Apr. 19, 1705, spon. by Hans Jacob Heckel and Marx Weimer, and Magdalene. He immigrated to America on the ship *Richard and Elizabeth* in 1733, and received a warrant for 200 acres in West Manchester Township on Oct. 18, 1738. He was naturalized in MD in Oct. 1743. He had the following children:
  - Anna Maria, b. on Mar. 30, 1741, bapt. by JCS on Aug. 21, 1741, and spon. by Andreas Hill and Catarina Kuntz.
- Hans Michael, b. on Dec. 3, 1707, and bapt. on Dec. 4, 1707. He immigrated to America on the ship *Francis and Ann* in 1741, and m. Susanna Reuscher on Dec. 14, 1741 (JCS). He was naturalized in MD on Sept. 21, 1763. His will was written in Frederick Co., MD, on Sept. 21, 1763, and probated on Nov. 20, 1764.

Biger - Godlib was taxed in 1762.

MANCHESTER TOWNSHIP

Bixler - Christian was taxed in 1762. He received a warrant for 200 acres in East Manchester Township on Oct. 30, 1736, that was surveyed on June 1, 1763, and patented on Sept. 26, 1763. His will was written in Manchester Township on Mar. 3, 1777, and probated on Mar. 10, 1777. He had the following children:
- John was taxed in 1762 (mentioned as eldest in will). He m. Susanna, dau. of Nicholas Bieri (see entry).
- Christian was taxed in 1762. His will was written in Manchester Township on Oct. 4, 1795, and probated on Nov. 5, 1795. He m. Magdalena, and had the following children:
  - Christian m. Elizabeth, and d. in Fairfield Co., OH, in 1813. His will was written on Nov. 5, 1812, and probated in Feb. 1813.
  - Jacob.
  - Joseph.
  - Michael.
  - John.
  - Conrad.
  - Magdalena, m. Peter Waltz/Welty.
  - Elisabeth, m. John Hoover.
  - Catherine m. Leonard, son of Casper Knab (see entry), at TLY on Mar. 6, 1796.
  - Eve.
- Christina m. Conrad Strickler (see entry). She is not mentioned in the will, but her will names her bros., John and Joseph Bixler.
- Barbara received the interest of her yearly share as long as she lived without Valentin Joacky (he is mentioned as a son-in-law).
- Joseph got his father's mill property.
- Jacob.
- Michael.

Blosser (Blasser) - John m. Catharina, dau. of Nicholas Bieri (see entry). They purchased 393 acres called *Dover*, and 397 acres in Greenfield located on the east side of the Monongahela and Cheat Rivers where they meet at what is now Point Marion, Fayette Co., Springhill Township, PA, in 1796. They were alive in 1813, when they are mentioned in the will of their son, Nicholas. They had the following children:
- John, b. about 1767, m. Mary, dau. of Jacob and Anna Barbara (Neff) Clemmer, and had his will probated in Fayette Co. on Feb. 10, 1829. She was b. in York Co., Hopewell Township, PA, on Dec. 14, 1767, and d. in Fayette Co., Springhill Township on Sept. 9, 1854.
- Anna, b. about 1769, m. Jacob Clemmer, and resided in Fayette Co., Springhill Township, PA. He was b. about 1766, and d. between 1850 and 1860.

- Nicholas, b. about 1774, m. Anna Cagey, and d. in Fayette Co. on Feb. 6, 1814. She d. in 1820.
- Jacob, resided in Fairfield Co., OH.
- Abraham, resided in Fairfield Co., OH.
- Isaac, m. Elizabeth Kauffman, and resided in Fairfield Co., OH.
- George, resided in Fairfield Co., OH.

Bohn - Jacob was taxed in 1762. He m. Elisabeth, and they were sponsors to the baptism of Agnes Opp at STR in 1769.

Bohn - Johan Nicholas m. Anna Maria about 1752, and Anna Elisabeth about 1755/56. His will was written in Manchester Township on Apr. 10, 1804, and probated on Oct. 5, 1804. He had the following children:
- Jacob.
- Maria Rebecca, b. on Nov. 26, 1753, and bapt. at CLY on Feb. 10, 1754.
- Elisabeth, b. about 1756, and m. Georg, son of Casper Lichtenberger (see entry).
- Maria Catharina, b. on Feb. 2, 1760, and bapt. at CLY on Apr. 27, 1760. She m. Jacob Knab (see entry).
- Rebecca Maria, b. on Nov. 16, 1762, and bapt. at CLY on Jan. 1, 1763.
- Margaret, b. about 1764, and m. Casper Knab (see entry).
- Ludwig, b. about 1766, and m. Elisabeth.
- Maria Barbara, b. on May 26, 1769, and bapt. at CLY on July 23, 1769. She m. Georg Ringer.

Bone - Valentine had his probate inventory filed in Manchester Township in 1780.

Boner - John was taxed in 1762.

Bott - Johann Henrich was taxed in 1762. He was b. in 1700, and d. in 1783. They arrived at Philadelphia on Sept. 7, 1748. His probate inventory was filed in Manchester Township in 1783. He m. Anna Maria Catharina Kunigunda, dau. of Peter and Anna Clara Christ, in Sonnenberg, Germany, on Nov. 22, 1724. She was b. on Nov. 22, 1701, and d. on Jan. 1, 1771. They had the following children (bapt. at Hessen-Nassau, Breithardt Steckenroth):
- Johann Jonas, b. on Oct. 8, 1725, bapt. on Oct. 14, 1725, and d. in 1793. He was taxed in 1762, and served in the Revolutionary War. His probate inventory was filed in Manchester Township in 1793. He m. Anna Catharina, dau. of Georg Heinrich and Anna Elisabeth (Herring) Joseph (see entry in Dover section under Herring), at

CLY on Sept. 16, 1760. She was b. in 1740, and d. in 1807. They had the following children:
- Christina, b. on Jan. 3, 1764, bapt. at WOL in Jan. 1764, and spon. by Johan Hennrich Bott and Anna Kristdina Josebin. She m. Conrad, son of Conrad Eissenhardt (see entry).
- Catharina Elisabeth, b. on Oct. 19, 1766, bapt. at WOL on Nov. 30, 1766, and spon. by Peter and Catharina Elisabeth Wolff.
- Johan Peter, b. in 1769, m. Elisabeth, dau. of Killian Ziegler (see entry), and d. in 1846. She was b. in 1773, and d. in 1820.
- Anna Catharina, b. on Sept. 30, 1771, bapt. at WOL on Feb. 22, 1772, and spon. by Frantz Jacob Romer and Catharina Wolfin.
- Anna Margaretha, b. on Jan. 1, 1774, bapt. at WOL on Apr. 17, 1774, and spon. by Johannes and Margaretha Eppelman.
- Johan Heinrich, b. in 1776.
- Maria Susanna, b. on Feb. 26, 1779, bapt. at WOL on Apr. 5, 1779, and spon. by Jacob and Susanna Stower.
- Anna Catharina Elnora, bapt. on Aug. 10, 1727, and m. Conrad Maul (see entry) at CLY on Jan. 24, 1749.
- Anna Margaretha, bapt. on Aug. 14, 1729, and d. before 1738.
- Catharina Elisabetha, bapt. on Mar. 25, 1732, and m. Peter, son of Peter Wolff (see entry), at CLY on Oct. 20, 1751.
- Anna Dorothea, bapt. on June 19, 1735, and was a sponsor to the baptism of Anna Dorothea Gap in 1755 (RJL). She m. Johan Peter Lindt, and had the following children:
  - Johan Peter, b. on June 26, 1766, and bapt. at CLY on July 13, 1766.
  - Johan Henrich, b. on Oct. 23, 1770, and bapt. at CLY on Nov. 19, 1770.
  - Catharina, b. on Oct. 18, 1777, and bapt. at CLY on Dec. 14, 1777.
- Anna Margaretha, bapt. on Sept. 13, 1738, and m. Johann Apfelman at CLY on Nov. 4, 1751 (see entry in Codorus section).
- Margaretha Elisabetha, bapt. on Feb. 9, 1740.
- Johann Henrich, bapt. on Mar. 7, 1743. He d. before 1780.

Bott - Kunigunde, b. about 1743, and m. Andreas Schreyer at STM on Aug. 21, 1764.

Bott - Elisabeth Margaretha, b. on May 3, 1731, and d. on Sept. 7, 1753 (CLY). She m. Georg Gerber at CLY on May 7, 1749. He was taxed in York in 1779, and his probate inventory was filed in York Boro in 1791. They had the following children:
- Catharina Barbara, b. on Feb. 26, 1750, and bapt. at CLY on Mar. 4, 1750. She m. Benjamin, son of Dieter Fahnestock, at STR on Oct. 29, 1770.

- Johan Bartholomew, b. on Nov. 11, 1751, and bapt. on Nov. 24, 1751.

Bott - Johan Wentel, b. about 1734, and m. Maria Christina Fischborn at CAN on May 5, 1755, and Magdalena about 1757. He had the following children:
- Johann Adam, b. on May 20, 1758, and bapt. at STJ on May 21, 1758.
- Johannes, bapt. by RJL on Oct. 12, 1760, and spon. by Johannes and Anna Maria Lehman.

Bott - Johan Emerich m. Anna Maria, and had the following children:
- Johan Philip, b. Aug. 24, 1748, and bapt. at CLY on Sept. 25, 1748.

Bott - Hermanus, b. in 1697, and immigrated to America with Peter Bott (b. 1708) and Hans Emerich Bott (b. 1701) on the ship *Loyal Judith* on Sept. 2, 1743. He was taxed in 1762. His will was written in Manchester Township on Oct. 9, 1764, and probated on July 28, 1772. He m. an unknown woman about 1722, and Anna Catharina Hahn at CLY on June 13, 1749. He had the following children:
- Maria Elisabeth, b. about 1723, and m. Johannes Guckes at CLY on Jan. 16, 1744, and had the following children:
  - Johannes, b. on Aug. 14, 1748, bapt. at STM on Sept. 4, 1748, and spon. by Hermanus Bott.
  - Sybilla Maria Elisabeth, b. on Sept. 26, 1751, and bapt. at CLY on May 16, 1752.
  - Maria Dorothea, b. on Mar. 13, 1753, and bapt. at CLY on Mar. 25, 1753.
  - Anna Maria, bapt. by RJL on Sept. 4, 1757, and spon. by Christian and Maria Elisabeth Groll.
  - Johan Georg, bapt. by RJL on May 6, 1759, and spon. by Georg and Barbara Meyer.
  - Johan Jacob, b. on Dec. 22, 1760, and bapt. at CLY on Dec. 30, 1760.
  - Johann Reinhard, b. on June 11, 1762, bapt. at TLY on June 19, 1762, and spon. by Johann Reinhard and Maria Elisabeth Bott.
- Johann Adam, b. about 1729. He served in the Revolutionary War. He m. Juliana Lauman at CLY on Aug. 4, 1750, and had the following children:
  - Catharina Elisabeth, b. on Aug. 25, 1751, and bapt. at CLY on Aug. 29, 1751.
  - Anna Catharina, b. on Feb. 22, 1753, and bapt. at CLY on Mar. 4, 1753.
  - Johann Adam, bapt. by RJL on Dec. 22, 1754, and spon. by Johannes and Christina Hay.

- Elisabeth, b. on Nov. 28, 1757, and bapt. at CLY on Dec. 3, 1757.
- Georg Peter, b. on Mar. 27, 1760, bapt. at CLY on Mar. 30, 1760, and d. on Feb. 18, 1761.
- Maria Ottillie, b. on Nov. 26, 1761, and bapt. at CLY on Dec. 6, 1761.
- Johannes, b. on Aug. 3, 1763, and bapt. at CLY on Aug. 14, 1763.
- Anna Maria Christina, b. on Jan. 1, 1765, and bapt. at CLY on Jan. 12, 1765.
- Herman, b. on Apr. 7, 1767, and bapt. at CLY on Apr. 12, 1767.
- Daniel, b. on Nov. 25, 1773, and bapt. at CLY on Aug. 21, 1774.
- Adam, b. on July 26, 1775, and bapt. at CLY on July 30, 1775.

- Johann Reinhardt, b. about 1731, and m. Maria Elisabeth. He served in the Revolutionary War. His will was written in Manchester Township on Apr. 19, 1790, and probated on July 5, 1790. They had the following children:
  - Maria Catharina, b. on Mar. 10, 1752, and bapt. at CLY on Mar. 22, 1752. She m. Francis Winkler.
  - Anna Barbara, b. in Oct. 1755, and bapt. at CLY on Nov. 23, 1755.
  - Johann Georg, bapt. at CLY on Jan. 13, 1758.

- Ottilia, b. about 1735, and m. Peter Lauer at CAN on Aug. 24, 1756, and John Hagener about 1764. Ottilia had the following children:
  - Juliana Lauer, b. on Oct. 28, 1758, and bapt. at CLY on Nov. 5, 1758. She d. on Aug. 8, 1759, and is bur. at CLY.
  - Johan Reinhard Hagener, b. on Feb. 8, 1764, and bapt. at CLY on Feb. 12, 1764.

- Johann Jacob, b. about 1738. He served in the Revolutionary War. He m. Maria Magdalena Lauman at CLY on Nov. 22, 1761, and had the following children (recorded at CLY):
  - Adam, b. on Sept. 8, 1762, and bapt. on Sept. 19, 1762.
  - Anna Maria, b. on Jan. 25, 1768, and bapt. on Feb. 1, 1768.
  - Susanna, b. on Apr. 21, 1770, and bapt. on Apr. 29, 1770.
  - Jacob, b. on Oct. 8, 1772, and bapt. on Oct. 25, 1772.
  - Jacob, b. on Dec. 23, 1773, and bapt. on Jan. 19, 1774.
  - Elisabeth, b. on Feb. 8, 1779, and bapt. on Apr. 18, 1779.
  - Catharina, b. on July 30, 1780, and bapt. on Aug. 27, 1780.
  - Daniel, b. on Oct. 20, 1783, and bapt. on Nov. 16, 1783.
  - Benjamin, b. on Sept. 3, 1785, and bapt. on Oct. 16, 1785

Bott - Conrad, b. about 1734. He was a saddler from Sonnenberg, when he m. Jacobina Dannbach at Trinity Lutheran Church in Lancaster on Nov. 12, 1754. They had the following children:
- Johann Conrad, bapt. by RJL on Dec. 16, 1759, and spon. by Johan Conrad and Anna Margaretha Kiefaber.

- Catharina, b. on Mar. 19, 1764, bapt. at St. John's Lutheran Church in Adams Co., Germany Township on May 20, 1764, and spon. by Georg and Anna Kunigunda Lehman.

<u>Botzman</u> - Georg was taxed in 1762.

<u>Bruckhardt</u> - Julius m. Anna Margaretha. He was taxed in Manchester Township in 1779. His will was written in Manchester Township on Apr. 17, 1793, and probated on June 10, 1793. Her probate inventory was filed in Manchester Township in 1805. They had the following children:
- Abraham, b. about 1757, and m. Maria Magdalena Kohler, at TLY on Sept. 3, 1780. He was taxed in Bott's Town in 1779.
- David, b. about 1759. He was taxed in Bott's Town in 1779.
- Daniel, b. about 1761.
- Elisabeth, b. about 1762, and m. Jacob Marty.
- Katharina, b. about 1764, and m. Michael Miller.
- Barbara, b. on June 3, 1766, and m. Ludwig, son of Ludwig Trieber (see entry in Codorus section).
- Heinrich, b. on Mar. 23, 1771, and bapt. at CLY on June 7, 1794. He m. Catherine.
- Maria, b. about 1773.

<u>Burkhardt</u> - Carl m. Anna Margaretha before 1716, and Anna Cunigunda. Anna Margaretha d. in Flomborn, Germany. Carl immigrated to America in 1736, and was living in 1758. Carl and Cuniginda were sponsors at the baptism on Cunigunda Schaffer at the First Reformed Congregation at Lancaster in 1750. Carl and Anna Margarthea had the following children:
- Paul, b. on May 1, 1716, and bapt. on May 17, 1716. He m. Anna Eva, dau. of Georg Schwob, in Earl Town, Lancaster Co., on Oct. 16, 1739 (JCS), and Anna Eva, dau. of Friedrich Stillinger, and widow of Henry Becker (see entry) on Feb. 22, 1757. Anna Eva Schwob d. on Dec. 11, 1756. He d. on Aug. 29, 1758, and is bur. in Henry Bott's burial ground. Paul had the following children (8 children 5 alive in 1758):
  - Maria Magdalena, b. on Oct. 13, 1740, and bapt. at CLY on Nov. 25, 1740. She m. Johan Adam Diehl (see entry in Shrewsbury section).
  - Catharina, b. about 1744, and m. Johan Georg Weinbrenner at STR on Mar. 14, 1765.
  - Anna Maria, b. on May 1, 1746, bapt. at STM on June 8, 1746, and spon. by Christoph Besserer and wife.
  - Margaretha, b. about 1749, and m. Vendel, son of Andreas Gross (see entry in Dover section), at STR on Mar. 13, 1770.

MANCHESTER TOWNSHIP   187

  - Johan Carl, b. on Sept. 7, 1751, and d. on Aug. 17, 1758 (CLY).
    He is bur. in Henry Bott's burial ground.
  - Mathias (probably Carl's son but not proven) m. Anna Maria, and
    had the following children:
    - Anna Maria, b. on Mar. 24, 1748, and bapt. at CLY on May 20,
      1748.
    - Maria Margaretha, b. on Dec. 26, 1749, and bapt. at CLY on June
      4, 1750.
    - Maria Barbara, b. on June 24, 1752,. and bapt. at CLY on Nov. 9,
      1752.
  - Frederick (probably Carl's son but not proven) was a sponsor with
    Mathias Burckhardt to the baptism of Magdalena Elisabeth
    Welschans at CLY in 1745).

Casner - Jacob was taxed in 1762.

Duer - Gabriel was taxed in 1762. He m. Catharina, and had the
following children:
  - Johann Georg, b. on Jan. 10, 1768, bapt. at TLY on Mar. 6, 1768,
    and spon. by Georg Rudi and wife.
  - Jacob, b. on Nov. 28, 1771, and bapt. at CLY on Dec. 25, 1771.

Ebert - Hans Michael was b. in Unter-Anfrach, Germany, in 1694,
immigrated to America on the ship *Brittania* on Sept. 21, 1731, and
was licensed (Blunston License) to settle on 500 acres located on the
West side of Codorus Creek opposite to the fork. He d. in Manchester
Township on Apr. 16, 1749, and is bur. in CLY churchyard. He had the
following sons:
  - Johan Michael of Unter-Anfrach and York Co., Manchester
    Township. He immigrated to America on the ship *Britania* on Sept.
    21, 1731, and d. in May/June 1785. His will was written in
    Manchester Township on Sept. 29, 1784, and probated on June 3,
    1785. He was naturalized on Sept. 25, 1751. He m. Eva
    Margaretha, dau. of Johann Adam Diehl (see entry in Shrewsbury
    Township). Michael was County Assessor from 1767 to 1770 and
    tax collector in Manchester Township in 1775. He was Supervisor
    of the Highways in 1757. At the time of his death, Michael owned
    780 acres in Manchester Township along the Codorus Creek. They
    had the following children in Manchester Township:
    - Johan Michael, b. on Dec. 28, 1742, and bapt. at Christ's
      Lutheran Church of York on Feb. 9, 1743. He m. Elizabeth, dau.
      of Jacob Rudisill (see entry), at CLY on Aug. 8, 1764, and d.
      about Apr. 1790. She d. in May 1791. Michael served in the
      Revolutionary War. They had the following children:

- Anna Maria, b. on July 28, 1765, bapt. on Aug. 11, 1765, and spon. by Johan Jacob and Anna Maria Rudisill. She m. Frederick, son of Andreas Hoke (see entry).
- Eva Margaretha, b. on May 20, 1767, bapt. on June 28, 1767, and spon. by Michael Ebert, Sr., and wife. She m. Henrich, son of Mathias Jacob Schmeisser (see entry).
- Michael, b. on Aug. 2, 1769, bapt. on Aug. 13, 1769, and spon. by Martin Ebert and Dorothea Rudisill.
- Johan Jacob, b. on Nov. 18, 1771, bapt. on Dec. 29, 1771, and spon. by Jacob Rudisill and wife. He m. Catharina. She d. on Jan. 6, 1862, aged 85 years, 6 months, and 6 days (bur. in BLY cemetery).
- Jonas, b. on Dec. 15, 1773, bapt. on Feb. 27, 1774, and spon. by Jonas Rudisill and wife.
- Johannes, b. on Feb. 9, 1776, bapt. on Apr. 4, 1776, and spon. by Nicholas Diehl and wife.
- Elisabeth, b. on Sept. 2, 1778, bapt. at CLY on Oct. 25, 1778, and spon. by Martin Ebert and wife.
- Susanna, b. on Feb. 11, 1781, bapt. on Apr. 8, 1781, and spon. by Andrew Schmidt and wife.
- Helena, b. on Dec. 5, 1744, bapt. at Christ's Lutheran on June 10, 1745, spon. by Jacob and Helena Billmeyer, and d. before 1757.
- Johan Jacob, b. on Oct. 2, 1746, bapt. at Christ's Lutheran on Oct. 4, 1746, spon. by Jacob and Helena Billmeyer, and d. before Mar. 1786.
- Maria Elizabeth, b. on Dec. 16, 1748, spon. by John Amendt and Maria Apollonia Paul, and bapt. at Christ's Lutheran on Feb. 2, 1749. She m. Zachariah, son of Zachariah and Margaret Shugart. He was an innkeeper in York, served in the Committee of Correspondence on Nov. 3, 1775, and was a 1st Lt. in Captain Michael Smyser's Company under Col. Michael Swope's Flying Camp. They moved to Alexandria, VA, between 1787 and 1790, and then moved to southwestern VA.
- Johan Martin, b. on Jan. 9, 1751, and bapt. at Christ's Lutheran on Feb. 24, 1751. He m. Anna Maria, dau. of Mathias and Anna Catharina (Koppenhoffer) Smyser (see entry), and d. in West Manchester Township in May 1814. She was b. on Nov. 10, 1756, and d. on Mar. 29, 1833. They are bur. in Zion Lutheran cemetery. Martin served in the Revolutionary War.
- Maria Margaret, b. on June 21, 1753, and bapt. at Christ's Lutheran on July 22, 1753. She m. Martin, son of Peter and Elisabetha (Kramer) Gaertner (see entry in Dover section under Kramer), and d. in Hellam Township on Apr. 14, 1824. He was b. on June 21, 1744, and d. on Mar. 30, 1818.

- Philip Adam, b. on July 2, 1755, bapt. at Christ's Lutheran on Sept. 2, 1755, and spon. by Adam and Maria Catharina Endler. He m. Susanna, dau. of Mathias and Anna Catharina (Koppenhoffer) Smyser (see entry), and d. in St. Louis, MO, on Dec. 6, 1803 (1805). She was b. on Mar. 31, 1760, and d. on Apr. 2, 1840. Philip served in the Revolutionary War, and was a merchant in St. Louis.
- Helena, b. on May 20, 1757.
- Daniel, b. on June 25, 1759, bapt. at Christ's Lutheran on July 29, 1759, spon. by Daniel and Elisabeth Diehl, and d. before Mar. 1786.
- Johannes, b. on June 26, 1761, bapt. at Christ's Lutheran on June 28, 1761, and spon. by Michael and Wilhelmina Margaretha Geisselman. He m. Elizabeth, probably a dau. of Col. Michael and Anna Maria (Hoke) Smyser (see entry), and Anna Weyle on Aug. 22, 1805, and d. in Huron Co., Norwalk, OH, on July 14, 1835. Elizabeth was b. about 1766, and d. in Dauphin Co., Harrisburg, PA, on Feb. 19, 1803. Anna was b. on Feb. 13, 1780, and d. on Apr. 11, 1806. Johannes moved to OH in 1820.
- Adam, b. on Sept. 15, 1763, bapt. at Christ's Lutheran on Oct. 10, 1763, and spon. by Adam and Anna Barbara Leitner. He m. Clara, dau. of Peter and Dorothea (Smyser) Hoke (see entry), at TLY on Oct. 18, 1785, and d. in York Co., PA, about Sept. 1808. She was b. in 1767, and d. on Apr. 13, 1838. She is bur. in CLY cemetery.

- Johan Martin was b. in Unter-Anfrach Anspach on Oct. 28, 1724, and came to America in 1732. He m. Eva Barbara, dau. of Casper Kerber (see entry), at CLY on Apr. 10/11, 1749. He was naturalized on Sept. 25, 1751. They moved to Wachau, North Carolina, on May 2, 1771. They had the following children in Manchester Township (recorded at FMY):
- Martin, b. on July 13, 1750, bapt. on July 24, 1750, and spon. by Michael and Eva Margaretha Ebert.
- Johan Georg, b. on June 4, 1752, bapt. on June 15, 1752, and spon. by Johan Georg and Anna Barbara Meier.
- Christian, b. on June 29, 1754, bapt. on July 5, 1754, and spon. by Godfrey Engel, Philip Rothrock, Lewis Brotzman, and John Heckdorn. He d. of smallpox on June 9, 1762, and is bur. at God's Acre cemetery.
- Anna Maria, b. on July 22, 1756, bapt. on July 25, 1756, and spon. by Anna Elisabeth Hons, Catharina Heckedorn, and Anna Maria Muller.
- Rosina, b. on Dec. 13, 1758, bapt. on Dec. 17, 1758, and spon. by Anna Maria Miller, Catharina Heckedorn, Elisabeth Hoens, and Walpurgis Kerber.

- Samuel, b. on Mar. 22, 1761, bapt. on Easter Monday, and spon. by Samuel Herr and John Heckedorn. He d. on Apr. 2, 1761, and is bur. in God's Acre cemetery.
- Christian, b. on Aug. 21, 1762, bapt. on Aug. 22, 1762, and spon. by Henry Lindemeyer, John Heckedorn, Georg Weller, and Marcus Hoens.
- Christina, b. on Feb. 19, 1765, bapt. on Feb. 21, 1765, and spon. by Elizabeth Hoens, Eva Weller, and Anna Herr.
- Catharina, b. on Nov. 21, 1769, and bapt. on Nov. 26, 1769. She d. in 1769.

Eichelberger - Philipp Friederich was bapt. at Ittlingen Lutheran Church (BNK) on Apr. 17, 1693 to Johannes and Maria Barbara Eichelberger. He m. Anna Barbara Dorners on Nov. 11, 1714, and immigrated to America on the ship *Albany* in 1728. After Barbara's death, he m. Maria Magdalena Becker in Conestoga, Lancaster Co., on Apr. 4, 1738 (JCS). He was naturalized on May 19, 1739. He was taxed in Manheim Township in 1762. His will was written in Hanover on Feb. 5, 1776, and probated on Oct. 22, 1776. Magdalena's will was written in Hanover on Nov. 17, 1789, and probated on Apr. 30, 1790. Friederich had the following children (the first 6 bapt. at Ittlingen (except Maria), and the rest at Trinity Lutheran Church of Lancaster, in Lancaster Co., PA:
- Johan Martin, b. on Nov. 16, 1716. He was naturalized on Apr. 10, 1760. He received a warrant for 350.28 acres in West Manchester Township on Oct. 8, 1746, that was surveyed as 348.65 acres on Sept. 24, 1764. He also received a warrant for 71.25 acres in West Manchester Township, that was surveyed on Apr. 7, 1752, and patented on Sept. 24, 1764. He was a tavern keeper in York from 1741 to 1751. His will was written in Manchester Township on Feb. 8, 1781, and probated on Apr. 28, 1781. He m. Anna Maria, and had the following children (recorded at CLY unless otherwise noted):
  - Georg, b. about 1740, and m. Lydia, dau. of Francis Worley.
  - Johan Friederich, b. about 1742, and m. Eva.
  - Philip Jacob, b. on Mar. 12, 1744, and bapt. on Apr. 18, 1744. He m. Barbara, dau. of Michael Barth at STR on Nov. 28, 1769.
  - Susanna, b. about 1746.
  - Johann Bernhard, b. on Mar. 3, 1748, and bapt. on May 20, 1748. His will was written on July 16, 1781, and probated on Aug. 2, 1781.
  - Benjamin, b. on Oct. 30, 1750, and bapt. on Nov. 10, 1750 (not mentioned in will).
  - Anna Maria, b. on Feb. 18, 1752, and bapt. on Feb. 23, 1752.

- Barbara, b. on Feb. 18, 1752, and bapt. on Feb. 23, 1752 (not mentioned in will).
- Anna Catharina, b. on May 6, 1754, and bapt. on May 13, 1754 (not mentioned in will).
- Johan Martin, bapt. by RJL on July 13, 1755, and spon. by Matheus and Catharina Schmeisser.
- Johann Martin, b. on Jan. 28, 1759, and bapt. on Feb. 25, 1759.
- Anna Margaretha, b. on Mar. 2, 1720. She m. Adam Vollmar at Lancaster Co., Conestoga on Jan. 24, 1738 (JCS), and Vincens Kieffer. Anna Margaretha and Vincens had the following children:
  - Magdalena.
  - Barbara.
  - Catharina.
  - Sabina.
  - Valentine.
- Johann Friederich, b. on Feb. 18, 1722, and d. on May 1, 1768. He m. Catharina. She had a child with Frederick Schaffer (while she was m. to Frederick Eichelberger), named Veronica Barbara (b. on Sept. 5, 1761, and bapt. at CLY on Sept. 27, 1761 (spon. by Frederick Basler and wife). She showed repentance and regret for her actions, but she also had a child with Frederick Bahler (a m. man (while she was m. to Frederick Eichelberger)), named Johan Frederick (b. on Dec. 25, 1764, and bapt. at CLY on Apr. 18, 1766).
- Margaretha Barbara, b. on Aug. 9, 1724.
- Maria, b. about 1726, and m. Hans Georg, son of Mathias Ness (see entry in Shrewsbury section), at the Moravian Church at Lancaster on Mar. 13, 1744.
- Anna Barbara, b. on Feb. 7, 1727.
- Johann Georg, b. on Dec. 22, 1729. He m. Christina Dorothea Pasch at Trinity Lutheran Church in Lancaster on June 18, 1751. He d. on Apr. 16, 1752, and was bur. at CLY on Apr. 17, 1752.
- Johann Adam, b. on May 27, 1739. He received a warrant for 200 acres in Shrewsbury Township with George Weis on Mar. 23, 1768, that was surveyed as 196.26 acres called *The Range* on Nov. 25, 1768 (improved 14 years). He was taxed in Manheim Township in 1762. He kept a tavern in Manheim Township. His will was written in Manheim Township on Nov. 25, 1787, and probated on Feb. 1, 1788. He d. on Dec. 2, 1787. He m. Magdalena Bechtel. She was b. on Dec. 5, 1743, and d. on Dec. 30, 1821. They had the following children:
  - Frederick.
  - Michael, b. on May 1, 1765, and m. Catharina, dau. of Mathias Jacob and Elisabeth (Eichelberger) Schmeisser, before 1790. Jacob and Elisabeth Schmeisser's dau., Catharina was b. on Sept. 19, 1782, and at CLY bapt. on Oct. 27, 1782. Either her birth

date is incorrect, or Michael m. two women by the name of Catharina, because Catharina Schmeisser would not have had her first child on Oct. 24, 1791 (a son, named Adam). Prowell's *History of York* does say Michael m. Catharina Schmeisser. Michael d. in 1801.
- Samuel, b. on Jan. 5, 1769, and m. Maria Catharina, dau. of Mathias Emeric Schmeisser (see entry), on Aug. 2, 1790, and d. in Heidelberg Township on Apr. 22, 1828. He owned a saw mill. She was b. on Feb. 27, 1772, bapt. at CLY on May 10, 1772, and d. in Heidelberg Township on Feb. 6, 1842 (1841).
- Elisabeth, b. on Jan. 11, 1770, and m. Michael, son of Johann Peter Hoke (see entry).
- Adam m. Susanna Schmeisser (see entry) before 1796, and the widow of ___ Forney. After Susanna's death, Adam moved to Cumberland Co., PA, and bought a farm and grist mill. He d. at age 48, and is bur. in Largsdorf graveyard near Kingston, PA.
- Joseph.
- Susanna.
- Salome.
- Hans Michael, b. on Oct. 16, 1740.
- Maria Barbara, b. on Jan. 15, 1743, and m. Andreas Hoog (see entry).
- Elisabeth, b. about 1745, and m. Mathias Jacob, son of Mathias Schmeisser (see entry).
- Jacob, b. about 1747. He was a tavern keeper in Hanover. He m. Catherine, and had the following children:
  - John, b. on Sept. 10, 1786, bapt. at Christ Church, Littlestown, Adams Co., on July 27, 1786, and spon. by Philip and Elisabeth Schmidt.
- Leonhardt, b. on July 14, 1750, and bapt. at Warwick Lutheran Church in Lancaster Co. He m. Elisabeth, dau. of Mathias Schmeisser (see entry), in 1775, and d. on Feb. 14, 1811. She was b. on Mar. 21, 1753, and d. on Jan. 26, 1817. He was a tavern keeper in Monaghan Township. They had the following children:
  - Jacob, b. in 1776, and d. on June 17, 1831. He m. Elisabeth Dinkle, widow of ___ Musser. She d. on Oct. 9, 1832. He was York County Sheriff, and member of the state legislature in 1809. He was Justice of the peace in 1829.
  - Mary M., b. on Jan. 22, 1778.
  - Sarah, b. in Apr. 1781.
  - Frederick, b. on Aug. 24, 1783.
  - George M., b. on Feb. 11, 1785.
  - John, b. on Feb. 5, 1787.
  - Elisabeth, b. on Mar. 3, 1789.
  - Lydia, b. on Nov. 7, 1792.

- Susan, b. in 1794.
- Catharine, b. on Apr. 6, 1796, and drowned on Aug. 12, 1810.
- Ludwig, bapt. by RJL on Jan. 26, 1755, and spon. by Joseph and Barbara Schmid. He d. in Hanover aged 83 years, 9 months, and 2 days. He m. Elisabeth, and had the following children:
  - Frederick, b. about 1782 (mentioned in his grandmother's will).
  - Magdalena, b. about 1784 (mentioned in his grandmother's will).
  - Johan Jacob, b. on Mar. 6, 1786, bapt. at St. John's Lutheran Church in Adams Co. on Apr. 30, 1786, and spon. by Jacob and Anna Maria Eichelberger.
  - Sarah, b. on Oct. 10, 1788, bapt. at St. John's Lutheran Church in Adams Co. on Mar. 22, 1789, and spon. by Nicholas and Barbara Jacobi.
  - Michael, b. on Oct. 22, 1791, bapt. at St. John's Lutheran Church in Adams Co., and spon. by John and Anna Maria Winterroth.
  - Johan Georg, b. on Dec. 14, 1793, bapt. at St. John's Lutheran Church in Adams Co. on Apr. 6, 1794, and spon. by Jacob and Anna Pfarr.
  - Hanna, b. on Dec. 23, 1797, bapt. at St. John's Lutheran Church in Adams Co. on May 13, 1798, and spon. by Nichol and Barbara Jacobi.
- Maria Magdalena, bapt. by RJL on Mar. 25, 1759, and spon. by Jost and Maria Elisabeth Wagner.

Eissenhardt - Conrad was taxed in 1762. He received a warrant for 160 acres in West Manchester Township on Apr. 3, 1767, that was surveyed on May 13, 1767. His will was written in Manchester Township on Dec. 25, 1781, and probated on Jan. 26, 1782. He m. Catharina. After his death, she m. Gottfried, son of Nicholas Koenig (see entry), in 1800, and Daniel Dift at TLY on Oct. 2, 1808. She d. before 1821. Conrad and Catharina had the following children (*Ancestry of the Eissenhart Family* by Willis Wolf Eisenhart (1951)):
- Johan Georg, b. in Aug. 1759, and bapt. at CLY on Sept. 2, 1759. He m. Eve, dau. of Killian and Anna Maria (Lischey) Ziegler, and d. in Feb. 1846 (bur. in Prospect Hill cemetery). She was b. on Sept. 9, 1770, and d. in 1857. He was a blacksmith, and served as a Private under Captain John Ehrman in 1781, and Captain George Geisselman in 1781/82. He was also a doctor.
- Johan Jacob, b. on Oct. 8, 1761, bapt. at CLY on Nov. 1, 1761, and spon. by Georg, son of Johan Jacob Eissenhardt. He m. Elisabeth, dau. of Henry and Freene Wohlgemuht, at TLY on Dec. 30, 1783. He was a blacksmith, and served as a Private in Captain Reinhard Bott's Company in 1783. He d. in Dover/West Manchester Township in 1812, and his estate was administered on Dec. 8, 1812.
- Anna Maria, b. about 1763, and d. between 1782 and 1790.

- Maria Elisabeth, b. on Sept. 17, 1765, and bapt. at CLY on Oct. 20, 1765.
- Conrad, b. in 1767, m. Christina, dau. of Jonas and Anna Catharina (Joseph) Bott (see entry), and Christina, dau. of John and Catharina (Maul) Joseph. He d. on May 25, 1858 (bur. at WOL). Catharina d. on Jan. 21, 1861.
- Johan Peter, b. on Jan. 17, 1772, bapt. at WOL on Feb. 22, 1772, and spon. by Peter Ottinger and Maria Witmeyer.

Eissenhardt - Johan Georg was taxed in 1762, and naturalized in Sept. 1764. He was said to be a son of Johan Jacob Eissenhardt, and Conrad was probably his bro. He moved to Frederick Co., MD, soon after his marriage, but returned to York Co., PA, in 1771. On Apr. 26, 1771, he purchased land in Shrewsbury Township, and was taxed there in 1779. He was a blacksmith, and moved to Bedford Co., PA, in 1789. He m. Anna Elisabeth, dau. of Jacob Ottinger (see entry). They had the following children (*Ancestry of the Eissenhart Family* by Willis Wolf Eisenhart (1951)):
- Anna Maria, b. on June 18, 1768, and bapt. at CLY on July 3, 1768.
- Anna Elisabeth, b. on Feb. 20, 1772, bapt. at FRI on Apr. 12, 1772, and spon. by Michael Ness, P. Jacob, and Clara Ottinger.
- Dorothea, b. on Sept. 23, 1776, bapt. at FRI on Nov. 10, 1776, and spon. by Dorothea, dau. of Jacob Ottinger.
- Johan Jacob, b. on Jan. 9, 1779, bapt. at FRI on Mar. 14, 1779, and spon. by Jacob and Magdalena Hess.
- Johan Georg, b. on June 18, 1784, bapt. at FIS, and spon. by Christian and Maria Catharina Mek.

Ellenbarger - Peter was taxed in 1762. His will was written in Manchester Township on Mar. 23, 1796, and probated on Apr. 6, 1796. He m. Eva. Her probate inventory was filed in 1802. An Ulrich Ellenbarger's probate inventory was filed in Windsor Township in 1782, but his relationship to Peter has not been proven. Peter and Eva had the following children:
- Christian.
- Peter, m. Mary, dau. of Johan Weltz of Manheim Township before 1793.
- Ulrich, received his father's loom.

Emig - Johannes was a nailsmith and journeyman at Uttenhoffen, Northern Alsace. He m. Anna Dorothea, dau. of Hans Georg and Anna Maria (Volckel) Rotter, in Gundershoffen on Nov. 21, 1717, and immigrated to America on the ship *John and William* in 1732. He received a warrant for 200 acres in West Manchester Township on May 24, 1746, that was surveyed as 454 acres on May 18, 1767. Johannes

was naturalized on Sept. 24, 1762. His probate inventory was filed in Manchester Township in 1787. He had the following children at Gundershoffen (see BNA):
- Johan Georg, b. on June 18, 1718, and bapt. on June 20, 1718.
- Nicolaus, b. on May 24, 1719, and bapt. on May 29, 1719. He m. Eva Margaretha Rausch, and had the following children:
  - Eva Barbara, b. on July 17, 1740, and bapt. at the First Reformed Congregation in Lancaster, PA, on July 19, 1740.
  - Philip, b. on Jan. 1, 1745, bapt. at the First Reformed Congregation at Lancaster, and spon. by Philip Roemig and wife.
  - Johannes, bapt. by RJL on July 5, 1753, and spon. by Johannes and Dorothea Emig.
  - Joseph, bapt. by RJL on Apr. 20, 1755, and spon. by Joseph and Barbara Schmid.
  - Friedrich, bapt. by RJL on May 13, 1759, and spon. by Adam Eichelberger and Lowis Erbin.
- Johan Georg, b. on Mar. 7, 1721, and bapt. on Mar. 9, 1721.
- Johannes, b. on Mar. 14, 1722, and bapt. on Mar. 15, 1722. He was naturalized on Sept. 24, 1762, and d. in Manchester Township in 1787. He m. Maria Margaretha, dau. of Valentine Krantz (see entry), at the First Reformed Church at Lancaster, on Dec. 15, 1745, and had the following children:
  - Valentin, b. on Nov. 14, 1748, bapt. by RJL on Jan. 22, 1749, and spon. by Valentine and Elisabeth Krantz. He d. on Apr. 15, 1833, and is bur. at WOL. He m. Barbara, dau. of Philip and Christina (Reiff) Gauff (see entry in Dover section). She d. on Dec. 24, 1812. He served in the Revolutionary War.
  - Anna Margaretha, bapt. by RJL on Nov. 11, 1750, and spon. by Zacharias and Anna Margareth Schuckert.
  - Johannes, b. on Feb. 19, 1753, and bapt. at CLY on Apr. 1, 1753.
  - Johan Georg, b. on Nov. 19, 1761, and bapt. at CLY on Jan. 1, 1762.
  - Anna Barbara, bapt. by RJL on Apr. 8, 1764, and spon. by Georg and Anna Barbara Meyer.
- Anna Maria, b. on July 6, 1723, and bapt. on July 8, 1723. She m. Anthony Kobel, and had the following children:
  - Johannes, b. on July 15, 1742, bapt. at the First Reformed Congregation in Lancaster, PA, on Oct. 4, 1742, and spon. by Johannes Emig.
- Johan Daniel, b. on Feb. 6, 1727, and bapt. on Feb. 9, 1727.
- Magdalena, b. on Sept. 28, 1731, and bapt. on Sept. 30, 1731.
- Mathias, b. on Feb. 28, 1737, bapt. at The First Reformed Congregation at Lancaster on Apr. 17, 1737, and spon. by Mathias Marker, Mathias Resser, and Frederick Strubel and wife. He m. Anna Margaretha in 1759, and had the following children:

- Eva Dorothea, bapt. by RJL on Dec. 16, 1759, and spon. by Johannes and Dorothea Emig.
- Niclaus, bapt. by RJL on Jan. 4, 1762, and spon. by Nicolaus and Eva Margaretha Emig.
- Elisabeth, bapt. by RJL on Nov. 20, 1762, and spon. by Peter Budinger and Maria Elisabeth Emig.
- Johan Philliph, bapt. by RJL on Jan. 12, 1766, and spon. by Philliph Emig and Elisabeth Bergerin.
- Maria Elisabeth, b. about 1737,

Endler - Philip Adam was b. to Johan Michael and Anna Catharina Endler, and bapt. at Ittlingen Lutheran Church on Jan. 23, 1717. He immigrated to America on the ship *Snow Molly* in 1737, and was naturalized on Apr. 10, 1760. He was taxed in 1762, and m. Maria Margaretha, dau. of Michael Gaiss (see entry) in Lancaster Co., Leacock Township, PA, on Apr. 10, 1739. She d. in York Co., PA, on Nov. 21, 1762, at 4:00 a.m. She is bur. at Christ's Lutheran Church. Philipp was alive in 1762. On July 27, 1765, he sold 180 acres in West Manchester Township to Matthew Smyser. They had the following children (6 sons and 3 daus. (5 sons and 2 daus. survive in 1762)):
- Johan Martin, b. on Mar. 28, 1742, bapt. at Christ's Lutheran on Apr. 7, 1742, and spon. by Martin Weigel and wife.
- Anna Maria, b. on Aug. 28, 1743, bapt. at Christ's Lutheran on Sept. 18, 1743, and spon. by Johan Martin and Anna Maria Eichelberger.
- Philip, b. about 1745, and m. Magdalena, dau. of Philip Peter before 1768.
- Johan Jacob, b. on Jan. 18, 1748, and bapt. at Christ's Lutheran Church of York, York Co., PA, on May 22, 1748. His probate inventory was filed at York in 1804.
- Juliana, b. on Jan. 7, 1750, and bapt. at Christ's Lutheran on Mar. 4, 1750.

Ertel - Valentine was taxed in 1762.

Eyster - Christian was b. in Stuttgart Neckar, Wurtemburg, in 1710 to Johan Jacob (1665-1745) and Catherine Eyster. Christian m. Anna Margarethe, dau. of Martin and Anna Barbara Schmeisser (see entry), in 1732. She was b. in 1711, and d. on Apr. 4, 1780 (after Christian's death, she m. Martin Miller (before 1749)). Christian received a warrant for 100 acres in Manheim Township on Oct. 28, 1746, and 500 acres in West Manchester Township on Oct. 30, 1736 (Blunston License/patented as 508 acres on Apr. 5, 1746). Christian d. in Manchester Township in 1747 (will dated Aug. 26, 1747). They had the following children in West Manchester Township:

- Elias, b. on Aug. 6, 1734, m. Anna Maria, dau. of Christian Lau (see entry), on Aug. 6, 1754, and d. in Manchester Township in 1833. He is bur. at WOL. She was b. in 1737, and d. in 1781. They had the following children:
  - Anna Maria Magdalena, b. on Nov. 16, 1755, bapt. by RJL on Dec. 14, 1755, and spon. by Christoph Laumann and Magdalena Lauin. She m. Christopher, son of Jacob and Mary Catharina (Klee/Clay) Slagle of Berwick Township, on Apr. 18, 1776, and d. on Oct. 1, 1793. He was b. on July 2, 1747, bapt. at STM in 1747, and d. on Sept. 21, 1831. She is bur. in STM cemetery, and he is bur. in Mount Olivet cemetery in Hanover.
  - Johan Georg, b. on Feb. 4, 1757. He m. Maria Magdalena, dau. of Jacob and Maria Catharina (Klee/Clay) Slagle of Berwick Township, on Nov. 14, 1780, and d. on June 9, 1836. She was b. on Dec. 16, 1763, bapt. at STM on Jan. 21, 1764, and d. on July 15, 1807. They resided in Adams Co., Straban Townsip, PA, and are bur. in Bender's cemetery in Butler Township.
  - Christian, b. in 1759, m. Margaret, dau. of Peter Wolf (see entry) about 1778, and Elisabeth Senseny on Oct. 25, 1788. Elisabeth was b. in 1765, and d. in 1814. Christian d. on Oct. 30, 1808.
  - Peter, b. on Feb. 28, 1761. He m. Margaret, dau. of David Slagle of Berwick Township, and d. on Feb. 19, 1836. She was b. in 1769, and d. in 1850.
  - Johan Michael, b. on Oct. 10, 1766, bapt. at WOL on Nov. 30, 1766, and spon. by Michael and Anna Maria Lau.
  - Elisabeth, b. on Apr. 10, 1770, bapt. at WOL on May 6, 1770, and spon. by Andreas, son of Peter Lau, and Elisabeth, dau. of Peter Amelot. She m. Daniel, son of David Slagle of Berwick Township, and d. on Dec. 16, 1850. He was b. in 1760, and d. in 1822.
  - Johan Adam, b. on Sept. 30, 1772, bapt. at WOL on Oct. 25, 1772, and spon. by Casper and Magdalena Kerber. He m. Elisabeth Emig on Nov. 21, 1797, and d. on Dec. 31, 1850. She was b. in 1776, and d. in 1843.
  - Maria Catharina, b. on Apr. 14, 1774, bapt. at WOL on May 28, 1774, and spon. by Peter and Catharina Menges. She d. in 1777.
  - Wilhelm, b. on Dec. 4, 1777, bapt. at WOL on Jan. 11, 1778, and spon. by Wilhelm Moymeyer and Catharina Schmidt. He m. Elisabeth Spangler on May 6, 1802, and d. on Sept. 6, 1824. She was b. in 1785, and d. in 1849.
  - Anna Maria, b. on Jan. 25, 1781, bapt. at WOL on Feb. 25, 1781, and spon. by Andreas Lau and wife. She m. John Emig on Apr. 4, 1802, and d. on Mar. 1, 1838. He was b. in 1780, and d. in 1842.
- Hannah, bapt. on Mar. 16, 1735, and m. Peter, son of Michael Sprenckel (see entry).

- Margaret, b. in 1737, and m. Johan Michael, son of Michael Sprenckel (see entry).
- Elisabetha, b. about 1739, and m. Jacob Heidler. They both d. before 1763, and had the following dau.:
  - Margaret, b. about 1761.
- Georg, b. in 1741, m. Anna Christina, dau. of Jacob Altland, and d. in West Manchester Township in 1810 (date of probate inventory). She was b. on Aug. 23, 1743, and d. on Dec. 4, 1825. They had the following children:
  - Johan Georg, b. on Aug. 30, 1762, and bapt. at CLY on Oct. 31, 1762.
  - Johann Peter, b. on Sept. 22, 1764, bapt. at WOL on Jan. 21, 1765, and spon. by Peter and Susanna Lau.
  - Anna Maria, b. on Oct. 14, 1767, bapt. at WOL on Nov. 1, 1767, and spon. by Elias and Anna Maria Eyster.
  - Magdalena, b. on Sept. 8, 1769, bapt. at WOL, and spon. by Casper and Magdalena Kerber.
  - Margaretha, b. on Mar. 20, 1773, bapt. at WOL on May 2, 1773, and spon. by Frederick and Margaretha Romer.
  - Elisabeth, b. on Feb. 25, 1776, bapt. at WOL on Mar. 24, 1776, and spon. by Peter and Maria Barbara Spiess.
  - Johannes, b. on Jan. 24, 1779, bapt. at WOL on Apr. 5, 1779, and spon. by Andreas and Catharina Hanss.
  - Anna Maria, b. on Mar. 11, 1782, bapt. at WOL on Apr. 19, 1782, and spon. by Elias Eister and wife.
- Christian, b. about 1743.
- Christina, b. in Jan. 1746, and m. Georg, son of Michael Sprenckel (see entry).

Fackler - Adam was taxed in 1762. He was son of Jacob and Magdalen Fackler of York Town (Jacob's will was probated on Oct. 9, 1775 (Jacob's son, Johannes, resided in Shrewsbury Township)). He immigrated to America on the ship *Charming Nancy* on Oct. 8, 1737. He received a warrant for 150 acres in West Manchester Township on July 26, 1765, that was surveyed as 197.120 acres on Oct. 23, 1765. Adam's will was written in York Town Township on May 7, 1771, and probated on May 15, 1771. Adam m. Maria Magdalena, and had the following children:
- Gottleib, b. about 1746. He resided in Manchester Township in 1779. He m. Barbara. He moved to Tuscarwas Co., OH, about 1812, and d. in 1816.
- Jacob, b. on Apr. 27, 1748, and bapt. at CLY on May 20, 1748.
- Johan Georg, b. on Feb. 21, 1750, and bapt. at CLY on Mar. 18, 1750.

- Maria Magdalena, b. on June 12, 1752, and bapt. at CLY on June 28, 1752.
- Eva Catharina, bapt. by RJL on July 23, 1755, and spon. by Georg Adam and Catharina Baur.
- Catharina, b. about 1757.
- Elisabeth, b. on June 16, 1760, and bapt. at CLY on July 6, 1760.
- Susan Maria, b. on Dec. 9, 1761, and bapt. at CLY on Jan. 1, 1762 (d. young).
- Johan Adam, b. on Aug. 31, 1763, and bapt. at CLY on Oct. 2, 1763 (not mentioned in will).

Fletcher - Jacob wrote his will in Manchester Township on Sept. 24, 1758, and it was probated on Oct. 17, 1758. He m. Anna Elisabetha, and had the following children (the will mentions sons that are minors, and that none of his children after his death are to be brought up in the Catholic faith but Lutheran or Calvinist):
- Anna Maria.
- Maria Elisabetha.

Frey - Johann Georg m. Elisabeth, dau. of Georg Hechler (see entry). His will was written in Manchester Township on Oct. 16, 1802, and probated on Feb. 14, 1804. They had the following children:
- Susanna, b. on Sept. 20, 1760, bapt. at TLY on May 29, 1763, and spon. by Johann Georg Hechler and Elisabeth Knoer.
- Anna Maria, b. on Mar. 13, 1762, bapt. at TLY on May 29, 1763, and spon. by Johann Jacob Hechler and Catharina Klein.
- Johann Andreas, bapt. at QUI on Oct. 26, 1767, and spon. by Andreas and Anna Florentina Klein.
- Conrad, b. on Apr. 10, 1769, bapt. at QUI on Apr. 30, 1772, and spon. by Conrad Klein and Catharina Elisabeth Meiern.
- Johann Jacob, b. on Jan. 26, 1772, bapt. at QUI on Mar. 15, 1772, and spon. by Jacob Hechler and Anna Maria Mayern.
- Maria Eva, b. on Feb. 4, 1774, bapt. at QUI on Apr. 4, 1774, and spon. by Eva Becker/Beherin and Andreas Klein.
- Johan Georg, b. on Mar. 21, 1776, bapt. at QUI on Apr. 14, 1776, and spon. by Peter Schaffer.
- Maria Elisabet, b. on Feb. 9, 1778, bapt. at QUI on Mar. 22, 1778, and spon. by Peter Schaffer and wife.

Freytag (Friday) - Nicholas was taxed in 1762. He m. Maria Catharina, widow of Nicholas Klingler, in Gonnheim, Germany, on May 7, 1720, and Anna Elisabeth in Gonnheim in 1733. He immigrated to America on the ship *Thistle* in 1738. He had the following children at Gonnheim (see BFG):

- Nicholas, bapt. on July 14, 1720, and spon. by Nicholas Coblentz and Anna Margaretha Klingler.
- Catharina Elisabetha, bapt. on Nov. 3, 1734, and spon. by Johan Jacob Pfarr and Catharina Elisabetha, dau. of Hans Martin Bohler.
- Johan Martin, bapt. on May 5, 1737, and spon. by Johan Martin and Anna Catharina Bohler.
- Catharina Elisabetha, bapt. by RJL on May 26, 1745, and spon. by Johan Adam Kramer and Anna Catharina Welshofer.
- Johan Martin, bapt. by RJL on Aug. 31, 1755, and spon. by Johan Martin and Catharina Bohler.

<u>Friedlein</u> (Friedland) - Johan Ludwig was taxed in 1762. He m. Anna Margaretha, and had the following children:
- Johan Ludwig, b. on June 5, 1756, and bapt. at CLY on July 18, 1756.
- Maria Elisabeth, b. on Oct. 26, 1758, and bapt. at CLY on Nov. 12, 1758.
- Johan Georg, b. on Oct. 23, 1760, and bapt. at CLY on Nov. 23, 1760.
- Anna Catharina, b. on Feb. 26, 1762, and bapt. at CLY on Apr. 18, 1762.
- Johan Peter, b. on Sept. 28, 1764, and bapt. at CLY on Nov. 18, 1764.
- Anna Maria, b. on Mar. 11, 1767, and bapt. at CLY on May 3, 1767.

<u>Gaiss</u> - Michael m. Rosina, and was a shoemaker in Lidolsheimin, Durlach, Germany. He d. in Germany before 1738, and had the following daus., who immigrated to America in 1738:
- Maria Margaretha, b. in Lidolsheimin on Mar. 13, 1715, and m. Philipp Adam Endtler (see entry) in Lancaster Co., Leacock Township, PA, on Apr. 10, 1739.
- Elisabetha, m. Johan Dieterich Uhler in Lancaster Co., Leacock Township, PA, (by Reverend Stoever) on July 10, 1739 (see entry).

<u>Geese</u> (Grees) - Hans Michael was taxed in 1762. He m. Anna Elisabeth, and had the following children:
- Johan Michael, bapt. by RJL on Sept. 28, 1755, and spon. by Heinrich and Catharina Ruck.

<u>Gemling</u> - Bernhard wrote his will on July 30, 1766, and it was probated on Aug. 11, 1766. He m. Anna Catharina, and had the following children:
- Catharina Margaretha, b. on Oct. 2, 1760, and bapt. at CLY on Nov. 22, 1760.

- Johan Bernhard, b. on Aug. 17, 1764, bapt. at STR on Sept. 5, 1765, and spon. by Andreas and Anna Florentina Klein.

Gentzler - Conrad m. Gertrude. He had 247 acres in West Manchester Township surveyed on Oct. 13, 1746. His will was written in York on Mar. 16, 1773, and probated on Apr. 11, 1778. His probate inventory was filed in Paradise Township in 1778. They had the following children:
  - Maria Magdalena, b. about 1722, and m. Johan Philip, son of Christian Lau (see entry), in 1742.
  - Philip W., b. in 1741, and d. in Lincoln Co., Lincolnton/Leeper's Creek, North Carolina, on Oct. 7, 1804. In 1767, he purchased land at High Schoals. He m. Juliana, dau. of Philip Wintermeyer (see entry), and had the following children:
    - Catharina, m. ____ Cline.
    - Anna Margaretha, b. on Sept. 24, 1760, and bapt. at CLY on Oct. 12, 1760. She d. on May 2, 1833. She m. Philip Devepaugh. He was b. in 1751, and d. on June 29, 1825.
    - Maria Catharina (Katie), b. on July 21, 1762, bapt. at CLY on July 22, 1762, and m. John Finger (listed separately from Catharina who m. ____ Cline, but may be the same person with two marriages).
    - Mary, m. ____ Garden.
    - Elisabeth.
    - Barbara, m. Henry Troutman in 1802.
    - John (Conrad), b. on Apr. 1, 1764, and bapt. at CLY on Apr. 15, 1764. He m. Barbara Rudisill (see entry), and resided in Rutherford Co., North Carolina.
    - Philip, m. Mary Quickel.
    - Georg, m. Magdalena, dau. of Peter Finger.
  - Georg Philip m. Maria Magdalena, dau. of Peter Lau (see entry), at Strayer's on Nov. 17, 1767. His probate inventory was filed in Codorus Township in 1816. They had the following children:
    - Johan Georg, bapt. at the Monocacy Lutheran Congregation in Frederick Co. on Oct. 2, 1768, and spon. by Isaac and Anna Jauler.
    - Susanna, b. on Mar. 3, 1774, bapt. at Wolf's in York Co. on Mar. 27, 1774, and spon. by Valentin Alt and Catharina Lau.
    - Anna Eva, b. on May 2, 1776, bapt. at Wolf's on May 16, 1776, and spon. by Johan Peter Lau and Eva Lau, single. She m. Michael, son of Michael and Magdalena Kessler. He was b. on Aug. 5, 1774, and d. in Codorus Township on Mar. 20, 1871. She d. on Oct. 30, 1839.
    - Conrad, b. on Oct. 4, 1777, bapt. at Wolf's on Nov. 22, 1777, and spon. by Andreas and Elisabeth Lau.

EARLY GERMAN SETTLERS OF YORK CO., PA

- Peter, b. on Jan. 24, 1782, bapt. at Wolf's on Feb. 24, 1782, and spon. by Georg Lau and wife.
- Conrad m. Maria Eva, and had the following children:
  - Michael, b. on Nov. 8, 1767, bapt. at Wolf's on Nov. 29, 1767, and spon. by Michael and Margaretha Fiesel.
  - Magdalena, b. on Jan. 1, 1771, bapt. at Wolf's on Jan. 20, 1771, and spon. by Casper and Magdalena Kerber.
  - Johan Philip, b. on Sept. 18, 1772, bapt. at Wolf's on Oct. 25, 1772, and spon. by Philip and Magdalena Lau.
  - Johan Georg, b. on June 30, 1774, bapt. at Wolf's on July 15, 1774, and spon. by Georg and Anna Maria Schwob.
- Johan Valentine, b. on Sept. 4, 1759, and bapt. at CLY on Sept. 10, 1759.
- Maria Elisabeth, b. on Aug. 8, 1761, and bapt. at CLY on Aug. 13, 1761.

Geyer (Keyer) - Jacob received a warrant for 300 acres in West Manchester Township on Oct. 28, 1746.

Graber - Henry was taxed in Manchester Township in 1779. He m. Christine, and had the following children:
- Philip, b. on Sept. 7, 1744, and bapt. at CLY on Sept. 14, 1744.
- Johan Adam, b. on Aug. 31, 1746, and bapt. at CLY on Oct. 28, 1746.
- Elisabeth May, b. on Aug. 4, 1748, and bapt. at CLY on Aug. 28, 1748.
- Catharine, b. on May 15, 1751, and bapt. at CLY on June 2, 1751.
- John, b. on Aug. 4, 1753, and bapt. at CLY on Sept. 29, 1753.

Graber - Philip was taxed in 1762. His will was written in Manchester Township on Jan. 22, 1797, and probated on Oct. 26, 1805. He was taxed in Manchester Township in 1779. He m. Maria Esther, and had the following children:
- Henry, b. on Jan. 14, 1746, and bapt. at CLY on May 8, 1746 (not mentioned in will).
- John, b. on June 17, 1749, and bapt. on July 17, 1749. He m. Maria Barbara.
- Jacob, b. on July 24, 1751, and bapt. at CLY on Aug. 25, 1751.
- Anna Margaret, b. on Dec. 6, 1747, bapt. at CLY on May 31, 1748, and m. Johan Adam, son of Erasmus Holtzappel (see entry), at STR on May 27, 1766.
- Susanna Maria, b. on Mar. 7, 1753, and bapt. at CLY on Mar. 25, 1753. She m. George Wetterrect.

- Catharina, bapt. by RJL on Aug. 10, 1755, and spon. by Peter and Catharina Stambach. She m. Balthasar, son of Valentine Hamm (see entry).
- Elisabeth, bapt. by RJL on Aug. 14, 1757, and spon. by Christian and Elisabeth Groll. She m. Mathias Klein.

Grass - Andreas d. before 1750. His probate inventory was filed in 1752. He m. Louisa. They had the following children:
- Johan Andreas, b. on Feb. 19, 1750, and bapt. at CLY on Mar. 20, 1750. He m. Maria Catharina about 1771. His will was written in Manchester Township on Jan. 22, 1818, and probated on Feb. 17, 1818.

Graybill (Krepill) - Jacob received a warrant for 200 acres in West Manchester Township on Oct. 30, 1736, that was surveyed as 361 acres on Apr. 8, 1746 (Blunston License). He immigrated to America on Aug. 19, 1729. He applied to keep a tavern in the town of York in July 1751, but was denied. He m. Catharina (she was alive in 1760), and had the following children:
- Susanna, b. about 1734, and m. Daniel Dewalt (see entry in Shrewsbury section).
- Michael, b. about 1736, and m. Jane Hair at STR on Feb. 13, 1770. He was a sponsor to the baptism of Daniel Dewalt in 1756 (FRI).

Graybill - Johannes wrote his will in Lancaster Co. (?Donegal Township) on Nov. 25, 1773, and it was probated in York Co. on Mar. 2, 1775. His probate inventory was filed in Manchester Township in 1774, and Donegal Township in 1775. He m. Anna, and had the following children:
- Christian.
- Barbara.
- Anna
- Johannes. He probably the John, who had his is probate inventory filed in Manchester Township in 1801.
- Eve.

Grove - Jacob was taxed in 1762.

Grunwald (Greenwald) - Christophel was taxed in 1762. He m. Anna Maria Grockrine at STM on Jan. 2, 1756, Anna Maria, dau. of Anthony and Margaret Grever of Manheim Township before 1769, and Maria, dau. of Frederick Becker (see entry), before 1781. He was taxed in Manchester Township in 1779. His will was written in Manchester Township on Oct. 5, 1805, and probated on Nov. 8, 1805. He had the following children:

- Abraham.
- John, m. Elisabeth, dau. of Frederick Ruhl (see entry in Codorus section).
- Frederick, m. Anna Maria before 1800.
- Johan Jacob, b. on Aug. 23, 1761, and bapt. at CLY on Oct. 4, 1761 (mother is Anna Maria).
- Anna.
- Catherine, m. John Heistand.

Gunther - Michael was taxed in 1762. He was a sponsor to the baptism of Michael Klein in 1756 (RJL). He m. Christina Elisabeth, dau. of Michael Kuntzel (see entry), and had the following children:
- Conrad, b. on July 23, 1758, and bapt. at CLY on Aug. 13, 1758.
- Jacob, bapt. by RJL on Apr. 5, 1761, and spon. by Jacob Kuntzel and Anna Maria Lowenstein.
- Michael, b. on Feb. 7, 1770, bapt. in July 1770, and spon. by Michael Quickel and wife.
- Andreas, b. on May 4 (9), 1773, bapt. at QUI on May 9, 1773, and spon. by Conrad Klein and Catharina Elisabetha Meyers.
- Anna Margaretha, b. on Mar. 16, 1781, bapt. at QUI on June 10, 1781, and spon. by Johan Scherp and wife.

Gutling - Peter was taxed in 1762. He m. Maria Catharina, dau. of Johann Henrich and Anna Maria (Herbach) Cherdron/Schetrone (see entry) (she is probably the Catharina Gutling that m. Johan Nichol Jacob at STR on July 18, 1771). Peter d. about 1764. They had the following children:
- Heinrich, bapt. by RJL on July 6, 1755, and spon. by Abraham and Margareth Schederon.
- Anna Maria, bapt. at STR on Mar. 27, 1757, and spon. by Heinrich and Anna Maria Schederon.
- Johan Peter, bapt. at STR on June 21, 1761, and spon. by Peter and Elisabetha Benss. He m. Barbara, dau. of Christian Stabler (see entry in Shrewsbury section), and d. in York Co., Springfield Township, PA, on Apr. 16, 1815.
- Maria Elisabetha, bapt. by RJL on Dec. 18, 1763, and spon. by Leonhard and Maria Elisabeth Schederon.

Hammer - Reinhart received a warrant for 350 acres in Manchester Township on Oct. 30, 1736, that was surveyed as 259 acres on Dec. 19, 1754 (Blunston License). He m. Susanna Maria, and Appolonica between 1743 and 1759. Appolonica's probate inventory was filed in Manchester Township in 1790. They had the following children:
- Maria, b. about 1717, and m. Ludwig Wysong (see entry).

MANCHESTER TOWNSHIP

Hanacle - John was taxed in 1762.

Haner - Philip Jr. was taxed in 1762.

Hoehns - Philip Henrich was taxed in 1762 (see entry in Codorus section).

Hechler - Hans Georg, son of Jacob and Margaretha Hechler, was b. in Birlenbach, Northern Alsace, on Apr. 14, 1708, and bapt. on Apr. 15, 1708. He moved to Ingelsheim by 1733, and immigrated to America on the ship *Barclay* in 1754. He was taxed in 1762. His probate inventory was filed in Manchester Township in 1774. His will was written on Apr. 12, 1773, and probated on Jan. 31, 1774. He m. Susanna, and had the following children (see BNA):
- Barbara, b. about 1731, and was confirmed at Hunspach in 1746.
- Anna Maria, b. in 1733, and d. on July 30, 1741.
- Hans Martin, bapt. at Birlenbach (in the church at Hunspach) on Jan. 27, 1735 (confirmed at Rott in 1749). He m. Anna Barbara. In 1774, they were sponsors to the baptism of a child of Georg Vogler at Zion Lutheran Church in Washington Co., Hagerstown, MD. They had the following children:
  - Johan Georg, b. on Apr. 31, 1761, bapt. at CLY on Sept. 19, 1761, and spon. by Johan Georg, son of Nicholas Vogel and the single dau. of Conrad Stuck.
- Elisabetha, b. about 1737, and was confirmed at Hunspach in 1750. She m. Johann Georg Frey (see entry).
- Samuel, b. on July 27, 1739, and bapt. at Rott Lutheran Church on Aug. 4, 1739.
- Johann Jacob, b. on June 8, 1741, and bapt. at Rott Lutheran Church on June 11, 1741. He m. Barbara about 1778, and had the following children:
  - Maria Elisabeth, b. on Dec. 27, 1778, bapt. at QUI on Feb. 30 (?) 1779, and spon. by Georg Frey and wife.
  - Catherine, b. on Sept. 2, 1781, and bapt. at CLY on Oct. 7, 1781.
  - Johann Jacob, bapt. at QUI on Apr. 18, 1784, and spon. by Johann Adam and Barbara Miller.
  - Maria Barbara, b. on May 19, 1786, bapt. at QUI on July 2, 1786, and spon. by Georg and Elisabeth Frey.
- Johann Georg, b. on June 13, 1743, and bapt. at Rott Lutheran Church on June 16, 1743. He was confirmed at the Lower Bermudian Church in Adams Co. on May 22, 1763. He m. Elisabeth, and had the following children:
  - Peter, b. on Mar. 6, 1771, bapt. at QUI on Mar. 17, 1771, and spon. by Peter Schaffer and wife.

- Johannes, b. on Apr. 6, 1773, bapt. at QUI on May 9, 1773, and spon. by Georg Frey and wife.
- Catharina, b. on Mar. 9, 1775, bapt. at QUI on Mar. 19, 1775, and spon. by Jacob Hechler and Catharine Kohler.
- Catarina Elisabeth, b. on Jan. 28, 1777, bapt. at QUI, and spon. by Velte Kohler and Catharina Becker.
- Susanna, b. on June 21, 1779, bapt. at QUI on July 10, 1779, and spon. by Susanna Frey.
- Conrad, b. on Apr. 4, 1782, bapt. at QUI on Apr. 7, 1782, and spon. by Conrad Klein and wife.
- Johann Michael, b. on Feb. 20, 1747, and bapt. at Rott on Feb. 24, 1747.

Heckert - Frantz was b. on Apr. 18, 1702, and d. on Jan. 23, 1752. He was bur. at CLY on Jan. 25, 1752. He m. Maria Greth. His will was written in Manchester Township on Nov. 1, 1751, and probated on Jan. 2, 1753. They had the following children:
- Jacob was taxed in 1762. He m. Anna Maria Magdalen Spickert at CAN on Apr. 22, 1755. His probate inventory was filed in Manchester Township in 1772. Her will was written on Sept. 29, 1810, and probated on Dec. 27, 1810. They had the following children:
  - Johan Philip, b. on May 18, 1756, and bapt. at CLY on June 27, 1756. He m. Dorothea. His will was written in York Borough on Oct. 30, 1811, and probated on Dec. 8, 1812.
  - Johan Jacob, b. on Aug. 8, 1759, and bapt. at CLY on Oct. 14, 1759. He m. Maria Updtegraf at TLY on Feb. 18, 1783.
  - Johan Georg, b. on Oct. 15, 1760, and bapt. at CLY on Dec. 25, 1760.
  - Catharine, b. on May 16, 1762, and bapt. at CLY on July 4, 1762. She m. Peter Reisinger at TLY on Sept. 3, 1786.
- Johan Peter m. Anna Maria Schumacher at CAN on May 5, 1755.
- Regina.
- Anna Margareth (was to come of age in June 1755).

Heid - Christian was taxed in 1762. He m. Anna Maria, and had the following children:
- Lowis Sophia, bapt. by RJL on Sept. 1, 1754, and spon. by Christo and Lowis Sophia Haubli.

Hens - Philiph was taxed in 1762. He received a warrant for 200 acres in West Manchester Township on Mar. 30, 1767. He m. Barbara about 1743, and had the following children:
- Philiph, b. about 1744. He received a warrant for 250 acres in West Manchester and Manchester Township on Mar. 13, 1767.

- Anna Catharina, bapt. by RJL on Mar. 8, 1746, and spon. by Heinrich and Anna Catharina Wolf.
- Johan Peter, bapt. by RJL on Feb. 16, 1755, and spon. by Philliph and Catharina Weber.
- Johan Martin, bapt. by RJL on July 31, 1757, and spon. by Martin and Susanna Baur.

Herman - Johan Nicholas was taxed in 1762. His will was probated on Apr. 5, 1764. He m. Ester Schwenk, and had the following children:
- Maria Margaretha, b. on Dec. 4, 1751, and bapt. at CLY on Dec. 15, 1751.
- Johan Jacob, b. on Aug. 15, 1754, and bapt. at CLY on Aug. 18, 1754.
- Johan, b. on Mar. 20, 1760, and bapt. at CLY on Apr. 6, 1760.
- Johann Philip, b. on Sept. 9, 1762, bapt. at TLY on Oct. 17, 1762, and spon. by Johann Philip Weiter and Catharine Schaedle.

Herris (Harry) - Johan Martin was taxed in 1762. He m. Anna Maria, and had the following children:
- John, b. on Feb. 18, 1760, and bapt. at CLY on Apr. 6, 1760.
- Johan Adam, b. on May 1, 1762, and bapt. at CLY on May 3, 1762.

Heyer - Johan Philip was b. in Rummershausen Hesse-Cassel, Germany (Rummelhausen Limeshain). He m. Anna Elisabetha Bergtold at Gonnheim on Jan. 6, 1711, and had the following children there (unless otherwise noted) (see BFG):
- Appolonia, bapt. at Friedelsheim on Nov. 8, 1711, and spon. by Johan Georg and Anna Barbara Sorg.
- Johan (Philip), bapt. on May 28, 1713. Philip Heyer, age 31, immigrated to America on the ship *Lydia* in 1743.
- Anna Barbara, bapt. on Aug. 21, 1718, and m. Christian Kramer (see entry in Dover section).
- Johan Friderich, bapt. on Apr. 1, 1720, and spon. by Johannes and Anna Margaretha Spannknebel. He immigrated to America on the ship *Lydia* in 1743. A Frederick Hayer m. Margaret Schmoker at Lititz Moravian Church in Lancaster Co., PA, in 1746. Frederick was m. to a Catharina in 1747, when they were sponsors at the baptism of a child of Christian Kramer.
- Anna Elisabetha, bapt. on Jan. 24, 1723.
- Johan Valentin, b. in 1725, and immigrated to America on the ship *Lydia* in 1743. He m. Anna Catharina, dau. of Jacob and Catharina Welschofer of Springettsbury Township. They had the following children (bapt. by RJL unless otherwise noted):
  - Johan Jacob, bapt. on Feb. 3, 1751, and spon. by Jacob and Anna Catharina Welshoffer.

- Maria Elisabetha, bapt. on Nov. 26, 1752, and spon. by Johannes Comfort and Maria Elisabetha Welshofer.
- Johannes, bapt. on Mar. 9, 1755, and spon. by Johannes Schultz and Eva Welschofer.
- Johan Georg, bapt. at Creutz Creek on Jan. 10, 1757, and spon. by Johan Georg Spengler and wife.
- Anna Maria, b. on Mar. 7, 1760, bapt. at CLY on June 4, 1760, and spon. by Anna Maria Schultz.
- Eva, b. on Feb. 26, 1763, bapt. at CLY on Mar. 20, 1763, and spon. by Killian Schmall and wife.

Hoffman - Johan was taxed in 1762. His probate inventory was filed in Manchester Township in 1773 (he is listed as John Sr.). He m. Maria Elisabeth. Her probate inventory was filed in Newberry Township in 1774. They had the following children:
- John. His probate inventory was filed in Newberry Township in 1780 (he is listed as John Jr.).
- Juliana, b. about 1751, and m. Johan Wilhelm Becher at STR on Jan. 16, 1772.
- Anna Maria, b. on Mar. 10, 1760, and bapt. at CLY on May 26, 1760.

Hoffman - Henry was taxed in 1762. He m. Maria Christina, and had the following children:
- Maria Christina, b. on July 23, 1761, and bapt. at CLY on July 30, 1761.
- Maria Christina, b. on Dec. 26, 1762, and bapt. at CLY on Jan. 1, 1763.
- Johan Henrich, b. on Apr. 9, 1768, and bapt. at CLY on May 1, 1768.

Hoh (Hoke) - Martin wrote his will in Manchester Township on Aug. 6, 1776, and it was probated on Nov. 18, 1776 (the probate inventory says his name is Hoke). He m. Elisabeth, and had the following children (all minors in 1776):
- Elisabeth.
- Margaret.
- Michael.
- Catharina.

Hoke (Hoog) - Johan Jacob was taxed in 1762. He immigrated to America on the ship *Mortonhouse* on Aug. 24, 1728, and was a ruling elder and lay preacher at Lancaster, PA, from 1733 to 1736. He purchased 100 acres in York Co. on Apr. 26, 1746, and was a weaver. He received a warrant for 100 acres in West Manchester Township on

MANCHESTER TOWNSHIP

Nov. 21, 1748, that was surveyed as 144.120 acres on Apr. 11, 1749, and patented on May 6, 1765. His will was probated on June 21, 1766, and his probated inventory was filed in Manchester Township in the same year. He m. an unknown woman, and Anna Margaretha about 1732. Anna Margaretha d. between Mar. 7, 1785 and Apr. 11, 1785. Jacob had the following children (see Hoke by Berlekamp and McConnell (1980)):
- Johan Georg, b. about 1720, and d. about Apr. 1762. He purchased a lot in York Borough in 1741. He m. Anna Barbara LeFevre, and had the following children:
  - Maria Magdalena, b. on Feb. 2, 1742, and d. in Huntingdon Co., Alexandria, PA, on Mar. 11, 1819. She m. Johan Conrad Bucher in Cumberland Co., Carlisle, PA, on Feb. 26, 1760. He was a minister. He was b. in Neukirch, Canton Schaffhausen, Switzerland, on June 10, 1730, and d. in Lebanon, PA, on Aug. 15, 1780. He served in the French and Indian War, and the Revolutionary War. She moved to Alexandria, PA, in 1812.
  - Benjamin, b. about 1744. He d. before Apr. 14, 1818. He resided in Beardstown/Bardstown, KY, in 1791.
  - Barbara, bapt. by RJL on Nov. 11, 1750, and spon. by Joseph and Magdalena Welschans. She m. Andreas Muller. He d. in Wayne Co. (four miles from Wooster), OH, in 1818. In 1790, they resided in Fayette Co., Union Township, PA. In 1804, they resided eight miles from Uniontown, PA. Barbara was living in Wayne Co., OH, in 1824.
  - Georg Thomas, bapt. by RJL on June 24, 1753, and spon. by Benedict and Susanna (Welcher) Schwob (m. after the baptism?). He d. before Apr. 11, 1785.
  - Johan Peter, bapt. by RJL on Dec. 1, 1754, and spon. by Peter and Agnes Wolff. He d. before Apr. 2, 1818. He resided in Fayette Co., Union Township, PA, in 1790, and in 1804 was a hatter at Uniontown, PA.
- Samuel, b. about 1722. He m. Maria Catharina, and they were sponsors to the baptism of Samuel Wild in 1750 (RJL). He purchased a lot in York Borough in 1741. he was taxed in Straban Township (now Adams Co.) in 1762. They had the following children:
  - Conrad, b. on Nov. 25, 1745, bapt. at Trinity Lutheran Church in New Holland, Lancaster Co., PA, on Feb. 19, 1746, and spon. by Johan Georg Hock.
  - Clara, bapt. by RJL on Mar. 11, 1757, and spon. by Johannes and Elisabeth Hartz.
- Susanna, b. about 1724, and m. Wilhelm Schroder at Trinity Lutheran Church of New Holland, Lancaster Co., PA, on Aug. 14,

1744. Wilhelm and Susanna had the following children (recorded by RJL):
- Philip Jacob, bapt. on July 2, 1749, and spon. by Jacob and Maria Catharina Ob.
- Arnold, bapt. on June 10, 1757, and spon. by Peter and Anna Maria Kramer.
- Juliana, bapt. on Aug. 22, 1762, and spon. by Ulrich and Juliana Eckler.

- Johan Jacob, b. about 1727. He was taxed in 1762. He was alive in 1766, and d. before the petition was made of Jacob's heirs on Apr. 11, 1785. He m. Susanna, and had the following dau.:
- Maria Catharina, bapt. by RJL on Feb. 13, 1757, and spon. by Samuel and Maria Catharina Hoog. She was mentioned in her grandfather's will in 1766, but not in the petition of 1785.

- Eva Dorothea, b. on July 14, 1730, bapt. at Trinity Lutheran Church in New Holland, Lancaster Co., PA, in Aug. 1730, and spon. by Johannes Heckmann and wife. She m. Jacob Brindli at CLY on May 18, 1752. He was taxed in Warrington Township in 1762. His probate inventory was filed in Warrington Township in 1785. She was alive in 1785. Jacob and Eva had the following children:
- Barbara, bapt. by RJL on Sept. 7, 1755, and spon. by Georg and Barbara Hoog.
- Catharina, bapt. by RJL on May 8, 1757, and spon. by Andreas Hoog and Catharina Holtzbaumin.
- Anna Maria Barbara, bapt. by RJL on Jan. 7, 1759, and spon. by Balthasar Spangler and Maria Magdalena Hoogin.
- Michel, b. on Oct. 20, 1762, bapt. at the Lower Bermudian Church in Adams Co., and spon. by Nicholas and Catharina Dotterer.
- Johan, b. on Sept. 26, 1764, bapt. at the Lower Bermudian Church, and spon. by Johann and Elisabeth Lehmer.

- Andreas, b. on Mar. 23, 1733, bapt. at Trinity Lutheran Church at New Holland, Lancaster Co., PA, on Sept. 20, 1733, and spon. by Andreas Holtzbaum. He was taxed in 1762. He was a Private in Captain Reinhardt Bott's Company, 3rd Battalion in 1780. He was at Trenton at the time of the Hessian defeat. He moved to KY between 1790 and 1796. He had 400 acres on Chenoweth Run in Jefferson Co., KY, on May 5, 1796; 400 acres on Beargrass in 1797, and 400 acres in Beargrass in 1799. He was granted a license to keep a tavern in his house in 1798. He d. near Jeffersontown (Jefferson Co.), KY, on Jan. 3, 1800. His will was written on Sept. 23, 1799, and probated on Jan. 7, 1800. He m. Maria Barbara a dau. of Frederick and Magdalena Eichelberger (see entry). She d. on Mar. 19, 1814 (possibly Mar. 9, 1817). They are bur. in Jeffersontown cemetery, and had the following children:

MANCHESTER TOWNSHIP   211

- Johan Adam, bapt. by RJL on July 6, 1760, and spon. by Johan
  Adam Eichelberger and Anna Maria Holtzbaumin. He m.
  Catharina Hoffheins before 1787, and Catherine, widow of ___
  Welch, in Bullitt Co., KY, on Jan. 31, 1825. He served in Captain
  Reinhardt Bott's Company, 3rd Battalion in 1780. He d. in
  Jeffersontown, KY, on Aug. 7, 1832.
- Maria Clara, b. on May 23, 1762, bapt. at the Lower Bermudian
  Church in Adams Co., and spon. by Conrad and Maria Clara
  Schwob. She m. Heinrich Spangler at TLY on Nov. 28, 1779, and
  John Miller of Baltimore. Henrich's will was written in York Co.
  on Jan. 18, 1791, and probated on Feb. 14, 1791 (see entry in
  Shrewsbury section).
- Johan Friedrich, bapt. at WOL on Sept. 21, 1766, and spon. by
  Johan Friederich and Eva Eichelberger. He m. Anna Maria, dau.
  of Michael Ebert (see entry).
- Elisabeth, b. about 1769. She m. John Pottorff in Jefferson Co.,
  KY, on Apr. 23, 1799 (divorced at Jeffersonville, IN, in 1805), and
  William Goose.
- Johann Jacob, b. on Oct. 22, 1771, bapt. at TLY on Dec. 25, 1771,
  and spon. by Jacob Eichelberger and wife. He m. Catherine
  Reisinger on Apr. 23, 1799, and Elisabeth (Reisinger) Wise
  (widow of Peter), on Aug. 30, 1832. He d. in Jefferson Co. before
  Dec. 1840. Catharine was b. on May 10, 1780, and d. on Apr. 15,
  1832. Elisabeth was b. on Aug. 10, 1789, and d. on Dec. 9, 1874.
- Peter, b. on Sept. 2, 1773, and m. Elisabeth Meyers, Susanna
  (Wise) Crist (widow of Abraham), on Jan. 21, 1815, Mary
  Pomeroy on Aug. 26, 1819, and Eleanor, dau. of Charles Easum
  (widow of John Waggoner), on May 30, 1827. He d. in
  Jeffersontown on Nov. 12, 1857, and is bur. in the Reformed
  Cemetery. Eleanor was b. on Nov. 30, 1790.
- Maria Barbara, b. on Mar. 9, 1776, bapt. at WOL on Apr. 28,
  1776, and spon. by Georg and Catharina Rudi. She m. Jacob
  Meyers (d. 1809), Leonard Harbold on Apr. 26, 1827, and Aaron
  Wilhite on July 1, 1830. She d. on Dec. 13, 1854.
- Leonard, b. on July 10, 1779, m. Barbara, dau. of Adam and
  Catharine (Hoffheins) Hoke (his niece), on Oct. 24, 1804, and d.
  in Jefferson Co., KY, on Aug. 9, 1823. She was b. on Dec. 12,
  1787, and d. on June 26, 1853. They are bur. in the Reformed
  Cemetery in Jeffersontown, KY. He was a Ensign of the 33rd
  Regiment Kentucky Militia in 1802. His will was written on Aug.
  13, 1823, and probated on Sept. 8, 1823.
- Maria Magdalena, b. about 1735. She was a sponsor to the baptism
  of Anna Maria Barbara Brinli in 1759 (RJL). She d. before 1766.
- Maria Clara, b. on July 8, 1737, and m. Johan Cunraudt, son of
  Johannes and Anna Dorothea (Line) Schwob (see entry).

- Johann Peter, b. on Oct. 6, 1739. He was a Sgt. in Captain
  Reinhardt Bott's Company from 1780 to 1782. He and his bro.,
  Johannes purchased their father's homestead, which fell to Peter
  after Johannes' death. Peter is bur. on this farm. His will was
  written in West Manchester Township on Dec. 12, 1804, and
  probated on Jan. 5, 1805. He m. Maria Dorothea, dau. of Mathias
  and Anna Catharina (Koppenhaffer) Schmeisser (see entry). She
  was b. on Mar. 19, 1747, and d. on Jan. 10, 1815. They had the
  following children:
  - Michael, b. on July 18, 1763, and m. Elisabeth, dau. of Adam and
    Magdalena (Bechtel) Eichelberger (see entry), at TLY on Apr. 21,
    1788. He d. in Franklin Co., Peters Township, PA, on Nov. 15,
    1846. She was b. on Jan. 11, 1770, and d. on Aug. 20, 1833. They
    are bur. in Mercersburg cemetery. He resided in Adams Co.,
    Mount Joy Township in 1790. He moved to Franklin Co. between
    Mar. 4 and May 30, 1796.
  - Maria Clara, bapt. at WOL on June 29, 1766, and spon. by
    Conrad and Maria Clara Schwob. She m. Adam Ebert (see
    entry).
  - Catharina, bapt. on Jan. 25, 1767, and m. John Rouss.
  - Sabina, b. about 1769, and m. John Pentz.
  - Peter, b. on Feb. 24, 1771, and bapt. at CLY on Apr. 7, 1771. He
    m. Elisabeth Krantz, Anna Maria Hubert, and Catharine.
  - Jacob, b. on Jan. 20, 1774, bapt. at TLY on Apr. 3, 1774, and
    spon. by Andreas Hock and wife. He m. Anna Maria Krantz.
  - Anna Maria, b. on July 31, 1776, bapt. at WOL on Sept. 29, 1776,
    and spon. by Frantz Jacob and Catharina Roemer. She m.
    Andrew Schreiber.
  - George, b. on Feb. 14, 1785, bapt. at TLY on May 8, 1785, and
    spon. by Georg and Catharina Rudi. He m. Susanna, dau. of
    Philip Adam and Susanna (Schmeisser) Ebert (see entry), and d.
    on Aug. 16, 1849. She was b. in 1789, and d. on Oct. 2, 1871.
- Conrad, b. about 1741. He was taxed in 1762. He m. Catharina
  Elisabetha, dau. of Georg Ament of Hellam Township, about 1769.
  He resided in York Co., Heidelberg Township, in 1800. His will was
  written in Adams Co., PA, on Feb. 8, 1822, and probated on Apr.
  30, 1823. She d. in Adams Co., Cumberland Township, PA, on Dec.
  7, 1831 (aged 82 years). Conrad had the following children:
  - Johan Jacob, b. on Apr. 28, 1771, bapt. at STM on June 3, 1771,
    and spon. by Conrad Schwop and wife.
  - Johann Conrad, bapt. at ERC on Feb. 25, 1776, and spon. by
    Casper Hoke and wife Elisabeth(?).
  - Elisabeth, b. on Jan. 8, 1780, bapt. at ERC on Feb. 6, 1780, and
    spon. by Georg Rudy and wife.

MANCHESTER TOWNSHIP 213

- Johannes, b. on Oct. 4, 1782, bapt. at ERC on Nov. 12, 1782, and spon. by Henry Hoock.
- Catharine, b. on Dec. 4, 1785, bapt. at ERC on Jan. 15, 1786, and spon. by J. Christoph and Elisabeth Gobrecht.
- Johan Georg, b. on Mar. 19, 1788, bapt. at ERC on May 11, 1788, and spon. by Johannes Schwob.
- Johannes, b. about 1741. His will was written in Manchester Township on Oct. 27, 1781, and probated on Nov. 14, 1781. He m. Maria Sabina, dau. of Johannes and Catharina Elisabetha (Graff) Schwob (see entry). In 1797/98, Sabina moved to North Carolina with her children. She d. near Lincolnton, North Carolina, on Aug. 9, 1826, and is bur. in the Lutheran cemetery at Lincolnton. Johannes and Sabina had the following children:
  - Henrich, b. on Feb. 19, 1764, and m. Catharine Ramsauer.
  - Johan Peter, bapt. at WOL on June 29, 1766, and spon. by Johan Peter and Catharina Elisabeth Wolf. He d. before 1781.
  - Johan Frederick, b. on Oct. 9, 1768, bapt. at WOL on Nov. 11, 1768, and spon. by Friederich and Eva Eichelberger. He m. Catherine Hafer, Elizabeth Lawrence on May 11, 1817, Elisabeth Stirewalt on Aug. 4, 1833, and Rebecca Kiblar/Wilson on Feb. 7, 1839. He d. in Catawba Co., North Carolina, on Jan. 1/8, 1844. Catharine was b. in York Co. on Feb. 11, 1768, and d. in Lincoln Co., North Carolina, on Nov. 24, 1816. Elizabeth Lawrence was b. in London, England in 1782, and d. in Lincoln Co. in 1820.
  - Maria Sabina, b. on Aug. 17, 1770 (or Apr. 17, 1771), bapt. at TLY on July 21, 1771, and spon. by Peter Hoock and wife. She m. Conrad Michael. She d. on July 21, 1850.
  - Daniel, b. on Nov. 20, 1773, bapt. at TLY on Apr. 3, 1774, and spon. by George Rudi and wife. He m. Barbara Ramsaur. She was b. on Feb. 5, 1780. He was a senator, and Captain in the War of 1812. In 1835, he moved to Jacksonville, Alabama, and d. in 1856.
  - John, b. on May 26, 1778, m. Barbara Quickel on Jan. 10, 1808, and d. in Lincolnton, North Carolina, on June 3, 1845. He was a Colonel in the Militia, and proprietor of Lincolnton Factory.
  - George.
- Casper, b. on Jan. 6, 1744, and d. in Paradise Township on July 16, 1821. His probate inventory was filed in Paradise Township in 1821. His will was written on Apr. 16, 1821, and probated on Sept. 17, 1821. He m. Anna Margaretha, dau. of Johann Philip and Maria Margaretha (Krantz) Emig (see entry). She was b. on Oct. 1, 1750, and d. on Oct. 31, 1831. Her probate inventory was filed in Paradise Township in 1831. They are bur. in Garber's Mennonite cemetery in Heidelberg Township. They had the following children:

- Johannes, b. on Dec. 1, 1771, bapt. at TLY on Dec. 12, 1771, and spon. by Johannes Emig and wife. He m. Eva Bederman, and d. in Knox Co., OH, in 1852. She d. in 1856.
- Catharina Elisabeth, b. on Feb. 18, 1774, bapt. at WOL on Apr. 17, 1774, and spon. by Conrad and Elisabeth Hoock. She probably d. before 1790.
- Georg, b. on Aug. 29, 1775, and m. Catharina Stambach. He d. at Menges, PA, on Oct. 18, 1844. She was b. on Mar. 12, 1784, and d. on Oct. 16, 1857. His will was written in Paradise Township on May 11, 1842, and it was probated on Nov. 24, 1844.
- Johan Jacob, b. on Jan. 24, 1780, bapt. at ERC on Feb. 27, 1780, and spon. by Johan Jacob and Clary Schwob. He probably d. before 1790.
- Samuel, bapt. on Feb. 22, 1783, and spon. by Valentine Emig and wife. He d. in Paradise Township on Apr. 27, 1826. He m. Elisabeth, dau. of Jacob Weist. She was b. in 1788, and d. in Richland Co., OH, in 1871.
- Michael, b. on July 16, 1785, bapt. at WOL, and spon. by Michael Welsch and wife. He m. Barbara Fishel and Susan Hershey. Barbara d. about 1828. Susan was b. on Apr. 27, 1800, and d. on Aug. 1, 1881. Michael and Susan are bur. in Garber's Mennonite cemetery.
- Anna Maria, b. on Feb. 17, 1746, and m. Johann Michael, son of Mathias Schmeisser (see entry).
- Frederick, b. about 1748. His will was written in Manchester Township on May 10, 1771, and probated on July 1, 1771. It named bros. Conrad, Casper, Henry, and Andrew (John and Andrew were execs).
- Johan Philip, b. on Jan. 8, 1752, and bapt. at CLY on Mar. 5, 1752. He d. before 1766.
- Johan Heinrich, bapt. by RJL on Mar. 16, 1755, and spon. by Heinrich and Catharina Wolf, and d. in Gettysburg, PA, on Feb. 24, 1826. He served in the Revolutionary War. He m. Hanna, dau. of Peter and Rachel (Shertz) Ferree (of Lancaster Co., Strasburg Township), on May 25, 1781. She was b. on Aug. 18, 1759, and d. on Aug. 28, 1830. They are bur. in Evergreen cemetery. They had the following children:
  - Anna Maria, b. on Sept. 18, 1782, bapt. at ERC on Dec. 15, 1782, and spon. by Conrad and Gloria (Clara) Schwob.
  - Jacob, b. on Oct. 10, 1783, bapt. at ERC on Dec. 25, 1783, and spon. by Conrad and Elisabeth Hoock. He m. Margaret Lohr on Nov. 23, 1809, and d. on Nov. 28, 1867. She was b. on Apr. 23, 1793, and d. on Oct. 10, 18?? in Epworth, Iowa. In 1826, Jacob was a potter near McConnelsburg, Bedford Co., PA (now Fulton Co., Bethel Township).

MANCHESTER TOWNSHIP 215

- Rebecca, b. on May 31, 1785, bapt. at ERC on July 24, 1785, and spon. by Frederick and Barbara Benss/Brusz. She m. William Buchannon, and d. on July 24, 1837.
- George, b. in 1789, and m. Mary Bohn.
- Henry, b. on Jan. 1, 1794, and m. Sarah E., dau. of George Eyster. He d. in McConnelsburg, PA, on 1878 (aged 84 years). She d. in Adams Co., PA, before 1840. He was a tinsmith.
- Hanna, b. on Sept. 18, 1795, and m. Adam, son of Michael Hoke.
- Elias, b. on Oct. 17, 1799, and d. on Jan. 12, 1822.
- Catharina, b. about 1757, and m. Georg, son of Daniel and Susanna Rudi of Lancaster Co., Manheim Township, on Apr. 11, 1785. He resided in York Co., Cumberland Township, PA, in 1775, when he received part of his father's 267 acre tract in York Co., Paradise Township. He was an innkeeper in 1783. On Feb. 27, 1795, he sold his land in Paradise Township, moved to KY, and d. in Jefferson Co. before Oct. 1806 (date of estate appraisal). On Dec. 1, 1795, they purchased 164 acres on Muddy Fork of Beargrass Creek. They had the following children (some may have been from a previous marriage):
  - Henry, b. about 1785, and m. Margaret Haywood on Feb. 19, 1807.
  - Lydia, b. about 1786, and m. William Edwards on Feb. 27, 1806.
  - Daniel, b. about 1787, and m. Mary Shively on Dec. 10, 1807.
  - Jacob, b. about 1788, and m. Mary Welshier Steele on Nov. 10, 1808.
  - John.
  - Frederick, b. on May 3, 1791, m. Ann Susan Owen on June 18, 1812, and d. in Paris, Illinois on Apr. 20, 1840.
  - Mary, b. about 1792, and m. Henry Wolf.
  - Susannah, b. about 1794, and m. John Herr on July 9, 1814.
  - Eliza, b. about 1796, and m. James M. Edwards.

Holtzappel - Johann Leonhard was b. to Jacob and Anna Maria Margaretha (Klein) Holtzapffel, at Michelfeld, Germany, on Feb. 21, 1683. He m. Anna Maria Barbara (b. 1674), and immigrated to America on the ship *Britannia* in 1731. They had the following children (see BNK):
- Anna Barbara, b. in 1707, and m. Adam Ruppert (see entry).
- Erasmus, b. on Sept. 21, 1710, and bapt. at Eschelbach on Sept. 27, 1710. He was taxed in 1762. He received a warrant for 100 acres in West Manchester Township on Apr. 3, 1767, and another 100 acres on the same date. He was naturalized on Sept. 24, 1763. His will was written in Manchester Township on Dec. 6, 1792, and probated on Dec. 10, 1793. He m. Christina Ruscher in Lancaster Co.,

Earltown, PA, on Feb. 14, 1738 (JCS), and had the following children:
- Johan Jacob, b. on Jan. 23, 1739, bapt. at CLY on Feb. 15, 1739, and spon. by Jacob and Elisabeth Rudisill.
- Johan Adam, b. on Aug. 25, 1740, and bapt. at CLY on May 17, 1741. He m. Margaret, dau. of Philip Graber/Kreber (see entry) at STR on May 27, 1766.
- Anna Maria, b. on Mar. 26, 1742, and bapt. at CLY on May 18, 1742.
- Johan Hendrick, b. on Mar. 26, 1742, and bapt. at CLY on May 18, 1742.
- Johan Jacob, b. on Oct. 11, 1744, and bapt. at CLY on Nov. 11, 1744.
- Johan Bernard, b. on Nov. 7, 1747, and bapt. at CLY on May 20, 1748. His probate inventory was filed in West Manchester Township in 1820.
- Ersamus, b. on May 5, 1749, and bapt. at CLY on June 25, 1749. His probate inventory was filed in Manchester Township in 1798.
- Elisabeth, b. on Apr. 5, 1751, and bapt. at CLY on May 13, 1751. She m. Henry Shock.
- Maria Barbara, b. on Jan. 7, 1753, and bapt. at CLY on Jan. 26, 1753. She m. Jacob Fackler.
- Catharina, bapt. by RJL on Mar. 2, 1755, and spon. by Bernhardt and Elisabetha Holtzinger. She m. Jacob Clingman.
- Anna Christina, b. on Jan. 23, 1761, and bapt. at CLY on Mar. 20, 1761. She m. David Stein.
- Maria Margaretha, b. on June 30, 1762, and bapt. at CLY on Aug. 4, 1762. She m. Frederick Hoober.

Homel - William was taxed in 1762.

Hornin - Leonardt was taxed in 1762. He m. Eva Margareth, and had the following children:
- Elisabeth Catharina, bapt. by RJL on May 1, 1758, and spon. by Michael and Elisabeth Catharina Gubler.

Hoss - Johan Philip was taxed in 1762. He received a warrant for 300 acres in West Manchester Township on Mar. 14, 1767, that was surveyed as 172.120 acres on Mar. 23, 1767. He was taxed in York Township in 1779. He m. Eva, dau. of Friedrich Stillinger, and widow of Heinrich Becker (see entry) in 1760. Anna Salome, dau. of Johan Martin Schoemaker, at STR on June 17, 1768, and Magdalena between 1784 and 1788. His will was written at York on Jan. 20, 1788, and probated on June 9, 1788. Philip had the following children:
- Jacob, b. about 1760.

MANCHESTER TOWNSHIP

- Elisabeth, b. about 1762, and m. George Fink about 1781.
- Eve, b. about 1764, and m. Philip Barker before 1788.
- Peter, b. about 1766.
- Johan Philip, b. on Feb. 8, 1769, bapt. at STR on Mar. 17, 1769, and spon. by Johan Philip and Ester Graber.
- Johan Dieter, b. on Jan. 29, 1770, bapt. at STR on Mar. 25, 1770, and spon. by Johan Dieter and Margareth Ruppert.
- Philip, b. on June 15, 1780, and bapt. at CLY on July 30, 1780.
- Catharine, b. on Mar. 3, 1783, and bapt. at CLY on Apr. 18, 1783.

Humrichhauss - Johannes was taxed in 1762. He moved to Montgomery Co., Germantown, PA, in 1771, and he d. there on May 27, 1771. His probate inventory was filed in Manchester Township in 1771. He m. Maria Barbara in Oct. 1750, and had the following children:
- Johannes, bapt. by RJL on Apr. 28, 1751, and spon. by Johannes and Margaretha Leib. He m. Maria Barbara, dau. of Georg Quickel (see entry in Dover section). His probate inventory was filed in Dover Township in 1819. In 1821, Barbara resided in Fairfield Co., OH.
- Peter, b. on Oct. 10, 1753. In July 1776, he was a Lieutenant in the Philadelphia Militia under Col. John Moore, Lt. Col. Smith, and Major Bush. He was a Captain in the 2nd Philadelphia Battalion. He was in the Battle of Germantown, and at the Battle of Trenton he was appointed Officer of the Day to bury the dead. He m. Maria, dau. of Maria Margaret (Miller) Hadelman (Stadleman/Stottleman), in Philadelphia Co., Springfield Township on Feb. 20, 1777. In 1798, he moved to Washington Co., Hagerstown, MD, where he d. on Feb. 13, 1837. She d. in 1839. They are bur. in Zion Reformed cemetery.
- Catharina, bapt. by RJL on May 27, 1756, and spon. by Johannes Wahl and Catharina Leibin. She m. Henry Dundore.
- Johann Georg, bapt. by RJL on July 1, 1759, and spon. by Johannes Wahl. He m. Elisabet Bruner at TLY on Dec. 11, 1780. He resided in Rockingham Co., VA, in 1788.
- Anna Maria, b. in 1761, m. Peter Bentz, and d. in 1842. He was b. in 1758, and d. in 1823. They are bur. at QUI cemetery.
- Johan Jacob, bapt. by RJL on Oct. 24, 1763, and spon. by Johan Jacob and Susanna Steeg. He d. young.

Immel - Johannes Leonhardt was taxed in York in 1762. He was b. to Martin Immel at Wernetz, Rothenberg, Bavaria, on Nov. 17, 1702, and d. on Dec. 29, 1777. He m. Maria, dau. of Andreas Burkhart, on Dec. 26, 1733 (JCS), Margaretha, dau. of Casper Kerber (see entry) before 1751, and Maria about 1760. Maria Burkhart was b. in Watzendorff,

Germany, on July 5, 1714, and immigrated to America in 1733. Leonhardt's will was written on Mar. 2, 1773, and probated on Apr. 7, 1778. His probate inventory was filed in York Town. Maria's probate inventory was filed in York in 1785. He had the following children (see *Immel/Imel Family in America* by Velma Byrum Keller (1974)):
- Georg Michael, b. on Feb. 18, 1735, bapt. at CLY on Feb. 23, 1735, and spon. by Michael Eberd, Jr. He m. Sophia Caroline Meissler at Old Goshenhoppen Lutheran Church in Montgomery Co. on Oct. 28, 1760, and Catharina Sidle on Jan. 9, 1775. He was a soldier in the Revolutionary War, and resided in Philadelphia in 1800.
- Maria Elisabetha, b. on June 17 (?), 1736, bapt. at CLY on July 3, 1736, and d. young.
- Anna Margaretha, b. on June 17 (?), 1736, bapt. at CLY on July 3, 1736, and spon. by Dorothea Weigelin. She m. Henry Amendt, and Georg Lewis Lefler. Henry d. in 1760/61.
- Barbara, b. on Apr. 10, 1738, bapt. at CLY on Apr. 22, 1738, and spon. by Dorothea Weigelin. She m. Henry, son of Johannes Beintzel (see entry in Dover section).
- Anna Maria, b. on July 25, 1739, bapt. at CLY on Mar. 15, 1740, and spon. by Michael Immel and wife. She was not mentioned in the will.
- Christina, b. on Mar. 22, 1742, and bapt. at CLY on Feb. 9, 1743. She m. Martin Hambrecht.
- Johannes, b. on Mar. 22, 1744, and bapt. at CLY on Apr. 15, 1744. He was taxed in York in 1779. He m. Dorothea, and d. in York Co. on May 16, 1788. He was a 1st Lt. under Captain Frederick Metzgar during the Revolution.
- Sebilla, b. on Mar. 25, 1748, and m. Michael, son of Peter Schriber, at STR on Dec. 24, 1769.
- Martin, b. on Nov. 11, 1752, bapt. at FMY on Nov. 22, 1752, and spon. by his father. He d. young.
- Maria Magdalena, b. on Apr. 4, 1754, bapt. at FMY on May 5, 1754, and spon. by Anna Maria Muller, Eva Barbara Ebert, and the Weller woman.
- Eva Maria, b. on Dec. 4, 1756, bapt. at FMY on Dec. 12, 1756, and spon. by Eva Barbara Ebert, Anna Eva Weller, and Anna Walpurg Kerber (the grandmother).

<u>Jauler</u> - Jacob was probably the Hans Jacob Jauler, son of Johannes and Anna Elisabetha Jauler, that was bapt. at Barbelroth, Pfalz, Bayern, Germany, on May 11, 1704. Jacob m. Maria C. in Winden Pfalz Bayern, Germany, about 1736, and had the following children there (unless otherwise noted):
- Jacob, b. about 1740. He m. Barbara, and moved to Frederick Co., MD, with his bro., Isaac.

- Isaac, b. about 1743. He m. Anna, probably a dau. of Casper Glattfelter (see entry). They moved from York Co., West Manchester/North Codorus Township, PA, to Frederick Co., Middletown, MD, between 1767 and 1768, and from MD to Bedford (now Somerset) Co., Elk Lick Township, PA, between 1775 and 1778. Isaac and Anna are sponsors to the baptism of Johan Georg, son of Georg Philipp and Maria Margaret (Lau) Genssler, at the Monocacy Lutheran Congregation in Frederick Co. on Oct. 2, 1768. Isaac took communion in Frederick Co. on Oct. 3, 1774, and was a signer of a petition from the Frederick Congregation that stated he would be subject to the Christian discipline and order according to the Resolution of Rev. Coetus, which met in Lebanon on May 10, 1775. The name Jauler evolved to Youler and finally Yowler. In 1787, Isaac was taxed with 100 acres 2 horses and 3 cattle in Elk Lick Township, and served in the Township Militia on Feb. 7, 1789. He d. in Aug. 1798, and his wife survived him.
- Anna Margaretha, b. about 1745. She m. Johan Jacob, son of Jacob and Anna Johanna (Josi) Ottinger, in Trinity Lutheran Church of York, York Co., PA, on Dec. 30, 1766 (marriage record says Janler (a common mistake for Jauler)). They resided in Manchester Township in 1789.
- Anna Dorothea bapt. by Reverend Jacob Lischy in York Co., West Manchester/North Codorus Township, PA, on May 16, 1756, and spon. by Adam and Anna Dorothea Bartmesse (Dover Township resident, but had land in North Codorus Township at this time).

Jorge - Jacob was taxed in 1762.

Jose (Josi) - Johann Martin m. Anna Johanna. He received a warrant for 300 acres in West Manchester Township on Oct. 30, 1736 (Blunston License). His probate inventory was filed in York Co. in 1763 (?in 1747). He had the following children:
- Anna Barbara, b. about 1718, and was the sponsor to the baptism of Maria Barbara Jung in 1735 (JCS).
- Anna Johanna, b. about 1720, and m. Jacob Ottinger (see entry).
- Nicholas, b. about 1722. His probate inventory was filed in York Co. in 1763. He may be the father of Nicholas Jose, who was b. on Dec. 11, 1748, and d. on Dec. 13, 1748 (CLY).
- Maria Magdalena, b. about 1725, and m. Johan Jacob, son of Mathias Ness (see entry in Shrewsbury section).
- Peter, b. about 1728, and m. Ottillia before 1749. They were sponsors to the baptism of Anna Ottilla Ottinger in 1749 (RJL).
- Johann Friederich, b. on July 26, 1731, and bapt. at Trappe Lutheran Church in Montgomery Co., PA.

Kagie - Henry received a warrant for 600 acres in Manchester Township on Mar. 4, 1736, and 600 acres on May 24, 1740, that was surveyed as 480 acres on Apr. 7, 1742.

Kastner - Georg Adam was taxed in 1762. He m. Maria Anna, and had the following children:
- Johan Michael, b. on Dec. 30, 1734, and bapt. at CLY on Nov. 16, 1735.
- Johan Georg, b. on July 22, 1737, and bapt. at CLY on Aug. 1, 1737.
- Maria Ursula, b. about 1740, m. Conrad Gunther, and had the following children:
  - John, b. on June 29, 1759, and bapt. at CLY on Aug. 12, 1759.
  - Dorothea, bapt. by RJL on Oct. 7, 1760, and spon. by Johannes and Dorothea Koch.
  - Anna Maria, b. on Oct. 2, 1762, bapt. at TLY on Oct. 24, 1762, and spon. by Georg Adam Kastner and wife.
  - Philip Jacob, b. on Sept. 29, 1761, and bapt. at CLY on Nov. 8, 1761.
- Andreas, bapt. by RJL on Sept. 7, 1755, and spon. by Andreas and Florina Klein.

Kenick - Gotfrit was taxed in 1762.

Kerber - Johan Casper d. intestate in West Manchester Township before Aug. 9, 1758. He had 300 acres on Codorus Creek on the West side of the Susquehanna River. He received a warrant for 300 acres in Spring Garden Township on Oct. 30, 1736 (Blunston License). He m. Anna Wahlburg, and had the following children:
- Anna Eva, b. in Wagendorf in the Mark of Anspach on Nov. 10 (Dec. 9), 1717, and m. Georg Matthias Weller in the fall of 1741, and d. one mile from York Town on Nov. 23, 1785. Georg's will was written on May 5, 1775, and probated on Jan. 17, 1780. He was b. in Hegenau, Wurtemberg, Germany, on Sept. 19, 1709, and d. on Jan. 2, 1780. They had the following children (recorded at CLY and FMY):
  - Maria Magdalena, b. on Oct. 29, 1742, and bapt. on Nov. 24, 1742.
  - Johan Georg, b. on July 25, 1744, and bapt. on Nov. 11, 1747.
  - Maria Barbara, b. on Apr. 16, 1747, and bapt. on June 4, 1747.
  - Eva Elisabetha, b. on June 3, 1749, and bapt. on July 4, 1749.
  - Johan Martin, b. on June 27, 1751, and bapt. on July 21, 1751. He served as a Private in Captain Godfrey Fry's Company during the Revolution, and d. in 1788. He is bur. in Prospect Hill cemetery.

MANCHESTER TOWNSHIP 221

- Johan Jacob, b. on May 10, 1754, bapt. on July 14, 1754, and d. on Jan. 7, 1761.
- Sabina, b. on Aug. 9, 1756.
- John, b. on Mar. 13, 1759, bapt. on Mar. 18, 1759, and spon. by Martin Ebert, John Heckedorn, Frantz Jacob Muller, and Marcus Hoens.
- Johan Michael, b. about 1719, and m. Elisabetha Klapper in Lancaster Co. on June 19, 1739 (JCS).
- Margaretha, b. about 1721, and m. Leonard Immel (see entry).
- Anna Elisabetha, b. in Reichenbach, Ansbach, on Jan. 30, 1727. She m. Marcus Hoehns (see entry in Codorus section).
- Eva Barbara, b. in Reichenbach, Anspach on July 25, 1729. She m. Martin, son of Hans Michael Ebert (see entry), on Apr. 10, 1749.
- Anna Wahlburg, b. on Dec. 14, 1734, bapt. at Christ's Lutheran on Jan. 1, 1735, and spon. by Margaretha Weybrechtin. She m. Peter Pfaff (see entry in Codorus section).
- Anna Barbara, b. on Dec. 15, 1735, bapt. at Christ's Lutheran on Jan. 1, 1735, and m. Georg, son of Georg Meyer (see entry).
- Johan Casper, b. on July 13, 1737, bapt. at Christ's Lutheran on Aug. 1, 1737, and spon. by Jacob Ziegler. He m. Maria Magdalena, dau. of Christian and Anna Cleva Lau (see entry). They had the following children:
  - Anna Eva, b. on Mar. 31, 1762, and bapt. at CLY on Apr. 18, 1762.
  - Johan Michael, b. on June 27, 1765, bapt. at WOL on July 14, 1765, and spon. by Michael and Anna Maria Lau.
  - Maria Magdalena, b. on Sept. 15, 1768, bapt. at WOL on Oct. 30, 1768, and spon. by Jacob Becker.
  - Maria Barbara, b. on Oct. 11, 1773, bapt. at WOL on Nov. 7, 1773, and spon. by Conrad and Eva Gensler.

Klein - Andreas was taxed in 1762. His probate inventory was filed in Manchester Township in 1778. He m. Anna Clementine Florentina about 1757, and had the following children:
- Eva Catharine, b. about 1743, and m. Philip, son of Georg Quickel at STR on Nov. 20, 1764.
- Michael, bapt. by RJL on Mar. 22, 1756, and spon. by Michael Gunther and Christina Kuntzlerin.
- Johan Reinhard, b. on Jan. 12, 1758, and bapt. at CLY on Apr. 23, 1758.
- Maria Elisabeth, b. on Oct. 28, 1760, and bapt. at CLY on Dec. 1, 1760.

Knab - Casper had his probate inventory filed in Manchester Township in 1781. He m. Maria Barbara, and had the following children:

- Johan Jacob, b. about 1754, bapt. by RJL on May 25, 1760, and spon. by Michel Lora. He m. Maria Catharina, dau. of Nicholas Bohn (see entry), at TLY on June 25, 1780. His probate inventory was filed in Manchester Township in 1811.
- Casper, b. about 1756, bapt. by RJL on May 25, 1760, and spon. by Casper Klember. He m. Margaret, dau. of Nicholas Bohn (see entry), at TLY on July 24, 1781. His probate inventory was filed in Manchester Township in 1823.
- Peter, b. about 1758, bapt. by RJL on May 25, 1760, and spon. by Johanes Schaffer. He m. Elisabeth.
- Anna Maria, b. on Nov. 25, 1760, and bapt. at CLY on May 17, 1761.
- Johan Leonard, b. on Aug. 11, 1767, and bapt. at CLY on Oct. 25, 1767. He d. before 1769.
- Johan Leonard, b. on Feb. 5, 1769, and bapt. at CLY on May 14, 1769. His probate inventory was filed in Manchester Township in 1817. He m. Catharina, dau. of Christian Bixler (see entry), at TLY on Mar. 6, 1796.
- Johann Wilhelm, b. on June 17, 1771, and bapt. at TLY on Oct. 6, 1771.
- Johan Yost, b. on Jan. 24, 1773, bapt. at TLY on May 20, 1773, and spon. by Yost Wahl and wife.
- Elisabeth, b. on Jan. 24, 1773, bapt. at TLY on May 20, 1773, and spon. by Yost Wahl and wife.

Koch - Johannes was taxed in 1762. He m. Dorothea, and had the following children:
- Johan Heinrich, bapt. by RJL on Nov. 9, 1755, and spon. by Conrad Gentzler.
- Johan Michael, b. on Jan. 12, 1759, and bapt. at CLY on Mar. 4, 1759.
- Catharine, b. on May 26, 1761, and bapt. at CLY on June 25, 1761.
- Christine, b. on July 22, 1763, and bapt. at CLY on Sept. 11, 1763.

Koenig (King) - Nicholas received a warrant for 200 acres in Manchester Township on Aug. 22, 1765, that was surveyed as 259 acres on Nov. 18, 1765. He was naturalized on Apr. 10/12, 1762, and m. Susanna, widow of Nicholas Vogeler (see entry in Codorus section), at TLY on Dec. 17, 1771. His will was written in York Town on Mar. 9, 1776, and probated on Mar. 29, 1776. He had the following children:
- Anna Elisabet, b. about 1738, and m. Simon Kronmuller (see entry).
- Gottfried, b. about 1740. He m. Anna Christina, dau. of Johan Philip Ziegler (see entry), about 1761, and Catharina, widow of Conrad Eissenhardt (see entry), in 1800. His will was written in

West Manchester Township on Oct. 19, 1805, and probated on Dec. 3, 1805. He was naturalized on Sept. 24, 1762.
- Barbara, b. about 1742, and m. Adam Wilhelm of Lancaster Co., PA.
- Philip Jacob, b. about 1744. He m. Maria Barbara about 1766, and Catharina, dau. of Johan Philip Ziegler (see entry), about 1772. His will was written in Manchester Township on Nov. 9, 1791, and probated on Feb. 23, 1792. He was naturalized on Sept. 24, 1762, and was the assessor for Manchester Township in 1777/78.

Kohler - Andreas was taxed in 1762. His will was written in Manchester Township on Dec. 26, 1786, and probated on Jan. 11, 1787. He m. Magdalena, and Maria before 1786. Andreas and Magdalena had the following children (9 children in all) (they were Catholics):
- Maria Magdalena, b. on July 4, 1748, and bapt. at CLY on July 10, 1748.
- Baltzer, bapt. by RJL on June 18, 1749, and spon. by Balthasar and Magdalena Spengler. His probate inventory was filed in Manchester Township in 1820. He was taxed in Manchester Township in 1779. He m. Elisabeth about 1776, and Christine about 1778, and had the following children:
  - Johan Philip, b. on Dec. 30, 1777, and bapt. at CLY on Mar. 22, 1778.
  - Johan Georg, b. on Nov. 6, 1779, and bapt. at CLY on Mar. 26, 1780.
  - Henry, b. on July 3, 1781, and bapt. at CLY on Aug. 5, 1781.
  - Catharine, b. on Mar. 5, 1786, and bapt. at CLY on June 4, 1786.
  - Johannes, b. on Oct. 12, 1790, bapt. at WOL on Feb. 16, 1791, and spon. by Jacob and Susanna Stober.
- Johan Georg, b. on Feb. 8, 1752, and bapt. at CLY on Mar. 15, 1752.
- Appolonia, b. about 1754, and was a sponsor to the baptism of Johan Michael Schedel at QUI in 1773.
- Child, b. about 1756, and is possibly the Jacob Kohler that m. Elisabeth Welshantz at TLY on Nov. 19, 1775.
- Joseph, b. about 1758. He was taxed as a single man in Bott's Town in 1779. His probate inventory was filed in Manchester Township in 1816. His will was probated on July 18, 1816, and the legatee was the Roman Catholic Church of York Borough.
- Valentine, b. about 1760. He was taxed as a single man in Bott's Town in 1779. He m. Magdalena, dau. of Conrad Becker (see entry in Dover section), and had the following children (recorded at QUI):
  - Johan Philip, b. on June 11, 1783, bapt. on June 29, 1783, and spon. by Philip Mohr and wife.

- Johannes, b. on Oct. 5, 1784, bapt. on Oct. 31, 1785, and spon. by his parents.
- Andreas, b. about 1762. He was taxed in Manchester Township in 1779. He m. Margaretha, and had the following children (recorded at QUI):
  - Jacob, b. on June 28, 1785, bapt. on Aug. 8, 1785, and spon. by George Eichelberger and wife.
  - Maria Catharina, b. on Nov. 26, 1788, bapt. on Jan. 10, 1789, and spon. by Conrad and Maria Catharina Becker.
  - Elisabeth, b. on Sept. 24, 1790, bapt. on Oct. 24, 1790, and spon. by Anna Elisabeth Becker.
- Susanna, b. about 1764, and was a sponsor to the baptism of Susanna Giess at QUI in 1785.

Krantz - Valentine received a warrant for 200 acres in Manchester Township on Oct. 20, 1738, that was surveyed as 248 acres on Oct. 29, 1746, and 276.100 acres on Dec. 11, 1773. His probate inventory was filed in Manchester Township in 1755. He m. Maria Elisabeth. Her will was written in York Town on Oct. 5, 1776, and probated on Dec. 14, 1776. They had the following children:
- Maria Margaretha, b. about 1725, and m. Johannes, son of Johannes Emig (see entry), at The First Reformed Church at Lancaster, on Dec. 15, 1745.
- Christina, b. about 1733, and m. Sebastian Fink before 1752 (see entry in Dover section).
- Catharina, b. about 1736.
- Susanna Elisabeth, b. on Sept. 15, 1739, bapt. at CLY on Nov. 14, 1739, and m. Killian Dipinger (see entry in Shrewsbury section).
- Valentine, b. on Dec. 7, 1741, bapt. at CLY on Dec. 16, 1741, and m. Christina about 1763.
- Elisabeth, b. about 1743, and m. Wendell Reissinger about 1763, and had the following children:
  - Elisabeth, b. on Nov. 29, 1764, and bapt. at CLY on Dec. 25, 1764.
  - Johan Georg, b. on Oct. 9, 1766, bapt. at TLY on Nov. 30, 1766, and spon. by Killian Tuebinger and wife.
  - Johann Jacob, b. on May 11, 1770, bapt. at TLY on July 23, 1770, and spon. by Peter Hock and wife.
- Georg, b. about 1745. His probate inventory was filed in Manchester Township in 1791. He m. Elisabeth, dau. of Georg Weimer at STR on Oct. 4, 1768. Her will was written in Manchester Township on Aug. 11, 1819, and probated on Aug. 31, 1819.

MANCHESTER TOWNSHIP 225

Kronmuller - Johan Martin was b. in Backnang, Wurtemburg, and immigrated to America on the ship *President* on Sept. 27, 1752. He was naturalized on Apr. 10/11, 1762, and received a warrant for 200 acres in Manchester Township on July 26, 1765, that was surveyed as 98.40 acres on May 12, 1767. He was taxed in York in 1762. His will was written in Manchester Township on May 3, 1770, and probated on Jan. 28, 1771. He m. Anna Elisabet, dau. of Nicholas Koenig (see entry) of York Town, at Trinity Lutheran Church in Lancaster, PA, on June 20, 1756, and had the following children:
- Johan Nicholas, b. on Sept. 8, 1759, bapt. at CLY on Sept. 2, 1759, and was bur. at CLY on Sept. 9, 1759.
- Johan Martin, b. on Jan. 29, 1761, and bapt. on Feb. 15, 1761. He m. Barbara Mayer at TLY on Sept. 21, 1784. During the Revolution, he was a Private in Captain John Ehrman's Company, 1st Battalion from 1780 to 1783. He was a blacksmith.
- Thomas, b. on Mar. 17, 1762, and bapt. at CLY on Mar. 28, 1762. In 1783, he had a illegitimate child with Margaret, who became the wife of Leonard Baumgartner about 1784. During the Revolution, he was a Private in the 7th Company, 1st Battalion from 1781-83.
- Maria Dorothea, b. on Nov. 23, 1763, bapt. at CLY on Jan. 1, 1764, and m. John Hess at TLY on May 22, 1783.
- Georg, b. in 1765.
- Jacob, b. about 1766.
- Johan Philip, b. in 1769.
- Maria Barbara, b. on July 1, 1770, and bapt. at CLY on Aug. 12, 1770.

Kuntzel - Jacob was taxed in 1762. His will was written on Nov. 4, 1759, and probated on Oct. 22, 1760. He had the following children:
- Christina Elisabeth, m. Michael Gunther (see entry).   -Jacob was taxed in 1762.

Lambert - Mathias wrote his will in Manchester Township on June 27, 1756, and it was probated on Mar. 16, 1757. He m. Anna Rosina. Her probate inventory was filed in 1758. They had the following children:
- Jacob was taxed in 1762 (?also in Dover Township). He m. Maria Margreth, and had the following children:
  - Johan Jacob, bapt. at STR on Dec. 28, 1755, and spon. by Jacob and Catharina Ob.
  - Matheus, bapt. at STR on Jan. 7, 1759, and spon. by Jacob and Catharina Ob.
  - Johannes, bapt. at STR on Oct. 30, 1761, and spon. by Johannes and Anna Sophia Zinn.
- Casper was taxed in Dover Township in 1762. He m. Elisabeth Barbara, and had the following children:

- Juliana, bapt. at STR on Oct. 20, 1757, and spon. by Michael and Barbara Spaar.
- Caspar, bapt. at STR on Jan. 22, 1763, and spon. by Anton and Maria Barbara Ulrich.
- Maria Elisabeth, bapt. at STR on Aug. 4, 1764, and spon. by Antony and Maria Barbara Ulrich.
- Johan Peter, b. on Jan. 11, 1766, bapt. at STR on Mar. 30, 1766, and spon. by Michael and Barbara Spaar.
- Catharina, bapt. at STR on Nov. 17, 1769, and spon. by Michael and Barbara Spaar.
- Maria Elisabeth, b. on Dec. 4, 1771, and bapt. at CLY on Jan. 19, 1772.
- Magdalena, b. on Feb. 3, 1774, and bapt. at CLY on Apr. 17, 1774.
- Magdalena, bapt. at STR on Mar. 14, 1778, and spon. by Friederich and Elisabeth Spaar.
- Susanna, b. on May 14, 1780, bapt. at STR on Aug. 13, 1780, and spon. by Maria Elisabetha Spaarin.
- George.
- Anna m. Jacob, son of Killian Schmidt (see entry).
- Catherine.

Lang (Long) - Johan Michael was taxed in 1762. His will was written in Manchester Township on Mar. 12, 1775, and probated on Mar. 18, 1778. He m. Maria Barbara Graff and Anna Regina Magdalena, widow of Michael Lohra (see entry in Dover section), at STR on Aug. 4, 1768 and had the following children:
- Johan Michael, bapt. at the First Reformed Congregation at Lancaster on Oct. 28, 1739. He was taxed in 1762, m. Maria Margareth Peterman at CLY on Jan. 1, 1760, and had the following children:
  - Elisabeth, bapt. at QUI on May 19, 1766, and spon. by Elisabeth Langin and Johan Georg Miller.
  - Johan Michael, bapt. at QUI on Aug. 4, 1768, and spon. by Michael Lang and Regina Lorain.
  - Andreas, bapt. at QUI on Oct. 19, 1771 (aged 5 weeks), and spon. by Andreas Lang and wife.
  - Maria Magdalena, b. on May 22, 1742, bapt. at the First Reformed Congregation at Lancaster on June 6, 1742, and spon. by Johan Storfinger and Maria Magdalena Schlepp. She m. Daniel Peterman, and had the following children:
    - Heinrich, b. on Nov. 13, 1762, bapt. at TLY on Dec. 26, 1762, and spon. by Michael Lang and wife.
    - Daniel, b. on Sept. 12, 1767, bapt. at TLY on Oct. 25, 1767, and spon. by Michael Peterman and wife.

- Georg, b. on Sept. 5, 1775, bapt. at TLY on Nov. 5, 1775, and spon. by Killian Tuebinger and wife.
- Andreas, b. about 1746, m. Anna Eva, dau. of Georg Rudi, at STR on Jan. 24, 1769. He had the following children:
  - Johan Andreas, b. on Feb. 9, 1770, bapt. at STR on May 13, 1770, and spon. by Michael and Anna Regina Lang.
  - Elisabeth, b. on Nov. 15, 1771, and bapt. at CLY on Dec. 25, 1771.
  - Johan Henrich, b. on Feb. 14, 1774, and bapt. at CLY on Apr. 1, 1774.
  - Johan Georg, b. on Nov. 16, 1781, bapt. at QUI on Dec. 29, 1781, and spon. by his parents.
  - Susanna, b. on Oct. 8, 1784, bapt. at STR on June 26, 1785, and spon. by Jacob and An Maria Rudi.
- Johan Peter, b. on Mar. 12, 1749, and bapt. at Christ's Lutheran Church of York on Mar. 26, 1749. He m. Elisabetha, dau. of David Schaffer (see entry in Shrewsbury section). They had the following children (recorded at CLY):
  - Regina, b. on Oct. 7, 1774, and bapt. on Dec. 4, 1774.
  - Elisabeth, bapt. on Oct. 20, 1776.
  - Peter, b. on July 16, 1778, and bapt. on Aug. 23, 1778.
  - Friedrich, b. on June 13, 1780, and bapt. on July 30, 1780.
  - Catharina, b. on Aug. 20, 1782, and bapt. on Nov. 17, 1782.
- Elisabeth, b. on June 2, 1751, and bapt. at CLY on June 23, 1751.

Lau - Lips was taxed in 1762.

Lau - Leps was taxed in 1762.

Lau - Hans Theobald was a smith at Sultzthal, Northern Alsace, and m. Margaretha. They had the following children (definitely Conrad, Susanna Catharina, Hans Peter, and probably Christian (see BNA)):
  - Susanna Catharina, b. in 1694, m. Johannes, son of Johann Michael Joho, in Lembach on Mar. 1, 1735, and immigrated to America on the ship *Two Sisters* in 1738. He was b. in 1701, and was a maker of wooden shoes. They had the following children:
  - Maria Christina, b. on Oct. 20, 1735, and d. before 1738.
  - Eva Catharina, b. on June 18, 1737, and d. before 1738.
  - Maria Christina, b. on Mar. 14, 1740, bapt. by JCS on May 22, 1740, and spon. by Janeslaus Wuchtel and Maria Christina Baumann.
  - Eva Catharina, b. on May 26, 1749, bapt. by JCS on June 25, 1749, and spon. by Werntzel Buchtrueckel and wife.

- Anna Maria, bapt. by RJL on Sept. 9, 1750, and spon. by Peter and Susanna Lau (mother is listed as Anna Maria).
- Christian, b. on Aug. 21, 1696 (a hoffman in Sulzthal in 1724). He m. Anna Cleophe, dau. of Johan Jacob and Anna Maria (Schaub) Frey, in 1722. She was b. on Apr. 27, 1696, bapt. at Wingen Lutheran Church in Northern Alsace, and d. circa 1773. Christian and his family immigrated to America on the ship *John and William* on Oct. 17, 1732, and d. in York Co., Manchester Township, PA, on Apr. 21, 1772 (bur. at WOL). His will was written on Jan. 11, 1770, and probated on May 13, 1772. He received a warrant for 150 acres on Apr. 10, 1750, and was appointed constable on Manchester Township in 1749. They had the following children (recorded at Lembach Lutheran Church in Northern Alsace unless otherwise noted(see BNA)):
  - Johan Philip, b. on Mar. 29, 1722, m. Magdalena, dau. of Conrad Gentzler (see entry), in 1742, and d. in July 1781. He was taxed in Codorus Township in 1762, and naturalized in Manchester Township on Sept. 24, 1763. His will was probated on Aug. 30, 1781. They had the following children:
    - Gertrude, b. on Mar. 17, 1761, and bapt. at Wolf's on Mar. 24, 1761. She m. Frederick Miller.
    - Henrich, b. in 1763.
    - Elisabeth, b. on Sept. 7, 1765, bapt. at Wolf's on Sept. 29, 1765, and spon. by Elias and Anna Maria Eyster. She m. Philip Rudisill, and d. in Lincoln Co., North Carolina, on Oct. 6, 1824.
    - Andreas, b. in 1767.
    - Michael, b. in 1771.
    - Magdalena, b. on Sept. 1, 1773, m. John, son of Hans Peter and Maria Catharina (Miller) Menges (see entry), on Mar. 15, 1792, and d. on Aug. 24, 1858. He was b. on Mar. 16, 1766, and d. on Dec. 12, 1839. They are bur. in Rodes cemetery in York Co., Jackson Township.
  - Catharina Juliana, b. on Oct. 8, 1724, bapt. on Oct. 10, 1724, and spon. by Philipp Hoch, Anna Catharina, wife of Hans Kachel, and Juliana Catharina (Frawinger) Droxel.
  - Son, b. on Feb. 19, 1727, and d. young.
  - Johan Peter, b. on Mar. 19, 1728, m. Susanna Ness, dau. of Mathias Ness (see entry in Shrewsbury section), in Codorus Township in 1748, and d. there on Mar. 7, 1806. Susanna was b. on Apr. 15 (June 10), 1732, and d. on Jan. 17, 1801 (both are bur. at Wolff's). They had the following children:
    - Maria Magdalena, b. on Aug. 22, 1749, and bapt. at CLY on Nov. 2, 1749. She m. Georg Philip, son of Conrad Gentzler (see entry), on Nov. 17, 1767. He was b. in 1750, and d. in 1816.

MANCHESTER TOWNSHIP   229

- Andrew, b. on Oct. 7, 1751, and bapt. at CLY on Nov. 3, 1751.
  He m. Elisabeth and Magdalena, and d. in Feb. 1822.
- Johan Georg, b. on Jan. 18, 1754, and bapt. at CLY on Feb. 17,
  1754. He m. Magdalena, dau. of Michael Hassler (see entry in
  Codorus section), and d. on Feb. 20, 1808.
- Anna Maria, b. about 1755, and m. Daniel, son of Daniel
  Rennolly (see entry in Codorus section).
- Catharina, b. about 1757, and m. Valentine, son of Valentine
  Alt (see entry in Shrewsbury section).
- Anna Eva, b. on Apr. 29, 1760, and bapt. at Wolf's on May 27,
  1760, and spon. by Heinrich, son of Matthias Ness and Eva,
  dau. of Georg Myer. She m. Johan Peter, son of Daniel
  Rennolly (see entry in Codorus section).
- Susanna, b. on Aug. 7, 1771, and m. Valentine Bergheimer.
- Anna Margaretha, b. in Nov. 1733, bapt. at CLY on Feb. 23,
  1735, and spon. by Johan Georg Schwab, Jr., and Anna Maria
  Eberdt.
- Johan Michael, b. on Oct. 30, 1735, bapt. at CLY on Nov. 6, 1735,
  and spon. by Johan Michael Eberdt and M. Magdalena Schwab.
  He m. Anna Maria in 1758, and d. on June 2, 1795. She was b.
  on Mar. 3, 1738, and d. on Aug. 13, 1815. Michael and Anna
  Maria had the following children in West Manchester Township:
- Peter, b. about 1760, m. Barbara, dau. of Daniel Rennolly (see
  entry in Codorus section), and d. in 1834.
- Maria Catharina, b. on Mar. 12, 1763, m. Christian, son of
  Daniel Rennolly (see entry in Codorus section), and d. on Aug.
  18, 1822.
- Anna Maria Magdalena, b. on Aug. 9, 1766, bapt. on Sept. 7,
  1766, and spon. by Casper and Maria Magdalena Kerber. She
  m. Henry Wehler on Aug. 23, 1789.
- Maria Elisabetha, b. on Oct. 13, 1768, bapt. at Wolf's on Oct.
  30, 1768, and spon. by Andreas, son of Peter Lau, and Maria
  Elisabetha, dau. of Peter Amelot. She m. Georg Heinrich
  Wonder, and d. on Apr. 5, 1855. He was b. in 1766, and d. in
  1831.
- Johan Michael, b. on Feb. 24, 1771, bapt. at Wolf's on Mar. 7,
  1771, and spon. by Elias and Anna Maria Eyster. He m.
  Margaret Eyster, and d. on July 16, 1839. She was b. in 1773,
  and d. in 1867.
- Anna Maria, b. on Aug. 30, 1773, bapt. at Wolf's on Sept. 13,
  1773, and spon. by Joseph Hassler and Anna Maria Lau. She
  m. Philip Gentzler, and d. on Mar. 30, 1819. He was b. in 1772,
  and d. in 1861.
- Anna Margaretha, b. on Sept. 10, 1775, bapt. at Wolf's on Oct.
  8, 1775, and spon. by Philip and Magdalena Lau.

- Christian, b. on Oct. 22, 1777, bapt. at Wolf's on Nov. 22, 1777, and spon. by Peter and Susanna Lau. He d. on June 12, 1792, and is bur. in WOL cemetery.
- Susanna, b. on Aug. 1, 1780, bapt. at Wolf's on Aug. 27, 1780, and spon. by Peter and Susanna Lau.
- Anna Maria, b. on Apr. 17, 1737, bapt. at CLY on June 20, 1737, and spon. by Johan Georg Schwab, Jr., and A. Maria Eberdt. She m. Elias, son of Christian Eyster (see entry), on Aug. 6, 1754, and d. on Mar. 17, 1811.
- Maria Magdalena, b. on Sept. 5, 1739, bapt. at CLY on Nov. 14, 1739, and spon. by Michael Ebert and M. Magdalena Schwab. She m. Casper Kerber in 1758 (see entry).

- Conrad, b. about 1699, and was a hoffman in Sultzthal in 1721. He m. Maria Barbara, dau. of Johan Jacob and Anna Maria (Schaub) Frey, at Lembach Lutheran Church on Feb. 25, 1721. She was b. in Wingen, Northern Alsace, on Apr. 21, 1701. They immigrated to America on the ship *John and William* in 1732. In 1743, Conrad and Christina Lau were sponsors to the baptism of John Loffer at SML. He was an exec. for the will of Nicholas Honing in 1752. He moved to Orange Co., North Carolina, and d. there in 1775. Conrad and Maria Barbara had the following children (recorded at Lembach Lutheran Church unless otherwise noted (see BNA)):
- Maria Catharina, b. on Nov. 28, 1722.
- Maria Barbara, b. on May 14, 1724, and d. young.
- Hans Peter, b. on Sept. 26, 1725, and d. young.
- Anna Barbara, b. on July 24, 1727, and bapt. at Oberbronn Lutheran Church on July 27, 1727.
- Anna Maria, b. on Mar. 18, 1729.
- Johann Peter, b. on Jan. 19, 1731, and d. young.
- Johann Peter, b. in Nov. 1733, bapt. at CLY on Feb. 15, 1735, and spon. by Jacob Ziegler.
- Maria Barbara, b. on Dec. 28, 1736, bapt. at CLY on Jan. 14, 1737, and spon. by Philipp Ziegler and M. Barbara Wittmer.
- Johann Friederich, b. on Oct. 9, 1739, bapt. at CLY on Nov. 14, 1739, and spon. by Johan Friederich Tranberg and his fiancee, Maria Eva Wittmer.

- Hans Peter, b. on Apr. 11, 1701, and bapt. at Lembach, Northern Alsace, on Apr. 14, 1701. He was a tailor, and m. Maria Elisabetha, dau. of the late Samuel Guthman, former citizen and baker at Strassburg, at Lembach on May 5, 1721. They immigrated to America before 1749, and soon moved to Orange Co., North Carolina. They had the following children (at Lembach unless otherwise noted (see BNA)):
- Johann Jacob, b. on Dec. 14, 1722, and bapt. on Dec. 16, 1722.

MANCHESTER TOWNSHIP 231

- Johann David, b. on Jan. 7, 1724. He was a sponsor at CLY in
  1749. He received a MD warrant for a tract called *Long Hill* in
  1752 (located just south of SLC), and was naturalized in Orange
  Co., North Carolina, on Apr. 10/11, 1761. He m. Anna Maria, and
  had the following children:
  - Son, b. about 1751, and d. in 1753 (SLC).
  - Maria Magdalena, b. on Mar. 25, 1753, bapt. at SLC on Apr.
    23, 1753, and spon. by Jacob Hauck and Catharina Gotzin.
  - Samuel, bapt. at SLC on Apr. 6, 1755, and spon. by Hans
    Georg Vogelmann and Catharina Gotz.
- Maria Elisabetha, b. on May 7, 1725, and bapt. on May 10, 1725.
  She m. Georg Albrecht at CLY on May 26, 1749.
- Hans Peter, b. on Feb. 9, 1727, and bapt. on Feb. 11, 1727. He d.
  before 1736.
- Maria Catharina, b. on Dec. 31, 1727, and d. young.
- Margaretha, b. on Mar. 11, 1731, and bapt. on Mar. 13, 1731.
- Johan Peter, b. on Feb. 8, 1736, and bapt. on Feb. 10, 1736.
- Catharina Elisabetha, b. on Sept. 9, 1738. She was a sponsor to
  the baptism of a dau. of Johan Nicholas Wolfgang in 1755 (SLC).
- Maria Magdalena, b. on Jan. 12, 1741, and bapt. at
  Langensoultzbach, Northern Alsace (her father was a day laborer
  at Cappenwoog at this time).

Lauterbach - Conrad was taxed in 1762. He m. (Elisabeth Barbara in
1752) Susanna Barbara, and had the following children:
  - Margareth, bapt. by RJL on Nov. 4, 1752, and spon. by her
    parents.
  - George, b. about 1760, and m. Anna Maria Jung at TLY on Oct. 10,
    1782 (not proven to be a son).
  - Michael, b. on Apr. 7, 1762, and bapt. at CLY on May 16, 1762.

Leather - Frederick received a warrant for 300 acres on Oct. 30, 1736
(Blunston License), that he sold to Nicholas Ob on Jan. 6, 1756.

Leib - Ulrich m. Veronica. They immigrated to America on the ship
Molly on Sept. 30, 1727, and settled in Lancaster Co., Manheim
Township, PA. They and had the following children:
  - Ulrich, b. about 1732, m. Elisabeth, dau. of John Huber, and had
    the following son:
    - Josef, b. on Sept. 13, 1766, and d. in Fairfield Co., Rush Creek
      Township, OH, on Aug. 26, 1839. He m. Elisabeth, dau. of
      Johannes Seitz (see entry in Shrewsbury section). Elisabeth d. in
      Rush Creek Township on Mar. 4, 1841, and is bur. beside her
      husband in Grandview cemetery. They moved to Fairfield Co. in

1801, and Josef built the second mill on Rush Creek. Josef purchased 300 acres in Rush Creek Township in Aug. 1817.
- Christian, b. about 1734. He was taxed in 1762. His will was written in Manchester Township on Nov. 25, 1793, and probated on Mar. 19, 1796. He m. Mary, dau. of Anthony and Margaret Grever of Manheim Township (this may have been a second marriage, a Christian Liebpe, hatmaker of Berlin m. Catharina Barbara Daubenberger at Trinity Lutheran Church in Lancaster, PA, on Nov. 29, 1757). He had the following children:
  - Anna Maria, b. about 1760, and m. Joseph Updegraf at TLY on Apr. 6, 1779.
  - Elisabeth, b. in 1762, and m. Christian Miller at TLY on May 24, 1785.
  - Abraham, b. in 1765, and m. Barbara Miller. He is probably the Abraham whose probate inventory was filed in Manchester Township in 1823.
  - Catharine, m. John Roth.
  - Juliana, m. Michael Miller.
  - Magdalena.
- Abraham, b. on Feb. 8, 1736, m. Anna Maria Kiesel, and resided in Lancaster Co., Manheim Township in 1770.
- Peter, b. about 1738.
- Henrich, b. about 1740.
- Barbara, b. on Aug. 16, 1743.
- John, b. about 1745.
- Daniel.
- Veronica, b. about 1749, and m. John Geib.
- Moses.

Leib - Johannes, son of Hans Rudolph (b. on Oct. 21, 1668) and Maria Agnes (Orth) Leib (m. on Nov. 2, 1689), and grandson of Melcher and Margareth (Muller) Leib, was b. in Reihen, Germany, on Aug. 5, 1696. He immigrated to America with his father on the ship *William and Sarah* in 1727. He was a baker, while he resided in Germany. He m. Anna Margaretha, dau. of Clemens Hiertzel, in Reihen on Nov. 2, 1724. They were sponsors to the baptism of Johannes Humrichhaus in 1751 (RJL). He d. on Jan. 1, 1754 (TLY). They had the following children (see BNK):
  - Johann Jonas, bapt. at Reihen Lutheran Church on Nov. 30, 1725. He was taxed in 1762. His will was dated on Oct. 28, 1763, and probated on Nov. 8, 1763. He mentions his widowed mother, who is residing with him. He m. Elisabeth, and had the following children:
    - Barbara, bapt. by RJL on Oct. 24, 1763, and spon. by Barbara Amma.

MANCHESTER TOWNSHIP 233

- Maria Elisabeth, bapt. by RJL on Oct. 24, 1763, and spon. by Elisabeth Ziegler.
- Johannes, bapt. by RJL on Oct. 24, 1763, and spon. by Nicholas Wild.
- Ester, b. about 1732, and m. Leonard Hartzell.
- Margaretha, b. in 1736, and m. Dieterich, son of Dionysius Meyer (see entry), between 1758 and 1763.
- Anna Elisabeth, b. about 1737, and m. Georg Philip, son of Philip Ziegler (see entry).
- Susanna Catharina, bapt. at Trinity Lutheran Church in Lancaster on Apr. 15, 1739, and m. Sebastian, son of Martin Weigel (see entry).
- Johann Gottfried, b. about 1741, and m. Barbara, dau. of Jacob Rudisill (see entry), at TLY on Dec. 22, 1761. They had the following children (he may have moved to Mecklenburg Co., North Carolina):
  - Jonas, b. on Feb. 6, 1763, bapt. at TLY on Apr. 10, 1763, and spon. by Jonas Freytag and Elisabeth Rudisill.
- Maria Barbara, b. on July 15, 1743, and bapt. at CLY on Aug. 28, 1743. She m. Jacob Ament.

Leidig - Michael was taxed in 1762. He m. Appolonia, and had the following children:
- Maria, b. about 1758, and was a sponsor to the baptism of Maria Magdalena Stein at QUI in 1773.
- Eva, b. about 1760, and m. Georg Maurer at TLY on Apr. 17, 1781.
- Johan Jacob, b. on Dec. 8, 1762, bapt. ar STR on June 19, 1763, and spon. by Jacob and Margaretha Weigel.
- Michael, b. about 1768, and m. Salome before 1789.
- Andreas, b. on Aug. 9, 1770, bapt. at QUI, and spon. by Michael Lang and wife.

Leineweber - Georg was taxed in Manchester Township in 1762, and Paradise Township in 1769. His probate inventory was filed in Manheim Township in 1771. He m. Catharina, and had the following children:
- Maria Eva Frene, b. on Mar. 3, 1768, bapt. at WOL on Apr. 17, 1768, and spon. by Valentine Kieffer, and Maria Frone, daugher of Peter Lanteman.

Leineweber - Philip was taxed in Paradise Township in 1762. He m. Catharina Elisabetha, and had the following children:
- Johann Philip, b. on July 29, 1764, bapt. at WOL on Sept. 9, 1764, and spon. by Philip Caspar and Margaretha Salome Spangler.

- Maria Margaretha, bapt. at Zion Lutheran Church in Middletown, Frederick Co., MD, on Dec. 10, 1775.

Lichtenberger - Johan Casper was taxed in 1762. He m. Maria Clara, and had the following children:
- Johan Killian, b. on Feb. 3, 1753, and bapt. at CLY on Mar. 18, 1753.
- Johan Georg, b. on Apr. 1, 1754, and bapt. at CLY on Apr. 21, 1754. He m. Elisabeth, dau. of Nicholas Bohn (see entry).
- Maria Christine, b. on Jan. 27, 1760, and bapt. at CLY on Mar. 30, 1760.

Liebenstein (Lowenstein) - Johan Georg was taxed in 1762. He was b. to Johan Heinrich and Eva Margaretha Liebenstein in 1713, and immigrated to America in 1731. His will was written in Manchester Township on May 17, 1771, and probated on Jan. 6, 1772 (the will book mentions that this abstract is incorrect, but not in what aspect). He m. Catharina, dau. of Jacob Rauscher of Alsace, on June 27, 1738, and had the following children:
- Johan Adam, b. on Feb. 16, 1739, and bapt. at CLY on Apr. 1, 1739.
- Maria Elisabeth, b. on Nov. 27, 1740, bapt. at CLY on Apr. 5, 1741, and spon. by Daniel Diehl and wife. She was a sponsor to the baptism of Maria Elisabeth Benner in 1765 (FRI).
- Johan Georg, b. on Apr. 6, 1742, and bapt. at CLY on May 18, 1742. He m. Elisabeth Barbara, dau. of Philip Lantz, at STR on Nov. 3, 1767. His probate inventory was filed in York in 1808. He was taxed in Manchester Township in 1779.
- Anna Maria, b. on July 24, 1743, and bapt. at CLY on Aug. 28, 1743. She was a sponsor to the baptism of Jacob Gunther in 1761 (RJL). She m. Johann Benner about 1764 (children recorded at FRI).
- Christina Catharina, b. on Aug. 5, 1746, and m. Johan Carl, son of Daniel Diehl (see entry in Shrewsbury section), at CLY on Oct. 11, 1763.
- Jacob, b. on June 2, 1748, and bapt. at CLY on July 17, 1748.
- Anna or Maria, b. about 1750.
- Anna Eva, b. on Apr. 7, 1753, and m. Georg, son of Daniel Diehl (see entry in Shrewsbury section).
- Christian, b. about 1755.
- Michael, b. about 1757. He m. Maria Elisabeth about 1780. He was taxed in Manchester Township in 1779.
- John, b. on Apr. 8, 1759, and bapt. at CLY on May 24, 1759. His probate inventory was filed in York in 1826. He m. Anna Barbara, dau. of Jacob Walter (see entry in Codorus section).

Maas - Lephart was taxed in 1762.

Maul - Conrad was b. in the Lower Palatinate, Germany, in 1723, immigrated to America on the ship *Hampshire* and took the oath of allegiance on Sept. 7, 1748. He m. Catharina Elnora, dau. of Johann Heinrich Bott (see entry), on Jan. 24, 1749, and had the following children:
- Catharina Elisabeth, b. on Feb. 16, 1750, and bapt. at CLY on Apr. 15, 1750. She m. Johan, son of Georg Henrich, and Anna Elisabeth (Herring) Joseph (see entry in Dover section under Herring). He was b. in 1748, and d. in 1840.
- Johan Philip, b. on Sept. 8, 1751, and bapt. at CLY on Oct. 20, 1751. He m. Maria, dau. of Georg Heinrich and Anna Elisabeth (Herring) Joseph (see entry in Dover section under Herring). She was b. in 1753.
- Susanna, b. in 1756, m. Jacob Stover, and d. in Paradise Township in 1830. He was b. in 1748, and d. in 1830.
- Conrad, b. in 1760, and d. in Adams Co., Abbottstown, PA, on Oct. 7, 1851.
- Dorothea, b. about 1763, and m. Peter Kidd (Kitt/Gitt).
- Johan Peter, b. on Sept. 5, 1768, bapt. at WOL on Oct. 30, 1768, and spon. by Peter and Cathrina Elisabeth Wolff. He m. Anna Oderman, and d. in 1851. She was b. in 1772, and d. in 1849.
- Jacob, b. in 1770, and m. Susanna. She was b. in 1802, and d. in 1851.
- Elisabeth, b. in 1775, and d. in 1845. She never m.

Mecker - Georg was taxed in 1762.

Menges - Johan Peter was taxed in 1779. He was b. on July 16, 1731, and d. on May 30, 1806 (bur. at WOL). He was a Private in the 5th Company during the Revolution. His will was written in West Manchester Township, and probated on June 7, 1806. He m. Maria Catharina Miller (1740-1806), and had the following children:
- Margaret, b. about 1764, and m. John Shaffer.
- John, b. on Mar. 16, 1766, m. Magdalena, dau. of Philip Lau (see entry), on Mar. 15, 1792, and d. on Dec. 12, 1839. She was b. on Sept. 1, 1773, and d. on Aug. 24, 1858. They are bur. in Rodes cemetery in York Co., Jackson Township.
- Elisabeth, b. about 1768, and m. John Fickes.
- Eve, b. about 1770, m. Jacob Eip.
- Catharine, b. about 1773, and m. Martin Ziegler.
- Jacob, b. about 1776, and m. Christina Leinbach at TLY on Nov. 6, 1798.

- Peter, b. in 1778, m. Sabina, dau. of Georg Philip Ziegler, and d. in 1848. She was b. in 1775, and d. in 1852.

Meyer - Dionysius, son of Hans Heinrich and Catharina Meyer, was bapt. on June 21, 1678. He m. Anna Maria, dau. of the late Hans Dorr at Sinsheim, Elsenz/Reihen (Northern Kraichgau, Germany, on Nov. 9, 1706. He received a Blunston License for 400 acres on the West side of the Susquehanna in West Manchester Township on Oct. 30, 1736. This land was surveyed at 394 acres on Mar. 14, 1757, and patented on June 18, 1762. He deeded this land to his son, Dieterich on June 18, 1762 (except for 19.117 acres that were sold to Peter Meyer in 1762). Dionysius and Anna Maria had the following children (BNK):
- Bernhardt, bapt. on Aug. 15, 1707, and d. before 1712.
- Anna Barbara, bapt. on Jan. 30, 1709, and d. in 1713.
- Anna Maria, bapt. on Feb. 9, 1711.
- Johann Bernhardt, bapt. on May 30, 1712, and d. before 1713.
- Johann Bernhardt, bapt. on Sept. 26, 1713.
- Anna Barbara, bapt. on Mar. 5, 1715, and d. before 1718.
- Hans Gorg, bapt. on June 23, 1716. He m. Christina, dau. of Philip Ziegler (see entry), in York Co., PA, on Nov. 21, 1737, and Barbara before 1745. Gorg received a Blunston License for 200 acres in West Manchester and North Codorus Township. This land was surveyed at 393 acres on Apr. 18, 1746, and was patented on Aug. 23, 1760. On Aug. 12, 1758, he sold the land he dwelt on in York, adjacent to Marcus Hains, Leonard Limble, and Codorus Creek. On May 27, 1760, he is listed as a Yeoman in Manchester Township, when he receives the mortgage of Michael Miller of Codorus Township for 220 acres. He warranted 25 acres in Codorus Township on Aug. 6, 1753. He was taxed in Manchester Township in 1762. Gorg's probate inventory was filed in York Co. in 1765. Gorg had the following children:
  - Johan Michael, b. on Aug. 23, 1738, bapt. at Christ's Lutheran Church of York on Nov. 19, 1738, and spon. by Johan Michael Kerber and Eva Kerber. He m. Anna Maria, and had the following children:
    - Elisabeth, b. on Sept. 12, 1775, bapt. at Wolf's on Oct. 8, 1775, and spon. by Heinrich and Agnes Ottinger.
  - Georg, b. about 1739. He Anna Barbara, dau. of Johan Casper and Anna Wahlburg Kerber (see entry). She was b. on Dec. 15, 1734, and bapt. at Christ's Lutheran on Jan. 1, 1735. He warranted 30 acres in North Codorus Township on Jan. 16, 1767. They had the following children:
    - Jacob, bapt. by Reverend Jacob Lischy on Jan. 21, 1759, and spon. by Michael and Wilhelmina Margaretha Geisselman.

MANCHESTER TOWNSHIP

- Maria Barbara, bapt. by Reverend Jacob Lischy on Dec. 3, 1761, and spon. by Johannes and Maria Elisabetha Guckes.
- Anna Maria, bapt. by Reverend Jacob Lischy on Feb. 13, 1763, and spon. by Jacob and Anna Maria Ziegler.
- Johan Jacob, bapt. at Wolf's on Feb. 13, 1763, and spon. by Jacob Ziegler and Anna Eva Uhlichin.
- Johan Heinrich, bapt. by Reverend Jacob Lischy on Jan. 13, 1765, and spon. by Heinrich and Anna Maria Greff.
- Catharina, bapt. by Reverend Jacob Lischy on Jan. 1, 1766, and spon. by Anna Wahlburg Kerberin.
- Elisabetha, bapt. at Wolf's on Jan. 9, 1767, and spon. by Frederick and Eva Eichelberger.
- Anna Barbara, bapt. on June 25, 1769, and spon. by Adam and Elisabeth Uhler.
- Sabina, b. in 1771, and bapt. on Mar. 17, 1771.
- Johannes, b. about 1741. He m. Margaretha, dau. of Jacob Ziegler (see entry), and had the following children:
  - Johannes, b. on Feb. 7, 1763, bapt. by Reverend Jacob Lischy on Apr. 10, 1763, and spon. by Johannes Ziegler and Eva Meyer.
  - Maria Barbara, bapt. at Wolf's on June 2, 1765, and spon. by Jacob and Maria Barbara Ziegler.
- Johan Martin, b. on Jan. 31, 1744, and bapt. at Christ's Lutheran on Feb. 26, 1744. He m. Christina, and had the following children:
  - Catharina, bapt. at Wolf's on Nov. 8, 1767, and spon. by Catharina Schultz.
- Anna Eva, bapt. by Reverend Jacob Lischy on Dec. 25, 1745, and spon. by Gorg and Anna Eva Weller.
- Johan Jacob, bapt. by Reverend Jacob Lischy on May 5, 1754, and spon. by Joseph and Magdalena Welshans.
- Elisabetha, bapt. by Reverend Jacob Lischey on June 22, 1755, and spon. by Wahlburg Kerberin.
- Anna Barbara, bapt. on Aug. 24, 1718.
- Johann Dieterich, bapt. on Mar. 10, 1721. He m. Anna Maria Magdalena about 1739, and Margaretha, dau. of Johannes Leib of Reihen (see entry), before Aug. 30, 1763. He was naturalized in Apr. 1762. He had the following children (bapt. at Christ's Lutheran Church of York):
  - Anna Margaretha, b. on Nov. 2, 1740, bapt. on Nov. 26, 1740, and spon. by Philip Ziegler, Jr., and his wife, Anna Margaretha.
  - Catharina Elisabetha, b. on Nov. 15, 1743, and bapt. on Nov. 30, 1743.
  - Johan Georg, bapt. by Reverend Jacob Lischy on Aug. 17, 1746, and spon. by Georg and Barbara Meyer.

- Johan Dieterich, bapt. by Reverend Jacob Lischy on Apr. 19, 1751, and spon. by Dewald and Susanna Maria Ehmig.
- Johannes, bapt. by Reverend Jacob Lischy on May 20, 1753, and spon. by Johannes and Charlotte Wolf.
- Johan Heinrich, bapt. by Reverend Jacob Lischy on May 17, 1756, and spon. by Georg Philip Ziegler and Anna Maria Durrin.
- Johan Michael, b. on July 28, 1758, and bapt. on Aug. 11, 1758.
- Susanna Maria, bapt. on June 27, 1723.
- Johan Jacob, bapt. on Apr. 13, 1727.

Meyer - Georg Ernst was taxed in 1762. He m. Eva Schultz, and d. in York Co., York, PA, in 1777. They had the following children bapt. at CLY:
- Maria Barbara, b. on June 5, 1747, and bapt. on June 28, 1747.
- Maria Elisabetha, b. on July 4, 1751, and bapt. on July 21, 1751.
- Sabina, b. on Apr. 11, 1758, and bapt. on May 15, 1758.

Miller - Hans Jacob was b. to Hans and ___ (Schneider) Miller, in 1628, and m. Vrenilli Gubleman. He immigrated to America on the ship *Mary Hope* from London on June 29, 1710, and arrived at Philadelphia in Oct. 1710. He had the following children (information from David Sprinckle):
- Rudliffe, b. in 1658. He m. Barbara, and d. in Lancaster Co., Conestoga Township, PA, in 1732. Rudliffe's wife d. sometime after that date. In 1719, Rudliffe was listed as an English settler in Conestoga Township. In 1720, he is listed as Rudith Miller (and son); in 1721, on the English assessments as Rudy; in 1722, as Ralph (and son); in 1724, Rudall (and son); and in 1725/26, as Rudy (and son). His will was written on Nov. 27, 1731, and probated on Feb. 1, 1732. Perhaps Barbara is the Bru Miller, whose estate was filed at Lancaster in 1740. Rudliffe and Barbara had the following children:
  - Henry, b. about 1796, and was taxed in Conestoga in 1719, 1721, 1722, 1724, 1725, 1726.
  - Jacob, b. about 1798 (possibly the Jacob whose estate was filed in Lancaster Co. in 1737).
  - Anna Margaretha, b. about 1700, and m. Michael Sprinckel (see entry). He was taxed in Conestoga Township in 1724 and 1726.
- Hans Jacob, b. on Mar. 20, 1663 (SWI?). He m. Magdalena on Apr. 2, 1693. In 1710, he had 1,000 acres surveyed in the Pequea Valley (+6% for roads). He was taxed in Lancaster Co., Conestoga Township in 1718; as Jacob and son in 1719; and Jacob Elder in 1725. He was naturalized in 1717. He d. on Apr. 20, 1739, and is bur. in Tchantz Graveyard. His estate was filed in Lancaster Co. in 1740. They had the following children:

MANCHESTER TOWNSHIP

- Jacob, b. about 1694. He was taxed in 1719 as freeman with his father; Jacob Jr. in 1720, 1725, 1726, 1724. He was naturalized in 1717. On Nov. 19, 1754, Jacob deeded 100 acres (part of a 1,000 acre patent to Jacob Miller on June 30, 1711) to his son, Martin in Strasburg Township. This land was adjacent to Jacob Miller, Jr., Amost Strettell, and Jacob Miller. He m. Catharina, and had the following children:
  - Jacob.
  - Martin was b. in Switzerland about 1720, m. Margareth Neff, and d. in Strasburg Township between Jan. 7, and Mar. 15, 1773 (will dates). On Dec. 1, 1744, Jacob and Catherine Miller deeded 100 acres in Strasburg Township to Martin that was part of the 150 acres that had been granted to them on Apr. 29/30, 1731.
- Hance, b. about 1796, and taxed in Conestoga in 1718, 1719.
- Martin, b. about 1798, and was taxed in Conestoga in 1719, 1725, 1726. He was naturalized in 1717, and his estate was filed in Lancaster Co. in 1743.
- Michael, b. about 1700 m. Barbara. He may be the Michael Miller that resided in York Co. on Oct. 16, 1727. His will was written on Mar. 23, 1737, and probated on Aug. 26, 1739. He was taxed in Conestoga in 1718, 1719, 1720, 1721, 1725, 1724, 1726. In May 1718, he had 1,200 acres on the northwest side of the Conestoga River. His will was probated in Lancaster Co. in 1739. He had the following children:
  - Jacob.

Mohr - Peter m. Maria Catharina, dau. of Johann Mattheis of Deux Ponts in the Palatinate, and immigrated to America in 1739. He d. in 1740 (after Feb.), and later in 1740, she m. Conrad Amman (see entry). She was b. in 1700, and d. on May 3, 1761. She was bur. in Henry Bott's burial ground on May 5, 1761 (CLY). Peter and Catharina had the following children (9 children 4 dead in 1761):
- Johan Jost m. Dorothea, and they were sponsors at the baptism of Johannes Quickel at STR in 1763. He may have been the Yost Mohr that m. Christina, dau. of John Lindy of York Town, before 1793. Jost had the following children:
  - Johan Philip, b. on Nov. 4, 1738, and bapt. at CLY on Dec. 16, 1738.
  - Eva Catarina, b. on July 3, 1741, bapt. by JCS at CLY on Aug. 20, 1741, and spon. by Marx Heus and Eva Catarina Iserlin.
  - Anna Catharina, b. on Aug. 8, 1748, and d. on Apr. 17, 1748. She was bur. at CLY on Apr. 17, 1748.
  - Maria Elisabeth, b. on Aug. 23, 1751, and bapt. at CLY on Aug. 25, 1751.

- Johan Georg, b. on May 13, 1752, and d. on May 14, 1752. He is bur. at CLY.
- John (not proven), b. about 1753, and m. Elisabeth Graff at TLY on Mar. 20, 1774.
- Peter (not proven), b. about 1758, and m. Gertrude Dinckel at TLY on Mar. 27, 1780.
- Elisabeth, m. Heinrich Luchenbach (see entry in Dover section).
- Charlotte, m. Johannes Wolff before 1750 (see entry).
- Philip Heinrich was taxed in Dover Township in 1762. His will was written in Dover Township on Oct. 28, 1776, and probated on Aug. 30, 1779. He m. Juliana Catharina about 1748 and Catharina. Juliana Catharina was b. on Jan. 15, 1716, and d. on Oct. 14, 1749. She was bur. at CLY on Oct. 15, 1749. Philip Heinrich had the following children:
  - Maria Dorothea, b. on Oct. 8, 1749, and bapt. at CLY on Oct. 9, 1749. She d. on Nov. 6, 1749, and was bur. at CLY.
  - Georg.
  - Maria.
  - Sophia, m. ___ Valentine.
  - Margaretha, b. on Nov. 5, 1730, m. Georg Ilgefritz (see entry in Dover section).
- Johan Nicholas was taxed in 1762. His will was written in Manchester Township on Aug. 2, 1791, and probated on Oct. 24, 1796. He m. Anna Margaretha, and had the following children:
  - Johan Georg, b. on Oct. 3, 1752, and bapt. at CLY on Oct. 29, 1752. He was not mentioned in the will.
  - Anna Margaretha, b. about 1755, and m. Anthony Desenberg. His will was written in Manchester Township on Nov. 1, 1804, and probated on Nov. 12, 1804.
  - Anna Maria, b. on Oct. 6, 1758, and bapt. at CLY on Nov. 12, 1758. She was not mentioned in the will.
  - Johan Peter, b. on Apr. 15, 1762, and bapt. at CLY on June 6, 1762. He m. Catharin about 1783.
  - Johan Christian, b. on May 27, 1760, and bapt. at CLY on July 19, 1760. He m. Catherine, dau. of Conrad Becker about 1788 (see entry in Dover section). His probate inventory was filed in Manchester Township in 1823.
  - Philip Christopher, b. on May 27, 1760, and bapt. at CLY on July 19, 1760. He m. Appolonia.
  - Katharina, b. about 1762, and m. Adam Schuler about 1784.
- Anna Engela Elisabeth, b. about 1734, and was a sponsor to the baptism of Anna Engela Leimbach in 1754 (RJL). She m. Tobias Hoetzel. His will was written in Paradise Township on Oct. 8, 1792, and probated on Nov. 28, 1792. They had the following children:

- Conrad, bapt. by RJL on July 23, 1755, and spon. by Conrad and Maria Elisabeth (Maria Catharina) Amman. He was not mentioned in the will.
- Charlotte, bapt. by RJL on Apr. 23, 1758, and spon. by Johannes and Charlotte Wolff. She m. Martin Schultz.
- Johannes, bapt. by RJL on Mar. 20, 1761, and spon. by Johannes Stubler and Eva Catharina Ammannin.
- Georg Heinrich, bapt. by RJL on Dec. 19, 1762, and spon. by Georg Heinrich and Anna Elisabeth Joseph.
- Johan Georg, bapt. by RJL on Jan. 8, 1765, and spon. by Johan Georg and Rosina Schelhammer. He was not mentioned in the will (unless he went by John).
- Philip.
- Eve, m. John Boss.
- Sophia, m. William Haines.
- Catharine, m. Jacob Geiger.
- Margaret.
- John.
- Tobias.
- Johan Peter, b. on Feb. 27, 1740, bapt. at The First Reformed Congregation in Lancaster Co., Lancaster, PA, on Feb. 25, 1740, and spon. by Johan Peter Doerr. He was taxed in 1762. He m. Anna Catharina before 1757, and Maria Magdalena about 1759. In 1760, Peter and Maria Magdalena were sponsors to the baptism of Anna Christina Appelman at WOL. His will was written in Paradise Township on Aug. 23, 1796, and probated on May 6, 1797. Peter had the following children:
  - Maria Eva, b. on Sept. 11, 1758, and bapt. at CLY on Nov. 12, 1758. She m. Daniel Jacobs at TLY on Oct. 7, 1783.
  - Eva Catharina, bapt. by RJL on Apr. 5, 1761, and spon. by Johannes Stubler and Eva Catharina Ammannin.
  - Johan Jacob, bapt. by RJL on Apr. 15, 1764, and spon. by Jacob and Barbara Amman.
  - Elisabeth, b. about 1766, and m. Samuel Jacob at TLY on Apr. 4, 1786.
  - Anna Barbara, bapt. at WOL on Nov. 11, 1768, and spon. by Heinrich and Anna Barbara Fissel.
  - John.
  - Magdalena.
  - Gertrude.
  - Margaret.

Morganstern (Morningstar) - John wrote his will in Manchester Township on Oct. 19, 1756, and it was probated on Nov. 30, 1756. He m. Anna Maria. They had the following children:

- Philip. He received his father's 375 acres on the island at Susquehanna, the 50 acres adjoining his (Philip's) land, and 300 acres on Pipe Creek. His will was written in Manheim Township on Feb. 2, 1789, and probated on Apr. 3, 1789. He was taxed in Manchester Township in 1779. He m. Anna Maria Eva, dau. of Johan Georg and Catharina (Jager) Kuntz of Heidelberg Township), on June 18, 1739 (JCS). She was b. on June 15, 1724, bapt. at Hatten Lutheran Church (BNA) on June 18, 1724, and immigrated to America on the ship *Pennsylvania Merchant* in 1732. They had the following children:
  - Johannes, b. on June 16, 1740, bapt. by JCS (STM) on June 30, 1740, and spon. by John Morgenstern, Johann Ebert, and Catarina Kuntz. His will was probated on Jan. 11, 1781, and executed by Valentine Fisher and Catharina Morningstar.
  - Johan Adam, b. about 1741, bapt. at STM, and spon. by Johan Adam Zanger, Johan Christian and Adam Hubert, and Catharina Kuntzing.
  - Maria Catharina, b. in Apr. 1743, bapt. at STM in May 1743, and spon. by Frederick Hasz and Catharina Kuntzing. She m. Peter Schultz.
  - Johanna Juliana Elisabetha, b. about 1745, bapt. at STM, and spon. by Juliana Morganstern and Johanna Kuntz. She m. Frederick Sauer on June 11, 1765.
  - Elisabeth, b. about 1747, and m. John Felty.
  - Anna Eva, b. in May 1750, bapt. at STM in 1750, and spon. by Christian Crolle.
  - Johan Philipp, b. in 1752, bapt. at STM in Nov. 1752, and spon. by Philip Croll and Juliana Frey.
  - Anna Maria, b. on May 14, 1754, bapt. at STM on June 1, 1754, and spon. by Christian Croll and wife. She m. Nicholas Hull.
  - Johan Georg, b. on Oct. 6, 1756, bapt. at STM in Nov. 1756, and spon. by Georg Meier and Catharina Hupperton. His will was written in Manheim Township on Aug. 4, 1804, and probated on Aug. 21, 1804.
  - Henrich, b. about 1758.
  - Anna Salome, b. on Jan. 19, 1760, bapt. at STM on Feb. 1, 1760, and spon. by Henry Holl and Anna Eva Hupperton.
- Maria Elisabetha, m. Johanes Hoffman at STM on May 22, 1744, and had the following children (recorded at STM):
  - John, b. in Aug. 1745, bapt. on Aug. 28, 1745, and spon. by John Morgenstern, Michael Lau, and J. Catharina Berkheimer.
  - Anna Maria, b. on Mar. 10, 1760, and bapt. at CLY on May 26, 1760.
- Ana Juliana Catarina Elisabeth, b. on July 2, 1733, and bapt. at Trappe Lutheran Church in Montgomery Co., PA. She was a

sponsor to the baptism of Juliana Kuntz in 1747 (STM). She was not mentioned in the will.

Moser - Samuel was b. in 1689, and d. on Feb. 22, 1755. He m. Catharina Weiss in Bischwiller, Bas-Rhin, France on May 14, 1714. She was b. in 1693. They had the following children in Birschwiller:
- Samuel, b. on Mar. 31, 1715. He was taxed in York Township in 1762. He m. Catharina Francois in Langensoultzbach, Bas-Rhin, France on Nov. 23, 1739. They arrived at Philadelphia in 1749, on the ship *Lydia*. They resided in York Co., Conewago Township, PA, and York Borough. Samuel may have been the Samuel who wrote his will on Feb. 2, 1796, probated in York Borough on June 2, 1796, and executed by Henry Tyson and John Herbach. The will referred to a wife Salome, son Samuel, and other children. Samuel and Catharina had the following children:
  - Maria Esther, b. in Bischwiller, France on Sept. 18, 1746, and m. Adam Kern at TLY on July 17, 1766.
  - Samuel, bapt. in York Co., PA, by Reverend Jacob Lischy on Mar. 3, 1750/1, and spon. by Christian and Anna Maria Leonhardt. He m. Eva Margaret, dau. of Michael and Margaret Geisselman (see entry in Shrewsbury section), sometime before 1780, and Anna Maria before 1787. He may be the Samuel who wrote his will on Aug. 1, 1811, probated in York Borough on May 20, 1816, and executed by Adam and George Moser. The will refers to a wife, Barbara, and children Adam, George, and Catharine.
  - Maria Elisabeth, bapt. in York Co. by Reverend Jacob Lischy on May 11, 1755, and spon. by Christian and Anna Maria Leonhardt.
- Hans Michael, b. on July 11, 1717. He was taxed in 1762. He m. Eva Maria, dau. of Melchior Elsasser, at Billigheim, Germany, on Jan. 16, 1741. She was b. in Billigheim on Sept. 11, 1717, and d. in Columbiana Co., OH, on June 27, 1807 (moved there with son Samuel in 1801). They arrived at Philadelphia in 1749 on the ship *Lydia* and settled in York Co., Manchester Township, PA. Michael d. there in 1789. They had the following children:
  - Hans Michael, b. in 1742. He m. Maria Anna Shaffer about 1771. Michael d. in 1811.
  - Peter, b. in 1744, m. Margaret Wortman (possibly the John Peter Moser that m. Margaret Wollmer at the First Reformed Congregation at Lancaster, PA, on May 21, 1765), and d. in 1808 (bur. in Petersburg, OH). In 1801, they moved to Jefferson Co., OH (now Mahoning Co.). During the Revolutionary War, he served as a Private in Captain Wright's Company in 1776, and Captain Smythe's Company Lancaster County Militia. She was b. in 1743, and d. in 1821.

- Samuel, b. on Feb. 16, 1746. He m. Elizabeth about 1766, and d. in Tuscarwas Co., Bolivar, OH, in 1808 (1810/12).
- Abraham, b. about 1748, and d. in 1822. He m. Barbara about 1775.
- Johannes, b. about 1750, and d. in 1826. He m. Catherine, dau. of John Lindy, before 1788.
- Johan Jacob, b. on Aug. 29, 1756. He m. Catherine before 1796, and resided in OH.
- Daniel, b. on Apr. 4, 1759, m. Catherine, and d. in Petersburg, OH, in 1817. He was a Private in Captain Strahler's Company, 6th Battalion Northampton County Militia, in the Revolutionary War. He was taxed as single in York Township in 1779. Daniel and his wife were sponsors at the baptism of Daniel Moser at BLY in 1792.
- Johan Peter, b. on July 16, 1724.
- Anna Maria, b. on Sept. 21, 1729.

Muller - Johan Conrad was taxed in 1762. He m. Maria Catharina Elisabeth about 1739, and had the following children:
- Maria Magdalena, b. on Aug. 3, 1740, and bapt. at CLY on Sept. 18, 1740.
- Margaretha, b. on Sept. 23, 1741, and bapt. at CLY on Sept. 27, 1741.
- Johan Andreas, b. on May 5, 1743, and bapt. at CLY on May 15, 1743.
- Barbara, bapt. at TLY on Mar. 17, 1745, and spon. by Georg and Barbara Meyer.
- Maria Susanna, bapt. by RJL on Apr. 18, 1746, and spon. by Johannes Wolff and Maria Susanna Meyer.
- Maria Margareth, bapt. by RJL on Jan. 28, 1750, and spon. by Johannes and Maria Margareth Emig.
- Johan Conrad, bapt. by RJL on May 10, 1752, and spon. by Conrad and Maria Catharina Amma.
- Anna Christina, bapt. by RJL on Dec. 22, 1754, and spon. by Heinrich and Margareth Gerhardt.
- Zacharias, bapt. by RJL on Feb. 20, 1757, and spon. by Zacharias and Anna Margaretha Schuckert.

Muller - Frederick was taxed in 1762. He m. Louisa, and had the following children:
- Johann Michael, bapt. by RJL on Nov. 9, 1757, and spon. by Johan Michael Schmeisser and Ottilla Hummelin.
- Anna Maria, b. on Mar. 4, 1767, bapt. at FMY on Mar. 8, 1767, and spon. by Anna Elisabeth Hoens and Elisabeth Meyer.

MANCHESTER TOWNSHIP

Muller - Herick was taxed in 1762.

Muller - Andreas was taxed in 1762. His probate inventory was filed in Manchester Township in 1779. He m. Maria Dorothea, dau. of Baltzer Knoertzer (see entry in Dover section). They had the following children:
- Johan Peter, b. on Mar. 12, 1759, and bapt. at CLY on Apr. 15, 1759.
- Dorothea, b. on Mar. 9, 1761, and bapt. at CLY on Apr. 12, 1761.
- Maria Barbara, b. on July 10, 1763, and bapt. at CLY on Aug. 21, 1763.
- Johannes, b. in Feb. 1766, bapt. at QUI on Mar. 16, 1766, and spon. by Johannes and Barbara Humrichhaus.

Muller - Phillip was taxed in 1762. His probate inventory was filed in Manchester Township in 1788. He m. Anna Maria, dau. of Martin and Magdalena Rhein (see entry in Shrewsbury section), in 1744. She was b. in Blanckenloch, Baden-Durlach, in 1720, and d. between 1763 and 1776. She immigrated to America with her parents in 1738. They had the following children:
- Anna Maria, b. about 1746, and m. Georg Schodde at STR on Nov. 14, 1769.
- Johan Georg, b. on Dec. 26, 1748, and bapt. at CLY on Mar. 26, 1749.
- Maria Elisabeth, b. on Apr. 28, 1751, and bapt. at CLY on May 19, 1751.
- Philip, b. on Sept. 1, 1753, and bapt. at CLY on Nov. 4, 1753.
- Maria Barbara, bapt. by RJL on June 27, 1756, and spon. by Georg and Maria Nes.
- Johan, b. on May 14, 1761, and bapt. at CLY on July 12, 1761.

Neiman (Neuman) - Christian was taxed in 1762. He m. Catharina, and had the following children:
- Johan Reinhard, b. on Apr. 15, 1759, bapt. at CLY on Apr. 29, 1759, and spon. by Reinhard and Maria Elisabeth Bott.
- Maria Elisabeth, b. on Apr. 17, 1761, bapt. at CLY on May 17, 1761, and spon. by Reinhard and Maria Elisabeth Bott.
- Herman, b. on July 18, 1768, bapt. at CLY on July 31, 1768, and spon. by Herman Guckes and Elisabeth Baurer.

Oberdorff - Casper was taxed in 1762. He m. Anna Catharina, and had the following children (he may also be the Casper Oberdorff who had his probate inventory filed in Hellam Township in 1768, m. Anna Elisabeth, and had Francis, b. on Oct. 4, 1751, and bapt. at CLY on Nov. 19, 1751 (there are other Oberdorff families in the area)):

- Johan Michael, b. on Dec. 18, 1761, and bapt. at CLY on Apr. 18, 1762.
- Johan Georg, b. on Feb. 12, 1764, and bapt. at CLY on Mar. 18, 1764.
- Dorothea, b. on May 28, 1766, and bapt. at CLY on July 13, 1766.

Ottinger - Jacob, son of Hans and Dorothea Ottinger, was b. at Elsenz, Germany, on Sept. 27, 1716, and immigrated to America on the ship *St. Andrew* on Oct. 27, 1738 (BNK). He was taxed in 1762, and naturalized in Apr. 1761. He was a tavernkeeper. His will was written in Manchester Township on Sept. 7, 1781, and probated on Sept. 17, 1781. He was a carpenter. He m. Anna Johanna, dau. of Johann Martin Josi (see entry), on Aug. 20, 1741 (JCS). She d. about 1801. They had the following children:
- Johan Jacob, b. about 1742, and m. Anna Margaretha, dau. of Jacob Jauler (see entry), at TLY on Dec. 30, 1766.
- Hanna, b. about 1745, and m. Michael Frederick. She was a sponsor to the baptism of Johan Jacob Ottinger in 1767.
- Anna Elisabeth, b. about 1747 m. Johan Georg Eisenhardt (see entry).
- Anna (Maria) Ottilla, bapt. by RJL on Mar. 26, 1749, and spon. by Peter and Ottillia Josi. She m. John Wild (see entry) at TLY on May 3, 1769. He is probably the John Wild that m. Catharina Schreiber at TLY on Apr. 13, 1779. She was not mentioned in the will, and probably d. before 1781.
- Johan Peter, bapt. by RJL on Mar. 1, 1752, and spon. by Peter and Catharina Elisabetha Wolff. He m. Maria Magdalena Romig at CLY on June 4, 1776, and Margaret Rubbert at TLY on Mar. 28, 1784.
- Anna Dorothea, bapt. by RJL on Nov. 17, 1754, And spon. by Johanna Boin and Philip Stambach. She m. John Dettemer.
- Henrich, b. about 1755, and m. Agnes before 1775. His probate inventory was filed in Dover Township in 1786.
- Maria Clara, b. about 1757, and was a sponsor to the baptism of Johannes Ottinger at WOL in 1774.
- Johannes, bapt. by RJL on Nov. 25, 1759, and spon. by Johannes and Anna Wolff. He m. Margaret Detterman at TLY on June 2, 1781.
- Anna Maria, b. on Apr. 24, 1762, and bapt. at CLY on Apr. 28, 1762.

Rhode - Anthony wrote his will in Manchester Township on Dec. 29, 1784, and it was probated on Feb. 8, 1785. He m. Magdalena, and had the following children:
- Henry.
- John.

- Franey, m. ___ Prinimen.
- Ann, m. ___ Strickler.
- Christian.
- Anthony.
- Frederick.
- Magdalena, m. ___ Culp.
- Elisabeth.

Roemer - Johann Frederick was taxed in 1762. He was b. in Stadecken, near Mainz, and was the great grandson of Jacob Roemer, mayor of Stadecken from 1650-1668. He immigrated to America on the ship *St. Mark* in 1741, and was naturalized in Apr. 1764. He m. Anna Dorothea Mueller in York Co., PA, on July 23, 1745, and Catharina, dau. of Jacob and Juluana (Bahn) Lanius (see entry in Dover Township section), in the First Moravian Church of York on Mar. 28, 1758. Dorothea, dau. of Felix Mueller (see entry in Codorus section), was b. in Leimen, near Heidelberg, in Oct. 1725, and d. on Sept. 12, 1757. Frederick purchased 310 acres in Manchester Township on Jan. 28, 1758. His will was written in Manchester Township on Dec. 30, 1782, probated on Apr. 15, 1784, and executed by John Rohmer and Jacob Lanius. Frederich had the following children:
- Franz Jacob, b. on Feb. 24, 1746, bapt. by RJL at Kreutz Creek on Easter, 1746, and spon. by Francis Jacob Mueller and Anna Maria Stambach. He d. in Franklin Co., Chambersburg, PA, in 1790, and is bur. in Zion Reformed Church cemetery. His will was written on Sept. 10, 1790, and probated on Dec. 22, 1790. He m. Catharina Wolff in York on Dec. 25, 1772, and served at a Lt. Col. of the 5th Battalion York County Militia from 1779 to 1783.
- Johan Henry, b. on Feb. 6, 1748, bapt. by RJL on Feb. 17, 1748, and m. Judita. He resided in Adams Co., PA, in 1776.
- Johan Frederick, b. on Mar. 24, 1750, bapt. in Apr., 4, 1750, and d. in Franklin Co., Chambersburg, PA, on Aug. 26, 1822. He is bur. in Zion Reformed Church cemetery. He m. Catherina Heitler in York on Dec. 25, 1772, and Magdalena. Magdalena was b. 1760, and d. in Chambersburg on Mar. 8, 1831. He was a Lt. of the 4th Battalion of the York County Militia during the Revolutionary War.
- Johan, b. on Mar. 1, 1753, bapt. on Mar. 5, 1753, and spon. by Johan Beitzel, Peter Binckele, and Francis Jacob Mueller. He d. in Washington Co., Conococheague, MD, in 1784. He m. Maria Barbara, dau. of Johann Nicolaus and Maria Barbara (Riedt) Schwingel. She was b. in Berks Co., PA, on Mar. 17, 1756, bapt. at Christ's Evangelical Lutheran Church of Stouchsburg on Apr. 4, 1756, and spon. by Johann Nicolas Riedt. Johan was a private in the 5th Company of York County Associators during the Revolutionary War.

- Anna Maria, b. about 1755, and m. Joseph, son of Michael and Margreta Hassler (see entry in Codorus section).
- Juliana, b. on Jan. 14, 1759, bapt. at the First Moravian Church on Jan. 15, 1759, and spon. by Anna Maria Miller, Eva Weller, Anna Maria Votring, and her grandmother, Juliana Lanius.
- Catharina, b. on Feb. 17, 1760, bapt. at the First Moravian Church on Feb. 21, 1760, and spon. by Rosina Schmidt, Eva Barbara Ebert, and Margaret Binckel. Elisabeth, b. on Oct. 28, 1761.
- Maria Magdalena, bapt. by Reverend Jacob Lischy on Feb. 26, 1764, and spon. by her uncle and aunt, Christophel and Catharina Weidner.
- Johan Adam, bapt. at Wolf's in Mar. 1765, and spon. by Johan Adam and Catharina Wolff.

Rors - Nicholas was taxed in 1762.

Rothrock - Philip was taxed in 1762. He was b. in Leiselheim, Germany, on Dec. 8, 1713, immigrated to America in 1733, and was received into the Moravian Society at Lancaster on Feb. 11/22, 1752. He had 139 acres surveyed in West Manchester Township on Oct. 28, 1746. His will was written on Feb. 28, 1798, and probated on Mar. 31, 1803. He m. Catharina Kuntz of Rothenbach on Mar. 11/22, 1740, and Eleanora, widow of Jacob Galatin, at FMY on Sept. 21, 1781. Catharina was b. in Mar. 11, 1720, immigrated to America in 1726, and d. on Nov. 10, 1777. Eleanora was b. in Schwarzenau, Witgenstern, Germany, on Aug. 14, 1724, came to America with her parents, and became a member of the Moravian Congregation at Lancaster on Jan. 31, 1751. Eleanora was alive in 1798. Philip and Catharina had the following children (recorded at FMY):
- Jacob, b. on May 14, 1741, and bapt. on May 25, 1741. He m. Barbara.
- Anna Maria, b. on Sept. 6, 1742.
- Johannes, b. on Feb. 7, 1744, and bapt. on Feb. 18, 1744. He m. Dorothea, dau. of Georg and Rosina Gump, on May 1, 1767, and Charity Worley in 1776. Dorothea was b. on Oct. 11, 1749, and d. on Dec. 18, 1775. Charity was b. on Feb. 20, 1759, and bapt. as Salome on Nov. 13, 1785. He served in the Revolutionary War as a Lieutenant, and d. on Aug. 28, 1805. He is bur. in Prospect Hill cemetery.
- Catharina, b. on Sept. 19, 1745, and bapt. on Sept. 22, 1745, and spon. by Johannes and Catharina Heckedorn.
- Philip, b. on Oct. 11, 1746, and bapt. on Oct. 22, 1746.
- Peter, b. on Oct. 11, 1746, and bapt. on Oct. 22, 1746.
- Infant, bapt. on Nov. 2, 1747.

MANCHESTER TOWNSHIP

- Georg, b. on Oct. 18, 1748, and bapt. on Oct. 29, 1748. He m. Louise Harttafel at FMY on Nov. 30, 1773, and Maria Walter at FMY on May 21, 1780.
- Valentine, b. on Oct. 6, 1751, bapt. at FMY on Oct. 17, 1751, and spon. by Francis Jacob Muller, John Peizel, Francis Beroth, John Heckedorn, and Peter Binckele.
- Benjamin, b. on Nov. 9, 1753, bapt. at FMY on Nov. 11, 1753, and spon. by John Heckedorn, Francis Lewis Beroth, Francis Jacob Miller, Georg Herbach, Peter Binckele, Marcus Hohns, and Lewis Brotzman.
- Joseph, b. on May 11, 1755, bapt. at FMY on May 14, 1755, and spon. by John Heckedorn, Lewis Brotzman, and Martin Ebert.
- Catharina, b. on May 18, 1757, bapt. at FMY on May 19, 1757, and spon. by Barbara Schlegel, Juliana Lanius, Catharina Heckedorn, and Eva Barbara Muller. She m. ___ Bentz.
- Anna Maria, b. on Mar. 1, 1759, bapt. at FMY on Mar. 4, 1759, and spon. by Anna Maria Muller, Catharina Heckedorn, and Eva Weller. She m. ___ Meissenkop.
- Frederick, b. on Sept. 30, 1760, bapt. at FMY on Oct. 4, 1760, and spon. by Heckedorn, Peizel, and Francis Jacob Muller.

Rudisille (Rudisilli) - Johan Jacob, son of Hans and Anna, was bapt. on Oct. 4, 1666, and m. Cleophe, dau. of Ulrich and Catharina (Endress) Neff, in Michelfeld, Germany, on Feb. 19, 1688, and d. there on Sept. 16, 1748. She d. in Michelfeld on Feb. 6, 1758. They had the following children at Michelfeld (see BNK):
- Anna Catharina, b. on Oct. 30, 1689 (at Eichtersheim).
- Hans Michael, b. on Mar. 11, 1692, and m. Anna Elisabetha, dau. of Andreas Vorreuter, and had the following children at Michelfeld:
  - Johann Jacob, b. Feb. 12, 1715, m. Anna Christina Regula on Feb. 2, 1740, and immigrated to America on the ship *Brothers* in 1752 (BNK mentions that the Jacob who immigrated to America, and settled in York Co. may have been the son (b. Aug. 12, 1715) of Hans Leonhard and Sophia (Keller) Rudisill, and grandson of Hans and Anna Rudisill). Jacob's will was written in Codorus Township, and probated on Apr. 20, 1802. They had the following children (b. at Michelfeld except the first and last two):
    - Johann Ludwig, b. in Leiman on Sept. 22, 1740. He m. Magdalena about 1766.
    - Anna Elisabetha, b. on Nov. 5, 1742. She m. Abraham Roth.
    - Johan Jacob, b. on Sept. 23, 1745, and d. on Mar. 27, 1748.
    - Johan Jacob, b. on Mar. 30, 1748. He was not mentioned in the will.
    - Johann Leonhard, b. on Aug. 15, 1751, and d. before 1754.

- Johann Leonhard, b. on Jan. 6, 1754, and bapt. at CLY on Jan. 13, 1754. He was not mentioned in the will.
- Johan, b. about 1756.
- Andreas, b. on Jan. 4, 1717, and immigrated to America on the ship *Phoenix* in 1749. He was naturalized in Manheim Township in Apr. 1762. He m. Maria Margaretha, and had the following children (recorded at CLY except the last):
  - Johann Jacob, b. on Sept. 20, 1750, bapt. on Oct. 18, 1750, and spon. by Jacob and Elisabeth Rudisill. He d. on Dec. 1 (Nov. 22), 1810 (bur. in STM cemetery). His will was written in Hanover Township on Aug. 28, 1808, and probated on Dec. 13, 1810. He m. Anna Eva, dau. of Adam and Catharina (Kuntz) Hubbert. She was b. on Mar. 17, 1751, and d. on Dec. 20, 1806. He served as a 1st Lieutenant in the Revolutionary War.
  - Maria Elisabeth, b. on Aug. 20, 1752, and bapt. on Aug. 21, 1752. She m. William Bear.
  - Charlotte, b. about 1754 (unmarried in 1808).
- Weyrich, b. on Aug. 7, 1695, and m. Anna Barbara, dau. of Hans Peter and Anna Magdalena (Bohli) Siegfried, at Michelfeld, Germany, on Sept. 13, 1718, and immigrated to America on the ship *Samuel* in 1737. She was b. at Elsenz, Germany, on May 9, 1696. He moved to North Carolina, and d. before June 4, 1764. Weyrich had the following children at Michelfeld (except the first, second, and last)(see BNK):
  - Johannes, b. about 1719, and was taxed in 1762. He m. Anna Catharina Wagner at the First Reformed Church of Lancaster, PA, on Jan. 21, 1746. He received a land grant for 200 acres on May 20, 1754. They had the following children (recorded at CLY unless otherwise noted):
    - Maria Barbara, b. on Dec. 25, 1746, bapt. on Feb. 24, 1747, and spon. by Weyerich and Barbara Rudisill. She m. Johan Georg, son of Michael Spaar (see entry in Dover section), at STR on Nov. 8, 1768.
    - Johann Weyrich, b. on Sept. 23, 1749, bapt. on Nov. 5, 1749, and spon. by Weyerich and Barbara Rudisill.
    - Elisabeth, b. on Apr. 27, 1752, and bapt. on May 18, 1752. She m. Jacob, son of Peter Schreiber at STR on Jan. 2, 1770.
    - Johannes, bapt. by RJL on Nov. 9, 1755.
    - Maria Margaretha, b. on Dec. 4, 1757, and bapt. on Feb. 4, 1759.
    - Susanna, b. on Aug. 26, 1762, and bapt. on Sept. 26, 1762.
    - Maria Barbara, b. on July 31, 1766, and bapt. at CLY on Sept. 14, 1766.

MANCHESTER TOWNSHIP   251

- Elisabetha, bapt. at Elsenz on Feb. 20, 1721, and m. Martin, son of Martin and Magdalena Rein (see entry in Shrewsbury section), at the Moravian Church at Lititz, Lancaster Co., on Nov. 22, 1744.
- Johann Michael, b. on Sept. 11, 1723. He was a sponsor to Catharina Barbara Nebinger in 1745. In 1750, he located on Leeper's Creek in North Carolina (Anson (now Gaston) Co.). On May 20, 1754, he purchased 200 acres (the deed record mentions bros. Philip and Weirich (Terrick)). Michael d. in the latter part of 1793. He had the following children:
  - Andrew, b. on Mar. 2, 1748, bapt. at STM on Apr. 10, 1748, and spon. by Andrew Madinger and wife.
  - Henry, m. Catharine Friday and Saloma Seitz.
  - Philip, m. Elizabeth Johnson in 1788.
  - Susanna, m. John Derr.
  - John m. Mary Ramsaur.
  - Jacob, m. Susanna, dau. of Michael Hoyle.
  - Catharine m. Jacob Link.
  - Hanna, b. in 1758, and m. Johan Godfrey Arndt.
  - Elizabeth, m. Matthias Davault.
  - Dorothy, m. John Early in 1798.
  - Barbara, m. Conrad (?John) Gensler (see entry in Dover section).
- Johann Weyrich, b. on May 29, 1726, and m. Magdalena. They later moved to North Carolina. They had the following children:
  - Eva Dorothea, bapt. by RJL on Feb. 10, 1751, and spon. by Nicholas and Eva Ehmig.
  - Maria Elisabeth, b. on Nov. 21, 1752, and bapt. at CLY on Nov. 26, 1752.
  - Maria Margareth, b. on Jan. 27, 1754, and bapt. at CLY on May 5, 1754.
- Anna Catharina, b. on May 12, 1729, and d. on July 1, 1730.
- Philipp Jacob, b. on July 25, 1731, and bapt. on July 26, 1731. He m. Mary, and moved to Anson (now Gaston) Co., between Friday Schoals and High Schoals, North Carolina, where his will was written on Aug. 4, 1792, and probated in 1794. Philip had the following children:
  - Elisabeth, m. Jacob, son of Jacob Costner.
  - Barbara, m. Michael, son of Jacob Costner.
  - Catharina, m. Jacob, son of Bastian Best.
  - Maria, m. Frederick, son of Georg Hovis.
  - Margaretha, m. David Costner.
  - Susanna, m. Adam, son of Peter Costner.
  - Michael, m. Mary Carpenter.
  - Philip, m. Elizabeth, dau. of Philip Lau.

- Wirely.
  - Johann Georg, b. on Feb. 8, 1734, and d. on Feb. 16, 1734.
- Johann Georg, b. on Nov. 3, 1735.
- Tobias, b. about 1737. He and Jacob Rudisill were sponsors to the baptism of Tobias Windnagel in 1756. He m. Louisa, and had the following children (recorded at CLY):
  - Johan Jacob, b. on Oct. 23, 1760, and bapt. on May 10, 1761.
  - Louisa, b. in Feb. 1783, and bapt. on Oct. 2, 1783.
- Anna Johanna, b. on Dec. 28, 1740, bapt. CLY on May 17, 1741, and spon. by Jacob Ottinger and Anna Johanna Igsin.
  - Philip Heinrich, b. on Sept. 24, 1697, and immigrated to America on the ship *William and Sarah* in 1727. He was a tailor at Weiler before coming to America. He m. Anna Maria, dau. of Georg Philip Schopff of Weiler, at Sinsheim on Apr. 14, 1722, and unknown woman about 1729, and Susanna Bayer at Lancaster Co., Conestoga, on Oct. 27, 1734 (JCS). He had the following children:
    - Georg Philip, b. on Mar. 30, 1723, bapt. at Sinsheim on Apr. 1, 1723, and d. before 1725.
    - Georg Philip, b. on Aug. 18, 1725, and bapt. at Sinsheim on Aug. 19, 1725.
    - Maria Barbara, b. on Apr. 12, 1730, bapt. at Trinity Lutheran Church in Lancaster on May 7, 1730, and spon. by Caspar and Maria Barbara Lochmann.
    - Anna Barbara, b. about 1732, and m. Johan Georg Christoph Stech at Trinity Lutheran in Lancaster on Jan. 29, 1751.
    - Anna Maria, b. about 1733, and m. Philipp Adam Brenner at Trinity Lutheran Church in Lancaster on Sept. 18, 1751.
    - Anna Catarina, b. on Aug. 19, 1735, bapt. at Trinity Lutheran Church in Lancaster on Sept. 14, 1735, spon. by Christoph and Anna Catarina Ulrich. She d. before 1750.
    - Johann Michael, b. on Sept. 1, 1737, bapt. at Trinity Lutheran Church in Lancaster on Sept. 25, 1737, and spon. by Johan Michael and Anna Catarina Beyerle. He m. Maria Angelica Schaefer at Trinity Lutheran Church in Lancaster on Apr. 30, 1765. He was a tailor.
    - Johan Melchior, b. on Oct. 11, 1738, bapt. at Trinity Lutheran Church in Lancaster on Oct. 29, 1738, and spon. by Johan Melchior Beyerle and Susanna Bartin. He m. Anna Christina Mezger at Trinity Lutheran Church in Lancaster on Oct. 16, 1759. He was a saddler.
    - Johan Jacob, b. about 1740, and m. Barbara Wegerlin at Trinity Lutheran Church in Lancaster on May 5, 1761. He was a blacksmith.

MANCHESTER TOWNSHIP 253

- Susanna, b. on Oct. 19, 1744, and bapt. at Trinity Lutheran Church in Lancaster.
- Catharina, b. in Aug. 1750, and bapt. at Trinity Lutheran Church in Lancaster on Oct. 12, 1758. She m. Heinrich Schenck at Trinity Lutheran Church in Lancaster on Mar. 27, 1758.
- Son, b. and d. in 1700.
- Hans Georg, b. on May 7, 1701.
- Maria Catharina, b. on Nov. 19, 1703, and d. young.
- Johann Jacob, b. on Apr. 10, 1706, and immigrated to America on the ship *Mortonhouse* in 1729. He was taxed in Manchester Township in 1762, and was naturalized in Apr. 1761. Jacob's will was written in Manchester Township on Nov. 10, 1785, and probated on Jan. 10, 1787. He m. Elisabeth, dau. of Tobias Amspacher (see entry in Codorus section). He had the following children:
  - Johan Jacob, b. about 1732, and m. Anna Maria Messerschmidt at CAN on Apr. 22, 1755. He was a wheelwright, and his probate inventory was filed in York Town in 1776. Jacob had the following children:
  - Tobias, b. on Mar. 10, 1756, bapt. on Apr. 18, 1756, and spon. by Tobias Rudisill. He d. on Aug. 29, 1758, and was bur. at CLY on Aug. 3, 1758.
  - Philip, b. on Feb. 3, 1759, and bapt. at CLY on Feb. 18, 1759.
  - Anna Elisabetha, b. on Apr. 7, 1760, and bapt. at CLY on Apr. 16, 1760.
  - Johan Jacob, b. on Dec. 7, 1762, and bapt. at CLY on Dec. 25, 1762.
  - Johan Jacob, b. on Apr. 17, 1777, bapt. at CLY on May 10, 1777, and spon. by his grandparents, Jacob Rudisil, Sr., and wife (this was a posthumous child).
  - Jonas, b. about 1734, and was taxed in 1762. He m. Maria Elisabeth Maul. His probate inventory was filed in Manchester Township in 1799. They had the following children:
    - Philip, b. on Apr. 4, 1756, and bapt. at CLY.
    - Maria Elisabetha, b. on Mar. 25, 1759, and bapt. at CLY on Apr. 22, 1759.
    - Maria Barbara, b. on Jan. 1, 1761, and bapt. at CLY on Feb. 8, 1761.
    - Johannes, b. on Feb. 25, 1763, and bapt. at CLY.
    - Susanna, b. on Nov. 8, 1765, and bapt. at CLY on Nov. 25, 1765.
    - Jonas, b. on Aug. 3, 1768, and bapt. at CLY on July 31, 1768. He m. Susanna, dau. of William and Susanna Clark of Mecklenburg Co., North Carolina. He d. in Mecklenburg Co.

on Aug. 31, 1830. Susanna was b. on May 22, 1773, and d. on
Feb. 1, 1852.
- Jacob, b. on May 9, 1770, and bapt. at CLY on Jan. 4, 1770.
- Rosina, b. on June 5, 1772, and bapt. at CLY on July 5, 1772.
- Anna Maria, b. on June 9, 1779, and bapt. at CLY on July 18,
1779.
- Baltazar, b. about 1736, and m. Maria Elisabetha. They had the
following children (recorded at CLY unless otherwise noted):
  - Jonas, b. on Dec. 18, 1769, and bapt. on Mar. 18, 1770.
  - Maria Eva, b. on July 5, 1771, and bapt. on Aug. 9, 1771.
  - Johannes, b. on Mar. 18, 1773, and bapt. on Apr. 25, 1773.
  - Jacob, b. on July 21, 1774, and bapt. on Aug. 28, 1774.
  - Johan Georg, b. on Oct. 20, 1776, and bapt. on Dec. 1, 1776.
  - Maria Elisabetha, b. on Jan. 2, 1780, and bapt. on Mar. 5,
  1780.
- Johan Philip was taxed in 1762. He was b. on Apr. 19, 1738,
and bapt. at CLY on May 21, 1738. He m. Elisabetha, dau. of
Adam Rupert (see entry), at CLY on July 28, 1761. They had
the following children (recorded at CLY):
  - Johannes, b. on May 13, 1762, and bapt. on May 16, 1762
  (not listed in North Carolina records).
- Anna Maria Catharina bapt. at the First Reformed Church at
Lancaster, Lancaster Co., PA, on May 5, 1742, spon. by
Balthasar and Anna Catharina (Wolf) Knoertzer, and m.
Johannes Reber about 1760 (see entry in Codorus section).
- Elisabetha, b. about 1742, and m. Johan Michael, son of Hans
Michael Ebert (see entry), at CLY on Aug. 7, 1764.
- Barbara, b. about 1744, and m. Gottfried, son of Johannes Lieb
(see entry).
- Susanna, b. about 1746, and was a sponsor to Susanna Reber
in 1765. She m. Andreas Schmidt, and had the following
children (recorded at CLY unless otherwise noted):
  - Andreas, b. on Apr. 3, 1774, and bapt. on May 8, 1774.
  - Johan, b. on Apr. 5, 1776, and bapt. on May 12, 1776.
  - Johan Jacob, b. on July 24, 1778, and bapt. on Aug. 9, 1778.
  - Catharina, b. on Aug. 24, 1780, and bapt. on Sept. 3, 1780.
  - Henrich, b. on Nov. 18, 1788, and bapt. on Feb. 1, 1789.
- Thomas, b. on Nov. 5, 1748, and bapt. at CLY on Dec. 18, 1748
(he is not mentioned in the will).
- Maria Dorothea, b. on Feb. 11, 1751, and bapt. at CLY on Mar.
17, 1751. She m. Georg Meyer, and had the following children:
  - Maria Elisabetha, b. on Mar. 23, 1773, and bapt. at CLY on
  May 30, 1773.
  - Johan, b. on Dec. 29, 1776, and bapt. at CLY on Apr. 6, 1777.
  - Susanna, b. on Dec. 21, 1778, and bapt. on Apr. 4, 1779

- Anna Maria, b. on Mar. 25, 1781, bapt. at QUI on Apr. 26, 1781, and spon. by Carle Heier and wife.
- Anna Maria, b. on Sept. 3, 1784/83, bapt. at QUI on Mar. 28, 1785/84, and spon. by Jacob and Sophia Gottwald.
- Johann Georg, b. on Feb. 10, 1790, bapt. at QUI on June 7, 1790, and spon. by Balthasar and Maria Elisabetha Rudisill.
- Rebecca, b. on June 16, 1753, and bapt. at CLY on Aug. 5, 1753. She is not mentioned in the will.
- Johan Heinrich, b. on Dec. 18, 1759, and bapt. at CLY on Feb. 3, 1760. He m. Judith Spengler at TLY on May 27, 1781.
- Anna Maria, b. on June 20, 1762, and bapt. at CLY on July 25, 1762. She m. Andreas Ritter.
- Catharina, b. on Aug. 17, 1708, and d. young.
- Johann Philip, b. on Mar. 27, 1711.
- Anna Catharina, b. on July 27, 1713.
- Matthaus, b. on Easter, 1718, and bapt. on Apr. 19, 1718.

Ruppert - Johann Adam, son of Adam Rupert, was b. in 1706. He was a smith at Rappenau, Germany, when he m. Anna Barbara, dau. of Leonard Holtzappel (see entry), at Michelfeld, Germany, on Apr. 25, 1730. He immigrated to America on the ship *Britannia* on Sept. 21, 1731, and was taxed Manchester Township in 1762. The administration bond for his estate was dated Nov. 17, 1781. They had the following children (see BNK):
- Anna Catharina, b. on Apr. 22, 1731, and bapt. at Michelfeld.
- Catharina, b. on June 4, 1733, bapt. at CLY on Sept. 17, 1733, and spon. by Maria Barbara Kalberman.
- Erasmus, b. on Apr. 6, 1736, bapt. at CLY on May 29, 1736, and spon. by Erasmus Holtzappel and wife.
- Christina, b. in May 1738, bapt. at CLY on Aug. 2, 1738, and spon. by Erasmus Holtzappel and wife. She m. Peter, son of Peter Becker (see entry in Shrewsbury section).
- Johan Dieterich, b. on Dec. 5, 1740, bapt. at CLY on Apr. 5, 1741, and spon. by Johan Dieterich Ulrich and wife. He was overseer of the poor for Manchester Township in 1771. He m. Maria Margaretha, dau. of Peter Schultz of Heidelberg Township, at CLY on Dec. 28, 1762.
- Elisabeth, b. on Mar. 5, 1743, bapt. at CLY on Mar. 29, 1743, and spon. by Dieterich Ulerich and wife. She m. Philip, son of Jacob Rudisill (see entry), at CLY on July 28, 1761.
- Margareth, bapt. by RJL on Oct. 27, 1745, and spon. by Philip and Anna Margaretha Endler and Dieterich and Elisabeth Uhler. She m. Jacob, son of Martin Weigel (see entry), at STR on Feb. 15, 1763.

- Johan Adam, b. on Apr. 13, 1748, bapt. at CLY on May 20, 1748, and spon. by Dieterich and Elisabeth Uhler. He was a Private in Captain Philip Albright's Company, Colonel Samuel Miles' Battalion of Riflemen in "camp near King's Bridge" in Sept. 1776. He and other soldiers mutinied and deserted later that month. He later signed a petition with the other soldiers stating that he did not leave New York for cowardice but for bad usage, and he was willing to fight to defend the Province. He was a Corporal in the 10th Regiment of the Pennsylvania Line from 1777-1781. He was granted a pension on Oct. 9, 1832, while he was residing in Columbiana Co., OH.
- Magdalena, b. on Feb. 4, 1751, bapt. at CLY on Apr. 7, 1751, and spon. by Elisabeth Uhler.

Schaffer - Serenus. His will was written in Manchester Township on May 30, 1769, and probated on Jan. 11, 1770. He m. Margaret. Their children were not named in the will.

Scheib (Shipe) - Jacob was taxed in 1762. He m. Maria Elisabeth Schneider, and had the following children:
- Infant, b. on Feb. 12, 1763, bapt. at TLY on Mar. 20, 1763, and spon. by Michael Lederman and wife.

Scheib (Shipe) - Martin was taxed in 1762.

Schmeisser - Martin was the second officer in command under Frederick V, and was mortally wounded at the Battle of Wurtemburg. He m. Anna Barbara. She was b. in Germany in 1681, and immigrated to America with her children on the ship *Britannia* on Sept. 21, 1731. She first settled in York Co., Kreutz Creek, and later in Manchester Township. They were members of the Lutheran Church in the Parish of Lustenau, Germany, and had the following children (see *History of the Schmeisser Family by Amanda Laucks-Xanders* (1931)):
- Anna Margarethe, b. in 1711, and m. Christian Eyster (see entry).
- Mathias, b. in Reigelbach Ansbach on Feb. 15, 1715. He received a warrant for 100 acres in Jackson Township Jan. 29, 1742, that was surveyed as 150 acres on May 5, 1743. He m. Anna Catharina, dau. of Johan Wolfgang and Anna Maria Copenhaver, on July 23, 1738. She was b. in Rueblingen, Germany, on June 5, 1717, immigrated to America with her parents on the ship *Pennsylvania* on Sept. 11, 1732. Wolfgang settled in Lebanon Co., PA. Anna Catharina d. on Feb. 13, 1763, and Mathias d. on Apr. 12, 1778. He was a weaver. During the Revolutionary War, he was a teamster, who conducted a baggage wagon. He was later promoted to Colonel. His will was

MANCHESTER TOWNSHIP 257

written in Manchester Township on Apr. 7, 1778, and probated on
May 1, 1778. They had the following children:
- Johan Georg, b. on Dec. 23, 1739, and bapt. at CLY on May 3,
  1740. He m. ___ Mulhaus at CLY in 1760, and d. in 1763. He
  had no children.
- Johan Michael, b. on Nov. 21, 1740, bapt. at CLY on Nov. 25,
  1740, and spon. by Johan Georg and Barbara (Stambach)
  Schmeisser. He m. Anna Maria, dau. of Jacob Hoke (see entry),
  and d. in West Manchester Township on July 7, 1810. He was a
  farmer and tavern keeper. He served during the Revolution as a
  Captain in Col. Michael Swope's Regiment, and was captured by
  the British at Fort Washington on Sept. 16, 1776. He was
  released and returned home in 1778, and in the same year was
  elected a member of the House of Representatives of PA. He was
  re-elected to this office 7 times through 1790. From 1790 to 1795,
  he served in the State Senate.
- Mathias Jacob, b. on Oct. 3, 1742, and bapt. at CLY on Oct. 15,
  1742. He m. Elisabeth, dau. of Frederick Eichelberger (see
  entry), and d. in 1793. He was Justice of the Peace, and was
  elected to the House of Representatives in 1789.
- Mathias Emeric, b. on Nov. 1, 1744, and bapt. at CLY on Nov. 15,
  1744. He m. Louisa, dau. of Jacob and Anna Catharina (Clay)
  Slagle, on Mar. 5, 1770, and d. in West Manchester Township on
  Feb. 21, 1829. She was b. on May 2, 1744, and d. on Aug. 26,
  1820. His will was written on July 5, 1814.
- Maria Dorothea, b. on Mar. 19, 1747, and bapt. at CLY on May
  10, 1747. She and m. Peter, son of Jacob Hoke (see entry).
- Rosina, b. on Feb. 12, 1749, and bapt. at CLY on Mar. 12, 1749.
  She m. Georg Moul, and d. in 1796/97.
- Maria Sabina, b. on Dec. 14, 1750, and bapt. at CLY on Apr. 7,
  1751. She m. Johan Jacob, son of Johannes Schwob (see entry).
- Elisabeth, b. on Mar. 21, 1753, and bapt. at CLY on May 20,
  1753. She and m. Leonhardt, son of Frederick Eichelberger (see
  entry).
- Anna Maria, b. in 1756, bapt. by RJL on May 29, 1757, and spon.
  by Martin and Anna Maria Eichelberger. She m. Martin, son of
  Johan Michael Ebert (see entry), and d. in 1833.
- Susanna, bapt. by RJL on June 26, 1760, and spon. by Martin
  and Anna Maria Eichelberger. She m. Philip Adam, son of Johan
  Michael Ebert, and d. in 1840.
- Johan Georg, b. in 1722, and received a warrant for land in
  North Codorus Township on Jan. 29, 1742, that was surveyed as
  138 acres on May 5, 1743. He m. Maria Barbara, dau. of
  Johannes Stambach (see entry in Codorus section) at CLY (or
  Trinity Lutheran in Lancaster Co.) on May 22, 1740. His will was

written in Newberry Township on Feb. 17, 1747. After Georg's death, Barbara m. Georg Muller (see entry in Codorus section) in 1748, and moved to Codorus Township. Georg and Barbara Schmeisser had the following children:
- Mathias, b. in 1741/42, and d. in MD in 1786. He m. Johanna Angela, dau. of Henry Leinbacher (see entry in Dover section). In 1763, Mathias Schmeisser and Georg Muller sold Georg Schmeisser's farm in Newberry Township. They moved to MD about 1773. After Mathias' death, she m. Joseph Tible/Bitle of KY.
- Johann, b. on July 17, 1743. he resided in Dover Township in 1773.
- Johan Jacob, b. on Mar. 19, 1747, and d. before Feb. 19, 1763.

Schmidt - Killian was b. in 1693, and m. Catharina, dau. of Andreas Frey, in 1715. She was b. in Stein, Germany, on Oct. 5, 1687, d. of Dysentery at 4 a.m., on Aug. 19, 1758, and was bur. at Henry Wolf's burial Ground on Aug. 20. He immigrated to America on Aug. 17, 1733, and received a warrant for 200 acres in Manchester and West Manchester Township on Oct. 30, 1736 (Blunston License). His probate inventory was filed in Manchester Township in 1763. They had the following children (7 children total (three were living in 1758)):
- Anna Margaretha, b. in 1716, and m. Philip Ziegler (see entry) on Nov. 21, 1737 (JCS).
- Anna Maria, b. about 1718, and m. Johan Georg, son of Peter Wolff (see entry), on May 22, 1738 (JCS), and Andreas Neppinger about 1744. His will was written in York Town on June 28, 1779, and probated on Oct. 26, 1779. Anna Maria was alive in 1779. They had the following children:
    - Catharina Barbara, bapt. by RJL on Mar. 17, 1745, and spon. by Killian and Catharina Schmidt, Michael Rudisill, and Barbara Facklerin. She m. Georg Weller.
    - Maria Elisabeth, b. on Jan. 4, 1749, and bapt. at CLY on Jan. 15, 1749. She was not mentioned in the will.
    - Andreas, b. on May 19, 1751, and bapt. at CLY on May 26, 1751. He d. on Aug. 20, 1752, and was bur. in York on Aug. 21, 1752 (CLY).
    - Anna Margaretha, b. on Apr. 27, 1753, and bapt. at CLY on Apr. 29, 1753. She was not mentioned in the will.
    - Georg, bapt. by RJL on May 18, 1755, and spon. by Georg and Anna Elisabetha Kuntz. He had an illegitimate son with Catharina Elisabeth Meyer in 1775, and m. Anna before 1777.
    - Andreas, b. on Aug. 26, 1757, d. on Apr. 7, 1759, and was bur. in the Lutheran church yard at York on Apr. 9, 1759. His godparents were Philip Ziegler and wife.

- Maria Agnes, b. about 1725, and m. Peter Wolff (see entry).
- Andreas, b. about 1727. He was taxed in 1762. His will was written in Manchester Township on Oct. 13, 1806, and probated on May 1, 1812. He m. Anna Barbara (she was not mentioned in the will). They had the following children:
  - Andreas, b. on Dec. 28, 1748, and bapt. at CLY on Jan. 20, 1749.
  - Johan Georg, b. on May 8, 1750, and bapt. at CLY on May 13, 1750.
  - Maria Eva, b. on Apr. 9, 1752, and bapt. at CLY on Apr. 26, 1752.
  - Anna Catharina, b. on July 27, 1754, and bapt. at CLY on Aug. 18, 1754.
  - Johan Jacob, bapt. by RJL on May 1, 1757, and spon. by Johann Jacob Wolff and Maria Eva Schultzin. He was not mentioned in the will, unless he went by John.
  - Maria Barbara, b. on July 15, 1759, and bapt. at CLY on Aug. 26, 1759.
  - Maria Magdalen, b. on Mar. 28, 1762, and bapt. at CLY on Apr. 18, 1762.
  - John, b. about 1764.
  - Heinrich, b. on July 12, 1767, and bapt. at CLY on Aug. 2, 1767.
- Jacob, b. about 1729. He was taxed in 1762. He m. Anna, dau. of Mathias Lambert (see entry). She d. in childbirth on Apr. 17, 1771. They had the following children:
  - Anna Magdalena, b. on Aug. 15, 1762, bapt. at TLY on Oct. 31, 1762, and spon. by Heinrich Walder and wife.
  - Jacobus, b. on Sept. 4, 1763, and bapt. at CLY on Apr. 15, 1764.
  - Anna, b. on Apr. 17, 1771, bapt. at QUI on Apr. 27, 1771, and spon. by Conrad Becker and wife.

Schneider - Peter was taxed in 1762. His will was written in Manchester Township on Mar. 15, 1802, and probated on Apr. 19, 1804. He m. Maria Rebecca about 1748, and Elisabetha, dau. of Franz Jacob Muller (see entry in Codorus section), at FMY on Sept. 15, 1767. He had the following children:
- Maria, b. about 1748.
- Johan Jacob, b. on Sept. 25, 1751, and bapt. at CLY on Nov. 10, 1751.
- Maria Catharina, b. on Apr. 6, 1754, and bapt. at CLY on Apr. 14, 1754.
- Maria Elisabeth, b. on May 10, 1756, and bapt. at CLY on June 6, 1756.

- Philip, b. about 1758.
- Maria Barbara, b. on Aug. 21, 1759, and bapt. at CLY on Mar. 25, 1750. She was not mentioned in the will.
- Johan Nicholas, b. on Apr. 7, 1760, and bapt. at CLY on Apr. 27, 1760.
- Johan Peter, b. on Feb. 21, 1763, and bapt. at CLY on Apr. 10, 1763. He d. before 1773.
- Maria Rebecca, b. on June 12, 1764, and bapt. at CLY on Aug. 12, 1764.
- Magdalena, b. about 1766.
- Maria Christina, b. on Apr. 7, 1768, and bapt. at CLY on June 5, 1768.
- Johan Peter, b. on May 23, 1773, bapt. at FMY on May 30, 1773, and spon. by Francis Jacob Muler, John Heckedorn, Sr., Francis Lewis Beroth, and Jacob Lanius, Sr. He d. on Sept. 3, 1773 (FMY).
- Peter, b. about 1775.

Schreyack - Johannes wrote his will in Manchester Township on May 17, 1785, and it was probated on Mar. 13, 1788. He m. Sabina about 1753, and Anna M. before 1785. He had the following children:
- Johan Leonard, b. on Jan. 26, 1738, and bapt. at CLY on May 12, 1738.
- Anna Barbara, b. on Sept. 22, 1741, and bapt. at CLY on Oct. 28, 1741. She was not mentioned in the will.
- Helena, b. on Sept. 22, 1743, and bapt. at CLY on Oct. 9, 1743. She m. Michael Fackler.
- Johan Jacob, b. on Feb. 8, 1745, and bapt. at CLY on Feb. 9, 1748.
- Johan, b. on Sept. 15, 1747, and bapt. at CLY on Oct. 21, 1747. He m. Maria Magdalena Rauhauser at STR on Dec. 27, 1768 (see entry in Dover section).
- Michael, b. about 1749.
- Anna Magdalena, b. about 1751.
- Christian, b. on May 26, 1754, and bapt. at CLY on June 1, 1754.

Schwab - Hans Georg immigrated to America from Sinsheim, Baden, on Sept. 21, 1727. He had land in West Manchester Township surveyed to him on Oct. 8, 1746. He was one of the organizers of Christ's Lutheran Church of York. He was a Justice of the Peace on Aug. 29, 1746 and Apr. 22, 1749. He d. in 1757. He m. Anna Eva, and had the following children:
- Hans Georg m. Anna Maria. He was taxed in Paradise Township in 1762. His will was written in Paradise Township on Mar. 11, 1780, and probated on May 27, 1782. They had the following children:
  - Johan Jacob, bapt. by RJL on Nov. 18, 1745, and spon. by Jacob Billbeyer.

MANCHESTER TOWNSHIP 261

- Dau.
- Anna Barbara, m. Johan Michael Ranck of Paradise Township. They had the following children:
  - Georg Michael, b. on Nov. 27, 1729, bapt. at Muddy Creek Lutheran Church in Lancaster Co. on ____ 24, 1730, and spon. by Johan Georg Schwab, Sr.
- Eva Elisabeth, m. Peter Yaeger of Paradise Township.
- Anna Eva, b. about 1718, and m. Paul, son of Carle Burckhardt (see entry), at Earl Town in Lancaster Co. on Oct. 16, 1739 (JCS).
- Anna Maria, m. Peter Huber. They had the following children:
  - Elisabeth, bapt. at Muddy Creek Reformed Congregation in Lancaster on Apr. 13, 1746, and spon. by Daniel Kellivin and Elisabeth Scher.

Schwob - Yost was the son of a Burger and Burgomaster of Leiman and Anna Katharina. He was b. in Sinsheim, Baden on Feb. 22, 1678, after the death of his father. He immigrated to America in 1720, settled in Lancaster Co., Upper Leacock Township, PA, and d. there in 1735. He had the following children (see *History of the Swope Family* by Gilbert E. Swope (1896)):
- Maria, b. in 1698.
- Anna Christina, b. in 1701.
- Johannes, b. at Leiman on May 28, 1704, bapt. on May 28, 1704, m. Anna Dorothea, dau. of John Line, in 1725 and Catharina Elisabetha Graff on May 25, 1742. Johannes d. in Upper Leacock Township on Dec. 18, 1780 (bur. in Old Heller's (Salem) cemetery). Anna Dorothea d. in 1740. Anna Dorothea d. in 1740. Catharina Elisabetha Nov. 2, 1725, and d. on Aug. 14, 1776. Johannes had the following children:
  - Johannes, b. on Sept. 27, 1726, and resided in Lancaster Co., PA.
  - Georg Michael, b. on Dec. 10, 1727, and d. in Lancaster Co. in 1758.
  - Elisabeth, b. on July 31, 1729, and d. young.
  - Anna Barbara, b. on Mar. 12, 1731, m. Philip Glonninger, and d. in Lebanon Co., Lebanon Township, PA, on Sept. 23, 1810. He was b. in 1719, and d. on Dec. 11, 1796.
  - Anna Maria, b. on Jan. 3, 1733.
  - Anna Catharina, b. on Mar. 15, 1734, m. Ludwig Schott, and resided in Lebanon, PA.
  - Johan Cunraudt, b. in Lancaster Co., Upper Leacock Township, PA, on May 22, 1736, bapt. at Trinity Lutheran Church in New Holland, Lancaster Co., on May 29, 1736, and spon. by Cunraudt and Anna Maria Templemann. He was taxed in Warrington Township in 1762. He was a potter, and d. in York Co., Hanover, PA, on Aug. 3, 1799. His will was written on July 29, 1799, and

probated on Sept. 5, 1799. He m. Maria Clara, dau. of Johan Jacob Hoke (see entry). She d. on Apr. 18, 1812, and is bur. with her husband in Emanuel Reformed cemetery. They had the following children:
- Johann Jacob, bapt. at the Lower Bermudian Church (Adams Co.) on Feb. 15, 1759, and spon. by Johann Jacob and Anna Margaretha Hoog.
- Anna Barbara, b. on Mar. 22, 1761, bapt. at the Lower Bermudian Church on Mar. 23, 1761, and spon. by Andreas and Barbara Hoog.
- Johann, b. on Oct. 1, 1763, bapt. at the Lower Bermudian Church on Oct. 10, 1763, and spon. by Johannes and Catharina Elisabetha (Graff) Schwob. He m. Catharine Karl, and d. on July 1/10, 1844. She was b. in Feb. 1770, and d. on Dec. 8, 1860.
- Henrich, b. on Sept. 26, 1767, m. Elisabeth Herr in 1792, and d. on Feb. 13, 1842. She was b. on Sept. 26, 1774, and d. on June 13, 1843. They moved to Carroll Co., Taneytown, MD, in 1793, and are bur. in the Lutheran Churchyard at Taneytown. He operated a general store.
- Georg, b. on Oct. 15, 1774, and never m.
- Adam, b. on Aug. 15, 1778, and m. Lydia, dau. of Henrich and Maria Clara (Hoke) Spangler. She was b. on Aug. 15, 1785, and d. on Dec. 20, 1841. He was a tanner at Gettysburg in 1806, and d. on Aug. 22, 1855.
- Margaretha, b. on Mar. 27, 1738, m. Georg Diehl, and resided in Lancaster Co.
- Anna Dorothea, b. on Jan. 4, 1740.
- Maria Juliana, b. on Mar. 17, 1743.
- Johan Jacob, b. on June 9, 1744, m. Maria Sabina, dau. of Mathias Schmeisser (see entry), on Dec. 16, 1750, and d. on June 10, 1811. She was b. on Dec. 16, 1750, d. on June 27, 1820. He served in the Revolution in Captain Roland's Company of Associators in July 1775. They are bur. in Old Heller's cemetery.
- Christina, b. on Nov. 10, 1745.
- Johan Heinrich, b. on Mar. 10, 1747, m. Barbara Wilder, and d. in Upper Leacock Township on Sept. 11, 1808. She was b. on Apr. 27, 1756, and d. on Jan. 13, 1826. He is bur. in Old Heller's cemetery.
- Maria Sabina, b. on Dec. 26, 1748, m. Johannes, son of Johan Jacob Hoke (see entry), and d. in Lincoln Co., North Carolina, on Aug. 9, 1826.
- Susanna, b. on May 22, 1750, and d. on Aug. 13, 1776 (bur. in Old Heller's (salem) cemetery).

- Johan Daniel, b. on Nov. 4, 1751, m. Elisabeth Graybill in 1781, and d. in Upper Leacock Township on Dec. 17, 1821. She was b. on Feb. 23, 1765.
- Anna Eliza, b. on Nov. 12, 1753, and d. on Feb. 12, 1773.
- Johan Adam, b. on May 2, 1756, m. Sarah Graybill, and d. on Feb. 7, 1821. She d. on Sept. 2, 1805.
- Johan Ulrich, b. in 1707.
- Anna Elisabeth, b. in 1713.

Seigrist - Hans Urich wrote his will in Manchester Township on Aug. 26, 1774, and it was probated on May 6, 1776. He had the following children:
- Barbara, m. Michael Teitcher.

Sesrang - Bartholomeus received a warrant for 200 acres in West Manchester and Manchester Township on Jan. 8, 1742.

Shedley - Jacob was taxed in 1762.

Spangler - Hans Georg immigrated to America on the ship *St. Andrew* on Sept. 14, 1751. He settled in Manchester Township, and his will was written there on Jan. 26, 1754, and probated on Mar. 16, 1754. He m. Rosina. Her probate inventory was filed in Manchester Township in 1767. They had the following children:
- David, resided in Germany.
- Elisabeth, resided in Germany.
- Georg Michael, b. on Mar. 20, 1732, and m. Maria Elisabeth about 1758, Anna Elisabeth, dau. of Jacob Probst about 1770, and Christina, dau. of Philip Voglesong of Warrington Township about 1791. He was an Ensign in the 4th Company (portion that became part of the New Jersey Flying Camp in 1776), and the 7th Company 3rd Battalion. He was a cordwainer, and in 1788, he was an inn keeper. He d. in Paradise Township on Oct. 2, 1810 (bur. at Prospect Hill in West Manchester Township). Georg Michael had the following children (see *Spangler History* by Edward W. Spangler):
  - Georg Frederick, b. on May 25, 1759, and bapt. at CLY on Aug. 5, 1759. He d. on Oct. 21, 1831, and is bur. in Prospect Hill cemetery in West Manchester Township. He served as a Private in Captain Like Irvine's Company during the Revolution.
  - Elisabeth, b. about 1769, and m. ____ Kesselring.
  - Georg Jacob, b. on Nov. 25, 1771, and bapt. at CLY on Dec. 8, 1771.
  - Rosina Catharina, b. on Dec. 11, 1773, and bapt. at CLY on Dec. 19, 1773.

- Johan Jacob, b. on Mar. 18, 1777, and bapt. at CLY on Mar. 30, 1777. He d. in Cumberland Co., Carlisle, PA, in 1852.
- Georg Philip, b. on Aug. 5, 1779, bapt. at CLY on Aug. 15, 1779, and resided in Abbottstown, PA. He was a hatter. He m. Christina Leab and Catherine Myers.
- Johannes, bapt. at CLY on Oct. 11, 1783, and resided in Abbottstown, PA.
- Johan Michael, b. on Apr. 12, 1787, and bapt. at CLY on May 27, 1787. He resided in East Berlin, PA.
- Susanna, b. on Jan. 28, 1789, bapt. by RGO, and spon. by Peter and Catharina Schultz.
- Carl, b. on Jan. 28, 1792, bapt. at CLY on Mar. 25, 1792, and resided in Paradise Township.
- Daniel, b. on Mar. 8, 1794, bapt. at CLY on May 22, 1794, and resided in Montgomery Co., Dayton, OH.

Spenith - John was taxed in 1762.

Sprenckel - unknown had the following children:
- Peter, b. about 1702. He supposedly had a 50 acre land warrant in West Manchester Township. He d. in York Co., PA, in 1759, and had the following sons, who moved to Rowan Co., North Carolina, in 1759:
  - Michael, b. about 1724.
  - George, b. about 1726.
  - Peter, b. about 1728.
- Michael, b. about 1704 (Germany or Switzerland). He m. Anna Margaret, dau. of Rudliffe and Barbara Miller (see entry). Michael appeared on the tax lists of Lancaster Co., Conestoga Township, in 1724 and 1726. On Apr. 6, 1734, Michael was granted a license from Samuel Blunston, Esq., agent of the Honorable Proprietaries of PA, for 500 acres of land west of the Susquehanna River situated in Hellam (now West Manchester Township). Lord Baltimore claimed this region of PA for MD at this time, and the Germans mistakenly allowed Colonel Cresap to survey this land for Lord Baltimore. When they realized their error, they sent a letter of apology to the PA government, a letter to Lord Baltimore, notifying him of the change (on Aug. 11, 1736), and voluntarily placed themselves under the PA government. Lord Baltimore issued warrants for the arrest of all 54 signers of this letter on Oct. 21, 1736 on grounds of "contriving, signing and publishing a seditious paper, and writing against his lordship and this government," but they could not be served until favorable weather in the spring. In May 1737, Lord Baltimore's officers rode up and seized eighteen Germans, including Michael Sprenckel. They were

taken to Annapolis, MD, and thrown into jail with fourteen others, who were engaged in what the MD government considered the "Revolt of the Germans." They were all later released, and allowed to return to their homes. On Oct. 25, 1736, Michael was one of the intended victims of the "Chester County Plot," in which settlers in Chester Co., PA, were offered the land of the York Co. Germans to remove the German settlement by force. The plot was organized by the MD government, but discovered before it could be enacted. On Oct. 28/Nov. 22, 1746, Michael was granted 200 acres on the Codorus Creek in Hellam (now West Manchester) Township, and North Codorus Township, bordering the first grant. This land area now lies west of York, south of route 30, on both sides of the Trinity Road, in the area of Braybill's Station, and old milk stop on the Pennsylvania Central Railroad. A large part of the land was purchased by the U.S. Government in 1920 as part of a flood control project called Indian Rock Dam. Michael d. in York Co., Manchester Township, PA, in June 1748. His will was written on June 6, 1748, the same date that George Mayer and Michael Tanner were appointed guardians of Michael's minor children, and probated on June 10, 1748. Michael and Margaret moved to York Co. between 1724 and 1727. After Michael's death, Margaret m. Henry Eberhart/Everhard (about 1750), and d. about 1770 in Manchester Township. They signed a release to her son George on Mar. 2, 1765. Michael and Margaret were the parents of the following children:
- Peter, b. about 1725. He m. Hannah, dau. of Christian and Anna Margarethe (Schmeisser) Eyster (see entry), and d. in York Co., West Manchester Township in 1789. Hannah was bapt. on Mar. 16, 1735, and d. in 1832. They had the following children in West Manchester Township:
  - Christina, b. in 1767.
  - Peter, b. in 1768.
  - Michael, b. on Jan. 28, 1770.
  - Daniel, b. in Aug. 1772.
  - Georg, b. in Aug. 1774.
  - Anna, b. on June 5, 1776.
  - Magdalena, b. in 1778.
  - Dorothea, b. about 1780.
- Elizabeth, bapt. at Lauck's Mennonite Church on May 7, 1727. She m. John Strickler (probably a son of Conrad), and resided in York Co., Hellam Township. They had the following children:
  - Jacob, b. about 1748, and d. in Fayette Co., PA, in 1832.
- Anna Barbara, b. in 1729. She m. Adam Hoffman (see entry) in York Co., PA, on July 17, 1743, and Ludwig Treiber about 1753 (see entry in Codorus section).

- Esther, bapt. at Lauck's on Aug. 2, 1730, and m. Johan Jacob Keller (see entry).
- Susannah, bapt. at Lauck's on Sept. 1, 1730, and m. Henry, son of Christian and Maria Landis. They resided in York Co., Newberry Township.
- Johan Michael, b. in 1732. He was taxed in 1762, and m. Margaret, dau. of Christian and Anna Margarethe (Schmeisser) Eyster. Margaret was b. in 1737, and d. in 1759. After Margaret's death, Michael m. Maria Elisabeth, dau. of Johan Martin and Anna Dorothea (Friedle) Weigel, about 1759/60. Michael was a tavern keeper in Manchester Township in 1779, and served in the York County Militia during the Revolutionary War. Michael d. on May 25, 1816. They had the following children:
  - Maria Christina, bapt. by Reverend Jacob Lischy on Mar. 15, 1758, and spon. by her uncle and aunt, Abraham and Christina Kieffer.
  - Anna Margareth, bapt. by Reverend Jacob Lischy on Mar. 9, 1760, and spon. by Gerg Meyer and Anna Barbara Dorothea Weiglerin.
  - Maria Elisabeth, bapt. by Reverend Jacob Lischy on Mar. 9, 1760, and spon. by Gerg Meyer and Anna Barbara Dorothea Weiglerin.
  - Johan Jacob, b. on Aug. 7, 1761, and bapt. at Christ's Lutheran on Sept. 6, 1761.
  - Maria Catherine, b. on Oct. 4, 1762, bapt. at Christ's Lutheran on Nov. 28, 1762, and d. on May 17, 1766. She is bur. in Henry Wolf's burial ground.
  - Johan Heinrich, b. on Jan. 7, 1764, and bapt. at Christ's Lutheran on Mar. 4, 1764.
  - Eva, b. on June 30, 1765, bapt. at Wolf's Reformed Church on Sept. 8, 1765, and spon. by Sebastian Weigel and wife.
  - Johan Michael, b. on Oct. 28, 1766 at 4:00 am, and d. on Jan. 23, 1772. He was bapt. at Wolf's on Jan. 25, 1767, and spon. by his uncle and aunt, Georg and Barbara Sprenckel.
  - Anna Barbara, b. on Apr. 18, 1771, and bapt. at Christ's Lutheran on May 5, 1771.
  - Michael, b. on Jan. 22, 1773, and bapt. at Christ's Lutheran on Apr. 25, 1773.
  - Peter, b. on Aug. 25, 1776, and bapt. at Christ's Lutheran on Oct. 20, 1776.
- Anna Margaretha, bapt. at Lauck's on Oct. 2, 1735, and m. Johan Ludwig, son of Casper Kieffer (see entry in Codorus section).
- Christina, bapt. at Lauck's on June 10, 1737, and m. Abraham, son of Casper Kieffer (see entry in Codorus section).

- Katrina, b. about 1739, and m. Johann Adam Trorbach (see entry in Codorus section).
- Georg, bapt. at Lauck's on June 2, 1741. He m. Christina, dau. of Christian and Anna Margarethe (Schmeisser) Eyster about 1761, and Anna Barbara Millican about 1765. Christina was b. in Jan. 1746, and d. on July 6, 1764. George d. on June 27, 1805. George had the following children in York Co., West Manchester Township:
  - Anna Maria, b. about 1767.
  - Johan Georg, bapt. at Wolf's on Jan. 6, 1769, and spon. by Georg Vogel and Susanna Muller. He m. Susanna.
  - Michael, b. about 1771.
  - Elizabeth, b. about 1773.
  - Johannes, b. on Aug. 11, 1776, bapt. at Wolf's on Sept. 29, 1776, and spon. by Johannes and Elisabeth Beyer. He m. Gertrude Gehlhaus on Dec. 9, 1800 at the First Reformed Church of York.
  - Anna Barbara, b. on Mar. 3, 1779, bapt. at Wolf's on Apr. 18, 1779, and spon. by Mary Murphy.
  - Maria Magdalena, b. on Oct. 17, 1781, bapt. at Wolf's on Dec. 26, 1781, and spon. by Johannes Beyer and wife.
  - Petter, bapt. at Wolf's on Mar. 12, 1785, and spon. by Vriderig Remer and wife. He d. before 1805.
  - Vriderig, bapt. at Wolf's on Mar. 12, 1785, and spon. by Vriderig Remer and wife.
  - Anna Catherina, b. on Feb. 12, 1786, bapt. at Wolf's on Apr. 9, 1786, and spon. by Elisabeth Beyer. She d. before 1805.
  - Daniel, b. about 1788.
- Eva, b. about 1743, and m. Michael Miller. He was taxed in Codorus Township in 1762 (see entry).
- Maudelina, b. about 1744, and d. about 1749 of smallpox.
- Heinrich, bapt. at Lauck's on June 14, 1745. He m. Anna Maria. She was b. in 1747, and d. in 1815. He d. in Adams Co., PA, on Oct. 14, 1823. They had the following children in York Co.:
  - Johan Peter, b. in 1764, and m. Margaret Kieffer. He was bapt. by Reverend Jacob Lischy on Aug. 17, 1765, and spon. Ulrich and Anna Maria Huber.
  - Anna Margareth, b. in 1766, bapt. by Reverend Jacob Lischy on July 22, 1766, and spon. by her uncle and aunt, Ludwig and Anna Margreth Kieffer. She m. Philip Kieffer.
  - Susanna, b. in 1770, and m. John Fox.
  - Henry, b. in 1772.
  - Michael, b. in 1775, and m. Mary Muntz.
  - Elizabeth, b. in 1779, and m. Daniel Wunder.
  - Catherine, b. in 1782, and m. Joseph Hayes.

- George, b. in 1784.
- Anna Maria, b. in 1788, and m. Christian Fortney.
- Maria, b. about 1746, and d. about 1749 of smallpox.
- William, b. about 1709. He was taxed in York in 1762. He m. Anna Catherina, and d. in York Co., York, PA, in 1772. His will was written on Jan. 16, 1772, and probated on Apr. 11, 1772. They were the parents of the following children:
  - Margaret, b. about 1731. She m. Tobias Hendrick (probably a son of Tobias), and had the following son:
    - Tobias, b. on June 14, 1759, and bapt. at Christ's Lutheran Church of York on Aug. 5, 1759.
  - Elizabeth, b. about 1733. She m. Johannes Bushong, and bapt. the following children at the First Reformed Church of York (the first two at Christ's Lutheran):
    - John Jacob, b. on Feb. 18, 1754, and bapt. on Mar. 16, 1754.
    - Elizabeth, b. on Jan. 4, 1759, and bapt. on Apr. 8, 1759.
    - Anna Maria, b. on May 22, 1763, bapt. on June 12, 1763, and spon. by Jacob Billmeyer and Salome Beck.
    - Wilhelm, b. on Dec. 16, 1765, bapt. on Dec. 23, 1765, and spon. by Jacob Billmeyer and wife.
    - Peter, b. on July 12, 1768, bapt. on Sept. 4, 1768, and spon. by Peter Duenckel and wife.
  - William, b. about 1735. He m. Catherine, and had the following children at York:
    - William, b. on Aug. 2, 1771, and bapt. at Christ's Lutheran on Aug. 11, 1771.
    - John, b. on Mar. 5, 1773, and bapt. at Christ's Lutheran on Apr. 4, 1773.
    - Elizabeth, b. on Sept. 5, 1774, and bapt. at Christ's Lutheran on Nov. 6, 1774.
    - Anthony, b. on Apr. 11, 1776, and bapt. at Christ's Lutheran on May 19, 1776.
    - Peter, b. on June 31, 1778, and bapt. at Christ's Lutheran on Sept. 6, 1778.
  - Catherine, b. about 1737. She m. Johan Georg, son of Johan Georg and Barbara Lang, in York Co., PA, on Jan. 8, 1758. They had the following children (recorded at CLY):
    - Anna Maria, b. on Mar. 22, 1760 (1 p.m.), and bapt. on Apr. 27, 1760.
    - Catharina, b. on Oct. 22, 1761 (9 p.m.), bapt. on Jan. 17, 1761, and spon. by Georg and Barbara Lang.
    - Elisabeth, bapt. on Dec. 11, 1763.
    - Georg Friedrich, b. on Oct. 24, 1770, and bapt. on Nov. 4, 1770.
    - Christina, b. on Jan. 22, 1773, and bapt. on Feb. 14, 1773.
    - Johannes, b. on May 10, 1775, and bapt. on May 28, 1775.

- Johann Jacob, b. on Feb. 2, 1779, and bapt. on Mar. 21, 1779.
- Magdalena, b. on Mar. 14, 1782, and bapt. on May 12, 1782.
- Charlotte, b. about 1739. She m. Nicholas, son of Johan and Sophia Zinn (see entry in Dover section).
- Henry, b. about 1741. He m. Catherine, and had the following children at York:
  - Catharine, b. on Jan. 11, 1770, and bapt. at Christ's Lutheran on May 6, 1770.
  - Henry, b. on Sept. 2, 1771, and bapt. at Christ's Lutheran on Nov. 7, 1771.
- Peter, b. about 1743. He m. Elizabeth, and had the following children in York:
  - Anna Maria, b. on Mar. 12, 1775, and bapt. at Christ's Lutheran on Apr. 16, 1775.
  - Peter, b. on Sept. 23, 1776, and bapt. at Christ's Lutheran on May 18, 1777.
  - Jacob, b. on May 22, 1800, and bapt. at Christ's Lutheran on July 6, 1800.
- Anna, b. about 1745.
- Eva, b. about 1747. She m. Abraham Immeler before 1772, and had the following children in York:
  - John William, b. on May 29, 1775, and bapt. at Christ's Lutheran on June 25, 1775.
- Anna Maria, b. on Apr. 22, 1749, and bapt. at Christ's Lutheran Church of York on Aug. 6, 1749. She m. Martin Schroder before 1772, and had the following children in York:
  - John Frederick, b. on Dec. 25, 1778, and bapt. at Christ's Lutheran on Jan. 31, 1779.
  - Catharine, b. on Nov. 2, 1781, and bapt. at Christ's Lutheran on Dec. 9, 1781.
  - Daniel, b. on Feb. 29, 1790, and bapt. at Christ's Lutheran on July 31, 1790.
- Johan Jacob, b. in Feb. 1751, and bapt. at Christ's Lutheran Church of York on May 27, 1751.
- Daniel, b. about 1753. He m. Christine, and had the following children at York:
  - Carl, b. on Apr. 28, 1779, and bapt. at Christ's Lutheran on May 30, 1779.
- Adam Heinrich received a land warrant for 50 acres in West Manheim Township on Mar. 9, 1753 (surveyed as 73 acres on July 13, 1753), and 50 acres in West Manheim Township on May 31, 1762 (he supposedly had a land warrant for 900 acres in West Manchester Township, but I have not found it).
- Georg, supposedly received a 50 acre land warrant in Lancaster Co., PA.

Strickler - Conrad was taxed in 1762 (he is probably a son of Conrad). He was taxed in Hellam Township in 1779. His will was written in Hellam Township on Sept. 18, 1790, and probated on Dec. 31, 1793. He m. Christina, dau. of Christian Bixler of Manchester Township (see entry). Her will was written in Hellam Township on Aug. 16, 1790, and probated on Nov. 9, 1798 (mentions bros. John and Joseph Bixler). They had the following children:
- Christian was exec. to Conrad's will, but was not named as a son.
- John was exec. to Christina's will, but was not named as a son.
- Barbara.

Uhler - Erasmus m. Sabina Friedlin, and had the following children (recorded at Ittlingen Lutheran Church (see BNK)):
- Johan Dieterich Uhler was bapt. on Nov. 30, 1711. He immigrated to America on the ship *Charming Nancy* in 1737. He m. Elisabetha Gaeiss (see entry) in Lancaster Co., Leacock Township, PA, (by Reverend Stoever) on July 10, 1739, and Anna Margaret about 1758. Dieterich's will was written in Manchester Township on Dec. 25, 1764, probated on Jan. 15, 1765, and executed by M. Eichelberger and Georg Myer. On Dec. 9, 1769, Jacob Ottinger, Adam Uhler, and Dieterich Ulher purchased 168 acres and 112.107 acres (+an additional 41.54 acres) and 217.80 acres respectively in West Manchester Township. The land was surveyed on Sept. 9, 1785, and patented on Mar. 6, 1804. On Feb. 7, 1812, the 217.80 acres went to the heirs of Dieterich Uhler, deceased. Dieterich had the following children (Dieterich and Elisabeth Ulher were sponsors at the baptism of Margareth, dau. of Johan Adam and Anna Barbara Rubert by Jacob Lischy in 1745):
  - Rosina, b. on Dec. 28, 1740, bapt. at Christ's Lutheran on Apr. 4, 1741, and spon. by Johan Adam and Anna Barbara Rupert. As Rosina Uhlerin/Ulrichin, was a sponsor with Bernhard Ziegler for the baptism of Bernhard Rudy by Rev. Jacob Lischy in 1759/61. She m. Bernard Ziegler (see entry).
  - Johan Adam, b. on Feb. 14, 1743, and bapt. at Christ's Lutheran on Feb. 23, 1743. He m. Elisabeth, dau. of Michael Geisselman (see entry in Shrewsbury section), at Strayer's on June 24, 1766. Adam's probate inventory was dated 1770. They had the following children (Elisabeth m. Frederick Rumel at Strayer's on Apr. 4, 1771, after Adam's death) (Adam and Elisabeth were sponsors to the baptism of Anna Barbara Meyer at Wolf's in June 1769):
    - Anna Barbara, b. on May 30, 1767, bapt. at Friedensaal on June 28, 1767, and spon. by Georg Geisselman and Maria Salome Korbmann.

- Johan Dieterich, b. on June 16, 1768, and bapt. at Christ's Lutheran on July 17, 1768.
- Maria Barbara, b. on Sept. 6, 1744, and bapt. at Christ's Lutheran on May 2, 1747.
- Andrew, b. on Apr. 9, 1747, and bapt. at Christ's Lutheran on May 2, 1747.
- Anna Eva, b. on July 6, 1749, and bapt. at Christ's Lutheran on Aug. 6, 1749. As Anna Eva Ulrichin, was a sponsor with Jacob Ziegler to the baptism of Johan Jacob Meyer at Wolf's in 1765. Mentioned as Eve in her father's will. She m. Georg Philip Ziegler (see entry).
- Erasmus, b. on Sept. 21, 1751, and bapt. at Christ's Lutheran on Nov. 3, 1751.
- Johan Valentine, b. on Mar. 3, 1754, and bapt. at Christ's Lutheran on Mar. 13, 1754.
- Dieterich, bapt. by Reverend Jacob Lischy on Apr. 3, 1757, and spon. by Paul and Anna Eva Burcket.
- Elisabeth, b. on June 6, 1759, and bapt. at Christ's Lutheran on July 15, 1759.
- Maria Sabina, b. on Jan. 21, 1761 at 6:00 p.m., and bapt. at Christ's Lutheran on Mar. 20, 1761.
- Andrew, b. on Sept. 21, 1762, and bapt. at Christ's Lutheran on Nov. 14, 1762.
- Catharina, b. on Sept. 18, 1764, and bapt. at Christ's Lutheran on Nov. 18, 1764.
- Johan Valentine, bapt. on May 4, 1715, and immigrated to America on the ship *Charming Nancy* in 1737. He was naturalized on Sept. 24, 1762 (residence was Northampton Co., Forks Township, PA).

<u>Wagner</u> - Jacob was taxed in 1762. He had 230 acres in Manchester and West Manchester Township surveyed on Oct. 10, 1747. His probate inventory was filed in Manchester Township in 1791. He m. Maria Barbara Bohn, and had the following children:
- Maria Catharina, bapt. by RJL on May 12, 1751, and spon. by Peter and Rebecca Schneider.
- Philliph, bapt. by RJL on Aug. 7, 1754, and spon. by Philliph and Barbara Hens.
- Anna Elisabeth, bapt. by RJL on Apr. 7, 1756, and spon. by Johan Nicholas and Anna Elisabeth Bohn.
- Maria, b. on Dec. 4, 1757, and bapt. at CLY on Sept. 28, 1758. She d. on Oct. 2, 1758, and was bur. at Henry Wolf's place on Oct. 4, 1758. Her godmother was Maria Catharina, widow of Georg Debold.
- Catharina, b. on July 16, 1759, bapt. at TLY on Nov. 2, 1762, and spon. by Philip Heintz and wife.

- Maria Barbara, b. on Feb. 16, 1762, bapt. at TLY on Nov. 2, 1762, and spon. by Philip Heintz and wife.

Weigel - Johan Martin was b. to Valentine Weigel of Saalbach, Brandenburg, Germany, on Nov. 11, 1703. In 1724, he trained as a carpenter at Wornitz, near Rothenburg, Germany, and immigrated to America in 1732, on the ship *Samuel*. He received a warrant for 200 acres in West Manchester and Dover Township on Oct. 30, 1736 (Blunston License). His will was written on Jan. 29, 1759, and probated on Feb. 3, 1759. He d. on Jan. 31, 1759, and was bur. at York on Feb. 2, 1759 (CLY). He m. Anna Dorothea, dau. of Nicholas Friedel (former master miller), at Hoffenheim, Germany, on July 11, 1729. They had the following children (see BNP):
- Johann Sebastian, bapt. at Helmstadt, Germany, on Nov. 12, 1730, and spon. by Johan Sebastian Hauck. He was taxed in 1762, and naturalized in Oct. 1765. His will was written in West Manchester Township on Dec. 31, 1804, and probated on Sept. 18, 1807. He m. Susanna Catharina, dau. of Johannes Leib (see entry), and had the following children:
  - Anna Margaretha, b. on Dec. 9, 1759, and bapt. at CLY on Apr. 27, 1760.
  - Maria Sabina, b. on June 16, 1761, and bapt. at CLY on Aug. 16, 1761.
  - Maria Elisabeth, b. on June 28, 1765, bapt. at WOL, on Sept. 8, 1765, and spon. by Michael and Elisabeth Sprenckel.
  - Catharina, b. on June 15, 1767, bapt. at CLY on Sept. 20, 1767, and spon. by Dorothea Weigel.
  - Susanna, b. on Mar. 25, 1770, bapt. at STR on Oct. 13, 1770, and spon. by Martin and Christina Weigel.
  - Anna, b. about 1772.
  - Magdalena, b. on Jan. 15, 1774, and bapt. at CLY on Mar. 20, 1774. She was not mentioned in the will.
  - Juliana, b. about 1772.
  - Peter, b. on Sept. 21, 1776, and bapt. at CLY on Nov. 3, 1776.
  - Henry, b. on May 10, 1780, and bapt. at CLY on July 30, 1780.
- Maria Juliana, b. on Oct. 22, 1733, and bapt. at CLY on Nov. 11, 1733.
- Johan Martin, b. on Sept. 11, 1735, and bapt. at CLY on Oct. 10, 1735. He was taxed in 1762. He m. Anna Catharina about 1761, Christina about 1766, and Margaretha, dau. of Peter Ob (see entry in Dover section), at TLY on May 10, 1772. He served as a Private in Captain Emannuel Herman's Company during the Revolution. He d. on Nov. 9, 1822, and is bur. in Neiman's cemetery. He had the following children:

MANCHESTER TOWNSHIP 273

- Maria Catharina, b. on May 9, 1762, and bapt. at CLY on June 6, 1762.
- Johan Martin, b. on Jan. 22, 1765, bapt. at STR on July 21, 1765, and spon. by Sebastian and Catharina Weigel.
- Elisabeth, b. on Mar. 5, 1770, bapt. at STR on Oct. 13, 1770, and spon. by Sebastian and Catharina Weigel.
- Christina, b. on Jan. 19, 1772, bapt. at STR on Feb. 9, 1772, and spon. by Sebastian and Catharina Weigel.
- Johan Jacob, b. on July 25, 1774, and bapt. at STR on Aug. 28, 1774, and spon. by Peter and Magdalena Weigel.
- Johan Peter, b. on July 17, 1780, bapt. at STR on Sept. 17, 1780, and spon. by Jacob and Margaretha Weigel.
- Maria Elisabetha, b. on Jan. 31, 1738, and bapt. at CLY on Apr. 22, 1738. She m. Michael, son of Michael Sprenckel (see entry), in 1759/60.
- Johan Jacob, b. about 1741. He was taxed in 1762. He m. Margaretha, dau. of Adam Rupert (see entry), at STR on Feb. 15, 1763, and had the following children:
  - Henry, b. on Nov. 9, 1763, and bapt. at CLY on Apr. 29, 1764.
  - Margaretha, b. on July 13, 1765, bapt. at STR on Aug. 18, 1765, and spon. by Dorothea and Martin Weigel.
  - Johan Jacob, b. on Feb. 7, 1767, bapt. at STR on Apr. 5, 1767, and spon. by Jacob and Maria Barbara Scheddron.
  - Johan Martin, b. on Mar. 13, 1769, bapt. at STR on Mar. 24, 1769, and spon. by Johan Martin and Christina Weigel.
  - Petrus, b. on Aug. 10, 1771, bapt. at STR on Sept. 22, 1771, and spon. by Peter and Magdalena Weigel.
  - Johannes, b. on Aug. 9, 1773, bapt. at STR on Sept. 10, 1773, and spon. by Carl and Eva Margaretha Albert.
  - Johan Georg, b. on Jan. 20, 1776, bapt. at STR on Jan. 28, 1776, and spon. by Johan Georg and Barbara Stauch.
  - Maria Elisabeth, b. on Aug. 23, 1778, bapt. at STR on Sept. 20, 1778, and spon. by Michael and Maria Elisabeth Sprenckel.
  - Michael, b. on May 5, 1783, bapt. at STR on June 29, 1783, and spon. by Michael and Catharina Pens.
- Johan Leonard, b. on Apr. 2, 1743, and bapt. at CLY on Apr. 28, 1743. He m. Rosina, dau. of Jacob and Helena (Holtzender) Biehlmajer, of York. She was b. on Mar. 21, 1749, bapt. at CLY on Apr. 9, 1749, and spon. by Andreas and Rosina (Biehlmajer) Schenck. They had the following children:
  - Susanna, b. on Sept. 16, 1779, bapt. at STR on Oct. 31, 1779, and spon. by Sebastian and Catharina Weigel.
  - John, b. on Jan. 19, 1789, and bapt. at CLY on June 9, 1789.
- Henrich, b. on Oct. 18, 1747, and bapt. at CLY on May 22, 1748.

- Wendel, b. about 1748, and m. Margaretha Elisabetha, and had the following children:
  - Johan Wendel, b. on Oct. 15, 1769, and bapt. at CLY on Oct. 29, 1769.
  - Maria Catharina, b. on Aug. 26, 1774, bapt. at STR on Sept. 24, 1774, and spon. by Anna Maria Messerle
- Margaretha, b. on Apr. 8, 1750, and bapt. at CLY on May 13, 1750.
- Peter, b. about 1752, and m. Magdalena, dau. of Simon Wittmeyer (see entry). They had the following children:
  - Maria Eva, b. on Oct. 30, 1772, and bapt. at CLY on Nov. 8, 1772.
  - Johan Peter, b. on Feb. 13, 1775, and bapt. at CLY on Mar. 5, 1775.
  - John, b. on Apr. 26, 1777, and bapt. at CLY on June 22, 1777.
  - Jacob, b. on Jan. 26, 1780, and bapt. at CLY on Mar. 26, 1780.

Welsch - Hans Jacob was b. to Michael Welsch (Burgermeister) of Baumholder, about 1685. He m. Anna Martha, dau. of Jacob Blum, at Baumholder, Germany, on Sept. 23, 1706. They had the following children (see BWP):
- Maria Elisabeth, bapt. on Jan. 24, 1708.
- Catharina Magdalena, bapt. on Apr. 19, 1710.
- Hans Wilhelm, bapt. on Aug. 22, 1712, and immigrated to America on the ship *Samuel* in 1737. He had the following children:
  - Johan Jacob, b. on Dec. 16, 1738, bapt. at CLY on Feb. 15, 1739, and spon. by Peter Wolf and Veronica Bassler.
  - Johan Peter, b. in Oct. 1740, bapt. at CLY on Apr. 5, 1741, and spon. by Jacob Welsch and wife.
- Johan Jacob, bapt. on Feb. 27, 1716, and immigrated to America on the ship *Samuel* in 1737. He received a warrant for 250 acres in West Manchester Township on Feb. 24, 1752. He was naturalized in Sept. 1762. He d. on May 30, 1773. His will was written in York Town on May 8, 1773, and probated on Aug. 25, 1773. He m. Anna Elisabeth, dau. of Peter Wolff (see entry) on Feb. 15, 1739 (JCS). She d. on Jan. 4, 1796. Her probate inventory was filed in York in 1796. They had the following children:
  - Johan Jacob, b. on May 20, 1741, bapt. at CLY on June 26, 1741, and spon. by Johan Jacob Ottinger and Hanna Jost.
  - Johan Michael, b. on Aug. 29, 1742, bapt. at CLY on Feb. 9, 1743, and spon. by Michael Welsch. He m. Maria Elisabeth Emig at TLY on Mar. 24, 1768.
  - Peter, b. on Apr. 24, 1744, and d. at Hanover, PA, on May 2, 1828. He m. Catharina, dau. of Adam and Catharina (Kuntz) Hubbert. She was b. in Dec. 1748, and d. on Mar. 15, 1812.
  - Johannes, b. about 1745, and m. Catharina about 1765.

- Johan Heinrich, b. on Dec. 22, 1748, bapt. by RJL on Feb. 5, 1749, and spon. by Johan Heinrich and Catharina Wolff, and Anna Wolffin. He m. Christina, dau. of Adam and Catharina (Kuntz) Hubbert, and d. at Hanover, PA, on Aug. 21, 1827. She was b. on Jan. 23, 1753, and d. on June 1, 1828.
- Johan Philip, bapt. by RJL on May 27, 1751, and spon. by Philliph Weber and Catharina Wolffin.
- Anna Catharina, bapt. by RJL on July 22, 1753, and spon. by Philliph and Catharina Weber.
- Vronica, bapt. by RJL on May 11, 1755, and spon. by Frederick and Veronica Bassler.
- Johan Adam, bapt. by RJL on Apr. 20, 1760, and spon. by Peter and Catharina Elisabetha Wolff.
- Johan Friedrich, b. on June 12, 1762, bapt. at TLY on June 17, 1762, and spon. by Frederick and Veronica Bassler.
- Georg, b. on Apr. 23, 1766, bapt. at TLY on May 11, 1766, and spon. by Peter Wolf and wife.
- Maria Barbara, bapt. on Aug. 21, 1718.
- Johan Michael, bapt. on Mar. 23, 1721. He was taxed in 1762. His will was written in York Borough on Sept. 14, 1789, and probated on Nov. 16, 1789. He m. Maria Margaretha Barbara. They had the following children:
  - Catharina Elisabeth, bapt. at TLY on Mar. 17, 1745, and spon. by Johannes and Catharina Wolf, and Jacob and Elisabeth Welsch. She m. David Cremer.
  - Johannes, b. about 1747, and m. Catharina Wolff at TLY on Aug. 1, 1773.
  - Jacob, b. about 1749.
  - Johan Michael, bapt. by RJL on Feb. 8, 1751, and spon. by Jacob Muller and Catharina Wolffin.
  - Henrich, b. on July 13, 1753, and bapt. at CLY on Aug. 13, 1753.
  - Elisabeth, bapt. by RJL on Mar. 26, 1758, and spon. by Johannes Welsch and Elisabeth Wolffin.
  - Maria Barbara, bapt. by RJL on Dec. 26, 1760, and spon. by Philip and Anna Maria Muller.
  - Johann Adam, b. on June 23, 1766, bapt. at TLY on July 6, 1766, and spon. by Johannes Welsch and wife. He was not mentioned in the will.
- Johan Anthoni, b. on Dec. 29, 1723.
- Johan Adam, bapt. on Oct. 24, 1725.
- Johan Abraham, bapt. on Nov. 27, 1729.

Weyer - Andrew was taxed in 1762. His will was written in West Manchester Township on Sept. 2, 1804, and probated on Nov. 6, 1804. He m. Sophia Elisabeth, and had the following children:

- Anton, b. on Sept. 20, 1761, and bapt. at CLY on Sept. 27, 1761.
- Michael, b. on Dec. 8, 1763, and bapt. at CLY on Dec. 11, 1763.
- John.
- Bernard.
- Elisabeth.
- Susanna.
- Anna Maria, b. on Aug. 31, 1776, bapt. at TLY on Oct. 4, 1776, and spon. by Catharina Pott.
- Margaretha.
- Jacob.
- Daniel.
- Lydia.

<u>Wild</u> - Nicholas was taxed in 1762. His will was written in Manchester Township on Sept. 1, 1784, and probated on Mar. 14, 1786. He m. Catharina, and had the following children:
- Maria Catharina, b. on Sept. 27, 1742, and bapt. at CLY on Oct. 14, 1743. She was not mentioned in the will.
- Valentin, b. on Sept. 26, 1743, and bapt. at CLY on Oct. 9, 1743. He m. Elisabeth, dau. of Heinrich Walther (see entry in Shrewsbury section), at STR on Apr. 7, 1768.
- Maria Elisabeth, bapt. by RJL on May 23, 1745, and spon. by Georg and Maria Elisabeth Kuntz.
- Johann, b. about 1746.
- Johan Adam, bapt. by RJL on Oct. 4, 1747, and spon. by Johannes and Barbara Schetlj.
- Barbara, bapt. by RJL on July 20, 1748, and spon. by Philip and Barbara Hens. She was not mentioned in the will.
- Samuel, bapt. by RJL on Mar. 25, 1750, and spon. by Samuel and Catharina Hog. He m. Margaret, dau. of Jeremias Beer (see entry in Dover section).
- Maria Magdalena, bapt. by RJL on Sept. 17, 1752, and spon. by Jacob and Maria Magdalena Fackler. She m. Johann Michael, son of Adam Seifert (see entry in Dover section). She was not listed in the will.
- Maria Margareth, bapt. by RJL on Sept. 15, 1754, and spon. by Ulrich and Maria Margareth Vollenweiller. She was not listed in the will.
- Johan Georg, bapt. by RJL on June 27, 1756, and spon. by Georg and Barbara Meyer.
- Anna Maria, b. about 1758, and m. Tobias, son of Carl Seib (see entry in Dover section).
- Anna or Maria, b. about 1760.

MANCHESTER TOWNSHIP

Wintermeier - Philip was taxed in 1762. His will was written in Manchester Township on Oct. 15, 1774, and probated on Jan. 6, 1775. He m. Anna Gertrude. They had the following children:
- Dorothea, b. about 1734, m. Peter Keiffer/Kauffer about 1755. His will was written in York Town on May 1, 1771, and probated on May 16, 1771. Her will was written in York Town on Dec. 18, 1811, and probated on Jan. 2, 1812.
- Julianna, b. about 1736, and was the sponsor to the baptism of Maria Catharina Kieffer/Kauffer in 1756 (RJL). She m. Philip W., son of Conrad Gentzler (see entry).
- Philip, b. about 1738. He was taxed in 1762. He m. Phillipina Schodle at STR on May 20, 1766. His probate inventory was filed in Manchester Township in 1807.
- Anthony, b. about 1740, and m. Anna Maria before 1762. His will was written in Dover Township on Nov. 9, 1796, and probated on May 5, 1798.

Wittmeyer - Simon immigrated to America on Sept. 25, 1751, and was taxed in Manchester Township in 1762. He received a warrant for 164 acres in West Manchester Township on Apr. 3, 1767, that was surveyed on May 13, 1767. His will was written in Manchester Township on Sept. 10, 1801, and probated on Feb. 5, 1806. He m. Maria, dau. of Conrad and Magdalena Klingemeyer, and had the following children:
- Magdalena, b. about 1752, and m. Peter, son of Martin Weigel (see entry).
- Anna Maria, b. on Dec. 12, 1755, and m. Andreas, son of Jacob Heg (see entry in Dover section).
- Simon, b. on Feb. 6, 1761, and bapt. at CLY on Apr. 19, 1761. He m. Elisabeth.

Wolff - Anthony was taxed in 1762. He and his wife were sponsors to the baptism of Georg Steeg in 1751 (RJL). He had the following children:
- Susanna Margaretha, b. about 1736, and m. John, son of Jacob and Barbara Gerber, in 1756, and d. in childbirth in 1757. He was b. in Mensingen, Wurtemburg, on June 10, 1726, immigrated to America with his parents in 1733, and d. on Nov. 4, 1759. They are bur. at the Lutheran Churchyard at York (CLY).

Wolff - Johann Jacob, was b. to Johann Peter and Susanna at Ratzweiler, Germany, and bapt. at Ulmet on May 3, 1694. He was from Ronneberg, when he m. Anna Barbara, dau. of Hans Jacob Orth of Weiler ander Noh, at Baumholder, Germany, on May 12, 1716. They immigrated to America on the ship *Samuel* in 1737, and were residing

in York Co. in 1750. His probate inventory was filed in 1750 (?). They had the following children, b. in Ronnenberg, and bapt. at Baumholder (see BWP):
- Maria Magdalena, b. on Feb. 3, 1717.
- Maria Barbara, b. on Oct. 29, 1718.
- Johan Peter, bapt. on Nov. 1, 1720. He had 429.105 acres in Manchester and West Manchester Township surveyed in 1767 (part of Killian Schmidt's warrant). His probate inventory was filed in York Town in 1771. He m. Maria Agnes, dau. of Killian and Catharina Schmidt (see entry), and had the following children:
  - Catharina, bapt. by RJL on Jan. 12, 1746, and spon. by Johannes and Catharina Wolff.
  - Anna Margaretha, b. on Dec. 20, 1746, and bapt. at CLY on Feb. 24, 1747. She m. Georg Marcus Hartman about 1767, and had the following children:
    - Johan Peter, b. on Apr. 2, 1768, bapt. at CLY on Apr. 24, 1768, and spon. by his grandparents, Peter Wolff and wife.
  - Johan Peter, bapt. by RJL on Mar. 5, 1749, and spon. by Killian and Catharina Schmidt.
  - Johann Jacob, bapt. by RJL on Apr. 29, 1750, and spon. by Johan Jacob and Anna Barbara Wolff.
  - Charlotta, b. on Jan. 29, 1752, bapt. by RJL on Mar. 22, 1752, and spon. by Johannes and Charlotte Wolff. She m. Henry Holl at TLY on Jan. 17, 1775, and d. in Adams Co., Abbottstown, PA, on Sept. 29, 1804.
  - Johan Georg, bapt. by RJL on Dec. 1, 1754, and spon. by Georg and Barbara Hog.
  - Maria Elisabeth, bapt. by RJL on Dec. 17, 1758, and spon. by Georg and Maria Elisabeth Fink. She m. Adam Paulus at TLY on June 2, 1778.
  - Andreas, b. about 1760, and chose Frederick Wolff of Berwick Township as his guardian.
- Johan Ludwig, bapt. on Mar. 5, 1723, and d. young.
- Anna Maria, b. on June 10, 1724.
- Johannes, bapt. on May 18, 1726. He was taxed in 1762. He m. Maria Charlotta, dau. of Peter Mohr before 1750 (see entry). He was a tailor, and d. in 1800. She was b. in 1725, and d. in 1798. They are bur. in Prospect Hill cemetery. They had the following children:
  - Johan Jacob, bapt. by RJL on Jan. 1, 1750, and spon. by Jacob and Anna Barbara Wolff.
  - Maria Catharina, bapt. by RJL on Dec. 1, 1751, and spon. by Conrad and Maria Catharina Amma.
  - Maria Magdalena, bapt. by RJL on May 20, 1753, and spon. by Dieterich and Magdalena Meyer.

- Eva, bapt. by RJL on Apr. 9, 1758, and spon. by Michael Schmeisser and Eva Ammin.
- Johannes, bapt. by RJL on Jan. 1, 1760, and spon. by Martin and Susanna Maria Bauer. He m. Anna Maria before 1782.
- Petrus, b. on Oct. 18, 1762, bapt. at TLY on Oct. 31, 1762, and spon. by Johannes Welsch and Margaretta Wolff.
- Johan Martin, b. on Apr. 5, 1766, bapt. at TLY on Apr. 20, 1766, and spon. by Martin Danner and wife.
- Johann Nickel, bapt. on Nov. 4, 1728. He was taxed in Adams Co., Berwick Township in 1762 and 1772.
- Maria Barbara, bapt. on Dec. 27, 1730.
- Maria Christina, b. on Jan. 12, 1733, and bapt. on Jan. 16, 1733.
- Johan Friederich, b. on Aug. 16, 1735, and bapt. on Aug. 21, 1735. He m. Maria Elisabeth about 1761, and Susanna, widow of Henrich Schuh between 1785 and 1791. He was taxed in Berwick Township in 1762. His will was written in Adams Co., Berwick Township on Mar. 17, 1803, and probated on May 28, 1803. He had the following children:
  - Christina, b. in 1758, m. Henry, son of Jacob Baltzley, and d. in 1848.
  - Frederick, b. in 1761.
  - Anna Catharina, bapt. by RJL on Apr. 12, 1762, and spon. by Heinrich and Catharina Weller. She d. young.
  - Elisabeth m. John Noll, and d. in Adams Co., Abbottstown in 1833.
  - Jacob, b. on Aug. 21, 1769, and d. in 1869.
  - Maria d. between 1803 and 1833.
  - Johan Georg, b. on Oct. 18, 1781, bapt. at Abbottstown Lutheran Church in Adams Co. on Jan. 6, 1782, and spon. by Heinrich and Susanna Schuh.
  - Andreas, b. on June 5, 1783, bapt. at Abbottstown Lutheran Church on July 27, 1783, and spon. by Henry and Charlotte Holl. He m. Mary, dau. of William Mummert.
- Johan Jacob, b. about 1737, and was taxed in Berwick Township in 1762. He was a sponsor to the baptism of Johan Jacob Schmidt in 1757 (RJL). He received a warrant for 266.5 acres in Paradise Township on Dec. 18, 1751, that was surveyed on Dec. 29, 1751. He purchased 100 acres in Berwick Township in Pigeon Hills on Feb. 27, 1754, that was deeded to Frederick Wolff on July 22, 1757/Dec. 13, 1762 (these land transactions may refer to Jacob Sr., and the 1750 probate inventory may refer to a different Jacob Wolff).

Wolff - Georg m. Anna Elisabeth. His will was written in Manchester
Township on Mar. 13, 1781, and probated on July 30, 1781. He had the
following children:
  - John (eldest son, not of age).
  - Elisabeth (eldest dau.).
  - George.
  - Catharine (youngest dau.).

Wolff - Johann Peter, son of Jacob and Catharina (Clauser) Wolff, was
bapt. at Elsenz, Germany, on Mar. 7, 1688, confirmed in 1703, and
immigrated to America on the ship *Dragon* in 1732. He m. Anna Maria
(they were alive in 1748), and had the following children at Elsenz
(except the last) (see BNK):
  - Johan Georg, bapt. on Dec. 6, 1716, and m. Anna Maria, dau. of
    Killian Schmidt (see entry), on May 22, 1738 (JCS), and d. about
    1743. After Georg's death, Anna Maria m. Andreas Neppinger
    about 1744. Georg and Anna Maria had the following children:
    - Johan Philip, b. on Feb. 26, 1739, and bapt. at CLY on Apr. 20,
      1739. He was taxed in 1762. He m. Maria Esther about 1761.
    - Johan Peter, b. on July 7, 1742, and bapt. at CLY on July 31,
      1742.
  - Johannes, bapt. on Sept. 11, 1718. He was taxed in 1762. His will
    was written in Manchester Township on June 1, 1773, and
    probated on June 19, 1773. He m. Anna (she d. before 1773), and
    had the following children:
    - Johan Jacob, b. on Feb. 18, 1739, and bapt. at CLY on Apr. 20,
      1739.
    - Elisabeth, b. on Dec. 9, 1740, bapt. by JCS, on Apr. 15, 1741, and
      spon. by Carl Eisen and wife. She m. Nicholas Schaffer (see entry
      in Codorus section).
    - Maria Catharina, b. on Aug. 17, 1743, and bapt. at CLY on Sept.
      18, 1743. She was unmarried in 1773.
    - Johan Peter, bapt. by RJL in May 1746, and spon. by Johan
      Peter and Anna Wolff.
    - Anna Maria, bapt. by RJL on Apr. 8, 1750, and spon. by Peter
      Wolff and Catharina Wolffin.
    - Barbara, bapt. by RJL on Nov. 17, 1751, and spon. by Philliph
      and Barbara Hens. She m. ____ Thomas.
    - Johannes, bapt. by RJL on Apr. 7, 1754, and spon. by Heinrich
      and Anna Wolff.
    - Margaret, b. about 1755, and m. Georg Shuck about 1776.
    - Heinrich, bapt. by RJL on June 27, 1756, and spon. by Jacob and
      Elisabeth Welsch. He was not mentioned in the will. He is
      probably the child that d. in 1758, and was bur. on his father's
      farm (CLY).

MANCHESTER TOWNSHIP 281

- Johan Georg, b. on Dec. 24, 1758, and bapt. at CLY on Jan. 5, 1759.
- Tobias, bapt. by RJL on May 10, 1761, and spon. by Jacob and Hanna Ottinger.
- Sabina, b. about 1763, and m. Joseph Welschans at TLY on Nov. 6, 1785.
- Martin, bapt. on Feb. 11, 1720.
- Anna Elisabetha, bapt. on May 18, 1721, and m. Jacob Welsch on Feb. 15, 1739 (JCS) (see entry).
- Johan Heinrich, bapt. on Dec. 15, 1723, and received a warrant for 200 acres in West Manchester Township on Dec. 20, 1751, that was surveyed on Nov. 14, 1752, and patented as 222.80 acres on Feb. 13, 1762. He m. Anna Catharina, dau. of Johan Georg Cammer at the First Reformed Church of Lancaster, PA, on Feb. 3, 1745, and had:
  - Anna, bapt. by RJL on Dec. 11, 1748, and spon. by Peter and Anna Wolff, and Catharina Wolffin.
  - Anna Elisabeth, bapt. by RJL on Jan. 27, 1751, and spon. by Jacob and Anna Elisabeth Welsch.
  - Anna Catharina, bapt. by RJL on Dec. 25, 1752, and spon. by Johannes and Anna Wolff.
  - Johan Heinrich, bapt. by RJL on Jan. 12, 1755, and spon. by Friedrich and Veronica Bassler
  - Johannes, bapt. by RJL on Dec. 7, 1760, and spon. by Johannes and Anna Wolff.
  - Johan Jacob, b. on Sept. 30, 1766, and bapt. at TLY on Oct. 5, 1766.
  - Benjamin, b. on Aug. 15, 1769, and bapt. at TLY on Aug. 26, 1769.
- Hans Peter, bapt. on Sept. 1, 1726, and d. before 1730.
- Caspar, bapt. on May 9, 1728.
- Johan Peter, bapt. on Oct. 4, 1730. He was taxed in 1762. His will was written in Manchester Township on Jan. 22, 1793, and probated on Mar. 11, 1796. He served in Captain John Ehrman's Company during the Revolution, and is bur. in WOL cemetery. He m. Catharina Elisabeth, dau. of Henrich Bott (see entry) at CLY on Oct. 20, 1751. She was b. in 1732, and d. in 1807. They had the following children:
  - Johan Adam, bapt. by RJL on June 14, 1752, and spon. by Johan Adam and Juliana Bott. He m. Anna Maria before 1780.
  - Anna Catharina, b. on Oct. 8, 1753, and bapt. at CLY on Oct. 28, 1753 (unmarried in 1793?).
  - M. Dorothea, b. about 1754, and m. Michael Ege before 1775.
  - Margaret, b. about 1758, and m. Christian Eyster (see entry) about 1778.

- Elisabetha, bapt. by RJL on Feb. 22, 1761, and spon. by Jacob and Elisabetha Welsch. She m. Georg Bard.
- Johan Heinrich, bapt. by RJL on Jan. 12, 1763, and spon. by Johan Heinrich and Catharina Bott. He m. Elisabeth before 1795.
- Anna Maria, b. about 1766, and m. Peter Becker at TLY on Sept. 20, 1787.
- Barbara, b. about 1768, and m. Peter Schmeisser about 1789.
- Sabina, b. on May 14, 1772, bapt. at WOL on June 8, 1772, and spon. by Philip and Catharina Weber. She was not mentioned in the will.
- Catharina, b. about 1732.
- Anna Barbara, b. on Apr. 10, 1737, bapt. at the First Reformed Church of Lancaster, Lancaster Co., PA, and spon. by Georg Keller and wife.

Wolff - Johannes m. Ester, and had the following children:
- Johannes, bapt. by RJL on Aug. 12, 1753, and spon. by Adam and Catharina Hubert.
- Henrich, bapt. by RJL on Jan. 2, 1763, and spon. by Heinrich and Hanna Neff.
- Elisabeth, bapt. by RJL on Mar. 2, 1765, and spon. by John and Elisabeth Bar.

Wolss - Peter was taxed in 1762. He m. Maria Elisabeth, and had the following children:
- Maria Magdalena, bapt. by RJL on Oct. 30, 1757, and spon. by Johannes and Maria Magdalena Kroll.

Wysong - Ludwig was taxed in 1762. He settled in Manchester Township in 1740, and received a warrant for 160 acres called *Digges Choice* on Aug. 19, 1766. His will was written in Heidelberg Township on Sept. 19, 1784, and probated on Sept. 29, 1784. He m. Maria, dau. of Reinhart Hammer (see entry), and had the following children (see *Some Descendants of Ludwig Wysong* by James Richard Sutton (1989)):
- Maria, b. in 1738, and m. Georg Bordman in Aug. 1757.
- Susanna Catharina, b. on Jan. 10, 1740, bapt. at CLY on May 19, 1740, and spon. by Georg Housman/Heinsman, and Reinhardt and Susanna Hammer.
- Johan Ludwig Reinhardt, b. on Feb. 4, 1743, bapt. at CLY on Feb. 9, 1743, and spon. by Reinhardt and Susanna Hammer. In the Revolutionary War, he served in Captain Georg Eichelberger's Company, 1st Battalion, in 1775 and 1776; Captain Christoph Laumen's Company, 3rd Battalion, in 1778; Camp Security in York in 1781; and Captain James Johnston's Company in 1782. He m.

MANCHESTER TOWNSHIP   283

  Anna Catharina Kitzmiller, and d. in Cambria Co., Loretto, PA, on
  Jan. 28, 1808. He is bur. in the Catholic cemetery in Loretto. She
  was b. in 1741, and d. in 1802.
- Valentine, b. in 1744. In the Revolutionary War, he served in the
  7th Class Associators of Heidelberg Township in 1781. He m.
  Elisabeth Albright in 1777, and was taxed in Heidelberg Township
  from 1779 to 1786. He was a tavern keeper from 1782 to 1787. In
  1787, he moved to the Potomac Valley then to White Horse Ford,
  and then into Berkley Co., Shepherdstown, VA. In 1788, he moved
  to Botetourt Co., VA, where he was a brick maker/mason. In 1794,
  he purchased land in Franklin Co., VA. On July 6, 1801, he had
  319 acres in Franklin Co. In the Fall of 1816, he moved to
  Montgomery Co., OH, and in 1817, to Randolph Co., White River
  Township, IN, where he purchased 80 acres on Feb. 25, 1818. His
  estate was administered on June 28, 1824. Her probate inventory
  was filed on Nov. 18, 1825.
- Joseph, b. in 1745. In the Revolutionary War, he served in Captain
  Rudolph Springer's Company, 1st Battalion, in 1776, and in
  Captain Michael Schmeisser's Company, Pennsylvania Battalion,
  Flying Camp. He was captured at Fort Washington on Nov. 16,
  1776, and d. in a British prison in New York in Winter of 1777.
- Henry, b. in 1747, and m. Catharina Dodd.
- Feidt, b. in 1752. In the Revolutionary War, he served in the
  Virginia Militia from Shepherdstown, VA, and at Fort McIntosh,
  and Ft. Laurens on the Muskingum River in OH. He served in the
  Fincastle (Botetourt Co.) Militia in July 1781, and was discharged
  in Oct. He served at Bottom's Bridge, and the Siege and Surrender
  of Cornwallis. He was a blacksmith, and proprietor of a wagon
  shop. He m. Elisabeth Phemach, and Susannah Coffman in
  Botetourt Co., VA, on Mar. 27, 1816. He d. in Botetourt Co.,
  Fincastle, VA, on Aug. 4, 1837.
- Franey, b. in 1753, and m. James Davis on July 1, 1771.
- Catharina, b. in 1754, and m. Henry Hattman on July 26, 1773.
- Jacob, b. in 1757. In the Revolutionary War, he served in Captain
  Swearewgen's Frontier Rangers in VA in 1778, and the 8th
  Virginia Regiment from Shepherdstown in 1779. He m. Mary Byers
  on Easter Monday, 1783, at Berkley Co., Shepherdstown, VA, and
  d. there on Sept. 7, 1823.

<u>Yodder</u> - Daniel was taxed in 1762. He m. Catharine, and had the
following children:
  - Maria Barbara, b. on Oct. 1, 1759, and bapt. at CLY on Oct. 28,
    1759.

Yoner - Jacob received a warrant for 1,000 acres (?) in West Manchester Township on Apr. 15, 1761, that was surveyed as 30 acres on June 2, 1767.

Ziegler - Georg Philip, son of Hans Georg and Sara Ziegler was bapt. in Sinsheim Lutheran Church in Germany, on Apr. 1, 1677. He immigrated to America on the ship *William and Sarah* in 1727. His probate inventory was filed in York Co. in 1756. He m. Anna, dau. of Jacob Mayer of Reyhen, at Weiler Lutheran Church in July 1702. They had the following children (recorded at Weiler and Sinsheim (see BNK)):
  - Johan Jacob, bapt. on May 15, 1703. He was taxed in 1762. He received a warrant for 150 acres in West Manchester Township on Oct. 30, 1736 (Blunston License), that was surveyed as 285 acres on Apr. 8, 1746, 2.80 acres on May 14, 1757 (to Jacob Ziegler and Peter Lau, trustees of the Lutheran Church), and 133 acres to Philip Ziegler, and 131 acres to Georg Ziegler (sons of Jacob deceased) on Oct. 10, 1765. He m. Anna Maria Barbara. Jacob and Maria Barbara were sponsors to the baptism on Maria Barbara Meyer in June 1765. He d. in 1765 (between June and Oct.). He had the following children (recorded at CLY):
    - Johan Georg Philip, b. on July 23, 1735, and bapt. on Aug. 21, 1735. He was taxed in 1762. He m. Anna Margaretha.
    - Johan Jacob, b. on Mar. 5, 1735 (?), and bapt. on Apr. 7, 1742. He m. Susanna Rudyn at Trinity Lutheran Church in Lancaster, PA, on May 19, 1766.
    - Philip, b. about 1737.
    - Johannes, b. about 1739, and was a sponsor to the baptism of Johannes Meyer in 1763. He was not mentioned in the will.
    - Margaretha, b. about 1741, and m. Johannes, son of Georg Meyer (see entry).
    - Anna Catharina, b. on Sept. 15, 1744, and bapt. on Nov. 11, 1744. She was not mentioned in the will.
  - Maria Catharina, b. on Mar. 1, 1705.
  - Barbara, b. on July 25, 1707, and d. in 1707.
  - Ludwig, b. on Oct. 28, 1708, and d. in 1708.
  - Hans Martin, bapt. on Mar. 12, 1710.
  - Johan Georg, bapt. on Feb. 2, 1712. He was taxed in Manheim Township in 1762. He received a warrant for 150 acres in West Manchester Township on Oct. 30, 1736 (Blunston License). His probate inventory was filed in 1764. He m. Anna Margaretha Amspacher on Jan. 17, 1738 (JCS) (see entry in Codorus section), and had the following children (recorded at CLY):
    - Johan Heinrich, b. on Oct. 19, 1739, and bapt. on Dec. 14, 1739.

MANCHESTER TOWNSHIP 285

- Johan Georg, b. on Dec. 12, 1742, and bapt. on Feb. 23, 1743. He was taxed in Manheim Township in 1762.
- Johan Philip, b. on Sept. 14, 1744, and bapt. on Nov. 11, 1744. He m. Elisabeth about 1765.
- Maria Elisabetha, b. on July 9, 1746, and bapt. on Oct. 4, 1746.
- Rebecca, b. on Jan. 7, 1750, and bapt. on Mar. 4, 1750.
- Johan Jacob, b. on Mar. 24, 1752, and bapt. on May 3, 1752. He is probably the Johan Jacob Ziegler that d. on Aug. 24, 1752, and bur. on Aug. 26, 1752 (CLY (says b. on Oct. 31, 1751)).
- Johan Philipp, b. on Aug. 24, 1713. He was taxed in 1762. He received a warrant for 200 acres in West Manchester, Franklin, and Dover Township on Oct. 30, 1736 (Blunston License), and 328.80 acres on Oct. 16, 1767, that was surveyed as 328.80 acres on Apr. 8, 1746, and patented on Oct. 23, 1767. He m. Anna Margaretha, dau. of Killian and Catharina Schmidt (see entry), in York Co., Codorus, PA (JCS), on Nov. 21, 1737. He d. in 1800, and she d. in 1783. They had the following children in Manchester Township:
  - Johan Bernhard, b. on Aug. 24, 1738, and bapt. at Christ's Lutheran on Nov. 19, 1738. He was taxed in Manchester Township in 1762. He m. Rosina, dau. of Dieterich Uhler (see entry). His probate inventory was filed in Codorus Township in 1797. Her probate inventory was filed in Codorus Township in 1819.
  - Georg Philip, b. on Aug. 7, 1739, and bapt. at Christ's Lutheran on Nov. 14, 1739. He d. before 1742.
  - Anna Christina, b. on Sept. 7, 1740, bapt. at Codorus by Rev. Stoever on Sept. 18, 1740, and spon. by Jacob Zeigler and Agnes Schmidt. She m. Gottfried, son of Nicholas Koenig (see entry).
  - Georg Philip, b. on Aug. 4, 1742, and bapt. at Christ's Lutheran on Oct. 24, 1742. He was taxed in 1762. He m. Anna Elisabeth, dau. of Johannes Leib (see entry), before 1763, and Eva, dau. of Dieterich Uhler, about 1769 (see entry). His will was written in West Manchester Township on Aug. 17, 1804, and probated on Sept. 7, 1804.
  - Killian, b. on Aug. 4, 1742, and bapt. at Christ's Lutheran on Oct. 24, 1742. He m. Anna Maria, dau. of Jacob Lischey (see entry in Codorus section), about 1767, and had his probate inventory filed in Paradise Township in 1808. She was b. in 1743, and d. in 1823.
  - Johan, b. on Jan. 8, 1744, and bapt. at Christ's Lutheran on Jan. 17, 1744. He m. Mary, and d. in 1799.
  - Johan Jacob, b. on Oct. 21, 1745, and bapt. at Christ's Lutheran on Feb. 9, 1746.
  - Anna Margaretha, b. on Mar. 29, 1747, and bapt. at Christ's Lutheran on May 3, 1747.

- Maria Catharina, b. on Mar. 10, 1749, and bapt. at Christ's Lutheran Church of York on Apr. 23, 1749. She m. Philip Jacob, son of Nicholas Koenig (see entry).
- Johan Henrich, b. on Aug. 17, 1753, and bapt. at Christ's Lutheran on Oct. 7, 1753. He m. Eva Kapp about 1776.
- Andreas, bapt. by Reverend Jacob Lischy on Apr. 25, 1756, and spon. by Andreas and Anna Maria Nebinger. He d. before 1758.
- Johann Peter, bapt. by Reverend Jacob Lischy on Apr. 25, 1756, and spon. by Peter and Anna Elisabeth Wolf. He m. Margaret Herbach at TLY on May 22, 1781.
- Andrew, b. on Sept. 7, 1758, and bapt. at Christ's Lutheran on Oct. 29, 1758. He m. Anna Maria.
- Maria Magdalena, bapt. by Reverend Jacob Lischy on Sept. 16, 1759, and spon. by Adam Eichelberger and Maria Susanna Fischerin.
- Anna Christina, b. on Dec. 15, 1715.

287

SHREWSBURY TOWNSHIP

<u>Ager</u> - William was taxed in 1762.

<u>Alt</u> - Valentine immigrated to America on the ship *Davey* on Oct. 25, 1738, and m. Anna Catharina, dau. of Martin and Anna Catharina Schmidt. They settled in Montgomery Co., PA, and moved to York Co. between Feb. 1755, and Apr. 13, 1755. Catharina was b. in Fenershausen in Osingen, Germany, (recorded in death records of CLY) on Dec. 1, 1722, and d. on June 8, 1759. Valentine d. in 1755. His will was written on July 18, 1755, and probated on Jan. 10, 1756. After Valentine's death, Anna Catharina m. Heinrich Conrad, and had one child. Valentine and Catharina had the following children (eight children, five alive at the time of Catharina's death):
- Adam, b. about 1738, and was taxed in 1762. His probate inventory was filed in Shrewsbury Township in 1779. He m. Susanna. They had the following children (recorded at FRI):
  - Eva, b. on July 24, 1762, and spon. by Johann and Eva Kleinfelter.
  - Elisabetha, b. on Jan. 19, 1764, and spon. by Jacob and Elisabetha Alt.
  - Salome, b. on Mar. 28, 1766, and spon. by Peter and Salome Korpman.
  - Johan Adam, b. on Feb. 17, 1768, and spon. by Johan Heinrich and Anna Maria Alt.
  - Daniel, b. on Nov. 22, 1770, and spon. by Daniel Korpman.
  - Susanna, b. on Feb. 29, 1772, bapt. on Apr. 12, 1772, and spon. by Heinrich and Juliana Merckel.
- Johan Heinrich, b. about 1740, and m. Anna Maria, dau. of Heinrich Walter (see entry), and widow of Peter Ness (see entry), about 1768. He m. Christina after 1789. His will was written in Shrewsbury Township on Aug. 14, 1816, and probated on Sept. 23, 1816. They had the following children (recorded at FRI):
  - Valentin, b. on Aug. 4, 1772, bapt. on Aug. 30, 1772, and spon. by Valentin Alt and Catharina Walter.
  - Johann Valentin Philipp, b. on Nov. 22, 1775, bapt. at FRI on June 23, 1776, and spon. by Heinrich Walter, the grandfather.
  - Johannes, b. on Feb. 13, 1781, bapt. at FRI on Apr. 15, 1781, and spon. by Johann and Barbara Schmidt.
  - Elisabeth, b. on Oct. 1, 1783, bapt. at FRI on Dec. 11, 1783, and spon. by Dorothea, dau. of Heinrich Walter (dec.).
  - Anna Maria, b. on Dec. 7, 1785, bapt. at FRI on Jan. 15, 1786, and spon. by Conrad and Juliana Hardt.
  - Frederick, b. on Apr. 6, 1788, bapt. at FRI on May 1, 1788, and spon. by Valentine and Elisabeth Wild.

- Ludwig, b. about 1791.
- Henry, b. about 1793.
- Cristina, b. about 1795.
- Jacob, b. about 1740, and m. Elisabetha Margaretha, dau. of Philip Schneider (see entry). Jacob had the following children (recorded at FRI):
  - Eva, b. on Aug. 3, 1764, bapt. on the 12 Sunday after Trinity, and spon. by Georg Hamspacher.
  - Johan Jacob, b. on Feb. 25, 1767, bapt. on Palm Sunday, and spon. by Jacob and Catarina Pfluger.
  - Christina, b. on Mar. 19, 1770, bapt. on Apr. 22, 1770, and spon. by Peter and Christina Behler.
- Anna Magdalena, b. on Apr. 9, 1742, and d. on July 9, 1745.
- Johan Friedrich, b. on Nov. 11, 1743, bapt. at New Hanover Lutheran Church in Montgomery Co., PA, on Feb. 5, 1744, and spon. by Johan Frederick Stempel and wife. He m. Eva Heins. They had the following children (recorded at FRI):
  - Johann Friedrich, b. on Jan. 30, 1764, and spon. by Jacob and Elisabetha Margaretha Alt.
  - Anna Catharina, b. on Aug. 19, 1766, bapt. on Sept. 7, 1766, and spon. by Peter and Catharina Hau.
- Anna Catharina, b. on Sept. 30, 1744, bapt. at New Hanover Lutheran Church in Montgomery Co. in 1745, and spon. by Henrich Krauss and wife.
- Conrad, b. on Dec. 18, 1746, and bapt. at Trappe Lutheran Church in Montgomery Co. on Mar. 14, 1747.
- Catharina, b. on Sept. 29, 1748, bapt. at New Hanover in Montgomery Co. on Dec. 4, 1748, and spon. by Catharina Krause.
- Valentine, b. on Mar. 22, 1750, bapt. at New Hanover Lutheran Church in Montgomery Co., and spon. by Valentin Vogt and wife. He and d. in 1826. He was a sponsor to the baptism of Valentin Alt in 1772. He m. Catharina, dau. of Peter Lau (see entry in Manchester section).
- Philip, b. on Oct. 12, 1752, bapt. at New Hanover Lutheran Church in Montgomery Co. on Mar. 25, 1753, and spon. by Philip Jost and wife.
- Elisabetha, bapt. by RJL on Apr. 13, 1755, and spon. by Johannes and Elisabeth Bouschmann.

<u>Amspacher</u> - George received a warrant for 50 acres in Springfield Township on Jan. 13, 1769, that was surveyed as 51.50 acres called *Port Hook* on Apr. 22, 1769 (see entry in Codorus section).

SHREWSBURY TOWNSHIP   289

Amspacher - Tobias received a warrant for 100 acres on Aug. 6, 1753, that was surveyed as 157.13 acres on May 20, 1765 (see entry in Codorus section).

Amspacher - Valentine received a warrant for 50 acres on Dec. 7, 1772 (see entry in Codorus section).

Baehli - Johannes Abraham m. Anna Maria. He is probably the Johannes Bolle that immigrated to America on the ship *Mortonhouse* on Aug. 24, 1728. He was residing in Berks Co., Albany Township, PA, in 1754. It is uncertain what religion he belonged to before he immigrated to America (possibly Anabaptist/Mennonite), because most of his children underwent adult Lutheran baptisms in Berks Co. He was probably of Swiss descent, because that name is prevalent there. Johannes and Anna Maria disappear from the records of Berks Co. after the baptism of their son Abraham in 1763. Johannnes and Anna Maria were the parents of the following children:
 - Annastass, b. about 1728, and bapt. by Reverend Daniel Schumacher on Jan. 28, 1755.
 - Frantz, b. in 1730. He was bapt. by Reverend Daniel Schumacher on May 25, 1755, and m. Christina about 1752. Frantz d. in Albany Township in Mar. 1805.
 - Daniel, b. about 1732. He m. Anna Rosina (Hoell). He resided in Berks Co., Windsor Township, PA, in 1754, 1757, 1759, and 1761. About 1765, Daniel and his bro. Jacob moved to York Co., Shrewsbury Township, PA. On Oct. 18, 1769 Daniel and Wendle Heys surveyed 126.80 acres in Shrewsbury Township (they had 97.48 of these acres resurveyed on June 22, 1798). On Sept. 30, 1789, Daniel warranted 25 acres in Shrewsbury Township (interest beginning on July 1, 1788). The land was surveyed on June 21, 1798, and patented on Nov. 8, 1808. On Mar. 23, 1769, Daniel warranted 200 acres in Shrewsbury Township. This land was surveyed as *Bayleys Plains* for 191.95 acres (improved about 2 years), and patented to George Hamscher on Oct. 19, 1791. In 1779 and 1780, Daniel had 100 acres, two horses and two cattle; in 1781, 100 acres, two horses and four cattle; in 1782, 100 acres, two horses, and five cattle; and in 1783, he had 100 acres and two inhabitants. Anna Rosina's maiden name is presumed to be Hoell because Daniel and Rosina appeared as sponsors on numerous baptisms of the Hoell family at Zion's Moselem Church in Richmond Township. Daniel d. in Shrewsbury Township in Jan. 1811, and Anna Rosina in May 1815. Daniel's will was written on June 5, 1798, and probated by Rosina Baehli and Henry Ruhl on Jan. 21, 1811. Rosina's will was written on Mar. 28, 1815, and probated on May 2, 1815 by Henry Ruhl and George Frederick.

The beneficiaries of Rosina's estate were Jacob Baehli, Henry Baker, Lydia Baker, Rosina Baker, and Henry Ruhl. Daniel and Rosina may have had the following children in Berks Co., Windsor Township, PA:
- Eva, It has not been proven, but it is possible that Daniel had a dau. named Eva, because a Rosina, Lydia and Henry Baker were the beneficiaries of Anna Rosina Baehli's will. She may be the Eva that m. Jacob Becker/Baker. His will was written on Jan. 6, 1808, probated in Shrewsbury Township on Feb. 6, 1808, and executed by Georg Gantz and Henry Ruhl (the will mentions children Anna Maria, An Rosina, Lydia, Jacob, and Henry).
- Jacob, b. on Sept. 1, 1734. He was bapt. by Reverend Daniel Schumacher on Oct. 29, 1755, spon. by Anthony and Elisabeth Pettersheimer. He was on the tax lists of Albany Township in 1754, 1758, and 1759. In 1758, he is listed as poor. He m. Anna Maria, had one dau., and m. Eva Elisabetha, dau. of Hans Peter and Eva Elisabetha (Kunckel) Kleinfelter (see entry), in Berks Co., PA, about 1759/60. Eva was b. in Florsbach, Hessen, Germany, in 1732, and m. Johan Gottleib Volck about 1754. Gottleib d. in Berks Co., Ruscomb Manner Township in 1759. Gottleib and Eva Elisabetha had the following dau. in Ruscomb Manner Township:
- Elisabetha, b. on July 22, 1755, bapt. at Mertz Church in Rockland Township on Aug. 31, 1755, and spon. by Michael and Elizabeth Homan. She was mentioned in her stepfather, Jacob Baehli's, will in 1812, as Elizabeth Folk. I believe she may be Elisabetha, wife of Wentel Heiss/Heuss, because they appear on numerous baptisms of the Baehli family. Wentel d. in Shrewsbury Township. His will was written on Mar. 11, 1815, probated on July 13, 1816, and executed by Daniel Heiss and Peter Kleinfelter. On Oct. 18, 1769, Daniel Baehli and Wendle Heys surveyed 126.80 acres in Shrewsbury Township (the had 97.48 of these acres resurveyed on June 22, 1798). He warranted 50 acres on Sept. 26, 1785, that was surveyed as 60.80 acres on Feb. 4, 1786. He warranted 125 acres in Shrewsbury Township with Michael Kinsler on Mar. 1, 1786. This land was surveyed as 176.31 acres on Oct. 21, 1786, and patented on Nov. 17, 1807. Elisabetha's probate inventory was taken in 1818.
- Jacob Baehli moved to York Co., Shrewsbury Township, PA, with his bro. Daniel in 1765. Jacob was a weaver and yeoman. On Oct. 16, 1767, he warranted 200 acres in Shrewsbury Township. This land was surveyed as 220.59 acres called *Bald Faced Hills* on Sept. 23, 1768, and 197 acres on May 31, 1775. The 197 acre tract was patented to Henry Bailey on Dec. 19, 1809. In 1779, he had 70 acres, two horses, and one head of cattle; in 1780 and 1781, 100 acres, two horses, and three cattle; in 1782, he had 50 acres, two

horses, and three cattle; and in 1783, 100 acres and four inhabitants. During the Revolutionary War, Jacob served as a Private in the York County Militia, Captain John Ehrman's Company in 1776 and 1778. Eva Elisabetha d. in Shrewsbury Township on June 24, 1809, and Jacob on Aug. 1, 1812. They are bur. in Fissel's cemetery. Jacob was the father of the following children:
- Anna Catharina, b. on Feb. 12, 1758. She was bapt. by Reverend Daniel Schumacher on Apr. 2, 1758, and spon. by Conrad Bielmann and Catherina Grimmen. It has not been proven, but she probably m. Michael, son of Adam and Catharina Roser. Michael was a Private in the 6th Company, 7th Battalion in 1778-80, and the 8th Company, 5th Battalion, as a Corporal 1782-83 during the Revolutionary War. He had a Land Draft called *Roseborough* consisting of 27 3/4 acres in Shrewsbury Township, on the MD line on Oct. 29, 1786. In 1783, he resided in Codorus Township. He was later considered a yeoman of Baltimore Co., MD.
- Jacob, b. about 1760. He m. Susanna about 1784. Jacob resided in Codorus Township with 10 acres, and one horse in 1779; 10 acres, and one head of cattle in 1780; 10 acres, one horse, and two cattle in 1781 and 1782; and 10 acres and five inhabitants in 1783. Jacob moved to Lycoming Co., Elmsport, PA, between 1812 and 1817. where Susanna d. before 1817, and Jacob d. in 1829. After Susanna's death, Jacob m. Elizabeth Conrad, widow of Michael Fisher. Michael d. in 1799. Elizabeth was b. in 1760.
- George, b. on Dec. 13, 1762. He m. Margaretha dau. of Peter and Anna Margaretha (Rudolph) Gerberich, and Catharine Eberhart in York Co. on June 9, 1800. In 1779, George had 100 acres, two horses, and one head of cattle in Shrewsbury Township; in 1780 and 1781, 100 acres, two horses, and three cattle; in 1782, 100 acres, two horses, and five cattle; and in 1790, one male over 16, three males under 16, and five females. George was a Private in the Revolutionary War. He was drafted into the York County Militia in July 1776, and served in Captain Long's Company and Col. Swope's Battalion for three months. He marched from York to Lancaster, and then to Philadelphia, Trenton, and Brunswick. He then marched to Amboy, and Newark, and then was discharged in Oct. 1776. He was drafted again in the fall of 1782. He served in Captain Furry's Company under Major Austin. He was assigned to guard (at Camp Security, York) British prisoners taken with Cornwallis for three months. He applied for pension in Jan. 1834. George d. in Codorus Township on Nov. 24 (23), 1843, and his estate was administered in Jan. 1845.

- Margaretha Barbara, b. on July 23, 1764, bapt. in Albany Township, Berks Co., PA, at the Allemangel Lutheran Church on Sept. 2, 1764, and spon. by Andreas Kunckell and Margaretha Barbara Probst. She m. Heinrich, son of Frederick Ruhl (see entry).
- Anna Barbara, b. on Apr. 17, 1766. She was bapt. at St. Jacob's on May 10, 1766, and spon. by Ludwig Hahnawaldt and Anna Barbara Gerberich. She m. Barnet Hamschear in Trinity Reformed Church of York, PA, on Dec. 24, 1780. Barnet d. in Shrewsbury Township in 1792.
- Anna Rosina, b. on Mar. 27, 1769, bapt. at St. Jacob's on May 28, 1769, and spon. by her uncle and aunt, Daniel and Anna Rosina Baehli. She m. Johan Georg, son of Johannes Ruhl(see entry).
- Susanna, b. about 1771. She probably m. Jacob Kerchner about 1787, but it has not been proven. After Susanna's death, Jacob m. Elisabetha, dau. of Georg and Margaretha (Gerberich) Baehli, at Christ's Lutheran Church of York on June 14, 1803. Jacob's estate was administered in York Co. on May 13, 1828.
- Johannes, b. about 1773. He d. in Codorus Township in Aug. 1841. His will was written on Feb. 4, 1841, and probated on Aug. 21, 1841 by John Ruhl and Jacob Kerschner. Johannes m. Margaretta.
- Peter, b. about 1738. He m. Margaretha and resided in Berks Co., Albany Township.
- Johan Nickel, b. about 1740. He m. Catharina, and resided in Berks Co., Greenwich Township, PA.
- Johann Abraham, b. in 1742. He was bapt. on Apr. 28, 1763 at Rosenthal Lutheran Church, and spon. by his bro., Jacob Baehli. Abraham m. Catharina, who d. about 1770, and then m. Margaretha in 1770. Abraham moved to Frederick Co., Middletown, MD, with his bro., Carl Ludwig, about 1770.
- Carl Ludwig, b. about 1744. He m. Anna Elisabeth. They moved to Frederick Co., Middletown, MD, with Carl's bro., Abraham, in 1770.

Bauer - Henry was taxed in 1762. He m. Elisabeth, and had the following children:
- Heinrich, bapt. by RJL on Jan. 19, 1749, and spon. by Conrad and Catharina Frey. He received a warrant for 100 acres in Shrewsbury and Hopewell Township on July 12, 1768.
- Anna Maria, b. on Apr. 18, 1754, and bapt. at CLY on June 9, 1754.
- Conrad, bapt. by RJL on Oct. 12, 1755, and spon. by Conrad and Catharina Holtzbaum.

Bauser - Johannes received a warrant for 50 acres in Springfield Township on May 11, 1776, that was surveyed as 96.14 acres on Mar. 23, 1787 (patented on Oct. 10, 1789). He m. Christina, and had the following children:
- Peter, b. on Aug. 12, 1770, bapt. at BLY on Aug. 16, 1772, and spon. by his parents.
- Barbara, b. in July 1772, bapt. at BLY on Aug. 16, 1772, and spon. by her parents.

Bechtle - Christian received a warrant for 200 acres on Oct. 27, 1767. He was an exec. of the will of Albertus Stuckslager in Cumberland Township (now Adams Co.) in 1777.

Becker - Peter was taxed in 1762. He received a warrant for 45 acres on Aug. 6, 1753, that was surveyed to Christopher Becker as 50.30 acres called *Stony Vane* (improved 16 years) on May 15, 1770. His probate inventory was filed in York Co. in 1774. He had the following children:
- Christophel was taxed in 1762. His probate inventory was filed in Shrewsbury Township in 1777. He m. Anna Maria, dau. of Philip Schneider (see entry). In 1778, she m. John Connor. They had the following children (recorded at FRI):
  - Philip, b. in 1762.
  - Maria Margaretha, b. on Aug. 21, 1764, bapt. on the 12th Sunday after Trinity, and spon. by Johan Schneider, single son of Philip Schneider.
- Peter received a warrant for 250 acres on Jan. 14, 1767, that was surveyed as 241.110 acres called *Long Meadows* on Mar. 27, 1768. His will was written in Shrewsbury Township on Mar. 14, 1815, and probated on July 22, 1819. He m. Christina, dau. of Adam Ruppert (see entry in Manchester section), and had the following children:
  - Johan Jacob, b. on Aug. 21, 1764, bapt. at FRI on the 12th Sunday after Trinity, and spon. by Jacob and Maria Magdalena Aest (not mentioned in will, unless he went by Johan).
  - Anna Barbara, b. on Feb. 25, 1770, bapt. at STJ on Apr. 22, 1770, and spon. by Daniel and Rosina Baehli (not mentioned in will).
  - John.
  - Catherine.
  - Margaret.
  - Elizabeth.

EARLY GERMAN SETTLERS OF YORK CO., PA

Blauser (Plauser) - Isaac received a warrant for 100 acres in Springfield Township on Sept. 23, 1762, that was surveyed as 139.18 acres called *Chestnut Hill* to John Blauser.

Blauser - John received a warrant for 25 acres in Springfield Township on Aug. 20, 1766.

Bobb - Mathias had his will written in Codorus Township on Aug. 1, 1792, probated on Apr. 1, 1793, and executed by John and Ludwick Bobb. He received a warrant for 25 acres in North Codorus Township on July 1, 1785. He had the following children:
- Johan.
- Adam m. Catharina Salome. They were sponsors to the baptism of Johan Jacob Schaffer at TLY in 1798. His probate inventory was filed in Codorus Township in 1837. They had the following children:
  - Catharina, b. on Aug. 27, 1791, bapt. at WOL on Sept. 25, 1791, and spon. by Jacob and Catharina Flieger.
- Ludwick m. Elisabeth. His probate inventory was filed in York in 1834. He had the following children (recorded at FRI):
  - Johann Bernhard, b. on Sept. 19, 1778, bapt. on Sept. 27, 1778, and spon. by Bernhard and Gertraut Bobb. He is probably the Bernard Bobb that m. Eve, dau. of Johann Bauman (see entry in Codorus section).
  - Elisabetha Catharina, b. on Dec. 6, 1782, bapt. on Dec. 29, 1782, and spon. by Johan Adam and Elisabeth Schaffer.
  - Ludwig, b. on June 27, 1784, bapt. at ZIE on July 25, 1784, and spon. by Michael Geisselman and wife.
  - Anna Maria, b. on Mar. 19, 1788, bapt. at STP on Apr. 2, 1788, and spon. by Friederich and Elisabeth Venus.
  - Johan Georg, b. on June 1, 1786, bapt. at STP on June 7, 1786, and spon. by Georg and Salome Geisselman.
- Bernhard. His will was written in Shrewsbury Township on July 1, 1799, and probated on Oct. 11, 1805. He m. Gertraut, and had the following children:
  - (not proven) Bernard m. Elisabeth, dau. of Georg Jacob Schafer (see entry in Codorus section), at TLY on Sept. 5, 1786.
  - Michael, m. Catharina before 1781.
  - Barbara, m. Christian Headrich about 1785 (see Codorus section).
  - Margaretha, m. Henry Baumgartner about 1786.
  - Eva Margaretha, b. on Jan. 21, 1778, bapt. at FRI on Feb. 15, 1778, and spon. by Eva Margaretha, dau. of Michael Geisselman. She m. Michael Geip about 1798.
  - Ludwig.

SHREWSBURY TOWNSHIP   295

- Henry.
- John, m. Elisabeth before 1799.

Bollinger - Jacob warranted 200 acres with John Graber on Nov. 24,
1768, that was surveyed as 151 acres called *Smith's Fancy* on Oct. 24,
1769 (improved 7 years) (see entry in Codorus section).

Couli (Coule) - Jacob received a warrant for 50 acres in Springfield
Township on Mar. 14, 1755.

Dagen - John received a warrant for 125 acres in Springfield Township
on Oct. 30, 1772, that was surveyed as 132.47 acres called *Little Value*
on Nov. 12, 1772. His will was written in Shrewsbury Township on Jan.
29, 1777, and probated on Feb. 16, 1791 (executed by Elizabet Dagen
and Peter Brillhart, and witnessed by Jacob Brillhart and Rudy Yund).
He m. Elizabeth, and had the following children:
- Elizabeth.
- Peter.
- Catharina.
- Barbara.

Diehl - Johan Adam, son of Hans Georg and Anna Catharina (Hertz),
Diehl was b. on Sept. 12, 1690, was confirmed at Herran-Sultzbach in
1704, and d. in York Co., PA, in Apr. 1755. He m. Maria Catharina,
dau. of Johan Daniel and Anna Catharina (Esch) Kreischer, of
Homberg on Dec. 4, 1712. She was bapt. on Oct. 28, 1696, and d.
before 1767. Johann Daniel, son of Georg Kreisher of Mertzweiler,
Gerichtsschoffe and Kirchencensor, m. Anna Catharina, dau. of
Abraham Esch of Deimberg, at Deimberg on Nov. 18, 1687. They
immigrated to America on the ship *Samuel* on Aug. 27, 1739, and
settled in York Co., PA. Adam's will was written on Mar. 31, 1755, and
probated on Apr. 16, 1755. They had the following children at
Homberg, Germany:
- Johann Daniel, b. in 1713. He m. Maria Elisabeth, dau. of Johan
  Nickel Simon (see entry), in Lancaster Co., Warwick Township,
  PA, on Dec. 26, 1740. He was b. near Homberg, Landkreis of
  Kusel, Pfaltz in 1713. He immigrated to PA, on the ship *Samuel* on
  Aug. 27, 1739. In 1751, Daniel received a land warrant in Codorus
  Township near Seven Valleys, and built a mill within a year. He d.
  intestate in Dec. 1761, and is bur. at Friedensaal Lutheran Church.
  At the time of his death he owned over 500 acres and four mills.
  He was naturalized on Apr. 10/11, 1761. Daniel and Maria bapt.
  the following children at Christ's Lutheran Church of York:
  - Johan Carl, b. on Oct. 19, 1742, and bapt. at Christ's Lutheran
    Church on Nov. 24, 1742. He d. in Adams Co., Cumberland

Township, PA, on Aug. 20, 1820. He m. Christina Catharina, dau. of Georg and Catharina (Rausher) Liebenstein (see entry in Manchester section), in Christ's Lutheran Church of York on Oct. 11, 1763. She was b. in Manchester Township on Aug. 5, 1746, and d. in Adams Co. on May 5, 1809. He inherited all of his father's mill property, and between 1768 and 1783, he built a brick addition to the original stone home. In 1783, he had 2 houses, 1 outhouse, 250 acres, 2 negroes, 4 horses, 8 horned cattle, 10 sheep, 1 grist mill, 1 saw mill, 1 hemp mill, and 2 stills. In addition to being a miller, he was a blacksmith. In 1773, he purchased, *Groundhog Hill*, in Shrewsbury Township, which he later sold part to Andrew Swartz. About 1787, he sold the mill property to Jacob Sitler, moved to Baltimore, MD, and purchased several town lots. In 1792, he sold the remainder of, Groundhog Hill, to Jacob Bowman. About 1805, he moved to Adams Co., PA, and purchased over 775 acres in Columbiana Co., OH, with intentions of moving there. His will was written on Mar. 15, 1812, and probated in 1851.

- Anna Maria, b. on Feb. 11, 1744, and bapt. at Christ's Lutheran on Mar. 17, 1744. She d. in York Co., York Township, on Jan. 10, 1800. She m. Frederick, son of Killian and Christina Fissel (see entry), and Captain John McDonald, probably son of John and Jane McDonald.
- Johan Adam, b. on Dec. 16, 1746, bapt. at Christ's Lutheran on Feb. 24, 1747, and d. in Aug. 1764.
- Georg, b. on Feb. 24, 1750. He d. in Codorus Township on July 28, 1804. He m. Anna Eva, dau. of Georg and Catharina (Rausher) Liebenstein (see entry in Manchester section), about 1774. She was b. in Manchester Township on Apr. 7, 1753, and d. on Oct. 19, 1835. Georg received his father's farm land. He was a tax assessor in 1781, and in 1783 had 300 acres. He was a Private in the 2nd Class of Captain George Geisselman's Company. When he d., he owned 484 acres.
- Maria Elisabeth, b. on Apr. 4, 1715, and m. Johan Adam Simon (see entry).
- Carl Adam, b. in 1717. He m. Maria Elisabeth, dau. of Johan Peter and Anna Margarethe (Becker) Ehrhardt, in Codorus Township on Nov. 24, 1742. She was bapt. at Staudernheim in the Palatinate on Nov. 30, 1716, and d. in Shrewsbury Township about 1795. On Mar. 1, 1755 (issued Apr. 10, 1749 and Oct. 18, 1753) he received a land warrant in Shrewsbury Township called *Diehl's Folly*. He applied for naturalization on Sept. 24, 1755, and was naturalized on Sept. 24, 1763. On Oct. 3, 1763, he purchased 118 acres and 40 perches (surveyed on Nov. 22, 1766) called *Diehl's Chance*. On Dec. 22, 1764, he had 394.5 acres called *Shrewsbury Town*, 344

acres 50 perches on a branch of Codorus Creek, and 249 acres on Deer Creek surveyed. On Apr. 4, 1769, he purchased a grist and saw mill on Deer Creek, which he sold to his bro. Peter in 1771. Carl also had a mill in Shrewsbury Township. He d. in Shrewsbury Township on Apr. 18, 1800. Carl and Maria Elisabeth had the following children:
- Adam, b. on Aug. 12, 1743, and bapt. at Christ's Lutheran Church on Sept. 18, 1743. He m. Anna Elizabeth Seyler, and d. in York Co., Windsor Township on Oct. 30, 1820. She d. in Chanceford Township on Mar. 7, 1831. Adam served under Captain Aquilla Wiley and John Ehrman in the Revolutionary War. In 1783, he was in Shrewsbury Township operating his father's mill on an 115 acre tract. On May 2, 1786, he purchased 71 acres 115 perches in Windsor Township. By 1795, he had a mill and 200 acres. The mill was located on Muddy Creek, and sold by Adam's execs. to his nephew Charles in 1823. Adam is bur. in Lebanon Lutheran cemetery.
- Eva Christina, b. in 1744. She m. Frederick Schinleber and Martin, son of Christopher and Philipena Kurtz. Frederick immigrated to America on the ship *Richmond* on Oct. 5, 1763, and d. about 1777. He took over Charles Diehl's mill on Deer Creek, and later Martin Kurtz took it over. Martin was b. in 1745, and d. in 1836. He was a teamster in the Revolutionary War, and one of the founders of Saddler's Church. Eva Christina d. in Shrewsbury Township on Aug. 22, 1828.
- Elizabeth, b. about 1746. She m. Jacob, son of Jacob and Catharina Scharer (see entry), and d. in Stark Co., Osnaburg Township, Mapleton, OH, in 1825. He was b. on Jan. 9, 1744, and d. in Stark Co. on Jan. 29, 1823. Jacob worked a mill he received from his father in Shrewsbury Township, until about 1805, when he moved to OH. Jacob was a Private in Captain George Long's 6th Battalion, during the Revolutionary War.
- Johan Carl, b. on Oct. 14, 1750. He m. Christina, dau. of Christian and Anna Stabler (see entry), about 1777. He d. in Shrewsbury Township on Aug. 1, 1817, and she d. there on ___ 18, 1811. In 1785, he received 356.11 acres from his father, and took over the family farm. He was overseer for Shrewsbury Township in 1780, and tax collector in 1783. Carl served in the York County Militia in the Revolutionary War under Captain Henry Ferree as a Private, 6th Class, and later in Captain John Ehrman's Company.
- Anna Catharina Elisabetha, b. on Dec. 3, 1752, and bapt. at Christ's Lutheran on Dec. 25, 1752. She m. Dewalt/Theobald, son of Jacob and Catherine Scharer (see entry). They resided on the border between Shrewsbury and Hopewell Township.

- Eva Margaretha, bapt. on Aug. 27, 1718. She m. Johan Michael, son of Hans Michael Ebert (see entry in Manchester section).
- Angelica Elizabeth, b. about 1721. She m. Johan Valentine, son of Johannes Verdriess, about Aug. 1742. He was b. in Fussengonheim in the Palatinate, and was residing in Frederick Co., MD, in 1779. Angelica was alive in 1772. Valentine received a land grant in Frederick Co., Monocacy, MD, in 1743, and settled on Little Hunting Creek. He was naturalized in MD in Oct. 1743. They had the following children:
  - Maria Catrina, b. on May 6, 1743, and bapt. at Monocacy Lutheran Church.
  - Johannes, b. on Mar. 11, 1744, bapt. at Monocacy, and was residing in Greenbriar Co., VA, in 1790. He m. Maria Catharina, dau. of Jacob Zither, in Frederick, MD, in 1772.
  - Maria Magdalena, b. in Jan. 1747, bapt. at Monocacy, and appears as a sponsor to a baptism of a child of Peter Diehl in Lancaster Co., PA, in 1767.
  - Valentine, b. about 1750.
- Nicholas, b. about 1724. He m. Maria Catherina, dau. of Johan Nicholas and Anna Barbara (Burkhart) Hantz, and d. in York Township in May 1790. She was b. in Sponheim, Germany, on Feb. 3, 1734, and d. in York in Oct. 1817. Nicholas worked for his father in the milling business, and received 230 acres and instructions to continue operating the mill with his bro. Peter, when his father d. On Oct. 8, 1767, he received a warrant in York Township, adjoining the land he received from his father in all consisting of 260 acres and 27 perches which he named Diehlsburg. He was overseer of the poor in 1757, tax assessor for York Township in 1769, and was Vestryman at Christ's Lutheran Church of York. In 1783, he had 245 acres, one horse and 2 horned cattle. Nicholas and Maria Catharina had the following son:
  - Peter, b. on Feb. 23, 1760, bapt. at Christ's Lutheran Church of York on Mar. 2, 1760, and d. young.
- Peter, b. about 1728. He m. Anna Maria Margaretha, dau. of Johan Nicholas and Anna Barbara (Burkhart) Hantz. She was b. in Sponheim on Sept. 5, 1737, and d. before Jan. 1801. Peter d. in York Township in Dec. 1812. When his father d., Peter received 130 acres and the mill property. On June 18, 1765, Peter had 160 acres and 94 perches surveyed. Peter and his bro., Nicholas, ran their father's farm and mill until 1762, when Peter sold the mill property to Casper Weaver who sold it the same day to Mathias Sitler. On Sept. 14, 1762, Peter purchased 96.5 acres in Lancaster Co., Donegal Township, and remained there until Feb. 5, 1771, when he purchased a mill property and 248 acres in Shrewsbury Township from his bro., Carl. He also purchased 72 acres and 90

perches in Hopewell Township. Peter and Maria Margaretha had the following children:
- Johan Peter, b. on Aug. 8, 1761, m. Susanna, dau. of George Krantz, and Catherine, dau. of Casper Diller on June 18, 1809. Susanna was b. on Aug. 14, 1769, and d. on Aug. 9, 1806. Peter served in the Revolutionary War as a Private in the 5th Class, Captain Frey's Company from 1777-1780. He served in Captain Peter Ford's Company from 1782 to 1783. He worked with his father in the mill business and 1801, he purchased a tract on the Little Conewaygo at the Ox Head Inn. He d. in Adams Co. on Aug. 1, 1839.
- Nicholas, b. on Feb. 4, 1765, bapt. at the First Reformed Congregation of Lancaster on Feb. 28, 1765, and spon. by Nicholas and Maria Catharina Diehl. He m. Elizabeth, dau. of George and Anna Maria (Holtsinger) Bentz, and d. in York Township on Oct. 11, 1847. She was b. in 1767, and d. on Jan. 14, 1818. He was a Private in Captain Godfrey's Company in the Revolutionary War from 1777 to 1780. He was a farmer in York Township, and later purchased lots in Freytown with his bro., Jacob. He was Director of the Poor for York Township from 1831 to 1834.
- Johan Adam, b. on Feb. 26, 1767, bapt. at Maytown Lutheran Church on Apr. 17, 1767, spon. by Andreas Arntz and Catharina and Mage. Verdruss, and d. young.
- Jacob, b. on Mar. 25, 1769, bapt. at Maytown Lutheran Church on Mar. 30, 1769, and spon. by Jacob and Elizabeth Kinter. He m. Anna Maria, dau. of Jacob Pflieger, on Apr. 13, 1797, and d. in York Township on June 3, 1854. He was Director of the Poor in York Township from 1826 to 1829. He purchased lots in Freystown with his bro. Nicholas. He inherited the mill property and adjoining land from his father.
- Elizabeth, b. on Nov. 26, 1771, m. Henry, son of Philip Jacob and Maria Catherina (Ziegler) King, and d. in York Co. in Dec. 1812.
- George, b. on Feb. 3, 1774, bapt. at Christ's Lutheran Church of York on May 8, 1774, and d. young.
- Catherine, b. on June 26, 1776, bapt. at Christ's Lutheran Church of York on Sept. 1, 1776, m. John Brillinger, and d. on Jan. 24, 1846. He was b. on Feb. 5, 1772, and d. on Apr. 5, 1820. They had 50 acres in Spring Garden Township, a mill property consisting of 160 acres in Manchester Township, 400 acres in Windsor Township, 50 acres in Hellam Township, and 2 lots in New Holland. He was one of the original directors of the York National Bank.
- Daniel, b. on June 11, 1779, bapt. at Christ's Lutheran Church of York on Aug. 8, 1779, m. Barbara, dau. of Jacob and Barbara

(Kohr) Stoehr, and d. on Mar. 10, 1824. She was b. on Feb. 1, 1786, and d. on Feb. 2, 1871. He inherited 44 acres and 77 perches from his father, which he sold to purchase land in Newberry Township (200 acres) and Conewaygo/Newberry Township (115 acres and a mill).
- Johan Georg, b. about 1732. He m. Christina, dau. of Heinrich and Susanna (Miller) Spengler (see entry), on May 30, 1758, and Maria Magdalena Kohler. Christina d. in York Co. about 1782/83. While in York Co., he resided in Dover Township, and his children were bapt. at Strayer's. He was naturalized on Apr. 1, 1765. He served in the Revolutionary War as a Private in Captain Godfrey Frey's Company, 3rd Battalion. He moved to Botetourt Co., VA, in the fall of 1787. He had the following children:
  - Susanna, b. about 1759, m. Carl, son of Philip Casper and Margaretta Salome Spengler (see entry), and d. in Botetourt Co. about 1803/4. He was b. in 1746, and d. on Sept. 16, 1833. Charles was a Private in Captain Philip Albright's Company, and later an Ensign in the 4th Company, 1st Battalion, during the Revolutionary War. On Apr. 9, 1790 he purchased 150 acres on the North Side of the James River in Botetourt Co. He was a blacksmith.
  - Johan Adam, b. on Jan. 28, 1763, and d. about 1783.
  - Eva Margaretha, b. on June 28, 1765, bapt. on Aug. 18, 1765, spon. by Michael and Eva Margaretha Ebert, and d. about 1783.
  - Nicholas, b. about 1768, and d. about 1810.
  - Johan Georg, b. on Nov. 17, 1770, bapt. on May 13, 1770, spon. by George, Susanna and Henrich Spengler, and d. about 1783.
  - Magdalena, b. on Feb. 23, 1774, bapt. at Christ's Lutheran Church of York on Apr. 3, 1774, and m. John Hinderleiter, and d. in Botetourt Co., VA. He was b. in Berks Co., PA, and d. in Botetourt Co. in 1844. He had land on Catawba Creek.
  - Peter, b. on Oct. 12, 1776, bapt. at Christ's Lutheran Church of York on Dec. 25, 1776, and m. Catherine, and d. in Botetourt Co. in Feb. 1827. She d. about Sept. 1843. He inherited land on Looney's Mill Creek (purchased by his father in 1791) from his father.
- Johan Adam, b. in Apr. 1734. He m. Maria Magdalena, dau. of Paul and Anna Eva (Schwab) Burkhart (see entry in Manchester section), on June 17, 1760. She was b. on Oct. 13, 1740. Adam was residing in York Co. in 1796. He worked in his father's mill with his bros. Peter and Nicholas after his father's death. He was naturalized on Aug. 23, 1764. He was an elder of Strayer's Church in 1767, and Supervisor of the Highways in 1775. He served in the York County Militia under Captain Adam Schaffer's Company, and Captain Christian Coffman's Company from 1777-79. He resided in

SHREWSBURY TOWNSHIP 301

Dover Township, and purchased 80 acres on Feb. 19, 1773. He probably went to live with one of his children, and it is uncertain which Township he d. in. Adam and Maria Magdalena had the following children:
- Anna Maria, b. on June 9, 1763, bapt. at Strayer's on July 24, 1763, and spon. by Michael Eberth and Anna Maria Eckert. She was alive on Dec. 25, 1778.
- Christina, b. on Sept. 28, 1765, bapt. at Strayer's on Oct. 19, 1765, and spon. by Johan Georg and Christina Diehl.
- Johan Nicholas, b. in 1766, m. Mary (1776-after 1850), and resided in York Co., Spring Garden Township in 1850. He had land in Manchester Township for a time.
- Johan Adam, b. on June 18, 1769, bapt. at Strayer's on Aug. 6, 1769, and spon. by Vendel Gross and Anna Margareth Burckert.
- Johan Peter, b. on Jan. 19, 1772, bapt. at Strayer's on Apr. 5, 1772, spon. by Peter and Barbara Weinbrenner, and d. on Jan. 22, 1775.
- Maria Catharina, b. on Aug. 25, 1774, bapt. on Sept. 24, 1774, and spon. by Vendel and Margaretha Gross.
- Peter, b. on Nov. 3, 1776, bapt. at Strayer's on Dec. 1, 1776, and spon. by Peter Diehl.

Deilman (Dillman) - Jacob received a warrant for 25 acres on May 26, 1774 (see entry in Codorus section).

Dewalt - Georg was taxed in 1762. He may have been a father or bro. to the following Dewalts:
- Daniel m. Susanna Krepil/Grebiel, and had the following children (recorded by RJL):
  - Daniel, bapt. on Aug. 15, 1756, and spon. by Michael Grebiel and Elisabetha Sohnin.
  - Maria Magdalena, b. on Apr. 13, 1758, and d. on Apr. 22, 1760. Her grandmother was Catharina, wife of Jacob Krepil.
  - Maria Magdalena, bapt. on July 6, 1760, and spon. by Catharina Grebillin.
- Heinrich Jacob m. Anna Maria Catharina, and had the following children (recorded by RJL):
  - Johan Frederich, bapt. on Apr. 27, 1766, and spon. by Frederich Berlinger and Anna Maria Bartesin.
  - Gabriel, b. on Sept. 26, 1767, bapt. at STM on 16th Sunday after Trinity in 1768, and spon. by Gabriel and Anna Elisabetha Graber.
  - Anna Elisabetha, b. on Sept. 26, 1767, bapt. at STM on 16th Sunday after Trinity in 1768, and spon. by Gabriel and Anna Elisabetha Graber.

Dipinger (Tuebinger) - Killian was taxed in 1762. He received a warrant for 50 acres in Springfield Township on Feb. 23, 1767. He m. Susanna, dau. of Valentine Krantz (see entry in Manchester section).

Ditenhauer (Dietenhoefer/Dietenheimer) - Georg was taxed in 1762. He received a warrant for 100 acres in Springfield Township, that was surveyed as 29.6 acres called *Elder Run* on Oct. 13, 1768. He had the following children:
- Georg had the following children:
  - Anna Maria, b. on Dec. 20, 1767, bapt. at BLY on Oct. 25, 1768, and spon. by Maria Elisabetha Valentin.
  - Maria Elisabetha m. Michael Wallendin/Valentine, and had the following children (recorded at CAN):
  - Juliana, b. on Sept. 27, 1755, bapt. on Oct. 26, 1755, and spon. by Johan Adam Paules and Juliana Dietenhofer.
  - Johan Jacob, b. on July 28, 1757, bapt. on Aug. 14, 1757, and spon. by Johan Jacob and Luise Sophia Hauble.
- Louisa Sophia m. Johan Jacob Hauble (Heibele/Haubly), and had the following children:
  - Christian, b. on Mar. 15, 1767, bapt. at FRI on Palm Sunday, and spon. by Baltzer and Maria Elisabetha Koller.
  - Johannes, b. on Sept. 15, 1769, bapt. at FRI on Oct. 22, 1769, and spon. by Johannes and Barbara Bauman.
  - Johan Jacob, b. on Mar. 26, 1774, bapt. at FRI on Apr. 24, 1774, and spon. by Frederick and Catharina Ruhl.
  - Anna Maria, bapt. by RJL on May 10, 1761, and spon. by Anna Maria Diettenhofferin.
- Juliana, was a sponsor to the baptism of Juliana Wallendin in 1755.
- Anna Maria, was a sponsor to the baptism of Anna Maria Hauble in 1761.

Ebert - Martin received a warrant for 100 acres in Shrewsbury and Hopewell Township on July 17, 1758 (see entry in Manchester section).

Eby - Christian received a warrant for 50 acres in Springfield Township on July 8, 1762, that was surveyed as 30.80 acres called *Poor Mill* on July 9, 1766, and patented on June 25, 1763. He received a warrant for 50 acres in Springfield Township on July 8, 1762, that was surveyed as 34.146 acres called *Stony Hallow* on Aug. 26, 1768. He was taxed in 1762. He was b. to Christian Eby in Lancaster Co., Manheim Township, PA, in 1743. He moved to Botetourt Co., VA, in 1792, returned to PA in 1795, and went back to VA in 1799, where he d. in 1835. He m. Catharina (?Huber), and had the following children:
- Elisabeth m. Charles Waltmire.
- Barbara m. Michael Specard, and resided in Botetourt Co., VA.

- Polly m. Jacob Heaston, and resided in Highland Co., OH.
- Catherine m. Joseph Heckman. He d. in Preble Co., OH, in 1826.
- Christian, b. on Dec. 28, 1777, m. Susannah, dau. of John and Jane (Wilson) McDonald, on Dec. 14, 1797, and d. in Preble Co., OH, on Dec. 10, 1859. She was b. on Apr. 10, 1781, and d. on May 11, 1866. They are bur. in Brower cemetery. He moved to Baltimore Co., MD, then to Carroll Co., MD, in 1828. In 1838, he moved to Montgomery Co., OH, and in 1853, moved to Preble Co.

Ehrhardt - Wilhelm received a warrant for 100 acres on Aug. 6, 1753, (application for 100 acres on Jan. 14, 1767) that was surveyed as 150.85 acres called *Codorus Head* on Aug. 19-29, 1766, (115.23 acres called *Straight Run* on Mar. 14, 1767 (the combined tracts are called *Ehrhart's Valley*)). He received a warrant for 100 acres on Jan. 14, 1767, that was surveyed as 114.146 acres called *Ehrhart's Fancy*. He received a warrant for a 100 acre tract and a 50 acre tract on May 31, 1763, that were surveyed as 120.102 acres called *Bow Run* and 60.29 acres called *Ehrhart's Choice* on Aug. 19-20, 1766 (both tracts are called *Ehrhart's Tavern*) (see entry in Codorus section).

Ehrman - unknown (possibly the Johannes Ehrmann that m. Elisabeth Huber, and had Anna Margaretha, b. on Oct. 31, 1739, bapt. at the First Reformed Church of Lancaster, Lancaster Co., PA, on July 13, 1740, and spon. by Nicholas Werret and Anna Margaretha Weidner) was the father of the following children (probably siblings):
- Anna Maria, b. about 1732, m. Gottfried Zillhard, and had the following children:
  - Catherine, b. on Nov. 17, 1752, and bapt. at CLY on Nov. 26, 1752.
  - Maria Margaretha, b. on Nov. 29, 1754, and bapt. at CLY on Dec. 8, 1754.
  - Anna Maria, b. on Sept. 28, 1758, and bapt. at CLY on Oct. 15, 1758.
  - Maria Elisabeth, bapt. by RJL on May 24, 1761, and spon. by Johannes and Maria Elisabeth Guckes.
  - Sophia, b. on Feb. 21, 1763, bapt. at TLY on Apr. 4, 1763, and spon. by Gotfried and Sophia Zwegiebel.
  - Johan Philip, b. on June 7, 1766, and bapt. at CLY on June 15, 1766.
- Johannes, b. about 1746 m. Margaretha, dau. of Frederick Frasher (see entry in Codorus section). He was a Captain in the Revolutionary War. She was b. about 1763. They had the following children:
  - Johan Georg, b. on Nov. 24, 1799, bapt. at FIS, and spon. by Johan Georg and Charlotte Gerberich.

- Johan Georg, b. about 1748, and m. Catharina, dau. of David
  Schaffer (see entry), before Dec. 1769. He received 220 1/2 acres
  called *Broad Spring*, in Shrewsbury Township, from her father,
  David, on Sept. 23, 1769. They had the following children in
  Shrewsbury Township:
  - Maria Magdalena, b. on Sept. 23, 1770, and bapt. at Friedensaal.
  - Michael, b. on Apr. 12, 1780, bapt. at Friedensaal on June 4,
    1780, and spon. by Georg and Catharina Hamspacher.
  - David, b. in Sept. 1781, bapt. at Friedensaal on Dec. 2, 1781, and
    spon. by his uncle and aunt, David and Anna Maria Schaffer.
  - Catharina, b. on Apr. 17, 1783, bapt. at Friedensaal on July 6,
    1783, and spon. by her grandmother, Catharina Schaffer.
  - Wilhelm, b. on Jan. 26, 1787, bapt. at Friedensaal on Apr. 29,
    1787, and spon. by his uncle and aunt, David and Anna Maria
    Schaffer.
  - Peter, bapt. at Friedensaal on June 15, 1789, and spon. by John
    and Elizabeth Schneider.
- Michael, b. about 1752, m. Anna Maria, dau. of David Schaffer (see
  entry), and had the following children in Shrewsbury Township:
  - Johannes, b. in 1782, bapt. at Friedensaal, and spon. by
    Johannes Schneider.

Fackler - Johannes was a son of Jacob and Maria Magdalen Fackler
(Jacob's will was probated in York Town on Oct. 9, 1775). He received
a warrant for 150 acres on Jan. 14, 1767, that was surveyed as 166
acres called *Pick Up* on Sept. 14, 1768, and patented as 258.120 acres
on Jan. 4, 1822. He received a warrant for 100 acres in Shrewsbury
and Hopewell Township on June 25, 1769, that was surveyed as 72.137
acres called *Poplar Spring* on Sept. 29, 1769. He m. Maria Eva
Kappler at CAN on May 13, 1755, and had the following children:
- Johann Georg, b. on Oct. 23, 1758, and bapt. at CLY on Nov. 19,
  1758.
- Maria Magdalen, b. on Feb. 13, 1761, bapt. at CLY on Feb. 22,
  1761, and spon. by her grandparents, Jacob and Maria Magdalen
  Fackler.
- Maria Barbara, b. on Feb. 24, 1767, and bapt. at CLY on Sept. 6,
  1767.
- Johann Peter, b. on Oct. 14, 1770, bapt. at FRI on Oct. 21, 1770,
  and spon. by Peter and Christina Behler.

Falkner - Melchior received a warrant for 100 acres in Springfield
Township on Nov. 15, 1746, that was surveyed as 161.80 acres on Oct.
20, 1761.

Feezler - William received a warrant for 50 acres in Springfield Township on July 12, 1750.

Fissel - Frederick was b. in Essenheim on the Maintz to Killian and Christina Fissel of Paradise Township (see entry in Dover section) on May 24, 1733, immigrated to America on the ship *Loyal Judith* on Sept. 3, 1742, and d. in Shrewsbury Township in Jan. 1778. He m. Anna Maria, dau. of Johan Daniel Diehl (see entry). She d. in York Township on Jan. 10, 1800. He purchased 170 acres and 116 perches in Shrewsbury Township on Nov. 1765, and in 1771 gave the land for Fissel's (Jerusalem) Union Church. He was a millwright/miller, and operated the Diehl Mill while Daniel's estate was settled. Frederick was naturalized on Apr. 3, 1763, and he served on the Committee for Defense during the Revolutionary War. When he d., he owned 250 acres and a mill tract consisting of 150 acres. John McDonald was b. in 1749, and d. in York Township on Mar. 19, 1813. During the Revolutionary War, he served as a Captain in Col. James Batt's Battalion. He received a warrant for 200 acres in Shrewsbury and Codorus Township on July 15, 1762, that was surveyed as 188.80 acres on June 22, 1786. Frederick and Anna Maria had the following children:
- Elizabeth, b. about 1762, and m. John, son of Johan Philip and Elizabeth (Flowers) Schneider (see entry).
- Henry, b. on Apr. 22, 1764. He m. Barbara, dau. Michael Fissel, and d. in Manheim Township in 1802. She d. in Paradise Township in Apr. 1823.
- Eva, b. in 1766. She m. Baltzer, son of John Faust of Lancaster Co., PA, on July 30, 1781. He founded the town of Shrewsbury, and had 150 acres, a grist mill and saw mill in Shrewsbury Township in 1780. He served in the Revolutionary War under Captain Henry Ferree in 1781.
- Margaret, b. on Dec. 12, 1768, m. Daniel, son of Daniel Reider, and moved to Wayne Co., OH, in 1816.
- Frederick, b. in 1769. He m. Phillippina Morgethal on Oct. 18, 1810, and d. in 1817. She d. in Paradise Township in Oct. 1837.
- Christina, b. in 1772.
- Daniel, b. in 1774, m. Elizabeth Frey, and d. in Codorus Township in Feb. 1824.
- Anna Maria, b. on Feb. 22, 1777.
- Catherine, b. on Dec. 28, 1782, and d. on Apr. 28, 1788.

Flauer (Flowers) - John m. Mary. His will was written in Shrewsbury Township on Mar. 3, 1772, and probated on Apr. 11, 1772. He had the following children:

- Elisabeth, b. about 1739, and m. Philip Schneider about 1759 (see entry).
- John received a warrant for 200 acres on Jan. 14, 1767, that was surveyed as 171.37 acres called *Codoras Falls*. His probate inventory was filed in York in 1775.
- Thomas was taxed in 1762.
- Ann.
- Sarah.
- David.
- James.
- Mary.
- Alice.

Frech (Fouk) - Conrad received a warrant for 150 acres on July 13, 1767, that was surveyed as 119.54 acres called *Shelven Rock* on Jan. 8, 1768.

Geisey - Conrad was b. in 1718, and immigrated to America on the ship *St. Andrew* on Oct. 2, 1741. He was taxed in York Township in 1762 and 1779. He m. Maria Agatha, dau. of Samuel and Elisabeth Wolff of Lancaster Co., Elizabeth Township (Baer according to Henricus' baptism), and Magdalena, widow of Heinrich Schwartz, on Feb. 15, 1791. Agatha was alive in 1770. Conrad d. on Feb. 5, 1802. He had the following children (*Giese, Geesey, Keesey Family in America* by T. C. Geesey (1935)):
- Jacob, b. about 1746, and m. Eva Catharina Frey at TLY on May 16, 1769. He was taxed in York Township in 1779. During the Revolutionary War, he served in the 6th Company, 3rd Battalion, under Captain George Long.
- Maria Elisabeth, b. about 1748, and m. Christianus, son of Georg Martin and Johanna Fridricca (Schmaltzhaff) Bleymeier. He was b. in Massenbach, Germany, on Apr. 3, 1741.
- Johan Conrad, b. on July 12, 1750, bapt. at The First Reformed Congregation at Lancaster on Aug. 5, 1750, and spon. by Ulrich and Maria Elisabeth Seiler. He m. Margaretha, dau. of John Inners, before 1775. He was taxed in York Township in 1779. He was a blacksmith, supervisor of the highways for York Township in 1773, and a 2nd Lt. in the 6th Company, 3rd Battalion, under Captain George Long in 1778.
- Maria Magdalena, bapt. by RJL on May 24, 1752, and spon. by Ludwig and Maria Magdalena Schreiner. She m. Bernhardt Cousler/Kaussler.
- Maria Margaretha, b. on Mar. 31, 1754, bapt. at CLY on May 20, 1754, and spon. by Johan Gottfried and Maria Margaretha Dietz. She m. Jacob Inners.

- Johannes, b. on Apr. 1, 1755, and m. Anna Catherine before 1781. He resided in York Township in 1779. He was overseer of the poor in York Township in 1795, and served in the 6th Company, 3rd Battalion, under Captain George Long, during the Revolutionary War. He d. on Apr. 4, 1830. Anna Catharina was b. on May 24, 1758, and d. on Dec. 10, 1830. They are bur. in Bleymeier's cemetery.
- Johan Christian, b. about 1757, and m. Mary, dau. of John Inners, and Elisabeth Flinschbach at TLY on Mar. 25, 1783. He was taxed in Shrewsbury Township in 1779. Elisabeth d. in 1831. He was a wagonwright.
- Catharina, bapt. by RJL on May 6, 1759, and spon. by Conrad and Catharina Holtzbaum. She was not mentioned in the orphan court docket on Mar. 24, 1803.
- Henricus, b. on July 2, 1762, bapt. at TLY on July 25, 1762, and spon. by Nicholas Schaffer and wife.

Geisey - Jacob d. in Lancaster Co., PA, before 1757. On Dec. 7, 1757, the guardian of his children applied for more money for them. Jacob had the following children:
- Maria Elisabetha, b. about 1729, and m. Ulrich Seiler in the First Reformed Congregation at Lancaster, PA, on Apr. 16, 1750. He was a linen weaver, and resided in Windsor Township in 1779. They had the following children:
  - Peter, b. on Nov. 28, 1753, and bapt. at CLY on Feb. 10, 1754.
  - Anna Barbara, b. on Jan. 1, 1763, bapt. at CAN on Mar. 20, 1763, and spon. by Jacob and Anna Sincke/Dineke.
  - Johan Georg, bapt. at Kreutz Creek Lutheran Church on Aug. 10, 1765, and spon. by Johan Georg and Anna Margareth Dee.
- Philip, b. in 1736, and was a communicant at the First Reformed Congregation at Lancaster in 1750 (listed as eldest son in Orphan's Court records).
- John, b. about 1738.
- Henry, b. about 1740.

Geisselman - Johan Michael was taxed in 1762. He received a warrant for 50 acres in Springfield Township on May 31, 1762, that was surveyed as 102 acres called *Mount Airy* on Nov. 15, 1766. He received a warrant for 50 acres in North Codorus and Springfield Township on May 31, 1762, and 200 acres on July 1, 1784 (interest began on Mar. 1, 1751), that was surveyed as 351 acres on Sept. 2, 1784. (patented as a 102 acre tract and a 249 acre tract on Oct. 18, 1784. His will was written in Shrewsbury Township on June 23, 1784, and probated on Sept. 16, 1784. He m. Catharina, dau. of Martin Rein (see entry) at the Moravian Church in Lancaster, PA, on Feb. 25, 1743, and Maria

Wilhelmina Margaretha Frinsh at the Moravian Church in Lancaster, PA, on Aug. 2, 1745. He had the following children:
- Maria Margaretha, b. on Nov. 8, 1743, and bapt. at CLY on Jan. 3, 1743. She m. Lorentz Kleinfelter (see entry), and d. on June 23, 1784.
- Johann Georg, b. on Jan. 27, 1747, m. Maria Salome Korbman in 1767, and Catharina Keller. He d. on Aug. 10, 1821/31. Georg and Salome had the following children (recorded at FRI):
  - Johann Adam, b. on Aug. 28, 1768, bapt. on Sept. 13, 1768, and spon. by Adam and Elisabeth Uhler. He m. Matina.
  - Maria Charlotta, b. on May 19, 1771, bapt. on June 9, 1771, and spon. by Jacob and Dorothea Kraft.
  - Maria Margaretha, b. on Dec. 14, 1772, bapt. on Dec. 20, 1772, and spon. by Maria Margaretha Korpman and P. Conrad Korpman.
  - Maria Eva, b. on Sept. 2, 1776, bapt. on Sept. 15, 1776, and spon. by Eva Margareth and Michael Geisselman.
  - Barbara, b. on Dec. 30, 1777, bapt. on Feb. 15, 1778, and spon. by Conrad and Catharina Corpman.
  - Anna Catharina, b. on Dec. 30, 1777.
  - Frederick, b. about 1779, m. Catharina Roser, and d. in 1866.
  - Michael, b. about 1781.
  - Georg, b. about 1783, and m. Catharine.
- Anna Elisabetha, b. on Feb. 12, 1749, bapt. at CLY on Mar. 26, 1749, and m. Adam Uhler at STR on June 24, 1766 (see entry in Manchester section). She m. Frederick Rummel before 1774.
- infant, bapt. at CLY in July 1750.
- Magdalen, b. in Jan. 1752, and bapt. at CLY on Apr. 19, 1752. She m. John Kunckel.
- Catharina Maria, b. on Dec. 25, 1754, and m. Johann Georg, son of Jacob Walter, about 1774 (see entry in Codorus section). She d. on Nov. 25, 1832.
- Eva Margaretha, b. in 1756, and m. Samuel Moser, Jr., in 1779 (see entry in Manchester section). She d. in 1786.
- Christina Maria, b. in 1758, m. Michael, son of Michael Hassler (see entry in Codorus section), on Dec. 1, 1777, and d. in 1847.
- Johan Michael, b. on Nov. 7, 1760, and d. on Sept. 29, 1823. He m. Anna Maria Frey about 1783, and Catharine Hershey about 1794. Catharine was b. on Oct. 9, 1773, and d. on Aug. 25, 1857.
- Frederick, b. on Sept. 28, 1761, m. Magdalena, dau. of Philip Venus (see entry), at TLY on May 4, 1786, and d. on Oct. 18, 1845 (bur. at FRI). She was b. on June 11, 1767, and d. on Jan. 11, 1831 (bur. at FRI).
- Susanna Christina, b. about 1763, and m. Johann Jacob, son of Johann Jacob and Magdalena (Schnazler) Correll, at TLY on Sept.

9, 1783. He was b. in York Township on July 5, 1759 (FMY). He was a Moravian, and a farmer in York Township.
- John, b. about 1765, and m. Rosina, dau. of Heinrich Korbman before 1793 (see entry).
- Jacob, b. about 1767, and d. in Wayne Co., OH, in 1825. He resided in Columbiana Co., OH.

Gemmel - William was taxed in 1762.

Gerlach - Johann Henrich received a warrant for 150 acres on Dec. 27, 1768. He received a warrant for 150 acres in Springfield Township on Oct. 15, 1762, that was surveyed as 212.120 acres called *Mount Peeble* on Aug. 16, 1766. He m. Maria Magdalena, dau. of Adam and Magdalena Schleppi, and widow of Phillip Frienst/Frensch (see entries in Codorus section), and had the following children:
- Johan Adam, bapt. by RJL on July 5, 1752, and spon. by Adam and Magdalena Schleppi.
- Johannes, b. on Dec. 17, 1762, bapt. at TLY on Feb. 6, 1763, and spon. by Killian Tuebinger and wife.

Glattfelter - Hans Peter was b. to Felix and Barbara (Glorius) Glattfelter, in Glattfelden, Switzerland in 1700, and bapt. on June 30, 1700. He m. Salome Am Berg/Amberg in Glattfelden on Nov. 23, 1721. The family (including his bro., Casper, see entry in Codorus section) set out for America on the ship *Francis and Elizabeth*, but Peter d. at sea before the ship's arrival (Aug. 30, 1743). Salome settled in York Co., PA, and d. there. They had the following children in Glattfelden, Switzerland:
- Elisabeth, b. on June 14, 1723, and m. Jacob Rein (see entry).
- Anna Barbara, b. on Aug. 12, 1725, and bapt. on Aug. 12, 1725. She m. Johannes Hildebrand (see entry).
- Felix, b. on Feb. 2, 1726/27. He was taxed in 1762. He m. Elizabeth about 1749, and Maria Sara Meyer at Christ's Lutheran Church of York on Oct. 25, 1750. They moved to Rowan Co., NC, between 1763 and 1768. Felix d. in Davidson Co., NC, on Jan. 18, 1814. Maria Sara was b. in Wurtemburg in 1731, and d. in Davidson Co. on Nov. 23, 1813. They are bur. in Bethany Reformed Church cemetery, near Midway. Felix had the following children:
  - Johannes, b. on Aug. 18, 1751, and bapt. at Christ's Lutheran on Sept. 8, 1751. He m. Catrine, dau. of Jacob and Derrodea Zinck, and d. in Davidson Co., NC, on Apr. 24, 1826. She was b. in Rowan Co., NC, on Feb. 22, 1755, and d. on Aug. 20, 1826.
  - Anna Maria bapt. by Reverend Jacob Lischy on July 22, 1753, and spon. by Casper and Anna Maria Gladfelter. She m. Martin

Jesse, son of Balthasar and Anna Barbara Neufong. He was b. in Berks Co., PA, about 1745, and d. in NC about 1775.
- Dorothea, b. on June 25, 1755, bapt. by Reverend Jacob Lischy on July 6, 1755, and spon. by Henrich and Dorothea Walther. She m. Peter Neufong before 1774, and Johannes, son of Michael and Elisabeth Kuntz, on Nov. 28, 1775. Johannes was b. in York (now Adams) Co., Conewago, PA, on Nov. 17, 1753, and d. in Davidson Co., NC, on Aug. 5, 1842. Dorothea d. in Davidson Co. on July 30, 1842.
- Johan Georg, bapt. by Reverend Jacob Lischy on Oct. 9, 1757, and spon. by Johan Georg and Sibilla Meyer. He served in the Revolutionary War, and d. in Rowan Co., NC, in 1837. He m. Elisabeth, dau. of Johan Paul and Elisabeth (Wallacher) Leonhardt. Elisabeth was b. in NC on Nov. 24, 1762, and was alive in 1785. After 1795, Georg m. Catharina Hochler.
- Susanna, bapt. by Reverend Jacob Lischy on Jan. 25, 1761, and spon. by Killian and Susanna Dipinger. She m. Johan Jorg, son of Balthasar and Anna Barbara Neufong, and d. in Rowan Co., NC, on Sept. 28, 1793. He was b. in Berks Co., PA, in 1753, and d. in Rowan Co. on Mar. 8, 1797. They are bur. in Bethany cemetery in Davidson Co.
- Johann Peter, b. on Mar. 13, 1763, m. Mary Amelia, dau. of Daniel and Elisabeth (Harman) Wagoner, on June 28, 1790, and d. in Davidson Co., NC, on Oct. 4, 1843. She was b. on July 2, 1772, and d. on Aug. 13, 1842. They are bur. in Bethany cemetery.
- Jacob, b. in Rowan Co., NC, on Jan. 1, 1770, m. Margaret, dau. of Johan Balthasar Hagge, in Rowan Co. on June 28, 1790, and d. in Davidson Co. on Feb. 1, 1837. He was a cabinet maker. She was b. in Rowan Co. on Sept. 4, 1771, and d. on Nov. 3, 1857. They are bur. in Bethany cemetery.
- Hans Rudolf, b. on Mar. 25, 1731. He m. Veronica Hitsberger/Hetzberger in Lancaster Co., PA, on Apr. 21, 1767, and d. in Davidson Co., NC, between 1804 and 1810. He lived in Shenandoah, Page, and Warren Counties, VA. On Nov. 3, 1787, he purchased 190 acres in Rowan Co., NC. They had the following children:
- Peter, b. about 1770.
- Elias, b. about 1775, and m. Susanna.
- Ann, b. about 1778, and m. Charles Leason, son of Charles and Ann Byrn.
- John C., b. in VA on Sept. 14, 1782 (or Rowan Co., NC), m. Catherine, dau. of Jacob Adam and Catherine (Myers) Bowers, and d. in Putnam Co., Russell Township, IN, on Aug. 19, 1831. She was b. in Davidson Co., NC, on Mar. 20, 1788, and d. in IN

on July 25, 1851. They are bur. in Parke Co., IN, in the Old
Lutheran cemetery in Greene Township.
- Jacob, b. about 1785, and m. Margaret.
- Magdalena, b. on Nov. 29, 1733.
- Casper, b. on July 17, 1740, and d. about 1743.

Goafman - Elizabeth received a warrant for 100 acres in Springfield
Township on Apr. 4, 1751 and 100 acres on Dec. 18, 1751.

Gobble (Gabel) - John was taxed in 1762. He received a warrant for
100 acres on Aug. 3, 1772, that was surveyed as 84.101 acres called
Stony Bottom on Oct. 19, 1787. He may be the John Gobel, b. to Johan
Georg Gobel on Aug. 28, 1734, and bapt. at CLY on Nov. 10, 1734. His
will was written in Shrewsbury Township on Mar. 26, 1789, and
probated on Mar. 5, 1791. John m. Gertraut, dau. of Peter Schneider
and widow of Philip Simon (see entry), and had the following children:
- Maria Christina, b. on Jan. 12, 1763, bapt. at FRI on Jan. 23, 1763,
and spon. by Johann Philip Schaffer and Catharina Diehl. She m.
Hans Gramer.

Gochenour - John received a warrant for 150 acres in Shrewsbury and
Springfield Township on Feb. 12, 1767, that was surveyed as 142.53
acres called *Timber Bottom* on June 19, 1767. He received a warrant
for 200 acres in Shrewsbury and Springfield Township on Oct. 15,
1762, that was surveyed as 203.38 acres on Nov. 16, 1764. He is the
son of Joseph Gochenour (see Dover section).

Graber (Greber) - Johannes warranted 200 acres with Jacob Bollinger
on Nov. 24, 1768, that was surveyed as 151 acres called *Smith's Fancy*
on Oct. 24, 1769 (improved 7 years). He m. Maria Barbara, and had
the following children:
- Wernhardt, bapt. by RJL on July 14, 1751, and spon. by Jacob and
Barbara Henn.
- Catharina Barbara, bapt. by RJL on Oct. 16, 1753, and spon. by
Valentine and Catharina Steinbrecher.

Grimm - Philip received a warrant for 250 acres in Springfield and
York Township on Mar. 14, 1767, that was surveyed as 194.120 acres
called *Ground Oak Plenty* on Oct. 14, 1767. His will was written on
Dec. 9, 1793, and probated on Dec. 24, 1793. His probate inventory was
filed in York Town in 1794. He m. Anna Barbara, and had the following
children (Barbara is probably the Barbara Grimm that m. Frederick
Eschbach at TLY on May 13, 1798):
- Christina, bapt. by RJL on Oct. 28, 1751, and spon. by Jacob
Bushon and Elisabeth Spenglerin.

- Johann Peter, b. on Nov. 20, 1753, and bapt. at CLY on May 5, 1754. He m. Anna Maria Schindler at TLY on Aug. 11, 1778.
- Philliph Ludwig, bapt. by RJL on Feb. 29, 1756, and spon. by Philliph Bier, Ludwig Kieffer, and Maria Margaretha Kiefferin. He m. Anna Maria about 1778, and Catherine about 1780.
- Michael, bapt. by RJL on Mar. 26, 1758, and spon. by Michael and Dorothea Barth. He m. Christina Weyerman at TLY on Mar. 28, 1785.
- Barbara, bapt. by RJL on Apr. 20, 1760, and spon. by Michael and Dorothea Barth. She was not listed in the will.
- Maria Dorothea, b. about 1762, and m. Conrad, son of Herman Muller (see entry), at TLY on Dec. 25, 1780.
- Jacob, b. on Oct. 26, 1764, and bapt. at CLY on Dec. 9, 1764. He m. Elizabeth before 1790.
- Daniel, b. about 1765, and m. Barbara Fols at TLY on Mar. 15, 1785.
- John, b. about 1767.

Groh - Jacob received a warrant for 100 acres in Springfield Township on June 9, 1763. He m. Susanna Siegrist, and had the following children:
- Friedericus, b. on July 26, 1762, bapt. at TLY on Aug. 29, 1762, and spon. by Frederick and Magdalena Stritmeyer.

Grouce - Jacob was taxed in 1762.

Hart - Martin received a warrant for 200 acres in Springfield Township on Aug. 10, 1768, that was surveyed as 102.62 acres called *Cold Hill* on Dec. 19, 1774. Martin and Catharina Hart were sponsors to the baptism of Catherine Stroer at FRI in 1794.

Hauk - Hans Martin, son of Blasius and Anna Margaretha (Vogler) Hauk, was b. at Ingelsheim, Northern Alsace, July 5, 1719, and bapt. at Hunspach Lutheran Church on July 9, 1719. He immigrated to America on the ship *St. Andrew* in 1752, and his father and bros., Michael and Bernard, immigrated to America on the ship *Ann* in 1749 (BNA). He was taxed in 1762. He received a warrant in Codorus and Shrewsbury Township for 40 acres on May 31, 1762. He m. Maria Magdalena, dau. of the late Theobald Billmann (of Igelsheim), at Hunspach, on Apr. 14, 1739, and had the following children (BNA bapt. at Hunspach unless otherwise noted):
- Maria Margaretha, b. on Oct. 9, 1740, bapt. on Oct. 16, 1740, and d. before 1759.
- Maria Elisabetha, b. on Dec. 14, 1742, and bapt. on Dec. 16, 1742.
- Johann Adam, b. on Dec. 18, 1746, and bapt. on Dec. 21, 1746.

- Johann Michael, b. on Dec. 29, 1749, and bapt. on Jan. 1, 1750.
- Maria Margareth, bapt. by RJL on Dec. 16, 1759, and spon. by Georg and Margaretha Ziegler.

Heinrich - Jacob received a warrant with Nicholas Yeakle for 100 acres in Springfield Township on Apr. 4, 1754, that was surveyed as 170 acres on Apr. 20, 1754. He had the following sons:
- Nicholas was taxed in 1762. He and Johan Nicholas Helle received a warrant for 25 acres in Springfield Township, that was surveyed as 8.110 acres called *Church Lot* on Apr. 5, 1769 (patented on Mar. 31, 1774 became the site of Friedensal (Schuster's) Lutheran Church. He received a warrant for 25 acres in Springfield Township on Feb. 12, 1767, that was surveyed as 41.44 acres called *Horsh Deyth* on Nov. 23, 1769. He m. Margaretha. They had the following children bapt. at FRI on Sept. 28, 1768:
  - Jacob, b. on Dec. 18, 1755, and spon. by Jacob Heinrich and Anna Maria Bremm.
  - Eva Elisabetha, b. on Feb. 16, 1759, and spon. by Georg and Eva Elisabetha Farch.
  - Christian, b. on July 30, 1760, and spon. by Jacob and Elisabetha Heinrich. He m. Eva Catharina, dau. of Tobias Muller (see entry).
  - Michael, b. on Aug. 6, 1762, and spon. by Michael Geiselman and wife.
  - Nicolaus, b. on Aug. 19, 1764, and spon. by Johannes Pfeiffer and wife.
  - Juliana, b. on Nov. 19, 1766, and spon. by Jacob and Eva Catharina Volgeme.
  - Johannes, b. on Sept. 27, 1768, and spon. by Johannes Pfrister and wife.
  - Daniel, b. on Dec. 24, 1778, bapt. at FRI on Jan. 6, 1779, and spon. by Johannes Pfeifer.
- Jacob, b. about 1741. He was a sponsor to the baptism of Jacob Heinrich in 1768. Jacob received a warrant for 100 acres in North Codorus Township on Oct. 1, 1762, that was surveyed as 116.80 acres, and 66.76 acres on Nov. 5, 1764. He was taxed in Codorus Township in 1762. He m. Anna Elisabetha, and had the following children:
  - Johan Jacob, bapt. at FRI on Apr. 5, 1768, and spon. by Nicholas and Margaretha Heinrich.

Helle - Johan Nicholas received a warrant for 25 acres in Springfield Township with Nicholas Heinrich, that was surveyed as 8.110 acres called *Church Lot* on Apr. 5, 1769 (patented on Mar. 31, 1774, and became the site of Friedensal (Schuster's) Lutheran Church).

Hess - Hans Ulrich was taxed in 1762. He received a warrant for 100 acres in Springfield Township on Jan. 16, 1767, and 150 acres on Feb. 18, 1773, that was surveyed as 261.59 acres called *Ursula* on Mar. 24, 1773. His will was written in Shrewsbury Township on Aug. 6, 1787, and probated on Aug. 26, 1790. He m. Ursula Schlatter (d. about 1795), and had the following children:
- Jacob, b. about 1751 (named as eldest in father's will). He received a warrant for 50 acres in Springfield Township on Feb. 18, 1773, that was surveyed as 39.133 acres called *Water Enough* on Mar. 24, 1773. He received a warrant for 100 acres in Springfield Township on Sept. 28, 1774, that was surveyed as 107.20 acres called *Pine Tree* on Oct. 21, 1774.
- Heinrich, bapt. by RJL on July 22, 1753, and spon. by Henrich and Dorothea Walther. He m. Elisabeth, dau. of Johann and Anna Barbara Bauman (see entry) in York Co. on May 13, 1782, and d. in Shrewsbury Township on Aug. 28, 1799. She was b. on May 13, 1757, and d. in Springfield Township on Feb. 26, 1844.
- Ursela, bapt. by RJL on May 4, 1755, and spon. by Henrich and Dorothea Walther. She m. John Menges on Nov. 9, 1779.
- Ulrich, bapt. by RJL on July 31, 1757, and spon. by Heinrich and Dorothea Walther.
- Anna Maria, bapt. by RJL on Aug. 5, 1759, and spon. by Casper and Anna Maria Glattfelter. She m. Michael, son of Casper and Anna Maria Glattfelter (see entry in Codorus section).
- Johan Ulrich, b. on May 23, 1762, bapt. at FRY on June 27, 1762, and spon. by Felix and Sarah Glattfelter.
- Kilian, b. on Apr. 27, 1766, bapt. at FRY on June 8, 1766, and spon. by Kilian Tuebinger and wife.

Hildebrand - Conrad received a warrant for 50 acres in Springfield Township on Dec. 7, 1749, that was surveyed as 96 acres to Conrad on Dec. 8, 1752, and 48.133 acres called *Deep Swamp* to John Hildebrand on Aug. 15, 1766 (land was adjacent to Johannes Hildebrand-see next).

Hildebrand - Johannes was taxed in 1762. He m. Anna Barbara, dau. of Peter Glattfelter (see entry). Johannes was b. in Eschenmosen, Bulach, Zurich, Switzerland on Mar. 2, 1714/15 to Hans Jacob Hildebrand, and d. in York Co., Shrewsbury Township, PA, on Apr. 2, 1782/83. She d. on Aug. 18, 1794. They are bur. in Bupp's cemetery. He received a warrant for 150 acres in Springfield Township on Aug. 16, 1769, that was surveyed as 86.68 acres called *High Land* on Oct. 17, 1769. He received a warrant for 50 acres in Springfield Township on Feb. 28, 1776, that was surveyed as 27.68 acres called *Small Run* on Apr. 18, 1776. Johannes and Anna Barbara had the following children in York Co., Shrewsbury Township, PA:

- Felix, b. on Nov. 14, 1749, bapt. by Reverend Jacob Lischy on May 13, 1750, and spon. by Felix and Elisabeth Glatfelder. He m. Maria Elisabeth, dau. of Johann Philipp and Anna Gertrude (Schneider) Simon (see entry), about 1772. He d. in Shrewsbury Township on Mar. 26, 1820. She d. in Shrewsbury Township on Oct. 31, 1820, and is bur. in Strine cemetery, beside her husband.
- Dorothea, bapt. by Reverend Jacob Lischy on June 21, 1751, and spon. by Heinrich and Dorethea Walther. She m. Jacob, son of Andreas and Anna Margaretha Swartz (see entry).
- Catharina, bapt. by Reverend Jacob Lischy on Dec. 22, 1751, and spon. by Johan Michel and Catharina Knotel.
- Johan Jacob, bapt. by Reverend Jacob Lischy on Nov. 12, 1752, and spon. by Jacob and Elisabeth Rein. He m. Maria Elisabeth Stiffler.
- Casper, bapt. by Reverend Jacob Lischy on Apr. 13, 1755, and spon. by Casper and Anna Maria Glattfelter. He m. Barbara Cramer at the First Reformed Church of York on June 3, 1783, and d. in Springfield Township on Oct. 22, 1841. She d. on Oct. 31, 1832. They are bur. in Bupp's cemetery.
- Heinrich, bapt. by Reverend Jacob Lischy on May 8, 1757, and spon. by Heinrich and Dorothea Walther. He m. Magdalene Kraut at the First Reformed Church of York on Nov. 14, 1787.
- Anna Maria, bapt. by Reverend Jacob Lischy on Sept. 14, 1760, and spon. by Casper and Anna Maria Glattfelter. She m. John Cheyry/Scheure/Scheiry in the First Reformed Church of York on Mar. 29, 1785.
- Sarah, b. about 1762. She m. John, son of Tobias and Maria Elisabetha Hartman, at the First Reformed Church of York on Jan. 21, 1783, and d. on Mar. 1, 1833. She is bur. in Prospect Hill cemetery.
- Anna Barbara, b. on Sept. 29, 1766, bapt. at Friedensaal on Oct. 19, 1766, and spon. by Conrad and Dorothea Swartz. She m. Ludwig, son of Tobias and Maria Elisabetha Hartman, at the First Reformed Church of York in Aug./Sept. 1787, and d. in York Co., Dallastown, on Apr. 8, 1831. He was b. in 1763, and d. on July 25, 1825.
- Maria Margaretha, b. about 1769, bapt. at Friedensaal between Dec. 1768 and July 1769, and spon. by Michael and Margaret Geisselman. She d. on Aug. 9, 1794.

Haman - Georg Michael was taxed in 1762. He received a warrant for 100 acres on June 1, 1762, that was surveyed as 188 acres on June 2, 1755. His will was written in Shrewsbury Township on Jan. 11, 1765, and probated on Jan. 3, 1769. He m. Catharina Elisabetha. They had the following children:

- Godleap.
- Anna Barbara, b. on Apr. 14, 1765, bapt. at STR on Apr. 28, 1765, and spon. by Johan Peter and Anna Barbara Streher.

Holtzbaum - Conrad received a warrant for 100 acres in Shrewsbury Township on Dec. 18, 1751, that was surveyed to him and Zachariah Shugart as 114 acres on June 9, 1757. He was taxed in York in 1762. His probate inventory was filed in York Town in 1775, and his widow was taxed in York in 1779. He m. Catharina, and had the following children:
- Catharina, b. about 1739, m. Johannes Schultz, and had the following children:
  - Anna Catharina, b. on Apr. 23, 1759, and bapt. at CLY on May 20, 1759.
  - Anna Maria, bapt. by RJL on Nov. 23, 1760, and spon. by Johan Jacob Welschover and Anna Maria Holtzbaumin.
  - John, b. on Nov. 21, 1761, and bapt. at CLY on Jan. 3, 1762.
  - Johann Jacobus, b. on July 15, 1763, bapt. at TLY on July 24, 1763, and spon. by Johan Jacob Schultz.
  - Maria Christina, b. on Jan. 2, 1765, bapt. at TLY on Jan. 27, 1765, and spon. by Georg Spengler and wife.
  - Susanna, b. on Mar. 21, 1768, bapt. at TLY on June 12, 1768, and spon. by Jacob Welsch and wife.
  - Susanna, b. on Mar. 8, 1771, bapt. at TLY in Apr. 1771, and spon. by Valentine Leiss and wife.
- Anna Maria, b. about 1740.
- Maria Barbara, b. on Sept. 25, 1754, and bapt. at CLY on Oct. 6, 1754.
- Johan Jacob, bapt. at WOL in Mar. 1765, and spon. by Jacob and Elisabeth Welsch.

Keener - Abraham received a warrant for 200 acres in Springfield Township on Sept. 23, 1762. He was taxed in 1762.

Kenler - Jacob was taxed in 1762.

Kersh (Kerst) - Jacob was taxed in 1762. He received a warrant for 50 acres in Springfield Township on May 31, 1762, that was surveyed as 100.52 acres called *Long Hill* on Jan. 17, 1767. He received a warrant for 40 acres on Feb. 12, 1769, that was surveyed as 40 acres called *Cherry Hill* on Mar. 25, 1786. He received a warrant for 50 acres in Codorus, Shrewsbury and Springfield Township on Mar. 28, 1774, that was surveyed as 43.156 acres called *Stony Batter* on Apr. 13, 1774. He may be the Jacob Kerth that m. Christina, and the following dau.:

SHREWSBURY TOWNSHIP 317

- Anna Maria, bapt. by RJL on June 14, 1761, and spon. by Ludwig and Anna Maria Weldner.

Kleinfelter - Hans Peter was b. to Hans Jorg and Margaretha (Rheinhardt) Kleinfelter, in Floersbach, Hesse Preussen, Germany, in 1702. He m. Eva Elisabetha Kunckel. She was b. in 1703, and d. in Berks Co., PA, sometime after 1754. Peter and his family arrived at Philadelphia in the ship *Duke of Bedford* on Sept. 14, 1751. The family settled in the Allemangel region of Berks Co., PA. No record has been found for Peter after his date of arrival in PA. Peter and Elisabetha had the following children in Florsbach, Hessen, Germany:
- Johan Georg, b. in 1725. He m. Anna Barbara, dau. of Antony and Maria Barbara Keller (see entry in Dover section), in York Co., PA, on Oct. 16, 1755. Georg Kleinfelter was paid for service during the Revolutionary War, and was a member of the 5th Class of inhabitants of Shrewsbury Township in 1780. He received a warrant for 50 acres on Feb. 12, 1767, that was surveyed as 43.35 acres called *Flower Garden* on June 19, 1767. He also received a warrant for 50 acres, adjacent to David Schaffer on June 1, 1762, that was surveyed as 29.19 acres called *Deer Valley* on June 19, 1767. He was a farmer in Shrewsbury Township, and d. there in June 1794. His will was written on Feb. 5, 1793, and probated on June 19, 1794. Anna Barbara d. sometime after 1794. They had the following children in Shrewsbury Township:
- Peter, b. in 1755. He m. Elizabeth. She was b. in York Co., Shrewsbury Township, PA, on Nov. 2, 1754, and d. there in 1842. Peter served in the Revolutionary War as a Private in the 5th (Capt. John Ehrman's) Company, 7th Battalion, York County Militia in 1778, and in the 5th (Capt. Henry Ferree's) Company, 5th Battalion, in 1779/80. He was fined for failure to perform his tour of Military duty within the period. He was a farmer in Shrewsbury Township, and d. there on Sept. 28, 1796.
- Georg, b. in 1758, d. in 1830, and m. Katherine. She was b. in 1767, and d. in 1831.
- Elizabeth, bapt. by Reverend Jacob Lischy on Feb. 15, 1761, and spon. by her uncle, Abraham Keller and Elisabeth Schneider. She m. Johan Adam Schaffer (possibly a son of David Schaffer see entry) about 1782. On Dec. 28, 1782, he served as a Private in Captain Henry Ferree's Company, 5th Battalion, York County Militia (from Shrewsbury Township). On Apr. 18, 1787, he received 113.25 acres in Shrewsbury Township from George and Barbara Kleinfelter, and on Nov. 24, 1787, received 25 acres in Shrewsbury Township from David Schaffer. On Jan. 3, 1791, Adam received 34.25 acres from Rudolph Spangler, and on June 20, 1794, Adam and Elizabeth signed a release of land Elizabeth

inherited from her father to Peter Kleinfelter. On Apr. 1, 1801, Adam and Elizabeth deeded the land they bought from Georg Kleinfelter in 1787, and a tract called *Fort Hill* to Jacob Koller.
- Melchior, b. in 1728. He m. Catharina Gernant. He resided in Berks Co., Maiden Creek Township in 1752, and had the following children:
  - Elisabetha, b. on Sept. 11, 1754, bapt. at Moselem Union on Oct. 8, 1754, and spon. by her uncle and aunt, Gottleib and Elisabetha Volk.
  - Eva, b. in 1758, and m. Georg Philip Eisenhauer in Berks Co., Stouchburg Township, PA, on Aug. 29, 1779. He was b. at Bethel, Lebanon Co., PA, to Johannes Eisenhauer on Dec. 19, 1754. He was bapt. on Jan. 13, 1755, and spon. by Georg Philip Schatterle.
- Eva Elisabetha, b. in 1732, and m. Johan Gottlieb Volk, and Jacob Baehli (see entry).
- Johannes Michael, b. on June 10, 1736. He m. Appolonia about 1760, and Maria Elisabeth about 1785. Appolonia d. sometime between 1780 and 1785 in York Co., Shrewsbury Township, PA. Maria Elisabeth was b. on June 15, 1760, and d. in Shrewsbury Township on Apr. 3, 1832. Michael served in the Revolutionary War as a Private in the 2nd (Capt. Aquilla Wiley's) Company, 5th Battalion, York County Militia. He received a warrant for 190 acres on Feb. 26, 1773, and 10 acres on Sept. 13, 1789, that was surveyed as 219.80 acres called *Vineyard* on Nov. 7, 1776. Michael was a farmer in Shrewsbury Township, and d. there on July 17, 1807. Michael was the father of the following children, b. in Shrewsbury Township:
  - Anna Barbara, b. in May 1761. She was bapt. on May 31, 1761 by Reverend Jacob Lischy, and spon. by her uncle and aunt, Georg and Anna Barbara Kleinfelter. She m. Johannes Kunckel.
  - Johannes, b. about 1763. He m. Margareta, dau. of Balthasar and Maria Elisabetha (Schaffer) Koller, about 1793.
  - Elisabeth Christina, b. on Jan. 13, 1765. She was bapt. at St. Jacob's on Mar. 3, 1770, and spon. by the widow, Christine Gerberich. She m. Johan Heinrich Kunckel. He was b. in 1751, and d. in 1827. She d. in 1815. Elisabeth Christina d. about Nov. 1832.
  - Eva Elisabetha, b. on Nov. 21, 1766. She was bapt. at St. Jacob's on Dec. 13, 1766, and spon. by her uncle and aunt, Jacob and Eva Elisabetha Baehli. She m. Johannes, son of Joseph and Elizabeth Seitz. Eva Elisabetha d. in Indiana Co., PA, in Nov. 1832.
  - Catherina, b. on Nov. 13, 1768. She was bapt. at St. Jacob's on Dec. 12, 1768, and spon. by Michael Kintzler and Catherine

Hohman. She d. in Sept. 1807. She m. Georg Jacob, son of Christian and Anna Stabler. He was b. on Dec. 26, 1768, and d. in 1830.
- Johannes Michael, b. on Feb. 20, 1770. He was bapt. at St. Jacob's on Mar. 27, 1770, and spon. by Peter and Anna Margaret Gerberich. He m. Barbara about 1789, and Maria Magdalena Garman the First Reformed Church of York on Mar. 27, 1796. Michael was High Sheriff of York Co., from 1808 to 1811, and kept a public house in Baltimore for a number of years. Barbara d. in York Co., Hopewell/Shrewsbury Township, PA, in 1796, and Michael d. in Baltimore Co., MD, on Sept. 20, 1850.
- Jacob, b. in 1772, and m. ___ Schaffer in York Co., York, PA, on Jan. 27, 1801.
- Margaret, b. in 1774. She m. Jacob Markey, and d. in 1809.
- Jean, b. about 1780, and d. sometime before 1832. She m. Frederick Grove. Some of her children resided in York Co., and some in Union Co., PA.
- Joseph, b. on June 15, 1786, and d. in Shrewsbury Township on Oct. 22, 1837. He m. Margaret Albright (Aug. 5, 1783-Oct. 28, 1877). Joseph d. on Oct. 22, 1837. They are bur. in the Evangelical Cemetery in Shrewsbury.
- Peter, b. in 1789. He m. Anna Maria Fisher, and d. in Shrewsbury/Codorus Township in 1830.
- Benjamin, b. in 1789, and d. in Shrewsbury Township on Aug. 14, 1849. He m. Christina Resinger in York Co., Hanover, PA, on Mar. 29, 1812.
- Johan Georg, b. on Aug. 11, 1790, and bapt. at Fissel's on Sept. 19, 1790, spon. by Joh. and Margaretha Gerberich. He d. in Shrewsbury Township in 1862, and m. Anna Marie Doudel.
- Susanna, b. about 1793, and m. Adam Baker.
- Adam, b. on Apr. 4, 1796. He m. Sarah/Maria Susanna, dau. of Jacob and Catherine (Dinkel) Doudel, in Adams Co., Gettysburg, PA, on June 1, 1819. He d. in Shrewsbury Township on May 1, 1871. Sarah/Maria Susanna was b. on Oct. 18, 1794, and d. on Nov. 30, 1867.
- Henry, b. about 1791. He m. Susan Reisinger at York Co., York, PA, on Nov. 22, 1812. He d. in Shrewsbury Township on Nov. 22, 1822.
- Daniel, b. in 1799, and d. in Shrewsbury Township on June 24, 1825. He owned two acres in Shrewsbury Township.
- Johannes, b. on Apr. 23, 1737. He m. Anna Margaretha, dau. of Hans Michael Gerberich. She was b. on Mar. 29, 1738, and d. in Shrewsbury Township on Mar. 16, 1813. Johannes was a Private in the 3rd (Captain John Miller's) Company, 7th Battalion, York County Militia in 1778, and the 2nd (Captain Aquilla Wiley's)

Company, 5th Battalion, York County Militia in 1779/80. He received a warrant for 100 acres on Apr. 30, 1765, that was surveyed as 131.85 acres called *Merry Mount/Fellowship* on Jan. 20, 1767 (patented as 111 acres on Apr. 26, 1785). He also received a warrant for 100 acres on Feb. 12, 1767, that was surveyed as 80.15 acres called *Black Oak Hill* and 44.66 acres called *Miller's Neighbor* on Apr. 30, 1790 (the 80.15 acre tract was patented on July 19, 1792). He farmed 300 acres in Shrewsbury Township. Later in their lives, Johannes and Margaretha moved in with their son, and during their stay, Reverend Jacob Albright was welcomed into the home. Jacob Albright founded the Evangelical sect, and the Kleinfelter home became one of the earliest and most notable places for assembly in Shrewsbury Township. Johannes and Margaret had attended St. Jacob's until 1771, when they began attending Fissel's, which Johannes had helped to build. After 1810, Johannes and Margaretha left the Fissel's congregation, and attended Reverend Albright's services. The Evangelical sect was frowned upon by Lutheran and Reformed congregations, and in 1813, when Margaretha d., Johannes sought to bury her in Fissel's cemetery, with other family members, but the church council refused him on religious grounds. Johannes made a plot for Margaretha on the farm of their son, and it eventually became the first Evangelical cemetery in York Co. He d. in Shrewsbury Township, one mile south of Glen Rock, PA, on Oct. 1, 1821, and is bur. the Kleinfelter burial ground, with his wife. They had the following children in Shrewsbury Township:

- Johann Jacob, b. on Aug. 4, 1767. He was bapt. at St. Jacob's on Aug. 16, 1767, and spon. by his uncle and aunt, Jacob and Eva Elisabetha Baehli. He m. Julianna, dau. of Johannes, and Helena Ruhl, in York Co., PA, in 1790. She was bapt. at St. Jacob's on Jan. 19, 1772, and spon. by Theobald Schneider and her cousin, Juliana Gans. Jacob d. in Shrewsbury Township on Apr. 30, 1830, and is bur. in the Kleinfelter burial ground. Juliana d. in Marion Co., Marion, OH, at the home of her son Jacob on Apr. 10, 1843, and is bur. in Pleasant cemetery.
- Anna Elisabetha, b. on Sept. 14, 1769, bapt. at St. Jacob's on Oct. 3, 1769, and spon. by John Koller and Elizabeth Gerberich.
- Adam, b. about 1771. He m. Maria Magdalena. He d. in Hopewell/Shrewsbury Township on Sept. 17, 1816.
- Joseph, b. about 1773.
- Lorentz, b. on Jan. 27, 1738/39. He m. Maria Margaretta, dau. of Johan Michael and Catharina (Rein) Geisselman, about 1766, and Susanna, dau. of Adam and Maria Heindel about 1780. Maria Margaretta was b. on Nov. 8, 1743, and bapt. at Christ's Lutheran on Jan. 3, 1743/44. Lorentz served in the Revolutionary War as a

Private in the 3rd (Capt. John Miller's) Company, 7th Battalion, York County Militia in 1778, and the 2nd (Capt. Aquilla Wiley's) Company, 5th Battalion, in 1779/80. He was a member of the 2nd Class of inhabitants of Shrewsbury Township in 1780. He received a warrant for 50 acres on Sept. 27, 1790, that was surveyed as 39.70 acres called *Blue Stone* on Apr. 2, 1791. He received a warrant for 50 acres on Sept. 27, 1790, that was surveyed (in two tracts) as 7.140 acres on Apr. 2, 1791. Lorentz d. in Shrewsbury Township on Jan. 27, 1830. He had the following children in Shrewsbury Township:
- Johannes, b. on Nov. 10, 1767. He was bapt. on Dec. 6, 1767, and spon. by his uncle and aunt, Johannes and Margaretha Kleinfelter. He m. Catherina. He d. in Shrewsbury Township in 1792.
- Jacob, b. on July 3, 1771. He m. Catherine, dau. of George Lutz. Jacob d. in Marion Co., OH, on Mar. 1, 1840. Catherine was b. on Aug. 9, 1780, and d. on Jan. 16, 1844.
- Maria, b. in 1781, and d. in Shrewsbury Township in 1810.
- Lorentz, b. on Jan. 10, 1784, bapt. at Fissel's on Jan. 17, 1784, and spon. by his uncle and aunt, Jacob and Eva Baehli.
- Susanna, b. on Feb. 20, 1788, bapt. at Fissel's on Mar. 20, 1788, and spon. by Wentel and Elisabeth Heuss.
- Christina, b. on June 21, 1790, bapt. at Fissel's on July 11, 1790, and spon. by Adam and Catharina.

Klick - John received a warrant for 50 acres on July 20, 1773, that was surveyed as 49.80 acres called *Addition* on Oct. 25, 1773.

Koller - Balthasar received a warrant for 25 acres on Aug. 27, 1772. He received a warrant for 50 acres on May 26, 1788, that was surveyed as 27.9 acres called *Blue Hill* on Dec. 13, 1788. He received a warrant for 50 acres on May 13, 1788, that was surveyed as 32.120 acres called *Green Bank* on Dec. 13, 1788. He received a warrant for 50 acres on Mar. 7, 1785, that was surveyed as 69.140 acres called *Cheapside* on Oct. 18, 1786. He received a warrant for 200 acres on Mar. 27, 1769, that was surveyed as 139.35 acres called *Hungry Hill* on Sept. 15, 1769. He m. Maria Elisabeth, dau. of David Schaffer (see entry). Baltzer was a tailor, received a farm in Shrewsbury Township from David Schaffer on Nov. 27, 1762. His probate inventory was filed in Shrewsbury Township in 1797. Baltzer and Maria Elisabeth resided in Shrewsbury Township, and had the following children:
- Johannes, b. on Aug. 25, 1763, bapt. at Friedensaal on the 19th Sunday after Trinity, and spon. by Lorentz and Margareta Kleinfelter. He m. Maria Elisabeth, dau. of Peter Gerberich (see

entry in Codorus section), about 1776. His probate inventory was filed in Shrewsbury Township in 1815.
- Johan Jacob, b. about 1764. He m. Anna Catharina Miller sometime before 1779, and Barbara about 1797. Jacob's heirs gave a release to their attorney on Nov. 24, 1845. His probate inventory was filed in Shrewsbury Township in 1832.
- Johann Georg, b. on Oct. 7, 1766, bapt. at Friedensaal on Nov. 9, 1766, and spon. by Georg and Anna Barbara Kleinfelter.
- Dau., b. about 1769, and m. Henry Rieman.
- Margareta, b. about 1772. She m. Johannes, son of Johannes Adam and Appolonia Kleinfelter (see entry), about 1773. He was b. in Shrewsbury Township about 1763.
- Adam, b. about 1775.

Korbman - P. Conrad had is probate inventory filed in Shrewsbury Township in 1785. He received a warrant for 150 acres in Springfield Township on Mar. 30, 1767, that was surveyed as 171.80 acres called *Kurfman Heim* on Oct. 19, 1774. Philip Heinrich Korpman, Anna Margaretha Korpman, and P. Conrad Korpman were sponsors to the baptism of Philip Heinrich Schwerth at FRI in 1771. Peter and Salome Corpman were sponsors at the baptism of Salome Alt at FRI in 1766. Maria Margaretha Korpman and P. Conrad Korpman were sponsors at the baptism of Maria Margaretha Geisselman at FRI in 1772. Maria Salome Korpman was a sponsor to the baptism of Anna Barbara Uller at FRI in 1767. Conrad and his wife, Catharina, were sponsors to the baptism of Barbara Geisselman at FRI in 1777. Conrad m. Anna Margaretha before 1742, and Catharina between 1773 and 1776. Conrad had the following children:
- Daniel, b. about 1742. He was taxed in 1762. He received a warrant for 150 acres in Springfield Township on Mar. 20, 1767, that was surveyed as 132.12 acres called *Beas Hallow* on Mar. 22, 1768. He m. Catharina, and had the following children:
  - Johannes, b. on July 20, 1771, bapt. on Aug. 4, 1771, and spon. by Johannes and Mar. Kleinfelter (FRI).
  - Anna Rebecka, b. on June 2, bapt. at FIS on Aug. 13, 1787, and spon. by Michael and Rebecka Kunssler.
- Peter, b. about 1744, and m. Maria Elisabeth about 1770 and Margaretha about 1776. Peter had the following children:
  - Anna Margaretha, b. in June 1771, bapt. at FRI on July 7, 1771, and spon. by Johan Adam and Anna Margaretha Lucas.
  - Johan Heinrich, b. on Apr. 6, 1777, and bapt. at STJ on May 8, 1777.
- Maria Salome, b. about 1746, and m. Jogan Georg, son of Michael Geisselman (see entry).
- Samuel, b. about 1748, m. Catharina, and had the following son:

- Johan Adam, bapt. at FRI on Mar. 13, 1770, and spon. by Adam and Susanna Alt.
- Philip Heinrich, b. about 1750, and m. Catharina. His will was written in York Borough on July 25, 1808, and probated on Apr. 14, 1809. They had the following children:
  - Rosina, b. about 1772, and m. John, son of Michael Geisselman (see entry), about 1793.
  - George.
  - Michael.
  - Catherine, m. Nicholas Welt.
  - Eve, m. George Metzgar.
  - Johannes, b. on Feb. 8, 1780, bapt. at FRI in Feb. 1780, and spon. by Carl and Christina Diehl.
  - Henry, b. on Mar. 21, 1783, and bapt. at CLY on May 23, 1783 (not mentioned in will).
- Jacob, b. about 1752, and m. Susanna, and had the following children recorded at FRI:
  - infant, b. in Dec. 1775, bapt. on Mar. 11, 1776, and spon. by Georg and Maria Salome Geisselman.
  - Anna Elisabeth, b. on Mar. 31, 1777, bapt. on Apr. 13, 1777, and spon. by Georg and Anna Elisabeth Schwerdt.
  - Eva, b. on July 22, 1783, bapt. at STP on Aug. 17, 1785, and spon. by Andreas and Eva Schetler.
  - Maria Magdalena, b. on July 25, 1785, bapt. at STP on Aug. 17, 1785, and spon. by Abraham and Magdalena Reber.

Kroll - Johan Christian was b. in Ringeshahn in the principality of Waldeck in 1707, and immigrated to America on the ship *Mortonhouse*, on Aug. 19, 1729. He received a warrant for 100 acres on Oct. 8, 1751, that was surveyed as 121.18 acres on Apr. 25, 1793. He also received a warrant for 100 acres with George Swope on June 1, 1762, that was surveyed as 102 acres. He was naturalized on Apr. 10/12, 1744. He d. of hectic fever and diarrhoea on Aug. 20, 1758 (bur. at CLY on Aug. 21, 1758), and his will was probated on Aug. 22, 1758. He m. Maria Elisabeth, dau. of Henry and Anna Maria (Resser) Kuerchner, in PA. They had the following children:
- Johan Philip, b. on Sept. 8, 1734, and bapt. at CLY on Feb. 23, 1735. He m. Maria Eva, and had the following children:
  - Christian, b. on Feb. 2, 1758, and bapt. at CLY on Mar. 26, 1758.
  - John, b. on Oct. 2, 1759, and bapt. at CLY on Nov. 11, 1759. He d. on Aug. 25, 1760, and was bur. at CLY on Aug. 26, 1760.
  - Johan Michael, b. on Jan. 23, 1762, and bapt. at CLY on July 7, 1762.
  - Johan Henrich, b. on Dec. 2, 1763, and bapt. at CLY on Mar. 11, 1764.

- Anna Maria, b. on Mar. 23, 1767, and bapt. at CLY on June 7, 1767.
- Johan Michael, b. on Feb. 9, 1738, and bapt. at CLY on Apr. 22, 1738.
- Johan, b. on July 31, 1740, and bapt. at CLY on Aug. 20, 1741. His will was written in Manchester Township on June 2, 1783, and probated on July 14, 1783. He m. Maria Clara, dau. of Martin and Susanna Stricker/Struecker, and had the following children:
  - John, b. on Aug. 19, 1767, and bapt. at CLY on Sept. 20, 1767.
  - Daniel, m. Catharine before 1791.
  - Magdalena, m. Frederick Hubly.
  - Susanna, b. on June 11, 1772, and bapt. at CLY on July 25, 1772.
- Maria Magdalena, b. on Mar. 9, 1743, and bapt. at CLY on Mar. 13, 1743.
- Maria Elisabeth, b. on Jan. 22, 1746, and bapt. at CLY on Feb. 9, 1746.
- Johan Henrich, b. on July 23, 1748, bapt. at CLY on July 31, 1748, and d. on Aug. 29, 1749. He was bur. at CLY on Aug. 31, 1749.
- Johan Heinrich, b. on Feb. 26, 1751, and bapt. at CLY on Mar. 17, 1751.

Lau - Philip received a warrant for a 25 acre tract on Sept. 2, 1745; 40 acre tract on Oct. 9, 1750; and a 50 acre tract on Apr. 4, 1751, that were surveyed as 78.129 acres called *Trout Pruna* on June 1, 1775. He also received a warrant for 25 acres on Sept. 2, 1745, and a 30 acre tract on Dec. 18, 1751, that was surveyed as 44 acres called *Rysocker* on June 1, 1775. He received a warrant for 60 acres in Codorus and Shrewsbury Township on Apr. 10, 1750, and 40 acres in the same on Oct. 9, 1750, that was surveyed as 69.71 acres called *Stainbaugh* on May 29, 1775 and 10.10 acres on June 1, 1775. He received a warrant for 60 acres in Codorus, Shrewsbury and Springfield Township on Sept. 10, 1750 (See entry in Manchester section).

Lauderman - Peter received a warrant for 45 acres in Codorus, Shrewsbury and Springfield Township on Mar. 10, 1775, that was surveyed as 29.64 acres called *Strawberry Hill* on May 15, 1791.

Leiss - Peter was taxed in 1762. He received a warrant for 200 acres in Springfield Township on Mar. 13, 1767, that was surveyed as 181.135 acres called *Cherry Garden* on June 23, 1767. He m. Elisabetha.

Lucas - Johan Adam was taxed in 1762. He m. Margaretha Heidel/Heydl, and had the following children:

SHREWSBURY TOWNSHIP

- Maria Elisabeth, b. on Nov. 9, 1751, and bapt. on Nov. 25, 1751, and spon. by Daniel Dieb and wife.
- Johan Jacob, b. on Sept. 18, 1765, bapt. at FRI on the 1st Sunday after Advent, and spon. by Jacob and Maria Magdalena Ness.
- Anna Christina, b. on Aug. 24, 1767, and bapt. at FRI on Sept. 13, 1767.
- Adam m. Catarina about 1789.

Lutz - Conrad was taxed in 1762. He m. Anna Maria Laub. They had the following children:
- Johan Jacob, b. on July 20, 1763, bapt. at FRI on Aug. 7, 1763, and spon. by Johan Jacob Kraft and Appollonia Hof.
- Johan Michael, b. on Feb. 15, 1766, bapt. on Good Friday, and spon. by Nicholas and Magdalena Schuster.

Michael - Heinrich was taxed in 1762. He m. Apolonica about 1752, and Christina Karges at CAN on Jan. 6, 1756. Heinrich had the following children:
- Johan Heinrich, bapt. by RJL on Sept. 30, 1753, and spon. by Michael and Anna Catharina Konig.

Merckel - Hans Martin, son of Hans Martin Merckel of Lampersloch, m. Maria Eva, dau. of Leonhardt Gack of Reimerswiller, Northern Alsace, in Feb. 1728. They immigrated to America on the ship *Peggy*, in 1754, and settled in York Co., Shrewsbury Township, PA. His land was referred to in a deed in 1760, but he does not appear in the tax list of 1762. Maria Eva d. in 1738. Martin and Maria Eva had the following children (recorded at Preuschdorf Lutheran Church in Northern Alsace (see BNA)):
- Maria Margaretha, b. on Nov. 23, 1728.
- Johan Heinrich, b. on Oct. 5, 1732, and bapt. on Oct. 8, 1732. He m. Juliana Shafftler. They had the following children (recorded at FRI):
  - Johann Georg, b. on June 28, 1763, bapt. on July 17, 1763, and spon. by Georg and Catharina Amspacher.
  - Michael, b. on Aug. 16, 1764, bapt. on the 12th Sunday after Trinity, and spon. by Michael Meyer and Georg Hamspacher.
  - Johann Heinrich, b. on Aug. 16, 1764, bapt. on the 12th Sunday after Trinity, and spon. by Michael Meyer and Georg Hamspacher.
  - Johann Martin, b. in Oct. 1766, bapt. on Nov. 9, 1766, and spon. by Jacob and Dorothea Kraft.
  - Johann Heinrich, b. on Jan. 12, 1772, bapt. on Jan. 26, 1772, and spon. by Heinrich Wilhelm and wife.

- Maria Catharina, b. on Mar. 1, 1778, bapt. on Mar. 27, 1778, and spon. by Georg and Catharina Amspacher.
- Margaretha, b. on Apr. 19, 1780, bapt. on June 4, 1780, and spon. by Michael and Margaretha Gerberich.
- Maria Barbara, b. on Apr. 27, 1736, and d. in 1738.
- Catharina, b. on Apr. 3, 1738. She m. Johan Georg Amspacher (see Codorus section).

Meckle (Meckel) - Christian received a warrant for 100 acres in Springfield Township on May 13, 1768, that was surveyed as 47.80 acres called *Swines Range* on July 27, 1768. His probate inventory was filed in Codorus Township in 1800. He m. Maria Catharina. Her will was written in Codorus Township on Oct. 5, 1806, and probated on Jan. 1, 1807. They had the following children:
- John.
- Christian.
- Jacob.
- Henry.
- Maria Catharina, b. on Oct. 16, 1774, bapt. at FRI on Nov. 27, 1774, and spon. by Michael and Maria Catharina Hengst. She m. John Binder.
- Georg, b. on Sept. 21, 1776, bapt. at FRI on Nov. 10, 1776, and spon. by Georg and Anna Elisabeth Eissenhard.
- Elizabeth, b. on Oct. 29, 1778, bapt. at FRI, and spon. by Elisabeth Bauman. She m. John Rudisil.
- Johann Michael, b. in Mar. 1781, bapt. at FRI on Apr. 15, 1781, and spon. by Michael Hengst.
- Maria Eva, b. in June 1783, bapt. at FRI in July, and spon. by Maria Catharina, wife of Michael Hengst. She was not listed in the will.
- Margaretha, b. on Aug. 19, 1785, bapt. at FRI on Oct. 16, 1785, and spon. by Margaretha, dau. of Michael Hengst. She was not listed in the will.
- Barbara.
- Anna, m. Jacob Stambach.

Mayer (Maeiger) - George received a warrant for 25 acres on Oct. 26, 1772, that was surveyed as 26.146 acres called *Pleasant Side* on Nov. 16, 1772.

Mayer (Maugher) - Michael received a warrant for 200 acres on June 25, 1768, that was surveyed as 32.5 acres on Sept. 29, 1789. He received a warrant for 200 acres on June 25, 1768. He received a warrant for 200 acres on June 23, 1768 (see entry in Codorus section).

Meyer - Henry received a warrant for 25 acres in Springfield, Hopewell and York Township on Mar. 29, 1756, that was surveyed as 63.29 acres on Sept. 17, 1756 (see entry in Codorus section).

Meyer - Christian was taxed in 1762 (see entry in Codorus section). He received a warrant for 50 acres in Springfield Township on Jan. 14, 1767, that was surveyed as 30.96 acres called *Frosty Valley* on Oct. 23, 1767. He received a warrant for 100 acres in Springfield Township on Aug. 10, 1768, that was surveyed as 177.111 acres called *Turkey Hill* on Oct. 5, 1768. He received a warrant for 100 acres in Springfield Township on Jan. 14, 1767, that was surveyed as 74.73 acres called *Long Hill* on Oct. 23, 1767. He received a warrant for 100 acres in Springfield Township on Jan. 16, 1746, that was surveyed as 135.80 acres on Jan. 4, 1754 and 106.85 acres called *Cold Bottom* on Aug. 8, 1766. He received a warrant for 25 acres in Springfield Township on Sept. 15, 1773, that was surveyed as 45 acres on Mar. 23, 1787. He received a warrant for 100 acres in Springfield Township on Sept. 23, 1762, that was surveyed as 98 acres called *Well Timbered* on Aug. 9, 1766.

Miller - Georg Adam received a warrant for 50 acres in Springfield and Hopewell Township on Oct. 31, 1771, that was surveyed as 55.49 acres called *Black Run* on Jan. 15, 1772.

Miller - Peter received a warrant for 400 acres in Shrewsbury and Hopewell Township on Nov. 27, 1762. He received a warrant for 400 acres in Shrewsbury and Hopewell Township on Nov. 27, 1762. He received a warrant for 200 acres on Nov. 27, 1762.

Moyer - John received a warrant for 100 acres in Springfield and York Township on Jan. 16, 1746, that was surveyed as 265 acres on Nov. 27, 1751.

Muller - Johan Herman received a warrant for 150 acres in Springfield Township on Feb. 20, 1767, that was surveyed as 138.80 acres called *Miller's Hills* on Feb. 6, 1775. His will was written in Windsor Township on July 22, 1783, and probated on Oct. 22, 1783. He m. Catharina, and had the following children:
- Michael, b. about 1735. He was the co-exec. of Tobias Muller's will in 1796.
- Tobias, b. about 1737. He was taxed in 1762. He received a warrant for 150 acres in Springfield Township on Nov. 3, 1768, that was surveyed on Apr. 21, 1769. He received a warrant for 150 acres in Springfield Township on Oct. 27, 1768, that was surveyed as 34.18 acres called *Little Swamp* on Apr. 21, 1769. His will was

written in Shrewsbury Township on May 19, 1795, and probated on Mar. 15, 1796. He m. Catharina Elisabeth Eisenhauer. They had the following children:
- Anna Catharina, b. on Dec. 24, 1758, and bapt. at CLY on Apr. 15, 1759. She m. Anthony Frey.
- Heinrich, b. about 1760, and m. Sophia about 1779.
- Elizabeth, b. about 1762, and m. Jacob Mier.
- Eva Catharina, b. on May 22, 1766, bapt. at FRI on July 6, 1766, and spon. by Wilhelm and Catharina Ehrhard. She m. Christian, son of Nicholas Heinrich (see entry).
- Susanna, b. on Sept. 18, 1768, bapt. at FRI, and spon. by Wilhelm and Catharina. She was not mentioned in the will.
- Sabina, b. on Sept. 4, 1770, bapt. at BLY on Oct. 4, 1770, and spon. by Herman Muller and wife. She was not mentioned in the will.
- Maria, b. about 1772.
- Johan Herman, b. on July 12, 1774, bapt. at BLY on Aug. 7, 1774, and spon. by Johan Herman Muller. He was not mentioned in the will.
- Christina, b. on May 28, 1777, bapt. on June 20, 1777, and spon. by Abraham and Elisabetha Schneider.
- Tobias, b. about 1779 (mentioned as youngest son in will).
- Frederick, b. about 1739. He m. Catharina. His will was written in Shrewsbury Township on July 30, 1802, and probated on Mar. 22, 1803. Frederick and Catharina had the following children:
  - Magdalena.
  - Elisabeth.
  - Christian, m. Chaterina before 1791.
  - Frederick.
  - Anna Maria, m. Jacob, son of Solomon Nunemacher (see entry), before 1790.
  - Catharina, m. Sal Bossert.
- Johannes Herman, b. about 1741, and m. Barbara. His will was written in Hopewell Township on Mar. 5, 1816, and probated on Feb. 21, 1817. They had the following children:
  - Maria Magdalena, b. on Jan. 3, 1767, bapt. at TLY on Apr. 12, 1767, and spon. by Heinrich Gerlach and wife.
  - Johan Henrich, b. on Feb. 20, 1768, bapt. at TLY on Apr. 4, 1768, and spon. by Johann Heinrich Gerlach and wife.
  - Herman, b. on Jan. 5, 1770, bapt. at BLY on Apr. 10, 1770, and spon. by his parents.
  - Susanna, b. on Sept. 21, 1771, bapt. at BLY on Jan. 26, 1772, and spon. by Mathias and Margaretha Streher. She was not mentioned in the will.

SHREWSBURY TOWNSHIP

- Elizabeth, b. on Dec. 28, 1775, bapt. at TLY on July 21. 1776, and spon. by Abraham Schneider and wife. She was not mentioned in the will.
- Regina, b. on Feb. 5, 1782, bapt. at BLY on May 31, 1782, and spon. by Abraham and Elisabeth Schneider.
- Johannes Herman, b. on Mar. 18, 1786, bapt. at TLY on June 9, 1786, and spon. by Conrad and Dorothea Miller.
- Johan Jacob, b. on Aug. 26, 1788, bapt. at FRI, and spon. by Tobias and Catharina Muller.
- Simeon, b. about 1748.
- Christian, b. about 1750.
- Johan Conrad, b. on Oct. 21, 1752, and bapt. at CLY on Dec. 3, 1752. He m. Maria Dorothea, dau. of Philip Grimm (see entry), at TLY on Dec. 25, 1780.

Muller - Wilhelm received a warrant for 50 acres in Springfield Township on Dec. 18, 1766. He m. Elisabeth, and had the following children:
- Wilhelm, b. on Sept. 27, 1769, bapt. at BLY on Nov. 12, 1769, and spon. by Wilhelm Kuge, P. Conrad, Maria Andres, and P. Gohns.
- John, b. on Nov. 24, 1774, bapt. at BLY on Mar. 19, 1775, and spon. by John Wilhelm.

Muller - Johannes received a warrant for 200 acres in Springfield Township on June 15, 1768, that was surveyed as 254.136 acres called *Stony Run* on Mar. 9, 1769 (improved 10 years). He m. Elisabetha, dau. of Michael Meyer (see entry in Codorus section), and had the following children (recorded at FRI):
- Johann Heinrich, b. on Oct. 7, 1765, bapt. at FRI on the 23rd Sunday after Trinity, and spon. by Heinrich and Magdalena Ness.
- Johann Michael, b. on Oct. 1, 1772, bapt. on Oct. 25, 1772, and spon. by Michael and Elisabeth Maier.
- Johannes, b. on June 9, 1774, bapt. on July 10, 1774, and spon. by Thomas and Rosina Ehrhardt.
- Elisabeth, b. on Feb. 26, 1776, bapt. on Apr. 8, 1776, and spon. by Christian and Elisabeth Kraus.
- Maria Catharina, b. on Apr. 19, 1778, bapt. at FRI on May 10, 1778, and spon. by Catharin, dau. of Jacob Beck.
- Johann Michael, b. on Feb. 21, 1780, bapt. on Mar. 26, 1780, and spon. by Michael, son of Michael Meyer.
- Jacob, b. on Dec. 21, 1782, bapt. on Dec. 29, 1782, and spon. by Jacob and Eva Lorch.
- Johann Peter, b. on Apr. 28, 1785, bapt. on May 15, 1785, and spon. by John and Rosina Frie.

Mueller - Martin was taxed in 1762. He received a warrant for 50 acres on May 23, 1748, and a warrant for 200 acres on Oct. 28, 1746, that was surveyed as 312 acres called *Martin's Choice* on Jan. 2, 1789. He m. Margaretha Barbara. They had the following children:
- Maria Salome, b. on Sept. 25, 1752, and bapt. at CLY on Dec. 3, 1752.
- Martin (probably), b. about 1743. His will was written in Shrewsbury Township on Mar. 4, 1790, and probated on May 22, 1790. He m. Anna Helena. They had the following children:
  - Anna Maria, bapt. by RJL on Apr. 22, 1764, and spon. by Conrad and Catharina Muller.
  - Eva, bapt. by RJL on Dec. 29, 1765, and spon. by Heinrich and Eva Brodbeck (mother is Veronica?).
  - Anna Barbara, b. on Mar. 20, 1767, and bapt. at STJ on Mar. 26, 1767.
  - Heinrich, b. on Feb. 20, 1769, and bapt. at STJ on June 4, 1769.
  - Catharina.
  - Margaretha.
  - Martin.
  - Elisabeth.

Musser - John received a warrant for 40 acres in Springfield Township on Mar. 4, 1771, that was surveyed as 45.80 acres called *Foul Play* on Apr. 18, 1771.

Ness - Matthias (b. in 1673) was citizen, smith, and Gerichtsschoffen at Mitschdorff, Northern Alsace. He m. Maria Barbara (b. in 1671), and immigrated to America on the ship *Britannia* in 1731. After Maria Barbara's death, Matthias m. Maria Barbara Hoerdter at Montgomery Co., Skippach, PA, on Nov. 28, 1733. His will was written in Philadelphia (now Montgomery) Co., Salford Township, PA, on Jan. 31, 1741/42. He was naturalized in 1740. They had the following children (see BNA):
- Jacob, b. in 1700.
- Hans Michael, b. in 1701. He m. Anna Dorothea, dau. of Hans Martin Pfeiffer of Preuschdorf at Mitschdorff on Feb. 3, 1728. Michael d. in Bucks Co., PA, before Feb. 22, 1745, when letters of administration were granted to his widow Dorothy. They had the following children:
  - Maria Margaretha, b. on Jan. 11, 1729, bapt. on Jan. 12, 1729, and d. young.
  - Hans Michael, b. on June 12, 1730, and bapt. on July 13, 1730.
- Matthias b. in 1704. He m. Anna Catharina, dau. of the late Hans Martin Motz, former citizen at Lampersloch, Germany, at Preuschdorf, Germany, on Jan. 6, 1722/23. Anna Catharina was b.

SHREWSBURY TOWNSHIP   331

in Lampertscloch on Oct. 20, 1701, and d. before June 1767. His
will was written in Manchester Township on June 30, 1767, and
probated on Sept. 24, 1767. He received a warrant for 50 acres in
Springfield Township on Mar. 18, 1746, that was surveyed as
173.80 acres on Jan. 22, 1754. He received a warrant for 50 acres
on Dec. 3, 1764. They had the following children:
- Maria Magdalena, b. on Dec. 26, 1723, and bapt. on Dec. 29,
  1723.
- Johan Jacob, b. in Mitschdorf on July 25, 1726, bapt. on July 27,
  1726, and spon. by his uncle, Johann Jacob Ness. He m. Maria
  Magdalena, dau. of Johan Martin and Anna Johanna Josi (see
  entry in Manchester section), in York Co., PA, on Nov. 22, 1748.
  He received a warrant for 100 acres in Springfield Township on
  May 25, 1749. He received a warrant for 50 acres in Springfield
  Township on Mar. 19, 1746 and 50 acres on June 1, 1767, that
  was surveyed as 235.48 acres called *Susannah* on Mar. 9, 1768
  (improved 18 years). He d. in Shrewsbury Township about 1782.
  They had the following children:
  - Margaretha, b. on Dec. 31, 1753, and spon. by Michael and
    Margaretha Geiselmann.
  - Michael, b. on Sept. 23, 1755, and spon. by Michael and
    Margaretha Geiselmann.
  - Magdalena, b. on Sept. 20, 1758, and spon. by Michael and
    Margaretha Geiselmann.
  - Wilhelm, b. on July 13, 1761, and spon. by Wilhelm and
    Catharina Ehrhard.
  - Johan Jacob, b. on May 26, 1766, bapt. at FRI on June 15,
    1766, and spon. by Peter and Anna Maria Ness. He m.
    Christina, dau. of Frederick and Anna Maria (Diehl) Fissel,
    about 1795, and d. in Shrewsbury Township in Dec. 1817.
  - Susanna, b. on Apr. 20, 1769, and spon. by Peter and Susanna
    Lau.
  - Johannes, b. on Sept. 30, 1771, bapt. at FRI on Oct. 27, 1771,
    and spon. by Johan Jacob and Maria Dorothea.
- Anna Catharina, b. on Apr. 25, 1729, and bapt. on Apr. 27, 1729.
- Susanna, b. on June (10), 1732, and m. Johan Peter, son of
  Christian Lau (see entry in Manchester section), in Codorus
  Township in 1748.
- Peter, b. about 1738, and m. Anna Maria, dau. of Heinrich
  Walther (see entry), in 1765/66. His probate inventory was filed
  in Shrewsbury Township in 1767. After Peter's death, she m.
  Heinrich Alt (see entry).
- Matthias, b. about 1740, and m. Maria Sophia. They had the
  following children (recorded at STJ):

- Rosina Magdalena, b. on Nov. 12, 1761, and bapt. on Nov. 21, 1761.
- Anna Elisabetha, b. on Mar. 18, 1765, and bapt. on Apr. 14, 1765.
- Veronica, b. on Jan. 16, 1767, and bapt. on Feb. 5, 1767.
- Johan Heinrich, b. on Oct. 23, 1768, and bapt. on Nov. 11, 1768.
- Juliana Salome, b. on Apr. 10, 1775, and bapt. on May 4, 1775.
- Susan, b. about 1742.
- Maria Dorothea, b. about 1744, m. Jacob Kraft, and had the following children:
    - Maria Magdalena, b. on Dec. 23, 1765, bapt. at FRI on Dec. 25, 1765, and spon. by Heinrich and Maria Magdalena Ness.
    - Johan Jacob, b. on Aug. 17, 1767, and bapt. at CLY on Aug. 23, 1767.
    - Maria Eva, b. on Sept. 6, 1769, bapt. at ELC on Oct. 1, 1775, and spon. by Joachim and Sara Leeman.
    - Michael, b. on Nov. 17, 1770, bapt. at FRI, and spon. by Michael Geisselman.
    - Georg, b. on Nov. 17, 1770, bapt. at FRI, and spon. by Johan Georg Geisselman.
    - Anna Maria, b. on Apr. 4, 1773, bapt. at FRI on Apr. 7, 1773, and spon. by Jacob and M. M. Ness.
- Henry, b. about 1746, and received a warrant for 100 acres on Jan. 13, 1768. He m. Maria Magdalena, dau. of Abraham Welschans (see entry), and had the following children:
    - Heinrich, b. on Sept. 2, 1766, bapt. at FRI on Dec. 25, 1766, and spon. by Jacob Welschantz and Anna Maria Williard.
    - Elisabetha, bapt. at FRI on Feb. 3, 1770, and spon. by Johannes and Elisabeth Muller.
    - Juliana, b. on May 15, 1776, and bapt. at CLY on June 16, 1776.
    - Catherine, b. on Nov. 5, 1779, and bapt. at CLY on Dec. 25, 1779.
- Johann, b. in 1705. He resided in Montgomery Co., PA.
- Dewald, b. in 1707. He resided in Montgomery Co., PA.
- Hans Georg, b. in 1710. He m. Anna Maria, dau. of Friederich Eichelberger (see entry in Manchester section), at the Moravian Church at Lancaster on Mar. 13, 1744. He was taxed in Manchester Township in 1762. They had the following children:
    - Maria Barbara, b. on Feb. 10, 1753, bapt. at CLY on Feb. 18, 1753, and spon. by Philip and Anna Maria Mueller.
- Johan Henrich, b. about 1734. He resided in Montgomery Co., PA.
- Johan Ulrich, b. about 1736. He resided in Montgomery Co., PA.

Neff - Henry was taxed in 1762, received a warrant for 30 acres in Codorus Township on May 28, 1775. He also received a warrant for 50 acres on Jan. 14, 1767, that was surveyed as 31.147 acres called *Pilgrim's Abode* on Apr. 17, 1767. His will was written in Codorus Township on Apr. 4, 1790, and probated on June 4, 1792. He m. Anna/Hanna, and Catharina after 1764. He had the following children:
- Henry.
- Mary.
- Anna Susanna, bapt. by RJL on Jan. 1, 1759, and spon. by Johannes and Anna Eberly.
- Magdalena.
- Elisabeth, bapt. by RJL on May 8, 1763, and spon. by Johannes and Elisabeth Meyer.

Neff - Jacob was taxed in 1762, and received a warrant for 150 acres in Codorus Township on Feb. 12, 1767, that was surveyed as 166 acres called *Neff's Folly* on Nov. 16, 1769. He also received a warrant for 50 acres on Apr. 3, 1770, that was surveyed as 39.154 acres called *Neff's Settlement* on Apr. 17, 1770 (interest began on Mar. 1, 1757 (settled about 13 years)). He is probably the Jacob Neff of York and Windsor Township, who had his probate inventory was filed in Windsor Township in 1792. He was taxed in York in 1762. He m. Elisabeth, and had the following children:
- Johan Georg, b. on Aug. 4, 1752, and bapt. at CLY on Oct. 22, 1752.
- Ulrich, b. on Oct. 8, 1754, and bapt. at CLY on Nov. 24, 1754.

Neswinger (Neuschwanger) - Jacob was taxed in 1762 (see Codorus section). He received a warrant for 100 acres in Springfield Township on Jan. 16, 1767, that was surveyed as 74.74 acres called *Current Spring* on Oct. 22, 1767. He received a warrant for 100 acres in Springfield Township on June 2, 1767, that was surveyed as 72.120 acres called *Trout Run* on Oct. 21, 1767.

Neswinger (Neuschwanger) - Peter received a warrant for 100 acres in Springfield Township on Apr. 4, 1772, that was surveyed as 118.37 acres called *Long Ridge* on Nov. 12, 1772, and patented on June 18, 1793.

Nunemacher - Johann Solomon was b. on Apr. 27, 1738, and d. on Aug. 13, 1810. He received a warrant for 50 acres on Dec. 4, 1770. His will was written on Aug. 11, 1810, and probated on Aug. 18, 1810. He m. Anna Maria. She was b. on Mar. 22, 1741, and d. on Dec. 22, 1813. Her probate inventory was filed in Shrewsbury Township in 1813. They had the following children:

- Barbara, m. David Schaffer. He was probably David, son of David and Anna Maria (Venus) Schaeffer (see entry), b. on Feb. 13, 1790, bapt. at Friedensaal on Apr. 25, 1790, and spon. by Conrad and Dorothea Swartz. David m. Margaretha. She was b. on Aug. 20, 1800, and d. on Sept. 20, 1863. David d. on Dec. 10, 1858, and is bur. in Fissel's cemetery. They had a dau., Hannah, b. before Aug. 1810 (mentioned in Solomon Nunemacher's will).
- George, m. Anna Maria about 1789.
- Jacob, b. on Jan. 18, 1768, m. Anna Maria, dau. of Frederick Miller (see entry), and d. on Feb. 24, 1852. She was b. on Mar. 22, 1768, and d. on Dec. 23, 1849.
- Daniel.
- Solomon.
- Ann.
- Mary.
- Catherine.

Olp - Ernest was taxed in 1762. He received a warrant for 15 acres in Springfield Township (interest began on Mar. 1, 1774), that was surveyed as 14.20 acres on Sept. 4, 1784, and patented on Aug. 3, 1809. He received a warrant for 200 acres on June 9, 1783 (settled 5-7 years ago/interest began on Mar. 1, 1756), that was surveyed as 200.120 acres, and patented on Aug. 3, 1809. He received a warrant for 100 acres in Springfield Township on Feb. 28, 1769, that was surveyed as 31.24 acres called *Gabes Thern* on Apr. 21, 1769, and patented on Aug. 2, 1809.

Peery (Bieri) - George received a warrant for 100 acres on Oct. 13, 1772, that was surveyed as 110.120 acres called *Peery's Liberties* on Mar. 4, 1773.

Peery (Bieri) - John received a warrant for 100 acres in Springfield Township on Feb. 12, 1767, that was surveyed as 70.4 acres called *Hold Fast* on June 22, 1767 (see entry in Manchester section).

Peery (Bieri) - Nicholas surveyed 150.62 acres in Springfield Township called *Pleasant Walk* on Jan. 16, 1754 (see entry in Manchester section).

Pfeifer - Johannes was taxed in 1762. He received a warrant for 100 acres in Springfield Township on Dec. 7, 1773, that was surveyed as 136.14 acres called *High Land* on Oct. 18, 1774. He received a warrant for 25 acres in Springfield Township on May 11, 1776, that was surveyed as 29.40 acres called *Pfiffers Desire* on Mar. 5, 1777. He m.

Margaretha, dau. of Philip Schneider (see entry). They had the following children:
- Anna Maria, b. on Nov. 2, 1765, bapt. at FRI on the 23rd Sunday after Trinity, and spon. by Peter Ness and Anna Maria Walter.
- Georg, b. on Mar. 24, bapt. at FRI in 1779, and spon. by Johannes Glattfelter and wife.

Ratz - Philip Heinrich immigrated to America on the ship *Edinburgh* on Sept. 16, 1751, and received a warrant for 50 acres in Springfield Township on Apr. 31, 1762, that was surveyed as 125.80 acres on Apr. 23, 1755. He was taxed in Paradise Township in 1769, and his probate inventory was filed there in 1773. He was a tailor. He m. Catharina Susanna. They were sponsors to the baptism of Catharina Susanna Schneider in 1755 (RJL). Heinrich and Catharina had the following children:
- Johann Peter, b. about 1744, and was taxed in Paradise Township from 1769 to 1782. He served in the 7th Battalion, York County Militia in 1778, and in Captain White's Company, 5th Battallion in 1780. He resided in Franklin Co., PA, in 1800. He m. Maria Elisabeth Geckler at STM on Oct. 16, 1764, and had the following children:
  - Catharina, bapt. by RJL on Nov. 25, 1767, and spon. by Heinrich and Catharina Ratz.
- Gottfried, b. about 1747, and m. an unknown woman about 1769, and Margareth Catharina, dau. of Lorentz and Catharina Elisabeth Schweisgute of Paradise Township, in York Co. in 1780. She was bapt. by RJL on Feb. 22. 1762, and spon. by Margaretha Saltzgeberin. He and Elisabeth Meyer were sponsors to the baptism of Catharina Stubler in 1767 (RJL). He purchased 96 acres in Rowan Co., NC, on Nov. 10, 1772, and was in Morris District in 1778, and Salisbury District in 1790. His will was written on June 17, 1803, and probated in 1804. He had the following children:
  - Henrich, b. on Oct. 14, 1770.
  - Gottfried, b. on Apr. 22, 1778.
- Johann Jacob, bapt. by RJL on Feb. 12, 1764, and spon. by Jacob Eyler and Esther Gecklerin.

Rein (Rhein) - Martin m. Magdalena, and had the following children:
- Anna Maria, b. in Blanckenloch, Baden-Durlach, in 1720, and d. between 1763 and 1776. She immigrated to America with her parents in 1738. She m. Phillip Muller (see entry in Manchester section).
- Catharina, b. about 1722, and m. Johan Michael Geisselman (see entry).

- Martin, b. about 1724, and m. Elisabetha, dau. of Weyrich Rudisill (see entry in Manchester section) at the Moravian Church at Lititz in Lancaster Co. on Nov. 22, 1744. His will was written in Shrewsbury Township on June 24, 1758, and probated on Sept. 23, 1758. They had the following children (recorded at CLY (unless otherwise noted)):
    - Thomas, b. on Aug. 19, 1745, and bapt. on Sept. 3, 1745. He m. Barbara Wise, and d. in Lincoln Co., NC, in 1837.
    - Jacob, b. on Dec. 26, 1746, and bapt. on Feb. 2, 1747. He m. Maria Elisabetha, dau. of Bastian Best, and d. in Lincoln Co., NC, in 1825.
    - Martin, b. on Jan. 1, 1752, and bapt. on Mar. 8, 1752.
    - Dorothea, bapt. by RJL on Mar. 2, 1756, and spon. by Thomas and Dorothea Grummerein.
- Jacob, b. about 1728, and m. Elisabeth dau. of Hans Peter Glatfelter (see entry), at Christ's Lutheran Church of York on Nov. 18, 1750. Jacob wrote his will in Lincoln Co., NC, on May 22, 1793, and it was probated in Jan. 1795. They moved to NC before 1764, and had 600 acres along Rudisill Creek. They had the following children:
    - Magdalena b. 5 weeks ago Wednesday, and bapt. at Christ's Lutheran Church of York on Sept. 8, 1751. She m. Adam Cloninger.
    - Peter, bapt. by Reverend Jacob Lischy on Mar. 16, 1755, and spon. by Jacob and Magdalena Ness. He m. Anna Magdalena, dau. of Garrett Wiltz/Wills.
    - Sarah Catharina, m. Johan, son of Georg Hovis.
    - Philip, m. Hanna, granddau. of Peter Hoyle.
    - Michael, m. Barbara, granddau. of Peter Hoyle (and sister to Hanna).
    - Mollie.
- Susan Mary, b. about 1730, and had the following dau. out of wedlock (recorded at CLY):
    - Maria Margaretha, b. on Sept. 3, 1751, and bapt. on Sept. 8, 1751.

Repanach - Casper received a warrant for 150 acres in Springfield Township on May 31, 1762.

Romig - Georg Michael was taxed in 1762. He received a warrant for 100 acres on May 30, 1759, that was surveyed as 112.3 acres on Apr. 25, 1793. He m. Catharina. They had the following children:
- Christina, b. on Apr. 22, 1753, and bapt. at CLY on May 20, 1753.
- Maria Dorothea, b. on Sept. 7, 1754, and bapt. at CLY on Sept. 28, 1755.

- Susanna, b. on June 9, 1769, and bapt. at STJ on Jan. 12, 1769.

Roser (Rose) - Adam departed from Singen, Baden, Germany, on Mar. 29, 1753, and arrived at Philadelphia on the ship *Edinburg* on Sept. 14, 1753. He received a warrant for 100 acres in Shrewsbury and Springfield Township on Feb. 12, 1767 (also 66 acres on Oct. 6, 1785), that was surveyed as 100.71 acres called *Ragged House* on June 23, 1767. He was a constable in Shrewsbury Township in 1780. His will was written in Shrewsbury Township on Mar. 4, 1786, and probated on Sept. 22, 1794. He m. Anna Catharina Kramer, and had the following children:
- Johann, b. about 1754, and m. Elisabeth. He was a Private from Shrewsbury Township in Captain George Eichelberger's Company in Dec. 1775. He was tried and acquitted for refusing to serve in the militia in Shrewsbury Township in 1780. He was taxed in Shrewsbury Township in 1779. Johann and Elisabeth had the following children:
  - Elisabeth, b. on Mar. 21, 1778, bapt. at FRI on Apr. 12, 1778, and spon. by Elisabeth, dau. of Adam Roser.
  - Magdalena, b. in Oct. 1785, bapt. at FRI on Nov. 13, 1785, and spon. by Magdalena, dau. of Adam Roser.
  - Philip, b. on Oct. 25, 1788, bapt. at BLY, and spon. by Nicholas and Eve Dibel.
  - George, b. on Dec. 3, 1798, bapt. at FRI, and spon. by George _____.
- Lorentz, b. about 1756, and was fined in 1777, for refusing military training. He served as a Private in the Revolutionary War in Captain John Ehrman's Company, 7th Battalion (1777-1780). He remained with this unit, when it became Captain Henry Ferree's Company, 5th Battalion, in 1780-1782. He was tried and acquitted for refusing to serve in the military in 1780. His estate was administered in Shrewsbury Township on Jan. 29, 1830. He m. Elisabeth, and had the following children:
  - Johann Georg, b. on Sept. 7, 1779, bapt. at FRI on Oct. 3, 1779, and spon. by Adam and Catharina Roser.
  - Anna Catharina, b. on Apr. 25, 1781, bapt. at FRI on May 13, 1781, and spon. by Johann and Maria Catharina Frey. She m. John Fry.
  - Elisabeth, b. on Mar. 17, 1784, bapt. at FRI on May 2, 1784, and spon. by George and Catherine Mayer. She m. Michael Fry.
  - Johan Philip, b. on Dec. 15, 1786, bapt. at FRI on Feb. 18, 1787, and spon. by Johan Philip, son of Adam Roser. He d. on June 23, 1845, and is bur. in FRI cemetery. He m. Margaret. She d. on May 11, 1880 (aged 91 years, 5 months, 8 days), and is bur. in FRI cemetery.

- Johan Lorentz, b. on Dec. 26, 1788, bapt. at BYL, and spon. by Lorentz and Susanna Heindel. He d. on Aug. 26, 1846, and is bur. in FRI cemetery.
- Conrad, b. about 1790.
- Adam, b. about 1792.
- Magdalena, b. about 1794, and m. George Beck.
- Michael, b. on Apr. 10, 1796, bapt. at FRI on May 23, 1796, and spon. by Michael and Catherine Ness. He d. on Sept. 4, 1867, and is bur. in FRI cemetery.
- John, b. on July 3, 1798, bapt. at FRI, and spon. by John and Elisabeth Frey.
- Susanna, b. on Nov. 20, 1800, and d. on Feb. 5, 1875. She never m., and is bur. in Bupp's Union Church cemetery. She had a illegitimate dau., named Susan Hamm according to her will written in Springfield Township on July 27, 1850, and probated on Mar. 19, 1875.
- Anna Maria, b. about 1802, m. Isaac Gibbs, and d. before 1830.

- Elisabeth, b. about 1758.
- Adam, b. about 1759, and was taxed in 1783. He served in the Revolutionary War as a Private in Captain John Ehrman's Company, 7th Battalion (1777-1780), and remained with the unit, when it became the Captain Henry Ferree's Company, 5th Battalion, in 1780. He served under Captain Simon Copenhaver from Aug. 10-Oct. 10, 1781, guarding prisoners at Camp Security in York (also under Captain James Edgar from Oct. 10-Dec. 10, 1781). He was indicted in Jan. 1780, for refusing to serve in the militia (tried and acquitted). He m. Anna Maria about 1788. Adam had the following children:
  - Catrina, b. in July 1789, bapt. at FIS in Sept. 1789, and spon. by Adam and Catrina Roser.
  - Lorenz, b. on Apr. 9, 1791, bapt. at FIS on May 22, 1791, and spon. by Lorenz and Elisabeth Roser.
  - Susanna, b. on Feb. 18, 1795, bapt. at FRI on May 3, 1795, and spon. by Jacob and Susanna Kerchner.
  - Johan Philip, b. on Dec. 25, 1798, bapt. at FRI, and spon. by Johan Philip.
- Michael, b. about 1761. He m. Anna Catharina, probably a dau. of Jacob Baehli (see entry). Michael was a Private in the 6th Company, 7th Battalion, in 1778-80, and the 8th Company, 5th Battalion, as a Corporal 1782-83 during the Revolutionary War. He had a Land Draft called *Roseborough*, consisting of 27 3/4 acres in Shrewsbury Township, on the MD line on Oct. 29, 1786. In 1783, he resided in Codorus Township. He was later considered a yeoman of Baltimore Co., MD. Michael and Catharina had the following children:

- Catharina, b. on Apr. 4, 1782, bapt. at Fissel's on May 18, 1782, and spon. by her grandparents, Adam and Anna Catherina Roser.
- Elisabetha, b. on Mar. 8, 1785, bapt. at Fissel's on May 1, 1785, and spon. by Jacob and Susanna Baehli.
- Eva, b. on Dec. 10, 1791, bapt. at Fissel's, and spon. by Georg Baehli and wife.
- Anna Rosina, b. on Jan. 20, 1793, bapt. at Fissel's, and spon. by Daniel and Rosina Baehli.
- Frantz, b. about 1763. He served in the Revolutionary War as a Private in Captain Henry Ferree's Company, 5th Battalion, in 1782. He m. Maria Gertraut, dau. of Jacob and Eva Lorich (see entry in Codorus section), and had the following children:
  - Jacob, b. on July 28, 1784, bapt. at FRI on Aug. 7, 1784, and spon. by his grandparents, Jacob and Eva Lorch.
  - Andreas, b. on Apr. 28, 1794, bapt. at SAD on June 1, 1794, and spon. by Andreas Zeller and wife.
  - Catharina, b. on Apr. 8, 1797, bapt. at Freysville Lutheran Church on Apr. 30, 1797, and spon. by Margred Kissinger.
  - Barbara, bapt. at SAD on July 29, 1799, and spon. by Barbara Decken (may be reversed, and Barbara Decken is the parent and Frantz Roser and wife are sponsors).
- Magdalena, b. about 1765.
- Johan Philip, b. about 1769, and m. Magdalena Reber at TLY on June 11, 1799.
- Conrad, b. on Jan. 6, 1771, bapt. at FRI on Feb. 3, 1771, and spon. by Jacob and Maria Magdalena Ness. He m. Elisabeth, and had the following children:
  - Susana, b. on Jan. 15, 1801, bapt. at FRI on Mar. 8, 1801, and spon. by Conrad and Susana Grindel.

Rothermel - Johann Christoph was b. in Ludwigshafen/Hassloch, Germany, in Dec. 13/18, 1721, and immigrated to Montgomery Co., Hanover Township, PA, with his parents, Johannes Peter and Anna Elisabetha (Weber) Rothermel, between 1721 and 1727. He was taxed Shrewsbury Township in 1762. He m. Juliana Stempel. They had the following children (recorded by RJL unless otherwise noted):
- Catharina, b. at Falkner Swamp in Montgomery Co. on Nov. 24, 1745, and m. Johan Adam, son of Hans Adam and Anna Catharina (Koch) Braus, at New Hanover Lutheran Church on July 2, 1765. He was b. on Dec. 17, 1739, and d. on Oct. 11, 1802. They resided in Northampton Co., Macungie Township, PA, until 1795, and then moved to Snyder Co., Kratzerville, PA.
- Johan Frederick, b. on July 1, 1747, and m. Barbara about 1773.
- Johan Leonard, b. on Oct. 24, 1750, and bapt. on Nov. 24, 1751.

- Felicitas, b. in Montgomery Co. on Sept. 1, 1752.
- Johannes, bapt. on May 4, 1755, and spon. by Johannes and Elisabetha Ott.
- Heinrich, bapt. at STJ about 1767.

Rush - Christian received a warrant for 25 acres in Springfield Township on Mar. 27, 1775, that was surveyed as 30.28 acres called *Chestnut Grubs* on Apr. 28, 1775.

Sangree - Christian was taxed in 1762.

Schaffer - Johann David was taxed in 1762. He was b. to Johan Jacob and Anna Maria (Biber) Schaffer, bapt. at Hirschland, Norther Alsace, France on Jan. 22, 1713, and spon. by David Schmith, Martinus Biber and Eva Schmid. He immigrated to America, and arrived at Philadelphia in the ship *Robert and Alice* in 1739. David m. Anna Catharina, dau. of Johann Nickel and Maria Margaretha (Von Marxheim) Simon (see entry), in York Co., Codorus Township, PA, on Mar. 13, 1742/43. David took the Sacrament on Sept. 18, 1763, and was naturalized on Sept. 24, 1763. He was the constable for Shrewsbury Township in 1754, and supervisor of the highways in 1761. He received a warrant for 100 acres adjacent to Georg Kleinfelter on Oct. 10, 1750 (interest began on Mar. 1, 1743), that was surveyed as 95.80 acres on Nov. 30, 1751. He received a warrant for 50 acres on Apr. 30, 1765, that was surveyed as 220.79 acres called *Broad Spring*. He also received a warrant for 50 acres on Mar. 15, 1749, and 50 acres on Sept. 10, 1750, that was surveyed as 203.131 acres called *Pleasant Orchard* on Dec. 24, 1766 (patented to Philip Schaffer on Jan. 2, 1810. He received a warrant for 100 acres on Jan. 14, 1767, that was surveyed as 33.101 acres called *Orchard Hill* on Mar. 9, 1769 (55.20 acres was surveyed to Philip Schaffer on Apr. 17, 1806, and patented to him on Dec. 20, 1809). He received a warrant for 50 acres on Apr. 30, 1765, that was surveyed as 107.47 acres called *Cold Spring* on Dec. 27, 1766 (patented to Philip Schaffer on Jan. 2, 1810. He received a warrant for 100 acres on June 1, 1762. On June 15, 1762, he sold the 50 acre tract in Shrewsbury Township that he purchased on Sept. 10, 1750 to George Kleinfelter. David was a farmer in Shrewsbury Township, and d. in Jan. 1770 (his will was written on Dec. 29, 1769, and probated on Jan. 9, 1770). In 1783, Catharina had 200 acres in Shrewsbury Township. Catharina d. in Jan. 1797, and her estate was administered by her son, Philip, on Jan. 2, 1797. They had the following children in Shrewsbury Township:
- Maria Elisabeth, b. on Jan. 16, 1743/44. She was bapt. at Christ's Lutheran Church of York on Mar. 17, 1743/44, and spon. by Johan Adam and Maria Elisabeth Simon. She m. Baltzer Koller (see

SHREWSBURY TOWNSHIP 341

entry). Baltzer was a tailor, received a farm in Shrewsbury Township from David Schaffer on Nov. 27, 1762.
- Johan Philip, b. on Apr. 5, 1745. He was bapt. by Reverend Jacob Lischy on May 23, 1745, and spon. by his uncle, Johan Philip Simon. In 1783, Philip had 350 acres in Shrewsbury Township. He was a Private in the 5th (Captain John Ehrman) Company, 7th Battalion, York County Militia in 1778, and continued in the same Company, 2nd Class, when it was reorganized (in 1779) as the 5th (Captain Henry Ferree) of the 5th Battalion in 1781, and Dec. 27, 1782. He received a warrant for 15 acres on July 23, 1788 (interest began on Mar. 1, 1780), that was surveyed as 54.114 acres on Dec. 22, 1788. He d. in Shrewsbury Township on June 21, 1824, and is bur. in Fissel's cemetery. His will was written on Aug. 27, 1821, and probated on June 26, 1824. He m. Anna Maria Barbara, dau. of Jacob and Maria Barbara (Keller) Scherer (see entry in Codorus section). She was b. on Nov. 11, 1755 (1753), and d. on Mar. 29, 1832. They are bur. in Fissel's cemetery.
- Catharina, b. about 1747. She m. Johan Georg Ehrman before Dec. 1769. He received 220 1/2 acres called *Broad Spring*, in Shrewsbury Township, from her father, David, on Sept. 23, 1769.
- Charles, b. about 1749. He was mentioned in his father's will, but must have d. before Nov. 1771, at least before Jan. 1786.
- Anna Magdalena, bapt. by Reverend Jacob Lischy on Oct. 19, 1751, and spon. by Joseph and Magdalena Welschans. She m. Henrich Swartz (see entry).
- Elisabetha, b. about 1753. She m. Johan Peter, son of Michael and Maria Barbara Lang/Long according to the release of David's children to their bro. David Jr. on Jan. 5, 1786 (see entry in Manchester section).
- Anna Maria, b. about 1755, and m. Michael Ehrman (see entry).
- Margaretha, b. about 1757, and m. Johannes Ehrhardt (see entry in Codorus section).
- David, b. on June 15, 1759, and had a guardian appointed for him on Nov. 27, 1771. He m. Anna Maria, dau. of Philip Venus (see entry), and Christina after 1808. David was a Private in the 5th (captain John Ehrman) Company, 7th Battalion, York County Militia in 1778, and a Private under Captain Henry Moore, assigned to guard prisoners at Camp Security in York from Aug. 20 to Sept. 20, 1781, and performed the same duty under Captain William Lindsay from Dec. 8, 1781 to Feb. 8, 1782. He received a warrant in Shrewsbury and Springfield Township for 60 acres (interest began on Mar. 1, 1760), that was surveyed as 73 acres on Mar. 25, 1786. He d. in Shrewsbury Township on Dec. 23, 1823, and is bur. in Keeny's cemetery. His will was written on Feb. 23, 1820, and probated on Sept. 30, 1823. He deeded 25 acres in

Shrewsbury Township to Adam Shaffer on Nov. 24, 1787. On Jan. 5, 1786, David's siblings Philip, Marilis wife of Baltzer Kohler, Margaret wife of John Ehrhard, Catharina wife of George Ehrman, Magdalena wife of Henry Schwartz, Elizabeth wife of Peter Long, and Anna Maria wife of Michael Ehrman, signed a release to David. Anna Maria was b. on Dec. 25, 1757, and d. on Aug. 30, 1808. Christina was b. on Aug. 22, 1790, and d. on Nov. 18, 1872. Christina petitioned for guardians to be appointed for Mary, George, Samuel, Rebecca, and Benjamin, minor children of David on Apr. 6, 1825.

- Johan Adam Schaffer, b. about 1761 (not proven to be a son of David). He was not listed as a son of David in David's will and the 1786 release, however, he had associations with David's family. He was previously believed to be the Johan Adam, son of Johannes and Maria Eva (Sat) Schaffer, of Northumberland Co., PA, who d. in Centre Co., PA, in 1840, but conflicting and insufficient information has led me to doubt this. Johan Adam Schaffer m. Elizabeth, dau. of Georg and Barbara Kleinfelter about 1782. She was bapt. by Reverend Jacob Lischy on Feb. 15, 1761, and spon. by her uncle, Abraham Keller and Elisabeth Schneider. On Dec. 28, 1782, Adam served as a Private in Captain Henry Ferree's Company, 5th Battalion, York County Militia (from Shrewsbury Township). On Apr. 18, 1787, he received 113.25 acres in Shrewsbury Township from George and Barbara Kleinfelter, and on Nov. 24, 1787, received 25 acres in Shrewsbury Township from David Schaffer. On Jan. 3, 1791, Adam received 34.25 acres from Rudolph Spangler, and on June 20, 1794, Adam and Elizabeth signed a release of land Elizabeth inherited from her father to Peter Kleinfelter. On Apr. 1, 1801, Adam and Elizabeth deeded the land they bought from Georg Kleinfelter in 1787, and a tract called *Fort Hill* to Jacob Koller.

Schaffer - Jacob received a warrant for 100 acres in Springfield Township on Apr. 5, 1754 (see entry in Codorus section).

Scharer - Jacob was taxed in York Township in 1762. He received a warrant for 100 acres in Springfield Township on Dec. 28, 1774. He received a warrant for 100 acres in Springfield Township on Oct. 24, 1767, that was surveyed as 45.71 acres called *Killian's Run* on Oct. 4, 1768. He received a warrant for 100 acres in Springfield and York Township on July 20, 1753, that was surveyed as 181 acres on July 31, 1753. His will was written in York Town on June 10, 1784, and probated on July 8, 1784. He m. Catharina, and had the following children:

SHREWSBURY TOWNSHIP

- Jacob, b. on Jan. 9, 1744, m. Elisabeth, dau. of Carl Adam and Maria Elisabeth (Ehrhardt) Diehl (see entry), and d. in Stark Co., Osnaburg Township, OH, on Jan. 29, 1823. He was a Private in Captain George Long's Company, 6th Battalion during the Revolutionary War. He was a miller in Shrewsbury Township.
- Philip, b. about 1746.
- Johan Dewald, bapt. by RJL in Mar. 1749, and spon. by Casper and Maria Agnes Kieffer. He m. Anna Catharina Elisabetha, dau. of Carl Adam and Maria Elisabetha (Ehrhardt) Diehl (see entry).
- Maria Eva, bapt. by RJL on May 12, 1751, and spon. by Georg Ernst and Maria Eva Meyer. She m. Francis Weinmuller.
- Maria Margareth, bapt. by RJL on May 24, 1752, and spon. by Abraham and Anna Barbara Kuffer. She m. Philip, son of Jacob Oberdier (see entry in Dover section).
- Anna, bapt. by RJL on Mar. 17, 1754, and spon. by Abraham and Christina Kieffer.
- Elisabeth, bapt. by RJL on July 6, 1755, and spon. by Christian and Maria Elisabeth Groll. She d. young.
- Maria Elisabeth, bapt. by RJL on Aug. 1, 1756, and spon. by Christian and Elisabeth Kroll. She m. Henry Dallman.
- Maria Catharina, b. about 1758, and m. George Hoffman.
- Anna Barbara, b. on Feb. 26, 1766, bapt. at TLY on Mar. 30, 1766, and spon. by Frederick Blier and wife. She m. George Anstine.

<u>Schinleber</u> (Schinleberger) - Feredeick received a warrant for 50 acres on Mar. 30, 1775. He received a warrant for 50 acres in Shrewsbury and Hopewell Township on Mar. 30, 1775. His probate inventory was filed in Codorus Township in 1777.

<u>Schmidt</u> - Peter (see entry in Dover section).

<u>Schneider</u> - Johan Philip was warranted 100 acres in Springfield Township on Apr. 4, 1751, and 100 acres on Feb. 12, 1767. He immigrated to America in 1741. He d. before 1780, and had the following children:
- Philip, b. about 1739, and m. Elizabeth, dau. of John Flaur (see entry), and d. in Shrewsbury Township about 1798. They had the following children:
  - Michael, b. about 1760, m. Maria Magdalena about 1781, and d. in Springfield Township about 1808.
  - John, b. about 1762, m. Elisabeth Fissel about 1780, and d. before 1815.
  - Abraham, b. on June 13, 1765, bapt. at FRI on July 7, 1765, and spon. by Abraham Schneider and Elisabeth Hasler. He m. Catherine.

- Johan Jacob, b. on June 15, 1769, bapt. at FRI, and spon. by Jacob and Maria Magdalena Nees. He m. Anna Maria.
- Hannah, m. James Long.
- Philip, m. Susanna, and d. in Hopewell Township in May 1815.
- Benjamin, b. on June 19, 1772, bapt. at FRI on July 5, 1772, and spon. by Carl and Maria Elisabeth Diehl. He m. Anna Palle in York Co. on July 24, 1793.

- Elisabetha Margaretha, b. about 1740, and m. Jacob Alt (see entry).
- Anna Maria, b. about 1742, and m. Christophel Becker (see entry).
- Margaretha, b. about 1744, and m. Johann Pfeifer (see entry).
- Johan Abraham, b. in Berks Co., Tulpehocken Township, PA, on Feb. 17, 1745/46, bapt. by JCS on Feb. 17, 1746, and spon. by Jacob and Maria Elisabetha Fischer and Heinrich Beyer and wife. He m. Elisabeth Hoesler in York Co. in 1769, and d. in Beaver Co., PA, before Apr. 1819. They had the following children (recorded at FRI):
  - Anna Catharina Elisabeth, b. on Apr. 1, 1770, bapt. on Apr. 22, 1770, and spon. by Philip Schneider the youngest and Catharine Schneider.
  - Maria Elisabeth, b. on Jan. 13, 1772, bapt. at FRI on Apr. 12, 1772, and spon. by Tobias and Catharina Muller.
  - infant, bapt. at FRI on Dec. 7, 1777, and spon. by Hermann and Barbara Muller.
  - Magdalena, b. on Aug. 31, 1787, bapt. at FRI on Oct. 14, 1787, and spon. by Michael Schneider and wife.
- Johannes, b. in Berks Co., Tulpehocken Township, PA, on June 12, 1748, bapt. by JCS on June 26, 1748, and spon. by Johannes Ramler and Maria Elisabeth Brenner. He m. Maria Margaretha, and had the following children (recorded at FRI):
  - Johann Georg, b. on Oct. 25, 1779, bapt. on Oct. 31, 1779, and spon. by Georg and Maria Salome Geisselman.
  - Eva, b. on Mar. 8, 1783, bapt. on Mar. 23, 1783, and spon. by John and Philippina Dunki.
- Jacob, b. about 1750, and m. Maria.
- Benjamin, b. about 1759, and appears on the tax list of Shrewsbury Township in 1780.

Schnell (Snell) - Philip received a warrant for 230 acres in Springfield Township on Aug. 6, 1773, that was surveyed as 226.60 acres on Aug. 16, 1773, and patented on Aug. 30, 1773.

Seitz - Johannes, son of Johann Andreas and Anna Dorothea (Welk) Seitz, was b. in Adelshofen, Germany, on Jan. 30, 1739/40, and m. Anna Catharina, dau. of Johannes and Anna Maria Ripp/Reub, at

Adelshofen on May 8, 1764. Johannes Ripp was a citizen and bricklayer of Adelshofen. Anna Catharina was b. on Oct. 21, 1741, and bapt. at Adelshofen on Oct. 22, 1741. Johannes and Anna Catharina, arrived at Philadelphia on the ship *Richmond* on Oct. 20, 1764. They settled in York Co., Shrewsbury Township sometime prior to 1773. He purchased 636 acres near Glen Rock on Apr. 28, 1786. Johannes taxed in Shrewsbury Township in 1773, and served during the Revolutionary War in 1777/78 in Captain John Erman's Company, 7th Battalion, 5th Company, York County Militia. Johannes d. in Apr. 1793, and is bur. in St. Peter's (Yellow) Reformed Church. His will was written in Shrewsbury Township on Dec. 21, 1792, and probated on Apr. 8, 1793. Anna Catharina d. in Shrewsbury Township on Feb. 20, 1820, and is bur. in Mt. Zion Evangelical Church cemetery. Johannes and Anna Catharina had the following children:
- Ludwig, b. on Jan. 5, 1763. He may have been the illegitimate son of Dorothea Welk and Johann Philipp Von Gemmingen. He was presumed to have been adopted by his first cousin once removed, Johannes Seitz, and his wife Anna Catharina, and assumed the name Ludwig Seitz (it has not been confirmed that Ludwig Seitz and Ludwig Von Gemmingen are the same person). If they are the same person, the adoption may have been done to insure he had the chance to grow up without the stigma surrounding his birth. The family immigrated to PA when Ludwig was about two years old on Oct. 20, 1764, in the ship *Richmond*. Ludwig m. Anna, dau. of John and Catharina (Hunsaker) Beery, in York Co., PA, in 1789. She was b. in York Co., PA, on Jan. 30, 1768, and d. in Fairfield Co., Rush Creek Township, OH, on Sept. 30, 1831. Ludwig was a farmer and a predestinarian minister in the Baptist church. After their marriage, they moved to Rockingham Co., Linnville District, VA, about 1789/90. In 1801, Ludwig moved to Fairfield Co., OH, and purchased land from the government. In 1802, he returned to VA, sold some of his household effects, placed the rest in wagons, and moved his family to OH. He received land from the government, located on the east side of the present location of Mt. Tabor Evangelical Lutheran Church. While in VA, Ludwig was an elder in the Whitehouse congregation, and in 1806, helped establish Pleasant Run Church, near Lancaster, OH. He was an ordained Baptist minister, and the first minister of Pleasant Run. In 1804, he was a Judge in Rush Creek Township. He d. while on a trip in Washington Co., PA, in 1824.
- Catharina, b. on Jan. 5, 1765, and m. Heinrich Keller.
- Anna Maria, b. on Dec. 12, 1766. She m. Christian, son of Christian and Anna Stabler (see entry), in York Co. on Apr. 11, 1812. He was b. on July 21, 1764, and d. in Baltimore Co., Stablerville, MD,

on Dec. 6, 1846. Anna Maria d. at Stablerville on Mar. 19, 1845. They are bur. in Stablerville cemetery.
- Elisabeth, b. on Dec. 10, 1769. She m. Josef, son of Ulrich, and Elisabeth (dau. of John Huber) Leib, and grandson of Ulrich and Veronica Leib (see entry in Manchester section). Ulrich and Veronica immigrated to America on the ship *Molley* on Sept. 30, 1727. Josef was b. on Sept. 13, 1766, and d. in Fairfield Co., Rush Creek Township, OH, on Aug. 26, 1839. Elisabeth d. in Rush Creek Township on Mar. 4, 1841, and is bur. beside her husband in Grandview cemetery. They moved to Fairfield Co. in 1801, and Josef built the second mill on Rush Creek. Josef purchased 300 acres in Rush Creek Township in Aug. 1817.
- Elenora, b. in 1771, and m. Georg Henrich, son of Heinrich and Anna Magdalena (Schaffer) Swartz (see entry), at York Co., Glen Rock, PA, in 1799. Georg Henrich was b. on May 30, 1781, bapt. at Friedensaal on June 10, 1781, and spon. by his uncle and aunt, Jacob and Dorothea Swartz. Georg purchased 34 acres and 146 perches in Shrewsbury Township from George Moor on May 17, 1798, and Georg and Elenora sold this land to Frederick Myers on Aug. 9, 1805. They moved to Fairfield Co., Berne Township, OH, in 1805. Georg was a yeoman, cooper, and miller. He operated a grist mill called *Swartz Mill*, which was connected to the Swartz Post Office. Swartz Mill Bridge was named for this mill. It was removed in 1962. He received a land grant in the East 1/2 of Section 36 of Berne Township on Feb. 3, 1807. This land was situated on Rush Creek. He d. on Apr. 6, 1821, and Elenora d. on Dec. 29, 1847. They are bur. in Delapp cemetery.
- Barbara, b. on Nov. 20, 1774. She m. Heinrich Einsel in York Co., PA, on Mar. 11, 1798. He was b. in Germany on Jan. 29, 1775, and may have d. in Seneca Co., OH. Barbara d. in Fairfield Co., Berne Township, OH, in Aug. 1851, and is bur. in Delapp cemetery. They moved to OH in 1801.
- Margaretha, b. Mar. 11, 1776. She m. John Zeller, and d. in York Co., PA, on Aug. 26, 1822. She was bur. in St. Peter's (Yellow) Reformed Church cemetery. He was murdered in York Co., PA, sometime after 1817.
- Johannes, b. on Mar. 22, 1778. He m. Eva, dau. of Adam and Christina Stabler, in York Co., PA, on Mar. 10, 1801. She was b. on Mar. 18 (15), 1785, bapt. at Friedensaal on Apr. 17, 1785, and spon. by Eva, dau. of Michael Kleinfelter. She d. on Oct. 3, 1856. Johannes was a Evangelical minister, and d. in Shrewsbury Township on July 4, 1856, and is bur. in Mt. Zion Evangelical Lutheran cemetery.
- Andreas, b. on Dec. 21, 1779. He d. in West Liberty, MD, on Apr. 19, 1835, and is bur. in West Liberty M. E. cemetery. He m. Anna

Catherine, dau. of Peter and Elisabetha Kleinfelter (see entry). She was b. on Aug. 25, 1784, bapt. at Friedensaal on Sept. 5, 1784, and spon. by Johan Jacob and Catherine Koller. Andreas was a miller and farmer at Gorsuch Mills, Baltimore Co., MD. Andreas and Anna Catherine had twelve children, all b. in Baltimore Co., MD. Anna Catherine d. on Aug. 21, 1859, and is bur. in Gooding's School House cemetery, near Glen Rock, PA.
- infant, b. about 1782, and d. in infancy.
- Michael, b. on Feb. 3, 1787, bapt. at Friedensaal on Mar. 18, 1787, and spon. by Michael and Elisabeth Meyer. He d. sometime before 1792.

Seitz - Johann Joseph, son of Johannes and Anna Christina Seitz, immigrated to America on the ship *Chesterfield* on Sept. 2, 1749, and m. Anna Elisabeth. He received a warrant for 21 acres in Springfield Township on Aug. 7, 1787 (interest began on Mar. 1, 1783). He received a warrant for 21 acres in Springfield Township on Aug. 7, 1787, that was surveyed as 9.73 acres called *Cold Hill* on Dec. 9, 1788. They were sponsors at the baptism of Elisabeth, dau. of Adam and Elisabeth Streher, at Friedensaal on Sept. 11, 1773. Joseph wrote his will on Sept. 1, 1794, and it was probated in Shrewsbury Township on Aug. 21, 1810. Joseph and Elisabeth had the following children:
- Johannes, b. about 1765. He m. Eva Elisabetha, dau. of Johannes Michael and Appolonia Kleinfelter (see entry), about 1786. She was bapt. at St. Jacob's on Dec. 13, 1766, and spon. by her uncle and aunt, Jacob and Eva Elisabetha Baehli. She d. in Indiana Co., PA, in Nov. 1832.
- Adam, b. about 1767. He m. Anna Elisabeth, dau. of Casper Hildebrand (see entry).
- Christiana, b. about 1768.

Shilling - Sebastian was taxed in 1762. He received a warrant for 100 acres on Mar. 28, 1768, that was surveyed as 126 acres called *White Rock Spring* on Nov. 26, 1768. He m. Maria Elisabeth Lang at STM on Nov. 21, 1754 (A Christian Shilling m. at STM on Jan. 19, 1755, and an Anna Maria Shilling m. Michael Newman at TLY on Oct. 27, 1766).

Shigley - Jacob was taxed in 1762.

Shinard - John was taxed in 1762.

Simon - Johann Nickel, son of Johan Peter and Maria Agnes (Meyer) Simon, was bapt. in Rheinland Herran-Sulzbach, Germany, on Oct. 3, 1677, and m. Maria Margaretha Von Marxheim at Herran-Sulzbach on Nov. 17, 1705. He followed his sons, Jacob and Adam, to America, and

arrived at Philadelphia in the ship *Samuel* on Aug. 27, 1739. Johann Nickel d. in Lancaster Co., Warwick Township, PA, sometime after Aug. 1739. Nickel and Maria Margaretha had the following children in Herran-Sulzbach:
- Johann Niclass, b. on Mar. 6, 1706/7. He immigrated to PA on the ship *Glasgow* in 1738 (age 31). He m. Maria Margaretha. They resided in Pfeffelbach before immigrating to America. They had the following children:
  - Elisabetha Catharina, b. on Jan. 25, 1731, and bapt. on Feb. 1, 1731.
  - Johan Nickel, b. on Apr. 19, 1733, and bapt. on Apr. 26, 1733.
  - Johan Peter, b. on June 29, 1735, and bapt. on July 3, 1735.
  - Maria Barbara, b. on Dec. 8, 1736, and bapt. on Dec. 16, 1736.
  - Johan Peter, b. on Sept. 24, 1746, bapt. in Berks Co., Atolhoe, PA, on Oct. 26, 1746, and spon. by Peter Hoffman and wife.
  - Johannes, b. on Mar. 5, 1749, and bapt. at Host Church in Berks Co.
  - Johan Michael b. in Lebanon Co., Jackson Township, PA, on Jan. 14, 1754, bapt. at Trinity Tulpehocken Church on Mar. 3, 1754, and spon. by Michael Spengler and wife.
- Johann Jacob, b. on Sept. 4, 1709, immigrated to America with his bro., Adam, in the ship *Charming Nancy* on Nov. 9, 1738. He resided in Lancaster Co., PA in 1760.
- Johan Adam, b. in 1716. He m. Maria Elisabeth, dau. of Johan Adam and Maria Catharina (Kreischer) Diehl, in Lancaster Co., Warwick Township, PA, on Dec. 26, 1740. Johan Adam Diehl was b. in Unden Cappeln, Germany, on Sept. 12, 1690, and d. in Apr. 1755. He m. Maria Catharina Kreischer on Dec. 4, 1712. Adam Simon arrived at Philadelphia on the ship *Charming Nancy* with his bro. on Nov. 8, 1738. He received a warrant for 200 acres on Jan. 12, 1746, and 50 acres on Apr. 1, 1751, that was surveyed as 195.40 acres on Apr. 16, 1747 and 59 acres called *Addition* on Dec. 12, 1752. He was granted 100 acres on a branch of the Codorus adjoining his bro.-in-law, Carl Adam Diehl's, land in Shrewsbury Township. On Mar. 6, 1760, Abraham Welty purchased Adam's land, and Adam moved to Franklin Co., Lurgen/Letterkenny Township, PA, nine mile southeast of Shippensburg. He moved to Washington Co., in 1776/77, and took out a land warrant in West Bethlehem Township in 1787, for 343 3/4 acres named *Dispair*. The land was patented on Mar. 19, 1788. Maria Elisabeth was b. in Hamberg, Germany, on Apr. 4, 1715, and d. in Washington Co., Bethlehem Township, PA, on Feb. 12, 1806. Adam d. intestate in Bethlehem Township on Mar. 28, 1788. They are bur. in Dutch Glory cemetery. They had the following children in York Co., Shrewsbury Township, PA:

- Michael, b. on Jan. 25, 1742. He d. in Mahoning Co., Boardman Township, OH, (bur. in Washington Co., Bethlehem Township, PA) on May 20, 1839. He m. Anna Ottillia, dau. of Valentine and Gertrude Schmeltzer, in York Co., PA, on Sept. 2, 1766, Anna Margaretha Rhoda Mohr, widow of ___ Althaus in Washington Co., PA, on Oct. 9, 1791, and Gertrude Schmidt, widow of John Dice. Anna Ottillia was b. on Feb. 2, 1741, immigrated to America on the ship *Royal Union* on Aug. 15, 1750, and d. on July 25, 1791. Anna Margaretha d. in childbirth about 1792. Gertrude was b. in 1750, and d. in 1837. Michael resided in Franklin Co., PA, near the MD line (he had some children bapt. in MD) until 1776/77, when he moved to Washington Co., PA. He received a warrant for a tract called *Blackberry* in West Bethlehem Township in 1787. He moved to OH and purchased 1200 acres in 1800. During the Revolutionary War, he was a Frontier Ranger under Captain Abner Howell, in the 3rd Battalion, Washington County Militia.
- Liese Catherine, b. on Jan. 6, 1744, and d. after 1797. She m. Philip Stark/Strong.
- Angelica Elizabeth "Agnes," b. on July 28, 1745, and d. after 1797. She m. Michael Beltz.
- Catharine, b. about 1748, and d. in Washington Co., PA, on Dec. 18, 1815. She m. George Densor in Cumberland Co., PA, on Apr. 6, 1769.
- Andreas, b. on Nov. 16, 1751, bapt. on Nov. 25, 1751, and spon. by Andreas and Dorothea Kuertzel. He d. in OH on July 9, 1828. He m. Maria Elisabeth Geckler. On Mar. 19, 1764, he was taken captive by Indians, adopted by them, and returned to his family eight months later, after being freed when Col. Henry Bouquet defeated the Indians at Bushy Run. He received a tract in West Bethlehem Township called *The Addition* in 1787. He d. in Columbiana Co., OH, in 1828.
- Margaret, b. about 1753, and resided in Franklin Co., PA, in 1800. She m. George Wright.
- Jacob, b. about 1755, and d. in Mahoning Co., OH, in Mar. 1845. He m. Catharine.
- Adam, b. about 1756, and d. before 1788.
- Anna Maria, b. about 1758, and resided in Trumbull Co., OH, in 1828. She m. James Stall, and Abraham Moser.
- Nicholas, b. in 1761, and d. in Portage Co., OH on Jan. 14, 1834. He m. Susan Geckler.

- Maria Elisabeth, b. about 1720, and m. Johan Daniel Diehl (see entry).
- Johann Philipp, b. on Mar. 3, 1722/23. He m. Anna Gertrude, dau. of Peter Schneider, in the First Reformed Church of Lancaster,

PA, on Feb. 2, 1745/46. Philipp received a land warrant in York Co., Shrewsbury Township on Mar. 9, 1753 for 150 acres that was surveyed as 251 acres on June 10, 1757. Philipp d. intestate in 1760, and Gertrude filed administration papers on Jan. 17, 1761. After Philipp's death, Gertrude m. John Gabel/Gobble (see entry), later in 1761. Gertrude d. in Shrewsbury Township in 1770. Philipp and Gertrude had the following children:
- Maria Elisabeth, b. on Dec. 3, 1746, and m. Felix Hildebrand (see entry).
- Hans Adam, b. about 1749.
- Elisabeth Catharina, bapt. by Reverend Jacob Lischy on Oct. 19, 1751, and spon. by Jacob Pfluger and Elisabeth Catharina Schneiderin.
- Anna Maria, bapt. by Reverend Jacob Lischy on Oct. 5, 1755, and spon. by Paul Schneider and Anna Maria Diehl.
- Anna Catharina, b. on Aug. 30, 1725, and m. Johan David Schaffer (see entry).

Schuster - Nicholas was taxed in 1762. He received a warrant for 150 acres in Jackson Township on Aug. 25, 1746. Nicholas and Maria Magdalena Schuster were sponsors at the baptism of Maria Magdalena Biegler in 1755 (RJL), and Johann Michael Lutz at FRI in 1766.

Sprinckel - Wilhelm received a warrant for 100 acres in Springfield and York Township on Oct. 28, 1746, that was surveyed as 244 acres (see entry in Manchester section). He received a warrant for 100 acres in Springfield Township on Mar. 7, 1768, that was surveyed as 24.157 acres on Mar. 8, 1769.

Spangler - Hans Rudolf, son of Jacob Spengler, m. Judith, dau. of Jacob Haegis of Beisassen, Sinsheim, Baden on July 16, 1678, and Marie Saeger of Duehren, Sinsheim, in 1691, and had the following children at Weiler Sinsheim, Baden, Germany, (information from *The Families of Caspar, Henry, Baltzer, and George Spengler* by Edward W. Spangler (1896)):
- Johannes, b. on Sept. 14, 1679.
- Anna Margaretha, b. on Mar. 5, 1682.
- Hans Kaspar, b. on Jan. 24, 1684, m. Judith, adopted dau. of Martin Ziegler, at Weiler on Feb. 9, 1712, and immigrated to America on the ship *William and Sarah* on Sept. 18, 1727. He settled in York Co., PA, in 1729. He received a warrant for 719 acres, on Oct. 16, 1738, that was patented to his son Rudolph as 363 acres and 154 perches. He d. in 1760, and his was will written on Apr. 27, 1759, and probated on Apr. 28, 1760. He is bur. in a

private family graveyard 1.5 miles east of York. Kaspar and Judith had the following children:
- Albrecht, bapt. on Nov. 20, 1712.
- Jonas, b. at Weiler on May 25, 1715. He settled on his father's land 2 miles west of Cordorus Creek on the Little Codorus Creek (warrant 1763/survey 1765). He d. in Paradise (now Jackson) Township in 1762 (date of probate inventory). He m. Maria (Stina), dau. of Martin Kindig (immigrated to America on Sept. 21, 1727). She was b. in 1718, and d. on Oct. 15, 1784. She is bur. in Pigeon Hills cemetery. They had the following children:
  - Anna Maria, bapt. by RJL on Sept. 22, 1745, and spon. by Michael Schwab and Anna Maria Spenglerin. She m. Christian Wiest on Oct. 27, 1768, and d. in Paradise Township on May 2, 1784. She is bur. in Pigeon Hills cemetery. He served in the 7th Company 7th Battalion in the Revolutionary War. He moved to Franklin Co., PA, between 1797 and 1836.
  - Joseph, b. in Paradise Township in 1745, m. Elizabeth Gardner, and d. in Washington Township in 1802. He was a 1st Lt. in Captain Michael Ege's Company, and a Major of the 5th Battalion York County Militia from 1775 to Apr. 5, 1778.
  - Bernhard, b. on Sept. 30, 1745, and d. in Jackson Township in 1802. He m. Eve/Frene, dau. Jacob Wist, at STR on Nov. 13, 1770, of Windsor Township. She d. on Dec. 25, 1818, aged 65 years. Bernard served in the 6th Company, 7th Battalion in the Revolutionary War.
  - Catharina, b. about 1747, and m. Jacob Wiest on Oct. 12, 1765. He was b. in 1741, and d. in Adams Co., Berwick Township on June 25, 1834.
  - Judith, b. about 1749, and m. Peter Erb. They resided in York Co., Manheim Township, and later, Frederick Co., MD.
  - Henrich, b. in 1750, and d. in Jackson Township in 1791. He m. Maria Clara Hoke on Oct. 28, 1779. She was b. in 1753, and d. in 1818. He served in the 7th Company 7th Battalion during the Revolutionary War.
  - Rudolph, b. about 1752, m. Christina, and d. in Adams Co., Berwick Township, PA, in Aug. 1830 he moved to Berwick Township in 1788.
  - Eve, b. about 1754, and m. Johan Emig. He was b. on Jan. 28, 1753, and d. on July 25, 1834. His second wife was Margaret Rudisill (1753-Mar. 31, 1839).
- Philipp, bapt. on July 18, 1717.
- Bernhard, b. in Weiler on Sept. 2, 1719, m. Anna Margaretha Gunnemer, and d. in York in 1804. He was naturalized on Sept. 24, 1762. He lived on a plantation of 326.5 acres which his father

acquired by occupation (1728) and improvement (patented to Bernhard). They had the following children:
- Jonas, b. in 1741, m. Catharine, and d. on Sept. 19, 1821. She was b. on Apr. 10, 1741, and d. on Feb. 4, 1812. He served in the 2nd Company 3rd Battalion in the Revolutionary War, and resided on his father's homestead in Springettsbury Township.
- Rudolph, b. on May 10, 1748. and bapt. at CLY on May 19, 1748. He d. in York Township on Jan. 4, 1816.
- Judith, b. on Sept. 1, 1754, m. Henry Rudisill on May 27, 1781, and d. before 1806.
- Henrich, b. on Jan. 29, 1758, bapt. at KRE on Apr. 2, 1758, and spon. by Henrich Becker and wife. He d. young.
- Anna Maria, b. on Feb. 19, 1760, m. John Wolf on Oct. 21, 1779. He was the church organ maker of York, and d. in 1804.
- Susanna, b. on Nov. 14, 1761, bapt. at TLY on June 20, 1762, and spon. by Susanna Serbach.
- Caspar, b. on Oct. 10, 1766, m. Catharina, dau. of Jost Harbaugh, and d. at his farm at Small's Mill 2 miles north east of York in 1804. She was b. on Dec. 8, 1769, and d. on Feb. 28, 1850. They are bur. in Prospect Hill cemetery.
- Maria Margaretha, b. on Nov. 26, 1768, bapt. at TLY on June 25, 1769, and spon. by Susanna Sarbach. She m. Jacob Creamer, and d. on Mar. 6, 1846. He d. on Jan. 7, 1836, aged 70 years.

- Rudolph, b. in Weiler on Mar. 1, 1721, and was naturalized in Paradise Township on Sept. 24, 1762. He resided on his father's land in Paradise (now Jackson) Township. He d. about 1782, and his widow, Barbara m. Philip Jacob. on Nov. 9, 1784, letters of administration were granted to Philip and Barbara Jacob. He m. Anna Maria about 1745, and Barbara after 1751. Rudolph had the following children:
- Anna Margaretha, bapt. by RJL on Apr. 28, 1746, and spon. by Bernhardt Spengler and Anna Magaretha Genemer.
- Catharina, b. about 1748, and m. Johan Georg, son of Georg Michael Kann (see entry in Dover section), at TLY on Oct. 27, 1767.
- Anna Maria, b. in 1750, and bapt. at CLY on Mar. 3, 1751. She m. Frederick Decker at TLY on July 19, 1778.
- Henrich, b. on Aug. 3, 1753, m. Catharina, dau. of Peter and Magdalena Mohr, and d. on Aug. 9, 1826. She was b. on Dec. 26, 1785, and d. on Dec. 18, 1835. They are bur. in Pigeon Hills cemetery. He served in the 7th Company 7th Battalion during the Revolutionary War.
- Bernhard, b. on Jan. 5, 1756, m. Elizabeth, and d. in Jackson Township on Mar. 10, 1828. She was b. on May 24, 1760, and

SHREWSBURY TOWNSHIP 353

d. on Jan. 22, 1789. They are bur. in Pigeon Hills cemetery. He
served in the 7th Company 7th Battalion during the
Revolution.
-Magdalena, m. John Ditti.
- Anna Maria, b. in Weiler on July 15, 1725, m. Michael Swope
(Schwob), and d. before 1765. He was coroner in 1761, justice of
the peace in 1764, and orphan's court judge in 1767. He was a
member of the State Assembly from 1768 to 1776, and was on
the Committee of Revolutionary Correspondence in 1775. He was
a Major of the 1st Battalion in 1775, and Colonel in 1776. He
formed a portion of the Flying Camp in East New Jersey in
1776, and was taken prisoner at Fort Washington in 1776
(exchanged in 1781). He was an inn keeper in 1753, shop keeper
in 1757, and merchant from 1779 to 1785. He was an Associate
Judge for the Courts of York Co. from 1767 to 1782, and in
1785, moved to Alexandria, VA. They had the following dau.:
- Anna Maria, b. on Feb. 24, 1752, and bapt. at CLY on Mar. 1,
1752.
- Balthasar, b. about 1727 (not proven to be a son, but seems to
fit nowhere else). He received a warrant for 100 acres in
Springfield Township on Nov. 28, 1746, that was surveyed as 148
acres on June 15, 1753 (there were two Balthasar Spenglers
taxed in York Township in 1779, one in York Town, and one in
Codorus Township. This Balthasar was probably one of the
Balthasars in York Township). He m. Anna Liebhard about 1745.
They had the following children:
- Balthasar, b. about 1746, and m. Catharina about 1767. He is
probably the Balthasar Spangler that was taxed in Codorus
Township in 1779. They had the following children:
- Infant, b. on Dec. 28, 1767, bapt. at TLY on May 17, 1768,
and spon. by Philip Casper Spengler and wife.
- Rudolph was b. on May 10, 1748, and bapt. at CLY on May 19,
1748. He m. Sophia about 1771, and had the following
children:
- Jonas, b. bapt. at TLY on Nov. 8, 1770, and spon. by Jonas
Spengler and wife.
- Bernhard, b. on Apr. 15, 1772, bapt. at TLY on June 28,
1772, and spon. by Bernhard Spengler and wife.
- Johannes, b. on May 22, 1777, bapt. at TLY on July 27,
1777, and spon. by his parents.
- Rudolf, b. on Sept. 27, 1785, bapt. at TLY on Apr. 9, 1786,
and spon. by his parents.
- Maria Elisabeth, b. on Apr. 22, 1796, bapt. at TLY on May 9,
1796, and spon. by Louisa Sophia Heibele.

- Maria Magdalena, b. on May 1, 1756, and bapt. at CLY on May 25, 1756.
- Philip Caspar, b. about 1730. He m. Margaretta Salome, dau. of Johann Daniel and Maria Ursula (Von Colmar) Dunckel, and d. in 1782 (date of probate inventory). He inherited 200 acres in York from his father. Margaretta was b. on Apr. 6, 1736, and d. on June 29, 1813. She is bur. in Zion cemetery. They had the following children:
  - Carl, b. about 1756, m. Susanna, dau. of Georg and Christina (Spangler) Diehl (see entry), and Ann Welsh (d. 1849). He moved to Botetourt Co., Botetourt, VA, between 1787 and 1792, and d. there in 1832.
  - Michael, b. on Oct. 13, 1758, and m. Catharina, dau. of Lorentz Schweisgood, on June 28, 1781. She was b. on Nov. 16, 1761. He served int he 2nd Company 3rd Battalion in the Revolution.
  - Johan Philip, b. on Mar. 17, 1761, and bapt. at CLY on Mar. 22, 1761. He m. Regina Stoever, and d. in Shenandoah Co., Strasburg, VA, in 1823. He served at a Lt. Col. of the 6th Regiment of the Virginia Militia in the War of 1812, and was a member of Virginia Legislature. He moved to VA about 1790.
  - Johann Frederick, b. on Apr. 17, 1763, bapt. at TLY on May 8, 1763, and spon. by Frederick Kuhn and wife. He moved to Shenandoah Co., Strasburg, VA, about 1790.
  - Elisabeth, b. on Nov. 19, 1767, bapt. at TLY on May 17, 1768, and spon. by Balthasar Spangler and wife. She m. John, son of John Herbach, on Oct. 1, 1786, and Robert Miller after 1801. John was b. on Dec. 5, 1762, and d. on Oct. 5, 1800.
  - Solomon, b. in 1770, m. ___ Taylor, served in the War of 1812, and d. in Shenandoah Co., Strasburg, VA, in 1830. She d. age 83.
  - Daniel, b. on Sept. 5, 1772, and bapt. at CLY on Apr. 2, 1775. He resided in Boone Co., KY, in 1817.
  - David, b. on Sept. 5, 1772 (?), and bapt. at CLY (?) on Apr. 2, 1775 (?). He moved Harrisonburg, VA, about 1790, and Franklin Co., Columbus, OH, about 1800.
  - Anthony, b. on Dec. 29, 1774, and bapt. at CLY on Apr. 2, 1775. He m. Catherine Kendrick on Feb. 27, 1796, and d. on June 29, 1834. She d. on Aug. 19, 1829.
  - Anna Maria, b. in 1777, m. Henry Imschwiller on Sept. 19, 1807, and d. at Bottstown on June 3, 1811.
- Judith, b. about 1735, and m. Henry Baker. He d. before 1766, and she m. Jacob Eichinberger on Mar. 25, 1766. On Sept. 3, 1767, Rudolph Spangler was appointed guardian of her children. Judith and Henry had the following children:

SHREWSBURY TOWNSHIP 355

- Maria, b. about 1758.
- Eva, b. about 1760.
- Catharina, b. about 1762.
- Anna, b. on Mar. 3, 1686.
- Anna Maria, b. on May 28, 1693, and m. Johan Bernard Brenneisen of Reihen.
- Rudolph, b. on Sept. 4, 1696.
- Jacob, b. on Sept. 12, 1698, and m. Sophia Dorothea Hoffman on June 14, 1729.
- Hans Georg, b. on Feb. 2, 1701, m. Katharina Laub, and d. in Philadelphia, PA, in 1744. He immigrated to America on the ship *Pleasant* on Oct. 11, 1732.
- Johan Heinrich, b. on July 1, 1703.
- Jorg Heinrich, b. on June 8, 1704, m. Susanna Muller of Meckersheim, at Weiler on Jan. 17, 1730, and immigrated to America on the ship *Pleasant* on Oct. 11, 1732. In 1732, they settled in York Co., Heigelberg Township. He was naturalized on Apr. 11, 1763. He purchased 165 acres on Aug. 6, 1746, and 165.119 in Spring Garden Township on May 14, 1764 (the latter patented to him on Apr. 14, 1768. He received a warrant on Apr. 14, 1767, that was patented on May 2, 1768. He had land in Windsor Township. His will was written in York on Feb. 25, 1773, and probated on July 9, 1776. He d. on July 6, 1776 (?same day as his son?). Susanna d. on Dec. 11, 1780. They had the following children:
  - Henrich, b. on Nov. 27, 1732, and was killed on July 6, 1776 (?) while serving in the 2nd Company 3rd Battalion in the Revolutionary War. He was not mentioned in his father's will.
  - Susanna, b. in Heidelberg Township near the Blue Mountains on May 14, 1735, bapt. by Rev. Muller at Caspar Spangler's on Dec. 17, 1735, and spon. by Rudolph Wilcke and wife. She d. on Nov. 29, 1809. She never m.
  - Christina, b. about 1737, and m. Johan Georg Diehl (see entry), on May 30, 1758.
  - Rudolph, b. about 1738. He m. Maria Catharina, dau. of Johan Hendrick and Eva (Kramer) Bahn (see entry in Dover section (under Kramer)), at CLY on Aug. 5, 1759. His will was written on Sept. 2, 1763, probated on Oct. 13, 1763, and executed by George Keentz and Adam Lightner. After his death, she m. Johan Peter, son of Peter and Catharina Schultz. Rudolph and Maria Catharina had the following children:
    - Johan Heinrich, bapt. by Reverend Jacob Lischy on Mar. 8, 1761, and spon. by his grandparents, Johan Heinrich and Eva Bahn. He m. Susanna, dau. of Ignatius and Margaret (Rutter) Lightner, and d. in Franklin Co., Mercersburg, PA, on Aug. 17,

1837. She was b. on Jan. 1, 1768, and d. on Sept. 5, 1855. He was a wagon manufacturer, and she kept a hotel.
- Maria Elizabeth, b. on June 29, 1763, bapt. at the First Reformed Church of York on July 24, 1763, and spon. by her uncle and aunt, Frederick Ruhl and wife. She m. Peter Streber on Dec. 26, 1782, and d. on Sept. 18, 1823. He d. in 1814. He was a carpenter, and contractor, and served in Captain Bailey's Company during the Revolution.
- Johan Georg, b. in 1740, and d. on July 15, 1797. He had no children, and left his estate to his sister, Susanna.
- Johan Balthasar, b. on Nov. 29, 1706, m. Maria Magdalena Ritter at Weiler on Apr. 29, 1732, and immigrated to America on the ship *Pleasant* on Oct. 11, 1732. In 1732, he purchased 200 acres, 1 mile east of Codorus Creek (in Springettsbury Manor). On Feb. 24, he had 487 acres in York Patented to him. He was the inn keeper of the Black Horse Inn (his wife took over after his death). His will was written on Oct. 9, 1770, and probated on Dec. 3, 1770. Magdalena's will was written on May 26, 1783, and probated on Nov. 9, 1784. They had the following children:
  - Johan Georg, b. in Baden on Mar. 20, 1732/33, m. Anna Maria, and d. on Oct. 2, 1810. She was b. on Jan. 3, 1735, and d. on Jan. 22, 1803. They had the following children:
    - Anna Maria, b. on May 29, 1757, bapt. at KRE on June 18, 1757, and spon. by Johannes Schultz and wife. She m. William McClean, and John Rouse. She d. on June 17, 1844. William d. on July 4, 1798.
    - Johan Georg, b. on Feb. 24, 1759, and bapt. at CLY on Mar. 18, 1759. He d. on Oct. 21, 1831. He served in Captain Georg Eichelberger's Company in 1775, and was a Lt. in the 2nd Company 3rd Battalion in 1776. He was a Colonel in 1799, and a Lt. Col. of the 113th Regiment in 1801. He was a member of the State Assembly in 1803, 1804, 1805, 1808, and 1809. He was Notary Public and Co. Treasurer from 1814-1817, and Director of the Poor in 1813, 1815, 1817, and 1818. He was a Colonel in 1816.
    - Maria Magdalena, b. on Oct. 30, 1761, and bapt. at CLY on Nov. 8, 1761. She m. Adam Wolf, and ____ Ellmore of Endenton, NC.
  - Johan Balthasar, b. on Apr. 16, 1735, and bapt. at CLY on Oct. 10, 1735. He succeeded his parents as inn keeper of the Black Horse Inn, and with his bro. Rudolph, was one of the original members of the Sun Fire Company of York (formed in Jan. 1771). He was a member of the Committee of Safety. He d. on Aug. 1, 1798, and is bur. in Prospect Hill cemetery. She was b. in

1739, and d. on Aug. 24, 1821. He m. Christina Messerschmeid, and had the following children:
- Daniel, b. on Nov. 20, 1761, bapt. at CLY on Dec. 25, 1761, and spon. by Daniel and Elisabeth, children of Balthasar Spangler. He was a sadler in 1794, and Co. Commissioner from 1799 to 1801. He m. Margaret Hahn on June 30, 1784, and d. on Feb. 11, 1813. She d. on May 28, 1810, aged 46 years, 7 months, and 9 days.
- Maria Elisabeth, b. on May 20, 1763, bapt. at TLY on June 19, 1763, and spon. by Philip and Anna Maria Albrecht. She m. Alexander Cobean on July 30, 1801. He was the first President of the York Gettysburg Turnpike in 1818.
- Maria Magdalena, b. on Jan. 31, 1768, m. William McClellan on Jan. 31, 1788, and d. in Adams Co., Marsh Creek, PA, on July 27, 1831. He was b. on June 21, 1763.
- John, b. on July 30, 1770, m. Margaret, dau. of Conrad Lederman on Feb. 28, 1805, and d. on July 22, 1831. She d. on Jan. 3, 1859, aged 73 years, 5 months, and 21 days. He was a Doctor, and served as surgeon of the 113th Regiment in 1807.
- Samuel, b. on July 30, 1773, bapt. at TLY on Sept. 26, 1773, and spon. by Johannes Spengler and wife. He m. Anna Maria, dau. of Peter and Elisabeth (Wolf) Duenkel, on Apr. 15, 1802. She d. on July 19, 1852, aged 68 years, 8 months, and 19 days. He was a soldier involved in suppressing the Whiskey Insurrection, and was inn keeper of the Black Horse Inn. He built the York House Tavern, conducted a tannery in Shrewsbury, and d. in Springfield Township on June 28, 1839.
- Jacob, b. on Jan. 3, 1776, bapt. on Feb. 18, 1776, and d. unmarried in Philadelphia in 1813.
- Georg, b. on Aug. 5, 1778, bapt. on Feb. 14, 1779, and d. in Philadelphia on Apr. 13, 1823. He was a merchant, and had no children.
- Maria, b. on Apr. 17, 1783, bapt. on Aug. 17, 1783, m. John, son of Jacob Dritt, on Mar. 16, 1813, and d. on June 28, 1858. He was b. on Apr. 18, 1793, and d. in 1844.
- Maria Juliana, b. about 1737, and m. Johan Frantz Wilhelm Bickel on Dec. 12, 1751, and had the following children:
  - Baltzer, b. on Oct. 5, 1757, and d. of convulsive fits on Oct. 4, 1762 (bur. at CLY on Oct. 5, 1762).
  - David, b. on Jan. 12, 1761, bapt. at CLY on Apr. 30, 1761, and spon. by Balthasar and Magdalena Spangler.
  - Johanna, b. on Mar. 19, 1762, bapt. at CLY on Mar. 28, 1762, and spon. by Balthasar and Magdalena Spangler.
- Rudolph, b. in 1738, m. Dorothea, dau. of Johan Daniel and Maria Ursula Duenkel, at TLY on Jan. 1, 1767, and d. on Aug. 5,

1811. She was d. on June 12, 1835, aged 87 years. He was a silversmith and clockmaker. He served in the Revolutionary War in Captain Georg Eichelberger's Company in 1775, and was a Captain in 1776. He had the following children:
- Johan Jacob, b. on Nov. 28, 1767, bapt. at TLY on Dec. 13, 1767, and spon. by Ursula Duenckel. He m. Susanna, dau. of John Hay, and Catherine A. Hamilton on May 23, 1820. He d. on June 17, 1843. Susanna was b. in 1779, and d. on Feb. 24, 1813. Catherine was b. on Nov. 13, 1792, and d. on June 12, 1873. He was Surveyor General of PA from 1818 to 1821 and 1830 to 1836.
- Catharina, b. on Jan. 1, 1770, bapt. at TLY on Jan. 28, 1770, and spon. by Ursula Hermsdorff. She m. George Barnitz, and d. on Dec. 27, 1824. He was b. on Feb. 18, 1770, and d. on Apr. 19, 1844.
- Elisabeth, b. on Feb. 23, 1773, m. William Nes, and d. on Apr. 14, 1844 (bur. at CLY). He was b. on July 13, 1761, and d. on July 19, 1828.
- Margaret, b. on Mar. 14, 1773, m. Joseph Slagle on Sept. 22, 1807, and d. in Frederick Co., Winchester, VA, on Apr. 15, 1852.
- Mary, b. about 1776, and m. Peter Small on Apr. 27, 1797. He d. on Apr. 30, 1823, aged 45 years.
- Jesse, b. about 1778, and m. Anna Maria.
- Daniel, b. on Oct. 9, 1781, bapt. at TLY on Oct. 20, 1781, and spon. by Balthasar Spangler and wife.
- Peter, b. on May 16, 1786, bapt. at TLY on June 2, 1786, and spon. by Johannes and Margaret Spengler.
- Helena Dorothea, b. about 1788, m. Charles Frederick Fisher on Oct. 2, 1808, and d. on May 15, 1842. He d. on Aug. 26, 1842, aged 59 years, 23 days.
- Elizabeth, b. in 1740, m. Frantz Kuntz and d. on Nov. 25, 1825. He d. on June 16, 1804, aged 64 years. They had the following children:
  - Maria Margaretha, b. on Oct. 10, 1765, bapt. at CLY on Oct. 20, 1765, and spon. by Maria Magdalena Spangler (her grandmother).
  - Michael, b. on Nov. 13, 1771, and bapt. at CLY on Dec. 8, 1771.
  - Magdalena, b. on Feb. 5, 1774, and bapt. at CLY on May 30, 1774.
  - Georg Adam, b. on Feb. 11, 1777, and bapt. at CLY on Mar. 30, 1777.
- Maria Magdalena, b. on Oct. 25, 1744, and bapt. at CLY on Nov. 11, 1744.

- Daniel, b. about 1746, m. Magdalena about 1766, and Maria Elisabeth, dau. of Nathaniel Leightner, after 1772. He d. about 1779, and his probate inventory was filed in York in 1780. His widow m. Dr. Charles Godfrey Ballan Wintersmith on Dec. 10, 1779. Daniel had the following children:
  - Magdalena (Helena), b. on Nov. 21, 1766, bapt. at TLY on Dec. 7, 1766, and spon. by Ignatius Leightner and wife. She m. John Rein.
  - Susanna (Hannah), b. on Oct. 9, 1771, bapt. at TLY on Oct. 7, 1772, and spon. by Michael Swope and wife. She m. Michael Keller.
  - Thomas, bapt. at TLY on Aug. 9, 1774 (mother is not named). He m. Anna Maria Funk. She was b. on Nov. 15, 1778, bapt. on Dec. 6, 1778, and d. on May 1, 1859 (bur. in Prospect Hill cemetery).
  - Joseph, bapt. at TLY on Mar. 30, 1775 (mother not named).
  - Sarah, b. in 1777.
- Johannes, b. on June 29, 1748, and bapt. at CLY on July 10, 1748. He m. Margaret Bahrth, and d. in Spring Garden Township on Oct. 11, 1796. She d. on Sept. 1, 1845. He served on the Committee Revolutionary Correspondence, and the Committee of Safety in 1775. He served in the 2nd Company 3 Battalion during the Revolution, and was Co. Commissioner from 1790-93. They had the following children:
  - Jacob, bapt. at TLY on Sept. 11, 1774, and spon. by Jacob Eichelberger and wife.
  - Zacherias, b. on Mar. 10, 1778, bapt. at TLY on Apr. 18, 1778, and spon. by Jacob and Barbara Eichelberger.
  - Johannes, b. on Nov. 1, 1779, bapt. at TLY on Dec. 31, 1779, and spon. by his parents.
  - Wilhelm, b. on Sept. 21, 1785, bapt. at TLY on Nov. 21, 1785, and spon. by his parents.
  - Rebecca, b. on Nov. 24, 1787, bapt. at TLY on Jan. 15, 1788, and spon. by Maria Magdalena and Elisabeth Spangler.
  - Margaretha Maria, b. on Jan. 8, 1790, bapt. at TLY on Apr. 5, 1790, and spon. by George Barth and wife.
  - Juliana, b. on May 20, 1794, bapt. at TLY on July 3, 1794, and spon. by her parents.
- Michael, b. about 1750. His will was written on May 3, 1790, and probated on Aug. 30, 1793.
- Anna Elisabeth, b. on Mar. 19, 1710, and m. Martie Moser of Rohrbach.
- Peter, b. on May 19, 1712, and immigrated to America on the ship *Samuel* on Dec. 3, 1740.

Spitler - Hans received a warrant for 100 acres in Springfield and York Township on Sept. 23, 1762, that was surveyed to Jacob Spitler as 144.58 acres called *Master Ground Oak* on Aug. 6, 1766. He m. Catharina, and had the following children:
- Jacob (probably), b. about 1746, and had the following children:
  - John, b. on Feb. 13, 1779, and bapt. at CLY on May 31, 1798.
- John, b. on Nov. 26, 1756, bapt. at FMY on Dec. 5, 1756, and spon. by John and Catharina Heckedorn. He d. of convulsive fits on Dec. 12, 1756, and was bur. on Dec. 13.

Stabler - Christian was taxed in 1762. He was b. in Musberg, Wurtemburg, Germany, on Feb. 5, 1726/27 to Georg and Agnes (Metzger) Stabler. He arrived at Philadelphia in 1752. He m. Anna, dau. of Michael and Barbara (Mueller) Fritz, in Hichberg, Wurtemberg, on May 8, 1752. She was b. in Plattenhardt, Wurtemberg, on July 25, 1726, and d. in Shrewsbury Township on Aug. 7, 1800. Christian d. in Shrewsbury Township on Dec. 13, 1783. They settled in Lancaster Co., Cocalico Township, PA, and 1761 moved to York Co., Shrewsbury Township, PA, in 1761. They had the following children:
- Anna Catharina, b. in Lancaster Co., Cocalico Township on Nov. 6, 1753, m. Andreas Muller about 1773, and d. in York Co. on Aug. 12, 1822.
- Anna Christina, b. on Nov. 3, 1757, bapt. on Jan. 8, 1758, and spon. by Alberech. She m. Johan Carl, son of Carl Adam and Maria Elisabeth (Ehrhardt) Diehl (see entry). She d. in York Co. on May 18, 1810.
- Johann, b. in Cocalico Township in 1759, m. Margaret Herschner at TLY on Oct. 21, 1781, and d. in York Co. on July 16, 1829.
- Maria Barbara, b. on Apr. 20, 1760. She m. Johan Peter, son of Peter and Catharina Gudling. He was bapt. at Strayer's on June 21, 1761, and spon. by Peter and Elisabeth Benss. She d. in Springfield Township on Oct. 9, 1862.
- Adam, b. Nov. 1, 1760 (?1761), m. Christina Diehl, and d. in Baltimore, MD, on Nov. 29, 1791.
- Johan Jacob, b. on Oct. 10, 1762, bapt. at CLY on Nov. 14, 1762, and m. Anna Catharina Fieser about 1788. He d. in North Hopewell Township on Sept. 5, 1837.
- Christian, b. on July 21, 1764. He m. Elisabeth Herschner in 1790, and Anna Maria, dau. of Johannes and Anna Catharina Seitz (see entry), in York Co. on Apr. 11, 1812. He d. in Baltimore Co., Stablerville, MD, on Dec. 6, 1846. Anna Maria d. at Stablerville on Mar. 19, 1845. They are bur. in Stablerville cemetery.
- Georg Jacob, b. on Dec. 26, 1768, and bapt. at CLY on Jan. 29, 1769. He m. Catharina, dau. of Johannes Michael and Appolonia

Kleinfelter (see entry). She was bapt. at St. Jacob's on Dec. 12, 1768, and d. in Sept. 1807. George d. in 1830.
- Anna, b. about 1770.

Stein - Johan Jacob received a warrant for 50 acres in Springfield Township on Nov. 25, 1766, that was surveyed as 45 acres called *Good Prospect* on Mar. 6, 1767. His will was written in Shrewsbury Township on Apr. 5, 1798, and probated on June 24, 1803. He m. Anna Maria, and had the following children (one of his daus. m. Theobald Schneider before 1798 (see entry in Codorus section)):
- Jacob, b. about 1764.
- Mathias, b. about 1766.
- Maria Catharina, b. on Nov. 6, 1768, bapt. at FRI in Dec. 1768, and spon. by Christian and Maria Catharina Michel.
- Anna Elisabeth, b. on Nov. 23, 1770, bapt. at FRI, and spon. by Georg Philip and Anna Elisabeth Venus.
- Andreas, b. on Apr. 6, 1773, bapt. at FRI on May 20, 1773, and spon. by Andreas and Catharina Muller.
- Magdalena, b. about 1775.
- Juliana, b. about 1777.
- Anna, b. about 1779.
- Johan Frederick, b. on Dec. 2, 1781, and bapt. at CLY on Apr. 13, 1782. His probate inventory was filed in Shrewsbury Township in 1827.

Swartz - Andreas was b. in Europe about 1720, m. Anna Margaretha about 1743. Andreas was a Yeoman in York Co., Shrewsbury Township, PA, as of 1745. He was Supervisor of Highways in 1759, and 1760, and Constable in 1768. He took the Sacrament on Apr. 4, 1763, and was naturalized on Apr. 11, 1763. Andreas or his son, Andreas, purchased 50 acres from Charles Diehl in Shrewsbury Township on Nov. 5, 1773. In 1783, he had 200 acres in Shrewsbury Township adjoining Jacob Henrich, Johannes Walter and Tobias Hartman. He received a warrant for 50 acres in Springfield Township on May 24, 1773, that was surveyed as 41.129 acres called *Swartz's Liberty* on Sept. 9, 1773. He received a warrant for 100 acres in Springfield and North Codorus Township on Nov. 20, 1771, that was surveyed as 105.20 acres called *Ground Eychlebergh* on May 22, 1772. He received a warrant for 100 acres in North Codorus and Springfield Township on Sept. 5, 1754, that was surveyed as 210.34 acres called *Second Fork* on Apr. 9, 1767. Andreas d. in May 1789, and Anna Margaretha d. sometime between 1786 and 1789. Andreas's will was written in Shrewsbury Township on Jan. 5, 1788, and probated on June 9, 1789. Andreas and Anna Margaretha had the following children:

- Conrad, b. on Dec. 4, 1744. He m. Dorothea Stein about 1767. She d. sometime after 1790, and he m. Elizabeth Raus. In the Revolutionary War, Conrad was a Private in the 5th (Captain John Ehrman) Company, 7th Battalion, York County Militia in 1778. He remained with this unit when it became the 5th (Captain Henry Ferree) Company, 5th Battalion in 1781. On Oct. 5-Dec. 5, 1781, he was in the detachment of the 6th Class of the previous Company under the command of Captain William Dodds guarding prisoners at Camp Security in York. He served until Dec. 28, 1782. In 1783, Conrad had 80 acres in Shrewsbury Township. He d. in Shrewsbury Township on Mar. 11, 1831. Conrad's will was written on Apr. 21, 1826, had a codicil added on June 7, 1830, and probated on Mar. 14, 1831. His beneficiaries were his siblings Margaret Schneider, Catharina Heinrich, and the children of his deceased bro. Henrich. His nephew, Henrich Swartz, Jr., was made exec. and trustee of the inheritance of the children of Henrich Swartz and the children of Henrich's deceased son Georg.
- Catharina, bapt. by Reverend Jacob Lischy at the First Reformed Church of York on Mar. 17, 1744/45, spon. by Mathies and Catharine Ness, and d. sometime before 1761.
- Jacob, b. in 1747. He m. Dorothea, dau. of Johannes and Anna Barbara (Glatfelder) Hildebrand (see entry), about 1771. She was b. on June 21, 1751, and is bur. in Stines cemetery. In the Revolutionary War, Jacob served as a Sergeant in the 7th (Captain George Geiselman) Company, 5th Battalion York County Militia in 1780, and in 1782, he was a Private in the 2nd Class of the same Company. In 1783, he had 100 acres in Shrewsbury Township. Jacob d. in Shrewsbury Township on Nov. 20, 1804, and he is bur. in Bupp's cemetery. His will was written on Feb. 21, 1804, and probated on Dec. 19, 1804.
- Anna Maria Margaretha, b. on Dec. 27, 1748, and was bapt. at Christ's Lutheran Church of York on Jan. 22, 1749, and spon. by Rebecca Hamspacker. She m. Dewalt Schneider (see entry).
- Henrich, b. on July 22, 1751. He was bapt. at Christ's Lutheran Church of York on Nov. 17, 1751, and spon. by Henry and Catharine Brehm. He m. Anna Magdalena, dau. of Johan David and Anna Catharina (Simon) Schaffer (see entry), about 1773. She was bapt. in Shrewsbury Township on Oct. 19, 1751, and d. sometime after Mar. 1801, when guardians were appointed for Henrich's minor children. Henrich was a yeoman in Shrewsbury Township, and served from 1778-1782 as a Private during the Revolutionary War. He served in Captain George Geiselman's Company, 7th Battalion, York County Militia in 1778, and remained a member of this unit in 1779, when it became the 7th Company, 5th Battalion under Captain Geiselman. He was listed in

the 7th Class of this Company in 1780 and 1782. He was a Private in a detachment of the 7th Class under Capt. Geiselman, in service guarding prisoners at Camp Security in York from Dec. 7, 1781 to Feb. 7, 1782. He was a member of the 6th Class on Jan. 30, 1781. In 1783, he had 80 acres in Shrewsbury Township. Henrich d. in Shrewsbury Township in Dec. 1799. His will was written on 12 Jan. 1799, and probated on Dec. 20, 1799.

- Andreas, b. about 1740, and d. in Shrewsbury Township in Jan. 1804. He served in the Revolutionary War in 1780-81. He named his siblings, and the children of his deceased bro., Henrich, as his beneficiaries. Theobald Schneider was granted administration on Jan. 30, 1804.
- Abraham, b. on June 26, 1758, and d. in Shrewsbury Township on Feb. 8, 1806. He is bur. in St. Paul's cemetery. He m. Anna Maria, dau. of John and Barbara Bauman of Codorus Township (see entry in Codorus section). He named his siblings and the children of his deceased bro., Henrich, as his beneficiaries. On June 21, 1800, Abraham and his wife, deeded 210 acres 34 perches in Shrewsbury Township to Bernhard Bope. The land had been given to Abraham by his father, and released by his siblings in 1798. His will was written on Jan. 15, 1805, and probated on Feb. 12, 1806. Anna Maria's will written on Mar. 21, 1818, and probated on Feb. 12, 1821. It named her sister, Eve (deceased), and her (Eve's) daus., Elizabeth, wife of Josophine Young, Catharina, Eve, Barbara, and Christina Bop. Anna Maria was b. on Oct. 28, 1759, d. on May 3, 1821, and is bur. in Friedensaal cemetery. Abraham served in the Revolutionary War, the following is a record of his service: Abraham Schwartz of Shrewsbury Township, fines 13.10 pounds by warrant dated May 10, 1777, while a resident of Hellam Township, for failure to "meet and exercise in order to learn the art of military," as was required in an Act of Assembly of Feb. 14, 1777. Private in 6th (Captain George Geiselman) Company, 7th Battalion, York County Militia according to an undated return assigned to the year 1778; he remained a member of this unit when (in 1779) it became the 7th (Captain George Geiselman) Company, 5th Battalion, York County Militia and in 1782 was listed in the 7th Class of this company. From Dec. 7, 1781 to Feb. 7, 1782 he saw actual service in a detachment of the 7th Class of the York County Militia under the command of Captain Geiselman, guarding prisoners of war at Camp Security in York Co. Abraham is bur. in St. Paul's cemetery in North Codorus Township.
- Anna Catharina, b. on Jan. 19, 1761. She was bapt. at Christ's Lutheran Church of York on Jan. 20, 1761, and spon. by Henry and Dorothea Walter, and Catharine, dau. of Conrad Mueller. She m. Jacob, son of Nicolus and Margarethe Heinrich (see entry). He

was b. on Dec. 18, 1755, bapt. at Friedensaal, and spon. by Jacob Heinrich, and Anna Maria Bremm.
- Johan Peter, b. on Jan. 19, 1761, and d. sometime before 1789. He was bapt. at Christ's Lutheran Church of York on Jan. 20, 1761, and spon. by Henry and Dorothea Walter, and Catharine, dau. of Conrad Mueller.

Swope - George received a warrant for 100 acres with Christian Kroll on June 1, 1762, that was surveyed as 102 acres.

Troerbach - Adam received a warrant for 200 acres in Springfield Township on Dec. 28, 1767, that was surveyed as 171.16 acres called *Berrick and Daule* on Mar. 8, 1769 (see entry in Codorus section).

Troerbach - Michael received a warrant for 300 acres in Springfield and York Township, that was surveyed as 210.122 acres called *Crum Wafer* on Mar. 7, 1769 (see entry in Codorus section).

Updegraff - Samuel received a warrant for 150 acres in Shrewsbury and Springfield Township on May 13, 1768.

Venus - Georg Philip was a master mason. He m. Dorothea about 1752, Maria Elisabeth, dau. of Peter Schmidt of Holtzbach, Simmern, Germany, about 1755, and Anna Elisabeth about 1761. Maria Elisabeth was b. in 1728, and d. on Sept. 29, 1760 (bur. CLY). She immigrated to America in 1754, m. Henry Zimmer in 1755 (two children). Philip d. without a will, and his estate was administered on May 22, 1777, by Elizabeth Venus and Conrad Schwartz. Philip had the following children:
- Johann Friederich, b. about 1751. He was taxed in York Township in 1779. His probate inventory was filed in Hopewell Township in 1820. He m. Elisabeth. Her probate inventory was filed in Hopewell Township in 1823. They had the following children:
  - Maria Elisabeth, b. in Mar. 1779, bapt. at FRI on Apr. 11, 1779, and spon. by Anna Maria, dau. of the late Philip Venus.
  - Johann Philip, b. on Aug. 26, 1780, bapt. at FRI on Oct. 1, 1780, and spon. by Samuel and Catharina Brenneman.
  - Johan Friedrich, b. on Nov. 18, 1789, bapt. at STP on Jan. 12, 1789, and spon. by Friederich and Magdalena Geisselman.
- Johan Georg, b. on Dec. 20, 1753, and bapt. at CLY on Dec. 26, 1753.
- Anna Maria, b. about 1756, and m. David, son of David Schaffer (see entry).
- Maria Eva, bapt. by RJL on Mar. 26, 1758, and spon. by Johan Georg Nees and Maria Eva Meyerin.

SHREWSBURY TOWNSHIP 365

- Maria Magdalena, b., bapt., and d. on Sept. 29, 1760 (bur. with Maria Elisabeth at CLY).
- John, b. on June 3, 1762, and d. on Aug. 15, 1762. He is bur. at CLY.
- Elisabeth, b. on July 11. 1763, and bapt. at CLY on July 31, 1763. She m. Michael Miller at TLY on Apr. 24, 1798.
- Maria Magdalena, bapt. at FRI on June 25, 1768, and spon. by Abraham Reber and Magdalena Weymuller. She m. Frederick, son of Michael Geisselman (see entry), at TLY on May 4, 1786.
- Dorothea, b. on Feb. 25, 1773, bapt. at FRI on Apr. 7, 1773, and spon. by Conrad and Dorothea Swartz.

Walter (Walther) - Peter received a warrant for 20 acres in Springfield Township on June 29, 1767. He was the sponsor of the baptism of Johannes Conel in 1776 (STR).

Walther - Heinrich was taxed in 1762. He received a warrant for 100 acres in Springfield Township on Dec. 20, 1769 (interest began on Mar. 1, 1757), that was surveyed as 109.51 acres called *Crooked Elbow* on Dec. 30, 1769. He received a warrant for 100 acres in Springfield Township on June 3, 1773, that was surveyed as 107.120 acres called *Walter's Addition* on Oct. 21, 1774. His will was written in Shrewsbury Township on Jan. 8, 1781, and probated on Feb. 17, 1781. He m. Dorothea Margareth Lauffer, dau. of Hans Jacob Lauffer, and immigrated to America from Zurich, Switzerland on the ship *Francis and Elizabeth* on Aug. 30, 1743. They had the following children (recorded by RJL):
- Anna Maria, bapt. on Aug. 31, 1745, and spon. by Casper and Maria Glattfelter. She m. Peter, son of Matthias Ness (see entry), and Johan Heinrich Alt (see entry).
- Elisabetha, bapt. on June 18, 1749, and spon. by Jacob and Elisabeth Rudysille. She m. Valentine Wild (see entry in Manchester section).
- Barbara, bapt. on July 12, 1752, and spon. by Johannes and Anna Barbara Hildebrand. She m. Johann Schmidt.
- Heinrich, bapt. on May 4, 1755, and spon. by Hans Ulrich and Ursula Hess.
- Salomon, bapt. on May 14, 1758, and spon. by Salomon Glattfelter and Anna Glattfelter.
- Dorothea, bapt. on Sept. 28, 1761, and spon. by Casper and Anna Maria Glattfelter. She m. Jacob, son of Georg Jacob Schaffer (see entry in Codorus section), on Jan. 4, 1785.
- Anna Margaretha, bapt. on Sept. 28, 1761, and spon. by Andreas and Anna Margaretha Swartz.

- Salomon, bapt. on Oct. 9, 1763, and spon. by Salomon Glattfelter and Anna Glattfelterin. He m. Catharina before 1785.

Weis - George received a warrant for 200 acres with Adam Eichelberger on Mar. 23, 1768, that was surveyed as 196.26 acres called *The Range* on Nov. 25, 1768 (improved 14 years).

Weishart - Christopher received a warrant for 100 acres on Oct. 5, 1772, that was surveyed as 82.128 acres called *Hugh's Lick* on Mar. 6, 1773. He m. Maria about 1769, and had the following son(s):
- John, b. on July 21, 1770, and bapt. at CLY on July 22, 1770.
- Johann Jacob, b. in Feb. 1780, bapt. at FRI on Apr. 9, 1780, and spon. by Georg and Anna Elisabeth Eissenhard (his mother was Susanna so it is not certain if this was by a second wife, or there was possibly a Christopher Jr, who m. Susanna).

Welschans - Jacob resided in Kirberg, and had the following sons:
- Abraham m. Anna, dau. of Isaac Haschard, on July 18, 1700. They had the following children (recorded at Diedendorf Lutheran Church in Northern Alsace (see BNA)):
  - Margaretha, b. on July 10, 1701.
  - Maria Johanna, b. on June 20, 1702.
  - Anna Judith, b. on Mar. 10, 1705.
  - Maria Magdalena, b. on Oct. 30, 1707.
  - Johann Henrich, b. on June 24, 1710.
  - Abraham, bapt. on Feb. 26, 1713, and spon. by Abraham Brion, Georg Hachar, Isaac Hachar, Susanna Georg, wife of Jacob Pilla. He m. Margaretha Brion, and immigrated to America on the ship *Robert and Alice* in 1739. They had the following children (recorded by RJL unless otherwise noted):
    - Anna Catharina, b. on Oct. 9, 1742, bapt. at the First Reformed Lutheran Church in Lancaster, PA, on Nov. 7, 1742, and spon. by Jacob and Elisabetha (Schleppi) Welschans.
    - Magdalena Elisabetha, bapt. on May 23, 1745, and spon. by Mathias Burckhardt, Friedrich Burckhardt, Magdalena Schleppi; and Elisabetha Kerber.
    - Maria Magdalena, bapt. on Apr. 30, 1749, and spon. by Joseph and Magdalena Welschans. She m. Heinrich, son of Matthias Ness (see entry).
    - Anna Maria, bapt. on Apr. 28, 1751.
    - Daniel, bapt. on June 24, 1753.
    - Johan Wilhelm, bapt. on May 25, 1755.
    - Elisabeth, bapt. on July 31, 1757.
    - Johan Heinrich, bapt. on Dec. 9, 1759.
    - Johannes, bapt. on June 3, 1764.

- Johan David, bapt. on Apr. 5, 1716.
- Johann Jacob, bapt. on Feb. 19, 1719. He immigrated to America on the ship *Lydia* in 1741. He m. Elisabeta, dau. of Johan Adam Schleppi in Rauwiller Lutheran Church on Oct. 27, 1740 (see entry). They had the following children:
  - Jacob, b. on Sept. 22, 1742, bapt. at the First Reformed Church of Lancaster, PA, on Oct. 10, 1742, and spon. by Jacob Schober and Abraham Hascher.
  - Balthazar, bapt. by RJL on July 6, 1746, and spon. by Balthasar and Magdalena Spengler.
  - Abraham, bapt. by RJL on May 13, 1750. He d. on Oct. 18, 1758.
  - Elisabeth, b. on Mar. 9, 1752, bapt. at CLY on Mar. 29, 1752, and spon. by Balthasar and Maria Magdalena Spengler.
  - Elisabeth, b. on Oct. 26, 1753, and bapt. at CLY on Dec. 25, 1753.
  - Johan Conrad, bapt. by RJL on Apr. 19, 1761 (mother is Eva Elisabeth).
- Johanneta, bapt. on June 3, 1721, and spon. by Thomas Fichter of Hellering, Jacob Frolich of Kirberg, Anna Grojean, Kirberg, and Johanneta Nagelin of Schonburg.
- Maria Elisabetha, bapt. on June 27, 1723.
- Hans Peter, m. Susanna, dau. of Abraham Fuhrmann of Berg on Dec. 6, 1705. They had the following children:
  - Joseph, bapt. at Diedendorf Lutheran Church in Northern Alsace on Dec. 9, 1714, and spon. by Peter Zeller of Kirberg, Joseph Schneider of Kirberg, and Anna, dau. of Isaac Georg. He immigrated to America on the ship *Robert and Alice* in 1739. He was naturalized on Apr. 10, 1760. He m. Magdalena about 1745. He had the following children (recorded by RJL unless otherwise noted):
    - Johan Jacob, bapt. on Apr. 28, 1746, and spon. by Jacob Ob and Maria Elisabetha Reiff. He m. Anna Maria, and had the following children (recorded at FRY):
      - Magdalena, b. on Nov. 14, 1767, bapt. at FRY on Jan. 24, 1768, and spon. by Joseph Welschans and wife.
      - Heinrich, b. on Dec. 31, 1769, and bapt. on Apr. 8, 1770.
      - Maria Elisabetha, b. on Mar. 29, 1773, and bapt. on June 13, 1773.
    - Anna Catharina, bapt. on Oct. 8, 1752, and spon. by Georg and Anna Barbara Meyer.
    - Joseph, bapt. on Mar. 2, 1755, and spon. by Georg and Elisabetha Schramm.
    - Elisabeth, bapt. on Oct. 9, 1757, and spon. by Ludwig and Catharina Kraft.

- Joseph, b. on Feb. 2, 1760, and bapt. at CLY on Feb. 24, 1760.
- Johan Peter, b. on Oct. 16, 1761, and bapt. at CLY on Nov. 22, 1761.

Weymueller - Johannes received a warrant for 100 acres in Codorus and Springfield Township on May 25, 1749, that was surveyed as 189.60 acres called *Weymiller's Desire* on Aug. 27, 1768. He received a warrant for 100 acres in Springfield Township on June 23, 1768, that was surveyed as 69.120 acres called *Gooseberry Hill* on Aug. 27, 1768. He m. Catharina, and had the following children:
- Johannes, b. on Nov. 9, 1742, and bapt. at CLY on Mar. 29, 1743.
- Magdalena, bapt. at CLY on Mar. 17, 1745, and spon. by Hans Georg and Magdalena Schwob.
- Johan Frantz, bapt. by RJL on July 5, 1753, and spon. by Frantz and Rebecca Hammer. He m. Eva, and had the following children:
  - Maria Eva, b. on Feb. 6, (1779), bapt. at FRI in 1779, and spon. by Christopher and Dorothea Hauble.
  - Abraham, b. on Nov. 14, bapt. at FRI on Nov. 29, 1781, and spon. by Abraham and Magdalena Rehler.

Wilhelm - Georg Heinrich was taxed in 1762. He received a warrant for 100 acres in Springfield Township on July 5, 1762, that was surveyed as 144 acres called *Poverty* on Aug. 25, 1766. He m. Christina. They had the following children:
- Heinrich m. Christina, and had the following children:
  - Anna Christina, b. on Apr. 5, 1772, bapt. at FRI on Palm Sunday 1772, and spon. by Frantz and Anna Kraft.
  - Johan Heinrich, b. in June 1773, bapt. at FRI on July 18, 1773, and spon. by Johannes and Margaretha Schneider.
  - Johan Peter, b. on Oct. 28, 1778, bapt. at FRI on Dec. 6, 1779, and spon. by Peter and Elisabetha Beiss,
  - Solomon, b. on Dec. 14, 1781, and bapt. at STJ on May 26, 1782.
- Anna Margaretha, bapt. by RJL on Dec. 9, 1753, and spon. by Johannes and Anna Margaretha Klein.
- Anna Barbara, bapt. by RJL on July 6, 1755, and spon. by Michael Groll and Maria Barbara Wilhelmin.

Wirick (Weirich) - Nicholas received a warrant for 100 acres in Springfield Township on Feb. 25, 1754. He received a warrant for 100 acres in Springfield Township on Jan. 25, 1754. He d. intestate in Aug. 1761, m. Elizabeth Margaretha, and had the following children:
- Katarina, m. John Flower of Shrewsbury (see entry).
- Elizabeth Margaretha, m. George Eppler of Winchester Co., Wood____, VA.

Yeakle - Nicholas received a warrant with Jacob Heinrich for 100 acres in Springfield Township on Apr. 4, 1754, that was surveyed as 170 acres on Apr. 20, 1754.

Yount - Rudolph was taxed in 1762. He received a warrant for 25 acres in Springfield Township on Sept. 23, 1762, that was surveyed as 83.65 acres called *High Ground* on Aug. 14, 1766. He received a warrant for 100 acres in Springfield Township on May 2, 1770, that was surveyed as 128.73 acres called *Yount's Choice* on June 27, 1770.

INDEX

-A-

Acker, 86, 112
Adam, 12, 113, 158, 339
Aest, 293
Ager, 287
Akenbogh, 95
Alberech, 360
Albert, 95, 127, 144, 156, 168, 273
Albrecht, 105, 231, 357
Albright, 67, 69, 283, 319
Alt, 43, 201, 229, 287, 288, 322, 323, 331, 344, 365
Althaus, 349
Altland, 115, 198
Altvater, 15
Amberg, 309
Amelot, 197, 229
Amend, 129
Amendt, 136, 188, 218
Ament, 212, 233
Amma, 232, 244, 278
Amman, 26, 176, 239, 241
Ammann, 159
Ammannin, 241
Ammin, 279
Amspacher, 1, 2, 253, 284, 288, 289, 325, 326
Andreas, 72, 104
Andres, 73, 329
Anspach, 115
Anspachin, 108
Anstine, 343
Anthony, 66
Apfel, 122
Apfelman, 2, 183
Apfler, 166
Appel, 95
Appelman, 241
Arndt, 251
Arntz, 299
Attich, 45
Aumiller, 72
Aumuller, 3

-B-

Babb, 19
Bachman, 51, 77, 93
Bachmn, 49
Baehli, 15, 19, 64, 65, 66, 67, 289, 290, 292, 293, 318, 319, 321, 338, 339, 347
Baer, 3, 49, 90, 306
Baesel, 173
Bahler, 191
Bahn, 63, 64, 136, 138, 146, 247, 355
Bahrth, 359
Bailey, 74, 290
Baist, 170
Baker, 99, 290, 319, 354
Balt, 7
Baltzley, 279
Banckert, 79
Baner, 176
Banman, 176
Banters, 110
Bar, 153, 282
Bard, 282
Barkdoll, 102
Barker, 217
Barner, 95, 156
Barnes, 156
Barnitz, 358
Barr, 4, 118
Bart, 107, 108
Bartel, 171
Bartemess, 3, 95, 167, 175
Bartesin, 301
Barth, 46, 59, 102, 108, 146, 190, 312, 359
Barthel, 91
Bartin, 252
Bartmess, 169
Bartmesse, 219
Basler, 36, 191

Bassler, 145, 161, 176, 274, 275, 281
Bauer, 147, 152, 166, 176, 178, 279, 292
Bauman, 3, 294, 302, 314, 326, 363
Baumann, 40, 101, 170, 227
Baumgartner, 10, 225, 294
Baur, 199, 207
Baurer, 176, 245
Bauser, 147, 293
Bayer, 33, 46, 79, 252
Bear, 49, 93, 153, 177, 250
Becher, 208
Bechtel, 191, 212
Bechtle, 293
Beck, 69, 268, 329, 338
Becker, 4, 12, 57, 64, 96, 97, 106, 107, 149, 177, 186, 190, 199, 203, 206, 216, 221, 223, 224, 240, 255, 259, 282, 290, 293, 296, 344, 352
Bederman, 214
Beer, 97, 102, 122, 177, 276
Beery, 131, 178, 345
Beherin, 199
Behler, 4, 5, 88, 288, 304
Behner, 74
Beier, 130
Beintzel, 218
Beisher, 178
Beiss, 368
Beisser, 14
Beitzel, 5, 98, 111, 140, 247
Beizel, 172
Beller, 75, 163
Beltz, 349
Bender, 109, 158
Bendter, 107
Benedick, 99, 151, 164
Benner, 78, 234
Bens, 106
Bensin, 100
Benss, 204, 215, 360
Bentz, 100, 150, 151, 177, 217, 249, 299
Bentzel, 100, 119
Berckheimer, 150
Berg, 309
Berge, 18, 68
Bergerin, 196
Bergheimer, 229
Bergheimerin, 126
Bergman, 156
Bergtold, 207
Berkheimer, 242
Berlekamp & McConnell, 117, 209
Berlin, 108
Berling, 25
Berlinger, 301
Bernard, 5
Berner, 95, 156, 170
Bernerin, 48
Bernhard, 352
Berot, 34
Beroth, 31, 32, 99, 249, 260
Besserer, 186
Best, 251, 336
Beyer, 178, 267, 344
Beyerle, 252
Biber, 340
Bickel, 357
Bidner, 105
Biegler, 350
Biegmann, 155
Biehlmajer, 65, 273
Bielmann, 291
Bier, 312
Bieri, 131, 178, 181, 334
Biger, 180
Bigler, 180
Billbeyer, 260
Billeten, 105
Billmann, 312
Billmeyer, 188, 268
Binckel, 34, 248
Binckele, 5, 28, 34, 50, 91, 247, 249
Binckely, 89

Binder, 326
Binkele, 28
Bischoff, 6, 79, 83
Bissecker, 110
Bitle, 258
Bitner, 98
Bitsche, 75
Bixler, 8, 179, 181, 222, 270
Blaize, 17
Blasser, 181
Blauser, 294
Blechart, 101
Blechhard, 149
Bless, 175
Bleymeier, 306
Blier, 343
Blocker, 17
Blosser, 179, 181
Blum, 274
Blunston, 264
Bob, 73
Bobb, 26, 90, 100, 294
Bock, 147
Bocket, 104
Boehl, 56
Bohler, 23, 35, 200
Bohli, 250
Bohn, 56, 150, 182, 215, 222, 234, 271
Boin, 82, 246
Bolle, 289
Bollinger, 6, 71, 154, 295, 311
Bolz, 136
Bombariere, 6
Bone, 182
Boner, 182
Bonge, 154
Bop, 3, 363
Bope, 363
Bopp, 4, 26
Bordman, 282
Bortner, 7, 16, 18, 24, 63, 68, 72, 80, 130
Boss, 241
Bossert, 38, 40, 142, 328

Bott, 2, 83, 119, 182, 183, 184, 185, 187, 194, 235, 245, 281, 282
Botzman, 186
Bouschmann, 288
Bower, 90, 165
Bowers, 310
Bowman, 296
Boyer, 82
Brady, 123
Brandy, 121
Brauer, 100
Braus, 339
Brehm, 362
Bremm, 313, 364
Brendlerin, 55
Breneman, 159
Brenneisen, 355
Brenneman, 153, 364
Brenner, 252, 344
Bricker, 3, 14
Briggs, 122
Brigner, 39
Brillhardt, 8
Brillhart, 8, 53, 295
Brillinger, 299
Brindel, 83
Brindli, 210
Brinli, 211
Brinton, 83
Brion, 366
Brishler, 148
Brodbeck, 9, 11, 30, 39, 330
Brodbeckin, 17
Brotzman, 5, 9, 32, 98, 99, 189, 249
Bruckerin, 133
Bruckhardt, 186
Bruecker, 78
Bruegger, 160
Bruner, 217
Brunner, 171
Brusz, 215
Brutzman, 98
Buatt, 165

Buchanan, 52, 93
Buchannon, 215
Bucher, 209
Buchtrueckel, 227
Buck, 124
Buehler, 135
Buhler, 10
Buinger, 196
Bunckely, 8
Bupp, 73
Burckert, 301
Burcket, 271
Burckhard, 127
Burckhardt, 116, 160, 187, 261, 366
Burckhart, 177
Burghart, 172
Burkhardt, 127
Burkhart, 86, 179, 217, 298, 300
Busch, 56
Bushon, 311
Bushong, 268
Busser, 38
Byers, 82, 283
Byrn, 310

-C-

Cagey, 182
Cammer, 281
Cansler, 153
Canto, 44
Cappell, 91
Carpenter, 251
Casner, 187
Cherdron, 204
Cheyry, 315
Childer, 97
Christ, 101, 182
Christie, 10
Christman, 5, 28, 34
Christy, 10
Clark, 253
Clauser, 280
Clay, 197, 257
Clemmer, 181

Cline, 201
Clingman, 216
Cloninger, 336
Closs, 2
Closter, 79
Cobean, 357
Coblentz, 200
Coffman, 53, 283
Colman, 112
Comfort, 79, 134, 208
Connell, 147
Connor, 293
Conrad, 42, 43, 84, 88, 287, 291, 329
Copenhaver, 256
Corel, 162
Corpman, 308, 322
Correll, 308
Costner, 251
Coule, 295
Couli, 295
Cousler, 306
Craddy, 24
Cramer, 43, 78, 315
Crawford, 142
Creamer, 352
Cremer, 46, 143, 275
Cremerin, 46
Cresap, 136, 264
Crist, 211
Croll, 242
Crolle, 242
Cronebach, 151
Croppach, 104
Crow, 136
Culp, 247
Culver, 135

-D-

Dagen, 295
Dallman, 343
Dannbach, 185
Danner, 10, 55, 101, 136, 150, 279
Dantzler, 107

Dattesmann, 112
Daubenberger, 232
Davies, 102
Davis, 102, 283
Debold, 271
Debus, 129
Decken, 339
Decker, 130, 352
Dee, 307
Degraff, 61
Degranche, 62
Dehoff, 3, 10, 11, 65, 74, 75, 19, 21, 39, 74, 78
Deilman, 301
Dellinger, 138
Denen, 28
Densor, 349
Dentzel, 174
Derr, 251
Dersteen, 130
Desch, 124
Desenberg, 240
Dettemer, 246
Detter, 101, 102
Detterman, 246
Detweiler, 11
Devault, 251
Devepaugh, 201
Devis, 112
Dewalt, 79, 203, 301
Dewes, 97, 98, 102, 119
Dibel, 337
Dice, 349
Dick, 11
Dieb, 325
Diederich, 77
Diehl, 12, 43, 90, 109, 117, 136, 158, 163, 186, 187, 188, 189, 234, 262, 295, 297, 298, 299, 301, 305, 311, 323, 331, 343, 344, 348, 349, 350, 354, 355, 360, 361
Diel, 170
Diellin, 170
Dietenheimer, 302

Dietenhoefer, 302
Dietenhofer, 302
Diettenhofferin, 302
Dietz, 79, 306
Dift, 193
Diller, 83, 299
Dillman, 11, 301
Dinckel, 240
Dineke, 307
Dinkel, 319
Dinkle, 192
Dipinger, 224, 302, 310
Ditenhauer, 302
Ditti, 353
Dodd, 283
Doerr, 241
Doll, 61, 109
Dorners, 190
Dorr, 236
Dotterer, 210
Doudel, 319
Drach, 124
Dresh, 124
Drexler, 45
Dritt, 357
Drorbach, 87
Droxel, 228
Dubbs, 57, 162
Duenckel, 268, 358
Duenkel, 357
Duer, 187
Dunckel, 354
Dundore, 217
Dunki, 344
Durrin, 238
Dussing, 163

-E-

Earhart, 12
Early, 251
Easum, 211
Eberd, 218
Eberdt, 229, 230
Eberhard, 98
Eberhardt, 41, 87

Eberhart, 265, 291
Eberly, 333
Ebert, 31, 32, 99, 128, 136, 173, 187, 188, 189, 211, 212, 218, 221, 230, 242, 248, 249, 254, 257, 298, 300, 302
Eberth, 301
Ebit, 173
Eby, 302
Echelbaur, 100
Eckart, 36
Eckert, 301
Eckler, 210
Edwards, 215
Ege, 281
Ehler, 45, 78
Ehmig, 238, 251
Ehrhard, 44, 57, 125, 328, 331, 342
Ehrhardt, 12, 39, 48, 144, 170, 296, 303, 329, 343, 360
Ehrman, 15, 303, 341, 342
Ehrmann, 303
Eichelberger, 190, 193, 195, 196, 210, 211, 212, 213, 224, 237, 257, 270, 286, 332, 366
Eichinberger, 354
Eichingers, 177
Eicholtz, 96, 102, 141, 152
Eickelberger, 359
Einsel, 346
Eip, 235
Eisen, 2, 280
Eisenhardt, 246
Eisenhart, 193, 194
Eisenhauer, 318, 328
Eisick, 73
Eislinger, 58
Eissenhard, 326, 366
Eissenhardt, 183, 193, 194, 222
Eissenhart, 193, 194
Eister, 198
Eisterin, 93
Elder, 238
Ellenbarger, 194

Ellmore, 356
Elsasser, 243
Elss, 105
Emig, 12, 13, 44, 83, 106, 114, 194, 195, 196, 197, 213, 214, 224, 244, 274, 351
Emler, 125
Emmerich, 18
Enders, 115
Endersen, 143, 144
Enderson, 144
Endler, 189, 196, 255
Endress, 249
Endtler, 200
Eners, 104
Engel, 31, 189
Engelman, 74
Engels, 98
Engle, 34
Ensminger, 153
Eppelman, 183
Eppleman, 2
Eppler, 368
Eppley, 13, 57
Eppli, 13
Erb, 82, 83, 88, 135, 351
Erbin, 195
Erek, 170
Erisman, 102
Ernst, 1, 157, 343
Ertel, 196
Erunst, 61
Erwin, 45
Esch, 295
Eschbach, 311
Eschelbach, 215
Esk, 140
Eslinger, 14
Esslinger, 57
Etter, 28
Evans, 139
Everhard, 265
Eychelpeyer, 100
Eyler, 335
Eyrich, 64, 65

Eyseck, 48
Eyster, 196, 198, 215, 228, 229, 230, 256, 265, 266, 267, 281

-F-

Fackler, 97, 198, 216, 260, 276, 304
Facklerin, 258
Faehr, 162
Fahnestock, 183
Failler, 22
Falkinstein, 12
Falkner, 304
Farch, 313
Farni, 135
Fass, 4, 26
Fast, 180
Faubel, 134
Faust, 69, 305
Fauster, 126
Feeser, 14, 51
Feezler, 305
Fehr, 162
Feiser, 5, 99, 103, 112
Feisser, 103
Felcker, 105, 132
Felty, 242
Fentzel, 112
Ferree, 214
Fetter, 177
Fettro, 113
Feusser, 103
Fichter, 367
Fickes, 235
Fiel, 105
Fiesel, 202
Fieser, 99, 128, 360
Fife, 67
Finck, 105, 107
Finckin, 107
Finger, 201
Fink, 41, 104, 106, 107, 153, 217, 224, 278
Fischborn, 130, 184
Fischbornin, 35

Fischel, 128, 135
Fischer, 5, 344
Fischerin, 78, 286
Fiser, 24
Fishel, 214
Fisher, 118, 242, 291, 358
Fissel, 1, 14, 44, 62, 93, 105, 108, 109, 126, 159, 160, 241, 296, 305, 331, 343
Fisser, 83
Flauer, 305
Flaur, 343
Flenschbach, 105
Fletcher, 199
Flickinger, 8, 55
Flieger, 294
Fliger, 165
Flinschbach, 307
Flohr, 110, 159, 173
Floor, 169, 171
Florentina, 221
Floucher, 7
Flower, 368
Flowers, 305
Folckner, 13
Folk, 290
Fols, 312
Fondorn, 148
Foobach, 116, 117
Forney, 192
Forny, 87
Forry, 86, 179
Fortney, 268
Fortune, 174
Foucks, 110
Fouk, 306
Fox, 267
Francois, 243
Frank, 179
Frantz, 95
Frasher, 15, 303
Frawinger, 228
Frech, 306
Frederick, 159, 177, 246, 289
Free, 54, 110

Freeland, 64
Freitag, 153
Frensch, 14, 21, 75, 309
Frescher, 130
Frey, 63, 111, 173, 199, 205, 206, 228, 230, 242, 258, 292, 305, 306, 308, 328, 337, 338
Freytag, 107, 199, 233
Frick, 112
Friday, 199, 251
Fridlein, 1
Frie, 329
Friedel, 272
Friedland, 200
Friedle, 266
Friedlein, 200
Friedlin, 270
Friedrich, 14
Friend, 21
Frienst, 14, 75, 309
Fries, 78
Frinsh, 308
Frisher, 16
Fritz, 360
Froescher, 15, 19, 72, 74
Frolich, 367
Frone, 233
Froschauer, 120
Fruh, 110
Fry, 111, 128, 153, 337
Frysinger, 107, 112
Fuchs, 103, 104
Fuesser, 51
Fuhrman, 25, 26
Fuhrmann, 367
Fulton, 69
Fultz, 16
Fulweiler, 89
Funk, 180, 359
Furhman, 25, 26

-G-
Gabel, 311, 350
Gack, 325
Gaeiss, 270
Gaertner, 135, 136, 138, 188
Gaiss, 196, 200
Galatin, 248
Gander, 25
Gans, 7, 8, 16, 19, 38, 63, 71, 319
Gansert, 113, 114, 160, 175
Gansshorn, 110
Gantsert, 158
Gantz, 16, 17, 18, 61, 66, 67, 69, 80, 290
Gantzert, 113, 139, 140, 160
Gantzertin, 160
Gap, 124, 183
Garber, 180
Garden, 201
Gardner, 351
Gares, 124
Garman, 319
Gartner, 157
Gartnerin, 33
Gauch, 168
Gauech, 155
Gauff, 114, 129, 130, 154, 195
Gaumuller, 7
Geberich, 319
Geckler, 335, 349
Gecklerin, 13, 335
Gedlinger, 151
Geese, 200
Gehlhaus, 267
Geib, 232
Geiger, 91, 241
Geil, 179
Geip, 294
Geiselman, 90, 313
Geiselmann, 331
Geisey, 67, 306, 307
Geisselman, 13, 24, 61, 90, 157, 158, 189, 236, 243, 270, 294, 307, 308, 315, 319, 322, 323, 332, 335, 344, 364, 365
Gemling, 151, 200
Gemmel, 309
Genemer, 352
Gennwein, 26

Gensler, 221, 251
Genssler, 219
Gentzler, 201, 228, 229, 277
Georg, 367, 368
Gerbach, 41, 57
Gerber, 83, 183, 277
Gerberich, 1, 7, 15, 18, 20, 66, 67, 68, 291, 292, 303, 318, 319, 321, 326
Gerecks, 20
Gerhard, 42
Gerhardt, 75, 105, 244
Gerlach, 15, 75, 309, 328
Gernant, 318
Gerot, 166
Gertraut, 169
Geschwy, 49
Gess, 96
Gettier, 25
Geyer, 202
Gibbs, 338
Giess, 224
Gilgen, 25
Ginter, 99, 114
Gippel, 89
Gischin, 69
Gitt, 235
Glabsatle, 175
Gladfelter, 309
Glasick, 20
Glasser, 46
Glassick, 11
Glat, 89
Glatfelder, 315, 362
Glatfelter, 21, 336
Glattfelder, 21
Glattfelter, 15, 21, 61, 219, 309, 314, 315, 335, 365, 366
Glattfelterin, 366
Gleim, 35, 55
Glink, 107
Glocker, 41
Glonninger, 261
Glorius, 21, 309
Goafman, 311

Gobble, 311, 350
Gobel, 311
Gobelet, 133
Gobler, 105
Gobrecht, 213
Gochenour, 114, 179, 180, 311
Gockelert, 158
Gohn, 74, 78
Gohnn, 46
Gohns, 329
Good, 179
Goose, 211
Gorsuch, 67
Gortman, 73
Gossler, 115, 126, 172
Gossner, 115
Gottleib, 23, 29
Gottwald, 58, 255
Gottwalt, 97, 107
Gotty, 26
Gotz, 231
Gotzin, 231
Grabell, 8
Graber, 98, 202, 216, 217, 295, 301, 311
Graeber, 50, 155
Graff, 213, 226, 240, 261, 262
Graibill, 31
Gramer, 311
Grass, 203
Gray, 4
Graybill, 203, 263
Greaves, 118
Greber, 116, 311
Grebiel, 31, 301
Grebillin, 301
Greenwald, 177, 203
Greenwalt, 64
Grees, 200
Greff, 141, 237
Grenn, 73
Greth, 206
Grever, 203, 232
Grim, 99
Grimm, 42, 106, 311, 329

Grimmen, 291
Grindel, 339
Gro, 179
Grob, 163
Grockrine, 203
Groff, 22, 70, 105, 153
Groh, 312
Grojean, 367
Grokes, 63
Groll, 118, 184, 203, 343, 368
Grooss, 97
Grosch, 29
Gross, 101, 115, 116, 144, 172, 186, 301
Grossin, 160
Grossmannin, 163
Grouce, 312
Grove, 203, 319
Gruber, 1
Gruen, 54
Grummerein, 336
Grunblad, 52
Grunewald, 177
Grunwald, 203
Gruss, 133
Gubleman, 238
Gubler, 216
Guckes, 184, 237, 245, 303
Gudling, 360
Gump, 32, 157, 248
Gunckel, 144
Gunnemer, 351
Guntel, 140
Gunther, 59, 99, 204, 220, 221, 225, 234
Gus, 96
Guscha, 115
Guthman, 230
Gutjahr, 157
Gutling, 160, 204
Guttelman, 121

-H-

Haas, 107, 116
Haber, 22
Hachar, 366
Hachelberger, 157
Hack, 138
Hackmann, 120
Hadelman, 217
Haegis, 350
Haentschi, 22, 27, 28
Hafer, 213
Haffner, 23, 55, 56, 62, 88
Hafner, 56
Hagener, 185
Hagge, 310
Hahn, 12, 184, 357
Hahnawaldt, 20, 292
Haines, 241
Hains, 236
Haintz, 100
Hake, 152
Hall, 71
Haller, 32, 101, 116
Haman, 315
Hambrecht, 218
Hamilton, 358
Hamm, 116, 117, 118, 119, 145, 203, 338
Hammann, 28
Hammer, 1, 23, 40, 107, 204, 282, 368
Hamschear, 292
Hamscher, 289
Hamspacher, 1, 2, 288, 304, 325
Hamspacker, 79, 362
Han, 93, 100
Hanacle, 205
Haner, 205
Hanewald, 30
Hanse, 173
Hanss, 198
Hanssin, 165
Hantz, 117, 298
Harbach, 79, 137
Harbaugh, 143, 352
Harbold, 211
Hardt, 287
Hari, 75

Haring, 119
Harman, 310
Harnisen, 33
Harring, 119
Harry, 207
Hart, 312
Hartman, 80, 90, 117, 124, 278, 315, 361
Hartmann, 23
Harttafel, 249
Hartz, 209
Hartzell, 233
Haschard, 366
Hascher, 367
Hasler, 343
Hassler, 7, 23, 68, 229, 248, 308
Hatten, 122
Hattman, 283
Hau, 288
Hauble, 302, 368
Haubli, 206
Haubly, 302
Hauck, 24, 57, 231, 272
Haug, 24, 25, 88
Haugin, 13, 25
Hauk, 24, 312
Haus, 145
Hause, 62
Hauser, 26, 30, 92
Hausman, 40
Hauss, 173
Hay, 184, 358
Hayer, 137, 138, 207
Hayes, 267
Haywood, 215
Headrich, 26, 294
Heans, 31
Hearken, 2
Heaston, 303
Hechler, 88, 199, 205, 206
Heck, 27, 117, 127
Heckdorn, 189
Heckedorn, 5, 22, 23, 27, 28, 29, 31, 32, 34, 50, 89, 98, 99, 128, 135, 140, 189, 190, 221, 248, 249, 260, 360
Heckel, 180
Heckert, 206
Heckman, 303
Heckmann, 210
Hedrich, 76, 77
Heeg, 27, 118
Heekin, 99
Heeritter, 30
Heg, 116, 117, 277
Heibel, 4
Heibele, 302, 353
Heid, 206
Heidel, 324
Heidler, 198
Heier, 255
Heilman, 22, 29, 42, 67
Heindel, 319, 338
Heiner, 173
Heinrich, 8, 16, 29, 40, 49, 313, 328, 362, 363, 364, 369
Heins, 288
Heinsman, 282
Heintz, 31, 150, 271, 272
Heiss, 155, 290
Heistand, 204
Heitler, 247
Hekedorn, 128
Helle, 313
Heller, 28
Hellman, 14, 29, 71, 82, 148, 165, 166
Hellwig, 40
Helmanin, 29
Heln, 30
Hendrick, 268
Hengst, 42, 326
Henick, 93
Henig, 30, 84
Henn, 87, 311
Hennig, 77, 84
Henrich, 121, 361
Hens, 206, 271, 276, 280
Henson, 163
Hentz, 172

381

Herbach, 5, 146, 160, 167, 204, 243, 249, 286, 354
Herbold, 100, 102, 119, 129
Hering, 119
Heriter, 30
Herleman, 26, 30
Herman, 91, 127, 173, 207
Hermsdorff, 358
Herr, 32, 169, 190, 215, 262
Herring, 54, 72, 98, 119, 120, 121, 122, 123, 124, 125, 126, 158, 165, 182, 235
Herris, 207
Herschner, 67, 360
Herschy, 84
Hersh, 121
Hershey, 6, 161, 214, 308
Hertz, 295
Hertzer, 144
Hertzog, 169
Hess, 1, 3, 22, 45, 152, 194, 225, 314, 365
Hessenduer, 164
Hetchler, 30
Hetrick, 70
Hetterich, 26
Hetzberger, 310
Hetzer, 115, 117
Heus, 239
Heuss, 290, 321
Heydl, 324
Heyer, 130, 139, 207
Heylmann, 9
Heys, 289, 290
Hiertzel, 232
Hildebrand, 22, 61, 309, 314, 347, 350, 362, 365
Hileman, 2
Hill, 180
Hiller, 72, 108, 109, 115, 118, 126
Hinam, 68
Hinderleiter, 300
Hinrim, 70
Hitsberger, 310
Hoch, 228

Hochler, 310
Hock, 99, 118, 209, 212, 224
Hoeheneise, 126, 152
Hoehns, 10, 31, 149, 205, 221
Hoell, 289
Hoeneis, 99, 128
Hoeneise, 32, 99, 128
Hoeneisen, 128
Hoens, 32, 99, 128, 189, 190, 221, 244
Hoerdter, 330
Hoesler, 344
Hoetzel, 240
Hof, 32, 325
Hoff, 5, 28, 30, 31, 33, 39, 50, 90
Hoffacre, 34
Hoffheins, 211
Hoffman, 34, 67, 85, 96, 100, 104, 118, 127, 145, 148, 164, 175, 208, 242, 265, 343, 348, 355
Hofman, 139
Hog, 276, 278
Hoh, 208
Hohman, 319
Hohns, 28, 249
Hoke, 117, 188, 189, 192, 208, 209, 211, 212, 215, 257, 262, 351
Hokin, 141
Holl, 48, 73, 242, 278, 279
Holtsinger, 299
Holtzapffel, 215
Holtzappel, 202, 215, 255
Holtzbaum, 210, 292, 307, 316
Holtzbaumin, 210, 211, 316
Holtzender, 273
Holtzin, 91
Holtzinger, 143, 216
Homan, 290
Homel, 216
Hommer, 105
Hommon, 158
Honeisen, 128
Honeisn, 128
Honig, 25, 34, 81

Honing, 230
Hons, 99, 189
Hoober, 216
Hoock, 126, 213, 214
Hoog, 85, 178, 192, 208, 210, 262
Hoogin, 210
Hooman, 162
Hoover, 127, 172, 181
Horn, 81
Hornig, 166
Hornin, 216
Hoss, 108, 216
Houck, 24
Housman, 282
Hovis, 251, 336
Hoyle, 251, 336
Hubbert, 250, 274, 275
Huber, 34, 35, 37, 39, 43, 72, 74, 126, 146, 147, 160, 166, 231, 261, 267, 302, 303, 346
Hubert, 48, 80, 86, 212, 242, 282
Hubly, 324
Hubman, 9
Hubmann, 77
Huckenberger, 36
Hull, 242
Hummel, 33
Hummelin, 33, 244
Hummerichhauser, 148
Humrich, 148
Humrichhaus, 107, 152, 232, 245
Humrichhauss, 96, 217
Hunsaker, 179, 345
Hupmann, 76
Hupp, 36
Hupperton, 242
Hutig, 145

-I-

Ickes, 82
Igsin, 252
Ilgefritz, 240
Ilgenfritz, 128
Immel, 100, 217, 218, 221
Immeler, 269

Imschwiller, 354
Inners, 306, 307
Iserlin, 239
Isler, 36

-J-

Jacob, 91, 194, 204, 241, 352
Jacobi, 193
Jacobs, 241
Jaeger, 10
Jager, 242
Janler, 219
Jauler, 22, 201, 218, 246
Jeki, 110, 172
Jenewein, 26
Joacky, 181
Jocki, 110
Johnson, 251
Joho, 227
Jonas, 57, 91
Jorge, 219
Jose, 219
Josebin, 183
Joseph, 119, 121, 182, 194, 235, 241
Josi, 219, 246, 331
Jost, 72, 169, 274, 288
Julisen, 129
Julius, 111, 119, 128, 129
Jung, 36, 219, 231

-K-

Kabel, 120
Kachel, 228
Kagie, 220
Kagy, 179
Kalberman, 255
Kalckreuter, 36
Kaltreiter, 36
Kann, 7, 15, 63, 64, 65, 72, 114, 129, 130, 155, 160, 352
Kapp, 286
Kappler, 304
Karges, 325
Karl, 262

Kastner, 220
Katzenbach, 23
Kauffer, 277
Kauffman, 83, 130, 131, 141, 167, 178, 182
Kaufman, 45
Kaufmann, 138
Kaussler, 306
Keagy, 85
Keawey, 46
Keel, 142
Keener, 316
Keentz, 137, 355
Kehr, 55
Keiffer, 28, 73, 277
Keifferin, 72
Keinardt, 83
Keintz, 166
Keller, 9, 17, 23, 35, 36, 37, 38, 39, 40, 48, 71, 73, 74, 77, 105, 131, 132, 168, 179, 249, 266, 282, 308, 317, 341, 342, 345, 359
Kellivin, 261
Kenick, 220
Kenler, 316
Kenner, 84
Kenrick, 354
Kerber, 31, 60, 189, 197, 198, 202, 217, 218, 220, 229, 230, 236, 366
Kerberin, 237
Kerbs, 14
Kercher, 40
Kerchner, 40, 292, 338
Kergerick, 40
Kern, 243
Kerr, 140
Kerschner, 292
Kersh, 316
Kerst, 316
Kerth, 316
Kesselring, 263
Kessler, 14, 24, 40, 171, 201
Keyel, 59

Keyer, 202
Kiblar, 213
Kidd, 235
Kiefaber, 185
Kiefer, 155
Kieffer, 15, 23, 30, 41, 42, 191, 233, 266, 267, 312, 343
Kiefferin, 106, 312
Kiesel, 232
Kindig, 351
King, 222, 299
Kinsler, 290
Kinter, 299
Kintzler, 318
Kirchner, 138
Kislin, 11
Kissel, 74
Kissinger, 339
Kitt, 235
Kitzmiller, 283
Kladi, 112
Klapper, 221
Klee, 78, 197
Klein, 58, 104, 106, 108, 125, 151, 152, 199, 201, 203, 204, 206, 215, 220, 221, 368
Kleindinst, 29, 42
Kleinfelter, 17, 19, 20, 22, 30, 44, 64, 65, 67, 68, 132, 287, 290, 308, 317, 318, 340, 342, 346, 347, 361
Klember, 222
Klemmasch, 87
Klick, 321
Klinefelter, 321, 322
Klingemeyer, 277
Klingler, 199, 200
Klopfer, 132, 167
Knab, 181, 182, 221
Knauf, 50
Kneier, 42
Knertzer, 152
Kneyer, 42
Knirtzer, 149
Knoer, 199

Knoertzer, 133, 150, 245, 254
Knortzer, 149
Knotel, 315
Knurtzerin, 149
Kobel, 33, 195
Kobelet, 133, 154
Koch, 220, 222, 339
Kochenour, 114
Koenig, 87, 193, 222, 225, 285, 286
Kohler, 96, 186, 206, 223, 300, 342
Kohmer, 98
Kohnz, 88
Kohr, 300
Koll, 22
Koller, 302, 318, 319, 321, 340, 347
Kolp, 115
Konig, 100, 325
Konrath, 42
Kontz, 132
Kontzin, 51
Koonsin, 106
Koppenhaffer, 212
Koppenhoffer, 188, 189
Korbman, 308, 309, 322
Korbmann, 270
Korpman, 287, 308, 322
Kowel, 33
Kraemer, 134
Kraft, 69, 308, 325, 332, 367, 368
Krah, 43
Kramer, 12, 28, 43, 44, 63, 74, 75, 79, 92, 96, 113, 134, 138, 139, 142, 146, 162, 188, 200, 207, 210, 337, 355
Krantz, 105, 106, 107, 146, 174, 195, 212, 213, 224, 299, 302
Kraus, 329
Krause, 288
Krauss, 18, 62, 288
Kraut, 53, 61, 315
Kreber, 216
Kreberin, 32

Krebs, 7, 14, 44, 72
Kreider, 153
Kreischer, 295, 348
Kreisher, 295
Kreiss, 68
Krepil, 301
Krepill, 203
Krob, 22
Kroin, 132
Kroll, 44, 118, 149, 174, 178, 282, 323, 343, 364
Kromer, 49
Kron, 29, 45, 77, 81, 137
Kronau, 123
Kronbach, 129, 139, 144, 169
Kronin, 45, 82
Kronmuller, 222, 225
Kruger, 105
Kuensli, 135
Kuerchner, 323
Kuertzel, 349
Kuffer, 25, 343
Kuge, 329
Kuhl, 142
Kuhn, 43, 46, 354
Kumforth, 134
Kunckel, 140, 290, 308, 317, 318
Kunckell, 292
Kunckle, 173
Kunssler, 322
Kuntz, 29, 47, 62, 79, 81, 89, 136, 180, 242, 243, 248, 250, 258, 274, 275, 276, 310, 358
Kuntzel, 204, 225
Kuntzing, 242
Kuntzlerin, 221
Kuntzli, 135
Kunzel, 28
Kurfman, 85
Kurtz, 96, 297
Kyner, 83

-L-

Lambert, 96, 149, 225, 259
Lammot, 27

Lampert, 167, 168
Lanchert, 173
Landis, 266
Lang, 140, 143, 226, 227, 233, 268, 341, 347
Langin, 226
Lanius, 28, 31, 32, 134, 137, 138, 247, 248, 249, 260
Lanteman, 233
Lantz, 234
Lau, 24, 25, 47, 62, 197, 198, 201, 202, 219, 221, 227, 228, 229, 230, 235, 242, 251, 284, 288, 324, 331
Laub, 325, 355
Lauderman, 324
Lauer, 114, 165, 185
Lauffer, 21, 365
Lauin, 197
Lauman, 184, 185
Laumann, 197
Laumeister, 156
Laur, 165
Lauterbach, 231
Lawrence, 213
Leab, 264
Leaseman, 82
Leather, 231
Lebber, 79
Lechner, 110
Lederman, 256, 357
Leeman, 332
Leer, 45
Lefevre, 209
Lefler, 218
Lehman, 184, 186
Lehmer, 210
Lehner, 80
Leib, 39, 217, 231, 232, 272, 285, 346
Leibi, 105
Leibin, 217
Leidig, 33, 144, 233
Leightner, 359
Leimbach, 240
Leinbach, 10, 140, 235
Leinbacher, 131, 140, 258
Leinbachin, 144
Leineweber, 233
Leininger, 141
Leiss, 138, 316, 324
Leitner, 8, 189
Lenhart, 142
Leonhardt, 138, 141, 243, 310
Lichte, 98
Lichtenberger, 86, 182, 234
Lickenfelder, 36
Lidey, 47
Lieb, 237, 254
Liebenstein, 90, 234, 296
Liebhard, 103, 353
Liebhardt, 67
Liebpe, 232
Lightner, 137, 355
Limble, 236
Linafelter, 35
Linckefelder, 40, 47, 71, 87
Linckelfelter, 95
Lindemeyer, 190
Lindt, 183
Lindy, 239, 244
Line, 211, 261
Linebaugh, 165
Lingfelder, 161
Linglefelder, 47, 48
Link, 251
Linn, 142
Lischey, 193
Lischey, 285
Lischy, 7, 15, 17, 22, 34, 37, 39, 40-43, 45, 48, 51, 74, 77-79, 126, 130, 132, 134-139, 145, 162, 163, 219, 236-238, 243, 248, 266, 267, 270, 271, 309, 310, 315, 317, 318, 336, 341, 342, 350, 355, 362
Lischyn, 83
Lochman, 117
Lochmann, 252
Loffer, 230

Lohr, 48, 49, 50, 51, 52, 92, 93, 214
Lohra, 143, 161, 226
Long, 226, 341, 342, 344
Lor, 79
Lora, 222
Lorain, 226
Loray, 46
Lorch, 329, 339
Lore, 49, 93
Lorich, 52, 339
Lorr, 49
Low, 56
Lowenstein, 204, 234
Lucas, 322, 324
Luchenbach, 240
Luckenbach, 103, 104, 119, 141, 143, 144
Luckenback, 143
Luffolt, 36
Luike, 100
Lutsch, 104
Lutz, 321, 325, 350

-M-
Maak, 52, 84, 124
Maas, 235
Mcclean, 356
Mcclelan, 67
Mcclellan, 357
Mcdonald, 296, 303, 305
Mackin, 124
Madinger, 251
Maeiger, 326
Mahl, 2
Mahon, 64
Maier, 329
Maisch, 138
Maitsch, 104
Maj, 127, 168
Majer, 98, 134, 163, 168, 172
Manchen, 67, 69
Marker, 195
Markey, 319
Markle, 8

Marter, 43
Martin, 1, 97
Marty, 186
Martz, 175
Mathies, 148
Matter, 57, 125
Mattheis, 176, 239
Maugher, 326
Maul, 119, 136, 183, 194, 235, 253
Maurer, 116, 144, 233
May, 116, 144, 147, 154, 160
Mayer, 52, 74, 133, 143, 145, 146, 147, 163, 225, 265, 284, 326, 337
Mayern, 199
Maysch, 139
Meckel, 326
Mecker, 235
Meckle, 326
Mehl, 137, 146
Meier, 189, 242
Meiern, 199
Meiley, 28
Meinhardt, 102
Meissenkop, 249
Meissler, 218
Meitsch, 103
Mek, 194
Melchior, 46
Meng, 39
Menges, 197, 228, 235, 314
Merckel, 1, 69, 287, 325
Merschel, 80
Messerle, 46, 146, 160, 171, 274
Messerschmeid, 357
Messerschmidt, 253
Messoncopp, 102
Metzgar, 97, 149, 323
Metzger, 124, 360
Metzler, 99
Meurer, 28
Mey, 96
Meyer, 1, 7, 13, 25, 52, 53, 54, 62, 81, 86, 87, 88, 90, 105,

111, 125, 131, 134, 148, 161,
163, 184, 195, 221, 233, 236,
237, 238, 244, 254, 258, 266,
270, 271, 276, 278, 284, 309,
310, 325, 327, 329, 333, 335,
343, 347, 367
Meyerin, 37, 148, 364
Meyers, 204, 211
Mezger, 252
Mezlerin, 166
Michael, 12, 73, 114, 139, 213, 325
Michel, 124, 125, 126, 361
Michlin, 166
Mickley, 110
Mier, 328
Miller, 19, 31, 33, 34, 37, 39, 41,
49, 54, 58, 77, 78, 85, 86, 90,
99, 107, 112, 113, 124, 125,
126, 128, 129, 140, 148, 151,
152, 153, 164, 178, 186, 189,
196, 205, 211, 217, 226, 228,
232, 235, 236, 238, 239, 248,
249, 264, 267, 300, 322, 327,
329, 334, 354, 365
Millican, 267
Milton, 24
Mitschele, 147
Mitschels, 156
Mittman, 146, 147
Mittmar, 96
Mochler, 57
Mockler, 57, 74
Mohr, 2, 96, 128, 143, 168, 176,
223, 239, 278, 349, 352
Mohrin, 141
Moller, 9
Moor, 346
Morgan, 137
Morganstern, 241, 242
Morgensten, 81
Morgenstern, 242
Morningstar, 241, 242
Moser, 243, 244, 308, 349, 359
Mott, 113

Motz, 330
Moul, 55, 257
Moyer, 327
Moymeyer, 197
Mueller, 16, 23, 54, 59, 170, 247,
330, 332, 360, 363, 364
Muhlheim, 26
Muler, 260
Mulhaus, 257
Mulleer, 62
Muller, 11, 13, 23, 28, 31, 32, 33,
34, 46, 54, 55, 56, 74, 82, 83,
87, 91, 98, 104, 111, 133,
148, 149, 152, 166, 189, 209,
218, 221, 232, 244, 245, 249,
258, 259, 267, 275, 312, 313,
327, 328, 329, 330, 332, 335,
344, 355, 360, 361
Mullheim, 57
Mumma, 91
Mummert, 279
Muntz, 267
Murphy, 267
Musser, 192, 330
Myer, 8, 56, 229, 270
Myers, 52, 264, 310, 346

-N-

Nagelin, 367
Nau, 72
Nebinger, 251, 286
Nees, 120, 175, 344, 364
Neff, 181, 239, 249, 282, 333
Neidig, 43
Neiman, 97, 118, 245
Neischwanger, 59
Neppinger, 258, 280
Nes, 245, 358
Ness, 1, 191, 194, 219, 228, 229,
287, 325, 329, 330, 331, 332,
335, 336, 338, 339, 362, 365,
366
Neswinger, 333
Neucommer, 57, 58
Neufong, 310

Neukommer, 14, 57, 76
Neuman, 53, 58, 175, 245
Neuschwanger, 59, 333
Newcomer, 58
Newman, 347
Newswanger, 59
Neyswanger, 59
Nicholas, 77, 127
Nichols, 102
Nickel, 348
Noll, 35, 55, 66, 279
Nonnemacher, 26
Notz, 59
Nunemacher, 328, 333, 334
Nutz, 59

-O-

Ob, 31, 32, 96, 100, 133, 141, 146, 147, 148, 149, 150, 174, 175, 210, 225, 231, 272, 367
Obbin, 160
Oberdier, 101, 109, 149, 150, 169, 172, 343
Oberdorff, 245
Oberlin, 165
Obin, 130, 149
Oblad, 116, 117
Ocker, 86
Oderman, 119, 235
Ohlinger, 26
Oler, 78
Olp, 334
Opp, 182
Orth, 232, 277
Ott, 40, 59, 62, 340
Ottenberger, 118
Ottinger, 171, 174, 194, 219, 236, 246, 252, 270, 274, 281
Ottman, 92
Owen, 126, 215

-P-

Paff, 31
Painder, 11
Palle, 344
Palli, 150, 178
Pasch, 191
Pather, 154
Paul, 188
Paules, 302
Paulus, 45, 138, 278
Pawer, 151
Peery, 334
Pegler, 4
Peissel, 113
Peitsel, 89
Peitzel, 167
Peizel, 128, 140, 249
Pengele, 89
Pens, 149, 166, 273
Pentz, 212
Perth, 102
Peter, 40, 101, 196
Peterman, 3, 39, 130, 226
Petri, 72
Petry, 36
Petter, 31
Petterscheimer, 290
Pfaff, 60, 140, 221
Pfarr, 193, 200
Pfeifer, 313, 334, 344
Pfeiffer, 313, 330
Pflieger, 41, 299
Pfluger, 41, 42, 288, 350
Pfrister, 313
Pfundt, 75
Phemach, 283
Philip, 65, 124
Philipp, 124
Piezel, 140
Pilla, 366
Platter, 176
Plauser, 294
Plessen, 112
Pomeroy, 211
Poole, 122
Pott, 36, 101, 276
Pottorff, 211
Prinimen, 247
Probst, 64, 263, 292

Prosser, 71
Protzman, 9
Prozman, 34
Prumbach, 151
Pudding, 45

-Q-
Quickel, 99, 100, 103, 127, 133, 151, 152, 153, 164, 201, 204, 213, 217, 221, 239
Quickelin, 152

-R-
Rachhauser, 129, 133, 139, 145, 153, 160
Rachhausser, 96
Racki, 154
Rader, 112
Radfang, 60
Rahauser, 101, 109, 116, 167, 174
Rahauserin, 166
Rahausser, 96
Ramler, 344
Ramsauer, 213
Ramsaur, 213, 251
Ranck, 261
Rankin, 142
Rathfon, 60
Ratscher, 52
Ratz, 335
Rauhauser, 260
Raulin, 138
Raus, 90, 362
Rausch, 195
Rauscher, 234
Rauser, 9
Rausher, 296
Reber, 55, 60, 61, 62, 65, 109, 254, 323, 339, 365
Reberin, 23, 55, 109
Rebmann, 88
Redfon, 60
Redvan, 60
Reese, 123
Regula, 249

Rehler, 368
Reib, 138
Reiber, 65, 170
Reibold, 61
Reidel, 101
Reider, 113, 305
Reiff, 86, 114, 130, 154, 195, 367
Reiffin, 114, 155
Reigert, 105
Rein, 22, 251, 307, 309, 315, 319, 335, 359
Reinecker, 46
Reinhard, 88, 184
Reinhardt, 11, 150, 282
Reisinger, 97, 156, 206, 211, 319
Reissinger, 25, 155, 156, 173, 224
Reitzel, 134
Remer, 267
Rennolly, 229
Rennoly, 22
Renolly, 23, 35, 37, 54, 56, 61, 84
Repanach, 336
Reppert, 1
Resch, 142
Resinger, 319
Resser, 195, 323
Reub, 344
Reuscher, 180
Reuter, 102
Rhein, 245, 335
Rheinhardt, 317
Rhode, 246
Ribi, 101
Richter, 95, 156, 170, 173, 174
Riedt, 247
Rieman, 322
Rife, 86, 179
Ringer, 182
Ripfel, 156
Ripp, 344, 345
Ritter, 102, 113, 255, 356
Rockey, 17, 154
Roemer, 23, 57, 212, 247
Roemig, 195
Rohmer, 5, 42, 135, 247

Rohrbach, 38, 62, 157
Roller, 170
Romer, 183, 198
Romig, 246, 336
Rors, 248
Rose, 337
Rosenberger, 144
Roser, 52, 291, 308, 337, 338, 339
Rosh, 53
Roth, 80, 232, 249
Rothermel, 30, 40, 48, 59, 62, 94, 339
Rothfan, 53
Rothrock, 31, 50, 98, 99, 128, 189, 248
Rotter, 194
Roudibousch, 111
Roudiboush, 129
Rouse, 356
Rouss, 212
Rubbert, 246
Rubel, 63, 160
Rubenthal, 75
Rubert, 270
Rubertin, 157
Ruck, 200
Ruddi, 213
Rudel, 155
Rudi, 143, 187, 211, 212, 215, 227
Rudisil, 253, 326
Rudisill, 2, 23, 36, 60, 145, 153, 157, 158, 168, 187, 188, 201, 216, 228, 233, 249, 250, 252, 253, 255, 258, 336, 351, 352
Rudisille, 249
Rudisillin, 60
Rudolph, 18, 66, 291
Rudrauf, 163
Rudy, 212, 270
Rudyn, 284
Rudysill, 149
Rudysille, 365
Ruhl, 7, 8, 16, 17, 18, 19, 20, 38, 61, 63, 64, 66, 68, 69, 70, 71, 76, 130, 137, 204, 289, 290, 292, 302, 319, 356
Ruisilli, 249
Rumel, 270
Rummel, 136, 157, 308
Runck, 30
Runk, 6, 40, 47, 71, 80, 82
Runkel, 57
Runkle, 4, 113
Rupert, 254, 255, 270, 273
Ruppert, 215, 217, 255, 293
Ruscher, 215
Rush, 340
Rutter, 355
Rybolt, 61

-S-

Sabel, 80
Saeger, 350
Saftler, 69
Sallmuller, 71
Salomonmuller, 71, 124, 125, 126
Saltzgeber, 114, 123, 158
Saltzgeberin, 335
Sangree, 340
Sappell, 44
Sarbach, 352
Sasseman, 178
Sat, 342
Sauer, 30, 242
Sauter, 7
Schack, 27
Schadlin, 174
Schaedle, 207
Schaefer, 130, 252
Schaeffer, 1, 99, 334
Schafer, 85, 132, 294
Schaffer, 12, 15, 41, 68, 72, 73, 74, 88, 102, 109, 110, 118, 122, 131, 158, 159, 160, 162, 172, 186, 191, 199, 205, 222, 227, 256, 280, 294, 304, 307, 311, 317, 318, 319, 321, 334, 340, 341, 342, 346, 350, 362, 364, 365
Scharer, 150, 297, 342

Schatterle, 318
Schaub, 228, 230
Schauck, 27
Schedderon, 113, 140, 146, 157, 158, 160, 161
Scheddron, 273
Schedel, 113, 223
Schederon, 106, 140, 204
Schedle, 141
Schedler, 141
Scheebler, 87
Scheib, 256
Scheifele, 25
Scheiry, 315
Schelhammer, 241
Schenck, 65, 161, 253, 273
Scher, 261
Scherer, 19, 34, 38, 39, 40, 43, 72, 73, 76, 78, 93, 341
Scherp, 204
Schetler, 323
Schetlj, 276
Schetrone, 204
Schettle, 161
Schettler, 118
Scheubel, 27, 135
Scheure, 315
Schilling, 83
Schindel, 117, 118, 169
Schindler, 312
Schinleber, 297, 343
Schinleberger, 343
Schitz, 80
Schlatter, 103, 314
Schleesman, 75
Schlegal, 31
Schlegel, 32, 99, 140, 249
Schlepp, 226
Schleppi, 14, 15, 75, 309, 366, 367
Schlesman, 75
Schmahlin, 14
Schmall, 208
Schmaltzhaff, 306
Schmeiser, 45, 46, 76
Schmeisser, 55, 81, 82, 141, 188, 191, 192, 196, 212, 214, 244, 256, 257, 258, 262, 265, 266, 267, 279, 282
Schmeltzer, 76, 349
Schmelzer, 138
Schmid, 91, 164, 193, 195, 340
Schmidin, 132
Schmidt, 1, 5, 6, 29, 31, 34, 43, 45, 50, 74, 76, 77, 78, 79, 80, 83, 97, 118, 135, 145, 146, 161, 162, 188, 192, 197, 248, 254, 258, 278, 279, 280, 285, 287, 343, 349, 364, 365
Schmith, 340
Schmoker, 207
Schnazler, 308
Schneider, 17, 36, 56, 67, 70, 79, 103, 104, 140, 144, 175, 238, 256, 259, 271, 288, 293, 304, 305, 306, 311, 315, 317, 319, 328, 329, 335, 343, 344, 349, 350, 361, 362, 363, 367, 368
Schneiderin, 350
Schneier, 342
Schnell, 344
Schnellbecker, 163
Schnug, 103, 104, 105
Schober, 367
Schodde, 245
Schodder, 106, 163
Schodle, 277
Schoemaker, 216
Schoerder, 56
Schopff, 252
Schott, 261
Schram, 139, 178
Schramm, 85, 114, 154, 155, 367
Schrammin, 154
Schreiber, 212, 246, 250
Schreiner, 12, 306
Schreyack, 154, 260
Schreyer, 124, 183
Schriber, 218
Schrimer, 30
Schriner, 50

393

Schroder, 209, 269
Schroms, 177
Schuch, 18
Schuckert, 195, 244
Schuggart, 149
Schuh, 279
Schuler, 104, 240
Schultz, 1, 6, 7, 80, 102, 111, 134,
 136, 137, 139, 146, 162, 174,
 208, 237, 238, 241, 242, 255,
 264, 316, 355, 356
Schultzin, 78, 130, 138, 259
Schulz, 18
Schumacher, 206
Schunck, 62
Schuster, 25, 325, 350
Schwab, 229, 230, 260, 261, 300,
 351
Schwartz, 18, 49, 92, 306, 342,
 363, 364
Schwartzwaelder, 164
Schweisgood, 354
Schweisgute, 335
Schwenk, 207
Schwerdt, 323
Schwerth, 322
Schwing, 157
Schwingel, 247
Schwob, 186, 202, 209, 211, 212,
 213, 214, 257, 261, 262, 353,
 368
Schwop, 212
Scoil, 62
Seel, 157
Seib, 32, 33, 100, 152, 163, 276
Seidedstricker, 173
Seifert, 164, 165, 166, 276
Seiffert, 156, 164
Seigrist, 263
Seiler, 306, 307
Seip, 163
Seitz, 131, 164, 179, 231, 251,
 318, 344, 345, 347, 360
Senseny, 197
Sepach, 80

Serbach, 352
Sesrang, 263
Seyler, 297
Shafer, 179
Shaffer, 235, 243, 342
Shafftler, 325
Shank, 161
Sharer, 38, 73
Shawer, 11
Shearer, 73
Shedderon, 114
Shederon, 149
Shedley, 263
Shertz, 214
Shettel, 99
Shettler, 85
Shigley, 347
Shilling, 83, 347
Shinard, 347
Shineman, 134
Shipe, 256
Shively, 215
Shock, 216
Shoemaker, 177
Shotter, 45
Shreyer, 17
Shuck, 280
Shuert, 80
Shugart, 188, 316
Shultz, 44, 137
Sidle, 218
Siegfried, 250
Siegrist, 14, 22, 36, 69, 105, 312
Siegristin, 105
Siford, 122
Simon, 12, 147, 295, 296, 311,
 315, 340, 341, 347, 348, 362
Sincke, 307
Sitler, 296, 298
Sittler, 177
Six, 164
Slagle, 197, 257, 358
Slesman, 75
Sloan, 142
Slothower, 99

Small, 46, 358
Smith, 70, 77, 78, 104, 161
Smyser, 188, 189, 196
Snavely, 152, 153
Snell, 344
Snellbecker, 103
Snyder, 40, 71, 79
Sohn, 166
Sohnin, 301
Solomonmuller, 92
Sopach, 80
Sorg, 207
Sowder, 167
Spaar, 95, 96, 98, 101, 117, 132, 133, 150, 167, 168, 169, 171, 172, 174, 226, 250
Spaarin, 157, 226
Spahr, 100, 159, 167
Spangler, 137, 197, 210, 211, 233, 262, 263, 317, 342, 350, 353, 354, 355, 357, 358, 359
Spanhauer, 81
Spannknebel, 207
Spar, 132
Specard, 302
Spenckel, 42, 54
Spengler, 129, 146, 208, 223, 255, 300, 316, 348, 350, 352, 353, 357, 358, 367
Spenglerin, 311, 351
Spenith, 264
Spessart, 81
Spessert, 81
Spickert, 206
Spieker, 10
Spiess, 56, 95, 139, 169, 198
Spitler, 22, 27, 360
Spitsberger, 169
Spodley, 169
Sponhauer, 29, 82
Sprenckel, 17, 34, 37, 41, 83, 85, 86, 87, 175, 197, 198, 264, 266, 272, 273
Sprenglerin, 41
Sprinckel, 238, 350

Sprinckle, 238
Stabler, 204, 297, 319, 345, 346, 360
Stadleman, 217
Stall, 349
Stambach, 6, 14, 34, 46, 55, 78, 81, 82, 83, 92, 203, 214, 246, 247, 257, 326
Stammin, 109
Stark, 349
Stauch, 159, 273
Stauedemeyer, 170
Stautenhauer, 104
Stech, 252
Steeg, 217, 277
Steele, 215
Steffie, 68
Steighletter, 92
Steiman, 49, 93
Stein, 80, 157, 161, 177, 216, 233, 361, 362
Steinbrecher, 311
Steltz, 84
Stely, 90
Stemen, 180
Stempel, 288, 339
Steng, 84
Stentz, 78
Stentzin, 77
Stewart, 102
Stich, 19
Stiefferlin, 109
Stiffler, 315
Stillinger, 177, 186, 216
Stina, 351
Stirewalt, 213
Stirtz, 179
Stober, 73, 223
Stocker, 162
Stoehr, 300
Stoever, 109, 354
Stohly, 130
Stohten, 43
Storfinger, 226
Stormer, 111

Stottleman, 217
Stouch, 156, 166, 170, 171, 172
Stouchenberger, 99
Stover, 235
Stower, 183
Straely, 165
Straher, 145
Straley, 173
Streber, 356
Streher, 95, 98, 111, 115, 128, 145, 147, 159, 170, 171, 172, 316, 328, 347
Streherin, 95
Strehly, 173
Strein, 112
Streithof, 52
Streithoff, 84, 85
Strettell, 239
Stricker, 324
Strickhauser, 84
Strickler, 136, 181, 247, 265, 270
Stritmeyer, 312
Stroer, 312
Strong, 349
Strubel, 195
Struebig, 104
Struecker, 101, 102, 324
Stubler, 241, 335
Stuck, 45, 72, 85, 205
Stucker, 54
Stuckey, 123
Stuckslager, 293
Study, 57
Stump, 49, 85, 93
Sturt, 102
Styvenson, 148
Summeraur, 85
Sunday, 158
Supinger, 35, 85
Suttle, 110
Swartz, 3, 23, 79, 173, 296, 315, 334, 341, 346, 361, 362, 365
Swartzin, 80
Switzgood, 158
Swope, 323, 353, 359, 364

-T-
Tanner, 265
Tauster, 126
Taylor, 67
Teitcher, 263
Templemann, 261
Tentzel, 112
Thiel, 91
Thomas, 280
Thompson, 142
Tible, 258
Tomas, 73
Tondorn, 148
Tranberg, 230
Trease, 77
Treiber, 34, 85, 265
Trein, 173
Trieber, 34, 186
Troerbach, 364
Trorbach, 47, 86, 87, 155, 267
Trorbachin, 87
Troutman, 201
Tuebinger, 73, 224, 227, 302, 309, 314
Tyson, 243

-U-
Ubachin, 155
Ubman, 39
Uhl, 109
Uhlem, 72
Uhler, 157, 200, 237, 255, 256, 270, 285, 308
Uhlerin, 270
Uhlichin, 237
Uhr, 152
Uhrich, 178
Ulerich, 87, 255
Ulius, 111, 128
Uller, 322
Ulmer, 77
Ulrich, 30, 109, 226, 252, 255, 276
Ulrichin, 270, 271
Uly, 166

Updegraf, 232
Updegraff, 63, 134, 364
Updtegraf, 206
Uppach, 148
Utz, 55

-V-

Valentin, 302
Valentine, 240, 302
Vaupel, 76
Velte, 116
Venus, 294, 308, 334, 341, 361, 364
Verdriess, 298
Verdruss, 299
Vogel, 25, 87, 88, 205, 267
Vogeler, 222
Vogelmann, 231
Vogler, 87, 180, 205, 312
Voglerin, 25
Voglesong, 263
Vogt, 59, 288
Vohl, 105
Volck, 290
Volckel, 194
Volgeme, 313
Volk, 318
Vollenweiler, 88
Vollenweiller, 4, 276
Vollmar, 191
Voltz, 18
Volz, 18
Von Colmar, 354
Von Gemmingen, 345
Von Marxheim, 340, 347
Vorreuter, 249
Votrin, 50, 88
Votring, 50, 248

-W-

Waggoner, 211
Wagner, 63, 71, 161, 193, 250, 271
Wagoner, 310
Wahl, 217, 222

Wahlburg, 220, 236
Walck, 174
Waldbauer, 170
Walder, 259
Wallacher, 310
Wallendin, 302
Walpurga, 60
Waltemeyer, 91
Walter, 53, 73, 75, 89, 90, 234, 249, 287, 308, 335, 361, 363, 364, 365
Walther, 22, 105, 106, 276, 310, 314, 315, 331, 365
Waltimier, 91
Waltmire, 302
Waltz, 181
Wampfler, 126
Wampler, 1
Wanner, 6
Ward, 122
Weaver, 298
Weber, 10, 101, 174, 207, 275, 282, 339
Wegerlin, 252
Wehler, 158, 229
Wehn, 102
Weickel, 93
Weidman, 90
Weidner, 134, 135, 139, 248, 303
Weigel, 101, 149, 171, 172, 173, 178, 196, 233, 255, 266, 272, 273, 277
Weigelin, 218
Weiglerin, 266
Weiman, 91
Weimer, 32, 174, 180, 224
Weinand, 156
Weinbrener, 98
Weinbrenner, 174, 175, 186, 301
Weinbrennerin, 174
Weiner, 143
Weinmuller, 343
Weirich, 368
Weis, 366
Weiser, 118

Weishart, 366
Weiss, 91, 243
Weissmueller, 49
Weist, 135, 214
Weiter, 207
Welch, 211
Welcher, 209
Weldner, 87, 317
Weldy, 144
Welk, 344, 345
Weller, 31, 32, 34, 89, 98, 99, 190, 218, 220, 237, 248, 249, 258, 279
Welsch, 45, 91, 160, 176, 214, 274, 275, 279, 280, 281, 282, 316
Welschans, 15, 41, 75, 76, 101, 114, 130, 154, 155, 187, 209, 281, 332, 341, 366, 367
Welschantz, 63, 332
Welschofer, 207, 208
Welschover, 316
Welsh, 154, 167, 354
Welshans, 237
Welshantz, 51, 223
Welshofer, 200, 208
Welshoffer, 207
Welshover, 136
Welt, 323
Welty, 114, 128, 146, 181, 348
Weltz, 63, 194
Wenen, 147
Wentel, 62
Wentz, 133, 134, 147, 156, 172
Werle, 5
Werner, 5, 9, 91, 172
Werret, 303
Wertz, 44, 92
Wetterrect, 202
Weyant, 10
Weybrechtin, 221
Weyer, 107, 108, 112, 275
Weyerman, 312
Weygand, 174
Weyl, 116

Weylandt, 156
Weyle, 189
Weymueller, 368
Weymuller, 61, 365
Weynand, 95
Wherly, 37, 39
Wibeling, 17
Wiest, 135, 351
Wigand, 47
Wil, 209
Wilcke, 355
Wild, 14, 98, 107, 161, 164, 165, 233, 246, 276, 287, 365
Wildasin, 36, 122
Wildbahn, 14
Wilder, 262
Wilhelm, 43, 92, 147, 223, 325, 329, 368
Wilhelmin, 368
Wilhide, 89
Wilhite, 211
Will, 51
Willhautin, 152
Willheut, 111, 128
Williard, 10, 158, 332
Wills, 336
Wilson, 213, 303
Wiltz, 336
Winck, 70
Windnagel, 103, 252
Winkler, 185
Wintermeier, 175, 277
Wintermeyer, 201
Winterroth, 193
Wintersmith, 359
Wintimier, 175
Wirick, 368
Wirth, 103, 104
Wirtz, 36
Wise, 211, 336
Wist, 351
Witmeyer, 194
Wittmer, 230
Wittmeyer, 118, 274, 277
Wodering, 88

Wohlgemuht, 193
Wolf, 73, 132, 155, 178, 197, 207, 213, 214, 215, 238, 254, 274, 275, 286, 352, 356, 357
Wolff, 2, 73, 133, 134, 138, 147, 176, 183, 209, 235, 240, 241, 244, 246, 247, 258, 259, 274, 275, 277, 278, 279, 280, 281, 282, 306
Wolffgang, 25
Wolffin, 23, 135, 178, 275, 280, 281
Wolfgang, 27, 77, 79, 93, 231
Wolfin, 183
Wollet, 122
Wollmer, 243
Wolss, 282
Wonder, 229
Worley, 112, 190, 248
Wortman, 243
Wottring, 88
Wright, 349
Wuchtel, 227
Wunder, 267
Wysong, 204, 282

-Y-

Yaeger, 261
Yeakle, 313, 369
Yodder, 283
Yoner, 284
Yost, 84
Youler, 219
Young, 3, 363
Yount, 8, 369
Yowler, 219
Yund, 295

-Z-

Zanger, 242
Zanklin, 72
Zasgin, 72
Zauck, 49, 51, 52, 73, 74, 92, 93, 172
Zech, 12
Zeck, 12
Zeel, 16
Zeigler, 70
Zeller, 339, 346, 367
Ziefer, 26
Ziegler, 1, 48, 76, 89, 93, 183, 193, 221, 222, 223, 230, 233, 235, 236, 237, 238, 258, 270, 271, 284, 285, 299, 313, 350
Zillhard, 303
Zimmer, 364
Zimmerman, 44, 93, 110, 123
Zin, 102, 165
Zinck, 309
Zinn, 96, 113, 127, 139, 149, 175, 225, 269
Zither, 298
Zouck, 49, 93
Zwegiebel, 303